Emerging Issues in
Financial Development

Emerging Issues in Financial Development

LESSONS FROM LATIN AMERICA

Tatiana Didier and Sergio L. Schmukler,
editors

THE WORLD BANK
Washington, D.C.

ISBN (paper): 978-0-8213-9828-9
ISBN (electronic): 978-0-8213-9956-9
DOI: 10.1596/978-0-8213-9828-9

Cover design: Bill Pragluski, Critical stages, LLC

Library of Congress Cataloging-in-Publication Data

Emerging issues in financial development : lessons from Latin America / [edited by] Tatiana Didier and Sergio L. Schmukler.
    pages cm
  Includes bibliographical references and index.
ISBN 978-0-8213-9828-9 (alk. paper) – ISBN 978-0-8213-9956-9
  1. Finance—Latin America. 2. Financial institutions—Latin America. 3. Monetary policy—Latin America. I. Didier, Tatiana. II. Schmukler, Sergio L. III. World Bank.
  HG185.L3E44 2013
  332.098—dc23   2013038521

Latin American Development Forum Series

This series was created in 2003 to promote debate, disseminate information and analysis, and convey the excitement and complexity of the most topical issues in economic and social development in Latin America and the Caribbean. It is sponsored by the Inter-American Development Bank, the United Nations Economic Commission for Latin America and the Caribbean, and the World Bank. The manuscripts chosen for publication represent the highest quality in each institution's research and activity output and have been selected for their relevance to the academic community, policy makers, researchers, and interested readers.

Advisory Committee Members

Titles in the Latin American Development Forum Series

Contributing Authors

Deniz Anginer, Economist, Development Research Group, Finance and Private Sector Development, World Bank.

Martín Auqui, Head, Bank Supervision Department, Superintendency of Banks, Insurance, and Pension Funds Administrators of Peru.

César Calderón, Senior Economist, Financial and Private Sector Development Vice-Presidency, World Bank.

Francisco Ceballos, Consultant, Development Research Group, Macroeconomics and Growth Team, World Bank.

Mariano Cortés, Lead Financial Sector Economist, Latin America and Caribbean Region, World Bank.

Augusto de la Torre, Chief Economist, Office of the Chief Economist for the Latin American and Caribbean Region, World Bank.

Katia D'Hulster, Senior Financial Sector Specialist, Financial Systems Department, World Bank.

Tatiana Didier, Senior Economist, Office of the Chief Economist for Latin American and Caribbean Region, World Bank.

Miquel Dijkman, Senior Financial Sector Specialist, Financial and Private Sector Development, World Bank.

Erik Feyen, Senior Financial Specialist, Financial and Private Sector Development, World Bank.

Eva Gutierrez, Lead Financial Sector Specialist, Latin America and Caribbean Region, World Bank.

Socorro Heysen, Former Superintendent, Superintendency of Banks, Insurance, and Pension Funds Administrators of Peru.

Alain Ize, Senior Consultant, Office of the Chief Economist for the Latin American and Caribbean Region, World Bank.

Eduardo Levy-Yeyati, Professor, Universidad de Buenos Aires and UTDT; Director, ELYPSIS Partners.

María Soledad Martínez Pería, Research Manager, Development Research Group, Finance and Private Sector Development, World Bank.

Claudio Raddatz, Economic Research Manager, Central Bank of Chile.

Sergio L. Schmukler, Lead Economist, Development Research Group, Macroeconomics and Growth Team, World Bank.

Steven A. Seelig, Consultant, Financial Systems Department, World Bank.

Luis Servén, Research Manager, Development Research Group, Macroeconomics and Growth Team, World Bank.

Tomás Williams, PhD student at Universitat Pompeu Fabra, Barcelona.

Contents

BOXES

FIGURES

TABLES

Acknowledgments

This book is related to a flagship study conducted at the Office of the Chief Economist for Latin America and the Caribbean (LAC) of the World Bank. This book contains a selection of the best background papers commissioned for that study and reflects the views of their authors, who are considered leading experts in the field. A separate flagship report, titled *Financial Development in Latin America and the Caribbean: The Road Ahead*, by Augusto de la Torre, Alain Ize, and Sergio Schmukler, binds together the key messages from these background papers and provides some policy recommendations. That report reflects the views of its authors and is at times different from the messages in this book.

The flagship study as a whole benefited from very detailed and substantive comments from many colleagues and experts, including: Aquiles Almansi, Timothy Brennan, Anderson Caputo Silva, Jorge Chan-Lau, Loic Chiquier, Martin Cihak, Stijn Claessens, Tito Cordella, Luis Cortavarría, Asli Demirguc-Kunt, Eduardo Fernández-Arias, Joaquín Gutierrez, Olivier Hassler, Tamuna Loladze, Marialisa Motta, Aditya Narain, Andrew Powell, Robert Rennhack, Roberto Rocha, Liliana Rojas Suárez, Heinz Rudolph, Pablo Sanguinetti, Sophie Sirtaine, Ilias Skamnelos, Craig Thorburn, and Rodrigo Valdés.

In addition, we received very useful feedback from participants at several presentations held at GDN 12th Annual Global Development Conference (Bogota), NIPFP-DEA (New Delhi), Bank of Korea (Seoul), ADBI (Tokyo), Bank of Spain (Madrid), LACEA 2011 (Santiago de Chile), Launch Event at Columbia University (New York), CAF-World Bank Workshop (Bogota), IMF (Washington, D.C.), American University (Washington, D.C.), Central Bank of Brazil (Rio de Janeiro), Casa das Garças (Rio de Janeiro), Foro Internacional de Economía (Lima), ITAM (Mexico DF), Central Bank of Uruguay (Montevideo), Central Bank of Paraguay (Asuncion), Ministry of Finance (Asuncion), ABIF (Santiago de Chile), Central Bank of Chile (Santiago de Chile), and University of Chile (Santiago de Chile).

The flagship study was also guided by an advisory group of LAC financial policy makers, who provided substantive comments. The members of the advisory group were:

• From Brazil: Alexandre Tombini (Governor, Central Bank) and Luis Pereira da Silva (Deputy Governor for International Affairs, Central Bank).

- From Chile: Luis Céspedes (former Head of Research, Central Bank).
- From Colombia: Ana Fernanda Maiguashca (Regulation Director, Ministry of Finance).
- From Costa Rica: Francisco de Paula Gutiérrez (former Governor, Central Bank).
- From Jamaica: Brian Wynter (Governor, Bank of Jamaica) and Brian Langrin (Chief Economist, Financial Stability Unit, Bank of Jamaica).
- From Mexico: Guillermo Babatz Torres (President, National Banking and Securities Commission) and Carlos Serrano (Vice President of Regulatory Policies, National Banking and Securities Commission).
- From Peru: Javier Poggi (Chief Economist, Superintendency of Banking, Insurance and Private Persion Funds) and Manuel Luy (Head of the Economic Research Department, Superintendency of Banking, Insurance and Private Pension Funds).
- From Uruguay: Mario Bergara (Governor, Central Bank).

Francisco Ceballos did an invaluable job of coordinating and putting together the material for this book. We also benefited from excellent research assistance at different stages of the project provided by Matías Antonio, Mariana Barrera, Patricia Caraballo, Francisco Ceballos, Luciano Cohan, Juan José Cortina, Juan Miguel Cuattromo, Federico Filippini, Ana Gazmuri, Julian Genoud, Julian Kozlowski, Laura Malatini, Lucas Nuñez, Paula Pedro, Virginia Poggio, Juliana Portella de Aguiar Vieira, Gustavo Saguier, Mauricio Tejada, Patricio Valenzuela, Luis Fernando Vieira, Tomás Williams, and Gabriel Zelpo. For competent administrative assistance, we thank Erika Bazan Lavanda and Ruth Delgado. For financial support we are grateful to the LAC region, the Spanish Fund for Latin America and the Caribbean (SFLAC), and the Knowledge for Change Program (KCP).

Abbreviations

AFP	Administradoras Privadas De Fondos De Pensiones
AMC	asset management company
ASBA	Asociación de Supervisores Bancarios de las Americas
ATM	automated teller machines
AUM	assets under management
BCBS	Basel Committee on Banking Supervision
BCP	Basel Core Principles for Effective Banking Supervision
BRS	Survey of Bank Regulation and Supervision around the World
CAF	Corporación Andina de Fomento
CDS	credit default swap
CGAP	Consultative Group to Assist the Poor
CNBV	National Banking and Securities Commission (Mexico)
CP	core principle
CRR	cash reserve ratio
DR	depository receipt
DTI	debt service to income
DXY	U.S. dollar index
EMBI	Emerging Market Bond Index
ETF	exchange-traded fund
FDI	foreign direct investment
FDIC	Federal Deposit Insurance Corporation
FM	frontier markets
FPC	first principal component
FSAP	Financial Sector Assessment Program
GDP	gross domestic product
GDPPC	gross domestic product per capita
GMM	Generalized Method of Moments
G-7	Group of Seven
HY	high yield
LAC	Latin America and the Caribbean
LMF	Lane and Milesi-Ferretti
LTV	loan-to-value ratio
marcap	market capitalization

MSCI	Morgan Stanley Capital International
MOU	memorandum of understanding
NAFIN	Nacional Financiera
NGO	nongovernmental organization
PC1	first principal component
PCE	peripheral core economy
PFA	pension fund administrator
PPP	purchasing power parity
SIFI	systemically important financial institution
SBS	Superintendencia De Banca, Seguros y AFP del Peru
SME	small and medium enterprise
VaR	value at risk

Overview

Emerging Issues in Financial Development: Lessons from Latin America

Francisco Ceballos, Tatiana Didier, and
Sergio L. Schmukler

Introduction

Since the 1990s, financial systems around the world, and especially those in developing countries, have gained in soundness, depth, and diversity, prompted in part by a series of financial sector and macroeconomic reforms aimed at fostering a market-driven economy in which finance plays a central role. Latin America and the Caribbean (LAC) has been one

The authors work for the World Bank in, respectively, the Development Economics Research Group (pancho.ceballos@gmail.com), the Office of the Chief Economist for Latin America and the Caribbean Region (tdidier@worldbank. org), and the Development Economics Research Group (sschmukler@worldbank. org). The views expressed here are those of the authors and do not necessarily represent those of the World Bank.

1

of the regions at the forefront of these changes, and it serves as a good laboratory for seeing where the challenges in financial development lie.[1] After a history of recurrent instability and crises (a LAC trademark), financial systems in the region appear well poised for rapid expansion. Indeed, since the last wave of financial crises that swept through the region in the late 1990s and early 2000s, the size of banking systems has increased (albeit from a low base), local currency bond markets have developed (both in volume and reach over the yield curve), stock markets have expanded, and derivative markets—particularly currency derivatives—have grown and multiplied. Institutional investors have become more important, making the financial system more complex and diversified. Moreover, important progress has been made in financial inclusion, particularly through the expansion of payments, savings, and credit services for lower-income households and microenterprises.[2] As evidence of their new soundness and resilience, LAC financial systems, with the exception of those in some Caribbean countries, weathered the global financial crisis of 2008–09 remarkably well.

The progress in financial development in LAC no doubt reflects governments' substantial efforts to provide an enabling environment. This includes lower macroeconomic volatility, more independent and better-anchored currencies, increased financial liberalization, lower currency mismatches and foreign debt exposures, enhanced effectiveness of regulation and supervision, and notable improvements in the underlying market infrastructure (trading, payments, custody, clearing, and settlement, for example).[3]

Despite all the gains in financial development, the intensity of financial sector reforms implemented over the past 20 years in many countries has not led to the expected increase in the size and depth of their financial systems. For example, LAC countries went through an aggressive financial liberalization process and worked vigorously to adopt internationally recognized regulatory and supervisory standards. Nonetheless, in many respects, the actual size and depth of LAC's financial systems remain underdeveloped by international comparisons—notably, bank credit to the private sector and liquidity in the domestic equity market. The expansion of bank credit, for instance, has been biased in favor of financing consumption rather than production. Furthermore, the provision of long-term finance—whether to households, firms, or infrastructure—remains below what many economists and policy makers desire.

This book studies the recent history of financial sector development and reforms in the LAC region and compares it to other developing and developed countries to shed light on the key obstacles to financial development, both past and future. This study is particularly timely in the wake of the global financial crisis that began in 2008, as our assumptions about the underpinnings of efficient and well-functioning markets undergo close scrutiny. The challenges for policy makers of ensuring a future of sustained development in a more globalized and possibly more turbulent world may have little to do with the challenges they faced in the past. Rather than going into sector-specific issues, the book focuses on the main architectural issues, overall perspectives, and interconnections. Its value thus hinges on its holistic view of the development process, its broad coverage of the financial services industry (not just banking), its emphasis on comparisons and benchmarking, its systemic perspective, and its explicit effort to incorporate the lessons from the recent global financial crisis. This book builds on and complements several overview studies on financial development both in LAC and in the developing world more broadly that have been published in the past decade, including those by the World Bank.[4]

This book is related to a separate Flagship Report entitled *Financial Development in Latin America and the Caribbean: The Road Ahead*, by Augusto de la Torre, Alain Ize, and Sergio Schmukler.[5] Although a reader may find similarities between this book and the Flagship Report, they complement each other in important ways. While much of the material for the Flagship Report draws on material in this book, the report ultimately reflects the views of its authors and thus differs at times from the messages here. This book selects the best background papers and reflects the views of their authors, who stand as experts in their individual fields, thus providing the reader with a set of valuable differing perspectives. The book also covers material not contained in the Flagship Report or anywhere else in the literature. It considerably extends the analyses and discussions of important topics for LAC's financial development, such as globalization, access to finance, the role of institutional investors, macroprudential policies, and systemic regulation and supervision. Furthermore, it covers additional aspects of the financial development process and focuses on the broader set of LAC countries. Finally, the audiences who benefit from the two products are likely to differ. While the Flagship Report will certainly benefit practitioners, policy makers, and specialized reporters, this book is likely to be of interest to academics and experts in the field eager to learn more about specific aspects of financial development in LAC that are relevant to other regions as well. Because the papers are presented as separate, self-contained chapters, the topics under discussion will be much more accessible to readers with varying interests.

The chapters in this book cover different issues related to financial development in LAC. Chapters 1 through 5 attempt to ascertain where the region's financial development lies, analyzing in detail some of the reasons and policy implications underlying its gaps in banking depth and equity liquidity, as well as the links between financial development and financial globalization. Chapters 6 and 7 consider two themes that are central to the region's financial development: long-term finance and the role of the state in risk bearing. Chapters 8 through 11 deal with regulation and supervision, first taking stock of the progress in the region and then analyzing the challenges LAC faces on three main facets of systemic oversight: macroprudential policy, microsystemic regulation, and systemic supervision. Taken together, the chapters offer a comprehensive analysis of the status, prospects, and challenges of sustainable financial development in the region.

The rest of the overview is structured as follows. Section 2 provides a very brief account of the different views that guided the financial development process in the LAC region and in many other countries around the world, putting in perspective the different chapters in the book while assessing LAC's current status. Section 3 describes the chapters related to where LAC stands in its financial development process. Section 4 summarizes the chapters that deal with promoting some aspects of financial development. Section 5 describes the chapters on regulation and supervision. Section 6 discusses some of the policy implications.

Perspectives on Financial Development

Two major LAC-specific historical experiences were critical to shaping the conventional wisdom on financial development in the region over the past 20 years. The first is the state dirigisme over the financial sector that dominated the continent during the era of import-substitution industrialization, especially during the 1960s and 1970s; that experience resulted in atrophied financial systems and large fiscal costs associated with mismanaged public banks. The second is the painful experience with the region's recurrent and often devastating currency, debt, and banking crises, particularly during the 1980s and 1990s. These crises illustrate the dangers that poor macroeconomic fundamentals pose for globalized financial systems. They set back financial development by years and had major adverse effects on growth, employment, and equity.[6] Moreover, as the 1990s unfolded, the wave of financial liberalization that heralded the shift away from state interventionism interacted in perverse ways with underlying macroeconomic vulnerabilities, exacerbating financial instability. This led the reform agenda to put an increasing emphasis on regulatory frameworks and the institutional enabling environment—an agenda on which LAC has embarked with great vigor, particularly since the second half of the 1990s.

These experiences—together with a worldwide intellectual shift in favor of free market economics—gave rise to a relatively strong consensus in the region on a financial development policy agenda based on four basic endeavors. The first was to *get the macro right,* which reflected the conviction that unlocking the process of financial development had to start with macroeconomic stability. It entailed, in particular, the cultivation of local currency as a reliable store of value that could underpin financial contracts. Over the past 20 years, ensuring stable and low inflation has thus become the first order of business in financial development. In addition, fiscal reform and the development of local currency public bond markets were viewed as natural complements to monetary reform.

The second endeavor was to *let financial markets breathe*. Initially, this was mainly manifested in a rapid process of financial liberalization.[7] Subsequently, it incorporated efforts to strengthen the multiple facets (institutional, informational, and contractual) of the enabling environment. All of this was accompanied by efforts to enhance market discipline, which included a sharp reduction or elimination of the direct intervention of the state in financial activities, including the state's tendency to move quickly to bail out troubled institutions.

The third endeavor was to *converge toward Basel-inspired standards of prudential regulation and supervision*. Before the global financial crisis, the focus was on idiosyncratic risks, not on systemic risks. The endeavor also favored limiting the perimeter of prudential regulation to deposit-taking institutions. The underlying assumptions were that the soundness of individual financial intermediaries implied the soundness of the financial system and that well-informed and sophisticated players outside the core banking system would discipline each other.

The fourth endeavor was to *promote the broadening of access to financial services* for the underserved (that is, small farmers, microentrepreneurs, small and medium enterprises, or SMEs, and low-income households). This was added to the policy agenda but only more recently and was spurred by enthusiastic support from multilateral development banks, nongovernmental organizations, and foundations (for example, the Gates Foundation). It was also boosted by the microfinance revolution, in which LAC played a prominent role.[8]

As the LAC region revisits its policy tenets, this book provides an in-depth stock taking of its financial systems and a forward-looking assessment of the main financial development issues. Many questions still remain on the extent and type of financial development. However, the reforms undertaken to secure macroeconomic stability and to promote market-friendly policies seem to have at least paid off handsomely during the recent global financial crisis.[9] In contrast to the G-7 countries, whose financial systems nearly collapsed, and, more important, to the troubled economic and financial history of LAC, no domestic banking system crisis occurred in the region.[10]

Although the global financial crisis did not wreak havoc on LAC's financial system, it has raised questions about the process of financial development. It illustrated that apparent *macroeconomic stability* (for example, the "great moderation" of low inflation and output volatility, accompanied by low interest rates) can potentially contribute to unsustainable financial development. The crisis showed that *market discipline* can fail even in financially developed economies, in the land of well-informed and sophisticated agents (such as commercial bank treasurers, investment bankers, fund managers, stock brokers, derivatives traders, and rating agencies). The crisis also demonstrated that the *Basel-inspired oversight program* had major flaws, partly because it was based on the great fallacy of composition—the soundness of the parts does not guarantee the soundness of the whole. The crisis also suggested that the links between financial stability and financial development are much more complex than previously thought. Finally, it raised red flags on policies that seek to broaden *financial access* too aggressively, uncovering significant tensions between financial inclusion (for example, the drive to make every household a homeowner) and financial sustainability. Researchers and policy makers, therefore, are left to reassess these four endeavors.

As the global financial crisis has taught us, the reassessment of the financial development process needs to consider at least two fundamental themes: first, that the financial development process itself can lead to financial instability and, second, that, to avoid such instability, the relationship between financial markets and the state needs to be rethought. Both themes are of significant and increasing relevance to LAC countries. The region's financial systems have experienced strong expansionary pressures, not least due to surging capital inflows, and this has posed risks of financial excesses and bubbles. In turn, the premium on quality financial development policies has been raised, thereby highlighting the need for a more effective complementarity between the role of markets and the role of the state. As summarized below, the discussion of these issues in subsequent chapters will help readers understand not only the current state of LAC's financial development process but also the state of its policy and reform agenda.

What Is the State of Financial Development in LAC?

Chapters 1 and 2 provide a foundation for the subsequent discussions by offering a comprehensive description of the current scope, depth, and composition of financial systems in LAC countries.

Chapter 1, by Tatiana Didier and Sergio Schmukler, systematically reviews the current state of financial development across seven of the largest countries in LAC, the so-called LAC7 group, comprising Argentina, Brazil, Chile, Colombia, Mexico, Peru, and Uruguay, and compares it with other regions and countries. Over the past two decades, financial systems in the region have become both more complex and deeper along several dimensions in ways that are consistent with the broad patterns described above. There has been a transition from a mostly bank-based model to a more complete and interconnected one in which bond and equity markets have increased in both absolute and relative sizes, institutional investors (mutual funds, pension funds, and insurance companies) have played a more central role, and the overall number and sophistication of participants have increased. Significantly, the strengthening of monetary management has allowed financing to shift toward the longer term and into local currency.

The authors also present some evidence that LAC's financial systems remain underdeveloped—relative to other emerging and developed regions—in some key respects. The stagnation of domestic bank financing has only been partially offset by other types of credit. Credit to households (that is, consumption financing) has expanded at the expense of firm and housing finance. Bond markets have developed but still remain small by several standards, especially private bond markets. Moreover, domestic equity markets in LAC have remained illiquid and highly concentrated, and insurance is still relatively underdeveloped. While institutional investors have become sophisticated and large, a significant share of their portfolios continues to be allocated to government bonds and bank deposits. There is nonetheless a large heterogeneity within the LAC region.

While a lack of funding does not seem to be a major problem in LAC (indeed, some countries have imposed or are considering controls on cross-country capital flows), there is still progress to be made in broadening and deepening participation. A central concern about participation—which has received much attention from academics, policy makers, and practitioners—involves extending the reach of financial services not only to SMEs but also to lower-income groups that have historically been excluded from the financial ecosystem.

Chapter 2, by María Soledad Martínez Pería, surveys the topic of financial inclusion in LAC. To distinguish *access to* financial services from *use of* financial services, she analyzes indicators that capture not only supply but also demand. At first glance, indicators of access to and use of banking services in LAC suggest that the region lags developed and other developing economies. However, this lag shrinks when income level and population density are accounted for, suggesting that LAC7 is not obviously underperforming its peers. As with domestic and international financial development, LAC7 countries rank ahead of their neighbors in the region both in access to and use of financial services.

Slack demand appears to be an important reason for the low use of banking services, with most households claiming either an absence of funds or joblessness as the main reason for not holding a savings account. Distrust of banks and aversion to the risks of bank borrowing and debt more broadly also seem to influence the extent to which firms and individuals use banking services in LAC. Financial fees could also be playing a role, since the analysis indicates that these tend to be higher in Latin America than in other regions.

In addition, the author provides a panorama of the prospects in this arena by considering the extent of public policy concerns toward financial inclusion issues. A majority of governments in LAC7 have adopted policies to promote financial inclusion, such as mandating low-fee accounts, using the banking sector to channel government transfers, or allowing for correspondent bank arrangements and for the use of mobile branches. The attention given to this agenda has, however, been spottier in the rest of the region. In general, LAC7 governments appear to be doing more along this dimension than those in Eastern Europe and in developed countries. Areas that still deserve some attention include SME financing, bringing down the cost of financial services, and reforming creditor rights.

Chapter 3, by Augusto de la Torre, Erik Feyen, and Alain Ize, complements the analyses in chapters 1 and 2 by putting the evidence in perspective relative to the overall process of financial development. To the extent that the development path of financial systems indeed generally follows the same broad dynamic patterns across countries and over time, a systematic benchmarking methodology using a broad array of cross-country financial indicators is possible. This approach sheds light on the relative standing of key measures of a country's (or group of countries') financial development, given not just its level of overall economic development (as proxied by income per capita) but also the structural factors (largely exogenous to policy) that may play a role in financial development, such as country size and demographic structure. The gaps in financial development, with respect to developed countries and other relevant developing countries, might then be interpreted as reflecting deficits in policy and policy-shaped institutions, as well as in other areas.

Consistent with the findings in chapter 1, the analysis in chapter 3 shows that LAC7 is broadly on track with respect to many financial development indicators but lags substantially in some important ones relative to other relevant countries. In particular, there is a substantial "banking gap." Banking depth indicators (deposits and private credit) lag significantly, and the gap has widened over time. Bank efficiency, as measured by net interest rate margins, also lags, but this gap has shrunk. There is also an important "equity gap." While LAC countries are approximately on track on the size of their stock markets, they trail far behind on the liquidity of their domestic markets, and such gaps have been widening. Overall, these gaps are of concern because they coincide with some of the financial indicators that have been shown to be the best predictors of future growth in output.[11]

On the banking gap, the findings in the chapter indicate that it reflects LAC's turbulent financial history to a large extent. The region has not yet fully recovered from the repeated credit crashes of the past. This puts the spotlight squarely on the need to ensure financial sustainability through an appropriate mix of oversight and development-oriented policies. But, consistent with the findings in chapter 2, a limited demand for credit (that is, a lack of bankable projects)—possibly reflecting LAC's mediocre output growth—also seems to explain a sizable portion of the gap. Here, the possible policy responses go much beyond the financial sector, of course. Growth-inducing financial policies, such as those that facilitate longer-maturity loans for SMEs or infrastructure projects, should also be called for. In addition, overcoming the banking gap has to do with addressing the remaining agency frictions. Interestingly, in LAC the main residual bottleneck is contractual (contract enforcement, creditor rights) rather than informational. The degree of competition (or lack thereof) and extent of informality in LAC vis-à-vis its benchmarks do not seem to account for a significant portion of the gap. Of course, this is not to say that a considerable improvement in these aspects would not have positive effects on the depth of the banking systems.

In relation to LAC's domestic trade in equities, the analysis in chapter 3 indicates that both agency and collective frictions contribute to explaining the observed gap. As also argued in chapters 1 and 4, the substitution of domestic markets by foreign ones under the pull of a bigger (more liquid and connected) marketplace is a first obvious explanation. However, because similar patterns are not observed in other regions, the obvious issue is why it may be true in LAC. While high concentration may also have played a role, determining the direction of causality is tricky, as a lack of liquidity also hinders the deconcentration of equity holdings. Chapter 1 argues that the large preponderance of buy-and-hold institutional investors also seems to have played some role, as further discussed in chapter 6, as LAC's turbulent history probably did as well, much as in the case of the banking gap. However, it is still puzzling that equity markets have not done better in recent years, despite the improved macrofinancial stability.

Chapter 4, by Tatiana Didier and Sergio Schmukler, explores the tight interplay between the financial development and the financial globalization processes. The evidence in the chapter shows that over the past decade, international financial integration has continued to increase in the developed and, to a lesser extent, most of the developing world. In the case of LAC, the financial internationalization process stabilized somewhat during the first decade of the 2000s, in contrast to the region's leading role in this process during the 1990s. Nevertheless, by the end of 2010, the region still showed a degree of financial globalization comparable to that of other emerging regions.

This increased financial globalization has been a widespread two-way process, with greater participation not only of foreigners in local markets but also of residents in foreign markets. Foreigners seem to act mostly as investors in emerging markets, as they typically do not seek financing in these markets. Emerging market residents, however, use foreign markets as investors as well as borrowers, tapping a much wider range of instruments. The evidence hints at a gradual but significant change in the nature of new bond and equity financing by the private sector in emerging countries and in LAC7 in particular, where international markets have become more important relative to domestic markets. Such a shift has been accompanied by increased liquidity abroad, possibly suggesting a shift of equity trading to foreign markets as well. However, in general most domestic borrowers seldom tap into foreign capital markets—which continue to show high concentration, with a few firms capturing the bulk of the financing activity—despite the fact that financing in foreign markets still boasts some positive developments, such as longer maturities and even incipient bond issuance denominated in local currency. In stark contrast, bond financing by the public sector has been shifting to local markets. These trends in the use of foreign markets by the public and private sectors of emerging economies in fact reinforce the developments in domestic markets documented in chapter 1.

A final interesting feature of the recent financial globalization process is the safer form of financial integration arising from the changing structure of external assets and liabilities. Emerging economies have typically become net creditors in debt assets and net debtors in equity assets. Such a composition of foreign assets and liabilities is particularly beneficial in times of turbulence, as balance sheet effects now typically work in their favor. In the case of LAC, the region has accompanied the global process of safer financial integration with lower debt liabilities and higher reserve assets, although equity liabilities continue to be dominated on average by foreign direct investment rather than by portfolio equity, consistent with the shortcomings of the local equity markets. Such a change in the structure of the external assets and liabilities might play a key contributing role in avoiding the downside risks of financial globalization.

Chapter 5, by Eduardo Levy-Yeyati and Tomás Williams also discusses the issue of financial globalization. Because of the way it is often measured, financial globalization is generally perceived to have grown in recent years, according to the available evidence. Contrary to this conventional belief, the authors argue that during the first decade of the 2000s, financial globalization both in LAC and in other emerging markets has grown only marginally and much more slowly than in more developed countries. In particular, once price effects are taken into account, the trend of growth in cross-border equity holdings weakens considerably, in contrast with the view of a proactive relocation of international capital toward emerging markets and in line with the discussion in chapter 4. Moreover, the authors argue that international portfolio diversification (a welfare-improving source of consumption smoothing) has been, at best, limited and declining.

The chapter also revisits the recent empirical literature on the implications of financial globalization for local market deepening, international risk diversification, and financial contagion more broadly. Financial globalization has indeed fostered domestic market deepening in good times, and it has been a driving force in the process of developing on-shore financial intermediation and financial de-dollarization. Hence, financial globalization has played a supporting role in the buildup of the growing resilience of the developing world, particularly in LAC7 countries. However, financial globalization does not seem to have yielded the dividends of consumption smoothing predicted by the theoretical literature. Moreover, the procyclical nature of portfolio flows, which typically retrench to core markets during episodes of turmoil, may amplify the effects of global business cycles on the emerging world in an undesirable way.

Promoting Financial Development

Chapters 6 and 7 shift gears and narrow the focus on two issues at the core of the sustainable financial development process: long-term finance and the risk-bearing role of the state. While LAC has made much progress in lengthening contracts, notably the maturity structure of public bonds as documented in chapter 1, much remains to be done. For example, policy makers had hoped that defined-contribution pension funds would help lengthen maturities and overcome the lack of liquidity, but, unfortunately, their portfolios continue to be concentrated in public sector bonds, short-duration bank deposits, and highly liquid securities. At the same time, with the demise of the monoline insurers, the public sector remains the only entity able to provide, guarantee, or enhance long-term debt finance. All of this is taking place in an environment in which the region is awash with investable funds, which is all the more puzzling. Clearly, going long is harder than often believed.

Chapter 6, by Claudio Raddatz, delves into this topic with a particular focus on institutional investors, discussing important issues such as the implications of their investment style on available assets, conflicts of interest between individual investors and the institutions channeling their savings, and the design of regulatory frameworks. As documented in chapter 1, nonbank financial intermediaries, such as pension funds, mutual funds, and insurance companies, are playing an increasing role in credit provision and asset management in LAC, with bonds and equities becoming more prominent sources of financing for firms and means of investment for households. The ensuing increase in complexity of financial instruments and in the intermediation process gives rise to a number of agency problems that are unfamiliar to individuals accustomed to operating in bank-based systems. The author describes these problems and discusses their relevance for LAC countries in light of the current (but evolving) financial environment. He also takes stock of the lessons learned in countries where these intermediaries have become systemically important (most notably the United States).

The evidence and discussion suggest that the incentives faced by institutional investors and other financial intermediaries matter for their asset allocation, including their risk-taking behavior and their investment horizon. In LAC, these incentives have so far led investors to favor low-risk and short-term assets. While restrictions to the supply of investable assets do not seem to explain the results fully, regulatory incentives appear to play an important role vis-à-vis direct and indirect market incentives, and especially for pension funds. These incentives are particularly noticeable in the way Chile's pension funds coordinate investment decisions around industry benchmarks. It points to the fact that the regulation of institutional investors has to deal with (perhaps unanticipated) trade-offs in an environment marked by asymmetric information and conflicts of interest. Central among these trade-offs is the regulators' short-term monitoring, which is intended to anticipate potentially large negative outcomes, and the ability and means of institutional investors to take advantage of (socially desirable) investments with high long-run but volatile short-run returns.

Finally, the author emphasizes the key role that conflicts of interest and related lending play in the region. Concentrated corporate ownership structures and the prevalence of financial conglomerates in several orbits of financial services make these issues particularly important for Latin American countries. The predominance of financial conglomerates in the LAC region also brings too-big-to-fail considerations to the forefront of the policy debate. Arguably, even in the presence of firewalls, troubles in one segment of the operations of a financial conglomerate may spread to other segments through contingent credit lines, equity values, or brand association, creating a systemic impact. A systemic approach to regulation that considers these interconnections would thus help reduce the possibility of "tunneling" (that is, the movement of resources within a given corporate structure from firms where the controller has relatively few cash flow rights to firms where those are higher), regulatory arbitrage, and systemic shocks to the financial system, all of which work against investors and in favor of the owners of the conglomerates. Chapter 10 returns to the issue of systemic supervision.

Chapter 7, by Deniz Anginer, Augusto de la Torre, and Alain Ize, revisits the role of the state in financial risk bearing, a topic that has gained greater visibility in the aftermath of the global financial crisis. The authors analyze this theme from the perspective of the underlying frictions. It starts by reminding the reader that over the past half-century or so, LAC has undergone large paradigm swings, from state dirigisme to market laissez-faire, and eventually to a more eclectic view. Throughout these phases, agency frictions and social externalities permeated the debate. At the same time, a parallel debate developed on public banks' second-tier role in the provision of guarantees.

The authors thus review in some depth the conceptual justifications for public financial risk bearing. They first argue that risk aversion is central to guarantees more broadly. Without risk aversion, no guarantee program, whether private or public, can be justified. In a context of risk aversion among financial system participants, externalities alone justify subsidies but not guarantees, whereas agency frictions alone justify private but not public guarantees. Thus, public guarantees can be justified only in the presence of risk aversion and agency frictions (that concentrate risk through skin-in-the-game requirements) when coupled with collective frictions (that limit the scope for spreading that risk among market participants). Hence, it is the state's natural advantage in resolving collective action (instead of agency) frictions that justifies public (rather than private) guarantees. The state is then naturally called to play to its strengths to complement markets rather than to substitute for them.

The authors conclude that focusing on the role of the state from this perspective raises a policy agenda that is as broad as it is thorny. A key implication is that states, before providing guarantees, should first exhaust efforts to spread risk through private guarantees and private risk sharing. The state can promote participation without taking risk itself through policies that directly ease the frictions (where, for instance, a development bank acts itself as coordinator) or through policies that mandate or gently coerce participation, as in the case of the mandatory contributions to privately administered pension funds. Given the positive externalities, the state can also use well-targeted subsidies as part of such interventions.

Dealing with Prudential Oversight

LAC's turbulent macrofinancial history has also stimulated efforts to overhaul regulation and supervision—that is, to improve prudential oversight. Indeed, when many developed country supervisors were bent on easing intermediation through more market-friendly regimes and less expensive capital and liquidity buffers, many LAC countries moved in the opposite direction.

Chapter 8, by Socorro Heysen and Martín Auqui, shows that progress has also been uneven, both within and across regions. They conduct an econometric analysis of assessments of compliance with Basel Core Principles over the past 13 years and find that LAC7 countries generally perform better than other countries in the LAC region, even after controlling for different levels of economic development.

The analysis also suggests that there are important differences across supervision areas, with some issues understandably more difficult to tackle than others. Two basic issues concerning the legal framework—the independence of bank supervisors and their legal protection—emerge as still problematic in many LAC countries. Moreover, there is some unevenness on regulatory issues as well. Many countries have still not fully met the minimum Basel I international standards on capital requirements, and the implementation of Basel II has been limited in the region. While LAC7 countries have recently taken some preliminary though important steps toward compliance with Basel III reforms, the rest of the region is markedly silent on its implementation. However, in many areas, including on the regulation of credit risk, there has been substantial progress. On the basic supervisory issues, LAC7 countries again tend to perform better than the rest of the LAC region, suggesting that effective implementation might be a problem mostly in the lower-income countries. Nonetheless, important progress has been made across the region, including a gradual shift to risk-based supervision. Finally, on consolidated and cross-border supervision, a complex issue that to some extent prefigures the challenges of systemic oversight, most LAC countries have had a harder time. While LAC7 again exceeds its benchmark, opaque conglomerate structures, high ownership concentration, and insufficient cooperation and coordination among supervisors combine to make the challenge even more difficult. Effective cross-border cooperation also remains a major challenge, all the more so in LAC, given the importance of foreign banking.

All in all, LAC now has a much better foundation on which to build and deal with the new challenges of systemic oversight in the aftermath of the global financial crisis—namely, connecting the parts and understanding how one may affect the other, building up a proactive capacity to deal with unstable market dynamics, and thinking about developmental and prudential policies as two sides of the same coin. In view of lead times and longer-term dynamics, now is the time to think about the future. LAC seems well poised for the road ahead. Its prudential buffers are currently high, supervisors across the region have made important strides toward improving traditional oversight, and LAC's numerous past crises have given its supervisors a definite edge.

Chapter 9, by César Calderón and Luis Servén, reviews the potential benefits and challenges of macroprudential policy in LAC. The chapter starts with a thorough comparative analysis of financial cycles around the world. The empirical evidence shows that LAC credit cycles are generally more protracted and abrupt than those in other emerging and developed countries. Likewise, cyclical fluctuations in bank leverage, housing prices, and real exchange rates are also more pronounced in LAC, especially in the downturn phases of the cycle. The unconditional probability of banking crises and the frequency of crash landings following lending booms are also higher in LAC. These facts echo the history of macroeconomic instability in the region. They imply that management of financial risks over the cycle represents an even larger policy concern in LAC than elsewhere.

In considering policies for managing systemic risk over the cycle, the authors argue that the main objective should not be to eliminate the financial cycle, but rather to make the financial system more resilient while tackling the externalities that amplify cycles and promote an excessive buildup of risk. A high priority should thus be placed on objectives such as removing any existing procyclicality in macroeconomic policies and traditional regulations, building financial system resilience to cyclical fluctuations, or dampening the cyclical fluctuations themselves. However, the authors note the need for much more research and testing. How to measure the buildup of risk is a particularly difficult challenge. In emerging regions, such as LAC, very close monitoring of credit accelerations is likely to be needed to disentangle hazardous credit booms from desirable long-term financial deepening. More broadly, the quest for developing a

robust macroprudential policy framework faces a number of other unre-
solved issues, including finding a proper balance between buffering the
financial system and dampening the cycle and between institution-specific
and systemwide triggers and targets, between price-based and quantity-
based tools, and between rules and discretion.

It is worth pointing out, however, that on many of these issues, LAC
is on a par with other regions. In fact, many LAC countries have already
introduced countercyclical provisioning or capital requirements. Several
countries in the region have used reserve requirements to help manage
capital inflows and the credit cycle. Furthermore, many LAC countries
have recently introduced regulations to limit the risks associated with
foreign currency exposures, which are also systemic in nature and similar
in spirit to the systemic regulations currently being debated to manage
credit cycles.

The authors also note that reforms in monetary management, as well
as macroprudential management, may be called for. In view of recent
evidence showing that low interest rates in the developed world promote
the search for yield among investors and encourage banks to push the risk
frontier, timely monetary tightening may also contribute to maintaining
prudent lending standards in the upswing phase of the cycle. However, it
is also worth noting that more active macroprudential management can
help relieve some of the pressures from monetary policy, thereby helping reconcile inflation and exchange rate targets in economies with open
capital accounts—an issue dear to the hearts of many central bankers in
LAC. Countercyclical deployment of fiscal policy would, of course, also
help achieve financial stability.

Chapter 10, by Mariano Cortés, Miquel Dijkman, and Eva Gutierrez,
shifts the focus from connecting the system through time to connecting
the parts to the whole, that is, from macroprudential management to
microsystemic regulation. The chapter starts by reviewing the key issues
associated with the setting of the outer perimeter of regulation. Although
regulatory perimeters are already widely extended in LAC, this issue
remains relevant. For starters, boundary concerns—the incentives to
migrate intermediation to the less regulated domains—continue to exist.
Important in this context is the issue of resource allocation. Spreading
resources too thinly may compromise the effectiveness of supervision,
providing an unwarranted sense of comfort and possibly breeding moral
hazard. To save on expenses, some countries have resorted to auxiliary models of delegated supervision for smaller credit cooperatives.
Another form of delegation could involve allowing those entities that
fund themselves only from regulated intermediaries to be exempt from
prudential regulation. Still another approach is to grant the supervisor
statutory authority to readily extend the perimeter as circumstances warrant (as in the Dodd-Frank Act). However, exercising such discretionary powers is particularly challenging, given the region's administrative

law framework. Another topic of discussion in the policy debate on the most appropriate boundary for regulatory supervision comes from the fact that systemic risk that builds up outside the financial system may end up contaminating the system through its impact on the markets in which both financial and nonfinancial firms participate or through common ownership.

The authors also argue that regulatory arbitrage can take place within the perimeter of regulation when different silos are regulated differently. Indeed, licenses granted to intermediaries in the LAC region tend to have a narrow scope of permissible activities, typically separating commercial from investment banking and insurance from banking more broadly. The current silo approach is hindered, moreover, by the weaknesses in consolidated regulation. The authors argue that one possible route for dealing with this issue is to pursue a fully uniform, risk-based approach in which all entities are similarly regulated, ultimately leading to universal licenses. There are, nonetheless, potential drawbacks to such a proposal: it is technically challenging; it could potentially lead to a loss of diversity, thus making the system more fragile; and it could foster the emergence of systemically important financial entities (SIFIs) that are deemed too big to fail.

Indeed, the region has many SIFIs, and there appears to be some consensus on the need to regulate them differentially. Implementing such a differential treatment will certainly be challenging in view of the data and analytical requirements. More important, the global financial crisis has highlighted the need to resolve unviable financial institutions, particularly SIFIs, in a nondestabilizing fashion. While the crises of LAC's past have led to the introduction of sophisticated frameworks for resolving bank failures in many countries in the region, these frameworks remain largely untested. In fact, crisis simulations conducted in several countries have revealed serious shortcomings in both tools and processes. Moreover, the development of systems for resolving the failure of financial conglomerates (including those that operate across borders) is still in its infancy.

Chapter 11, by Steven A. Seelig and Katia D'Hulster, discusses systemic supervision, an issue that has probably not received sufficient attention thus far in the public debate but that is nonetheless central to effective systemic oversight. The authors start by looking at the interface between regulation and supervision. The inherent tensions and complementarities between regulation and supervision are an essential part of the "rules versus discretion" debate. Hence, one of the main challenges of policy makers is to build sufficient discretion into the supervisory process (in a context of appropriate accountability) without relaxing regulations so much that prudential oversight loses its "teeth." The latter is an even greater challenge in civil law countries, such as those in LAC, where supervisors can usually take only those actions specified in laws and regulations.

Another key issue is how best to combine a top-down perspective with a bottom-up analysis. To be sure, one of the weaknesses in the financial stability analyses published by central banks has often been the absence of the supervisors' perspective on what is happening at individual institutions. The chapter argues that the necessary coordination—down to the technical staff level—for this process to succeed is certainly not trivial, particularly in countries where bottom-up supervision is conducted outside the central bank. A closely related (but conceptually distinct) issue is the relative emphasis on off-site versus on-site supervision. While one might think that—because it involves the forest more than the trees—systemic supervision is more about off-site, this is unlikely to be the case. Instead, systemic supervision calls for a review of on-site supervision, stressing its complementarities with off-site analysis.

According to the authors, the global financial crisis has called for a review of the role of market-based financial indicators and the reliance on market discipline. A key question arising from the crisis is not whether market discipline is good or bad, but instead how supervisors can make better use of market signals. For instance, when weak market signals constitute a severe limitation, policy makers may be significantly constrained in developing instruments (such as subordinated debt) that help price the risk and thereby facilitate risk discovery. Unless supported in some fashion by the state (and perhaps even subsidized), these instruments may simply be too expensive to see the light of day. The authors thus argue that an important research agenda for the region is to help design, introduce, and support the development of these instruments. Overall, an important requirement for proper market discipline is analysis and information. Because much information is a public good, one can easily argue that supervisory agencies should provide more of it, including information on (and better analysis of) the system as a whole, how it is wired and interconnected, and what the risks ahead are. When risks are detected, supervisors need not only to inform and guide but also to act.

Finally, the authors conclude that successfully implementing systemic supervision will require building up skills, which involves a quantum leap, not a marginal improvement. It will also require suitable organizational arrangements. The need for better coordination between monetary and prudential management with a systemic perspective naturally suggests that central banks will have to play a leading role. As central banks assume this role, however, it seems important not to compromise their independence. In the end, putting in place appropriate decision-making and interagency coordinating arrangements seems to deserve top priority. If a systemic oversight or financial stability council is set up, ensuring its accountability is crucial. Last but not least, cooperation across agencies needs to be encouraged. In addition to coordinating at home, supervisors will also need to coordinate better across borders. In LAC, the importance of foreign banks makes this an even greater priority.

Policy Implications

The chapters that follow yield many lessons and raise several issues for further research, many of them on the policy front. As the evidence presented in various chapters shows, LAC has made substantial progress in financial system development. First, there was a general financial deepening, with capital markets and institutional investors playing an increasingly important role and new markets and instruments springing up and making inroads. Consistent with this general deepening, the maturities of fixed-income instruments have lengthened considerably, yield curves have extended further into the long term, and there has been a broad-based, albeit certainly not yet complete, return to local currency (both in banking and in bonds). At the same time, the patterns of financial globalization have become safer, with lower debt liabilities and higher reserve assets. There has also been substantial progress in financial inclusion, particularly in LAC7 countries, which, in fact, now appear to be at least not behind and sometimes even ahead of their peers in this respect.

Yet significant gaps in LAC's financial development remain. First, the commercial banking sector underperforms both in size and in efficiency. Second, while there has been a substantial increase in consumer credit, this seems to have occurred largely at the expense of other types of lending, including the mortgage market, where LAC lags the most, but also firm financing. Third, the domestic equity market also underperforms in trading activity, if not in capitalization. Finally, the insurance industry lags in scope and size of assets. These gaps matter to the extent that they can constrain a country's growth potential, as well as its access to finance more broadly. By limiting intertemporal consumption smoothing, the gaps may also reduce welfare.

Moreover, there is substantial unevenness across the region. On the more positive side, important success stories—such as banking, corporate bonds, and insurance in Chile; equity and mutual funds in Brazil; or public debt in Brazil, Colombia, and Mexico—provide worthy examples to study and follow. Nonetheless, LAC countries, including those just mentioned, still face substantial challenges in establishing deep markets for long-term finance. In spite of the strong development of (and high fees charged by) asset managers, they continue to concentrate their portfolios in the shorter-term and more liquid securities. Moreover, they trade little. While the annuities industry in some countries, such as Chile, is a potential success story of how to help channel demand toward the longer and the less liquid securities, there are difficulties at the interface between pensions and annuities that most countries (to a greater or lesser extent) need to address.

A number of issues merit consideration in future research. A developmental policy agenda for the LAC region surely needs to aim at a better understanding of the nature and implications of LAC's gaps. Dealing with the banking gap should be the first order of business of this agenda. To what extent and in what ways are SMEs actually affected by a lack of credit? To what extent does the problem reside in the lack of bankable projects? Is lack of competition part of the problem? If so, what can be done about it? While research explores these questions, the policy agenda needs to focus on promoting productivity-oriented credit (firms, infrastructure, low-income households), which might include state interventions aimed at overcoming coordination failures, as well as interventions that offer well-targeted and well-priced credit guarantees to foster longer-term investments (including asset-backed securities or infrastructure bonds). Most important, however, sustainability is the name of the game: a slower but more sustainable, less fiscally risky approach is preferable to a more ambitious program of financial sector expansion that may overreach and therefore end badly.

On the equity gap, while a strengthening of the contractual environment would certainly help, more research is clearly needed to assess its impacts and uncover possible solutions. In addition, the ramifications of the link between the lack of stock trading and the efficiency of stock price discovery need to be ascertained. Research is also needed to assess how the lower liquidity of the stocks of smaller firms affects their price. As for solutions, while the region's atypically low turnover relative to the benchmark cannot be explained by size, size seems to matter immensely when it comes to policies for the development of local stock markets. With the exception of Brazil, this is the major challenge for LAC. While regional integration of stock exchanges might help overcome the constraints of market size, it does not necessarily solve the constraints associated with the small size of stock issues. Furthermore, additional research is needed to ascertain whether regional integration of stock markets can achieve any special benefits that could not, perhaps, be more effectively achieved through global integration. There is also a need to identify the governance frameworks that are appropriate to the larger as well as to the smaller stock markets. While further improvements in market infrastructure are, of course, welcome, they will probably help only at the margin. It might be the case that more can be done through venture capital funds (that is, through relationship-based, nonliquid equity finance) than through traditional market-based equity finance. If so, the emphasis should be put on ways to promote the growth of such funds. In the end, however, and in light of the dominance of institutional investors in the financial systems of the region, the restrictions set by regulators on the holding of stocks from smaller companies may considerably impair the feasibility of this approach.

With respect to the goal of lengthening financial contracts, there might be room for strengthening regulations that encourage longer-term investing. For life insurance companies, prudential regulation that encourages a matching of maturities may suffice. For pension funds, life-cycle funds or regulations that nudge defined-contribution funds into mimicking the investment behavior of defined-benefit funds could perhaps help lengthen their portfolios. In some cases, pension fund regulations may need to be revised to encourage investments in long instruments, such as infrastructure bonds, possibly with some partial public guarantees. Clearly, however, there is a line not to be crossed between internalizing the positive externalities of long-term finance and undermining pension funds' fiduciary responsibility by obliging them to invest in the pet political projects of the day. In view of consumers' and workers' bounded rationality and behavioral biases, regulations that, by default, channel their savings into investment portfolios that are the most appropriate for them might also be desirable. However, the scope of state intervention again clearly needs to be limited. A proper balance must be found between protecting those consumers who are clearly not equipped to manage their portfolios and encouraging those who are to do so, thereby enhancing market discipline.

In putting forward a financial development agenda, understanding the trade-offs between financial stability and financial development is key. While much has been written on stability issues since the global financial crisis, very little has been said on the links between stability and development. Indeed, despite such efforts as the establishment of the Financial Stability Board and the G-20, the international financial architecture is still exclusively focused on financial stability and is thus clearly unable to tackle the issues at the interface of financial development and financial stability. Finding the right balance between these two dimensions—a global challenge—takes on special characteristics in LAC. The current hands-on, silo-based, broad regulatory perimeter, innovation-cautious oversight has served the region well. However, some realignment may be needed as financial systems continue to mature and the intensity of cross-border competition increases. The more room LAC opens for markets to play and innovations to be introduced, though, the more it will need to rely on a well-targeted ex ante internalization of systemic risks and an ex post capacity to provide liquidity and absorb risks. The current developmental gaps are likely to complicate finding the proper trade-off, not least because they might feed resistance to the regulatory tightening associated with Basel III.

This trade-off is particularly important in promoting the nexus of finance and growth. It will involve the question of how to promote the "bright side" of financial development (more financing activity that spurs innovation and growth) without generating further problems with the "dark side" (the facets of financial activity that may engender "excessive" risks and may lead to crises). In LAC, with its large developmental gaps, one could take the view that the region is far from reaching a threshold where finance might be harmful (rather than beneficial) to growth, should one exist. Taking this view too strongly, however, would be unwise, given the growing interconnectedness and globalization of LAC's financial systems. Moreover, one can also argue that potential perils down the road should guide current policies. It is worth emphasizing that in LAC (and in other regions as well), the causality between finance and growth appears to be a two-way street. LAC's financial development gaps in part reflect the mediocre growth of the past. Therefore, much of the improvement of the regional underperformance in finance needs to take place outside finance, particularly in the growth, productivity, and competitiveness arenas. The history of mediocre growth also implies a need to focus more on financial policies that can help promote growth, as the latter will in turn help resolve the region's financial development gaps.

On the dark side of finance, much will need to be done on the regulatory front to deal adequately with the growing interconnectedness of financial markets and institutions. The starting point should be a revisiting of the outer perimeter of regulation. As for the inner perimeter, improvements in the oversight of conglomerates will in turn need to be paired with a revisiting and, possibly, a major overhaul of the regulatory and resolution framework for financial conglomerates as well as for the SIFIs. The improvements (as yet largely untested) that have already been introduced across the region in the resolution of individual financial institutions will now need to be extended to the resolution of financial groups and SIFIs, including those across borders. As for the SIFIs, while they will undoubtedly require tighter oversight, the region might want to avoid the U.S. example of formally anointing them as SIFIs. Instead, the intensity of supervision and tightness of regulation could be adjusted continuously (without sharp boundaries) according to criteria that apply to everyone. At the same time, the region will need to revamp its liquidity regulations to reflect a more systemic perspective, following to a large extent the emerging guidelines provided by Basel III.

Dealing with financial system dynamics will be another major component of LAC's systemic oversight reforms. The region will need to set its macroprudential policy objectives across a menu of progressively more ambitious goals, ranging from simply correcting the distortions brought about by traditional prudential norms to the most ambitious objective of dampening "excessive" fluctuations and passing through the intermediate goal of simply making financial systems more resilient to fluctuations. The goals and design of macroprudential tools and policies will also need to reflect the fact that LAC's financial cycles have been more frequent and pronounced and have ended badly more often than in other regions. The region's recurrent exposure to a potentially lethal mix of capital inflows and commodity price booms further raises the premium on quickly establishing or consolidating its macroprudential capacity.

On the brighter side, however, the floating exchange rate regimes that now prevail in much of LAC should help cushion shocks and enhance the scope for more active monetary and macroprudential home policies, even when the latter are asynchronous with those of the rest of the world. Nonetheless, macroprudential policy should clearly not be regarded as a magic bullet. While it can assist monetary policy, particularly by smoothing out the potential conflicts between monetary and exchange rate policies, it should be viewed as a complement to (not a substitute for) monetary (or fiscal) policies.

Notes

1. Throughout this book, we focus mostly on Latin America. However, we also present some evidence on Caribbean countries. Overall, we use the term *LAC* to refer to the region in general.

2. LAC has in fact been an important player in the worldwide microfinance revolution, which decisively shifted microfinance from a grant-intensive activity of nongovernmental organizations to a profitable, commercially viable banking business.

3. Financial sector reform agendas in LAC were often aided by Financial Sector Assessment Programs (FSAPs), undertaken jointly by the International Monetary Fund (IMF) and the World Bank in several countries in the region since 1998, as well as by technical assistance (including in the context of loan operations) provided by these institutions. Comprehensive FSAP documentation, including country reports and reviews of the program, can be found at http://worldbank. org/fsap. A fairly detailed documentation of the capital markets–related reforms undertaken by LAC during the 1990s and early 2000s can be found in de la Torre, Gozzi, and Schmukler (2007a, b). Chapter 8 of this book documents the progress in LAC with respect to banking supervision.

4. Other overview studies of LAC's financial sector include the following: the Inter-American Development Bank's 2005 report *Unlocking Credit: The Quest for Deep and Stable Bank Lending*, which focuses on the banking sector; the 2006 book by de la Torre and Schmukler, *Emerging Capital Markets and Globalization: The Latin American Experience*, which focuses on securities markets; the 2006 book by Stallings and Studart, *Finance for Development: Latin America in Comparative Perspective*; the Inter-American Development Bank's 2007 report *Living with Debt: How to Limit the Risks of Sovereign Finance*; and the Corporación Andina de Fomento's 2011 report *Servicios Financieros para el Desarrollo: Promoviendo el Acceso en América Latina*, which focuses on access to finance. Relevant overview studies by the World Bank on financial sector development issues with a global (rather than a LAC) focus include the following: the 2001 report *Finance for Growth: Policy Choices in a Volatile World*; the 2007 report *Finance for All? Policies and Pitfalls in Expanding Access*; and the 2013 *Global Financial Development Report, Rethinking the Role of the State*.

5. The Flagship Report, a set of presentations with graphs and tables for specific countries, and a press release are available at the LCR Chief Economist Office's website (www.worldbank.org/laceconomist) and a dedicated website (www.worldbank.org/lacfinancereport).

6. The uncertainty resulting from macroeconomic volatility—particularly high and unpredictable inflation—was deleterious to financial development, most of all for financing at the longer maturities. It corroded the role of money as a store of value, leading to a gradual buildup of currency and duration mismatches. The inflexible exchange rate regimes that were adopted in part to control inflation expectations instead exacerbated currency mismatches and made countries vulnerable to self-fulfilling currency attacks. This compounded the region's vulnerability

to currency crashes associated with unsustainable fiscal positions. Widespread mismatches, for their part, increased the fragility of financial systems to currency upheavals, interest rate volatility, and bank runs. In addition to their major—and well-known—adverse effects on growth and employment, financial crises have proven highly regressive for income and wealth distribution (see, for example, Halac and Schmukler 2004).

7. For a characterization of the financial liberalization sequencing debate, along with the relevant references, see chapter 4 of de la Torre and Schmukler (2006).

8. See, for instance, Robinson (2001), Yunus (2003), Armendáriz de Aghion and Morduch (2005), and Sengupta and Aubuchon (2008).

9. See, for example, Porzecanski (2009), IMF (2010), de la Torre et al. (2010), and Didier, Hevia, and Schmukler (2012).

10. According to IADB (2005), in recent history, LAC has been the geographical region of the world with the highest incidence of banking crises. In particular, 27 percent of LAC countries (35 percent excluding the Caribbean) experienced *recurrent* banking crises during the 1974–2003 period, compared to 13 percent in Sub-Saharan Africa, 11 percent in Eastern Europe and Central Asia, and 8 percent in East Asia and the Pacific.

11. See, for example, Beck and Levine (2004).

References

Armendáriz de Aghion, B., and J. Morduch. 2005. *The Economics of Microfinance.* Cambridge, MA: MIT Press.

Beck, T., and R. Levine. 2004. "Stock Markets, Banks, and Growth: Panel Evidence." *Journal of Banking and Finance* 28 (3): 423–42.

Corporación Andina de Fomento (CAF). 2011. *Servicios Financieros para el Desarrollo: Promoviendo el Acceso en América Latina.* Reporte de Economía y Desarrollo. Corporación Andina de Fomento. Bogotá, Colombia: CAF.

de la Torre, A., C. Calderón, T. Didier, T. Kouame, M. I. Reyes, and S. L. Schmukler. 2010. *The New Face of Latin America and the Caribbean: Globalized, Resilient, Dynamic.* World Bank Annual Meetings Report. Washington, DC: World Bank.

de la Torre, A., J. C. Gozzi, and S. Schmukler. 2007a. "Financial Development in Latin America: Big Emerging Issues, Limited Policy Answers." *World Bank Research Observer* 22 (1): 67–102.

———. 2007b. "Stock Market Development under Globalization: Whither the Gains from Reforms?" *Journal of Banking and Finance* 3 (16): 1731–54.

de la Torre, A., and S. Schmukler. 2006. *Emerging Capital Markets and Globalization: The Latin American Experience.* Washington, DC: World Bank; Palo Alto: Stanford University Press.

Didier, T., C. Hevia, and S. Schmukler. 2012. "How Resilient and Countercyclical Were Emerging Economies during the Global Financial Crisis?" *Journal of International Money and Finance* 31 (8): 2052–77.

Halac, M., and S. Schmukler. 2004. "Distributional Effects of Crises: The Financial Channel." *Economia* 5 (1): 1–67.

International Monetary Fund (IMF). 2010. *Meeting New Challenges to Stability and Building a Safer System.* Global Financial Stability Report. Washington, DC: IMF.

Inter-American Development Bank (IADB). 2005. *Unlocking Credit: The Quest for Deep and Stable Bank Lending.* Economic and Social Progress Report. Washington, DC: IADB.

———. 2007. *Living with Debt: How to Limit the Risks of Sovereign Finance.* Economic and Social Progress Report. Washington, DC: IADB.

Porzecanski, A. 2009. "Latin America: The Missing Financial Crisis." ECLAC Washington Office Studies and Perspectives Series 6, UN Economic Commission for Latin America and the Caribbean, Washington, DC.

Robinson, M. 2001. *The Micro Finance Revolution: Sustainable Finance for the Poor.* Washington, DC: World Bank; Baltimore: Open Society Institute.

Sengupta, R., and C. Aubuchon. 2008. "The Micro Finance Revolution: An Overview." *Federal Reserve Bank of St. Louis Review* (January/February). http://research.stlouisfed.org/publications/review/article/6256.

Stallings, B., and R. Studart. 2006. *Finance for Development: Latin America in Comparative Perspective.* Washington, DC: Brookings Institution; UN Economic Commission for Latin America and the Caribbean, Santiago, Chile.

World Bank. 2001. *Finance for Growth: Policy Choices in a Volatile World.* World Bank Policy Research Report. Washington, DC: World Bank; Oxford, UK: Oxford University Press.

———. 2007. *Finance for All? Policies and Pitfalls in Expanding Access.* World Bank Policy Research Report. Washington, DC: World Bank.

———. 2013. *Global Financial Development Report: Rethinking the Role of the State.* Washington, DC: World Bank.

Yunus, M. 2003. *Banker to the Poor: Micro-Lending and the Battle against World Poverty.* New York: Public Affairs.

1

Financial Development in Latin America and the Caribbean: Stylized Facts and the Road Ahead

Tatiana Didier and Sergio L. Schmukler

Abstract

In this chapter, we document the major trends in financial development in Latin America and the Caribbean (LAC) since the early 1990s. We compare trends in LAC with those in Asia, Eastern Europe, and

The authors work for the World Bank in, respectively, the Office of the Chief Economist for the Latin America and the Caribbean Region (tdidier@worldbank.org) and the Macroeconomics and Growth Team of the Development Research Group (sschmukler@worldbank.org). The chapter benefited from very helpful comments by Augusto de la Torre, Cesar Calderon, Asli Demirgüç-Kunt, Alain Ize, Eduardo Levy Yeyati, Guillermo Perry, Claudio Raddatz, Rodrigo Valdes, and participants at presentations held at the Bank of Korea International Conference 2011 (Seoul), the 12th Global Development Network Annual Meeting (Bogotá), the NIPFP-DEA Workshop (Delhi), ADBI (Tokyo), the World Bank (Washington, DC), IMF (Washington, DC), American University (Washington, DC), Central Bank of Brazil (Rio de Janeiro), Casa das Garças (Rio de Janeiro), Foro Internacional de Economía (Lima), ITAM (Mexico, DF), Central Bank of Uruguay (Montevideo), Central Bank of Paraguay (Asuncion), Paraguay Ministry of Finance (Asuncion), and University of Chile (Santiago de Chile). The authors are grateful to Francisco Ceballos, Luciano Cohan, Juan Cuattromo, Gustavo Meza, Paula Pedro, Virginia Poggio, Andres Schneider, Patricio Valenzuela, Luis Fernando Vieira, and Gabriel Zelpo for outstanding research assistance at various stages of this project. For help in gathering unique data, the authors wish to thank Mario Bergara (Central Bank of Uruguay), Samuel Fox (Fitch Ratings), Fabio Malacrida (Central Bank of Uruguay), and Carlos Serrano (National Banking Commission, Mexico), among many others. The views expressed here are those of the authors and do not necessarily represent those of the World Bank.

advanced countries, and we also compare countries within LAC. We show that financial systems in the LAC region, as in many other emerging economies, have become more diversified and more complex. In particular, domestic financial systems have become less bank based, with bond and stock markets playing a larger role; institutional investors have gained some space in channeling domestic savings, thus increasing the availability of funds for investment in capital markets; and several LAC economies have started to reduce currency and maturity mismatches. Nonetheless, a few large companies continue to capture most of the domestic savings. And because these trends have unfolded more slowly than promarket reformers had envisioned, broad, market-based financial systems with dispersed ownership have yet to materialize fully in LAC. As a result, convergence is still largely failing to happen, and the region's financial systems remain not only less developed than those of the advanced economies but also less developed than those of several other emerging economies, most notably those in Asia.

Introduction

Since the early 1990s, many economies in Latin America and the Caribbean (LAC) have undertaken significant efforts to expand the scope and depth of their financial systems. The literature suggests several reasons for doing so. Financial development has long been linked to faster growth and greater welfare (see, for example, Levine 1997, 2005; Luintel and Kahn 1999; Levine and Zervos 1996; King and Levine 1993a, 1993b). Increased access to financing has beneficial effects, especially for historically underserved segments, such as small and medium enterprises (SMEs) (see, for example, de la Torre, Martínez Pería, and Schmukler 2010; Beck, Demirgüç-Kunt, and Martínez Pería 2011; Beck and Demirgüç-Kunt 2006). A deep financial system has usually been perceived as more resilient to shocks and less prone to volatility and financial crises (see, for example, Easterly, Islam, and Stiglitz 2000; Aghion, Banerjee, and Piketty 1999; Acemoglu and Zilibotti 1997). These policy efforts have involved, among other things, improving access to banks (for savings, credit, and financial transactions in general) and developing capital markets as an alternative and competitor to the bank model, which is usually viewed as more costly.

The policy approach of countries in the LAC region to financial development has basically followed a model of dispersed ownership, or what can be called "the U.S. model." In this model, household savings are channeled directly into the capital markets, either through the retail market or, more generally, through financial intermediaries, such as pension funds, mutual funds, and insurance companies, that manage their savings. At the same time, firms can go directly to these markets to raise capital, which allows them to undertake riskier, longer-term investments than they would if they could raise funds only from banks. To entice households to put their savings in capital markets, firms protect shareholder rights, and market discipline helps punish firms (and financial intermediaries) that deviate from what is optimal for shareholders. In this model, risk is dispersed, idiosyncratic, and diversified. Banks play a less central role, competing with capital markets and financing projects that require more relationship lending. The role of the state in this model is to provide an enabling environment by safeguarding the investors and ensuring the stability of the financial system through regulation and supervision. The model entails a fundamental faith in free markets and competition.

Efforts at financial development have not been unique to LAC in this period, of course, as many emerging countries have also implemented significant promarket reforms. Initially, there were large-scale privatizations of state-owned companies (see, for example, de la Torre and Schmukler 2008; de la Torre, Gozzi, and Schmukler 2007a; Perotti and van Oijen 2001). Widespread pension system reforms, among others, introduced and established institutional investors, generating a significant supply of funds for the financial system. Financial markets were liberalized, and foreign banks were allowed to operate in domestic markets with the intention of channeling foreign savings into the domestic economy. Following the numerous financial crises of the 1990s and early 2000s, prudent macroeconomic and financial policies to foster growth, stability, and resilience were implemented. The goal was to adopt well-regarded international standards and to reduce mismatches, such as currency and maturity mismatches, while at the same time withdrawing the state from the markets and avoiding crowding out.

LAC's record on achieving reforms is mixed—the region has been at the forefront of implementing many reforms, although it has been lagging in others. For example, LAC has been a pioneer in pension fund reforms, switching from a defined-benefit, pay-as-you-go system to a defined-contribution one, where workers save by investing in financial instruments (see, for example, Kritzer, Kay, and Sinha 2011; Dayoub and Lasagabaster 2007). Countries in the region have also been leaders among emerging economies in opening up their financial markets to cross-border flows and to the entry of foreign financial institutions (see, for example, Cull and Martínez Pería 2010; Kaminsky and Schmukler 2008). Several LAC countries have tried to stabilize inflation by following floating exchange rate regimes and adopting inflation-targeting policies (see, for example, Schmidt-Hebbel and Corbo 2002; Mishkin 2000). Finally, many countries have actively fostered the development of long-term bond markets and a benchmark yield curve for the private sector by issuing debt in their domestic currencies. In contrast, a number of countries in the region have a long road ahead on regulatory issues. Many have still not fully met the minimum Basel I international standards on capital requirements, and the implementation of Basel II has thus far been limited in the region. While the LAC7 countries—Argentina, Brazil, Chile, Colombia, Mexico, Peru, and Uruguay—have recently taken some preliminary though important steps toward compliance with Basel III reforms, the rest of the region is markedly silent on its implementation (see chapter 8 in this volume).

The two decades of financial sector and macroeconomic reforms and, more recently, the global financial crisis provide us with a uniquely rich tapestry of themes and issues through which to review (and ponder) Latin America's financial development and its potential vulnerabilities, both present and future. The time is thus ripe for an in-depth evaluation of the returns on those efforts by taking stock of how these financial systems have developed and where they stand.

The conclusions in de la Torre and Schmukler (2008) and in other papers were based on data up to the early 2000s and suggested that outcomes did not match expectations and reform efforts. At that time, we were somewhat pessimistic about the prospects for financial sector improvement, given the difficulty of overcoming high systemic risk and volatility, the slow progress of financial development, and the large mismatches in currencies and maturities, all of which were the result of inherent deficiencies in emerging economies (see de la Torre and Schmukler 2004, 2008; de la Torre, Gozzi, and Schmukler 2007b). Other economists shared our pessimism, focusing on the metaphor of "original sin" in emerging economies—that is, the inability to issue long-term debt in their own currencies—as well as on outright dollarization and "sudden stops" that would subject the economies to frequent shutdowns of foreign financing (see, for example, Hausmann and Panizza 2003; Calvo and Reinhart 2000; Eichengreen and Hausmann 1999; Hausmann et al. 1999).

More recently, however, new data from the mid- to late-2000s and several anecdotal accounts suggest some reasons for optimism. Emerging economies have improved their macroeconomic performance, lowered inflation, and reduced fiscal deficits (Gourinchas and Obstfeld 2011). These policy achievements, together with high liquidity in international markets, have allowed emerging economies to issue long-term bonds in domestic markets, as foreign investors have expected further appreciations of local currency and entered local markets in search of higher yields. In addition, these economies weathered the storms of the recent global financial crisis relatively well, indicating the strength and resilience of their financial systems (see, for example, Didier, Hevia, and Schmukler 2011; Eichengreen 2009).

Even with these reasons for optimism, the path ahead will certainly be challenging, especially for policy makers. In particular, the old model of convergence to international standards is being questioned precisely because those standards are being revised in the wake of the 2008–09 global financial crisis. One example is the housing finance model fostered by public institutions like Freddie Mac and Fannie Mae in the United States, which other countries, such as Mexico, have also followed. Another example is the definition of the limits of regulation when banks and shadow banks are interconnected and when banks pose too high a systemic risk to be allowed to fail. This situation—wherein assets are excluded from banks' balance sheets through securitization and special-purpose vehicles—evolved in several emerging economies as capital markets were developing and other financial intermediaries arose. A third example is the need to provide better services to savers and investors, while monitoring the degree of risk, given the prevalence of global shocks. A fourth example is the increasing role of public banks as a way to foster access to finance in good times and bad.

The main goal of this chapter is to document some basic trends in the development of financial systems in LAC and in emerging economies more broadly. The primary value of this exercise is to put in perspective the absolute and relative size and the evolution of different components of the financial system using traditional and new indicators. We analyze both the borrowers' (firms, government, and households) and the savers' (households) side but focus on the perspective of the companies that are trying to raise capital and households that are trying to channel their savings. We also investigate how the nature of financial activity (currency, maturity, and scope of credit) has developed and to what degree changes in the size of markets have implied greater availability of financing for corporations (proxied by the concentration of capital market activity by the top firms). Our objective is to present a bird's-eye view of the financial system, although we provide many details for the interested readers. Since it is very difficult to evaluate the extent of financial development, given the lack of clear benchmarks, we provide comparisons over time and across regions relative to gross domestic product (GDP) and relative to different measures of market size. Chapter 3 of this book (by de la Torre, Feyen, and Ize) presents an analysis that takes into account other factors that can influence financial development. To our knowledge, no other publication has conducted this type of analysis.

We systematically analyze the evolution of the financial development of the LAC region during the 1990s and the 2000s. While we provide some evidence on the banking sector, most of the new evidence focuses on capital markets, at which many of the recent reforms were aimed and where most of the expectations were laid. We also document the evolution of the main financial intermediaries aside from banks: pension funds, mutual funds, and insurance companies. We focus on seven of the largest countries in LAC, the so-called LAC7; as noted, this group includes Argentina, Brazil, Chile, Colombia, Mexico, Peru, and Uruguay. In addition, in cases where patterns differ from the broad trends documented, we present evidence for specific countries within LAC7.[1] We also compare the patterns observed in the LAC7 countries with those in other developed and emerging regions. Among developed countries, we consider the G-7 countries (Canada, France, Germany, Italy, Japan, the United Kingdom, and the United States) as well as other advanced economies that are typically regarded as being somewhat more similar to emerging markets (Australia, Finland, Israel, New Zealand, Norway, Spain, and Sweden). As comparable emerging economies, we focus on two main regions: Asia (Indonesia, the Republic of Korea, Malaysia, the Philippines, and Thailand; and separately, because of their distinct natures, China and India) and Eastern Europe (Croatia, the Czech Republic, Hungary, Lithuania, Poland, the Russian Federation, and Turkey).

The main findings of the chapter provide a mixed, nuanced picture of the main trends in financial development and can be summarized as follows. The financial systems of emerging economies, including those in Latin America, have effectively developed over the past two decades, becoming in many respects and by several standard measures deeper and more complex. In particular, there has been a transition from a mostly bank-based model to one that is more complete and interconnected. Nonbank markets—namely, bonds and equities—have increased in absolute and relative sizes. New markets are also forming, albeit somewhat timidly. Nonbank institutional investors now play a much more central role, channeling a large part of the savings, and the number and sophistication of participants are increasing (even without taking into account the additional increasing participation of cross-border investors). The nature of financing is also changing to some extent, in general for the better, but at a slow pace. For instance, there is a longer maturity of bonds from both the private and the public sectors in domestic markets. The extent of the dollarization of loans and bonds has also declined. However, not all regions have moved in the same direction. For example, Eastern Europe increased its foreign currency debt before the global financial crisis, which was linked to the higher transmission of the crisis to the countries in that region.

In the case of Latin America, despite these new developments, financial systems still remain underdeveloped in comparison to other regions. Bank credit has stagnated. Consumer credit has increased, apparently at the expense of firm financing. Bond markets have expanded but not as fast as those in the rest of the world. Private bond markets have increased in size but remain relatively small. Equity markets remain small, illiquid, and highly concentrated in large firms. While institutional investors are sophisticated and large, most of the savings are still channeled to government bonds and deposits, and as a result, large amounts of private savings are not being channeled directly to firms. In other words, we do not observe a convergence of the region's indicators of financial development with those of more developed regions. In fact, developed countries have expanded their degree of financial development much more than emerging economies. Nevertheless, there is a large heterogeneity within the region. LAC7 countries are still substantially more developed than the rest of the region. Within LAC7, Brazil and Chile show some progress in particular areas (equity and bond markets, respectively), which, though incomplete, look encouraging.

The rest of the chapter is organized as follows. The next section documents and gives a broad overview of where LAC and emerging economies stand on commonly used and simple measures of financial sector development. The chapter then analyzes whether and how the nature of financing has changed over time and describes recent developments in alternative markets and products. The following section examines the main players in the financial system. The final section discusses the challenges ahead for financial sector development.

Financial Sector Development

We start by providing some basic stylized facts showing where LAC countries stand on commonly used broad indicators of financial sector development, comparing them with other emerging and developed countries over the past two decades. More specifically, we focus on the depth of the financial sector, analyzing the size of bond and equity markets and that of the banking sector. Overall, we observe that financial systems in LAC countries have developed significantly over the past two decades, typically transitioning from an "old" mostly bank-based model to a "new" more complex and interconnected model in which nonbank institutions play a more central role. Despite these improvements, financial systems in LAC remain underdeveloped compared to other developed and emerging regions.

Regarding the banking system, one perhaps surprising fact is that LAC7 lags behind developed and developing countries not only in relative size (as measured by total banking claims over GDP) but also in growth. The banking sector in developed countries is deeper to start with and has typically expanded faster than the banking sectors in many emerging economies over the past three decades. In the G-7 economies, for example, bank size increased more than 20 percent, growing from 96 percent to 115 percent of GDP, on average, between 1980–89 and 2000–09. In stark contrast, the banking system in LAC7 countries saw very little or no expansion in total assets as a percentage of GDP during the same period, even though it started from much lower bases (figure 1.1a). At the same time, also starting with more shallow banking sectors than the developed world, Asia and Eastern Europe had strong growth, with total bank assets having expanded as much as 47 percent in the former and 25 percent in the latter over the same period. Within the LAC region, the Caribbean countries and Central and South America show trends similar to LAC7. Offshore centers in LAC, such as the Bahamas, Barbados, and Panama, are exceptions, showing an impressive, almost twofold growth between the decades of the 1980s and the 2000s.

The patterns of financial development are strikingly different for bond markets across developed and developing countries over the past two decades. Bond markets have grown significantly in developing economies—by almost 80 percent in LAC7 countries (figure 1.1b)—but far less in developed countries. For example, bond market capitalization in Asia and Eastern Europe grew, respectively, 57 percent and 66 percent, on average, in the

Figure 1.1 Market Size of Banks, Bonds, and Equities in Selected Regions and Economies, 1980–2009

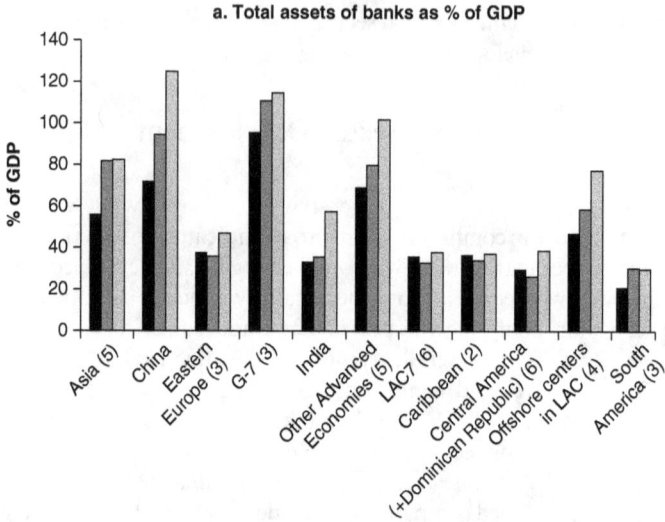

a. Total assets of banks as % of GDP

Countries and regions

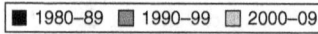

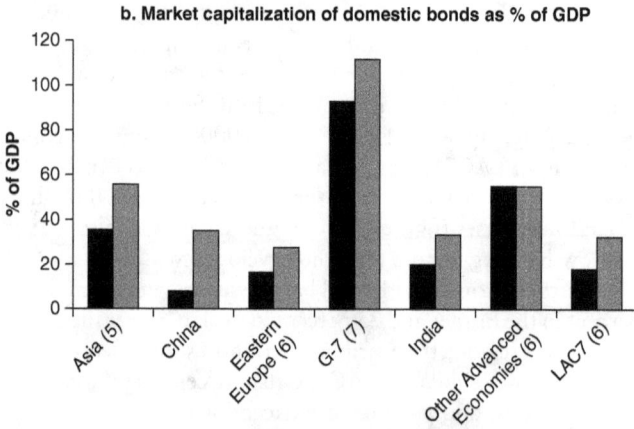

■ 1980–89 ■ 1990–99 □ 2000–09

b. Market capitalization of domestic bonds as % of GDP

Countries and regions

■ 1990–99 ■ 2000–09

(continued next page)

Figure 1.1 (continued)

c. Market capitalization of domestic equities as % of GDP

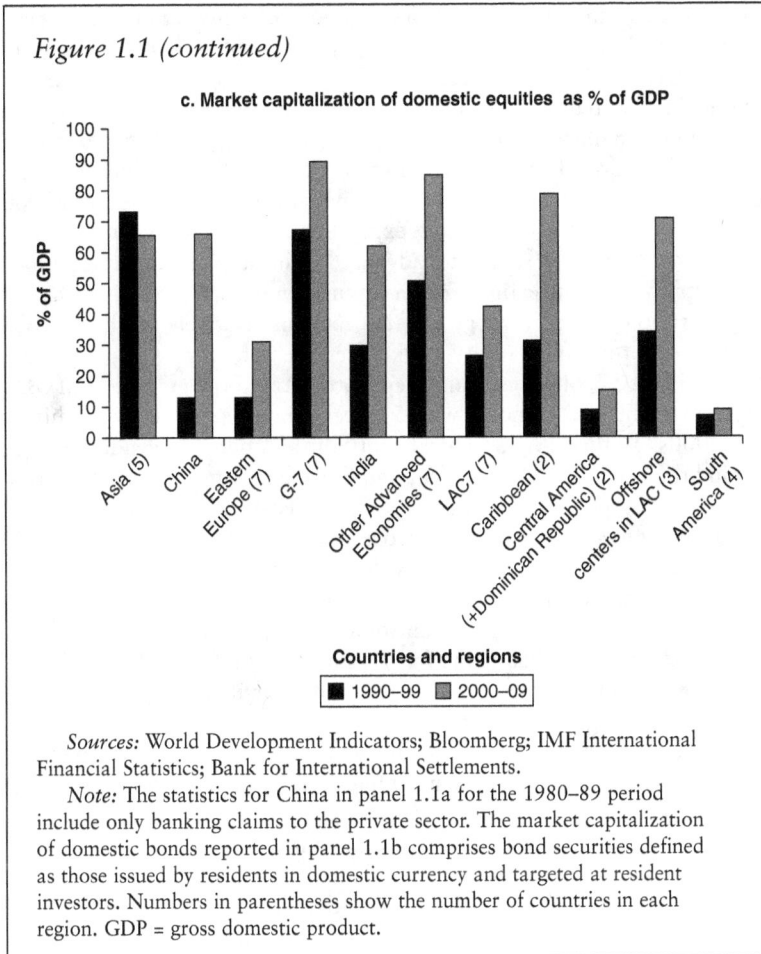

Countries and regions

■ 1990–99 ■ 2000–09

Sources: World Development Indicators; Bloomberg; IMF International Financial Statistics; Bank for International Settlements.

Note: The statistics for China in panel 1.1a for the 1980–89 period include only banking claims to the private sector. The market capitalization of domestic bonds reported in panel 1.1b comprises bond securities defined as those issued by residents in domestic currency and targeted at resident investors. Numbers in parentheses show the number of countries in each region. GDP = gross domestic product.

2000s relative to the 1990s, whereas other advanced countries experienced no growth, on average. Despite the fast growth, bond markets in LAC7 countries remain particularly small, at 32 percent of GDP, on average, during 2000–09, compared to about 56 percent for Asia and 112 percent for G-7 countries. Within LAC7, Peru and Colombia are at the bottom of the distribution, with 15 percent and 23 percent of GDP, respectively, whereas Brazil and Chile are at the top with 40 percent and 59 percent, respectively. The heterogeneity is even greater across the broad set of countries in LAC.

Somewhat similar patterns are also observed in the development of equity markets—equity market capitalization has typically grown faster in developing countries than in developed ones during the past decade, although there is greater heterogeneity across countries. For example, equity market capitalization across LAC7 countries expanded 60 percent in the 2000s vis-à-vis the 1990s, whereas it increased only 3 percent across G-7 countries (figure 1.1c). However, increases in equity prices can explain this trend, at least in part; that is, after adjusting market capitalization for changes in equity prices, a much more modest expansion of equity markets is observed around the world. For instance, equity markets in Eastern European and LAC7 countries expanded just 3 percent per year on average between 2000 and 2009. Similarly, equity markets expanded about 1 percent and 3 percent, respectively, in the G-7 and other advanced countries over the same period.

Despite its significant growth in nominal terms, equity market capitalization as a percentage of GDP remains relatively small in LAC7 countries. For instance, equity markets represented on average 42 percent of GDP in LAC7 countries, while they represented about 66 percent of GDP in Asian countries and more than 85 percent in developed countries during the 2000s. Within LAC, Central and South America considerably lag behind the LAC7, with 15 percent and 9 percent of market capitalization over GDP, respectively, during the 2000 decade. The Caribbean and offshore centers, however, have more developed equity markets, at 79 percent and 71 percent, respectively, for the same period.

These differences in the relative size of equity market capitalization are even larger once we attempt to control for differences in the availability of shares for investors, that is, the free float. Dahlquist et al. (2003) provide evidence that most firms in countries with poor investor protection are controlled by large shareholders, so that only a fraction of the shares issued by firms in these countries can be freely traded and held by portfolio investors. In other words, closely held shares typically represent a larger fraction of total market capitalization in emerging countries than in advanced ones. Once the percentage of closely held shares is taken into account, equity market capitalization becomes significantly smaller in LAC7 countries, and in emerging countries more broadly, than in developed ones.

Although LAC countries are closing the gap in financial sector development relative to advanced economies in many respects, they are still lagging behind, particularly in comparison with the developing countries in Asia. To shed light on the extent of underdevelopment of the LAC7, we compare the size of its financial systems in 2005–07 with those of Asia in 1989–91, when their per capita incomes were similar (figure 1.2). We also include a comparison with developed economies in 1989–91. These comparisons suggest that the financial systems in LAC7 might be 20 years or more behind those of more advanced economies. The depth of LAC7's banking system in the late 2000s is significantly lower than that observed on average in Asia and in developed countries in the early 1990s. Brazil and Chile stand as notable exceptions, with banking sectors similar in size (as a percentage of GDP) to those of developed countries like Australia, Italy, and Norway. Similar patterns are observed in bond markets. In equity markets, the patterns are more encouraging,

Figure 1.2 Depth of Financial Systems and Income per Capita in Selected Countries and Regions, 1989–2007

a. Banks

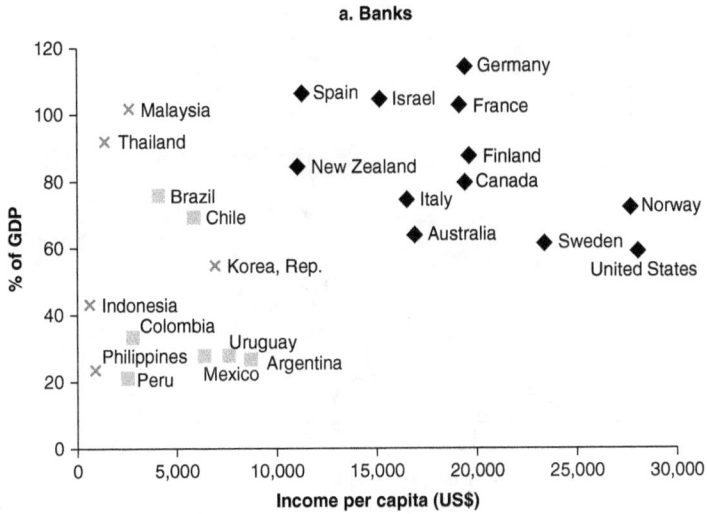

b. Bonds

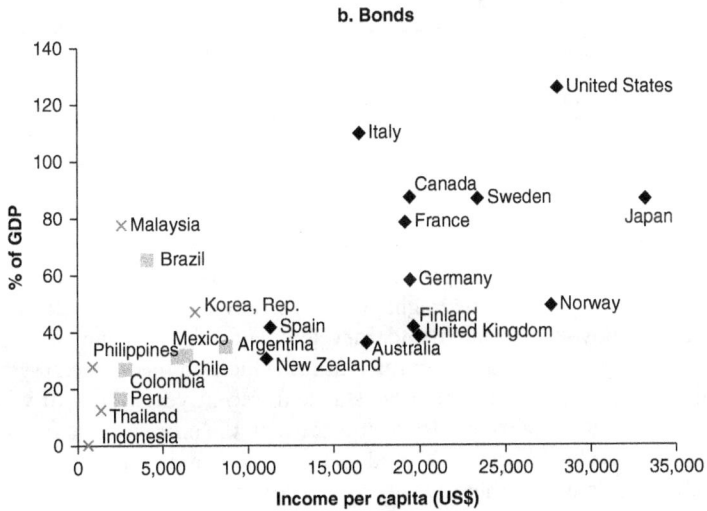

◆ G-7 and Other Advanced Economies (1989–91) ▨ LAC7 (2005–07) ✕ Asia (1989–91)

(continued next page)

Figure 1.2 (continued)

c. Equities

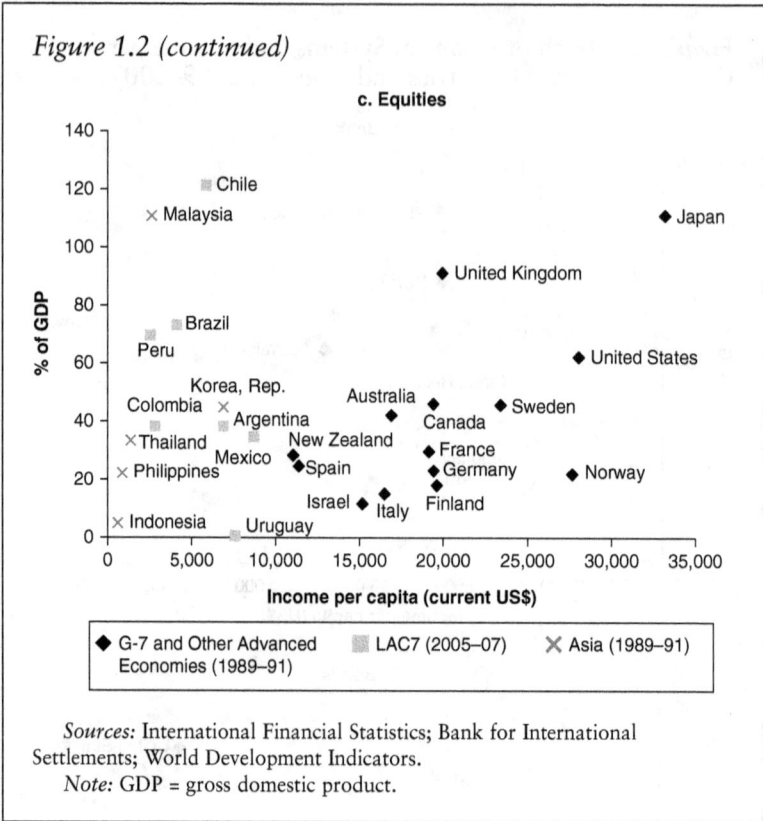

Sources: International Financial Statistics; Bank for International
Settlements; World Development Indicators.
Note: GDP = gross domestic product.

as stock markets in many LAC7 countries are comparable in size (relative
to GDP) to those in developed and developing Asian countries during the
early 1990s, although this might be driven only by valuation effects, as
discussed above. The relative underdevelopment of LAC7 countries seems
surprising, given the number of reforms introduced in the financial system
and the improved macroeconomic stance in recent years, both of which
were expected to yield closer convergence with the more mature financial
systems of developed countries and emerging economies in Asia.

On the bright side, there has been some convergence—a transition from
a mostly bank-based model to a more complete and complex model has
been a broad trend in the LAC region as well as in many other developing
countries (figure 1.3). For example, bond and equity markets in LAC7
countries now account for 64 percent of their financial systems, on average,
in contrast to 54 percent observed in the 1990s. Similarly, these markets
have grown from 45 to 55 percent of the size of the financial system in
Eastern European countries and from 18 to 45 percent of the financial

Figure 1.3 Size of Different Financial Markets in Selected Countries and Regions, 1990–2009

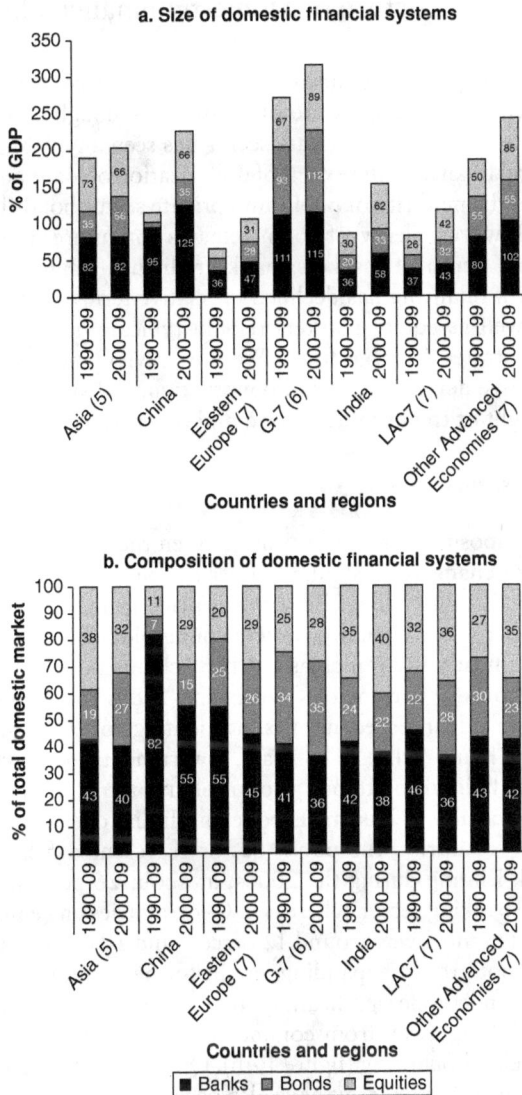

a. Size of domestic financial systems

b. Composition of domestic financial systems

■ Banks ■ Bonds □ Equities

Source: IMF International Financial Statistics; the Bank for International Settlements; World Development Indicators.

Note: Numbers in parentheses show the number of countries in each region. GDP = gross domestic product.

system in China. In developed countries, these markets typically account for about 60 percent of the financial system.

Changing Structure of Domestic Financial Systems

The increased depth of financial systems in LAC7 countries has come along with changes in the nature of financing—though slowly—toward the better: for example, the private sector has seen an expansion in local currency bond financing, the extent of dollarization of loans and bonds has declined, and the maturity of public and private sector bonds has typically increased. However, plenty of room remains for future development of the scope and depth of markets: bank credit has stagnated in various countries; firm financing has declined in relative terms; and private bond markets as well as equity markets remain typically small, illiquid, and highly concentrated in large firms. We now review more systematically these qualitative developments in domestic financial systems in emerging markets in light of trends in developed and other developing countries.

Banking Systems

While the composition of bank credit between the public and the private sector has not changed substantially over the past two decades in LAC7 countries, significant changes have taken place in the rest of the world. The large expansion of banking systems in developed countries has been concentrated mostly in an increase of their claims on the private sector, which rose from 50 percent of GDP in the 1980s to 98 percent in the 2000s in other advanced economies, accounting for 97 percent of total bank lending (figure 1.4a). In contrast, governments increased their borrowing not only in absolute but also in relative terms in many emerging markets, particularly in Eastern Europe and India, over the same period. Across LAC7 countries, the public sector represented a larger fraction of total bank lending during the 2000s, at about 26 percent of the total claims by the banking sector, whereas in G-7 countries and emerging Asian countries that number was around 12 percent and 10 percent, respectively.

Although not greatly expanding, credit to the private sector in LAC7 countries has undergone significant qualitative changes in its composition, with credit shifting away from commercial lending and mortgage credit toward household financing (figure 1.4b). Qualitative changes in the composition of private sector credit have also occurred in some other emerging markets, although mortgage lending has increased in the case of Eastern European countries and China. In contrast, the composition of bank credit has remained relatively stable in developed countries.

In a context of somewhat stagnant private sector credit in a number of developing countries, these patterns may indicate an unbalanced expansion

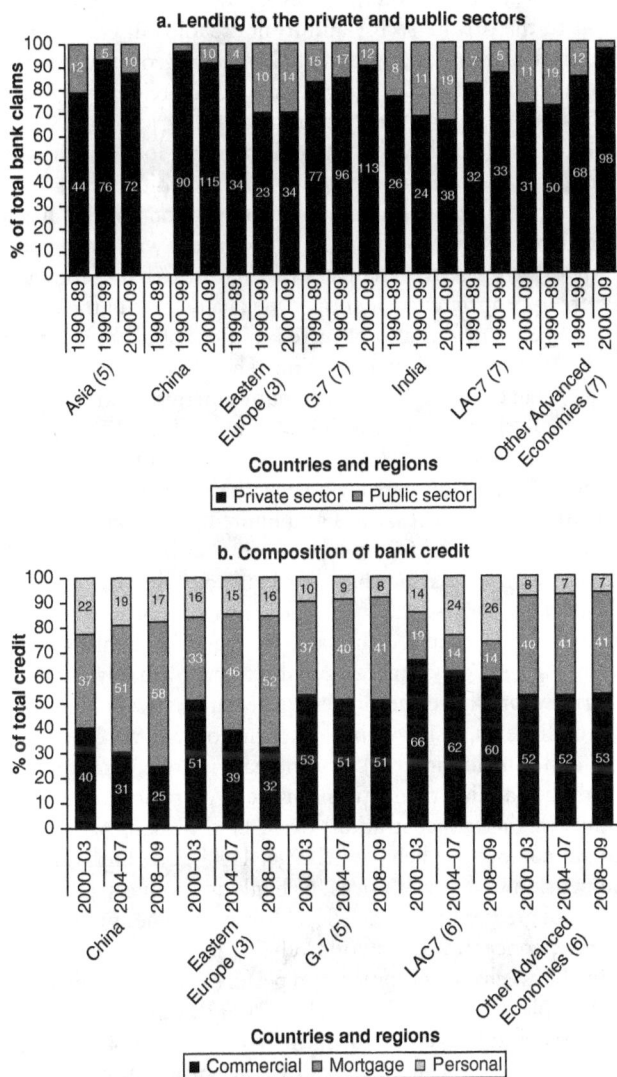

Figure 1.4 Nature of the Credit by Banks in Selected Countries and Regions, 1980–2009

Source: Local sources; International Financial Statistics.

Note: On panel 1.4a, the percentages shown within the bars represent the size of both public and private claims as a percentage of GDP. For China, the data on claims on the public sector are not available for 1980–89. Numbers in parentheses show the number of countries in each region.

of credit in a particular segment at the expense of the underdevelopment of others. For example, mortgages seem comparatively small across LAC countries. For LAC7 countries, these patterns in the development of banking systems indicate that as countries have grown over the past two decades, bank credit to the private sector and to households in particular has also expanded, thus alleviating any potential financial constraints. These patterns also suggest that banks have expanded, in relative terms, in areas where it has been easy for them to grant credit at low risk, such as consumer credit through credit cards and collateralized loans, such as car loans and housing (not to mention the expansion of credit to the government). The increased use of capital markets by corporations, which has lessened demand for bank finance, would also be consistent with these patterns.

Two other key qualitative changes in the nature of bank lending in LAC7 countries are appropriate to mention. One is a decline in the dollarization of loans—indeed, this has also occurred in most other emerging markets, although Eastern Europe is an exception. The other is a decline in the percentage of foreign currency deposits in many emerging markets, although it remains particularly high in Eastern European and LAC7 countries (figure 1.5). These developments are likely a consequence of the emerging market crises of the 1990s, when currency mismatches rendered the private sector vulnerable to currency fluctuations and limited policy options.

Banking systems in LAC7 countries are also becoming slightly more concentrated, with increasing shares of loans and deposits in the top five banks (figure 1.6). Surprisingly, the opposite trend is occurring in a number of other emerging markets. At the same time, foreign banks are increasing their presence in LAC7 and emerging markets more broadly; the LAC region and Eastern Europe have the highest penetrations, which are noticeably larger than those in Asia, China, and the other advanced economies (Claessens and van Horen 2013). The increase in concentration might raise concerns about banking competition in the LAC region. When fewer and larger banks (higher concentration) exist, banks might be more likely to engage in anticompetitive behavior (Berger 1995). The literature has linked bank competition with lower prices for banking products, increased access to finance, and greater bank efficiency. However, some studies have shown that, at times, concentration is not a reliable measure of competition and that the link between concentration and performance is not always negative (see, for example, Cetorelli 1999; Jackson 1992). Empirically, Anzoategui, Martínez Pería, and Rocha (2010) show that although banking systems in LAC countries exhibit a high degree of concentration, competition does not seem to have declined during the 1990s and 2000s.

Bond Markets

Despite their considerable expansion between 2000 and 2009, private (corporate and financial institutions) bond markets in LAC7 countries

Figure 1.5 Dollarization of the Banking System in Selected Countries and Regions, 1991–2009

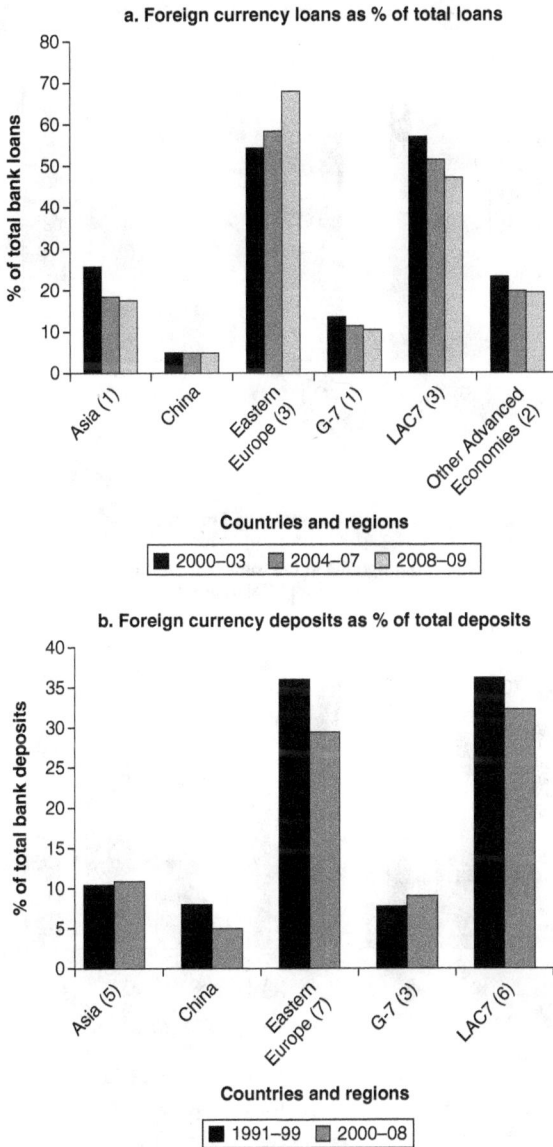

a. Foreign currency loans as % of total loans

y-axis: % of total bank loans

x-axis (Countries and regions): Asia (1), China, Eastern Europe (3), G-7 (1), LAC7 (3), Other Advanced Economies (2)

Legend: ■ 2000–03 ■ 2004–07 □ 2008–09

b. Foreign currency deposits as % of total deposits

y-axis: % of total bank deposits

x-axis (Countries and regions): Asia (5), China, Eastern Europe (7), G-7 (3), LAC7 (6)

Legend: ■ 1991–99 □ 2000–08

Source: IMF, International Financial Statistics.
Note: Numbers in parentheses show the number of countries in each region.

Figure 1.6 Concentration of Banking Systems in Selected Countries and Regions, 2000–10

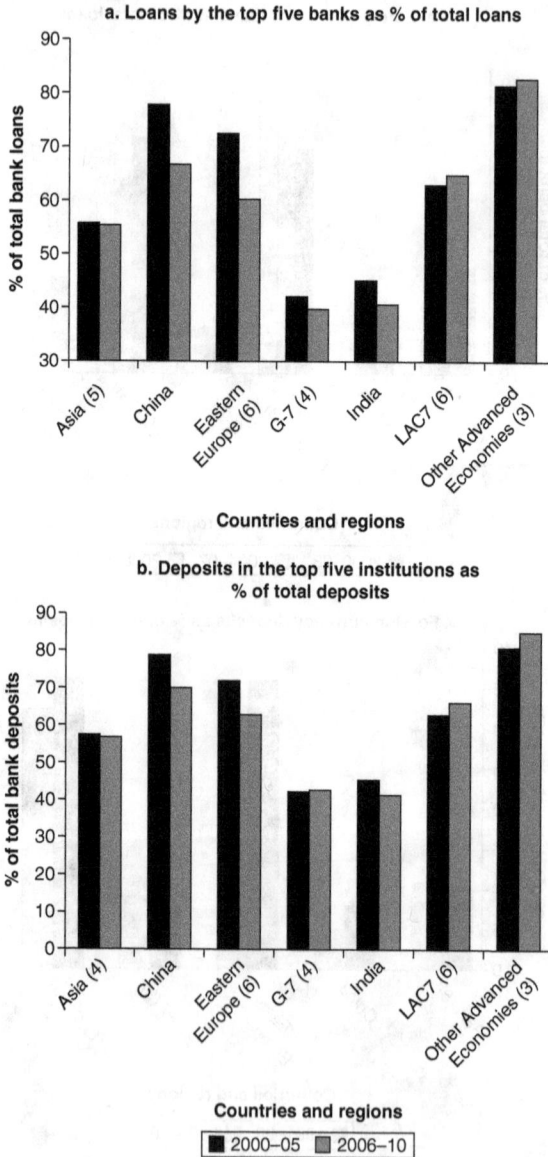

a. Loans by the top five banks as % of total loans

(y-axis: % of total bank loans; x-axis categories: Asia (5), China, Eastern Europe (6), G-7 (4), India, LAC7 (6), Other Advanced Economies (3))

Countries and regions

b. Deposits in the top five institutions as % of total deposits

(y-axis: % of total bank deposits; x-axis categories: Asia (4), China, Eastern Europe (6), G-7 (4), India, LAC7 (6), Other Advanced Economies (3))

Countries and regions

■ 2000–05 ▨ 2006–10

Source: Bankscope.
Note: Numbers in parentheses show the number of countries in each region.

remained relatively small in comparison to those in more developed countries and to public bond markets. For example, private bond market capitalization typically represented around 40 percent of GDP in developed countries during the 2000s, whereas it stood at only 10 percent and 23 percent across LAC7 and Asian countries, respectively, over the same period (figure 1.7a). A positive development is that private bond markets across LAC7 countries have grown more as a percentage of GDP than government bonds, gaining space in relative terms and hinting at less crowding out by the public sector. Issuance data also suggest a significant size difference between private and public bond markets. While issuance of bonds by the private sector stood at around 1 percent of GDP per year in LAC7 countries, public sector bond issuance was around 5 percent of GDP on average for most of the 2000s.

Figure 1.7 Bond Markets in Selected Countries and Regions, 1990–2009

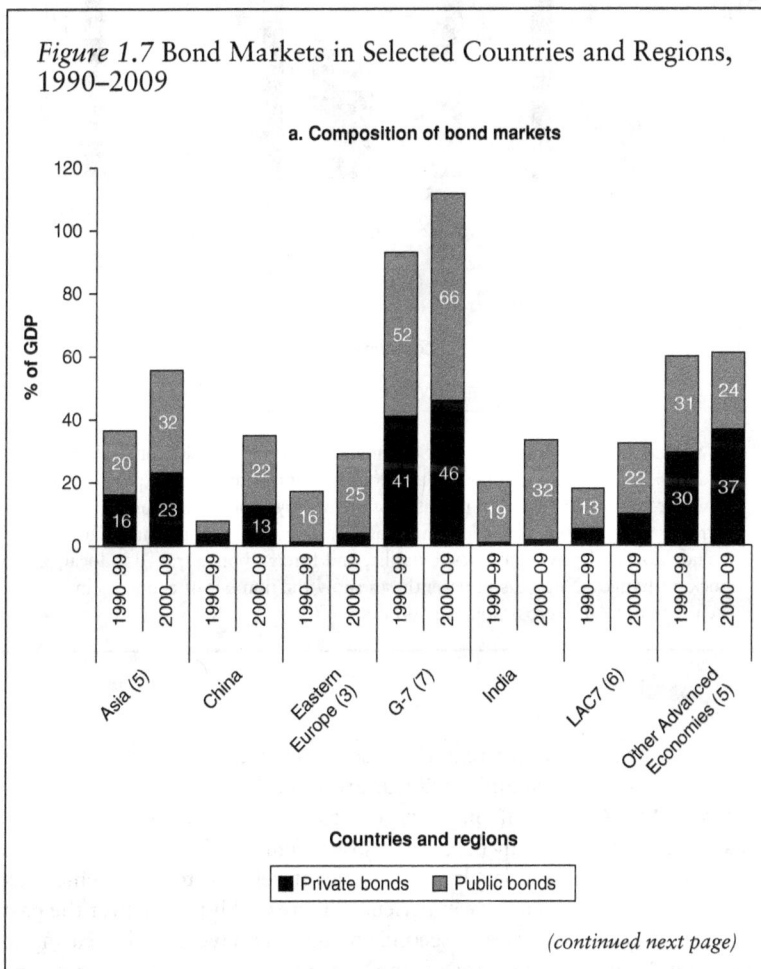

a. Composition of bond markets

(continued next page)

Figure 1.7 (continued)

b. Bond market turnover

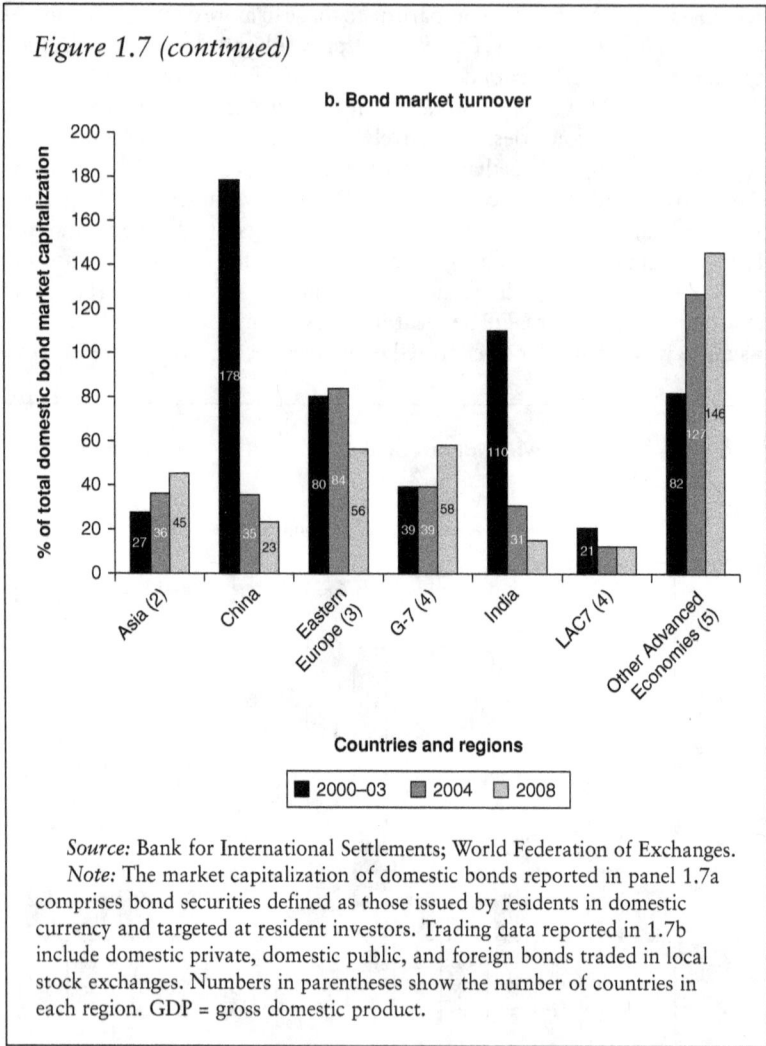

Countries and regions

■ 2000–03   ■ 2004   □ 2008

Source: Bank for International Settlements; World Federation of Exchanges.
Note: The market capitalization of domestic bonds reported in panel 1.7a comprises bond securities defined as those issued by residents in domestic currency and targeted at resident investors. Trading data reported in 1.7b include domestic private, domestic public, and foreign bonds traded in local stock exchanges. Numbers in parentheses show the number of countries in each region. GDP = gross domestic product.

Bond market liquidity remains a concern in LAC7 countries. While turnover between 2008 and 2009 was around 60 percent in G-7 countries and reached 146 percent on average across other developed nations, it was merely 12 percent in LAC7 countries (figure 1.7b). In addition, the differences in turnover levels are significant relative to other emerging markets, some of which have experienced increased liquidity over the past 10 years. Trading volumes in secondary markets have been increasing in emerging Asian countries, for example, growing from 27 percent during

2000–03 to 45 percent in 2008–09. These patterns suggest that primary bond markets have developed substantially more than secondary markets, and they are broadly consistent with the evidence that institutional investors hold bonds to maturity and do little trading (Raddatz and Schmukler 2008).

Not only are private bond markets in LAC7 countries, and in emerging countries in general, small in size, but also they have a limited reach, remaining a restricted source of firm financing. Only a small number of firms access bond markets for new capital in comparison to developed countries. For example, during the 2000s, 19 firms on average issued bonds in LAC7 countries, compared to 21 and 27, respectively, for Asia and other advanced economies, and an astounding 432 firms in G-7 countries (figure 1.8a). Moreover, this indicator even declined from its 1990 reading. At the same time, LAC7 markets remain largely concentrated, with the top five issuers capturing 43 percent of new bond financing during

Figure 1.8 Participation in Domestic Private Bond Markets in Selected Regions, 1991–2008

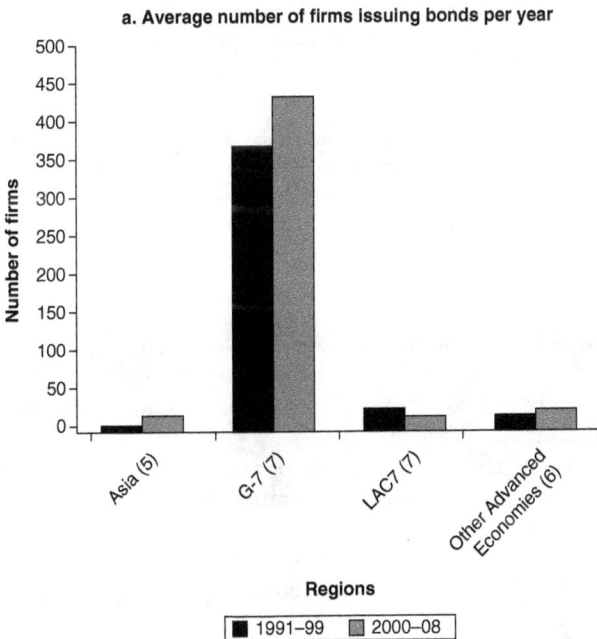

a. Average number of firms issuing bonds per year

(continued next page)

Figure 1.8 (continued)

b. Concentration (amount raised by the top five issuers as % of total amount raised)

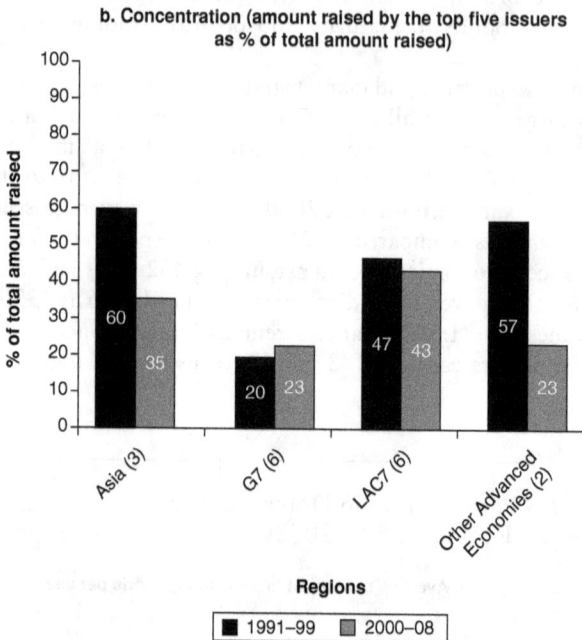

Source: SDC Platinum.

Note: The average number of firms issuing bonds per year in domestic markets is reported at the bottom of the bars in panel 1.8b. Numbers in parentheses show the number of countries in each region.

the 2000s (figure 1.8b). In other words, a few firms (typically the larger ones) capture the bulk of the new bond financing. These patterns seem to be intrinsically related to the behavior of institutional investors in local markets, as discussed below.

On a positive note, the profile of new bond issues across LAC7 countries has been improving considerably over the past two decades. As in developments in the composition of bank debt, and most likely as a consequence of a series of financial crises in the 1990s, LAC countries (in keeping with a broader trend across emerging countries) have on average made a conscious effort to try to reduce currency and maturity mismatches, minimizing concerns about credit risk and rollover difficulties. In particular, the maturity profile of both public and private sector bonds has been extended during the 2000s, and the degree of domestic currency debt has increased significantly. For example, relative to the 1990s, the private sector of LAC7 countries has increased the average maturity of domestic bonds from 6.1 years to 7.7 years. The increase in the average maturity of public debt is more striking, but it is not uniform across the LAC7 countries: between the 2000–03 and the 2008–09 periods, Brazil, Peru, and Uruguay showed significant increases in the maturity of public bonds, while Argentina's and Chile's public debt maturity remained somewhat unchanged or even declined (figure 1.9b).

At the same time, bonds denominated in foreign currency in local markets have declined significantly in the private and public sectors. For instance, such bonds represented about 25 percent of total outstanding private

Figure 1.9 Average Maturity of Bonds at Issuance in Domestic Markets in Selected Countries and Regions, 1991–2009

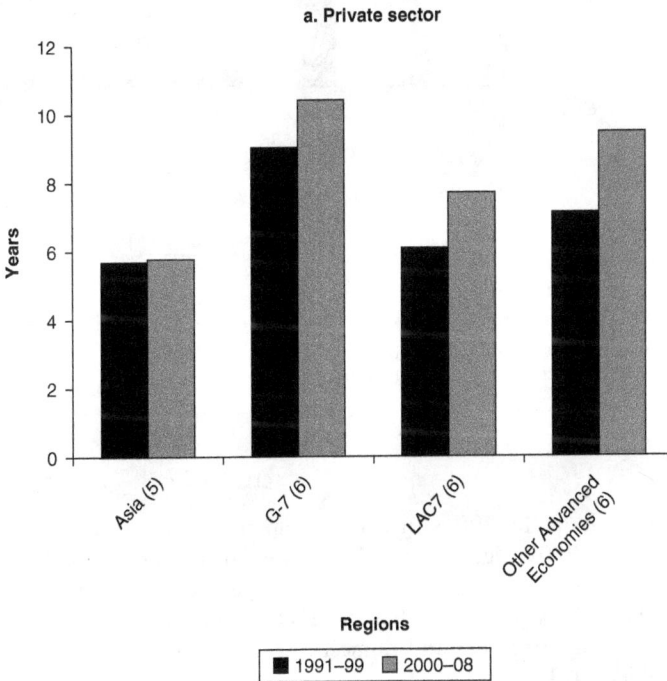

a. Private sector

(continued next page)

Figure 1.9 (continued)

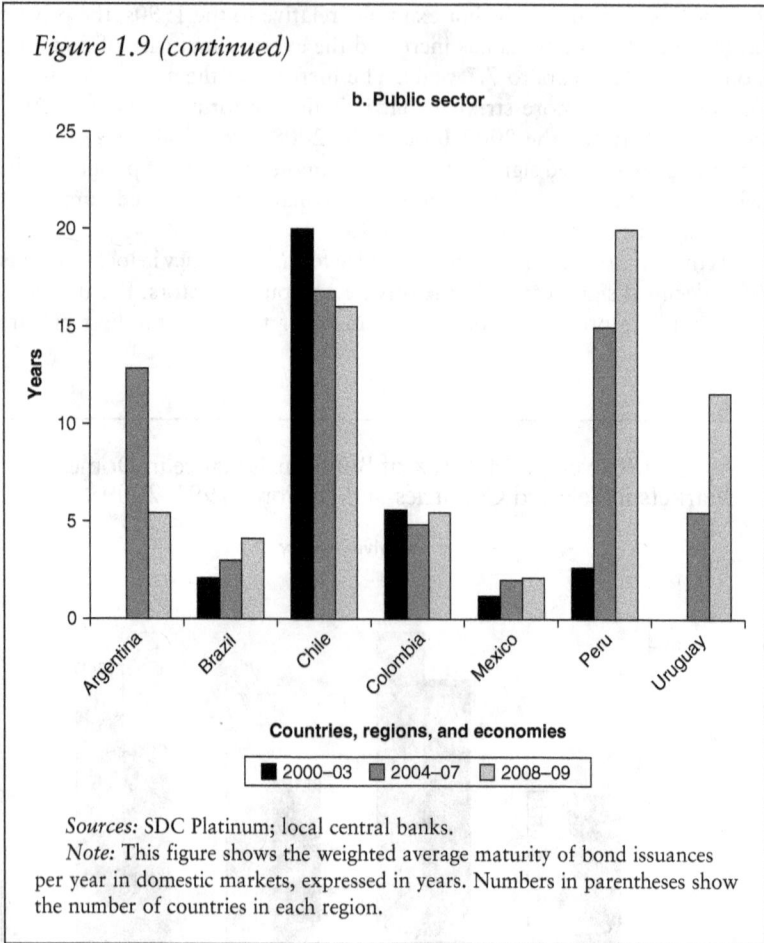

b. Public sector

Sources: SDC Platinum; local central banks.
Note: This figure shows the weighted average maturity of bond issuances per year in domestic markets, expressed in years. Numbers in parentheses show the number of countries in each region.

sector bonds in the 2000s in LAC7 countries, down from 33 percent during the 1990s (figure 1.10). These overall trends probably reflect a conscious effort by governments to change the profile of their debt, given the serious rollover difficulties that mismatches generated during earlier periods of global and domestic shocks (Broner, Lorenzoni, and Schmukler 2013).

Equity Markets

Figure 1.1c showed a sizable increase in equity market capitalization in LAC7 countries between the 1990s and the 2000s. In contrast, figure 1.11a shows that the value of capital-raising activities in equity markets actually fell between those periods. For example, new capital raised through equity markets increased between 26 percent and 31 percent on average in developed countries, whereas it actually declined between the 1990s and the 2000s in developing countries—by about 70 percent in LAC7. As we suggested above, these results may not be inconsistent, as the expansion of market capitalization might be partly explained by the increasing equity valuations around the world during the 2000s.

Furthermore, trading activity is consistent with this less than rosy picture of equity markets in LAC7 countries. Domestic markets are not only relatively illiquid in the region, but liquidity has also been declining over time, unfortunately confirming trends documented with data up

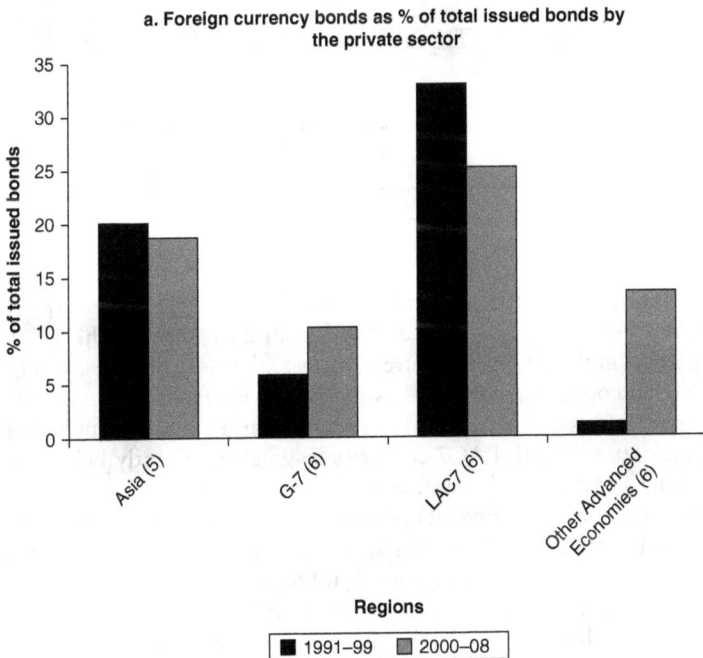

Figure 1.10 Currency Composition of Bonds at Issuance in Domestic Markets in Selected Countries and Regions, 1991–2009

(continued next page)

Figure 1.10 (continued)

**b. Public sector-issued local currency, foreign currency, and
inflation-linked bonds as % of total outstanding bonds**

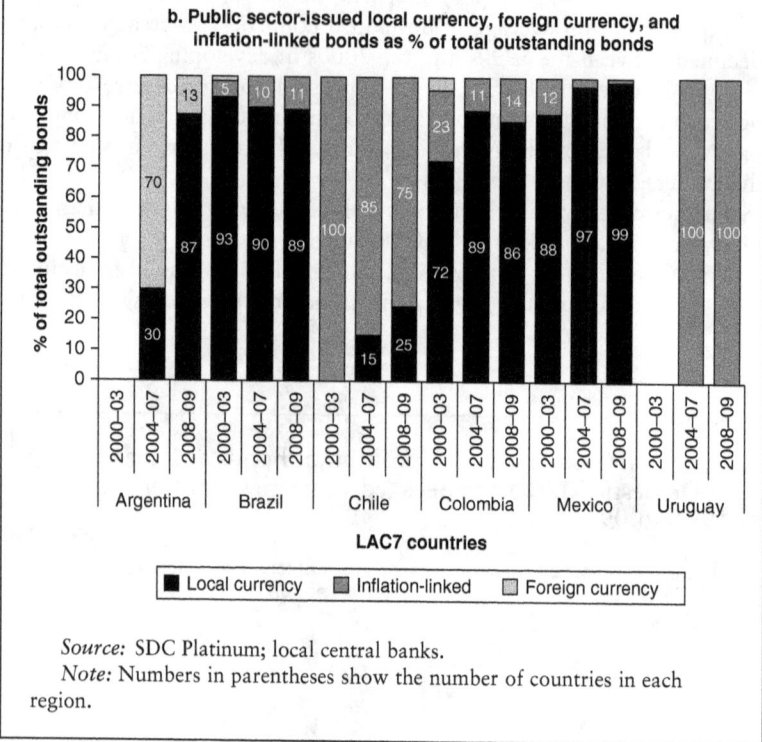

Source: SDC Platinum; local central banks.
Note: Numbers in parentheses show the number of countries in each
region.

to the early 2000s (de la Torre and Schmukler 2004). Turnover rates in LAC7 equity markets have declined from 25 percent in the 1990s to 17 percent in the 2000s. In contrast, in Asia, the G-7 countries, and other developed countries, turnover has increased significantly (figure 1.11b). Turnover ratios calculated with free-float market capitalization suggest similar patterns, with LAC7 countries lagging significantly behind other emerging and advanced countries.

Despite some improvements in depth, the use of equity markets remains limited in LAC7 countries, with only a few firms capturing most of the (primary and secondary) market. One reason is that the number of listed firms is rather small compared to developed and other developing countries, and it has been declining over the past decade (figure 1.12a). In addition, the number of firms using equity finance on a regular basis is typically small in LAC7 countries; for instance, on average, only six firms issued equity in any given year during the 2000s in LAC7 compared to

Figure 1.11 Activity in Domestic Equity Markets, 1990–2009

a. Value of new capital-raising issues

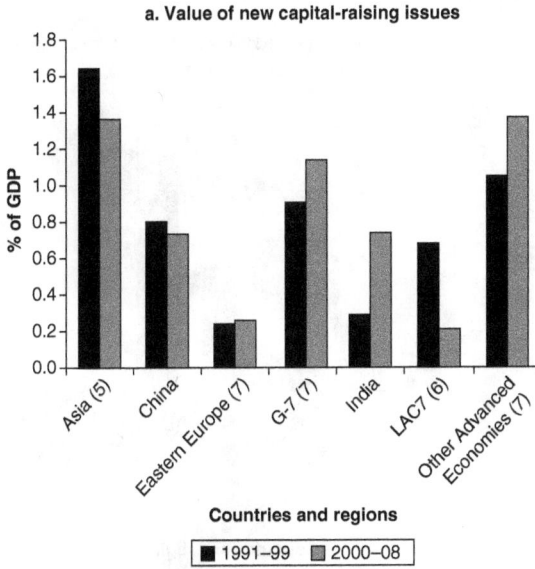

Countries and regions

■ 1991–99 ▨ 2000–08

b. Turnover ratio in domestic equity markets

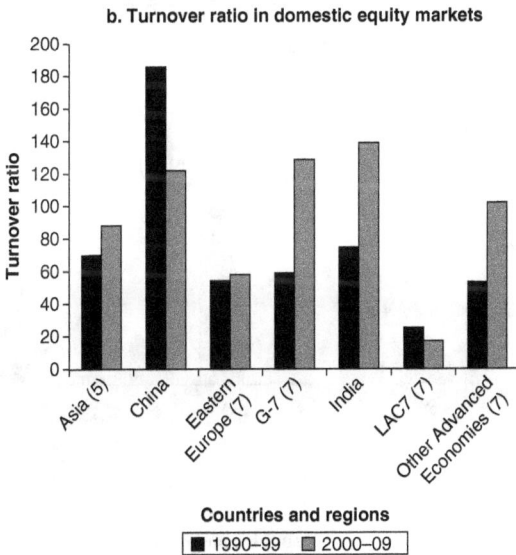

Countries and regions

■ 1990–99 ▨ 2000–09

Source: SDC Platinum; World Development Indicators.
Note: Numbers in parentheses show the number of countries in each region. GDP = gross domestic product.

Figure 1.12 Firm Activity in Domestic Equity Markets in Selected Countries and Regions, 1990–2009

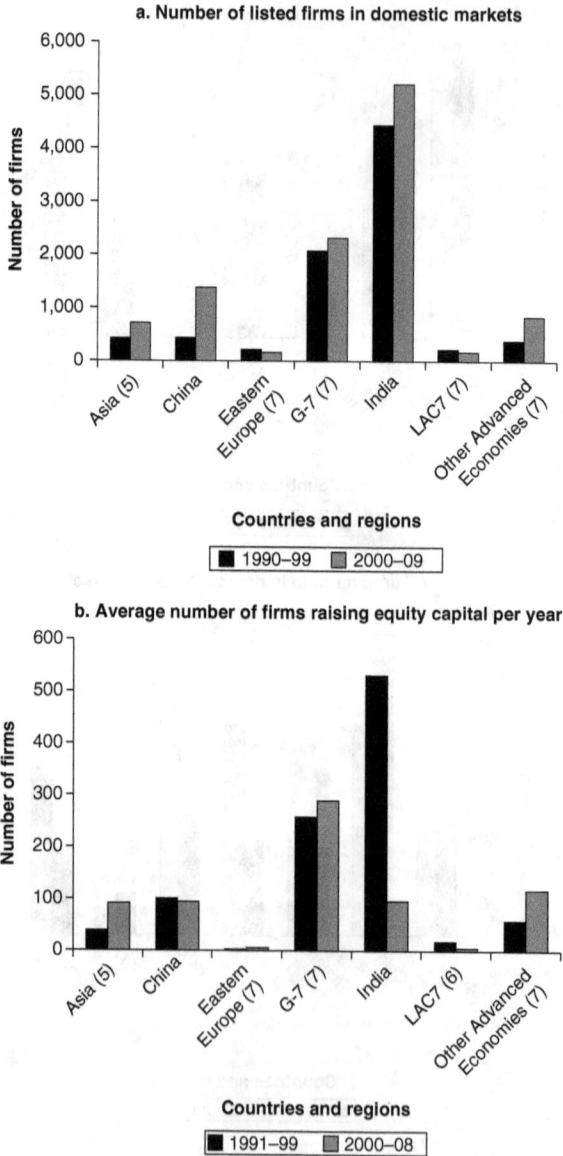

a. Number of listed firms in domestic markets

1990–99 ■ 2000–09 ■

b. Average number of firms raising equity capital per year

1991–99 ■ 2000–08 ■

Source: World Development Indicators; SDC Platinum.
Note: Numbers in parentheses show the number of countries in each region.

more than 290 in the G-7 countries, over 110 in other developed countries, and over 90 firms in Asian countries (figure 1.12b). Third, the bulk of equity financing is concentrated in a few firms; in fact, the share raised by the top five issuers increased in LAC7 countries from 72 percent to 82 percent between the 1990s and the 2000s (figure 1.13a). Last, trading in equity markets is highly concentrated in a few firms as well, with the top five firms capturing almost 60 percent of the trading in LAC7 countries (figure 1.13b). Again, within the region equity markets are most liquid in LAC7 countries, while other countries have generally much smaller and more illiquid markets—with fewer than 50 listed firms on average and turnover rates below 5 percent. These patterns suggest that if there were any deepening of equity markets, it did not bring about a greater breadth

Figure 1.13 Concentration in Domestic Equity Markets in Selected Countries and Regions, 1991–2009

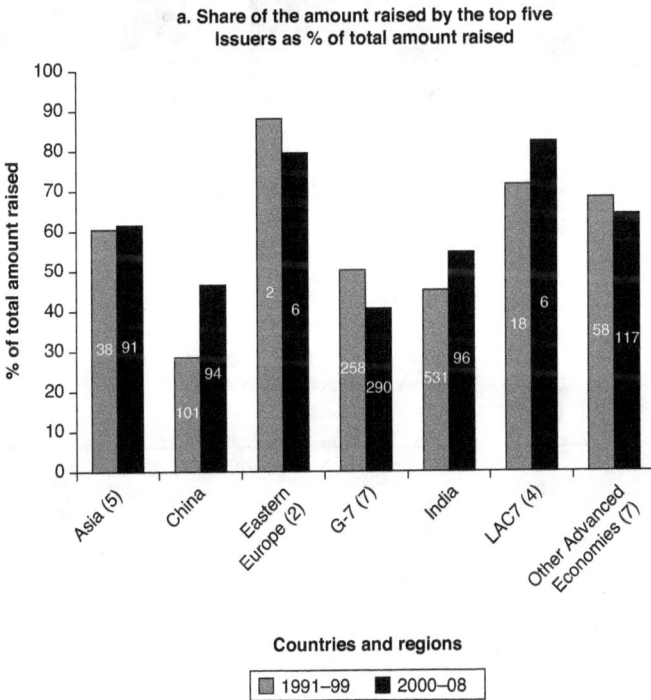

a. Share of the amount raised by the top five
Issuers as % of total amount raised

(continued next page)

Figure 1.13 (continued)

**b. Share of the value traded by the top five companies
as % of total value traded**

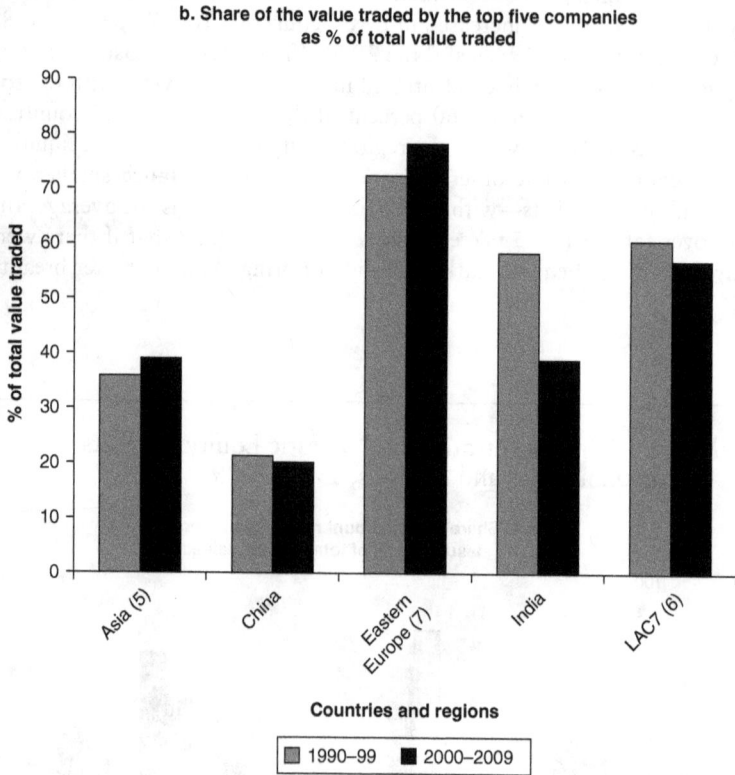

Source: Emerging Markets Database; World Development Indicators; SDC
Platinum.

Note: Numbers at the base of the bars in 1.13a represent the average
number of firms raising equity capital per year. Numbers in parentheses show
the number of countries in each region.

of access for firms. Equity markets seem to remain small, illiquid, and
highly concentrated in a few firms across the region.

Which Firms Access Capital Markets?

While the description above shows that few firms access bond and equity
markets, it provides little information about which firms do so. It is well
known that larger firms have greater access to capital markets, due at least

in part to cost and liquidity considerations. In practice, these considerations render the minimum issue size rather large for smaller firms (see Beck et al. 2006). Furthermore, firm-level data on publicly listed companies (generally the largest firms in an economy) across emerging markets show that not all public firms actually raise capital in bond and equity markets regularly, suggesting that an even more restricted set of firms uses financing from capital markets. Typically, firms that raise capital through either bonds or equity are larger (in assets), are growing faster (as represented by sales growth), are more profitable (greater return on assets), and are more liquid (that is, they have higher cash-to-current-asset ratios) than publicly listed firms that do not issue bonds or equities over a given period. There are, however, some differences across emerging regions: firms raising capital in some LAC7 countries (Brazil and Chile, for example) tend to be more leveraged than firms that do not use capital markets, while the opposite is true on average in a number of Asian countries, like China, Indonesia, and Malaysia. The fact that only a restricted set of firms uses capital markets can be partly explained by supply factors. For instance, the restricted investment practice of institutional investors is one possible explanation. As documented in a number of papers, institutional investors tend to invest in larger and more liquid firms, thereby limiting the supply of funds to smaller and less liquid firms (see, for example, Didier 2011; Didier, Rigobon, and Schmukler 2010; Edison and Warnock 2004; Dahlquist and Robertsson 2001; Kang and Stulz 1997).

Promising Spots in LAC? The Cases of Brazil and Chile

While the patterns documented so far focus mostly on LAC7 countries, we have shown at times that the broad picture is even more dismal in other LAC countries, reflecting the region's heterogeneity. However, the adoption of a more capital market–based approach is relatively more advanced in Brazil, Chile, Colombia, and Mexico. The cases of Brazil and Chile in particular are worth noting and show important progress in key areas that, though still incomplete, look encouraging, as documented below.

Bond Markets in Chile Private bond markets in Chile grew from 13 percent of GDP during the 1990s to 21 percent in the 2000s (figure 1.14a). Moreover, the private sector now accounts for a greater share of total outstanding bonds than the public sector—51 percent of total outstanding bonds on average in the 2000s compared to 33 percent on average during the 1990s. Consistent with these trends, primary markets are also highly active in Chile, with new bond issues by the private sector of 3.4 percent of GDP on average on an annual basis between 2000 and 2008. In contrast, the second largest primary market for bond issues by the private sector among LAC7 countries is Brazil, with annual amounts issued of about 1.4 percent of GDP on average (figure 1.14b).

Figure 1.14 Public and Private Bond Markets across LAC7 Countries, 1990–2009

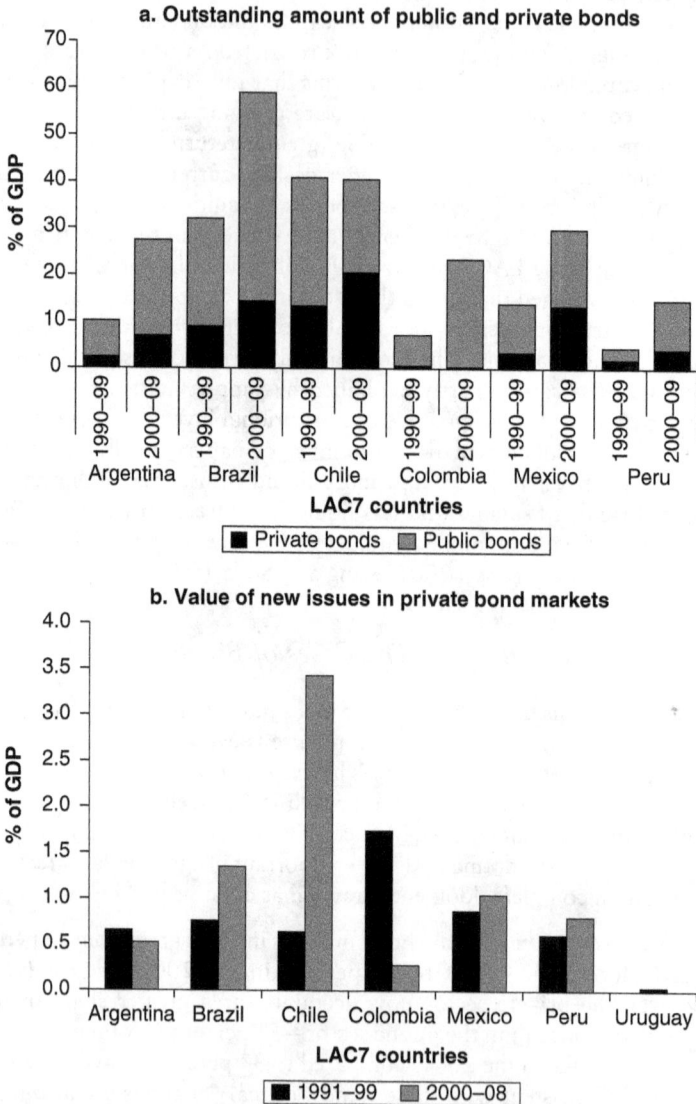

a. Outstanding amount of public and private bonds

b. Value of new issues in private bond markets

Source: Bank for International Settlements; SDC Platinum.
Note: The market capitalization of domestic bonds reported in 1.14a comprises bond securities defined as those issued by residents in domestic currency and targeted at resident investors. GDP = gross domestic product.

The use of primary bond markets by firms in Chile is also growing. In the 1990s, on average, 8 firms issued bonds in local markets in a given year, and in the 2000s the average increased to 23, or almost 1.4 firms per million inhabitants (figure 1.15a). Although small compared to G-7 countries, which boast 6.5 firms per million inhabitants, this is a greater number of firms raising capital than seen in many other emerging economies. Moreover, state-owned enterprises correspond to only 3 percent of outstanding amounts of corporate bonds, according to LarrainVial (2011), one of the largest brokerage firms in Chile. Concentration in Chile is also less a concern than it is in other emerging countries, with statistics comparable to those of G-7 countries (figure 1.15b). Nevertheless, the minimum issue size is, in practice, still quite high, and firms that use bond markets have, on average, US$173 million in outstanding bonds, which suggests how restricted access is for smaller firms.

The maturity structure of private bonds in Chile is surprisingly long for an emerging market—15.5 years at issuance, significantly longer than the observed average of 6.2 years in the other LAC7 countries and the 10 years

Figure 1.15 Activity in Domestic Private Bond Markets in LAC7 Countries, 1990–2008

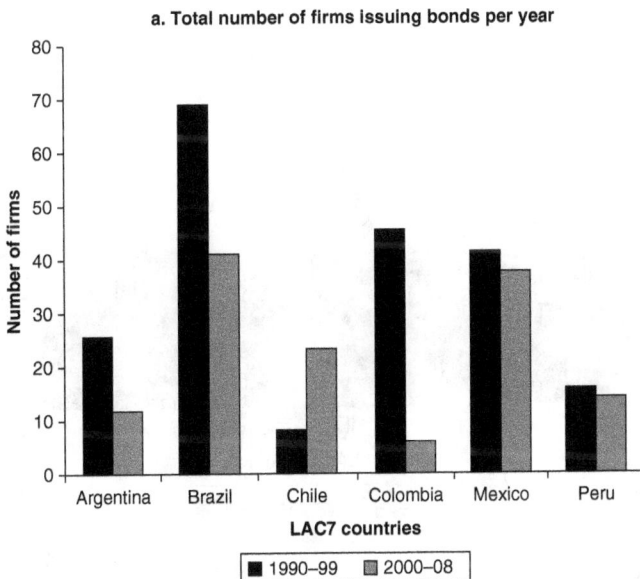

a. Total number of firms issuing bonds per year

(continued next page)

Figure 1.15 (continued)

**b. Share of the amount raised by top five issuers
as % of total amount raised**

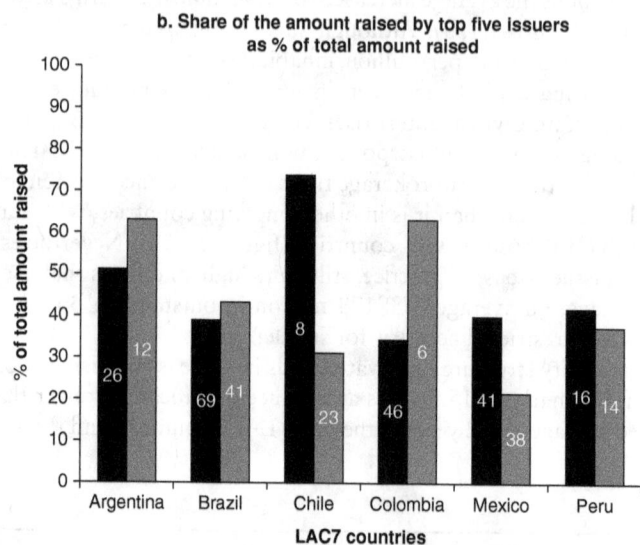

c. Average maturity at issuance in years

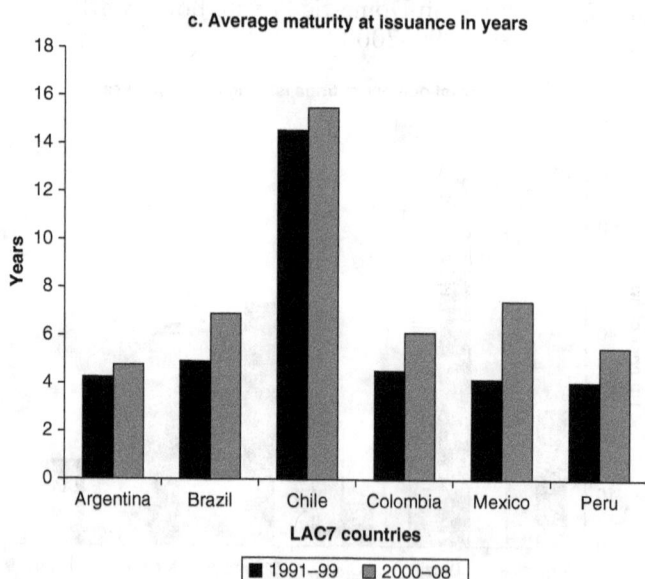

■ 1991–99   ■ 2000–08

Source: SDC Platinum.

Note: Numbers at the bottom of the bars represent the average number of issuers per year.

typically seen in a number of developed countries (figure 1.15c).[2] The long maturities in Chile are generally linked to indexed, high-grade bonds. In December 2005, 97.7 percent of issued bonds were inflation-linked bonds, and 1.5 percent were linked to the U.S. dollar. In December 2010, a similar composition was observed, when almost 94 percent of bonds were linked to inflation and 1.5 percent were linked to the exchange rate.[3] Domestic bonds are also mostly rated at investment grade, with very few high-yield issues. Non-investment-grade bonds correspond to 0.2 percent of issues, and by the end of 2010 the percentage of bonds rated BBB or below was about 3 percent, which is significantly lower than those in developed countries: high-yield bonds have reached almost 40 percent of issues in Japan and around 10 percent in the United States (statistics from LarrainVial 2011).

Although primary bond markets for the private sector seem highly developed, liquidity in secondary markets remains limited. According to LarrainVial (2011), trading of corporate bonds in Chile corresponds to about 20 percent of the total value traded in domestic bond markets, a disproportionate amount given its size relative to government bonds. Even though turnover ratios increased consistently in the 2000s, going from about 30 percent in 2002 to almost 60 percent in 2010, they stood in marked contrast to a turnover ratio of 294 percent for government bonds in 2010.[4] Liquidity in corporate bond markets in Chile also seems limited when compared to other LAC countries: about 463 percent in Mexico, 123 percent in Brazil, and 75 percent in Colombia.

These developments in Chilean corporate bond markets need to be viewed in light of their main institutional investors, pension funds, insurance companies, and, to a lesser extent, mutual funds. These investors, particularly pension funds, provide stable demand for corporate bonds, given their sheer size (about 65 percent of GDP for pension funds and 20 percent for insurance companies in 2010). Pension funds, for instance, held about 50 percent of the stock of bonds in 2010, while insurance companies held 32 percent. Given their status as large market players in corporate bond markets, their investment behavior will be tightly linked to developments in this market. For example, their large size implies that investments are usually made in large amounts, which limits the potential demand for smaller issues. These investors typically pursue buy-and-hold strategies, keeping bonds in their portfolios until maturity, as shown in Opazo, Raddatz, and Schmukler (2009) and Raddatz and Schmukler (2011), which can explain the low liquidity of the secondary private bond markets. In addition, current restrictions on pension fund investments limit their exposure to non-investment-grade issues, thus possibly explaining the low fraction of outstanding high-yield corporate bonds. The long maturity of corporate bonds can also be associated with the maturity structure of the liabilities of pension funds and insurance companies, which allows them to make longer-term investments.

The nature of their liabilities, mostly indexed to inflation, also implies a significant demand for inflation-linked bonds.

Regulatory changes that took place in the early 2000s may also be related to the timing of these developments in local currency bond markets. For instance, capital market reforms allowed pension funds and insurance companies more flexibility in their investments. The combination of sound macroeconomic and financial frameworks with price stability and credible fiscal and monetary policies, along with reduced macroeconomic volatility, might also have been important. Yet significant challenges remain in addressing some of the limitations of corporate bond markets in Chile. More specifically, greater access for smaller firms and more liquid secondary markets are particularly important goals.

Equity Markets in Brazil Equity markets in Brazil have gone through significant changes over the past 10 years with clear improvements in corporate governance. According to Nenova (2003), by the end of the 1990s Brazil had poor investor rights, low enforcement of contract law, and weak accounting standards. However, in December 2000, the São Paulo Stock Exchange (Bovespa) created three new corporate governance listing segments through which issuers could voluntarily adopt corporate governance practices beyond those required by Brazilian corporate law and capital market regulation more generally. Bovespa listing segments include the traditional Bovespa, Level 1, Level 2, and Novo Mercado, with each of these market segments requiring progressively stricter standards of corporate governance.[5] The main goal of creating these distinct segments, and of Novo Mercado in particular, was to reverse the weakening of the equity markets in Brazil that was taking place at the end of the 1990s by fostering good corporate governance practices, such as disclosure, transparency, and accountability.[6] According to Bhojraj and Sengupta (2003) and Shleifer and Vishny (1997), good governance practices increase investor confidence as they tend to reduce agency and information risks. Therefore, companies are likely to have access to capital at lower costs and better conditions, to increase the value and liquidity of their shares, and to improve their operating performance and profitability.[7] In fact, since then, equity markets have become more liquid and less concentrated, and a greater number of firms have been issuing equities; hence, larger amounts are being raised in Brazil (figure 1.16). These trends suggest that the improvements in the investor protection environment might have indeed paid off.

In spite of a timid beginning, due mostly to a number of external shocks, the Novo Mercado had taken off by the mid-2000s. The number of companies listed in these new corporate governance segments of Bovespa rose steadily, while the number of companies listed in the traditional segment of Bovespa decreased during the 2000s. By December 2010, 168 companies were listed in the three segments: 38 companies in Level 1,

Figure 1.16 Activity in Domestic Equity Markets across
LAC7 Countries, 1990–2009

a. Average number of firms issuing equity per year

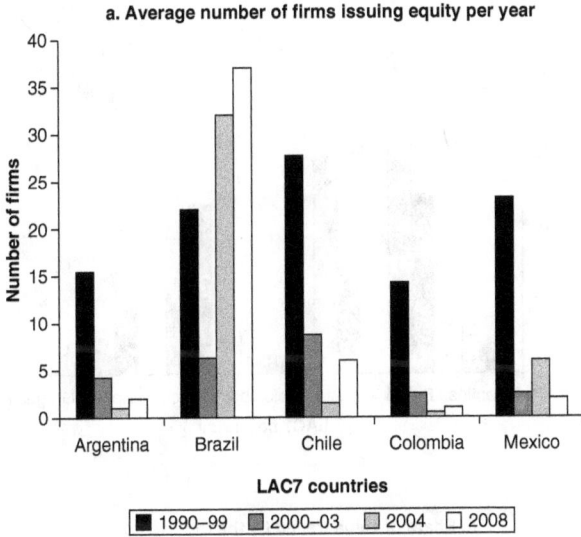

LAC7 countries

■ 1990–99   ▨ 2000–03   ▨ 2004   ☐ 2008

b. Average amount of new issues per year as % of GDP

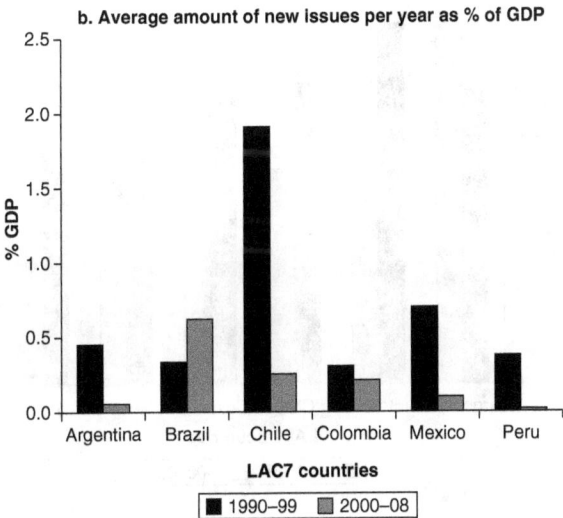

LAC7 countries

■ 1990–99   ▨ 2000–08

(continued next page)

Figure 1.16 (continued)

c. Total value traded per year as % of GDP

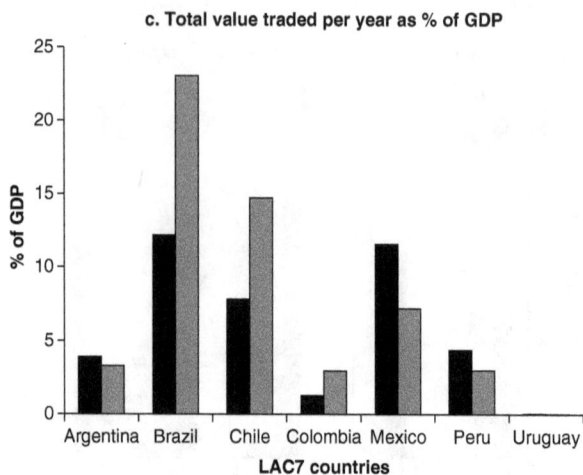

**d. Share of value traded by the top five companies
as % total volume traded**

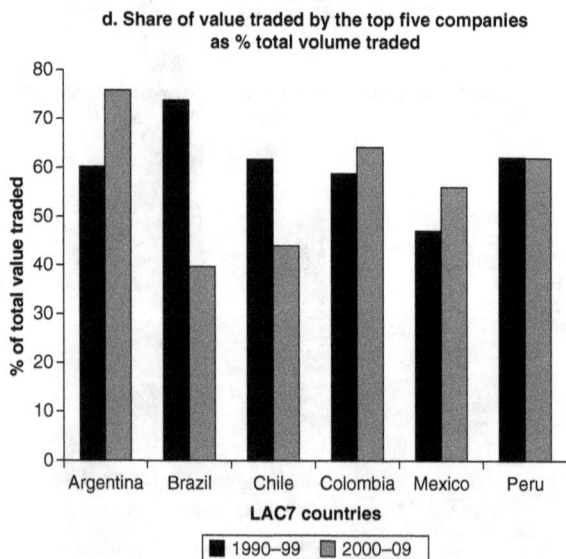

■ 1990–99   ■ 2000–09

Source: SDC Platinum; World Development Indicators; Emerging Markets Database.

Note: GDP = gross domestic product.

18 in Level 2, and 112 in Novo Mercado. These trends suggest a migration from the traditional segment to the corporate governance segments.[8] According to Gorga (2009), by 2007 the large, established, and successful corporations with alternative sources of financing tended to migrate to segments that required small changes in corporate governance (Levels 1 and 2), while the vast majority of companies listed in the Novo Mercado were new entrants looking at the equity market as a viable option to raise capital.[9] Moreover, the improved corporate governance segments of Bovespa have gained market participation, in 2010 representing more than 65 percent of market capitalization and almost 80 percent of value traded (figure 1.17).

The implementation of the Novo Mercado has been well received by foreign investors as well. During 2004–06, on average, foreign investors bought 70 percent of the new stock offerings in this segment of the market (Santana 2008). Similar patterns occurred during 2008–10. Santana (2008) has also argued that the Novo Mercado has allowed Brazilian companies,

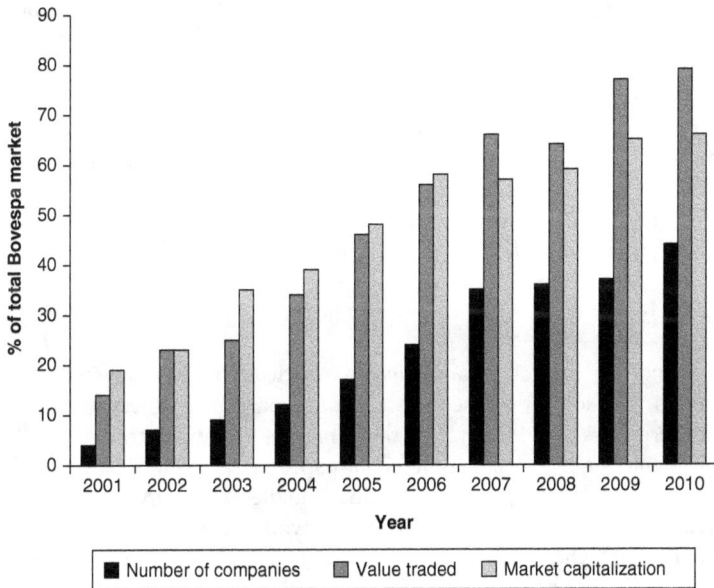

Figure 1.17 Relative Size of the New Corporate Governance Segments as a Percentage of Total Bovespa Market, 2001–10

Source: Bovespa.

and particularly new entrants, to access foreign capital without having to cross-list on international stock markets. For example, among Bovespa's 27 initial public offerings between 2004 and the first half of 2006, only two companies were listed simultaneously on the New York Stock Exchange.

Alternative Markets and Products

In recent years, LAC countries have seen the development of less traditional forms of financing; for example, factoring has deepened along with derivative markets and credit by retailers. Quantifying these new developments is, however, not an easy task as cross-country data are typically not available. Therefore, we focus instead on specific country studies or particular datasets that allow us to shed some light on recent trends in these nontraditional markets.

Derivative Markets

Since the late 1990s, trading of exchange rate derivatives in LAC7 countries has grown in dollar terms and as a percentage of GDP, particularly in Mexico.[10] Trading of interest rate contracts in LAC7 more than doubled as a percentage of GDP in the 2000s compared to the 1990s. Nevertheless, derivatives remain relatively illiquid in most emerging markets: turnover rates remain very small in comparison with those in developed countries. For example, the turnover in exchange rate contracts stands at about 1.1 percent of GDP in LAC countries, whereas the turnover in G-7 countries stands at 7.3 percent of GDP. Turnover figures also suggest that foreign exchange derivatives are largely concentrated in U.S. dollar contracts across developing countries, with U.S. dollar contracts representing about 98 percent of the turnover in LAC7.

Factoring

Factoring is a financial transaction in which accounts receivable (that is, invoices) are sold at a discount to a third party.[11] Invoices are typically short term (less than 90 days), so that a market for invoice trading would be equivalent to a high-yield commercial paper market. This is a particularly important market for SME financing. Smaller firms are typically more opaque (as credible information is less available and more limited) and riskier (with higher mortality rates, lower growth, and less profitability), and they usually do not have adequate collateral. Consequently, their access to bank financing is more restricted. Factoring helps them overcome a number of these constraints, allowing them access to short-term financing, mostly for working capital. These operations offer smaller firms financing without collateral, albeit small guarantees might be charged in some cases, as the underlying credit risk of the transaction belongs to the issuer of the invoice. In addition, factoring can lower the cost of capital for SMEs, because, in many emerging markets, issuers are larger firms with lower credit risk (due, at least in part, to a better credit history) than the SMEs seeking financing.

Factoring is an expanding industry, particularly in LAC countries and emerging markets more broadly. According to the International Factors Group, the worldwide industry turnover in 2008 was estimated at €1.2 trillion (the total amount of assigned receivables), and it has been growing—worldwide volumes increased 3.75 percent in 2008 and 15 percent in 2007.[12] This expansion in factoring volumes, although slowed during the global financial crisis of 2007–08, has been concentrated mostly in emerging markets and particularly in China, Eastern Europe, and LAC7 countries. Nevertheless, factoring is typically less important in emerging markets than in developed countries. In LAC7, for example, factoring represented 2.6 percent of GDP in 2008–09 compared to about 4 percent for developed countries (figure 1.18a).

Chile and Mexico are notable examples in the LAC region where factoring services have developed significantly in recent years and where invoices can actually be traded on organized exchanges or online markets. Factoring in Chile, for example, is one of the largest among emerging markets. In 2009, it had an accumulated volume of €12 billion (10.7 percent of GDP) and about 14,000 users of factoring services, according to the International Factors Group and the Chilean Association of Factoring. Moreover, nonbank factoring companies represent almost 10 percent of this total, according to the Central Bank's Financial Stability Report (2008). In Mexico, total industry turnover was estimated to be almost €11 billion in 2007 (almost 2 percent of GDP). Nonetheless, factoring is still relatively small compared to bank loans or credit lines.

As an alternative to the factoring services typically offered by banks in Chile, Bolsa de Productos is a new initiative that might actually become an important source of SME financing in the near future.[13] Although still in its earlier stages, with volumes of about US$100 million per month in 2011, Bolsa de Productos has been growing fast recently—more than 150 percent in 2010 over 2009. This exchange allows some form of reverse factoring, whereby invoices can be discounted and the credit risk borne by the investor is that of the issuers of the invoice. Moreover, no collateral is needed from SMEs posting the invoice.[14] Critical to the success of this initiative is the fact that discounting invoices in Bolsa de Productos is cheaper than factoring through banks, and it provides investors with a higher yield than they can get in money markets.

Bolsa de Productos is a well-designed initiative with clear solutions for most of the problems affecting SME financing: procedures for clearing and notification of invoices are standardized; insurance companies are active in this market and can guarantee the credit risk of smaller companies; securitization of invoices is also possible, and the "bundling" of invoices

Figure 1.18 Alternative Markets and Products in Selected
Countries and Regions, 2005–10

a. Total annual volume of factoring

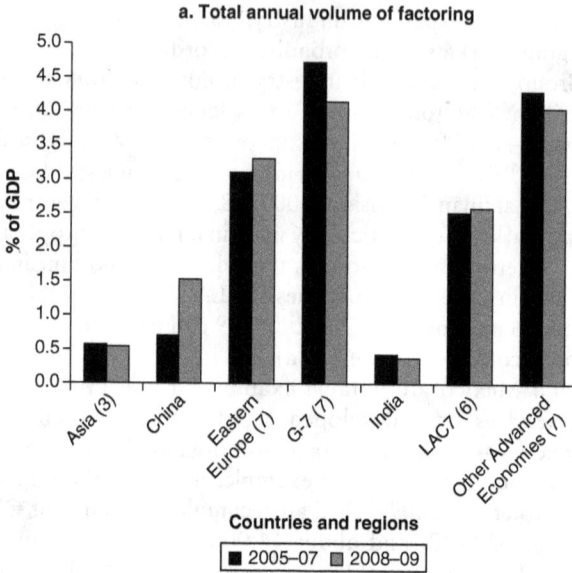

Countries and regions

■ 2005–07 ■ 2008–09

**b. Total annual credit provided by financial
cooperatives and credit unions**

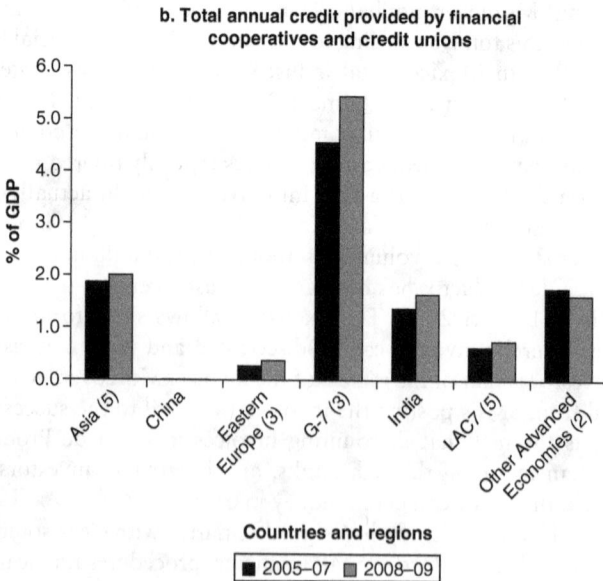

Countries and regions

■ 2005–07 ■ 2008–09

(continued next page)

Figure 1.18 (continued)

c. Annual gross issuance of securitized assets

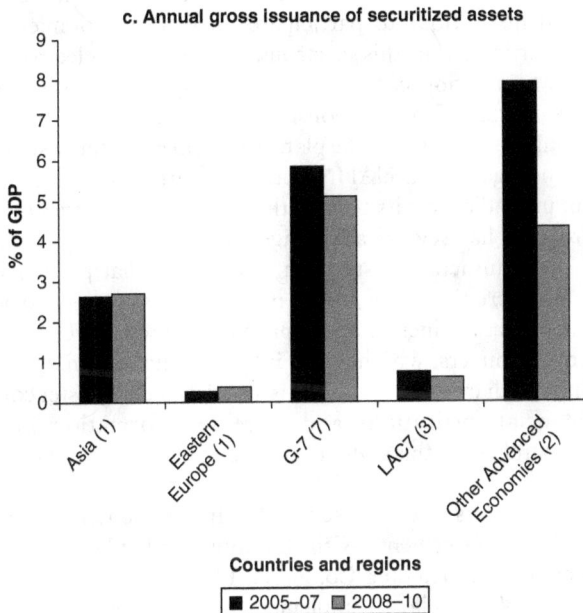

Source: Factors Chain International; World Council of Credit Unions; Reserve Bank of Australia; Bank of Canada; Fitch Ratings; Thomson Reuters; TheCityUK Securitization; SIFMA; Moody's Investors Service.

Note: Numbers in parentheses show the number of countries in each region.

could increase the volumes, making the investment attractive to large institutional investors (pension funds, for example); and competition can be created through an open trading platform.[15] Nevertheless, many of these solutions are not yet implemented due to small trading volumes.

Since 2001, Mexico, has had an online market for factoring services developed by the Mexican development bank NAFIN (Nacional Financiera), called Cadenas Productivas (Productive Chains).[16] This market provides reverse factoring services to SMEs through the creation of chains between large buyers and their suppliers.[17] This reverse factoring program is relatively large, having extended US$11.8 billion in financing in 2008, according to NAFIN; and now it represents a significant share of the factoring market in Mexico. According to Klapper (2006), as of mid-2004, the program included 190 large buyers (45 percent of which were private firms) and more than 150,000 suppliers (about 70,000 of which were SMEs), with a turnover of about 4,000 transactions processed daily.

All transactions are carried out on an electronic platform, which allows NAFIN to capture economies of scale, since most of the costs of the system are fixed and electronic access enables a large number of firms and financial institutions to participate. In fact, all commercial banks are able to participate in this electronic market. This electronic trading also reduces transaction costs, increases the speed of transactions, and improves security. NAFIN is responsible for the development, production, and marketing costs related to the platform. It operates the system and also handles all the legal work. NAFIN does not charge a fee for the factoring services but instead covers its costs with the interest it charges on its loans.

This program has several advantages in dealing with principal-agent problems and transaction costs. First, the buyers that participate in the program, large creditworthy firms, must invite suppliers to join their chain. This reduces principal-agent problems by effectively outsourcing screening to the buyers, who have an informational advantage relative to financial intermediaries. The program is also designed to foster competition among financial institutions and increase information availability, giving transparency to the system and the same access possibility to all intermediaries.

The program has been so successful in Mexico that NAFIN has also entered into agreements with development banks in several Latin American countries, including Colombia, El Salvador, and the República Bolivariana de Venezuela, to implement similar programs, while other development banks in the region are also considering replicating this model.

Financial Cooperatives and Credit Unions

As an alternative to bank financing, financial cooperatives and credit unions are typically financial institutions owned and controlled by their members and operated with the purpose of providing credit and other financial services to them. Hence, they aim mostly at credit provision to households as well as micro, small, and medium enterprises, either formal or informal. Financial cooperatives and credit unions vary significantly in size, ranging from small cooperatives with few members to some that are as large as commercial banks. Not all of these financial institutions are regulated and supervised by central banks and financial regulators. Loans from financial cooperatives and credit unions represent only a small fraction of financial systems in LAC7 countries, particularly compared to G-7 countries.[18] Specifically, credit by credit unions represented 5.4 percent of GDP in G-7 countries in 2008–09 and 0.7 percent in LAC7 countries (figure 1.18b).

Securitization

Structured finance is, in its simplest form, a process in which assets are pooled and transferred to a third party, commonly referred to as a special-purpose vehicle, which, in turn, issues securities backed by this asset pool. In other words, structured finance transactions can help convert illiquid assets into tradable securities. Typically, several classes of securities (called tranches) with distinct risk-return profiles are issued. Across LAC countries, securitized instruments have shown increasing signs of depth in different asset classes. In particular, gross issuance for LAC countries rose from US$2 billion in 2000 to US$24.4 billion in 2010, with Brazil and Mexico as the largest issuers. As a percentage of GDP, however, they declined during the 2008–10 period relative to 2005–07. Compared to developed countries, the structured finance markets in LAC7 countries remain relatively small and underdeveloped. While issuance in LAC7 countries represented less than 1 percent of GDP, gross issuance of securitized assets represented on average 6 percent of GDP per year in G-7 countries and almost 8 percent in other advanced economies between 2005 and 2007 (figure 1.18c).[19]

Although some of these issues are cross-border—typically between US$2 billion and US$4 billion over the past five years for LAC7 countries and mostly on futures—domestic markets represent the largest share of this market. For instance, issues in domestic markets represented almost 90 percent of total issuance in 2010 and more than 97 percent in 2009, when cross-border activity was at its lowest point in the 2000s. In addition, the securitization of different asset types has greatly developed—particularly in Brazil and Mexico, where the largest variety of securitized assets is available. The first deals in the region were cross-border futures transactions involving export receivables. Later deals involved financial receivables. More recently, the region has experienced the development of sophisticated asset-backed securitizations, such as new and used car loans, consumer loans, credit card receivables, equipment leases, and mortgage-backed securities. In 2010, most new issues were asset-backed issues (83.1 percent), followed by residential and commercial mortgage-backed securities (11.5 percent and 5.4 percent, respectively).

Credit by Retailers: The Case of Chile

Retail stores as credit providers seem to be on the rise. Chile is a notable example of this development. Retailers—and, in particular, the largest department stores in the country—have become nontrivial providers of household credit in recent years, and they have been so successful that they are exporting this experience to other countries in the LAC region. Although banks are still the main providers of household credit in Chile, representing 68 percent of total household financial debt, retailers are playing an increasingly important role. Household credit by retailers accounts for 11 percent of total household financial debt, 17 percent of total consumer debt, and 35 percent of nonbank debt (figure 1.19). In addition, the financing that retailers have extended to their customers is 3 percent of GDP.

Figure 1.19 Providers of Household and Consumer Credit in Chile, 2008

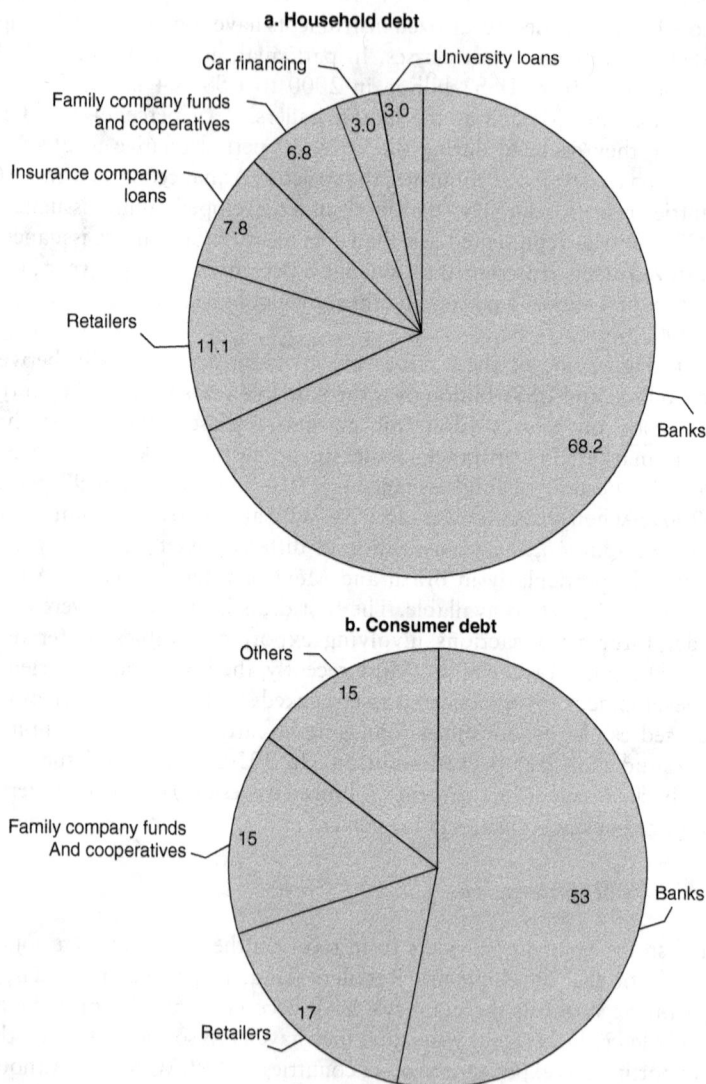

a. Household debt

Car financing

University loans

Family company funds and cooperatives — 6.8

3.0 3.0

Insurance company loans — 7.8

Retailers — 11.1

Banks — 68.2

b. Consumer debt

Others — 15

Family company funds And cooperatives — 15

Banks — 53

Retailers — 17

Source: Local sources.

This high penetration of the retail sector in Chile is related to the introduction of in-house credit cards.[20] These credit cards issued by department stores became popular in Chile because they offered consumer credit, especially to the middle-income segment of the population, when the bank credit market serving this segment was still in its early stages. Ripley was the first department store to introduce a system of credit in 1976, followed by Falabella and Paris, which launched their credit cards in 1980, and La Polar in 1989. Nowadays, retailers are shifting their focus beyond the middle class to include all segments of the population. For example, La Polar has targeted the middle- and low-income segments that typically do not have access to bank credit and thus depend largely on retailer credit. These cards are used by customers mainly to pay for merchandise purchased at these stores, and they can also be used to get cash advances and to make payments at other outlets, such as drugstores, supermarkets, and gas stations, with which the retailers have entered into alliances.

The Chilean retailer card industry now has 16.35 million valid cards—almost one card per inhabitant and about four cards per household. The main providers of credit through credit cards in the retail industry are Falabella, Cencosud, and Ripley. During the first quarter of 2010, Falabella's credit card was used for 59 percent of sales at its department stores, 28 percent of sales at its home improvement stores, and 18 percent of sales at its supermarkets.

Using this acquired expertise in providing consumer credit to households, Chilean retailers are exporting their success and presence in the financial sector to other countries in Latin America. Currently, Falabella operates in Argentina, Colombia, and Peru; Cencosud has already entered the Argentinean, Brazilian, Colombian, and Peruvian markets; Ripley has stores in Peru; La Polar started operating in Colombia in 2010. One notable example of this expansion is Falabella, which, by March 2010, had 775,000 active credit cards in Argentina, 522,000 in Colombia, and 937,000 in Peru. Peru has been the main market for Falabella's foreign credit business, where it started operating through Financiera CMR S.A. in 1997 (Banco Falabella since 2007). With US$432 million in outstanding loans, today Falabella's loans represent around 6 percent of total consumer loans in Peru.

Exchange-Traded Funds

Exchange-traded funds (ETFs) are a relatively recent and increasingly popular type of product traded on stock exchanges. They are traded portfolios composed of stocks as well as of commodities and bonds. They provide a greater scope for portfolio diversification and at the same time possess stock-like features, such as transparency, frequent pricing, and ease of trading, which are associated with low trading costs.

Currently, the number of ETFs in developed countries is larger than in emerging countries, most likely because of the greater depth and liquidity of their financial systems, as well as the greater sophistication of institutional investors in these markets. Nevertheless, these products have been on the rise in some LAC7 countries like Mexico. Moreover, ETFs are gaining space in secondary markets, with an increasing share of total trading in stock markets. In LAC7 countries, they accounted for 2.2 percent of the trading in 2008–09 compared to 0.1 percent during 2000–03.

Players in the Financial System (Saver's Perspective)

LAC's financial systems have also become more complex from the saver's perspective. In the past, banks interacted directly with borrowers and lenders, but now there is a greater diversity of players with a broader set of institutions, such as pension funds, mutual funds, and insurance companies, that are intermediating savings, providing economy-wide credit, and offering a broader variety of products, as shown briefly in the section on financial development. In fact, in some emerging countries institutional investors have become even more important than banks. This rise of nonbank intermediaries has been a significant factor in the development of local markets across financial systems of developing countries, and particularly those in LAC, to the extent that they provide a stable demand for financial assets. Nevertheless, as argued below, LAC still has a long way to go in raising the sophistication of its institutional investors, as most of the savings are still channeled to government bonds and bank deposits.

Main Financial Intermediaries

Although banks continue to play a significant and stable role, nonbank financial intermediaries, such as pension funds, mutual funds, and insurance companies, have been gaining considerable space in LAC7 countries and in other emerging markets around the world (figure 1.20). For instance, pension fund assets represent 19 percent of GDP in LAC7 countries and 15 percent in Asian countries, while mutual funds and insurance companies are usually larger on average in Asian countries than in LAC7 countries. Eastern European countries have smaller but also fast-growing institutional investors. As with most other features of the markets examined so far, these intermediaries are still smaller on average in LAC7 countries than in developed countries, reflecting, to some extent the developed countries' advanced financial systems.

Figure 1.20 Assets of Pension Funds, Mutual Funds, and Insurance Companies in Selected Countries and Regions, 2000–09

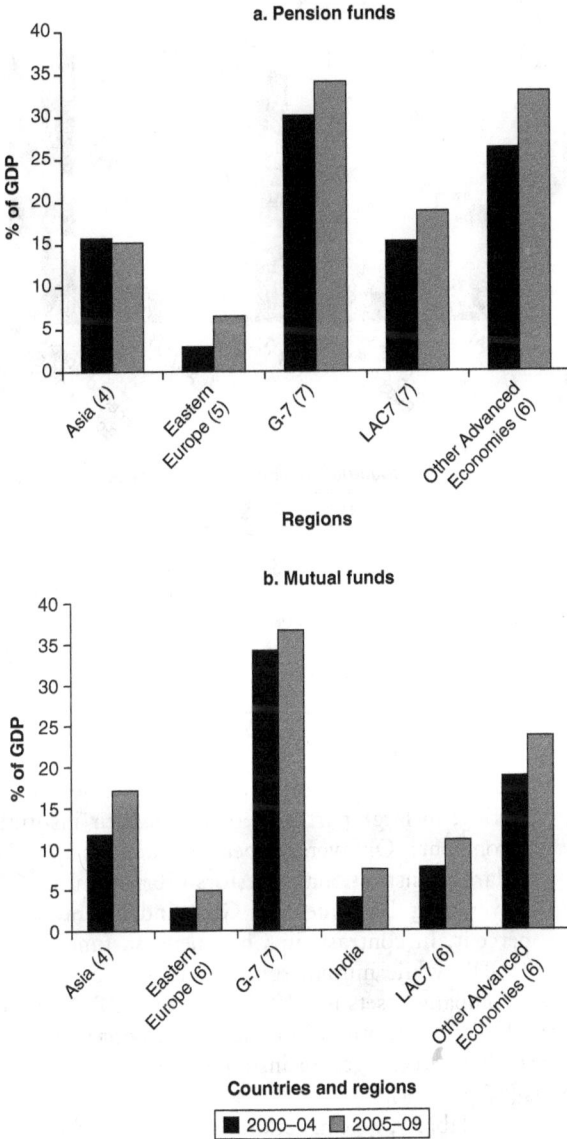

a. Pension funds

b. Mutual funds

2000–04   2005–09

(continued next page)

Figure 1.20 *(continued)*

c. Insurance companies

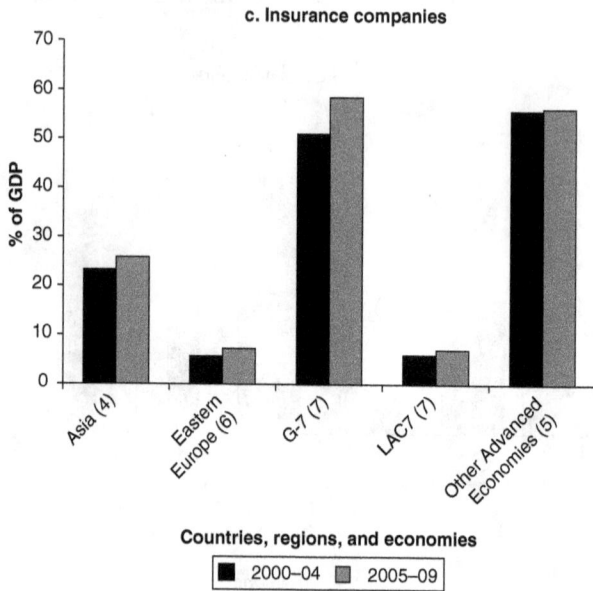

Sources: Asociación de Supervisores de Seguros de Latinoamérica; OECD; local sources; Investment Company Institute; Asociación Internacional de Organismos de Supervisión de Fondos de Pensiones.

Note: Numbers in parentheses show the number of countries in each region. GDP = gross domestic product.

The size of each type of institutional investor varies among LAC7 countries, reflecting, in large part, differences in their institutional and regulatory environments. On average, pension funds in LAC7 countries are usually the largest institutional investors (20 percent of GDP), with mutual funds averaging 10 percent of GDP and insurance companies averaging 6 percent. In contrast, in Chile pension funds reach almost 70 percent of GDP, while mutual fund assets are 15 percent of GDP and insurance company assets are 19 percent of GDP. Mutual funds in Brazil are the largest institutional investors (42 percent of GDP), with significantly smaller percentages for insurance companies (8 percent) and pension funds (16 percent).

Due to data availability, we can get only a glimpse of the private equity and venture capital funds. These funds, through which investors acquire a percentage of an operating firm, are particularly important for the financing of SMEs. Unsurprisingly, however, private equity and venture capital funds are still relatively underdeveloped in LAC countries. Private equity funds raised on average US$4.9 billion per year in LAC, a strong contrast to the almost US$46 billion raised in Asia between 2003 and 2009.[21] Moreover, over the same period LAC represented only 1.1 percent of total worldwide private equity fund raisings, compared with almost 10 percent for Asian countries, with the rest taking place in the United States and in Europe. Venture capital funds are even less represented in emerging markets in general, with a total of US$12 billion per year raised on average outside the United States and Europe during this period. Albeit smaller in absolute size, these funds have a relatively larger presence in emerging markets: fund raising outside the United States and Europe represented 25 percent over the same period. Although significantly smaller than other institutional investors, private equity and venture capital funds have been growing in the LAC region. In the first half of the 2000s, US$1.2 billion was raised on average in LAC countries, with the number rising to US$7.7 billion in the second half of the decade. Nevertheless, continuing growth for these funds in coming years will require adequate regulatory systems and rigorous disclosure standards. The latter are viewed as a particular issue in LAC countries, as accessing accurate and objective information for nonpublic firms is not straightforward. In this context, effective ex ante due diligence activities, valuation analysis, and ex post business monitoring, which are key for this industry, can be rather difficult.

The Nature of the Asset Side

Pension funds, mutual funds, and insurance companies provide a stable demand for domestic financial assets, given regulatory limits on their foreign investments, and thus have a potential role in deepening local capital markets across LAC countries. For instance, pension funds in LAC countries typically have less than 11 percent allocated abroad; Chile is the exception, with almost 45 percent allocated abroad in 2009. Surprisingly, however, institutional investors in the region, and in emerging markets more broadly, concentrate a significant fraction of their asset holdings in fixed-income instruments such as bonds and deposits and particularly in government bonds. These investment practices, which currently limit the role of institutional investors in the development of corporate bond and equity markets, are evident in figure 1.21a. Government securities and deposits (and other financial institution assets) accounted for more than 60 percent of the holdings of LAC7 pension funds during 2005–08. Nevertheless, as the figure also shows, this concentration by pension fund portfolios has declined.[22]

Figure 1.21b illustrates the heterogeneity within LAC countries. Pension funds in some countries (Argentina, Mexico, and Uruguay, for example) are heavily invested in government securities, while in others (like Chile and Peru) pension funds account for a greater share of deposits in their portfolios. Yet declines in both types of assets have taken place. At the same time, the shares of equity and foreign securities have been slowly increasing over the same period. Portfolio allocations to corporate bonds, however, have been relatively stable.

Comparable patterns are also observed in the investment structure of mutual funds in LAC countries.[23] Funds invest on average a large fraction of their portfolios in government bonds and money market instruments. Like trends in the pension fund industry, funds have been gradually shifting their portfolios toward equity investments (figure 1.22). In Brazil, for example, the share of public sector bonds declined from 73 percent to 48 percent between 2003–04 and 2005–09 on average. In Chile, this fraction declined from 14 percent to 6 percent, although deposits are a stable and substantial share of its portfolio, 63 percent on average

Figure 1.21 Composition of Pension Fund Portfolios in Latin America, 1999–08

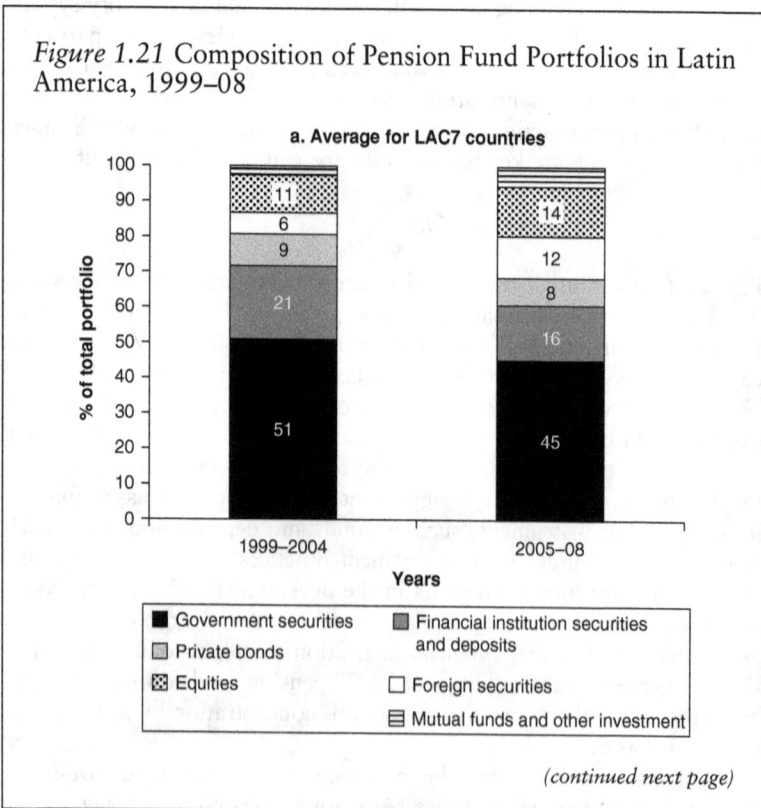

a. Average for LAC7 countries

Legend:
- ■ Government securities
- ▨ Financial institution securities and deposits
- ▥ Private bonds
- ▨ Equities
- □ Foreign securities
- ▤ Mutual funds and other investment

(continued next page)

Figure 1.21 (continued)

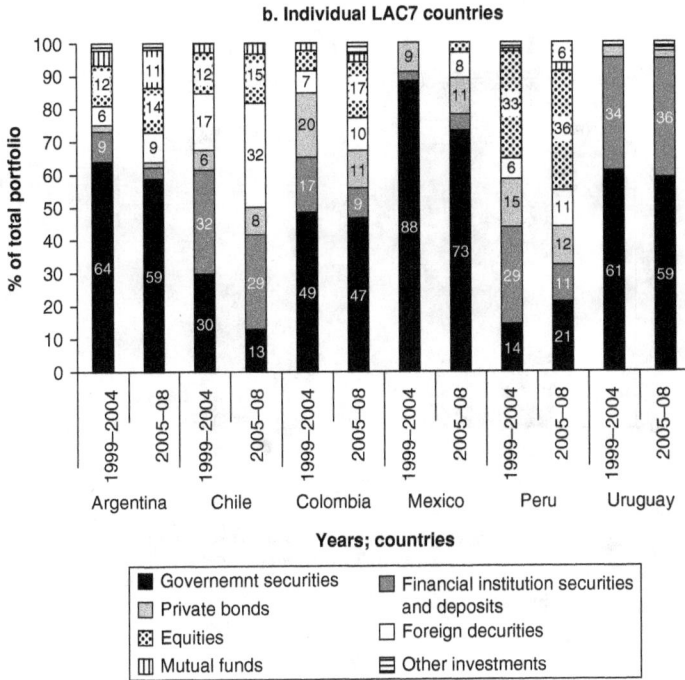

b. Individual LAC7 countries

Source: OECD; AIOSFP; FIAP; local sources.

over the same period. This composition of available mutual funds in the region raises the question of whether financial intermediaries or households themselves are responsible for these patterns. For instance, bond and money market funds account for 70 percent of existing mutual funds in LAC7 countries. In contrast, in G-7 and other developed countries, these funds correspond to about 35 percent of all funds. In those countries, equity funds are much more prominent, accounting for between 41 percent and 48 percent of existing funds, whereas in LAC7 countries equity funds typically account for 17 percent of available mutual funds, on average.

These trends suggest that institutional investors have not contributed to the development of local markets as much as expected in the LAC region. At the same time, one has to consider that relatively small and illiquid domestic markets can be viewed as unattractive by these investors, particularly by mutual funds that are subject to sudden withdrawals by clients. In other words, asset managers' incentives can explain, at least in

Figure 1.22 Composition of Mutual Fund Portfolios of Five Countries in LAC, 2000–09

a. Brazil

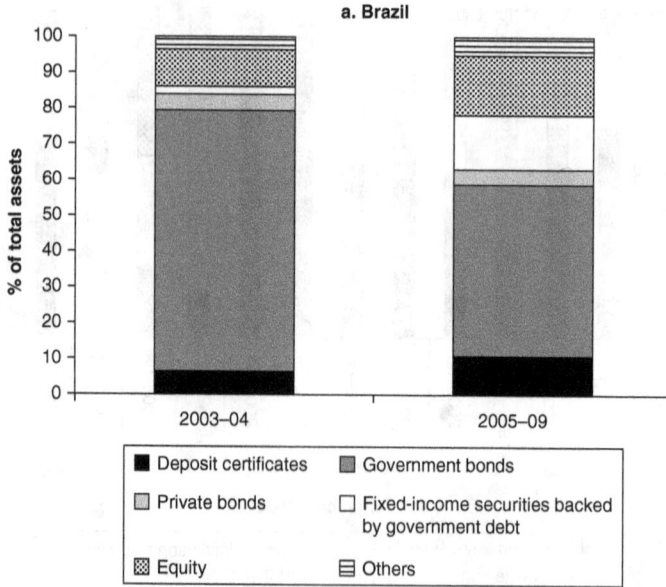

Legend:
- Deposit certificates
- Government bonds
- Private bonds
- Fixed-income securities backed by government debt
- Equity
- Others

b. Chile

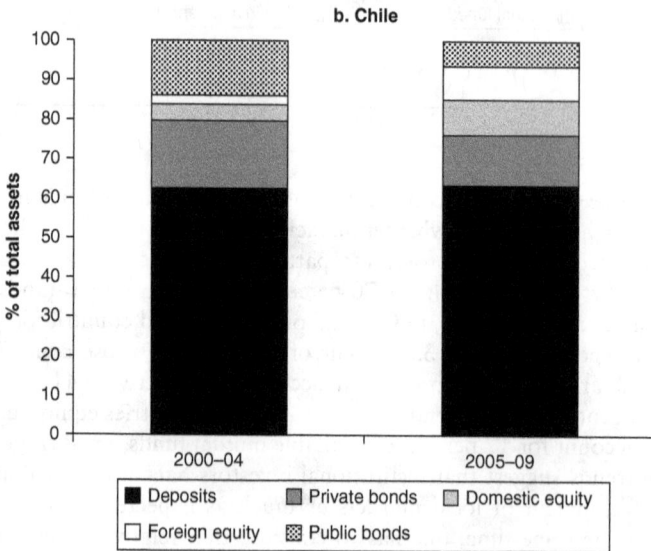

Legend:
- Deposits
- Private bonds
- Domestic equity
- Foreign equity
- Public bonds

(continued next page)

Figure 1.22 (continued)

c. Colombia

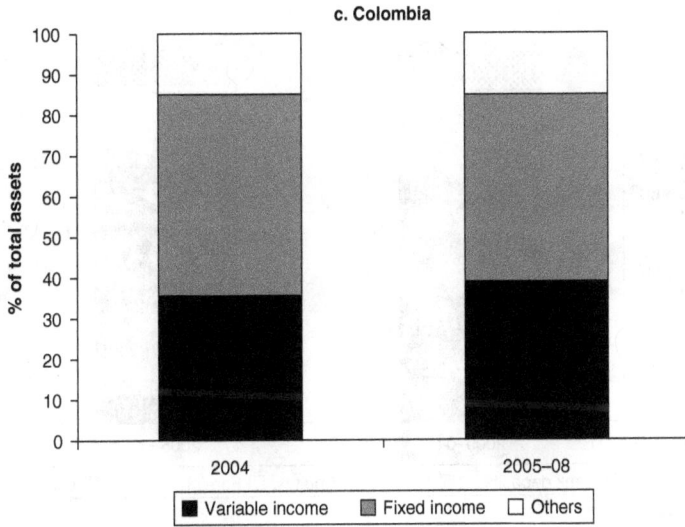

Legend: ■ Variable income   ▨ Fixed income   □ Others

d. Mexico

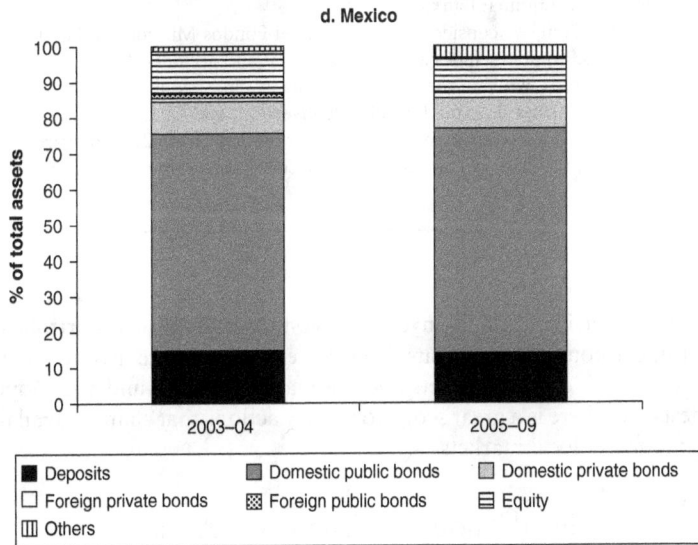

Legend: ■ Deposits   ▨ Domestic public bonds   ▨ Domestic private bonds
□ Foreign private bonds   ▨ Foreign public bonds   ⊟ Equity
▥ Others

(continued next page)

Figure 1.22 *(continued)*

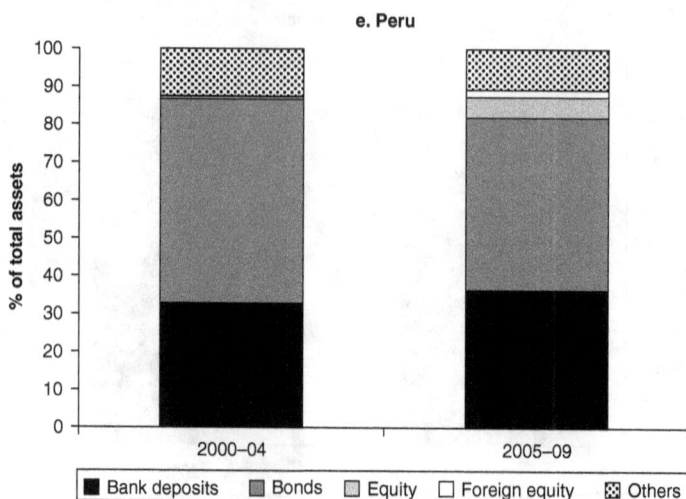

e. Peru

Source: International Financial Statistics; FGV-Rio; Conasev;
Superfinanciera; Andima; Banxico.
Note: For Peru, we consider the portfolios of Fondos Mutuos and Fondos
de Inversiones. Equity includes acciones de capital and acciones de inversion
for fondos mutuos, while in the case of investment funds, equities are
composed de acciones de capital, fondos de inversion, and otras participaciones
until 2002 and "Derechos de participacion patrimonial" from 2004 onward.
For Colombia, Fondos Vigilados and Fondos Controlados are reported in
different tables for 2002.

part, why large institutional investors invest the bulk of their portfolios in
government bonds and deposits. This current trap, where investors avoid
local corporate capital markets and the markets remain underdeveloped,
suggests that there is a great scope for policy actions that channel available
funds to foster local markets.

Final Thoughts: The Road Ahead

This chapter presents a systematic and detailed account of where emerging
economies and Latin America in particular stand with respect to financial
development. The evidence overall suggests that these countries are in a
substantially better position than in the past, even along such dimensions as
susceptibility to volatility and crises due to currency and maturity mismatches.

In general, domestic financial systems have continued developing since the 1990s, at the same time that standard measures indicate that international financial integration deepened and that foreign investors continued investing in emerging economies. As a result, more resources have become available in these economies relative to their size—that is, more savings are available for use, especially for the private sector, since governments have been reducing crowding out by demanding fewer funds due to fiscal consolidation. Furthermore, financial systems are becoming more complex and somewhat more diversified. Financing does not depend as much as before on banks, as bonds and equity play a larger role. Among bonds, corporate bonds are also increasing in importance. Regarding financial intermediaries, institutional investors have become much more prominent, most notably pension funds and mutual funds. Moreover, traditional markets and institutions are no longer the sole providers of financing, as other types of financing, like retail chain credit, seem to be gaining momentum. This, in turn, suggests that consumers might be better served now. Moreover, the nature of financing also seems to be changing. Debt is moving toward longer maturities and increasingly being issued in local currencies, which reduces mismatches, while domestic markets seem to be gaining some ground. Overall, these trends suggest safer financial development in emerging economies, which is accompanying the safer international financial integration.

Despite all the improvements, one can argue that many emerging economies are still relatively underdeveloped financially. In fact, the countries that have developed the most in recent years are the advanced economies. Therefore, the gap between industrial and emerging economies in financial development has widened even further. As a result, one might expect that the financial sectors of emerging economies will continue to expand in the years to come.

There is a notable heterogeneity in the indicators of financial development across emerging economies, including Latin America. While financial development has progressed in LAC, the region lags behind not only developed countries but also other emerging economies, most notably those in Asia. This observation holds true for all sectors of the financial system—banks, bond markets, and equity markets. The only area that appears relatively developed is the institutional investor side, in particular, pension funds. But even there, the assets held by these institutions are concentrated to a large extent in deposits and government bonds. Therefore, Latin America's financial system is unfortunately less developed than might have been expected, given its intensive reform efforts and improved macroeconomic performance. Moreover, it appears that the region will need many years to overcome the relative underdevelopment of its financial sector. A couple of countries, however, seem to be doing better: Brazil in its equity market and Chile in its corporate bond market. Furthermore, there are some nascent positive changes in the nature of domestic financial markets, with their reduced currency and maturity mismatches.

Nonetheless, to a large extent, only a few firms seem to be able to use capital market financing. Latin America has not become a place with finance for all, at least based on the data analyzed in this chapter.

What explains the lagging financial development in emerging economies and in Latin America in particular? What explains the persistent mismatch between expectations and outcomes? In this final part of the chapter, we discuss and speculate on some of the possible reasons, based on evidence from various pieces of other work. We also discuss some of the possible avenues for the future.

While it is difficult to answer the question of whether the problems lie in the supply or in the demand side of funds, the findings in this chapter suggest that the insufficient financial development does not seem to be determined just by the lack of available funds. In fact, financial underdevelopment seems to coexist with a large pool of domestic and foreign funds in the economy, not least because domestic residents are sometimes induced to save in market-based instruments targeted to domestic markets only. Moreover, funds are also available from foreign investors eager to invest in emerging economies.[24] The availability of funds will naturally provide a continuing deepening of some markets. There also may be problems on the demand side, but there is not enough evidence to confirm this. Some surveys indicate that SMEs are not well served, but many owners do not want to lose the control of their firms and do not wish to subject their companies to market forces. Moreover, even when firms complain about poor access to financing, it is not clear that they have worthwhile investment projects.

The burden does not seem to rest on aggregate factors alone. The macroeconomic performance and institutional framework have likely hampered financial development in the past, but many developing countries have substantially improved their macroeconomic and institutional stances, and yet financial development has not progressed as expected. In the 2000s, there has been much less crowding out by the government in the financial sector, especially in bond markets and banking. Moreover, corporate governance and other institutional indicators have improved and are not likely to explain the cross-regional and cross-country variation in financial development.

Financial globalization could, in principle, be behind the poor domestic development if financial activity (of domestic assets) moved overseas. In a world of financial integration, transactions do not have to take place domestically; that is, firms and households can transact in any market, domestic or foreign. But this does not seem to be the whole story. Some of the domestic development indicators take into account the activity that happens both domestically and abroad. Moreover, internationalization does not seem to be compensating for poor domestic development. Internationalization is positively correlated with financial development within and across regions. Thus, it complements rather than substitutes for domestic markets. Furthermore, globalization is important for many other countries and regions and thus does not explain the cross-country or cross-regional differences. And developed countries, with more domestic financial development than emerging economies, are even more globalized.

Part of the problem seems to lie in the financial intermediation process, since many assets available for investment are not purchased by banks and institutional investors. These institutions hold large resources that were expected to be invested long term and in many parts of the financial sector, not just in a few firms. However, institutional investors seem to shy away from risk, investing short term and following herding and momentum trading strategies, among other practices. Moreover, banks have moved from financing large corporations to financing standardized retail products and some specific lines of credit to SMEs that are easy to commoditize, that can be done on a large scale, and that involve relatively low risk, like leasing and collateral lending. Part of this trend might be due to a regulatory emphasis on stability. However, managers' risk-taking incentives seem to play an important role. For example, evidence from Chile on mutual funds, pension funds, and insurance companies seems to reinforce this point. In sum, while it could be the case that more assets would help those investors take more risk, the evidence and the literature indicate that the overall functioning of financial systems is not contributing to the degree of financial development envisioned by the promarket reformers.

To the extent that part of the problem lies in the financial intermediation process, policy makers face a difficult road ahead. The role of institutional investors is emblematic in this respect. For example, it is not clear how to generate incentives for more risk taking to foster innovation and growth while preserving the stability of the financial system. This problem is particularly acute because households are often forced to allocate a substantial portion of their savings to pension funds. On the one hand, to the extent that funds invest too conservatively, they will underperform relevant benchmarks. On the other hand, generating more risk taking would put households' funds at higher risk. And riskier behavior makes monitoring of financial intermediaries more difficult. In other words, there is a strong trade-off between stability and development, and it is not clear where the socially optimal outcome lies. To complicate matters more for policy makers, the global financial crisis led to a devaluation of the international paradigms and a questioning of the international regulatory framework.

Eventually, emerging economies will need to catch up, grow their financial systems, and take more risk, as they proceed to become more like developed nations. The challenge is how to do so without undermining financial stability. Macroprudential policies that limit expansions constitute a clear example of the dilemma policy makers face. It is difficult to distinguish spurious booms from leapfrogging for the same reasons that it has been difficult to spot bubbles in the financial systems of many developed countries.

Notes

1. In complementary work, we took a deeper look within Latin America and compared LAC7 to other South American countries (Bolivia, Ecuador, Paraguay, and República Bolivariana de Venezuela), Central America (Belize, Costa Rica, El Salvador, Guatemala, Honduras, Nicaragua, and, exceptionally, due to the characteristics of its economy, the Dominican Republic), the Caribbean (Jamaica and Trinidad and Tobago), and offshore financial centers (Aruba, the Bahamas, Barbados, Bermuda, the Cayman Islands, the Netherlands Antilles, and Panama).

2. Bonds whose maturity is less than one year (commercial paper mostly) are excluded from these statistics due to data availability.

3. Notice, however, that while nominal bonds are still a very small fraction of total issued corporate bonds, they have increased significantly over the past five years.

4. The trading of bonds issued by banks accounts for a large fraction of total trading in secondary bond markets in Chile—60 percent, on average, during 2010.

5. The main requirement for equity listings in Novo Mercado is the issuance of common voting stocks (that is, the so-called one-share-one-vote rule). This requirement was a response to the predominance of nonvoting stocks known as "preferred stocks" among Brazilian companies, allowing holders of voting stocks to take control of companies by owning small percentages of the total equity. In addition, Novo Mercado also required complying with a number of other good corporate governance practices such as a minimum 25 percent free float, U.S. GAAP reporting, and 100 percent tag-along rights, with all shareholders getting the same conditions in the event that a company was sold. The corporate governance listing segments Level 1 and Level 2 are intermediate segments between the traditional listing segment and the Novo Mercado, their main goal being to facilitate a gradual migration from traditional markets to Novo Mercado. A detailed description of the rules governing these different segments is available on Bovespa's webpage (http://www.bmfbovespa.com.br).

6. Glaser, Johnson, and Shleifer (2001) and La Porta et al. (1997) show that protection of minority shareholders is fundamental to the development of a country's capital market. In addition, Klapper and Love (2004) show that good governance practices are more important in countries with weak investor protection and inefficient enforcement.

7. Ashbaugh-Skaife, Collins, and LaFond (2006), for example, find that better corporate governance practices improve corporate credit ratings and reduce bond yields. De Carvalho and Pennacchi (2012) argue, for the case of Brazil, that migration from traditional markets to the Novo Mercado brings positive abnormal returns to shareholders and an increase in the trading volume of shares. Klapper and Love (2004) find that better corporate governance is associated with higher operating performance and higher Tobin's Q. Joh (2003) concludes that firms with a higher control-ownership disparity exhibit lower profitability.

8. It is important to note that some firms with a traditional Bovespa listing have public debt but not public equity.

9. This argument is consistent with data on the financial reports of Bovespa's listed companies that show that companies listed in the corporate governance segments, on average, are larger than companies in the traditional market but that companies listed in Levels 1 and 2 are larger than firms listed in the Novo Mercado.

10. The Bank for International Settlements publishes the "Triennial Central Bank Survey of Foreign Exchange and Derivatives Market Activity," which provides comprehensive and internationally consistent information on turnover in foreign exchange and interest rate derivative markets for over 50 countries.

11. See de la Torre, Gozzi, and Schmukler (2007c) and Klapper (2006) for a detailed discussion of factoring per se, as well as for a few case studies around the world.

12. The statistics, however, were significantly influenced by a strong euro. Most notably, a large market, such as that in the United Kingdom, actually increased when expressed in British pounds, while it decreased by 4.84 percent when expressed in euros.

13. Currently, main investors in Bolsa de Productos are institutional investors such as mutual funds, investment banks, and portfolio managers. Pension funds are expected to be added to this list soon.

14. Issuers of invoices need to be registered with the exchange. Currently, there are about 170 qualified issuers, out of which about 90 are active, according to Bolsa de Productos. Issuers can also negotiate the extension of their own contracts, and hence Bolsa de Productos is a source of financing for both issuers and holders of invoices. There are restrictions on becoming a qualified issuer—very large firms as well as medium-size firms on the other end can become qualified issuers. Any firm with an invoice from a qualified issuer can use the Bolsa de Productos.

15. For SMEs, discounting invoices in Bolsa de Productos is a cheaper alternative than factoring through banks, for instance, and for investors, it provides a higher yield than money markets.

16. This initiative is similar in nature to Bolsa de Productos in Chile.

17. Once a supplier delivers goods to the buyer and issues an invoice, the buyer posts an online "negotiable document" equal to the amount that will be factored on its NAFIN webpage. Participant financial institutions that are willing to factor this particular receivable post their interest rate quotes for this transaction. Finally, the supplier can access this information and choose the best quote. Once the factor is chosen, the discounted amount is transferred to the supplier's bank account. The factor is paid directly by the buyer when the invoice is due.

18. We consider credit unions as cooperative financial institutions that are owned and controlled by their members, providing credit and other financial services to them.

19. Net issuance includes issues sold into the market and excludes issues retained by issuing banks, while gross issuance includes those retained issues.

20. In-house credit cards have been an important source of retailers' profits, and more specifically interest on credit purchases. An example of this is Falabella—operating profits from CMR (its credit card unit) were US$43.9 million in the first quarter of 2010, making the credit business one of the main sources of Falabella's profit and its most profitable area, with an operating profit margin of 37.4 percent.

21. These statistics are from Preqin, the industry's leading source of information where country-level information is not available. Therefore, regional statistics cited include all countries geographically located within each region, making them different from the rest of this chapter.

22. The numbers in figure 1.21 are not directly comparable to those in figure 1.22 due to differences in the classification of assets and the sample coverage in countries and years.

23. Data availability prevents us from providing a broader analysis.

24. One could argue that international financial markets are very volatile and that foreign investors are not reliable. But this is the case across countries, and it is difficult to explain the cross-country or cross-regional volatility. Furthermore, international investors seem to be favoring emerging economies in relative terms even in a period of global crisis, although they did pull back from all countries in the wake of the global financial crisis.

References

Acemoglu, D., and F. Zilibotti. 1997. "Was Prometheus Unbound by Chance? Risk, Diversification, and Growth." *Journal of Political Economy* 105: 709–51.

Aghion, P., A. Banerjee, and T. Piketty. 1999. "Dualism and Macroeconomic Volatility." *Quarterly Journal of Economics* 114: 1359–97.

Anzoategui, D., M. S. Martínez Pería, and R. R. Rocha. 2010. "Bank Competition in the Middle East and Northern Africa Region." *Review of Middle East Economics and Finance* 6 (2): 26–48.

Ashbaugh-Skaife, H., D. W. Collins, and R. LaFond. 2006. "The Effects of Corporate Governance on Firms' Credit Ratings." *Journal of Accounting and Economics* 42: 203–43.

Asociación de Supervisores de Seguros de Latinoamérica. http://www.assalweb .org/.

Asociación Internacional de Organismos de Supervisión de Fondos de Pensiones. http://www.fiap.cl/prontus_noticia/site/artic/20121108/ pags/20121108095528.html.

Bank for International Settlements. http://www.bis.org/.

Bank of Canada. http://www.bankofcanada.ca/.

Bankscope. https://bankscope2.bvdep.com/version-2013614/home .serv?product=scope2006.

Beck, T., and A. Demirgüç-Kunt. 2006. "Small and Medium-Size Enterprises: Access to Finance as a Growth Constraint." *Journal of Banking and Finance* 30: 2931–43.

Beck, T., A. Demirgüç-Kunt, L. Laeven, and V. Maksimovic. 2006. "The Determinants of Financing Obstacles." *Journal of International Money and Finance* 25 (6): 932–52.

Beck, T., A. Demirgüç-Kunt, and M. S. Martínez Pería. 2011. "Bank Financing for SMEs around the World: Drivers, Obstacles, Business Models, and Lending Practices." *Journal of Financial Services Research* 39: 35–54.

Berger, A. 1995. "The Profit-Structure Relationship in Banking: Tests of Market Power and Efficient Structure Hypotheses." *Journal of Money, Credit, and Banking* 27 (2): 404–31.

Bhojraj, S., and P. Sengupta. 2003. "Effect of Corporate Governance on Bond Ratings and Yields: The Role of Institutional Investors and Outside Directors." *Journal of Business* 76: 455–75.

Broner, F., G. Lorenzoni, and S. Schmukler. 2013. "Why Do Emerging Economies Borrow Short Term?" *Journal of the European Economic Association* 11 (1): 67–100.

Calvo, G., and C. Reinhart. 2000. "When Capital Flows Come to a Sudden Stop: Consequences and Policy." In *Key Issues in Reform of the International Monetary and Financial System*, edited by P. K. Kenen and A. K. Swoboda, 175–201. Washington, DC: International Monetary Fund.

Cetorelli, N. 1999. "Competitive Analysis in Banking: Appraisal of the Methodologies." *Economic Perspectives* 23: 2–15.

Claessens, S., and N. van Horen. 2013. "Foreign Banks: Trends and Impact." *Journal of Money, Credit, and Banking*.

Cull, R., and M. S. Martínez Pería. 2010. "Foreign Bank Participation in Developing Countries: What Do We Know about the Drivers and Consequences of This Phenomenon?" Policy Research Working Paper 5398, World Bank, Washington, DC.

Dahlquist, M., L. Pinkowitz, R. Stulz, and R. Williamson. 2003. "Corporate Governance and the Home Bias." *Journal of Financial and Quantitative Analysis* 38 (1): 87–110.

Dahlquist, M., and G. Robertsson. 2001. "Direct Foreign Ownership, Institutional Investors, and Firm Characteristics." *Journal of Financial Economics* 59: 413–40.

Dayoub, M., and E. Lasagabaster. 2007. "General Trends in Competition Policy and Investment Regulation in Mandatory Defined Contribution Markets in Latin America." Policy Research Working Paper 4720, World Bank, Washington, DC.

De Carvalho, A. G., and G. Pennacchi. 2012. "Can a Stock Exchange Improve Corporate Behavior? Evidence from Firms' Migration to Premium Listings in Brazil." *Journal of Corporate Finance* 18 (4): 934–52.

de la Torre, A., J. C. Gozzi, and S. L. Schmukler. 2007a. "Stock Market Development under Globalization: Whither the Gains from Reforms?" *Journal of Banking and Finance* 31: 1731–54.

———. 2007b. "Financial Development: Emerging and Maturing Policy Issues." *World Bank Research Observer* 22 (1): 67–102.

———. 2007c. "Innovative Experiences in Access to Finance: Market Friendly Roles for the Visible Hand?" Policy Research Working Paper 4326, World Bank, Washington, DC.

de la Torre, A., M. S. Martínez Pería, and S. L. Schmukler. 2010. "Bank Involvement with SMEs: Beyond Relationship Lending." *Journal of Banking and Finance* 34 (9): 2280–93.

de la Torre, A., and S. L. Schmukler. 2004. "Coping with Risks through Mismatches: Domestic and International Financial Contracts for Emerging Economies." *International Finance* 7 (3): 349–90.

———. 2008. *Emerging Capital Markets and Globalization: The Latin American Experience*. Washington, DC: World Bank; Palo Alto, CA: Stanford University Press.

Didier, T. 2011. "Information Asymmetries and Institutional Investor Mandates." Policy Research Paper 5586, World Bank, Washington, DC.

Didier, T., C. Hevia, and S. L. Schmukler. 2011. "How Resilient Were Emerging Economies to the Global Crisis?" Policy Research Working Paper 5637, World Bank, Washington, DC.

Didier, T., R. Rigobon, and S. L. Schmukler. 2010. "Unexploited Gains from International Diversification: Patterns of Portfolio Holdings around the World." NBER Working Paper 16629, National Bureau of Economic Research, Cambridge, MA.

Easterly, W., R. Islam, and J. E. Stiglitz. 2000. "Shaken and Stirred: Explaining Growth Volatility." In *Annual World Bank Conference on Development Economics 2000*, edited by B. Pleskovic and J. E. Stiglitz, 191–211. Washington, DC: World Bank.

Edison, H., and F. Warnock. 2004. "U.S. Investors' Emerging Market Equity Portfolios: A Security-Level Analysis." *Review of Economics and Statistics* 86 (3): 691–704.

Eichengreen, B. 2009. "Lessons of the Crisis for Emerging Markets." *International Economics and Economic Policy* 7 (1): 49–62.

Eichengreen, B., and R. Hausmann. 1999. "Exchange Rates and Financial Fragility." *Federal Reserve Bank of Kansas City Proceedings*: 329–68.

Emerging Markets Database (EMDB).

Glaser E., S. Johnson, and A. Shleifer. 2001. "Coase and Coasians." *Quarterly Journal of Economics* 108: 853–99.

Gorga, E. 2009. "Changing the Paradigm of Stock Ownership from Concentrated towards Dispersed Ownership? Evidence from Brazil and Consequences for Emerging Countries." *Northwestern Journal of International Law and Business* 29 (2): 439–554.

Gourinchas, P. O., and M. Obstfeld. 2011. "Stories of the Twentieth Century for the Twenty-First." *American Economic Journal* 4 (1): 226–65.

Hausmann, R., M. Gavin, C. Pages-Serra, and E. Stein. 1999. "Financial Turmoil and the Choice of Exchange Rate Regime." Working Paper 400, Inter-American Development Bank, Washington, DC.

Hausmann, R., and U. Panizza. 2003. "On the Determinants of Original Sin: An Empirical Investigation." *Journal of International Money and Finance* 22: 957–90.

Jackson, W. 1992. "The Price-Concentration Relationship in Banking: A Comment." *Review of Economics and Statistics* 74: 373–76.

International Financial Statistics (IMF). International Monetary Fund, Washington, DC. http://elibrary-data.imf.org/FindDataReports.aspx?d=33061&e=169393.

Investment Company Institute. http://www.ici.org/.

Joh, S. W. 2003. "Corporate Governance and Firm Profitability: Evidence from Korean Firms before the Economic Crisis." *Journal of Financial Economics* 68: 287–322.

Kaminsky, G. L., and S. L. Schmukler. 2008. "Short-Run Pain, Long-Run Gain: The Effects of Financial Liberalization." *Review of Finance–Journal of the European Finance Association* 12 (2): 253–92.

Kang, J. K., and R. Stulz. 1997. "Why Is There a Home Bias? An Analysis of Foreign Portfolio Equity Ownership in Japan." *Journal of Financial Economics* 46: 3–28.

King, R. G., and R. Levine. 1993a. "Finance, Entrepreneurship, and Growth." *Journal of Monetary Economics* 32: 513–42.

———. 1993b. "Finance and Growth: Schumpeter Might Be Right." *Quarterly Journal of Economics* 108: 717–37.

Klapper, L. 2006. "The Role of Factoring for Small and Medium Enterprises." *Journal of Banking and Finance* 30 (11): 3111–30.

Klapper, L., and I. Love. 2004. "Corporate Governance, Investor Protection, and Performance in Emerging Markets." *Journal of Corporate Finance* 10: 703–28.

Kritzer, B. E., S. J. Kay, and T. Sinha. 2011. "Next Generation of Individual Account Pension Reforms in Latin America." *Social Security Bulletin* 71 (1): 35–76.

La Porta, R., F. Lopez-de-Silanes, A. Shleifer, and R. Vishny. 1997. "Legal Determinants of External Finance." *Journal of Finance* 52: 1131–50.

LarrainVial. 2011. "El Mercado de Renta Fija en Chile." Mimeo.

Levine, R. 1997. "Financial Development and Economic Growth: Views and Agenda." *Journal of Economic Literature* 35: 688–726.

———. 2005. "Finance and Growth: Theory and Evidence." In *Handbook of Economic Growth*, vol. 1, edited by P. Aghion and S. Durlauf, 865–934. Amsterdam: Elsevier.

Levine, R., and S. Zervos. 1996. "Stock Market Development and Long-Run Growth." *World Bank Economic Review* 10 (2): 323–39.

Luintel, K. B., and M. Khan. 1999. "A Quantitative Reassessment of the Finance-Growth Nexus: Evidence from a Multivariate VAR." *Journal of Development Economics* 60: 381–405.

Mishkin, F. S. 2000. "Inflation Targeting in Emerging-Market Countries." *American Economic Review* 90 (2): 105–09.

Moody's Investor Service. http://www.moodys.com/.

Nenova, T. 2003. "The Value of Corporate Voting Rights and Control: A Cross-Country Analysis." *Journal of Financial Economics* 68: 325–51.

OECD. http://www.oecd.org/.

Opazo, L., C. Raddatz, and S. Schmukler. 2009. "The Long and the Short of Emerging Market Debt." Policy Research Working Paper 5056, World Bank, Washington, DC.

Perotti, E., and P. van Oijen. 2001. "Privatization, Political Risk, and Stock Market Development in Emerging Economies." *Journal of International Money and Finance* 20: 43–69.

Raddatz, C., and S. L. Schmukler. 2011. "Deconstructing Herding: Evidence from Pension Fund Investment Behavior." Policy Research Working Paper 5700, World Bank, Washington, DC.

Reserve Bank of Australia. http://www.rba.gov.au/.

Santana, M. H. 2008. "The Novo Mercado." In *5 Focus Novo Mercado and Its Followers: Case Studies in Corporate Governance Reform,* edited by M. H. Santana, M. Ararat, P. Alexandru, B. B. Yurtoglu, and M. R. Cunha, 2–39. Washington, DC: International Finance Corporation.

Schmidt-Hebbel, K., and V. Corbo. 2002. "Inflation Targeting in Latin America." Documentos de Trabajo 230, Instituto de Economia. Pontificia Universidad Católica de Chile.

SDC Platinum. http://thomsonreuters.com/sdc-platinum/.

Shleifer, A., and R. W. Vishny. 1997. "A Survey of Corporate Governance." *Journal of Finance* 52: 737–83.

SIFMA. http://www.sifma.org/.

The CityUK Securitization. http://www.thecityuk.com/research/our-work/articles-2/net-global-securitisation-issuance-up-by-a-half-in-2010/.

Thomson Reuters. http://thomsonreuters.com//.

World Council of Credit Unions. http://www.woccu.org/.

World Development Indicators (database). World Bank, Washington, DC, http://data.worldbank.org/data-catalog/world-development-indicators.

2

Financial Inclusion in Latin America and the Caribbean

María Soledad Martínez Pería

Abstract

Building inclusive financial systems has become an important policy objective, given evidence suggesting that financial inclusion brings significant welfare effects. This chapter evaluates where Latin America stands on this issue. At first glance, access to and use of banking services in Latin America appear to be low. However, financial inclusion is not lower than what is predicted based on the region's income and population density, and lack of demand—documented in household and Enterprise Surveys—appears to be an important reason for low use. Financial fees could also be playing a role, since they tend to be higher in LAC. There are significant differences in firms' access to and use of banking services, depending on the size of the enterprise, with access and use being lower among smaller businesses. There are also significant disparities in financial inclusion within Latin America. LAC7 countries rank ahead of their neighbors in the region. LAC7 governments also appear to be doing more than those in Eastern Europe and in developed countries to promote financial inclusion. However, LAC7 countries lag behind those in Asia. Areas that need more government attention include increasing finance to small and

The author works for the World Bank's DECFP unit. The author is grateful to Diego Anzoategui, who provided excellent research assistance.

medium businesses, bringing down the cost of financial services, and reforming creditor rights.

Introduction

Improving access to finance and building inclusive financial systems that cater to the needs of a large segment of the population have become an important policy objective. In 2005, the United Nations adopted the goal of building inclusive financial systems across countries, designating that year as the Year of Microcredit. A survey recently conducted by the Consultative Group to Assist the Poor (CGAP) shows that 88 percent of regulators in 120 economies that responded to the survey have a legal responsibility to promote at least some aspect of financial inclusion (CGAP 2010).[1]

The increased interest in financial inclusion comes from a heightened awareness among academics and policy makers of the benefits of having inclusive financial systems. Theoretical studies (Banerjee and Newman 1993; Galor and Zeira 1993; Aghion and Bolton 1997) have shown that financial market frictions that prevent financial inclusion can inhibit human and physical capital accumulation and affect occupational choices, leading to persistent inequality or poverty traps. Moreover, recent empirical research has confirmed that there are positive welfare effects from firms' and individuals' gaining access to finance. In particular, studies show that access to credit products increases households' income and consumption (Pitt and Khandker 1998; Khandker 2005; Karlan and Zinman 2010); diminishes income inequality, hunger, and poverty (Burgess and Pande 2005; Khandker 2005; Beck, Levine, and Levkov 2010; Karlan and Zinman 2010); and fosters businesses' investments and profitability (Karlan and Zinman 2009; Banerjee et al. 2009). Moreover, other studies show that access to savings products increases savings (see Aportela 1999), empowers women (Ashraf, Karlan, and Yin 2010), and promotes productive investments and consumption (Dupas and Robinson 2009).

Where does Latin America stand with regard to financial inclusion? This chapter examines this question from various perspectives. First, the chapter characterizes financial inclusion in the region and compares it to that in other regions, using supply-side data obtained from bank regulatory authorities. In particular, we examine indicators such as the number of branches, automated teller machines (ATMs), loans, and deposits per capita. Second, we analyze barriers (monetary and nonmonetary) to the use of banking services from a survey of banks and compare Latin America to other regions. We focus on indicators like minimum balances and documentation requirements to open accounts, fees charged on deposits and loans, the number of places where bank customers can apply for loans and open deposit accounts, and the number of days to process loan applications. Third, the chapter examines demand-side data from firm-level surveys conducted by the World Bank across developing countries and from household surveys done by the Corporación Andina de

Fomento (CAF) in the largest Latin American cities. Using firm-level data, we examine the percentage of firms that have deposit accounts and, separately, loans, as well as the shares of fixed assets and working capital financed by banks. Using household demand-side data, we analyze the share of households that have an account or a loan and the reasons why households do not have access or choose not to use these services. Finally, the chapter analyzes the role of governments in the region in promoting financial inclusion. In particular, we try to establish how Latin America compares to other regions when it comes to adopting policies to promote financial inclusion.

We concentrate on analyzing access to and use of banking services because banks dominate the financial sector in Latin America and because data for the banking sector are more readily available across countries, facilitating the comparison of financial inclusion in Latin America to that in other regions. However, wherever possible we also present data on nonbanks and refer to initiatives that include them.

There are a number of caveats and limitations to our analysis. First, as mentioned above our analysis centers on banks and largely ignores nonbank institutions. Second, we focus on savings and credit services and, due to lack of data, ignore insurance services. Third, indicators on financial inclusion like the number of deposits or loans per capita may overestimate the extent of outreach, since some individuals and firms might have more than one account. Fourth, the supply-side data do not distinguish between the use of banking services by individuals and by firms. Finally, in analyzing the role of the government in promoting financial inclusion, we are able to document only efforts and policies, but we cannot conduct a welfare analysis of the impact of these policies.[2]

The rest of the chapter is organized as follows. We next discuss the complexities of defining and measuring financial inclusion. We then examine supply-side indicators of financial inclusion, comparing Latin America to other developing and developed countries. The following section compares barriers to the use of financial services in Latin America to those in other developing and developed countries. Next, we analyze demand-side data from firms and households on the use of and access to financial services in Latin America and explore the role of the government in promoting financial inclusion. The last section offers concluding observations.

Measuring Financial Inclusion

Financial inclusion—or broad access to financial services—is hard to measure in practice. A basic challenge in measuring it is to distinguish between access to and use of financial services. Individuals may choose not to open an account or to borrow, even if services are available at reasonable prices, due to cultural or religious reasons or because they have no demand, reducing use relative to access. Hence, access refers primarily to the supply of services, whereas use is determined by demand as well as supply. Voluntary self-exclusion does not constitute a problem of access. Similarly, financial inclusion does not mean that the supply of financial services always needs to meet the demand. In particular, we do not expect borrowers without profitable investment opportunities or with a bad credit history to be granted loans. Therefore, inferences about financial inclusion from measures of use of financial services do not necessarily imply the existence of market failures that warrant government intervention. Nonetheless, measuring use of financial services is the first and most readily available way to assess financial inclusion.

There are two main approaches to quantifying financial inclusion. Perhaps the most informative approach is to survey individuals and firms about their use of financial services. To the extent that surveys are nationally representative, they can provide reliable information about the percentage of the population or the share of firms that is financially included. One example of such efforts is the Enterprise Surveys that the World Bank has conducted in over 120 countries since 2002. Household surveys that measure the use of financial services, however, are available for only a relatively small subset of countries.[3] Moreover, it is usually difficult to compare the results of these surveys across countries due to differences in wording and methods, plus there are also some questions about the reliability and representativeness of survey results.[4] In the case of Latin America, in recognizing the limitations of the existing surveys, the CAF has recently conducted its own surveys to document access to and use of financial services in the region. However, because such surveys are not available for countries outside the region, it is difficult to benchmark the region against others using these data. Also, these surveys cover only the largest cities in the region.

An alternative approach to measuring the extent of access to and use of financial services is to rely on more easily collected supply-side information provided by financial institutions and gathered by regulators on the number of branches, ATMs, deposit accounts, and loans per capita.[5] While available for a large number of countries, this information is not without its own limitations. Unlike survey data, these data do not provide details on the characteristics of households and firms that use financial services. Also, aggregate figures may be only rough proxies for the extent of the use of financial services. For instance, the total number of deposit accounts in a country may differ significantly from the number of actual users, since individuals may have more than one account. In addition, most countries do not distinguish between corporate and individual deposit accounts. Nevertheless, aggregate indicators tend to be closely correlated with the share of households that use financial services estimated from household surveys when available (Beck, Demirgüç-Kunt, and Martinez-Peria 2007; Honohan 2008).

In the analysis that follows, we make use of both demand (survey-based) and supply-side data to characterize financial inclusion in Latin America. Our analysis distinguishes between a core group of larger and more developed countries in the region, which we call LAC7 (Argentina, Brazil, Chile,

Colombia, Mexico, Peru, and Uruguay), and the rest of Latin America, which we separate into two groups: Central America (Costa Rica, the Dominican Republic, El Salvador, Honduras, and Nicaragua) and South America (Bolivia, Ecuador, Paraguay, and the República Bolivariana de Venezuela). We also compare the LAC7 group to G-7 countries (Canada, France, Germany, Italy, Japan, the United Kingdon, and the United States), to other developed countries (Australia, Finland, Israel, New Zealand, Norway, Spain, and Sweden), to developing countries in Asia (China, India, Indonesia, the Republic of Korea, Malaysia, the Philippines, and Thailand), and to Eastern European countries (Croatia, the Czech Republic, Hungary, Lithuania, Poland, the Russian Federation, and Turkey).

Supply-Side Evidence on Financial Inclusion

Traditionally, the presence of a branch or an ATM has typically been considered a prerequisite for financial inclusion, as gateways for individuals and firms to access financial services.[6] The median number of branches (13) and ATMs (37) per 100,000 adults in LAC7 (figure 2.1) is smaller than that in

Figure 2.1 Median Number of Bank Branches and ATMs per 100,000 Adults in Selected Countries and Regions, 2009 (or latest available year)

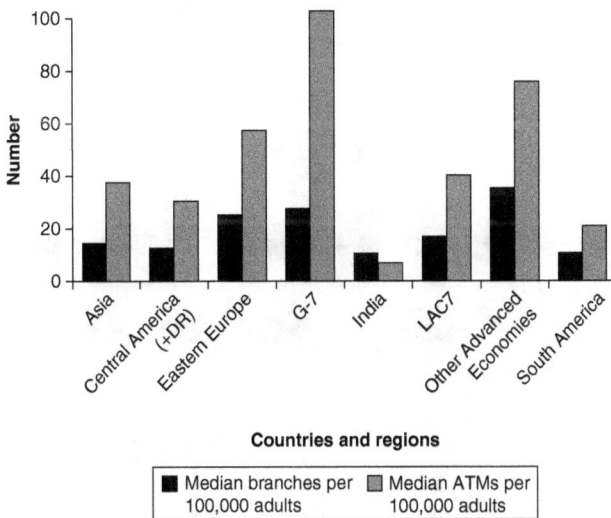

Source: CGAP 2009, 2010.

Note: LAC7 = Argentina, Brazil, Chile, Colombia, Mexico, Peru, and Uruguay; ATM = automated teller machine; DR = Dominican Republic.

Eastern European countries (22 branches and 54 ATMs per 100,000 adults), in G-7 economies (24 branches and 118 ATMs), and in other developed countries (32 branches and 73 ATMs). As shown in figure 2.1, however, the number of branches and ATMs for LAC7 countries is similar to that in the comparator Asian economies (11 branches and 34 ATMs). In a comparison of LAC7 countries to the rest of Latin America, LAC7 countries are clearly ahead when we consider differences in medians without controlling for other factors. At the same time, figures for Central American countries exceed those for the group of South American countries.

We characterize the use of banking services across countries by examining data on the number of deposit accounts and the number of loans outstanding per 1,000 adults. Figure 2.2 shows that the use of deposit services in LAC7 countries, where the median is 906 deposit accounts per 1,000 adults, is comparable to that observed for Asia (977) and for non-G-7 developed countries (918), but that it is below the median for economies in Eastern Europe (1,700) and for the G-7 countries (2,022). Use of deposit accounts within Latin America varies considerably, especially if we compare South American countries to those in Central America and in LAC7. The median number of deposit accounts per 1,000 adults in South America (453) is half that observed for LAC7 countries (906) and for Central American economies (825).

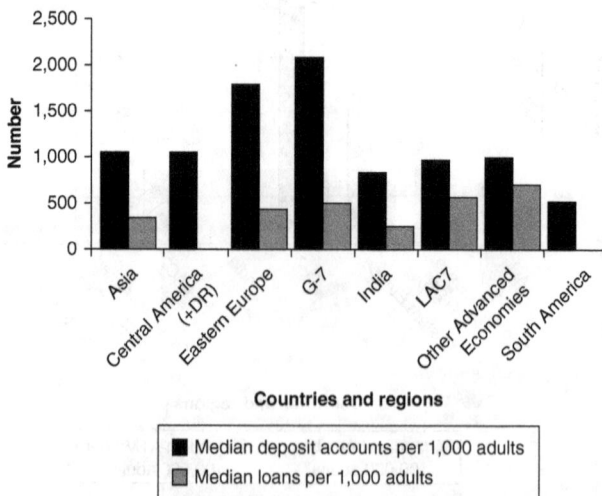

Figure 2.2 Median Number of Bank Deposit Accounts and Loan Accounts per 1,000 Adults in Selected Regions and Economies, 2009 (or latest available year)

Source: CGAP 2009, 2010.
Note: DR = Dominican Republic.

The use of loans in LAC7 countries, with a median of 498 loans per 1,000 adults, exceeds that observed for most groups of comparator countries, including G-7 economies (for which the median number of loans per 1,000 adults is 439). The only exception appears to be non-G-7 countries, where the median number of loans is 633. It is important to note, however, that data on the number of loans are available for a small number of countries—certainly fewer than the number of countries for which we have data on deposits, branches, and ATMs.

Are the differences we document in the number of branches, ATMs, deposits, and loans between Latin America and the rest of the world significant once we control for differences in income and population density? Figure 2.3 plots the actual versus the predicted number of branches per 100,000 adults from a regression of log branches controlling for log gross domestic product (GDP) per capita and log population density. Figure 2.4

Figure 2.3 Actual versus Predicted Number of Branches per 100,000 Adults in LAC and Comparators, 2009 (or latest available year)

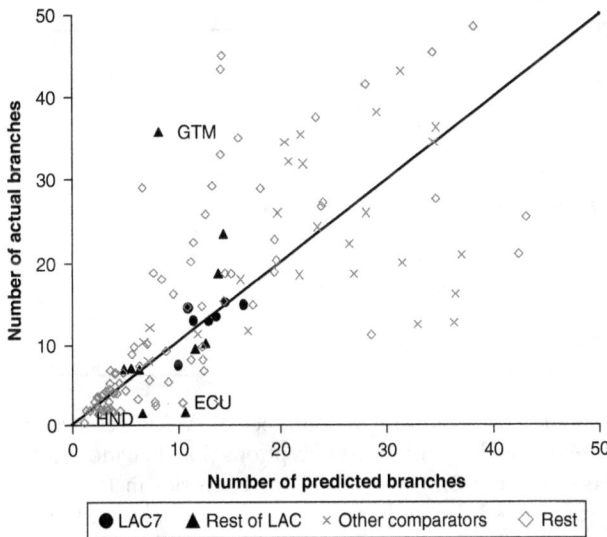

Source: Calculations based on CGAP 2009, 2010.

Note: Predicted numbers were obtained regressing the log of branches per 100,000 adults on the log of gross domestic product per capita in constant purchasing power parity terms and the log of population density. LAC = Latin America and the Caribbean; HND = Honduras; ECU = Ecuador; GTM = Guatemala. "Rest" refers to all countries with available data not in LAC or included in the "other comparators" group.

Figure 2.4 Actual versus Predicted Number of ATMs per 100,000 Adults in LAC and Comparators, 2009 (or latest available year)

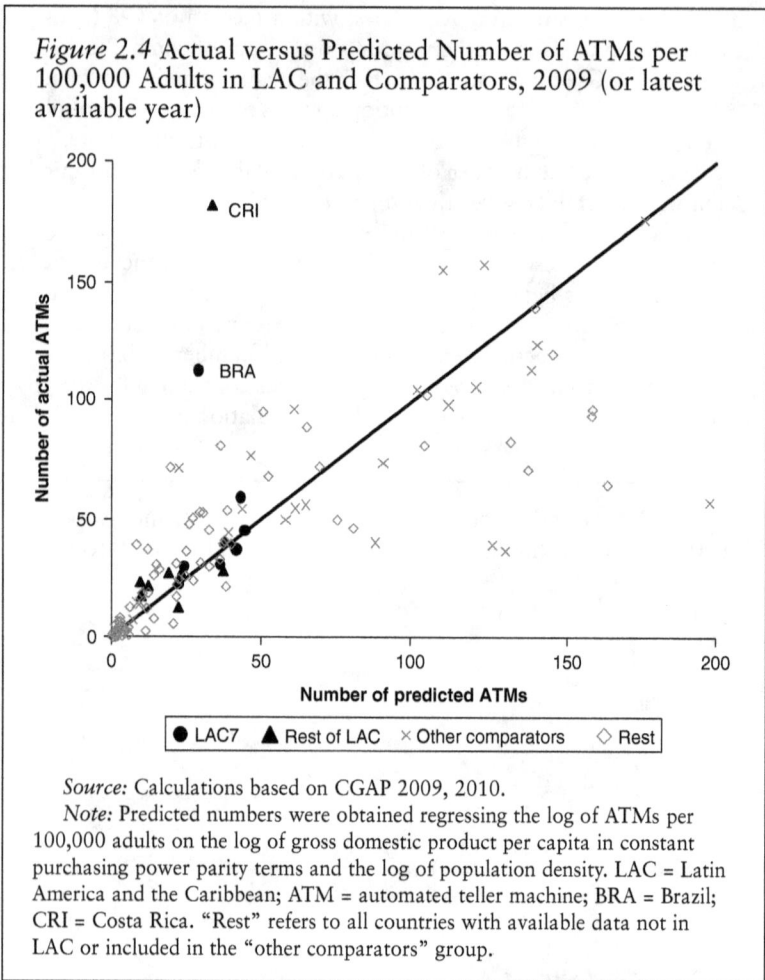

Source: Calculations based on CGAP 2009, 2010.

Note: Predicted numbers were obtained regressing the log of ATMs per 100,000 adults on the log of gross domestic product per capita in constant purchasing power parity terms and the log of population density. LAC = Latin America and the Caribbean; ATM = automated teller machine; BRA = Brazil; CRI = Costa Rica. "Rest" refers to all countries with available data not in LAC or included in the "other comparators" group.

shows a similar regression for the number of ATMs per 100,000 adults. Both figures show that with some exceptions (like Ecuador and Honduras in the case of figure 2.3), the values for countries in Latin America are not far from the 45-degree line. Hence, although the median number of branches and ATMs in the region is lower than that observed for other regions (primarily for the G-7, other developed countries, and Eastern Europe), the availability of branches and ATMs is fairly close to what we would predict, given the region's income and population density.

The use of deposits and loans in Latin American countries also does not seem to deviate much from what we would expect based on the region's income and population density. Figure 2.5 plots the actual versus the predicted number of deposit accounts per 1,000 people from a regression

Figure 2.5 Actual versus Predicted Number of Deposits per 1,000 Adults in LAC and Comparators, 2009 (or latest available year)

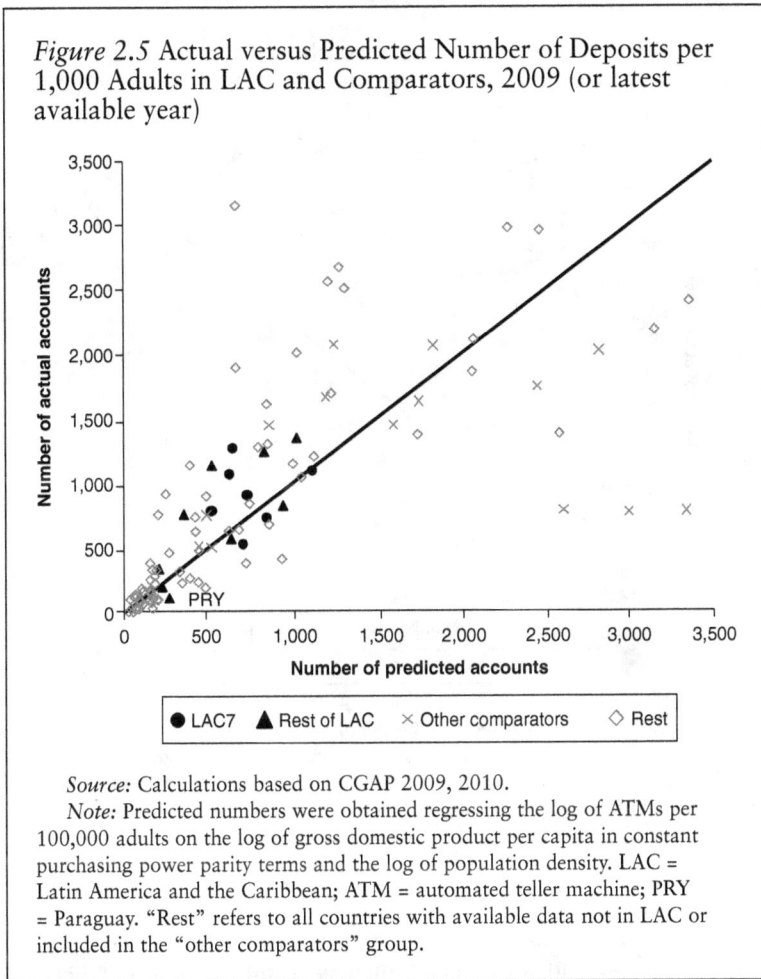

Source: Calculations based on CGAP 2009, 2010.

Note: Predicted numbers were obtained regressing the log of ATMs per 100,000 adults on the log of gross domestic product per capita in constant purchasing power parity terms and the log of population density. LAC = Latin America and the Caribbean; ATM = automated teller machine; PRY = Paraguay. "Rest" refers to all countries with available data not in LAC or included in the "other comparators" group.

controlling for GDP per capita and population density. Figure 2.6 shows similar results for the number of loans per 1,000 people. With few exceptions (in particular Paraguay), most countries in Latin America lie above the 45-degree line, plotting actual versus predicted deposit and loan accounts.

Overall, the raw statistics on the number of branches, ATMs, and deposits suggest that countries in LAC are on a par with economies in Asia but lag behind developed countries and developing economies in Eastern Europe. However, once we control for income and population density—variables that are bound to affect the availability and the use of financial services— these differences do not appear to be significant. In the case of the number of loans, we find that the use of loans in Latin America appears to exceed that for most other regions, even when we do not control for differences

Figure 2.6 Actual versus Predicted Number of Loans per
1,000 Adults in LAC and Comparators, 2009 (or latest
available year)

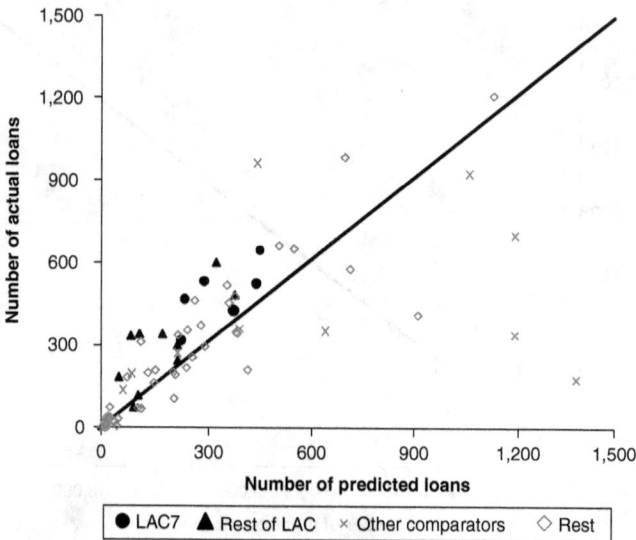

Source: Calculations based on CGAP 2009, 2010.
Note: Predicted numbers were obtained regressing the log of ATMs per
100,000 adults on the log of gross domestic product per capita in constant
purchasing power parity terms and the log of population density. LAC = Latin
America and the Caribbean; ATM = automated teller machine.

in income and population density. Note, however, that the data on loan
use are available only for a small sample of economies. Furthermore, it is
important to keep in mind that our proxies for the use of loans and deposits
are likely to overestimate the true use of banking services, since more than
one firm or individual could have more than one bank account or loan.

Supply-Side Barriers to Financial Inclusion

In characterizing financial inclusion, we must examine the degree to which
there are barriers to the use of financial services. These could refer to monetary barriers (such as fees or minimum balances) but also to nonmonetary
obstacles (like documentation requirements, the number of locations where
individuals can open accounts or apply for loans, the number of days to process a loan application, and so forth). Barriers matter for financial inclusion

because, to the extent that they increase the cost or affect the convenience of using banking services, they can reduce individuals' or firms' demand for such services. In what follows, we use data from a survey of financial institutions conducted by the World Bank (see Beck et al. 2008) during 2004–05 to quantify barriers to the use of financial services. Because these data are available only for the largest countries in Latin America, we are not able to compare LAC7 countries to the other Latin American regions.

Figure 2.7 shows the minimum amount needed to open a deposit account (expressed as a percentage of GDP per capita) across regions.

Figure 2.7 Minimum Amount to Open and Maintain a Deposit Account, as a Percent of GDP per Capita in Selected Countries and Regions, 2009 (or latest available year)

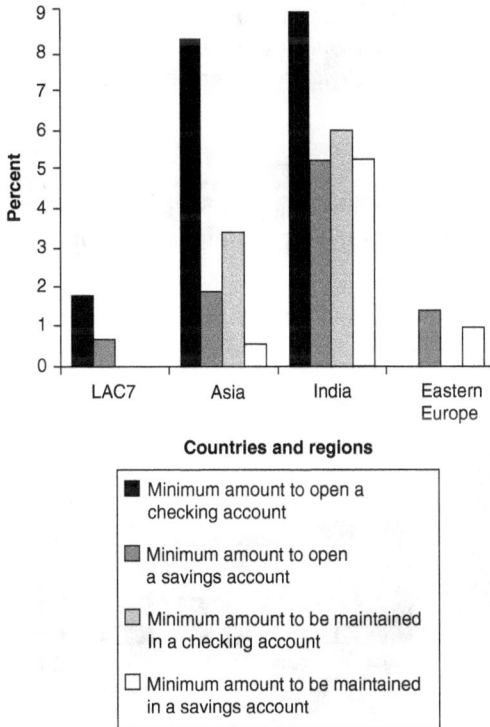

Legend:
■ Minimum amount to open a checking account
▨ Minimum amount to open a savings account
▢ Minimum amount to be maintained in a checking account
□ Minimum amount to be maintained in a savings account

Source: Beck et al. 2008.
Note: For most of these countries, there are no minimum requirements (or the requirements are very low relative to GDP). China, the G-7, and other advanced countries are not shown because the values for the variables are zero. GDP = gross domestic product.

At 2 percent for opening checking accounts and at 1 percent for savings accounts, the median balances required by banks in LAC7 countries are generally in line with those in most developing countries, although they exceed the median balances for developed countries. The minimum balances required for maintaining savings and checking accounts (approximately 0 percent of GDP per capita), however, are lower than those required in most developing countries and are in accord with practices in developed economies.

Deposit fees in Latin America tend to be higher than those observed in other regions (figure 2.8). While the median annual fees on checking (savings) accounts amount to 1.4 percent (0.5 percent) of GDP per capita in LAC7 countries, fees elsewhere range from 0.7 (0.3) in Asia, 0.2 (0) in Eastern Europe, and 0.2 (0) in G-7 countries.

Fees on consumer and residential (mortgage) loans in Latin America, which amount to 1.8 percent of GDP per capita and 1.4 percent, respectively, significantly exceed those in most comparator countries (figure 2.9). For example, consumer loan fees are 1.4 percent in Asia and Eastern Europe, while they are closer to 1 percent in G-7 countries. Fees on

Figure 2.8 Median Checking and Savings Accounts Annual Fees as a Percent of GDP per Capita, 2009 (or latest available year)

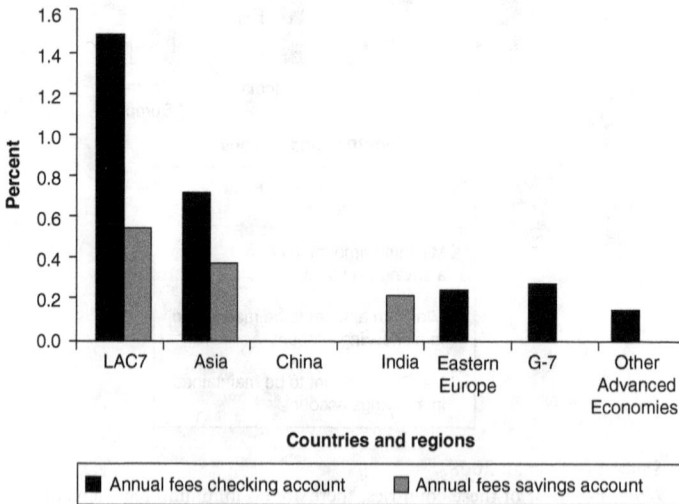

Source: Beck et al. 2008.
Note: GDP = gross domestic product.

Figure 2.9 Median Loan Fees as a Percent of GDP per Capita, 2009 (or latest available year)

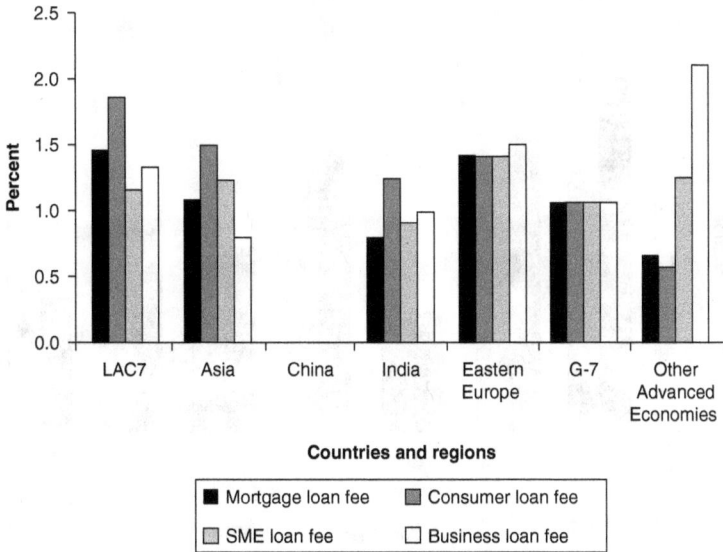

Source: Beck et al. 2008.
Note: GDP = gross domestic product.

other types of loans in LAC7 countries, however, are quite close to those observed in other regions. Fees on small and medium enterprise (SME) loans in LAC7 are 1.1 percent, while they are 1.2 percent in developing Asia, 1.4 percent in Eastern Europe, and 1 percent in G-7 countries.

As for nonmonetary barriers to the use of financial services, we find that the number of documents required to open deposit accounts in Latin America exceeds what is required in most other countries (figure 2.10). Most notably, while three documents are required in Latin America to open a checking account, two documents are required in G-7 countries, and only one document is needed in other advanced economies.

The number of locations where bank customers can open a deposit account or apply for a loan, however, is comparable to other developing countries or greater, even compared to G-7 economies (see figure 2.11). The median number of locations where banks in LAC7 countries allow customers to apply for loans is 4.2 (headquarters, branches, nonbranch outlets, or electronically), while it is close to 3 in the case of most other comparators. Among LAC7 countries, like in most other countries outside

Figure 2.10 Number of Documents Required to Open a Bank Account in Selected Countries and Regions, 2007 (or latest available year)

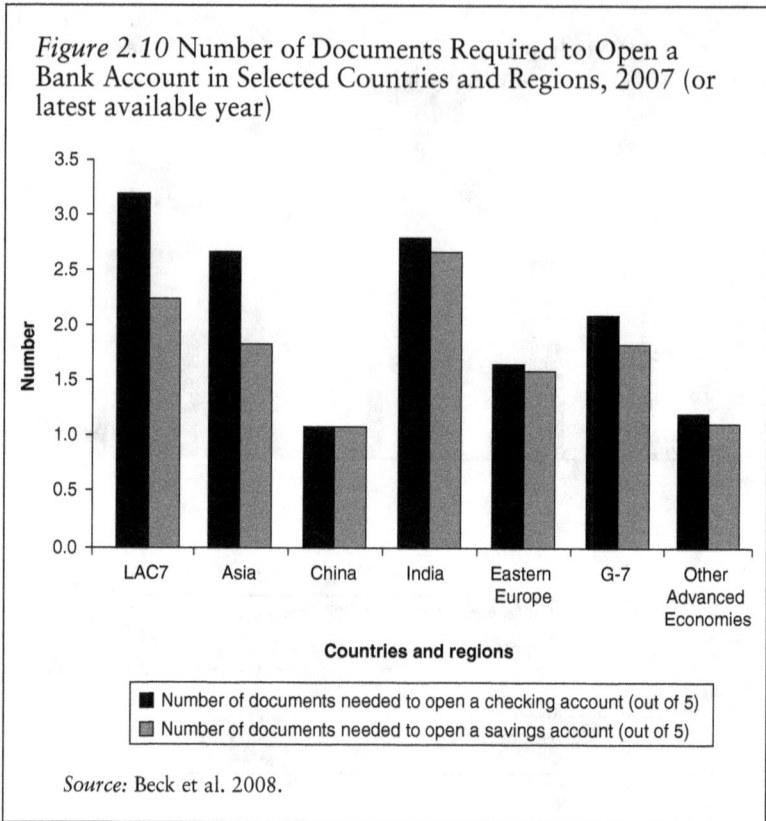

Source: Beck et al. 2008.

the region, bank customers have two types of locations (headquarters or branches) where they can go to open accounts.

The time it takes for a bank to process a financial contract (for example, a loan application) can also be perceived as a hurdle to using banking services. The World Bank survey reveals that with the exception of residential mortgages, which generally take 14 days to process, the number of days required to process other loans in LAC7 countries is in line with that in other developing regions (figure 2.12).

Overall, the main barriers to the use of financial services in Latin America appear to be monetary costs or fees. Table 2.1 shows regressions of deposit and residential mortgage loan fees against a number of possible determinants, including a dummy for LAC7 countries. We find that even after controlling for differences in banking sector structure, in the institutional environment, and in per capita income across countries, fees charged by banks in Latin America are higher.

Figure 2.11 Number of Locations to Submit Loan Applications or Open Deposit Accounts in Selected Countries and Regions, 2007 (or latest available year)

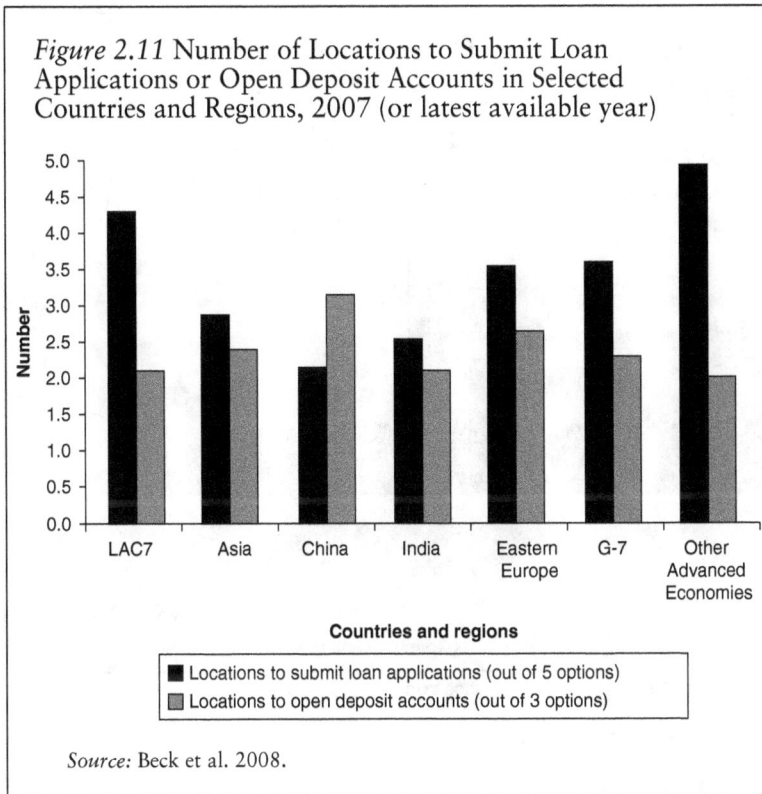

Source: Beck et al. 2008.

Demand-Side Evidence on Financial Inclusion

To characterize the demand for financial services and to provide demand-side evidence of the use of financial services, we rely on firm-level and household-level data collected through surveys. In particular, we analyze data available from the World Bank Enterprise Surveys for Latin America, Asia, and Eastern Europe and from recent household surveys conducted by the CAF in 17 cities in nine countries in Latin America.

We characterize firms' use of and access to banking services through a number of indicators constructed from the Enterprise Surveys database. First, we examine the percentage of firms that have a deposit account. Second, we examine the use of credit products. Then, we construct an indicator variable that equals 1 if the enterprise has an overdraft, loan, line of credit, or any bank financing for working capital or for fixed-asset purchases. We also look at the median percentage of working capital and separately at fixed assets financed by banks.

Figure 2.12 Number of Days Required to Process a Loan Application in Selected Countries and Regions, 2007 (or latest available year)

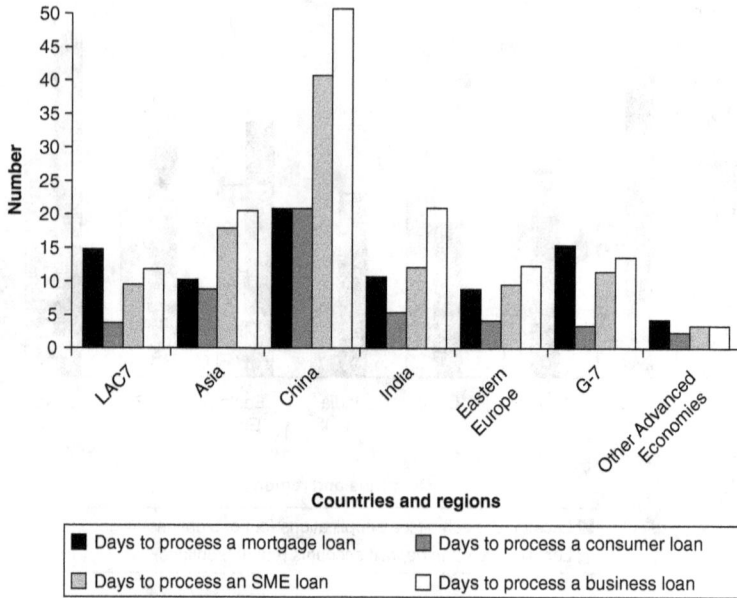

Source: Beck et al. 2008.
Note: SME = small and medium enterprise.

In analyzing the data from Enterprise Surveys, we distinguish between large firms and SMEs. Large firms are those with 100 or more employees, while SMEs are those that employ between 5 and 99 workers. Because SMEs tend to be more opaque and more vulnerable to economic volatility, they are generally expected to face more constraints in accessing banking services.

The vast majority of large firms and SMEs in Latin America have a bank account. Among LAC7 countries, almost 100 percent of large firms and 95 percent of SMEs have a bank account (figure 2.13). The use of bank accounts is also widespread among firms in Central America, where 99 percent of large firms and 87 percent of SMEs use bank accounts. In comparison, 100 percent of large firms and 98 percent of SMEs in Eastern Europe use bank accounts.

The use of bank credit among large firms in Latin America is more pervasive than among firms in Asia and Eastern Europe (figure 2.14).

Table 2.1 Regressions for Deposit and Loan Fees

Variables	Annual fees checking account (% of GDPPC)			Annual fees savings account (% of GDPPC)			Fee mortgage loan		
LAC7	2.47 [3.30]***	3.014 [2.11]**	4.222 [2.16]**	2.153 [3.18]***	1.203 [2.62]**	1.132 [2.27]**	2.501 [1.88]*	2.348 [1.85]*	2.852 [1.81]*
Countries outside comparator group	4.141 [2.96]***	0.892 [1.01]	0.158 [0.13]	1.454 [1.95]*	0.431 [1.15]	-0.251 [-0.56]	4.608 [1.54]	1.311 [1.64]	0.729 [0.69]
Concentration (% of assets held by top 5 banks)		0.019 [0.72]	0.058 [1.62]		-0.009 [-0.90]	0.014 [1.62]		-0.021 [-0.80]	-0.013 [-0.36]
Legal rights index		0.242 [1.08]	0.307 [1.01]		0.014 [0.18]	-0.007 [-0.10]		-0.052 [-0.27]	-0.09 [-0.45]
Credit information index		-0.409 [-1.01]	-0.533 [-1.04]		0.137 [0.99]	0.203 [1.72]*		-0.049 [-0.16]	-0.053 [-0.20]
Cost of enforcing contracts		0.077 [3.11]***	0.068 [2.56]**		0.013 [1.46]	0.014 [2.61]**		0.029 [0.84]	0.048 [1.26]
Heritage index of financial freedom		0.089 [1.84]*	0.074 [1.14]		0.023 [1.59]	0.017 [0.93]		0.053 [2.12]**	0.064 [1.41]

Table 2.1 Regressions for Deposit and Loan Fees *(continued)*

Variables	Annual fees checking account (% of GDPPC)			Annual fees savings account (% of GDPPC)			Fee mortgage loan		
Log of GDPPC (PPP)	-1.51	-2.157		-0.549	-0.967		-0.665	-1.053	
	[-1.97]*	[-2.31]**		[-2.05]**	[-3.06]***		[-1.36]	[-1.92]*	
Share of bank assets held by government banks		-0.027			-0.011			-0.003	
		[-0.57]			[-1.03]			[-0.12]	
Share of bank assets held by foreign banks			0.03			-0.002			0.001
			[1.17]			[-0.36]			[0.07]
Constant	-0.906	5.809	9.756	-1.588	2.637	5.699	0.607	5.182	7.384
	[-1.38]	[0.82]	[1.14]	[-2.41]**	[1.21]	[2.15]**	[0.93]	[1.21]	[1.55]
Observations	69	59	45	69	59	45	66	58	44
Pseudo R^2	0.0152	0.122	0.142	0.0265	0.166	0.296	0.00291	0.0552	0.0967

Note: Table 2.1 shows tobit estimations for deposit and mortgage loan fees against country dummies along with a series of variables proxying for bank structure, institutional environment, and income per capita. In particular, *LAC7* is a dummy that equals 1 for Argentina, Brazil, Chile, Colombia, Mexico, Peru, and Uruguay; *Countries outside comparator group* is a dummy that takes the value of 1 for countries other than those in the comparator group, which includes G-7 countries (Canada, France, Germany, Italy, Japan, the United Kingdom, and the United States), other developed countries (Australia, Finland, Israel, New Zealand, Norway, Spain and Sweden), comparable countries in Asia (China, India, Indonesia, the Republic of Korea, Malaysia, the Philippines, and Thailand), and in Eastern Europe (Croatia, the Czech Republic, Hungary, Lithuania, Poland, the Russian Federation, and Turkey). Robust t-statistics are in brackets. *, **, and *** denote significance at the 10, 5, and 1 percent significance level. GDPPC = gross domestic product per capita.

Figure 2.13 Firms' Use of Bank Accounts in Selected Regions, 2010 (or latest available year)

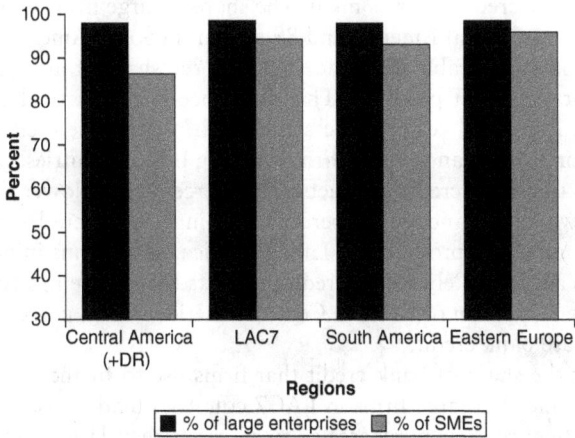

Source: Enterprise Surveys database.
Note: DR = Dominican Republic; SME = small and medium enterprise.

Figure 2.14 Firms' Use of Credit Products in Selected Regions, 2010 (or latest available data)

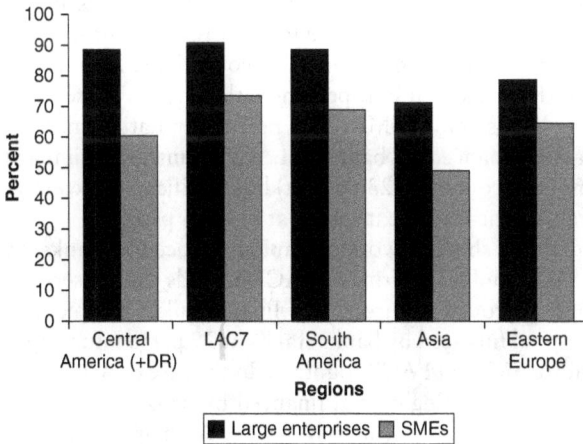

Source: Enterprise Surveys database.
Note: DR = Dominican Republic; SME = small and medium enterprise.

While 91 percent of large firms in LAC7 countries use bank credit to finance their operations, only 71 percent of firms in Asia and 79 percent in Eastern Europe use bank credit. In Latin America, the percentage of large firms that use credit is very similar. The share of large firms with credit is 90 percent in Central America and 89 percent in South America.

There is a noticeable difference between the share of large and small firms that use credit products. This difference is not particular to Latin America. Across all regions, the share of firms that use credit is much smaller for SMEs than for large firms. Among LAC7 countries, 73 percent of SMEs use bank credit products. This percentage is lower in Eastern Europe, where it stands at 65 percent, and in Asia, where less than half of SMEs use credit products. In Latin America, small firms in non-LAC7 countries are less likely to use credit products than those in LAC7 countries: only 64 percent of SMEs in Central America and 68 percent in South America use bank credit.

As for the share of bank credit that firms use to finance their operations, we find that large firms in LAC7 countries tend to use more bank credit to finance their purchases of fixed assets than large firms in Asia, Eastern Europe, and the rest of Latin America (figure 2.15). Among large firms in LAC, the median share of fixed assets financed by bank credit is 38 percent, while it is 28 percent among large firms in Eastern Europe and 22 percent for the same type of firms in Asia. In Latin America, the median share of fixed assets financed by bank credit among large firms is 27 percent in South America and 23 percent in Central America.

With the exception of Eastern Europe, the median share of fixed assets financed by banks among SMEs is lower than that for large firms. In the case of LAC7 countries, the median share of fixed assets financed by banks among SMEs is 24 percent, 14 percentage points lower than the median among large firms. Relative to other regions, the median share for LAC7 countries is higher than for Asian countries (21 percent), but lower than for SMEs in Eastern Europe, where the median share of fixed assets financed by banks among SMEs is 33 percent. In Latin America, the share of fixed assets financed by banks in LAC7 countries is similar to that in South American countries (23 percent) but significantly exceeds that share for Central America, where it stands at only 13 percent.

Regarding the share of working capital financed by banks, the median for both SMEs and large firms in LAC7 exceeds that observed across all other country groups (figure 2.16). In particular, the median share of working capital financed by banks stands at 29 percent for large firms and 19 percent for SMEs in LAC7 countries. In the case of Asian countries, the median share of working capital financed by banks is 20 percent among large firms and 16 percent among SMEs. Among countries in Eastern Europe, the median is 15 percent for large firms and only 9 percent for SMEs. In Latin America, the share of working capital financed by banks among large firms is greater in South America (25 percent) than it is in

Figure 2.15 Percentage of Fixed Assets Financed by Banks in Selected Regions, 2010 (or latest available year)

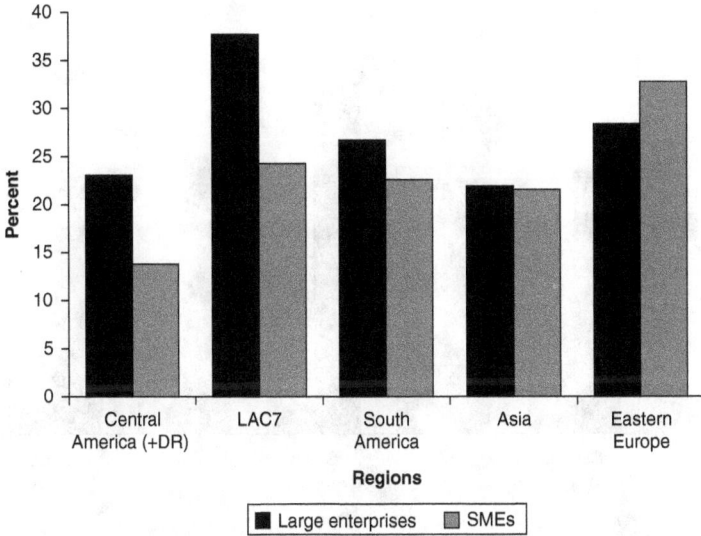

Source: Enterprise Surveys database.
Note: DR = Dominican Republic; SME = small and medium enterprise.

Central America (19 percent), but the opposite is true when it comes to SMEs. The median share of working capital financed by banks among SMEs is 15 percent in Central America and 12 percent in South America.

Overall, the Enterprise Surveys indicate that the use of bank deposit products is widespread in Latin America. However, the use of and access to credit are less pervasive, especially among SMEs. Firms in Latin America (especially those in LAC7 countries), though, do not appear to be lagging firms in other developing countries in their access to and use of bank credit.

Contrary to the case of firms, where comparable surveys documenting their access to and use of financial services exist for many countries, information at the household level is very limited and hard to compare across countries because the survey instruments and the samples vary from country to country. However, the CAF has recently attempted to remedy this problem for Latin America by conducting a survey of households in nine countries and 17 cities in the region. Below, we reproduce some of the tables from their study (see CAF 2011), showing the use of saving and credit services across cities in the region (see tables 2.2 and 2.3).

Figure 2.16 Percentage of Working Capital Financed by
Banks in Selected Regions, 2010 (or latest available year)

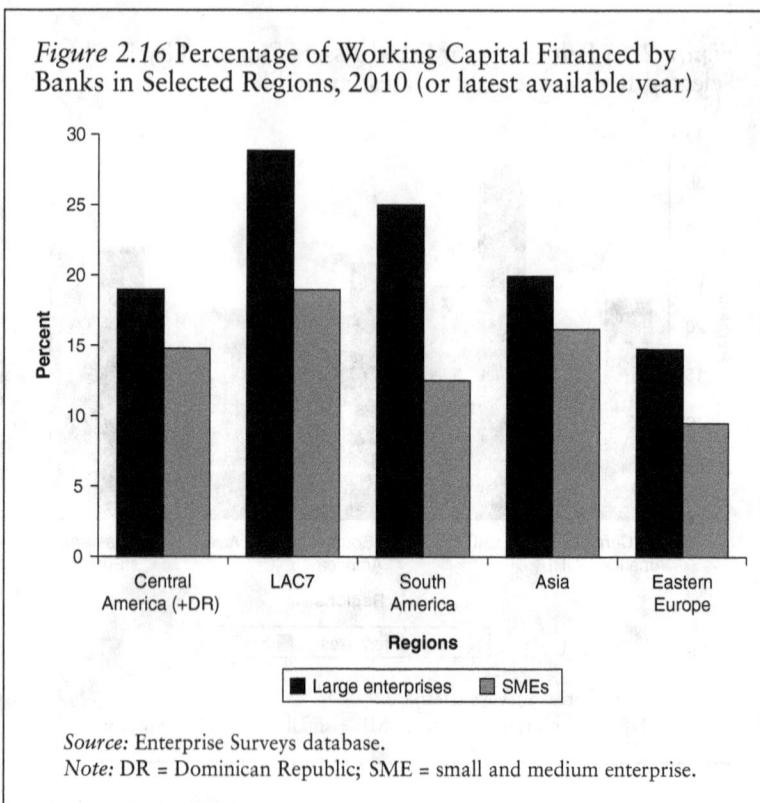

Source: Enterprise Surveys database.
Note: DR = Dominican Republic; SME = small and medium enterprise.

Household surveys were conducted by the CAF in five of the LAC7 countries: Argentina, Brazil, Colombia, Peru, and Uruguay—the LAC5. The surveys revealed that 51 percent of households in LAC5 countries have an account (table 2.2). Among households that do not have an account, the main reasons cited include lack of funds (61 percent) or absence of a job (19 percent). Only 11 percent of households gave not trusting financial institutions or not being able to meet the requirements to open an account as reasons for not having an account, and 7 percent complained about high fees. The statistics on the use of bank accounts among households in countries outside the LAC5 are very similar to those described above. Approximately 52 percent of households have an account, and, among those that do not, 72 percent mention lack of money as the main reason for not having an account. Only 5 percent of households complain about high fees, and 13 percent mention not meeting the requirements to open an account. Overall, demand considerations seem to be the main explanation for half of households not using an account.

Table 2.2 Household Use of Deposit Accounts in Latin America

Country	City	Do you have an account with a financial institution? (%)	Reasons for not having an account						
			Does not have enough money (%)	Does not have a job (%)	Prefers to hold funds in other ways (%)	Does not trust financial institutions (%)	Does not see the advantages of having an account (%)	Cannot meet the requirements to open an account (%)	High fees (%)
Argentina	Buenos Aires	42.1	53.8	21.1	19.1	15.2	7.6	17.2	1.7
	Córdoba	46.5	55.0	17.9	4.6	7.8	22.8	10.7	1.6
Bolivia	La Paz	35.7	72.9	16.6	16.3	16.8	12.6	12.1	8.2
	Santa Cruz	34.1	56.9	9.5	20.3	15.4	5.4	8.5	10.0
Brazil	San Pablo	72.5	51.2	14.0	5.5	1.8	28.7	13.4	14.6
	Río de Janeiro	65.6	54.6	19.5	12.7	4.9	17.1	13.2	12.2
Colombia	Bogotá	51.6	62.7	24.4	15.3	16.7	19.5	9.1	9.4
	Medellín	41.9	75.1	30.5	35.8	5.9	28.7	11.2	4.7
Ecuador	Quito	70.7	71.4	18.3	19.4	34.9	13.1	13.1	6.3
	Guayaquil	36.9	82.5	27.1	16.2	22.3	19.4	10.9	3.7

(continued next page)

Table 2.2 Household Use of Deposit Accounts in Latin America (continued)

Country	City	Do you have an account with a financial institution? (%)	Reasons for not having an account						
			Does not have enough money (%)	Does not have a job (%)	Prefers to hold funds in other ways (%)	Does not trust financial institutions (%)	Does not see the advantages of having an account (%)	Cannot meet the requirements to open an account (%)	High fees (%)
Panama	Ciudad de Panamá	52.7	68.6	27.6	19.2	6.5	2.7	14.6	7.7
Peru	Lima	38.4	59.1	21.0	23.2	21.6	14.3	8.7	16.5
	Arequipa	38.9	56.6	13.8	31.5	19.9	2.5	4.7	9.9
Uruguay	Montevideo	55.4	69.5	15.8	10.9	10.5	7.5	9.0	1.1
	Salto	55.4	74.7	13.6	7.9	1.9	7.9	14.3	2.3
Venezuela, RB	Caracas	81.6	74.3	37.6	30.3	21.1	19.3	20.2	0.0
	Maracaibo	50.4	78.8	21.2	19.8	20.1	1.4	8.5	2.7
	Average LAC5	50.8	61.3	19.2	16.7	10.6	15.7	11.2	7.4
	Other LAC	51.7	72.2	22.5	20.2	19.6	10.5	12.6	5.5

Source: CAF 2011.

Table 2.3 Household Use of Credit Accounts in Latin America

Country	City	Has loan or credit instrument (%)	Never applied for a loan (%)	Reasons for not applying for a loan (%)			Have you ever been denied a loan? (%)	Reasons why a loan was denied (%)			
				Too risky/ does not like to be in debt (%)	Does not have enough income or collateral requirements (%)	Does not know (%)		Insufficient income (%)	No collateral or guarantees (%)	No credit history (%)	Lack of documentation requirements (%)
Argentina	Buenos Aires	9.7	78.5	80.0	25.7	22.7	23.8	40.0	3.3	3.3	6.7
	Córdoba	14.2	71.5	66.6	31.0	24.2	15.7	65.4	7.7	3.8	0.0
Bolivia	La Paz	23.4	57.4	77.9	27.6	34.7	36.0	47.3	38.5	4.4	14.3
	Santa Cruz	25.2	59.2	69.4	22.7	34.7	26.7	18.8	39.1	10.9	12.5
Brazil	San Pablo	21.7	61.0	73.3	16.2	7.7	23.3	40.7	14.8	13.0	0.0
	Rio de Janeiro	15.5	77.0	69.3	17.7	10.6	13.0	50.0	5.6	22.2	0.0
Colombia	Bogotá	21.9	56.6	66.7	12.6	21.1	29.9	35.9	6.4	19.2	9.0

(continued next page)

Table 2.3 Household Use of Credit Accounts in Latin America (continued)

Country	City	Has loan or credit instrument (%)	Never applied for a loan (%)	Reasons for not applying for a loan (%)			Have you ever been denied a loan? (%)	Reasons why a loan was denied (%)			
				Too risky/ does not like to be in debt (%)	Does not have enough income or collateral (%)	Does not know requirements (%)		Insufficient income (%)	No collateral or guarantees (%)	No credit history (%)	Lack of documentation requirements (%)
	Medellín	16.0	71.0	54.4	33.3	25.6	26.9	45.7	8.7	15.2	4.3
Ecuador	Quito	22.3	57.5	73.0	27.9	17.0	31.4	50.0	20.0	12.5	8.8
	Guayaquil	17.1	75.5	74.5	30.2	16.3	14.4	28.6	38.1	14.3	4.8
Panama	Ciudad de Panamá	12.5	65.3	68.1	24.1	17.9	20.1	31.7	17.1	24.4	7.3
Peru	Lima	17.7	67.5	74.5	29.4	34.2	41.1	26.6	29.1	15.2	12.7
	Arequipa	30.0	50.8	66.9	25.9	35.2	31.6	23.7	25.8	8.6	20.4
Uruguay	Montevideo	30.3	39.3	74.7	25.3	35.6	26.9	33.7	21.1	28.4	7.4
	Salto	28.2	46.4	75.7	26.7	25.9	19.7	62.9	16.1	9.7	9.7

Table 2.3 (continued)

Country	City	Has loan or credit instrument (%)	Reasons for not applying for a loan (%)				Have you ever been denied a loan? (%)	Reasons why a loan was denied (%)			
			Never applied for a loan (%)	Too risky/ does not like to be in debt (%)	Does not have enough income or collateral requirements (%)	Does not know (%)		Insufficient income (%)	No collateral or guarantees (%)	No credit history (%)	Lack of documentation requirements (%)
Venezuela, RB	Caracas	7.5	62.6	51.4	40.6	3.5	26.5	42.4	5.1	15.3	3.4
	Maracaibo	6.7	88.0	48.7	28.2	22.6	25.7	11.1	5.6	5.6	5.6
	Average LAC5	20.5	62.0	70.2	24.4	24.3	25.2	42.5	13.9	13.9	7.0
	Other LAC	16.4	66.5	66.1	28.8	21.0	25.8	32.8	23.3	12.5	8.1

Source: CAF 2011.

Loan use is even less pervasive than the use of bank accounts. Only about 21 percent of households in LAC5 countries have a loan, and 62 percent have never applied for one (table 2.3). In the case of the other Latin American countries (Bolivia, Ecuador, Panama, and the República Bolivariana de Venezuela), only 16 percent of households have a loan, and 66 percent have never applied for one. Among the reasons cited for not applying for a loan, 70 percent of households in LAC5 and 66 percent in other LAC countries indicate that they consider borrowing too risky and prefer not to be in debt. Only 24 percent in LAC5 countries did not apply because of insufficient income or collateral. Among other countries in the region, 29 percent of households have not applied because of insufficient income or collateral. Hence, across Latin America, households that do not apply for loans appear to opt out of using credit services primarily because they have a strong aversion to being in debt.

Among households from LAC5 countries that applied for a loan, 25 percent were rejected. In the case of the other LAC countries, 26 percent were rejected. The main reasons for loan rejections include insufficient income (42 percent for LAC5 and 33 percent for other LAC countries), lack of collateral or guarantees (14 percent for LAC5 and 23 percent for other LAC countries), lack of credit history (14 percent for LAC5 and 13 percent for other LAC countries), and lack of documentation requirements (7 percent for LAC5 and 8 percent for other LAC countries).

Overall, the household-level data reveal that the use of banking services is rather limited in Latin America. Significantly, households' responses to questions about why they do not use services suggest that lack of income and self-exclusion play a stronger role than supply-side considerations like high fees and stringent documentation requirements. It is important to note, however, that these surveys are based on a small sample of households that reside only in urban areas. Nationally representative surveys that include rural areas might provide a different picture of the level of use and the reasons behind it. Furthermore, because these surveys were done only for Latin America, we are unable to compare their results to what might be observed in other developing countries.

The Role of the Government in Promoting Financial Inclusion

Analyzing the role of the government in promoting financial inclusion is difficult since it can encompass many different aspects: from documenting whether the government has an explicit mandate to promote financial inclusion, to examining specific government programs or interventions targeted at improving financial inclusion, to evaluating the adequacy of the financial sector infrastructure and the contractual environment. Furthermore, assessing the welfare impact of government policies designed to promote financial inclusion is particularly hard, since it requires isolating the impact of these policies from other factors that can also affect welfare. A full evaluation of government policies is beyond the scope of this chapter. Instead, we focus exclusively on documenting the efforts and policies in place to promote financial inclusion in Latin America and on comparing them to those enacted by governments in other regions.

Regulators in LAC7 countries are more likely to have a mandate to increase financial inclusion (including having a document laying out a strategy to promote access) than those in developed countries and emerging economies in Eastern Europe (figure 2.17). Eighty-six percent of the LAC7 countries (six out of seven) have developed a strategy document to promote inclusion,[7] while 29 percent of the countries in Eastern Europe and only one country among the G-7 (14 percent) have a similar document

Figure 2.17 Governments' de Jure Commitment to Financial Inclusion in Selected Countries and Regions, 2010 (or latest available year)

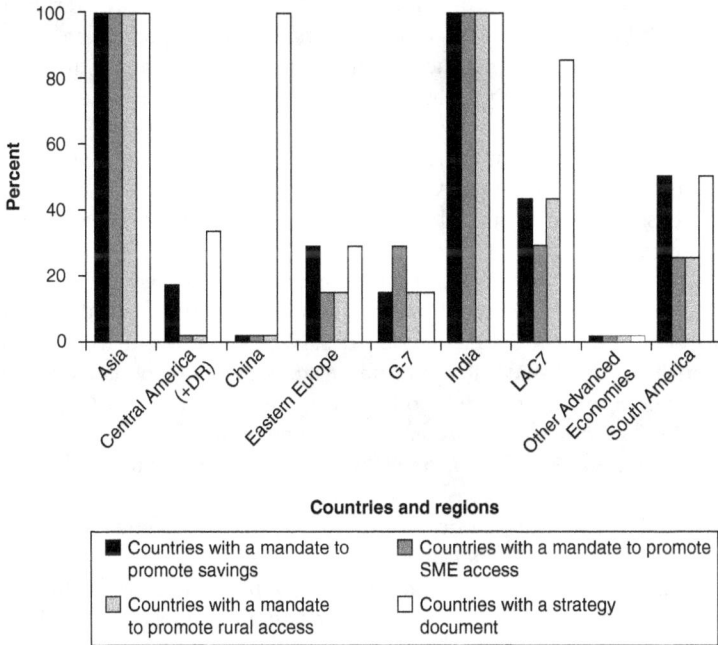

Countries and regions

- ■ Countries with a mandate to promote savings
- ▦ Countries with a mandate to promote SME access
- ▨ Countries with a mandate to promote rural access
- ☐ Countries with a strategy document

Source: CGAP 2009, 2010.
Note: DR = Dominican Republic; SME = small and medium enterprise.

in place. Similarly, while more than 40 percent of LAC7 countries have an explicit mandate to promote savings and access in rural areas (Argentina, Brazil, and Peru), 29 percent of countries in Eastern Europe and 14 percent among the G-7 have adopted such policies. LAC7 countries, however, lag behind Asia in their de jure commitment to financial inclusion, given that all emerging countries in this group have a strategy document and a formal mandate to promote access to finance.

Regulators in other Latin American countries are less likely than those in LAC7 countries to have adopted a mandate for financial inclusion or to have in place a strategy document to pursue that mandate. In South America, half the countries have a strategy document (Ecuador and the República Bolivariana de Venezuela) or a mandate to promote savings (Bolivia and the República Bolivariana de Venezuela). Among countries in Central America, only a third has a strategy document (Guatemala and Honduras), and only one country (El Salvador) has a mandate to promote savings.

Aside from examining governments' de jure commitment to financial inclusion, we analyze information on their de facto commitment to this goal. In particular, we consider (a) whether countries have dedicated units to promote their mandate of financial inclusion; (b) whether governments mandate that low-fee accounts be offered; and (c) whether governments use bank accounts to pay cash transfers. LAC7 countries lag behind those in Asia in having dedicated units to promote financial inclusion, but they are more likely to have basic accounts and to pay government transfers through accounts (figure 2.18). Furthermore, LAC7 countries outperform countries in Eastern Europe as well as developed economies in all three areas. Among LAC7 countries, 57 percent mandate that banks offer basic accounts, and 71 percent use bank accounts to pay government transfers.

As with the indicators of de jure commitment to financial inclusion, de facto indicators in South America, and especially in Central America, rank below those for the LAC7 countries. None of the countries in Central America has dedicated units to promote access, and no country mandates low-fee accounts. Only two countries in Central America (Costa Rica and Honduras) use bank accounts to pay government transfers. Among countries in South America, only Bolivia and the República Bolivariana de Venezuela have dedicated units to promote access, and Ecuador and the República Bolivariana de Venezuela are the only countries where the government pays transfers using bank accounts.

Access to financial services in many developing countries is hampered by the lack of a widespread network of banking outlets. In many rural areas, there are no bank branches or other delivery channels for financial services because financial intermediaries do not find it profitable to operate in those areas. Correspondent banks and mobile branches can play a significant role in expanding the outreach of financial services.

Figure 2.18 Governments' de Facto Commitment to Financial Inclusion in Selected Countries and Regions, 2010 (or latest available year)

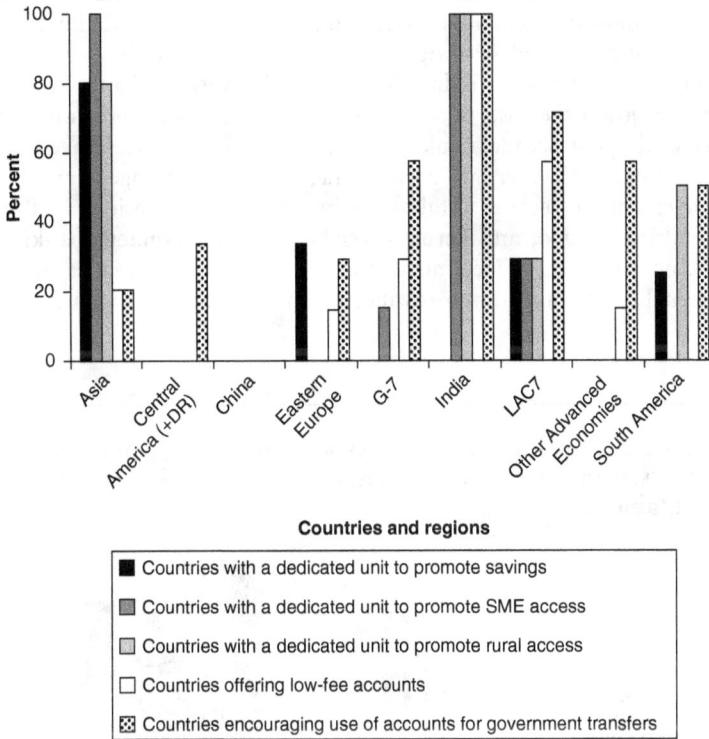

Countries and regions

- ■ Countries with a dedicated unit to promote savings
- ▨ Countries with a dedicated unit to promote SME access
- ▨ Countries with a dedicated unit to promote rural access
- □ Countries offering low-fee accounts
- ▨ Countries encouraging use of accounts for government transfers

Source: CGAP 2009, 2010.
Note: DR = Dominican Republic; SME = small and medium enterprise.

Correspondent banking arrangements are partnerships between banks and nonbanks with a significant network of outlets, such as convenience stores, post offices, drugstores, and supermarkets, to distribute financial services. These arrangements allow banks to provide their services in sparsely populated areas or in regions with low economic activity at significantly lower costs than opening and maintaining a full branch. Moreover, correspondent arrangements can also achieve broader financial inclusion by allowing banks to serve some customer segments that may not be profitably served through branches due to their lower transaction values, and correspondent arrangements may also be an effective way of providing services to people who are not familiar with the use of traditional banking facilities.

"Mobile branches" refer to any offices of a bank at which banking business is conducted that is moved or transported to one or more predetermined locations on a predetermined schedule. Like correspondents, mobile branches allow banks to offer services to poor and rural areas at lower costs than those associated with operating brick-and-mortar branches. Also, because mobile branches reduce the distance between the bank and its clients, they lower the costs of access to financial services for potential users.

Over the past decade, bank regulators in LAC7 countries have started to allow banks to enter into correspondent banking arrangements. These arrangements have been established by financial institutions in Brazil, Colombia, Mexico, and Peru. Nevertheless, correspondent banking is less common in LAC7 countries than it is among economies in Asia, Eastern Europe, and other advanced non-G-7 countries (figure 2.19).

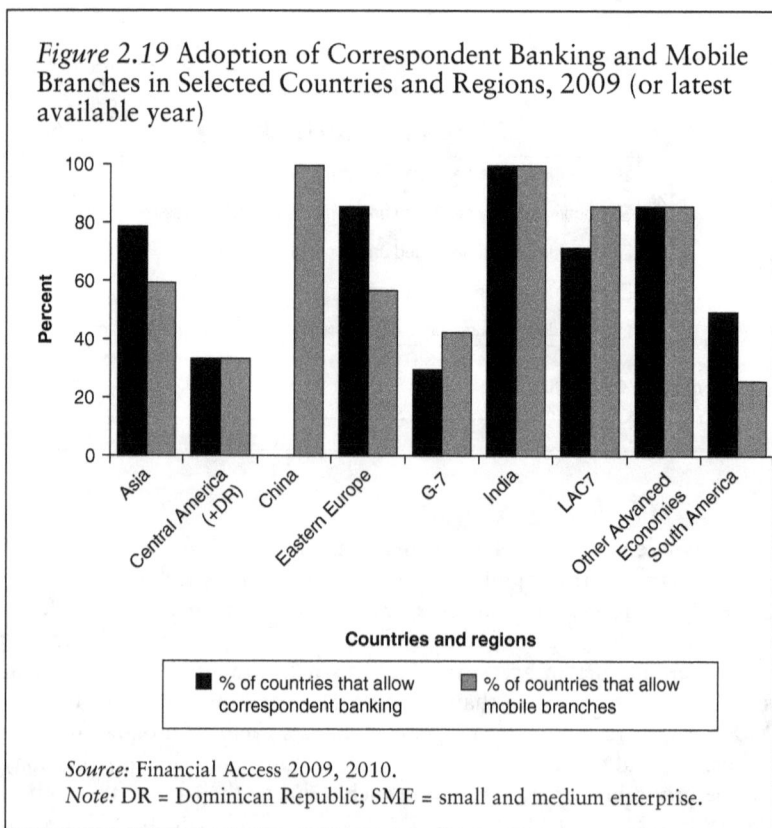

Figure 2.19 Adoption of Correspondent Banking and Mobile Branches in Selected Countries and Regions, 2009 (or latest available year)

Source: Financial Access 2009, 2010.
Note: DR = Dominican Republic; SME = small and medium enterprise.

While 71 percent of countries in LAC7 allow for correspondent banking, 80 percent of countries in Asia and 86 percent of countries in Eastern Europe and of advanced non-G-7 economies have adopted such practices.

In contrast, with the exception of China and India, where mobile branching is allowed, this practice is more common among LAC7 countries than among countries in the rest of Asia, Eastern Europe, and G-7 economies. Among LAC7 countries, 86 percent allow for mobile branches, while mobile branches have been adopted by 60 percent of the countries in Asia, 57 percent of those in Eastern Europe, and 43 percent of G-7 countries.

Similarly to what we found in the case of other policies, LAC7 countries are way ahead of their neighbors in the region when it comes to correspondent banking and mobile branches. Only one-third of the countries in Central America allow for either correspondent banking (Honduras and Nicaragua) or mobile branches (Costa Rica and Honduras). Among South American countries, half allow for correspondent banking (Bolivia and Ecuador), and only Bolivia has adopted the use of mobile branches.

Aside from adopting policies for promoting outreach among specific groups (like SMEs, the poor, or rural inhabitants), governments can influence the extent to which financial services are provided by financial institutions and used by the population at large by ensuring that the appropriate financial sector infrastructure and regulations are in place. In particular, the supply and the use of credit services will be influenced by the degree to which credit information is widely available to banks and the extent to which creditors feel that their rights are protected.

Based on an index measuring rules and practices affecting the coverage, scope, and accessibility of credit information available through either a public credit registry or a private credit bureau, LAC7 countries are ahead of comparator developing countries (figure 2.20).[8] Furthermore, the score obtained by LAC7 countries is identical to that assigned to G-7 economies. But when it comes to the legal rights index, which measures the degree to which collateral and bankruptcy laws protect the rights of borrowers and lenders and thus facilitate lending, LAC7 countries underperform most developed and developing countries. Clearly, legal rights reform should be a priority for LAC7 governments.

Comparing LAC7 countries to others in the region, we find that Central American countries have the same value on the credit information index and outrank LAC7 countries on the laws protecting the rights of creditors. Countries in South America other than the LAC7, however, appear to be lagging behind on the credit information index and especially on legal rights.

A complete analysis of the role of the government in promoting financial inclusion is beyond the scope of this chapter. In particular, we are unable to draw any conclusions about the welfare implications of different government policies. Nonetheless, the evidence presented indicates that a majority of governments in LAC7 countries have an explicit and

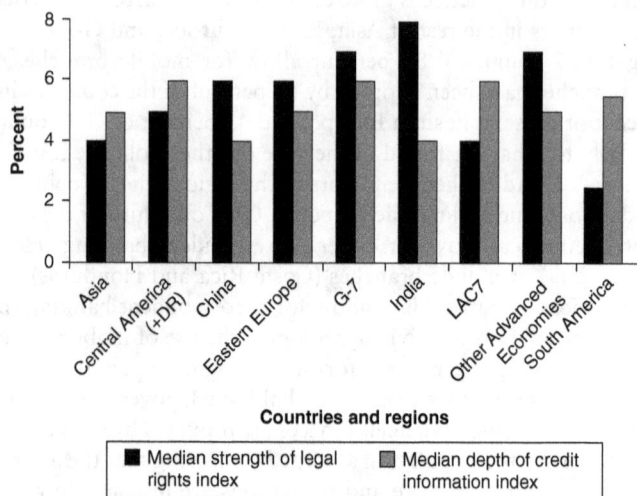

Figure 2.20 Index of Credit Information and Legal Rights in Selected Countries and Regions, 2009 (or latest available year)

Source: Doing Business database.
Note: DR = Dominican Republic.

formal commitment to financial inclusion and have adopted targeted policies to achieve this objective. Governments in LAC7 countries lag those in Asia but appear to be doing more than those in Eastern Europe and in developed countries. The rest of Latin America, though, lags behind LAC7 countries when it comes to adopting specific policies to promote financial inclusion. Finally, our analysis reveals that while the credit information environment in LAC7 countries compares favorably to that in other regions, governments throughout Latin America need to strengthen creditor rights.

Conclusions

At first glance, access to and use of banking services in Latin America appear to be low. Indicators of the numbers of bank branches, ATMs, and deposit accounts for the region are below those of developed countries and of some developing economies. However, our analysis suggests that the overall use of banking services is not lower than what is predicted based on the region's income and population density and that lack of demand appears to be an important reason behind the low use of banking services. Household surveys, for example, show that only half of households have an account. But most of those that do not have accounts are out of a job or do not have enough income to save. Distrust of banks and aversion to bank borrowing also seem to influence the extent to which firms and individuals use banking services in Latin America. Financial fees could also be playing a role, since our analysis indicates that these tend to be higher in Latin America than in other regions.

Across firms in Latin America, there are significant differences in the extent to which they access and use banking services, depending on the size of the enterprise. In general, access to and use of banking services are significantly lower for SMEs than for large firms. This is true across most countries within and outside of Latin America.

There are also significant disparities in financial inclusion in Latin America. LAC7 countries rank ahead of their neighbors both in access to and use of banking services and in the degree to which governments in these countries promote financial inclusion.

A majority of governments in LAC7 have adopted policies to promote financial inclusion such as mandating low-fee accounts, using the banking sector to pay government transfers, allowing for correspondent bank arrangements, and permitting the use of mobile branches. In general, LAC7 governments appear to be doing more than those in Eastern Europe and in developed countries. However, LAC7 countries lag behind Asia when it comes to the adoption of policies to promote financial inclusion. Areas that need more government attention include increasing SME finance, bringing down the cost of financial services, and reforming creditor rights. Outside of LAC7 countries, governments in the rest of Latin America need to step up their efforts to foster financial inclusion.

Notes

1. The topics related to financial inclusion considered in the CGAP survey include consumer protection, financial literacy, regulation of microfinance, savings promotion, small and medium enterprise finance promotion, and rural finance promotion.

2. CAF (2011) offers a more comprehensive picture of financial inclusion in Latin America.

3. Household surveys that compile data on the use of financial services are surveyed in Peachey and Roe (2004) and Claessens (2006). Also, Honohan and King (2009) analyze surveys from 11 African countries and Pakistan.

4. See Barr, Kumar, and Litan (2007) for more discussion of these issues.

5. Beck, Demirgüç-Kunt, and Martinez Peria (2007) collect aggregate data on the use of financial services around the world. These data were subsequently updated and augmented by CGAP (2009, 2010) and Kendall, Mylenko, and Ponce (2010).

6. In past decades, other important distribution channels—especially bank correspondents—have rapidly expanded throughout a number of developing economies, greatly contributing to financial inclusion. We discuss such alternative channels in the sections below.

7. Argentina, Brazil, Colombia, Mexico, Peru, and Uruguay.

8. A score of 1 is assigned for each of the following six features of the public credit registry or private credit bureau (or both): (a) both positive credit information (for example, outstanding loan amounts and pattern of on-time repayments) and negative information (for example, late payments, number and amount of defaults and bankruptcies) are distributed; (b) data on both firms and individuals are distributed; (c) data from retailers and utility companies as well as financial institutions are distributed; (d) more than two years of historical data are distributed; credit registries and bureaus that erase data on defaults as soon as they are repaid obtain a score of 0 for this indicator; (e) data on loan amounts below 1 percent of income per capita are distributed; note that a credit registry or bureau must have a minimum coverage of 1 percent of the adult population to score a 1 on this indicator; and (f) by law, borrowers have the right to access their data in the largest credit registry or bureau in the economy.

References

Aghion, P., and P. Bolton. 1997. "A Theory of Trickle-Down Growth and Development." *Review of Economic Studies* 64: 151–72.

Aportela, F. 1999. "Effects of Financial Access on Savings by Low-Income People." Chapter 1, PhD diss., Massachusetts Institute of Technology.

Ashraf, N., D. Karlan, and W. Yin. 2010. "Female Empowerment: Further Evidence from a Commitment Savings Product in the Philippines." *World Development* 38 (1): 333–44.

Banerjee, A., E. Duflo, R. Glennerster, and C. Kinnan. 2009. "The Miracle of Microfinance? Evidence from a Randomized Evaluation." Mimeo. MIT Department of Economics and Abdul Latif Jameel Poverty Action Lab.

Banerjee, A., and A. Newman. 1993. "Occupational Choice and the Process of Development." *Journal of Political Economy* 101: 274–98.

Barr, M., A. Kumar, and R. E. Litan. 2007. *Building Inclusive Financial Systems: A Framework for Financial Access.* Washington, DC: Brookings Institution Press.

Beck, T., A. Demirgüç-Kunt, and M. S. Martinez Peria. 2007. "Reaching Out: Access to and Use of Banking Services across Countries." *Journal of Financial Economics* 85: 234–66.

———. 2008. "Banking Services for Everyone? Barriers to Bank Access and Use around the World." *World Bank Economic Review* 22: 397–430.

Beck, T., R. Levine, and A. Levkov. 2010. "Big Bad Banks? The Impact of US Branch Deregulation in Income Distribution." *Journal of Finance* 65: 1637–67.

Burgess, R., and R. Pande. 2005. "Do Rural Banks Matter? Evidence from Indian Social Banking Experiment." *American Economic Review* 95: 780–95.

CAF (Corporación Andina de Fomento). 2011. *Servicios Financieros para el Desarrollo: Promoviendo el Acceso en América Latina: Reporte de Economía y Desarrollo.* CAF- Banco de Desarrollo de América Latina.

CGAP (Consultative Group to Assist the Poor). 2009. *Financial Access 2009.* Washington, DC: CGAP.

————. 2010. *Financial Access 2010*. Washington, DC: CGAP.

Claessens, S. 2006. "Access to Financial Services: A Review of the Issues and Public Policy Objectives." *Journal of Financial Transformation* 17: 16–19.

Doing Business (database). International Finance Corporation and World Bank, Washington, DC. http://www.doingbusiness.org/rankings.

Dupas, P., and J. Robinson. 2009. "Savings Constraints and Microenterprise Development: Evidence from a Field Experiment in Kenya." NBER Working Paper 14693, National Bureau of Economic Research, Cambridge, MA.

Enterprise Surveys (database). International Finance Corporation and World Bank. http://www.enterprisesurveys.org/.

Galor, O., and J. Zeira. 1993. "Income Distribution and Macroeconomics." *Review of Economic Studies* 60: 35–52.

Honohan, P. 2008. "Cross-Country Variation in Household Access to Financial Services." *Journal of Banking and Finance* 32: 2493–2500.

Honohan, P., and M. King. 2009. "Cause and Effect of Financial Access: Cross-Country Evidence from the Finscope Surveys." Paper prepared for the World Bank Conference "Measurement, Promotion and Impact of Access to Financial Services," Washington, DC, March.

Karlan, D., and J. Zinman. 2009. "Expanding Microenterprise Credit Access: Using Randomized Supply Decisions to Estimate the Impact in Manila." CEPR Discussion Paper DP7396, Center for Economic Policy Research, Washington, DC.

————. 2010. "Expanding Credit Access: Using Randomized Supply Decisions to Estimate Impacts." *Review of Financial Studies* 23 (1): 433–64.

Kendall, J., N. Mylenko, and A. Ponce. 2010. "Measuring Financial Access around the World." Policy Research Working Paper 5253, World Bank, Washington, DC.

Khandker, S. 2005. "Microfinance and Poverty: Evidence Using Panel Data from Bangladesh." *World Bank Economic Review* 19 (2): 263–86.

Peachey, S., and A. Roe. 2004. *Access to Finance: A Study for the World Savings Institute*. Oxford: Oxford Policy Management.

Pickens, M., D. Porteous, and A. Rotman. 2009. "Banking the Poor via G2P Payments." CGAP Focus Note 58, Consultative Group to Assist the Poor, Washington, DC.

Pitt, M., and S. Khandker. 1998. "The Impact of Group-Based Credit Programs on Poor Households in Bangladesh: Does the Gender of Participants Matter?" *Journal of Political Economy* 106: 958–96.

3

Benchmarking LAC's Financial Development: The Banking and Equity Gaps

Augusto de la Torre, Erik Feyen, and Alain Ize

Abstract

This chapter uses a broad benchmarking methodology to assess LAC's financial development, identify the main developmental gaps, and detect the possible factors underlying those gaps. The chapter finds that LAC's financial development lags substantially on certain indicators, particularly banking depth and efficiency (the "banking gap") and stock market liquidity (the "equity gap"). LAC's turbulent financial history, mediocre growth, and residual weaknesses in the contractual (rather than the informational) environment all seem to have contributed to the banking gap. Regarding the equity gap, the offshore trading of the larger stocks mostly explains their lower domestic trading. The low trading of the smaller stocks appears to be related to the negative spillovers of the offshore migration of the larger stocks, the regional predominance of pensions funds over mutual funds, the lingering weaknesses in corporate governance and the contractual environment, and

The authors work for the World Bank as, respectively, chief economist for Latin America and the Caribbean (adelatorre@worldbank.org), senior financial specialist (efeijen@worldbank.org), and senior consultant (aize@worldbank.org). The chapter benefited from valuable comments by the various discussants of LAC's financial sector flagship.

the region's turbulent macrofinancial history. However, more research is needed to ascertain the relative importance of these various factors and infer from the evidence a robust policy agenda.

Introduction

When discussing the impact of financial structure on economic growth, the literature has, at least until very recently, generally concluded that function matters more than form.[1] Financial development has typically been understood as a relatively smooth and predictable march from "relationship-based finance" to "arms-length finance," involving a systematic process of market completion driven by a gradual reduction of frictions.[2] However, the global financial crisis showed that financial development has a "dark side" that can make it both nonlinear and bumpy. Thus, what may appear as financial development can in fact exacerbate market failures and thereby undermine financial sustainability.

De la Torre, Feyen, and Ize (2013) propose a conceptual framework of financial development based on a typology of the frictions that hinder financial contracting. They separate these frictions into agency frictions, which restrict the scope for delegation, and collective frictions, which restrict the scope for pooling and participation. Each of these two classes of frictions is, in turn, broken down into two paradigms, depending on the completeness of information and the extent of rationality. Thus, the two agency paradigms are costly enforcement and asymmetric information; the two collective paradigms are collective action and collective cognition. Financial structure reflects economic agents' efforts to find the path of least resistance around these four classes of frictions and paradigms. In turn, financial development (the evolution of financial structure over time) reflects the gradual erosion of frictions, quickened by innovation, returns to scale, and network effects.

This framework implies that the process of financial development is broadly predictable and can be explained by the gradual grinding down—under the push of competition, financial innovation, returns to scale, and network effects—of agency or collective frictions. Based on cross-sectional development paths, the authors indeed find that public debt, banking, and capital markets develop sequentially and under increasingly convex paths. However, the dynamic development paths followed by specific country groups can deviate substantially from the cross-sectional paths. This pattern may reflect country-specific development policies, path dependence, innovation-induced leapfrogging, or cycles and crashes.

These underlying regularities suggest that one can benchmark countries and compare their financial development performance using the broadest available dataset of cross-country financial indicators. This benchmarking approach can shed light on the question of where we would expect key measures of a country's (or a group of countries') financial development to be, given not only the level of economic development (as proxied by income per capita) but also the structural factors that matter for financial development but are largely exogenous to policy, such as country size and demographic structure. The financial development gaps that emerge from this exercise then largely reflect deficits in policy and policy-shaped institutions. In this chapter, we use this benchmark methodology to assess the financial development of Latin America and the Caribbean (LAC), to identify the main developmental gaps, and to detect the possible factors underlying those gaps.

We find that, whether we include all countries or only the largest seven, LAC is broadly on track with respect to many financial development indicators but that it lags substantially on some important ones. In particular, there is a substantial "banking gap." Banking depth indicators (deposits and private credit) lag markedly, and the gap has worsened rather than improved over time. Bank efficiency, as measured by net interest rate margins, also lags, albeit in this case the lag has receded rather than expanded. There is also an important "equity gap." While LAC is approximately on track on the size of its stock and bond markets, it lags dramatically on the liquidity of its *domestic* stock market, and the gap has been widening over time. These gaps are of concern because they coincide with some of the financial indicators that have been shown to be the best predictors of future output growth (see Beck and Levine 2005).

We then explore the possible causes underlying the banking and equity gaps. On the banking gap, the largest fraction of it simply reflects LAC's turbulent macrofinancial history. With the notable exception of Chile, large credit bubbles and crashes have affected all its largest countries in the past 20 years, leaving scars on their financial development that endure to this day. Financial sustainability is therefore essential to the ability of LAC's financial systems to catch up. Limited demand for credit, reflecting LAC's mediocre output growth, explains another substantial fraction of the gap. While this link between output growth and credit goes in the opposite direction from the one generally emphasized in the recent finance literature, ultimately it also puts the spotlight on productivity-enhancing credit policies. Finally, we find that contractual gaps, particularly enforcement and creditor rights, rather than informational gaps, have also contributed significantly to the banking gap. Hence, further progress in improving the judiciary and legal frameworks is called for.

On the equity gap, we find that the very large offshoring of stock market trading generally explains the underperformance in the domestic trading of the larger firms. However, it does not directly explain the low domestic trading of the smaller firms since the latter are not traded abroad. The evidence suggests, however, that as the large stocks move abroad, they leave the smaller stocks in shallower domestic markets. This adverse implication for the liquidity of the domestic stock market comes indirectly through various channels, including negative spillover effects. Additional factors behind the gap in domestic stock market liquidity include the dominance of buy-and-hold pension funds over more active institutional traders such as mutual funds; weaknesses in corporate governance (particularly with respect to minority shareholder rights and protections); and shortcomings in the general enabling environment (particularly in property rights). For reasons that remain to be fully elucidated, the region's history of macroeconomic and financial turbulence also seems to have something to do with the lack of domestic equity trading. Besides the obvious improvements in macrostability, stock market infrastructure, and the general enabling environment (which should all help but at the margin), developing a proper policy agenda remains thorny, particularly for the smaller countries and the smaller firms, given the decisive importance of scale (size of markets and of issues) and network effects in stock market development.

The rest of this chapter is structured as follows. In the next two sections, we briefly present the benchmarking methodology and its main results. We next review the possible causes of the banking gap and then go on to discuss the equity gap. The final section concludes by flagging the key policy issues and challenges for the future.

The Benchmarking Methodology

We measure domestic financial development based on a set of depth indicators:[3] bank deposits and private credit; insurance companies' premiums (life and nonlife); assets of mutual funds and pension funds; public and private debt securities (domestic and foreign); and equity market capitalization. We complement these depth indicators with several indicators of efficiency and liquidity for which there is sufficient cross-country data, specifically banks' net interest margin and equity market turnover. We complete this battery of financial development indicators with four indicators of bank soundness: leverage (ratio of unweighted capital to assets); capital adequacy (ratio of risk-weighted capital to assets); profitability (returns on assets); and liquidity (share of liquid assets in total bank assets).

To make the data as comparable as possible across countries, we control for economic development—both the level and the square level of gross domestic product (GDP) per capita—as well as for various other factors that can be considered as policy exogenous (at least in the short term). These include demographic (population size, density, young and old dependency ratios) and country-specific characteristics (dummies for fuel exporter, offshore financial center, and transition country).[4]

To better capture the underlying financial development patterns, we employ quantile (median) regressions, which are less influenced by outliers.

Moreover, rather than undergoing a panel estimate, which would blend variations across countries and across time, we conduct our analysis in two stages. In the first stage, we take each country's median financial indicators over the whole sample period and then conduct a cross-sectional estimate over the medians. In the second stage, we compare this cross-sectional aggregate development path with the individual dynamic development paths followed by specific regional groups of countries.

Where Is LAC?

Table 3.1 provides a synthetic view of LAC's financial development relative to its benchmark.[5] It compares the 1990s to the 2000s and contrasts the LAC7 countries (Argentina, Brazil, Chile, Colombia, Mexico, Peru, and Uruguay) with the region as a whole.[6] Figure 3.1 reports the performance of each of the LAC7 countries relative to their benchmarks for a subset of financial indicators.

On banking indicators, LAC's banking intermediation (both deposits and private credit) substantially lags its cross-sectional benchmarks (by over 20 percentage points of GDP in the case of the LAC7 countries), a trend that is worsening over time. On a country-by-country basis, Chile is the only LAC7 country that meets its benchmark on private credit to GDP. All other LAC7 countries are widely below their benchmarks. LAC's private sector bank credit has undergone a steep cycle, rising in the late 1980s and early 1990s, peaking in the mid-1990s, and collapsing thereafter. Bank deposits have followed a rather similar pattern, albeit less dramatic. When credit is decomposed into its commercial, mortgage, and personal components, we can see that the gaps in commercial and mortgage lending have worsened. The gap in consumer lending, however, has substantially diminished, following the very rapid expansion of personal lending over the past decade, particularly in the LAC7 countries (table 3.2 and figure 3.2).[7]

The efficiency of LAC's banking systems, measured as net interest margins, also seems to underperform in relation to its peers. However, in this case the lag has been closing rather than growing. Bank margins have narrowed to just below one percentage point in the past decade, down from over three percentage points during the previous decade. On the positive side, LAC banks largely exceed their benchmark on key prudential buffers (profitability, solvency, and liquidity). Indeed, the region currently has the highest reported prudential buffers in the world.

With respect to capital market indicators, LAC's equity market capitalization is broadly on track relative to its comparators, albeit somewhat on the low side (particularly for the LAC7 countries). On a country-by-country basis, Chile clearly stands out again, followed by Brazil. In contrast, the liquidity of LAC's equity markets, as proxied by

Table 3.1 Benchmark Model for LAC's Financial Development Indicators, 1990–99 and 2000–08

| | Median actual values (%) | | Workhorse median residuals | | | |
| | Rest of LAC | LAC7 | Rest of LAC | | LAC7 | |
	2000–08	2000–08	1990–99	2000–08	1990–99	2000–08
Bank private credit	36.0	24.2	-3.9***	-0.8**	-13.6***	-22.5***
Bank claims on domestic financial sector	1.1	2.6	-1.3***	-0.4***	-1.1***	-0.2
Bank credit to government	3.7	10.0	-5.2***	-5.3***	-4.3***	-1.1
Bank foreign claims	8.6	2.5	-0.5	2.0	-4.4***	-5.7***
Bank domestic deposits	37.4	25.4	-10.9***	-4.0***	-13.6***	-20.8***
Bank nondeposit funding	18.4	24.3	-3.1	-1.4	-5.1*	-6.5**
Net interest margin	4.9	4.8	0.0	1.0***	3.3***	0.9***
Noninterest income/total income	25.6	33.5	-9.4***	-4.2***	3.9	1.9**
Total bank financial assets/GDP (excluding reserves)	55.5	65.5	-17.6***	-0.7	-16.7***	-19.5***
Life insurance premiums	0.3	0.7	-0.3***	-0.3***	-0.7***	-0.4***
Nonlife insurance premiums	1.3	1.1	-0.1	0.1***	-0.2***	-0.3***
Pension fund assets	7.5	11.7		-4.3***		-0.7*

Table 3.1 Benchmark Model for LAC's Financial Development Indicators, 1990–99 and 2000–08 (continued)

	Median actual values (%)		Workhorse median residuals			
	Rest of LAC	LAC7	Rest of LAC		LAC7	
	2000–08	2000–08	1990–99	2000–08	1990–99	2000–08
Mutual fund assets	1.1	5.9		−9.8**		−5.9
Insurance company assets	2.1	4.0		−2.9***		−7.7***
Stock market turnover	2.3	12.6	−3.7	−10.6***	−18.4***	−28.8***
Stock market capitalization	15.7	33.6	−8.5	−7.7***	−7.7	−0.6
Domestic private debt securities	0.6	9.0	−10.1	−12.3	−1.6***	−3.0*
Domestic public debt securities	28.5	19.7	−17.6**	0.7	−21.3***	−12.2***
Bank foreign claims	17.2	24.5	−2.5**	−3.4	−4.0	0.0*
Foreign private debt securities	1.8	4.0	−1.6*	−2.4**	−1.9**	−2.5***
Foreign public debt securities	9.6	8.9	−3.0	1.3**	0.9	2.6***
Gross portfolio equity assets	0.2	3.1	−4.9***	−0.6***	−0.1	2.4
Gross portfolio debt assets	3.7	1.3	−1.0	1.2	0.1	0.0**
Gross portfolio equity liabilities	0.4	5.4	−2.3*	−2.2***	1.2**	1.8
Gross portfolio debt liabilities	9.2	12.2	¡16.1***	2.7	−4.9	3.2**
Capital/total assets	10.1	11.5	−0.2**	0.5**	0.6***	2.3***

(continued next page)

Table 3.1 Benchmark Model for LAC's Financial Development Indicators, 1990–99 and 2000–08 (continued)

| | Median actual values (%) | | Workhorse median residuals | | | |
| | Rest of LAC | LAC7 | Rest of LAC | | LAC7 | |
	2000–08	2000–08	1990–99	2000–08	1990–99	2000–08
Liquid assets/total assets	3.6	12.5	-4.8***	-5.9***	2.4***	5.0***
Regulatory capital/RWA	14.1	14.4		0.1		2.0***
Bank capital/assets	10.0	9.8		0.7		2.2***
Return on assets	1.5	1.3	-0.4	0.1	0.4***	0.5**

Source: de la Torre, Feyen, and Ize 2011.

Note: This table shows the results of a benchmark model for LAC's financial development indicators. It presents the 2000–08 median for all LAC countries and the median LAC residual for the 1990–99 and 2000–08 periods, respectively, derived from the workhorse median regression model of the financial indicator of interest on GDP per capita (squared), population size and density, fuel exporter dummy, age dependency ratio, offshore financial center dummy, transition country dummy, and year fixed effects. The asterisks correspond to the level of significance of Wilcoxon rank sum tests for distributional differences of the residuals between LAC and the rest of the world.

***, **, and * represent significance at 1 percent, 5 percent, and 10 percent, respectively. LAC = Latin America and the Caribbean; GDP = gross domestic product; RWA = risk-weighted asset.

Figure 3.1 LAC7 Financial Indicators against Benchmark

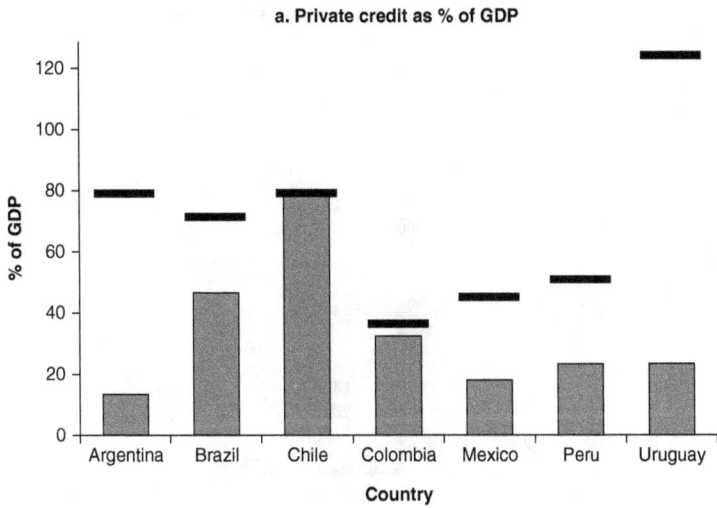

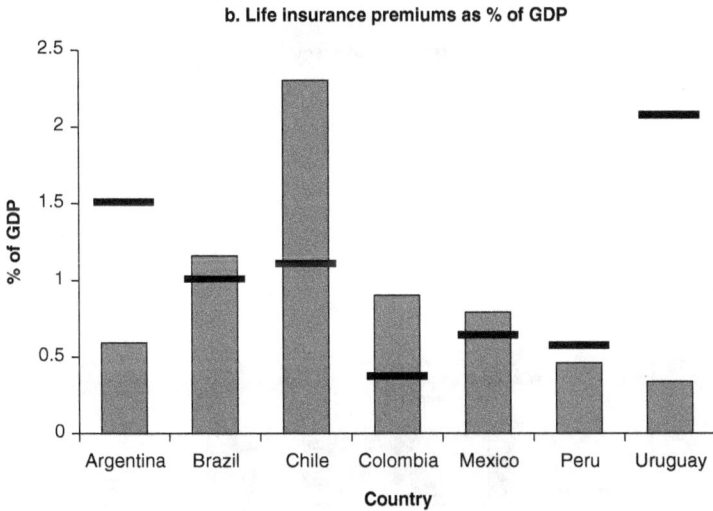

a. Private credit as % of GDP

b. Life insurance premiums as % of GDP

(continued next page)

Figure 3.1 *(continued)*

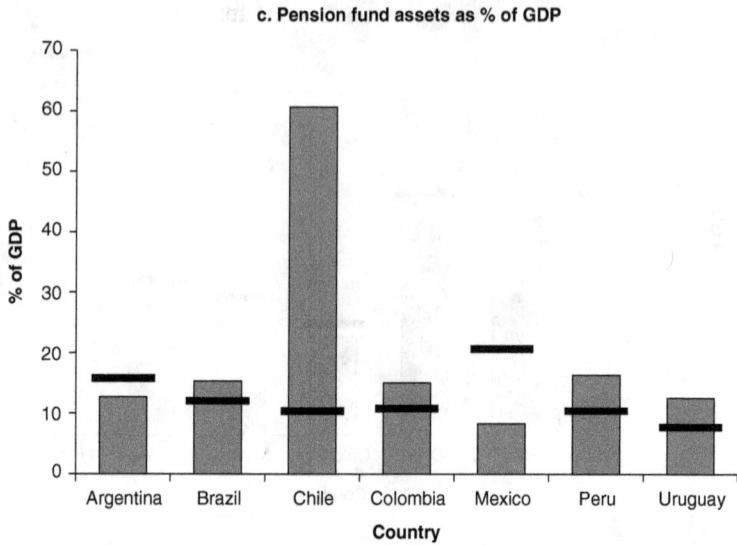

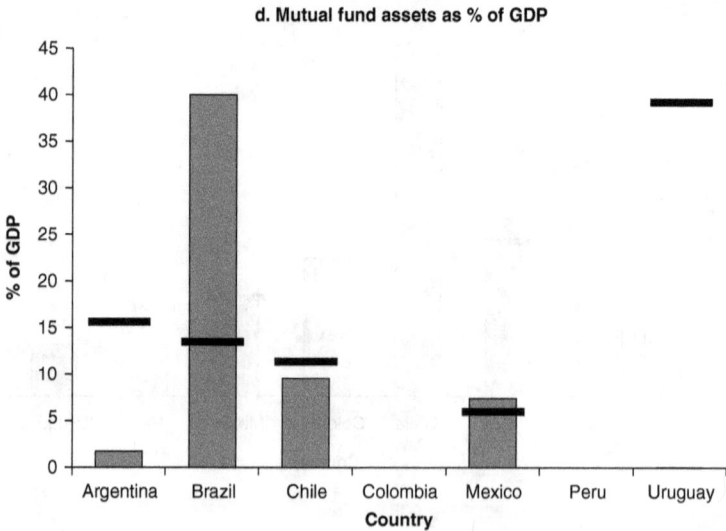

c. Pension fund assets as % of GDP

d. Mutual fund assets as % of GDP

(continued next page)

Figure 3.1 (continued)

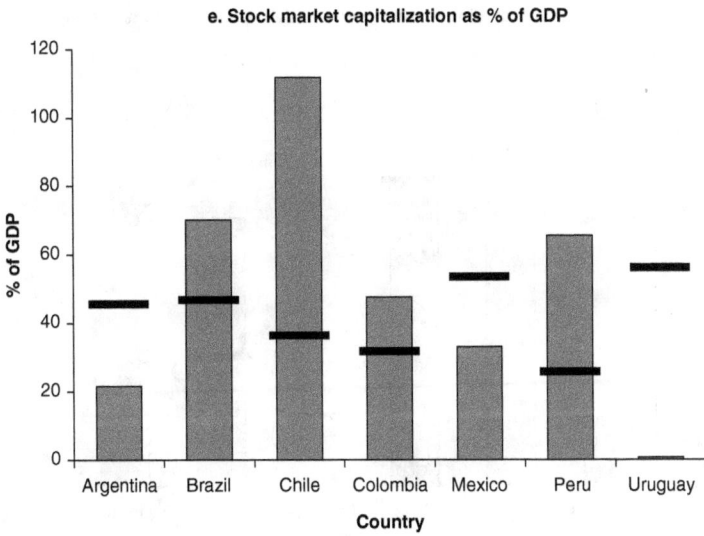

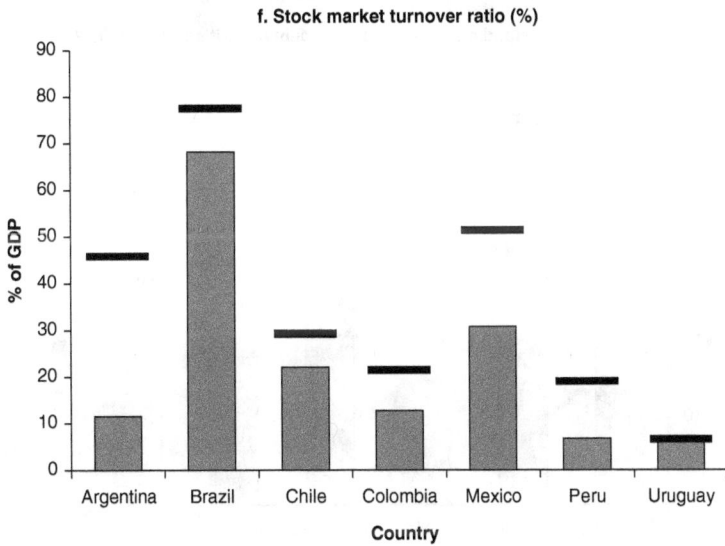

e. Stock market capitalization as % of GDP

f. Stock market turnover ratio (%)

(continued next page)

Figure 3.1 (continued)

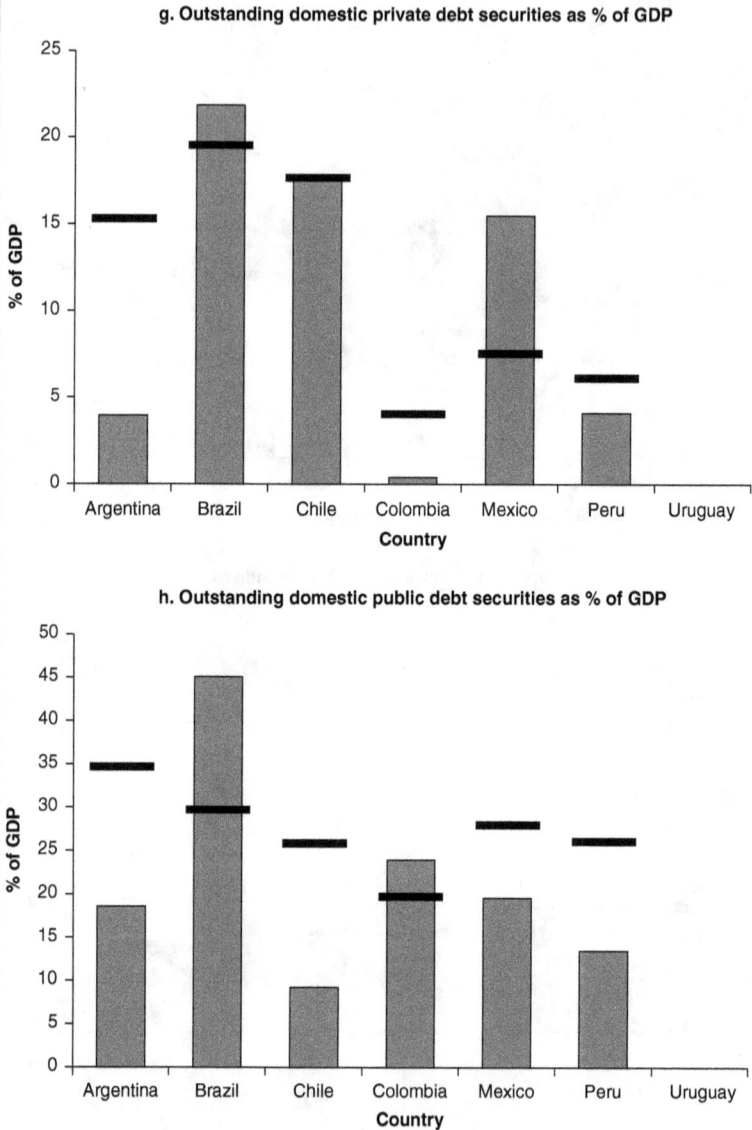

g. Outstanding domestic private debt securities as % of GDP

h. Outstanding domestic public debt securities as % of GDP

Source: de la Torre, Feyen, and Ize 2011.
Note: This figure shows financial indicators for individual LAC7 countries against their respective benchmark, represented by the horizontal bars. GDP = gross national product.

Table 3.2 LAC Credit Gap by Type of Credit, 1996 and 2007

	Expected	Actual	Gap	Gap/expected
Year: 1996				
Credit to the private sector as % of GDP				
Commercial	24.7	19.4	5.2	21.1
Mortgage	8.4	5.4	3.0	35.7
Consumer	8.8	3.4	5.4	61.4
Total	41.8	28.2	13.6	32.5
Year: 2007				
Credit to the private sector as % of GDP				
Commercial	22.9	14.5	8.4	36.7
Mortgage	12.6	3.1	9.5	75.4
Consumer	11.2	6.5	4.7	42.0
Total	46.7	24.2	22.5	48.2

Source: de la Torre, Feyen, and Ize 2011.
Note: This table shows the results of a benchmark model for LAC7 banking credit indicators. GDP = gross domestic product.

turnover, is lagging dramatically, and this lag has been steadily worsening. Except for Uruguay (which just meets its benchmark), all LAC7 countries fall short of their benchmarks.

Bond markets, both domestic and foreign private market capitalization, are a bit on the low side, although not exceedingly so. Moreover, on a country-by-country basis, Brazil, Chile, and Mexico all meet or exceed their benchmarks. In addition, LAC's public debt capitalization lags its benchmark substantially for domestic markets but exceeds it slightly for foreign markets, which suggests that LAC still has a long way to go in developing its local currency public debt markets and limiting its reliance on dollar-denominated foreign debt. This being said, on a country-by-country basis, both Brazil and Colombia exceed their domestic debt benchmarks.

Finally, on indicators related to institutional investors, LAC pension funds seem to be on track, with Chile having by far the most developed pension fund system in the region. Moreover, LAC7 mutual funds appear to have largely caught up with their benchmark, albeit with huge cross-country disparities. While Brazil's mutual funds industry exceeds its benchmark by an ample margin, and Chile and Mexico are

Figure 3.2 Average Composition of Private Credit by Type of
Credit in Chile, Colombia, Mexico, and Peru, 1996–2009

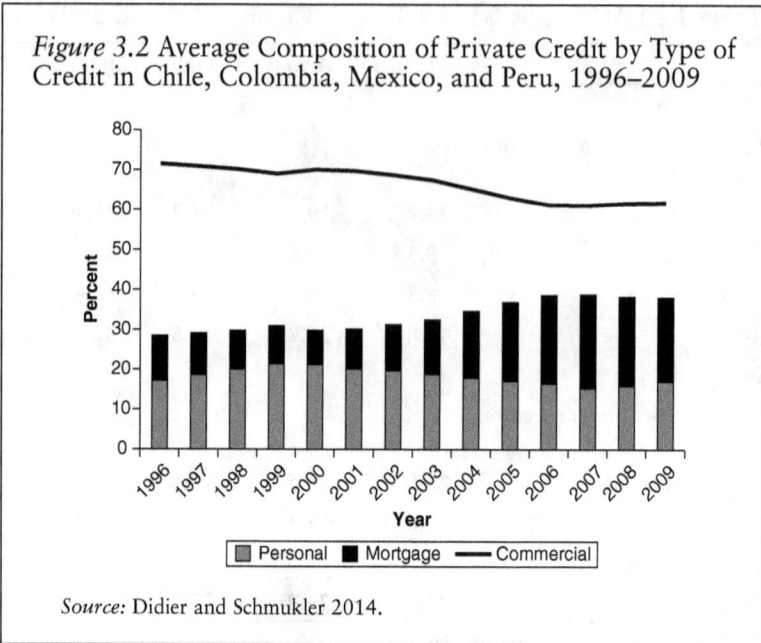

Source: Didier and Schmukler 2014.

close to their benchmarks, other LAC countries are far below their
peers. Regarding the insurance industry, insurance premiums (both life
and nonlife) lag significantly in both LAC and LAC7. Chile is again the
regional star performer, largely because of its well-developed annuities
industry.

What Explains LAC's Banking Gap?

In principle, the banking gap could reflect just a measurement problem,
particularly if foreign financing largely offsets the lack of domestic bank
financing. Because of data limitations, it is not straightforward to rule
this out. Nonetheless, balance of payments data provide some clues.
They suggest that the fluctuations in private sector domestic credit for
four of the LAC7 countries were generally matched by opposite (albeit
much dampened) changes in gross debt liabilities abroad (figure 3.3).
However, while the correlation is significantly negative (close to minus
40 percent), the two series are clearly orders of magnitude apart. Thus,
while there is evidently some substitution, it is quite limited. At the
same time, foreign private debt securities issued by LAC7 corporations

abroad (that is, nonbank credit to corporations) do not outperform the benchmark (see table 3.1). Therefore, one can safely conclude that while cross-border credit (from markets or intermediaries) may have substituted for domestic bank credit *at the margin*, it clearly did not do so *on average*.

Alternatively, the lack of bank credit could reflect a lack of demand for lendable funds rather than a lack of supply. Or perhaps the low volume of commercial credit reflects a lack of bankable projects. LAC's lackluster growth could, in turn, be a reflection of a lack of investment rather than a lack of savings. And a lack of investment could reflect low productivity rather than a high cost of funds. Indeed, a sizable literature emphasizes LAC's structural bottlenecks in productivity and growth, which derive from institutional weaknesses as well as overvalued real exchange rates.[8] To test for such demand effects, we add to the benchmarking model average growth of past output as an additional control and find that it indeed explains a sizable part of LAC's current banking underperformance (table 3.3).

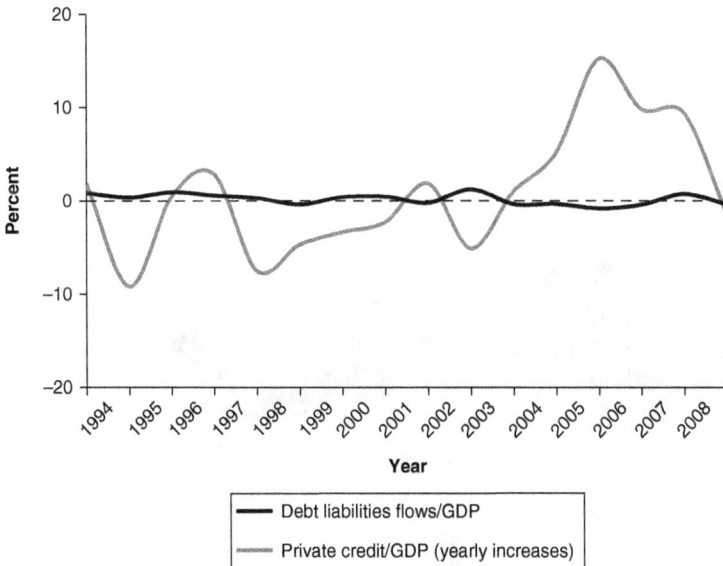

Figure 3.3 Offshore and Onshore Credit to the Private Sector in Brazil, Chile, Colombia, and Mexico, 1994–2009

Source: International Financial Statistics.
Note: GDP = gross domestic product.

Table 3.3 LAC Credit Gap: A Decomposition by Source

Source	Dependent variable: Bank private credit (% of GDP)			
	(1)	(2)	(3)	(4)
Enforcement contract index	-4.047*			-5.318**
	(-1.864)			(-2.358)
Legal rights index	1.662			1.671
	(-1.547)			(-1.385)
Credit information index	-0.526			
	(-0.379)			
Property rights index	0.235			0.069
	(-1.301)			(-0.335)
Annualized average sample GDP growth		7.450***		5.59**
		(2.935)		(-2.433)
Credit crash dummy (% of period)			-86.92***	-77.69**
			(-2.816)	(-2.042)
Workhorse controls	Yes	Yes	Yes	Yes

Table 3.3 LAC Credit Gap: A Decomposition by Source *(continued)*

Source	Dependent variable: Bank private credit (% of GDP)			
	(1)	(2)	(3)	(4)
Explained credit gap based on LAC7 median values				
Contract enforcement index	1.51			1.98
Legal rights index	0.64			0.65
Credit information index	0.47			
Property rights index	1.15			0.34
Annualized average sample GDP growth		3.70		2.80
Credit crash dummy (% of time)			7.02	6.27
Total explained gap	3.77	3.70	7.02	12.04
Gap	20.9	20.1	18.9	15.7
Percent of total gap explained	18%	18%	37%	77%

Sources: de la Torre, Feyen, and Ize 2011; Heritage Foundation; *Doing Business.*
Note: This table shows regressions of bank credit to the private sector against different explanatory variables. The contract enforcement index is the principal component of the following indicators from *Doing Business:* contract enforcement costs, number of days to enforce a contract (in logs), and number of procedures to enforce a contract. The legal rights index and the credit information index are from *Doing Business.* The property rights index is from the Heritage Foundation. Robust *t*-statistics are shown in parentheses.
*, **, and *** denote significance at the 10 percent, 5 percent, and 1 percent levels. LAC = Latin America and the Caribbean; GDP = gross domestic product.

An additional check on whether the lag in bank credit is supply based or demand based consists in looking at real interest rates. If the low credit primarily reflected a lack of demand for credit (rather than a lack of supply of funds), real interest rates should be low. On the bank lending side, this is clearly not the case as real lending rates in LAC have exceeded U.S. rates by close to 800 basis points, on average, over the past decade (figure 3.4). However, on the deposit side, real interest rates have exceeded U.S. rates by only 100–200 basis points over the past decade. Moreover, the deposit rate differential has always been below the country risk differential, as measured by the Emerging Markets Bond Index premiums. Overall, this does not seem to suggest a burning scarcity of funds.[9]

The obvious follow-up question, therefore, is, What is behind the fat bank margins? One possible answer is lack of competition. However,

Figure 3.4 Real Lending Rate, Real Deposit Rate, and Emerging Market Bond Index: Differentials between LAC7 and the United States, Five-Year Moving Averages, 1984–2010

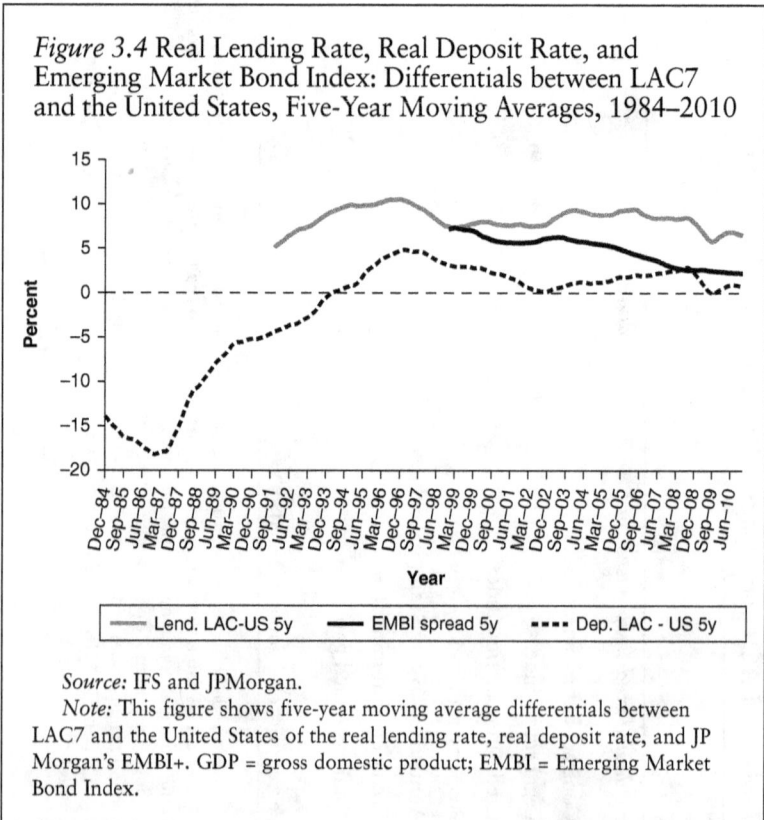

Source: IFS and JPMorgan.
Note: This figure shows five-year moving average differentials between LAC7 and the United States of the real lending rate, real deposit rate, and JP Morgan's EMBI+. GDP = gross domestic product; EMBI = Emerging Market Bond Index.

recent studies of bank competition, based on an analysis of Panzer-Rosse or the Lerner index (Gelos 2009; Anzoategui, Martínez Pería, and Rocha 2010) do not support this hypothesis.[10] In fact, LAC appears to outperform (rather than underperform) both of these indexes. Alternatively, the high bank overheads (which account for most of the high margins) could reflect a problem of insufficient scale. Indeed, including the ratio of private credit to GDP (a proxy for scale) as an additional control in the benchmark regressions explains about two-thirds of the current excess margin (table 3.4). Hence, the evidence suggests, perhaps not surprisingly, that the high margins and the limited scale of intermediation are largely mirror images of each other.

This finding, in turn, prompts us to explore the reasons for LAC's underperformance, given the size of its banking intermediation. Adding a basic set of enabling-environment indicators—contract enforcement costs, creditor rights, property rights, and credit information—to the basic benchmark regressions for private bank credit shows that some of them (enforcement costs and creditor rights) have a significant impact. Since LAC significantly underperforms on both of these indicators, the two variables together explain only a modest fraction—about 2.6 percentage points of GDP, or 17 percent of the credit gap (see table 3.3). Although that number is small, measurement noise is likely to bias this result downward. Its share of the total explained component of the gap (nearly one-fourth) probably provides a more accurate sense of the magnitude of its importance.

To examine the roots of the banking gap a bit further, we also check whether the low amount of private credit can be at least partly explained by two additional variables that are often mentioned as important for the region: the degree of bank competition and the size of the informal sector. Regarding bank competition, one would expect the depth of intermediation to be positively related to the extent of competition, as banks should compete more aggressively for market share the more competition there is. However, one would expect the depth of intermediation to be negatively related to informality, as it naturally becomes more difficult for banks to lend as informality grows. Bank competition can be measured in a variety of ways, including the assets of the three or five largest commercial banks as a share of total commercial banking assets, the H-statistic, the Lerner index, or the Boone indicator. Informality is measured as the share of informal employment in total nonagricultural employment. Table 3.5, which inserts these two additional controls into various regressions of private credit, shows that although the signs are generally (albeit not always) correct (competition generally expands credit; informality always reduces it), neither of the two new controls is significant in any definition of the variable or specification.

Nonetheless, to have a better feel for the possible magnitude of the effects, we use the regression coefficients for either variable—in the case

Table 3.4 Bank Net Interest Margins, Bank Overheads, and Private Credit

	Net interest margins	Net interest margins	Overheads	Overheads
Private credit (% of GDP)	−0.0261***	−0.0236***	−0.0247***	−0.0229***
	(−8.280)	(−6.314)	(−9.833)	(−8.390)
Contract enforcement index		−0.247*		−0.072
		(−2.224)		(−0.724)
Legal rights index		0.0538		0.0653
		(−0.976)		(−1.395)
Credit information index		−0.0161		−0.0153
		(−0.214)		(−0.276)
Property rights index		0.00697		−0.00324
		(−0.883)		(−0.467)
Constant	4.669	15.90**	5.172	17.92***
	(1.087)	(2.426)	(1.519)	(2.956)
No. of observations	1,280	459	1,280	459
R^2	0.36	0.49	0.35	0.48

Sources: de la Torre, Feyen, and Ize 2011; Heritage Foundation property rights index; *Doing Business*.

Note: This table shows full sample regressions of bank net interest margins and overheads against different explanatory variables. The contract enforcement index is the principal component of the following indicators from *Doing Business*: contract enforcement costs, number of days to enforce a contract (in logs), and number of procedures to enforce a contract. The legal rights index and the credit information index are from *Doing Business*. The property rights index is from the Heritage Foundation. Robust *t*-statistics are shown in parentheses.

*, **, and *** denote significant at the 10 percent, 5 percent, and 1 percent levels. GDP = gross domestic product.

of competition, we use the H-statistic in equation (4) of table 3.5 because it is the most significant; in the case of informality, we pick equation (6) because it has the same set of basic controls as equation (4)—to compute by how much private credit would increase in the median LAC7 country if (a) the degree of bank competition were increased from 0.751 (its current median value) to 1 (perfect competition); and (b) informality were reduced from 50.6 (its current median value) to zero (that is, if it were eliminated). Table 3.6 shows the results. It indicates that LAC7 private credit would rise by 8 percent in one case (full competition) and 23 percent in the other

Table 3.5 Determinants of Private Credit

	(1)	(2)	(3)	(4)	(5)	(6)	(7)	(8)
				Dependent variable: Bank private credit (% of GDP)				
Enforcement contract index								0.271
Legal rights index								1.928
Credit information index								
Property rights index								0.378
								(0.893)
Assets held by top 5 banks (% of total)	−0.133							
	(−0.491)							
Assets held by top 3 banks (% of total)		−0.188						
		(−0.879)						
Boone indicator			−1.188					
			(−0.137)					
H-statistic				33.32				
				(1.603)				
Lerner index					62.31			
					(1.303)			

(continued next page)

149

Table 3.5 Determinants of Private Credit (continued)

				Dependent variable: Bank private credit (% of GDP)				
	(1)	(2)	(3)	(4)	(5)	(6)	(7)	(8)
Annualized average sample GDP growth	9.395***	9.503***	8.494***	8.205**	7.662**	7.004	−0.477	4.19
	(−2.859)	(−3.121)	(−2.915)	(−2.171)	(−2.093)	(0.943)	(−1.265)	(0.614)
Informality index						−0.456	0.012	
						(−0.969)	(0.028)	
Credit crash dummy (% of period)							−1.133	−1.412
							(−1.130)	(−1.096)
Constant	240	256.5*	187.1	295.2	108.1	224	388.5	214.5
	(1.593)	(1.874)	(1.489)	(1.402)	(0.585)	(0.799)	(1.656)	(0.84)
No. of observations	106	117	118	73	93	67	77	67

Source: International Financial Statistics.

Note: This table shows regressions of bank private credit as percentage of GDP against different explanatory variables. *t*-statistics are shown in parentheses.

*, **, and *** denote significance at the 10 percent, 5 percent, and 1 percent levels. GDP = gross domestic product.

(zero informality). This finding suggests that while competition seems to have only a limited effect, the impact of reducing informality would be more substantial. In either case, however, the low levels of significance suggest caution. More research is clearly needed before these results can be taken at face value.

A last potential explanatory factor is LAC's turbulent macrofinancial history. Indeed, LAC was the region where crises were both the most frequent and the most encompassing, featuring a full range and mix of currency, banking, and debt crises (table 3.7). A bird's-eye view of events is provided by figure 3.5, which contrasts the dynamics of real interest rates in LAC with those of real bank credit since the late 1970s, based on medians for Brazil, Mexico, Argentina, Chile, Colombia, and Peru.[11] There were three clear credit cycles: one during the early 1980s, one lasting most of the 1990s (with an interruption in 1995 due to Mexico's "tequila crisis"), and one that is still ongoing after a brief interruption due to the global financial crisis.[12]

In view of this eventful background, a key question is whether the comparatively low levels of credit in the region today are a lasting reflection of the sharp collapses of credit during the 1980s and 1990s. At the same time, debt monetizations are likely to have undermined the credibility of local currencies, thereby boosting domestic financial dollarization. Hence, unless countries allowed dollarization to take hold—despite its drawbacks—one would also expect a lasting impact on the capacity of banking systems to intermediate.

To test for these effects, a worldwide credit crash variable—reflecting mild, strong, and severe annual drops in the ratio of private credit to GDP—is included in the basic benchmark regressions of private bank credit. To test for induced dollarization effects, a deposit dollarization variable is added, as well as a variable that interacts inflation with dollarization.[13] The credit crash variable is indeed very significant, explaining as much as a third of the current credit gap in LAC (see table 3.3). Inflation and its interaction with financial dollarization are also jointly significant (table 3.8).

Table 3.6 LAC Credit Gap: Effect of Changes in Competition and Informality

	Competition	Informality
LAC7 private credit predicted value	55.31	38.37
LAC7 adjusted value	59.90	47.22
Differences (%)	8.3	23.1

Source: Calculations based on data from de la Torre, Feyen, and Ize 2011.

Note: The adjusted value is the private credit increase in the median LAC7 countries if (a) the degree of bank competition is increased to 1 (perfect competition) and (b) informality is reduced to zero (no informality). LAC = Latin America and the Caribbean.

Table 3.7 Number of Crises by Type in Selected Countries and Regions, 1970–2007

	External debt crises	Domestic debt crises	Banking crises	Currency crises	Any type of crisis
Asia (5)	5	0	14	17	27
China	0	0	3	2	5
Eastern Europe (7)	6	2	13	15	28
G-7 (7)	0	0	16	1	17
India	0	0	1	1	2
Other advanced economies (7)	0	0	9	10	18
LAC	47	13	53	72	149
Caribbean (2)	5	0	3	7	14
Central America (+DR) (6)	11	2	13	14	33
LAC7 (7)	16	7	21	36	63
Offshore centers in LAC (3)	2	1	1	0	3
Other South America (4)	13	3	15	15	36

Source: Broner et al. 2013.
Note: This table shows the number of different types of crises taking place across several regions from 1970 to 2007. Numbers in parentheses indicate the number of countries covered.

Figure 3.5 Real Credit to the Private Sector and Compounded Real Deposit Rate Index, Medians in Six LAC Countries, 1978–2009

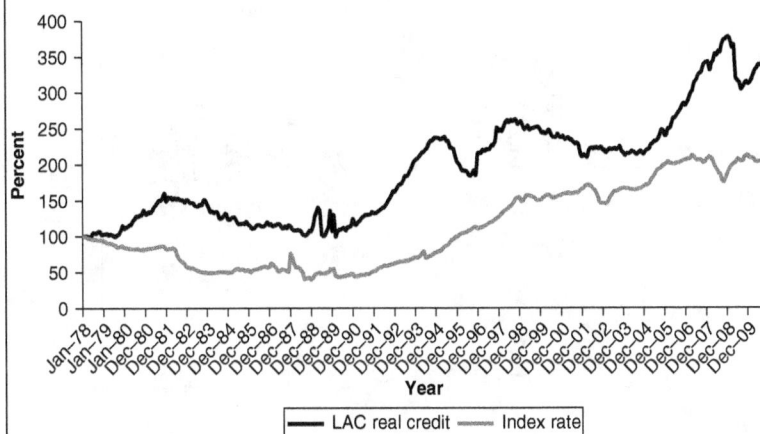

Note: This figure shows the evolution since the late 1970s of medians for the index of the compounded real deposit rate and the index of real bank credit in Argentina, Brazil, Chile, Colombia, Mexico, and Peru. LAC = Latin America and the Caribbean.

Hence, the evidence appears to lead to the following set of conclusions: (a) the banking crises of the past have taken a very significant toll on LAC's financial intermediation, and the region is still paying for the sins of its abrupt cycles;[14] (b) inflation has had a significant negative impact, not because it weakened balance sheets, but because it made financial contracting more difficult, particularly at the longer time horizons required for housing finance; and (c) the latter effect was at least partly offset, for the countries that allowed it, by financial dollarization.

Remarkably, the credit crash variable also helps explain banks' high interest margins as well as their comfortable financial soundness indicators (profitability, capital, and liquidity) (table 3.9). This suggests that banks that underwent crises were able to raise their margins (thereby raising their profitability), reflecting a forward reassessment of risks as well as perhaps a need to recoup the losses incurred during the crisis. At the same time, they became more prudent in managing risk, which led to less lending and higher prudential buffers. While this result is not too surprising, it is rather remarkable that these effects still linger a decade or two after the crises.

Table 3.8 Private Credit, Financial Dollarization, and Inflation, 2005–08

	Dependent variable: Average private credit to GDP in 2005–08				
	(1)	(2)	(3)	(4)	(5)
Dollarization: Period mean	-17.73*		49.93*		
	(-1.770)		(-1.851)		
Dollarization: Latest				55.77**	62.59*
				(-2.002)	(-1.774)
Log period inflation: Period mean		-6.380***	-15.16***	-15.27***	-17.81***
		(-2.952)	(-3.572)	(-3.690)	(-2.988)
Dollarization (mean)*log inflation (mean)			23.23**		
			(-2.249)		
Dollarization (last)* log inflation (mean)				24.84**	29.45*
				(-2.261)	(-1.893)
Constant	176.6**	167.2***	118.4	103.1	133.6
	(-2.321)	(-2.653)	(-1.557)	(-1.347)	(-1.234)
No. of observations	128	162	128	128	86
R^2	0.68	0.73	0.72	0.72	0.73

Source: de la Torre, Feyen, and Ize 2011.
Note: This table shows full sample regressions of bank credit to the private sector against variables capturing the level of dollarization and inflation between 2005 and 2008. Robust t-statistics are shown in parentheses.
*, **, and *** denote significance at the 10 percent, 5 percent, and 1 percent levels. LAC = Latin America and the Caribbean; GDP = gross domestic product; ROA = return on assets.

Table 3.9 Banks, Interest Margins, Financial Soundness, Enabling Environment Indicators, and Credit History in LAC: Growth and Crashes

	Net interest margin	ROA	Capital/total assets	Liquid assets/total assets	Regulatory capital
Enforcement contract index	-0.155	0.0438	0.353	2.366	0.247
	(-0.713)	(-0.42)	(-0.857)	(-0.726)	(-1.326)
Legal rights index	0.156	0.051	-0.192	0.787	0.312***
	(-1.318)	(-0.931)	(-0.903)	(-0.496)	(-3.131)
Property rights index	0.0246	0.00367	0.0659*	-0.0129	0.0347**
	(-1.192)	(-0.387)	(-1.769)	(-0.0502)	(-2.481)
Annualized average sample GDP growth	-0.0971	0.00887	-0.0202	0.156	-1.054***
	(-0.471)	(-0.108)	(-0.0642)	(-0.0504)	(-8.303)
Credit crash dummy (% of period)	20.83**	5.068**	17.52*	13.39	27.90***
	(-4.332)	(-2.266)	(-1.897)	(-0.183)	(-7.092)
Constant	7.914	9.730**	-19.96	187.9	12.26
	(-0.958)	(-2.504)	(-1.170)	(-1.408)	(-1.611)
No. of observations	88	88	98	98	78
Pseudo R^2	0.48	0.32	0.21	0.19	0.27

Sources: de la Torre, Feyen, and Ize 2011; Doing Business; Heritage Foundation.

Note: This table shows full sample regressions of banking indicators against different explanatory variables. The contract enforcement index is the principal component of the following indicators from Doing Business: contract enforcement costs, number of days to enforce a contract (in logs), and number of procedures to enforce a contract. The legal rights index and the credit information index are from Doing Business. The property rights index is from the Heritage Foundation. Robust t-statistics are shown in parentheses.

*, **, and *** denote significance at the 10 percent, 5 percent, and 1 percent levels. LAC = Latin America and the Caribbean; GDP = gross domestic product; ROA = return on assets.

What Explains LAC's Equity Gap?

To better understand the equity gap documented above, we begin by analyzing whether the lack of liquidity (low turnover) in the domestic equity markets can be due to the offshoring (migration abroad) of stock market activity. Figure 3.6 shows the "total turnover" for the stocks of (large) firms with depository receipts in the New York Stock Exchange—obtained as the sum of onshore and offshore trading divided by their market capitalization reported for the onshore market.[15] It also shows the domestic turnover for these same (large) firms and the turnover for all firms in the domestic market. The striking result is that once offshore trading is taken into account, the turnover of the large LAC firms nearly triples. Indeed, for the large LAC firms, turnover abroad dominates turnover at home, much more than in other regions. The effect is so strong that for the large LAC firms with depository receipt programs there does not seem to be an equity gap. Thus, offshoring does appear to be largely responsible for the atypically low domestic trading for these LAC firms. However, the story for the smaller LAC firms, which do not have access to foreign stock markets, is remarkably different. Their domestic equity turnover is extremely low compared to that in other regions. Moreover, it has remained broadly stable even as the total turnover of the large firms has increased substantially (figure 3.7).

A further check on the importance of foreign trading for LAC can be obtained by introducing the share of foreign trading as an additional control in the benchmark regressions of turnover (table 3.10). Once this new variable is introduced, the LAC dummy ceases to be significant. This provides additional support to the view that much of the apparent LAC equity gap can be explained by the region's extraordinary reliance on offshore trading.

The predominance of pension funds among institutional investors could also contribute to LAC's equity gap, as pension funds do not engage in active trading but instead mostly buy and hold.[16] Indeed, current regulations tend to reinforce the preference for buy-and-hold investment strategies, which can be detrimental to market liquidity (see Gill, Packard, and Yermo 2004). More generally, institutional investors tend to invest in larger and more liquid firms, hence limiting the supply of funds to smaller and less liquid ones.[17]

To determine the impact of pension funds, we regress the data with GDP per capita and population and plot the residuals along with the fitted regression line (figure 3.8). Remarkably, the regression line is flat for funds but clearly upward sloping for mutual funds and insurance companies. This finding is consistent with the fact that the growth of pension funds has a strong policy component, whereas the growth of other institutional investors occurs endogenously with economic and financial development.

Figure 3.6 Average Turnover Ratio in Selected Countries and Regions, 2000–10

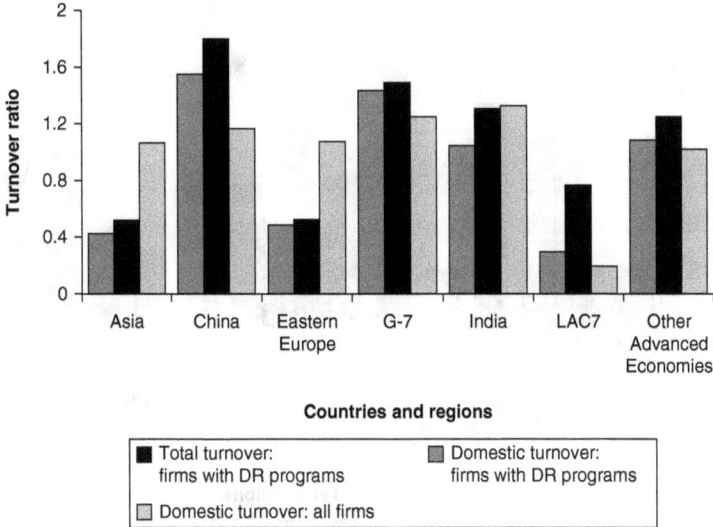

Source: Didier and Schmukler 2012.

Note: This figure characterizes domestic and foreign equity markets. It shows the average between 2000 and 2010 of the turnover ratios in domestic markets for firms with depository receipt programs as well as the total turnover ratios, which consider domestic and foreign trading activity. It also shows the aggregate turnover ratio in domestic markets for all listed firms. All depository receipts identified in the Depository Receipt Directory of the Bank of New York, with trading data reported in Bloomberg, are considered in this figure. DR = depository receipt.

However, if one interprets the causality in the other direction, it could also suggest that, in contrast with other institutional investors such as mutual funds, pension funds do not contribute much to stock market liquidity because they mostly buy and hold. In this interpretation, the fact that most LAC countries are bunched up under the regression line for mutual funds but are more evenly distributed around the line for pension funds would suggest that the low equity turnover could have something to do with the predominance of buy-and-hold pension funds in the region and the relative underdevelopment of mutual funds (which are presumably more active traders).

Weak corporate governance practices are also a commonly cited explanation for the low development of stock markets. Following the

Figure 3.7 Domestic and International Value Traded as a Percent of Domestic Market Capitalization in Selected Countries and Regions, 2000–10

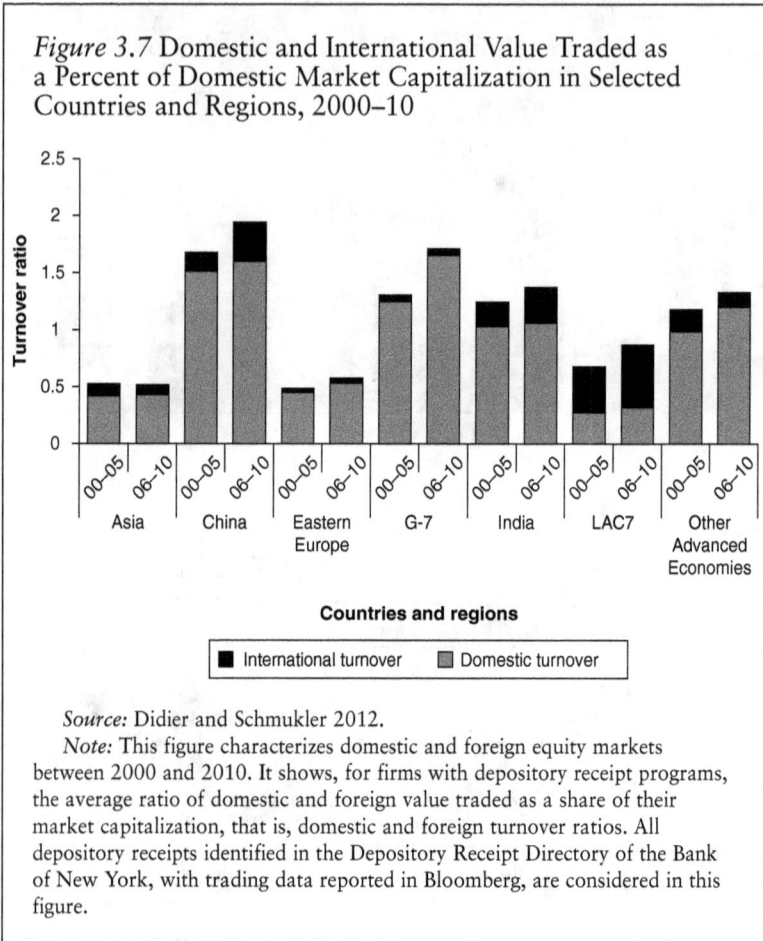

Source: Didier and Schmukler 2012.

Note: This figure characterizes domestic and foreign equity markets between 2000 and 2010. It shows, for firms with depository receipt programs, the average ratio of domestic and foreign value traded as a share of their market capitalization, that is, domestic and foreign turnover ratios. All depository receipts identified in the Depository Receipt Directory of the Bank of New York, with trading data reported in Bloomberg, are considered in this figure.

same procedure as that described above for pension funds, the plotting of the controlled residuals of the anti-self-dealing index and the anti-director-rights index—two widely used corporate governance indicators—suggests a possible link between low turnover and weak governance (figure 3.9). The regression line for the anti-self-dealing indicator is clearly upward, which suggests that it is more closely connected with market development. At the same time, most LAC countries are bunched up under the regression line, which confirms LAC's strong underperformance on this indicator and indicates that it might have something to do with LAC's equity gap.[18] Given the difficulties in measuring corporate governance and the multidimensionality of this concept, however, some caution is warranted.[19]

Table 3.10 Trading Activity in LAC

	Dependent variable: Value traded over GDP				
	(1)	(2)	(3)	(4)	(5)
LAC7 dummy	−50.54***	−72.62*	−26.13	−101.4**	−75.71**
	(−2.756)	(−1.766)	(−0.559)	(−2.501)	(−2.458)
Foreign value traded as % of total value traded			−114.9*		
			(−1.827)		
Foreign market capitalization as % of total market capitalization				411.5**	
				(2.143)	
Amount raised by top 5 equity issues as % of total amount raised					−31.85
					(−0.604)
Constant	−40.89	194.5	54.84	−417.4	407.9
	(−0.186)	(0.181)	(0.0535)	(−0.402)	(0.557)
Workhorse controls	Yes	Yes	Yes	Yes	Yes
No. of observations	86	34	34	34	47
R²	0.613	0.435	0.509	0.532	0.444

Source: de la Torre, Feyen, and Ize 2011.
Note: This table shows regressions of bank credit to the private sector against different explanatory variables and a dummy for LAC7 countries. LAC = Latin America and the Caribbean. Robust t-statistics are in shown in parentheses.
*, **, and *** denote significance at the 10 percent, 5 percent, and 1 percent levels.

Figure 3.8 Domestic Turnover and Institutional Investors

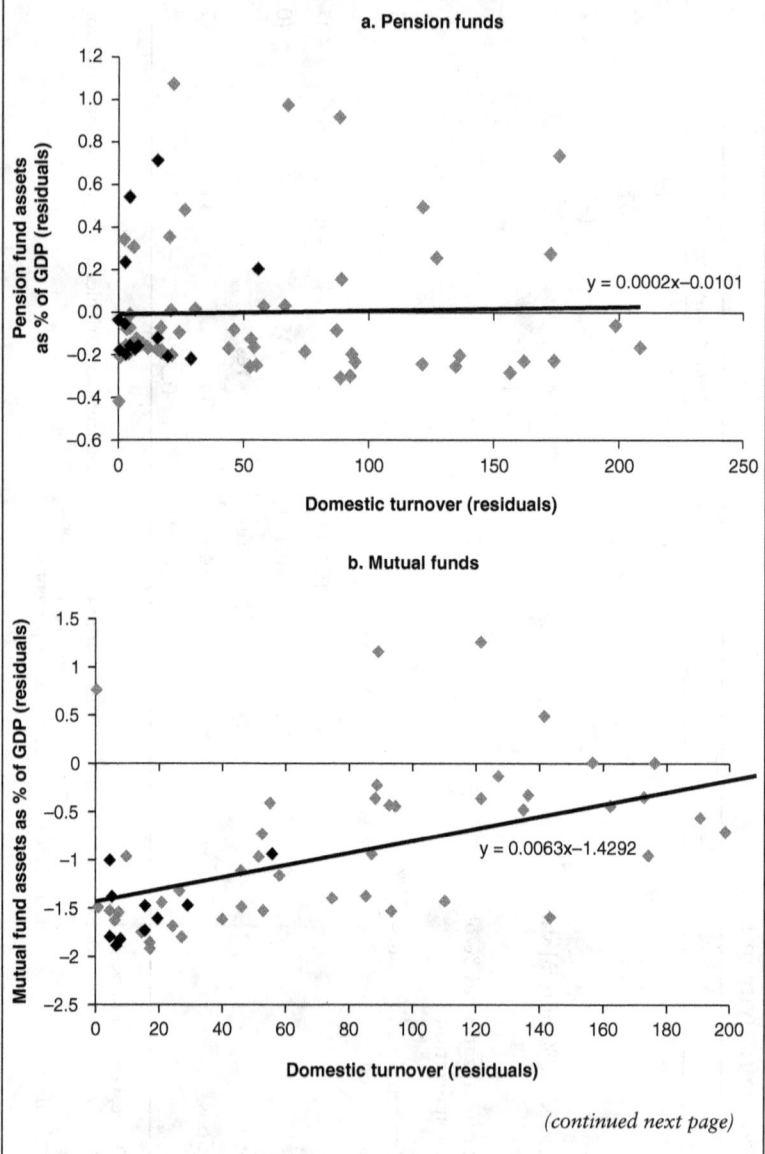

a. Pension funds

$y = 0.0002x - 0.0101$

b. Mutual funds

$y = 0.0063x - 1.4292$

(continued next page)

Figure 3.8 (continued)

c. Insurance companies

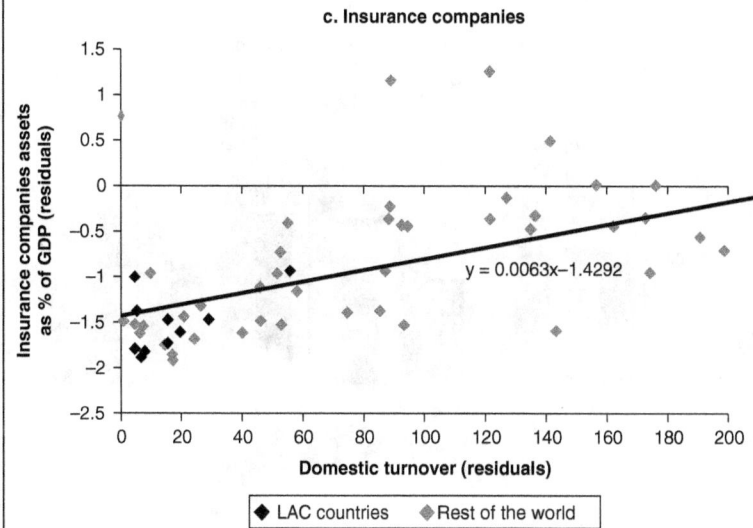

$$y = 0.0063x - 1.4292$$

Y-axis: Insurance companies assets as % of GDP (residuals)

X-axis: Domestic turnover (residuals)

Legend: ◆ LAC countries   ◆ Rest of the world

Source: Based on Didier and Schmukler 2014, 2012.
Note: This figure shows scatterplots of the 2005–09 average residuals of institutional investors' assets relative to GDP against the average residuals of the domestic turnover ratio. Figure 3.8a shows the assets of pension funds as a percentage of GDP. Figure 3.8b shows the assets of mutual funds as a percentage of GDP. Figure 3.8c shows the assets of insurance companies as a percentage of GDP. The turnover ratio is defined as the total value traded per year in domestic markets over domestic market capitalization. Residuals are obtained from ordinary least-squares regressions of the variables on GDP per capita and population. LAC countries are shown in dark color. LAC = Latin America and the Caribbean; GDP = gross domestic product.

Finally, LAC's low growth, turbulent macro- and financial history, and remaining weaknesses in its enabling environment might also contribute to explaining its low turnover in domestic equity markets. To check for such effects, we add to the benchmarking regressions proxy measures of economic prospects (average GDP growth for the past three decades) and macrofinancial turbulence (credit crash dummy, as defined above). We also add some measures of the quality of the enabling environment (contract enforcement, property rights, and credit information).

The results (table 3.11) are tentative as they do not fully survive robustness tests, but they do hint in some specific directions while underscoring the need for more research. In particular, financial crashes

Figure 3.9 Domestic Turnover and Corporate Governance in Selected Countries and Regions

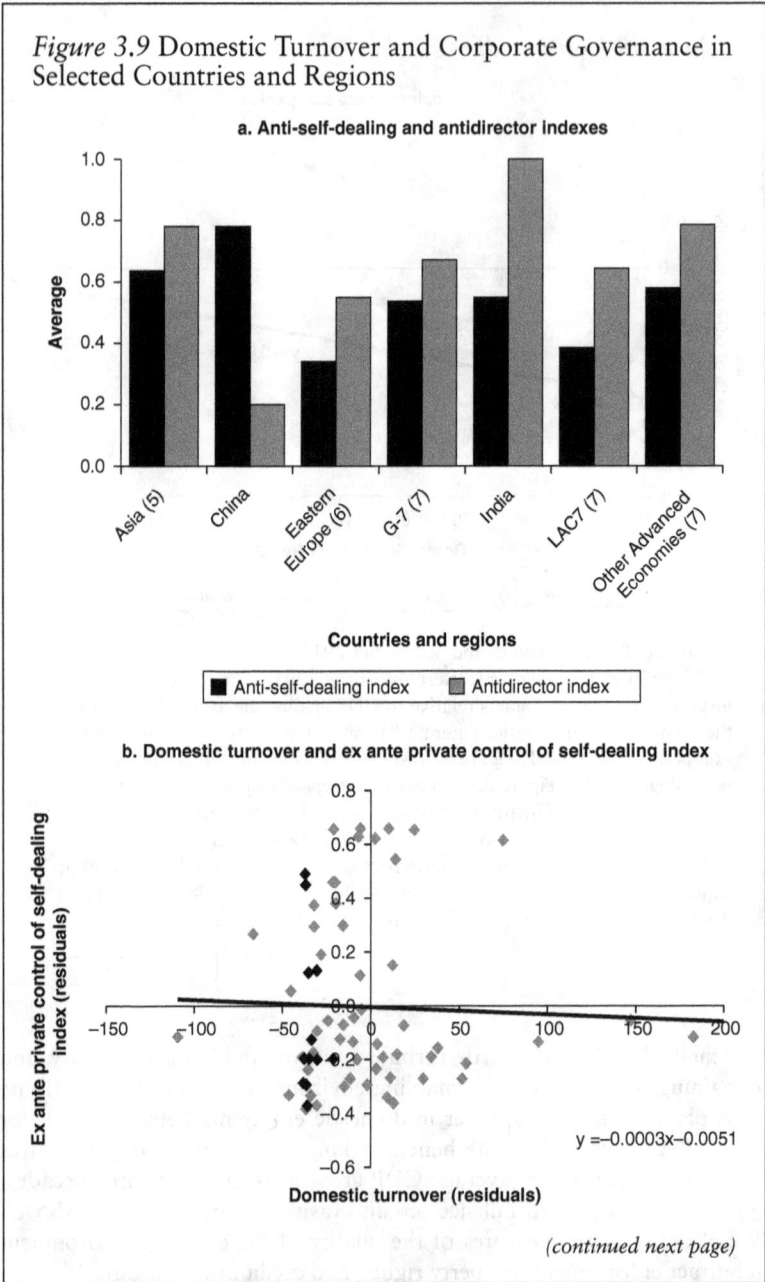

a. Anti-self-dealing and antidirector indexes

Countries and regions

■ Anti-self-dealing index   ▨ Antidirector index

b. Domestic turnover and ex ante private control of self-dealing index

$y = -0.0003x - 0.0051$

(continued next page)

Figure 3.9 (continued)

c. Domestic turnover and anti-director-rights index

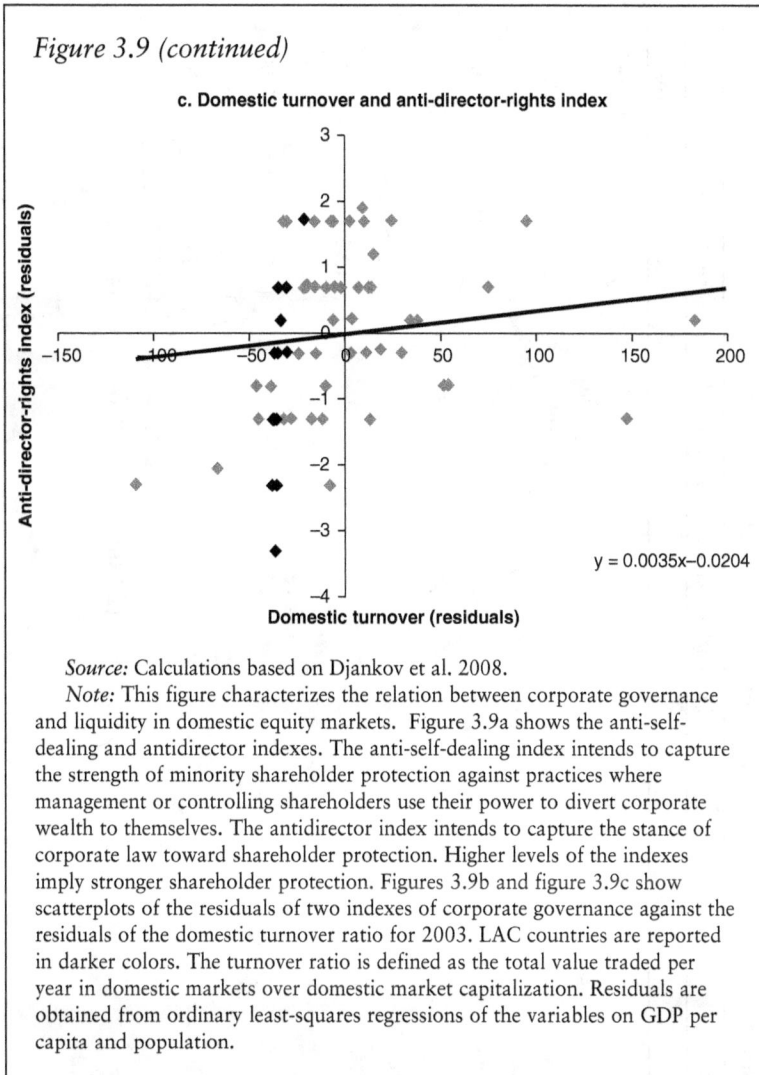

y = 0.0035x–0.0204

Domestic turnover (residuals)

Source: Calculations based on Djankov et al. 2008.

Note: This figure characterizes the relation between corporate governance and liquidity in domestic equity markets. Figure 3.9a shows the anti-self-dealing and antidirector indexes. The anti-self-dealing index intends to capture the strength of minority shareholder protection against practices where management or controlling shareholders use their power to divert corporate wealth to themselves. The antidirector index intends to capture the stance of corporate law toward shareholder protection. Higher levels of the indexes imply stronger shareholder protection. Figures 3.9b and figure 3.9c show scatterplots of the residuals of two indexes of corporate governance against the residuals of the domestic turnover ratio for 2003. LAC countries are reported in darker colors. The turnover ratio is defined as the total value traded per year in domestic markets over domestic market capitalization. Residuals are obtained from ordinary least-squares regressions of the variables on GDP per capita and population.

---

and low growth are significantly associated with the low turnover in domestic stock markets when introduced separately. Interestingly, however, they lose their significance when the LAC7 dummy is added. This could suggest that while financial crashes and low growth affect many other countries outside the LAC region, they have had special consequences in the case of LAC, so much so that they have become tightly interwoven with LAC specificities (the LAC7 dummy). Our econometric test for the

Table 3.11 LAC's Domestic Equity Turnover and Enabling-Environment Indicators

	Dependent variable: Stock market turnover					
	(1)	(2)	(3)	(4)	(5)	(6)
LAC7 dummy	-35.83***			-27.02**		-32.12**
	(-4.837)			(-2.505)		(-2.635)
Credit crash dummy (% of period)		-134.0*		-109.2	-125.7***	-72.19
		(-1.902)		(-1.524)	(-3.049)	(-1.042)
Annualized average sample GDP growth			6.315**	3.164		0.440
			(2.424)	(1.385)		(0.225)
Contract enforcement index					-4.298*	-1.477
					(-1.970)	(-0.495)
Credit information index					4.452***	2.091
					(2.738)	(0.976)
Property rights index					0.592***	0.510**
					(3.211)	(2.153)
Constant	306.9***	359.3**	353.9***	296.0***	445.7***	319.3**
	(4.010)	(2.390)	(2.786)	(2.730)	(4.343)	(2.348)

(continued next page)

Table 3.11 LAC's Domestic Equity Turnover and Enabling-Environment Indicators (continued)

		Dependent variable: Stock market turnover				
	(1)	(2)	(3)	(4)	(5)	(6)
Workhorse controls	Yes	Yes	Yes	Yes	Yes	Yes
No. of observations	107	107	86	86	103	84
Pseudo R^2	0.46	0.44	0.49	0.54	0.47	0.55

Sources: de la Torre, Feyen, and Ize 2011; Heritage Foundation; Doing Business.

Note: This table shows regressions of domestic equity turnover ratio aga contract (in logs), and number of procedures to enforce a contract. The credit information index is from Doing Business. The property rights index is from the Heritage Foundation. Robust t-statistics are shown in parentheses.

*, **, and *** denote significance at the 10 percent, 5 percent, and 1 percent levels. LAC = Latin America and the Caribbean; GDP = gross domestic product.

enabling-environment indicators also suggests that contract enforcement costs, property rights, and information are also part of the story of the low turnover in LAC's domestic stock markets (these variables retain statistical significance even when introduced together with the also significant financial crashes variable). However, like the financial crashes and growth variables, the enabling-environment indicators also lose significance once the LAC7 dummy is added. Again, this might suggest that the effects of low growth, financial crashes, and enabling-environment weaknesses are wrapped up tightly in the region's history and are crucial in shaping LAC's current state of financial development.

Policy Directions

The results in this chapter point toward a number of possible policy directions worth exploring. We briefly review them, starting with the banking gap. Altogether, the evidence suggests that the domestic banking gap, although partly offset by alternative channels of debt finance, particularly cross-border channels, is nonetheless real enough. LAC banks lend less and charge more than they should. One can safely assume that any remaining gap should affect SMEs more than large corporations, since the latter are able to switch sources of finance (whether at home or abroad) rather easily, depending on cost and availability. Even here, however, as shown in chapter 2, the evidence on whether LAC's SMEs have a particularly hard time getting financing is not particularly conclusive. Clearly, assessing in further depth the impact on SME financing of LAC's banking gap is therefore an area for priority research. Of particular value would be an analysis of credit information that provides more insight into lending to marginal borrowers. More research is also needed to ascertain the possible impact of the lack of credit on firms' leverage, activity, and investment, based on available enterprise-level financial accounts data. Similarly, in the case of mortgages, the gap also looks real. Yet not enough is known about the extent to which other forms of housing finance (including from public provident funds) may be offsetting the lack of bank credit.

The largest fraction of the banking gap simply reflects LAC's turbulent history. Even though much time has passed, LAC has not yet fully recovered from the repeated credit crashes of its past. Past turbulence also accounts for banks' still-high interest margins, high capital and liquidity buffers, and high profitability. The main policy lesson here is that financial sustainability is the name of the game. The long-run costs of financial crashes are too large to be taken lightly. The spotlight is thus squarely on macroprudential policy and good systemic prudential oversight.

The historically low demand for credit appears to explain another substantial portion of the gap. To the extent that output growth is affected by other (nonfinancial) policies, such as macropolicy or supply-side structural policies for enhancing productivity and competitiveness, the possible policy responses go beyond the financial sector. However, one can also argue that financial policies focused on overcoming the limited marginal productivity of capital by lowering the cost of finance could spur growth of output (and, hence, ultimately strengthen financial depth); that is, policy might increase the number of bankable projects by increasing their profitability.

Finally, a significant share of the banking gap also has to do with remaining weaknesses in the enabling environment. Much progress has been made in resolving informational frictions. Indeed, LAC is ahead of many emerging markets in the development of credit bureaus, for example. But the region still has a long way to go in addressing contractual frictions, particularly the enforcement of contracts and the preservation of creditor rights. While there are some indications that LAC's banking systems may also face efficiency issues associated with insufficient competition, the available evidence is inconclusive. Should the issue be confirmed through further research, a policy agenda to address it would need to be developed.

Our first clear conclusion on LAC's equity gap is that offshoring accounts for much of the region's sluggish turnover in its domestic equity markets. That gap probably does not matter much for the larger firms: whether their stock is traded in Mexico City or in New York is largely immaterial; and, when it matters, being traded in New York may actually be good because it yields reputational benefits. However, the domestic trading gap does matter for the smaller firms that cannot rely on international markets and are thus constrained by the lack of access to equity financing at home. Even if these firms' access to debt financing at home were adequate (which is probably not the case in view of the banking gap), that would not substitute for the lack of access to capital through equity, as the latter plays a unique role in long-term business expansion.

Two interrelated but clearly distinct questions spring up in this regard: Why is the offshoring of equity turnover so large in the case of LAC? and Why has offshoring seemingly had such a depressing impact on the liquidity of domestic equity markets? Levine and Schmukler (2007) shed light on the second question, providing some evidence on the channels through which the adverse effects of offshoring on domestic trading may work.[20] Yet there are no solid answers to the first question. LAC's history of low economic growth (to the extent that it is associated with uninspiring expected returns to investment) and, perhaps more important, its history of financial crashes may have something to do with the low trading. However, it is more difficult to understand why they might have caused the high offshoring.

A second conclusion is that the preponderance of pension funds over other institutional investors—as well as the remaining weaknesses in corporate governance, contract enforcement, and property rights—may have all contributed to some extent to LAC's turnover gap in domestic equity markets. Yet caution is also needed in interpreting the evidence. The policy-induced growth in pension funds, for example, may have displaced mutual funds by giving investors an alternative savings channel. However, pension funds may also help mutual funds develop by investing part of their portfolios in them. Moreover, as shown in the companion chapter by Raddatz in this same volume, it is not clear that the asset management behavior of LAC's mutual funds differs much from that of pension funds.

As for the possible impact on the equity market of LAC's weaknesses in corporate governance, one might take the view that this is of first-order importance considering the experience of Brazil's Novo Mercado, which appears to have been instigated by the tightening of governance norms. Yet, much of the success of the Novo Mercado may have more to do with Brazil's comparative size advantage than with governance reforms. Indeed, an alternative for the smaller countries might be to follow a "lighter governance" path that is more suited to the smaller firms, while accepting the trade-off of having a reduced scope for minority shareholders (who would be more willing to own stock under lighter governance arrangements). Such a light version might be characterized by more benign accounting and public disclosure standards, more private equity placements and over-the-counter activity, less reliance on centralized local exchanges, and concentrated (rather than atomized) stock ownership.

To overcome the constraints imposed by the small size of the markets, many have recommended the cross-border integration of LAC's stock markets. Indeed, Chile, Colombia, and Peru have recently reached an agreement of this sort, which focuses on integrating such functions as listing, order routing, and execution. Yet, despite the potential benefits of integrating securities markets in terms of scale and network effects, these attempts have thus far tended to fail (Lee 1999).[21] Moreover, as discussed in de la Torre, Gozzi, and Schmukler (2007), there remain some fundamental doubts about whether regional integration of stock exchanges would be better than deeper and better integration with the developed stock markets.[22]

In any event, ascertaining the policy path for stock market development in LAC, especially for the smaller countries, is fiendishly difficult, much more than is commonly recognized. Of course, there are enabling-environment reforms (in property rights and corporate governance frameworks, for example) that everyone agrees should help. And even for the small countries, there are many improvements in stock market infrastructure that can also help, including those aimed at reducing fragmentation in issuance and trading, enhancing securities clearance and settlement arrangements, organizing securities lending and borrowing facilities, improving valuation methods, promoting contract standardization, and upgrading financial reporting. However, such reforms would at best correct for only a modest part of the low turnover in the domestic equity markets.

Thus, the larger questions remain. Should the smaller countries simply "throw in the towel," forget about developing a local stock market, and accept the conclusion that equity funding is available primarily for their large resident corporations and mainly through listing on the international stock markets? Or should they persevere in developing local markets for the sake of their smaller firms? The only thing one can know for certain is that LAC will need to look beyond the simplest conventional wisdom: macrostability and compliance with international standards might help, but they will not suffice.

Notes

1. See Demirgüç-Kunt and Levine (2001) or Allen and Gale (2000). More recent papers (such as Demirgüç-Kunt, Feyen, and Levine 2011) have come closer to recognizing that banks and markets play different roles at different stages of economic development, that is, that form might also matter.

2. An earlier strand of thought viewed financial development as driven by the steady mitigation of asymmetric information failures such as moral hazard and adverse selection (see, for instance, Akerlof 1970; Spence 1973; Stiglitz and Weiss 1981). A more recent strand has emphasized enforcement costs and lack of collateral leading to problems of limited pledgeability (see Holmstrom and Tirole 1998; Geanakoplos 2009). Rajan and Zingales (2003) present a more complete narrative rooted in the same basic threads.

3. The data are from FinStats 2009, a worldwide financial database put together by the World Bank, which covers 40 key financial indicators for the period 1980–2008 (coverage quality varies between variables). The data come from a variety of sources including IFS, BIS, WDI, S&P, Bankscope, Axco, and national sources.

4. The controls were selected iteratively, based on individual statistical significance and collective explanatory power.

5. This section touches upon a number of issues already covered in chapter 1 of this book. However, this overlap is necessary for motivating the subsequent analysis and establishing a common ground with other financial development indicators introduced in this chapter. In addition, the benchmarking methodology developed in this chapter provides an alternative perspective on the same issues.

6. In de la Torre, Feyen, and Ize (2011), we assess LAC's progress over time and compare its performance to that of the G-7, other high-income countries, a subset of Eastern European countries, and a subset of Asian countries. To obtain a better feel for the evolution of the financial indicators relative to their benchmark, we plot regional median indicators against the underlying time and cross-sectional development paths.

7. Due to the limited coverage of the data currently available on the breakdown of private credit, we were unable to perform meaningful controls. Hence, we present only the raw data.

8. See, for example, McMillan and Rodrik (2011) for a discussion emphasizing the low growth of output and employment in LAC's higher-productivity sectors.

9. Recent work on emerging sovereign bond rates (Broner, Lorenzoni, and Schmukler 2013) shows that in normal times LAC faces a fairly elastic supply of foreign funds. Except at the longer end of the maturity range in times of world market turbulence, bond rates are basically determined by the world appetite for risk, with LAC behaving like other regions. The gradual shrinking of country premiums and their increased dependence on global fluctuations in risk appetite (rather than idiosyncratic factors) tell a similar story.

10. The H (Panzar-Rosse) statistic contrasts the elasticity of a firm's revenue with that of its input costs (under perfect competition, an increase in input prices should lead to a one-for-one increase in output prices and, hence, revenue). The Lerner index calculates the disparity between prices and marginal costs (a measure of the markup). The Boone indicator relates performance (measured in terms of profits) to efficiency (measured as marginal costs).

11. We include the compounded real (deposit) interest rate in the figure because it provides some indication of "autonomous" changes in credit that are simply driven by the compounding of interest rates.

12. The first cycle started with a period of easy money and low real U.S. rates. It ended brutally in 1982 with U.S. interest rates rising sharply in the wake of Volcker's stabilization efforts and LAC's rates going in the opposite direction, as the region's inflation rates went through the roof. The second cycle started with LAC's mostly failed exchange-rate-based stabilizations that resulted in high real interest rates, strong currency appreciations, and large capital inflows; that cycle ended with twin crises in most countries. The third cycle started in the early years of the millennium under the dual impetuses of domestic macrostabilization and the strongly stimulative world environment resulting from China's accelerated growth and large U.S. deficits.

13. These links between financial depth, inflation, and dollarization were first explored in de Nicolo, Honohan, and Ize (2005).

14. Interestingly, when adding a simple credit volatility variable (the year-to-year variance of private to GDP credit) as an additional control in the benchmark regressions of credit, it is not significant. Hence, it is credit crashes—but not volatility per se—that leave a substantial and lasting imprint on financial development.

15. The domestic market capitalization of these firms includes all the stocks issued at home even if they are completely traded abroad (through depository receipts).

16. Raddatz and Schmukler (2013) show that Chilean pension funds trade infrequently. On average, a pension fund trades only 13 percent of its assets, and the monthly changes in asset positions correspond to just 4 percent of the initial total value of the assets. This contrasts sharply with the 88 percent mean turnover ratio found in Kacperczyk, Sialm, and Zheng (2008) for a sample of 2,543 actively managed U.S. equity mutual funds between 1984 and 2003.

17. See, for example, Kang and Stulz (1997), Dahlquist and Robertsson (2001), Edison and Warnock (2004), Didier, Rigobon, and Schmukler (2011), and Didier (2011), among many others.

18. Of the individual countries, Argentina, Mexico, and Uruguay have the weakest corporate governance indicators. Brazil is an interesting case, as its anti-director index takes the maximum possible value while its self-dealing index is one of the lowest in the region. This might be a result of the recent developments in the Brazilian stock market whereby firms can adhere to stricter corporate governance rules by choosing where to list. While this might have boosted the value

of the antidirector index, which measures the extent of legal protection, it might not have had an immediate effect on actual self-dealing practices.

19. In unreported results on two more corporate governance indicators (ex ante private control of the self-dealing and public enforcement index), LAC7 seems to be overperforming, to the point of being even slightly ahead of the G-7 countries.

20. Offshoring can shift the trading of firms that issue abroad out of the domestic market—the "liquidity migration" effect. In addition, it can lead to a drop in the trading and liquidity of the stocks of the remaining domestic firms. This, in turn, can happen through two effects. The first effect ("negative spillovers") is linked with the increase in cost per trade at home due to fixed costs. The second effect ("domestic trade diversion") follows from the fact that the internationalization of stock issuance and trading induces improvements in reputation, disclosure standards, analyst coverage, and the shareholder base that induce investors to shift their attention from firms trading onshore to firms trading offshore.

21. Many reasons have been given for this lack of success, including legal and regulatory differences across countries, the adverse effects of different national currencies in the absence of sufficiently developed currency derivatives markets, informational barriers across markets (including differences in accounting and disclosure standards), and larger than expected difficulties in integrating market infrastructures.

22. While it is true that regional financial integration may reduce trading and issuance costs because of economies of scale, it seems doubtful that such cost reductions would be greater than those that could be achieved by global integration. Similarly, while it is true that neighboring investors may have informational advantages on regional firms compared to more remote foreign investors, it is not clear that such advantages would be better exercised by trading in a regional market than in a global one. Likewise, the conjecture that regional stock exchanges would facilitate access for medium enterprises needs to be reexamined, for these firms are segmented out of the international *and* local stock markets mainly because of the small size of their potential issues and not because of the size of the markets. The solution, therefore, is arguably not with bigger markets, regional or global, but with bigger issue sizes.

References

Akerlof, G. 1970. "The Market for 'Lemons': Quality Uncertainty and the Market Mechanism." *Quarterly Journal of Economics* 84 (3): 151–72.

Allen, F., and D. Gale. 2000. *Comparing Financial Systems*. Cambridge, MA: MIT Press.

Anzoategui, D., M. S. Martinez Pería, and R. R. Rocha. 2010. "Bank Competition in the Middle East and Northern Africa Region." *Review of Middle East Economics and Finance* 6 (2): 26–48.

Axco. http://www.axcoinfo.com/.

Bankscope. http://www.library.hbs.edu/go/bankscope.html.

Beck, T., and R. Levine. 2005. "Legal Institutions and Financial Development." In *Handbook of New Institutional Economics,* edited by C. Ménard and M. M. Shirley, 257–78. New York: Springer.

BIS. http://www.bis.org/.

Broner, F., G. Lorenzoni, and S. Schmukler. 2013. "Why Do Emerging Economies Borrow Short Term?" *Journal of the European Economic Association* 11: 67–100.

Dahlquist, M., and G. Robertsson. 2001. "Direct Foreign Ownership, Institutional Investors, and Firm Characteristics." *Journal of Financial Economics* 59: 413–40.

de la Torre, Feyen, and Ize 2011. "Financial Development: Structure and Dynamics." *Policy Research Working Paper No.5854, World Bank.*

———. 2013. "Financial Development: Structure and Dynamics." *World Bank Economic Review.*

de la Torre, A., J.C. Gozzi, and S. Schmukler. 2007. *Innovative Experiences in Access to Finance: Market Friendly Roles for the Visible Hand?* Washington, DC: Brookings Institution; Washington, DC: World Bank.

de Nicolo, G., P. Honohan, and A. Ize. 2005. "Dollarization of Bank Deposits: Causes and Consequences." *Journal of Banking and Finance* 29 (7): 1697–1727.

Demigürç-Kunt, A., E. Feyen, and R. Levine. 2011. "The Evolving Importance of Banks and Securities Markets." Policy Research Working Paper 5805, World Bank, Washington, DC.

Demigürç-Kunt, A., and R. Levine. 2001. "Bank-Based and Market-Based Financial Systems: Cross-Country Comparisons." In *Financial Structure and Economic Growth: A Cross-Country Comparison of Banks, Markets, and Development,* edited by A. Demigürç-Kunt and R. Levine, 81–140. Cambridge, MA: MIT Press.

Didier, T. 2011. "Information Asymmetries and Institutional Investor Mandates." Policy Research Working Paper 5586, World Bank, Washington, DC.

Didier, T., R. Rigobon, and S. Schmukler. 2011. "Unexploited Gains from International Diversification: Patterns of Portfolio Holdings around the World." NBER Working Paper 16629, National Bureau of Economic Research, Cambridge, MA.

Didier, T. and S. L. Schmukler. 2012. "Financial Globalization in Emerging Countries: Diversification vs. Offshoring." In New Paradigms for Financial Regulation: Emerging Market Perspectives, edited by Mario B. Lamberte and Eswar Prasad, 110–28. Washington, DC: Brookings Institution; Tokyo: ADBI.

———. 2014. Financial development in Latin America and the Caribbean: Stylized facts and the road ahead. In Didier, T. and Schmukler, S. L. (eds.) Emerging Issues in Financial Development. Washington, DC: The World Bank.

Djankov, S., R. La Porta, F. Lopez-de-Silanes, and A. Shleifer, 2008. "The Law and Economics of Self-dealing." *Journal of Financial Economics* 88(3): 430–465.

Doing Business (database). World Bank and International Finance Corporation. http://www.doingbusiness.org/.

Edison, H., and F. Warnock. 2004. "U.S. Investors' Emerging Market Equity Portfolios: A Security-Level Analysis." *Review of Economics and Statistics* 86 (3): 691–704.

FinStats. http://www.interactivedataclients.com/content/view/38/155/.

Geanakoplos, J. 2009. "The Leverage Cycle." In *NBER Macroeconomics Annual 2009 No. 24*, edited by D. Acemoglu, K. Rogoff, and M. Woodford. Chicago: University of Chicago Press.

Gelos, G. 2009. "Banking Spreads in Latin America." *Economic Inquiry* 47 (4): 796–814.

Gill, I., T. Packard, and J. Yermo. 2004. *Keeping the Promise of Social Security in Latin America.* Palo Alto: Stanford University Press; Washington, DC: World Bank.

Heritage Foundation. http://www.heritage.org/about.

Holmstrom, B., and J. Tirole. 1998. "Private and Public Supply of Liquidity." NBER Working Paper 5817, National Bureau of Economic Research, Cambridge, MA.

IFS (International Financial Statistics). International Monetary Fund. http://elibrary-data.imf.org/FindDataReports.aspx?d=33061&e=169393.

JP Morgan. http://www.jpmorgan.com/pages/jpmorgan.

Kacperczyk, M., C. Sialm, and L. Zheng. 2008. "Unobserved Actions of Mutual Funds." *Review of Financial Studies* 21 (6): 2379–416.

Kang, J. K., and R. Stulz. 1997. "Why Is There a Home Bias? An Analysis of Foreign Portfolio Equity Ownership in Japan." *Journal of Financial Economics* 46 (1): 3–28.

Lee, R. M. G. 1999. *What Is an Exchange? The Automation, Management and Regulation of Financial Markets.* Oxford, UK: Oxford University Press.

McMillan, M., and D. Rodrik. 2011. "Globalization, Structural Change, and Productivity Growth." NBER Working Paper 17143, National Bureau of Economic Research, Cambridge, MA.

Raddatz, C., and S. Schmukler. 2013. "Deconstructing Herding: Evidence from Pension Fund Investment Behavior." *Journal of Financial Services Research* 43 (1): 99–126.

Rajan, R., and L. Zingales. 2003. *Saving Capitalism from the Capitalists: Unleashing the Power of Financial Markets to Create Wealth and Spread Opportunity.* New York: Random House.

S&P. http://www.standardandpoors.com/home/en/us.

Spence, M. 1973. "Job Market Signaling." *Quarterly Journal of Economics* 87 (3): 355–74.

Stiglitz, J. E., and A. Weiss. 1981. "Credit Rationing in Markets with Imperfect Information." *American Economic Review* 71 (3): 393–410.

WDI (World Development Indicators). World Bank, Washington, DC. http://data.worldbank.org/data-catalog/world-development-indicators.

4

Financial Globalization: Some Basic Indicators for Latin America and the Caribbean

Tatiana Didier and Sergio L. Schmukler

Abstract

For a number of reasons, financial globalization has become increasingly relevant for developing countries. In this chapter, we address two particularly important aspects of financial globalization: (a) financial diversification, that is, the cross-country holdings of foreign assets and liabilities; and (b) financial offshoring, that is, the use of international markets by firms and governments. The evidence suggests that financial

The authors work for the World Bank in, respectively, the LCRCE unit (tdidier@worldbank.org) and the DECRG unit (sschmukler@worldbank.org). The authors received very helpful comments from Augusto de la Torre, Cesar Calderon, Asli Demirgüç-Kunt, Alain Ize, Eduardo Levy Yeyati, Guillermo Perry, Claudio Raddatz, Rodrigo Valdes, and participants at presentations held at the Global Development Network Annual Meeting (Bogotá), the NIPFP-DEA Workshop (Delhi), and the World Bank (Washington, DC). They are grateful to Francisco Ceballos, Luciano Cohan, Juan Cuattromo, Gustavo Meza, Paula Pedro, Virginia Poggio, Andres Schneider, Patricio Valenzuela, Luis Fernando Vieira, and Gabriel Zelpo for outstanding research assistance at different stages of this project. For help in gathering unique data, the authors wish to thank Mario Bergara (Central Bank of Uruguay), Samuel Fox (Fitch Ratings), Fabio Malacrida (Central Bank of Uruguay), Carlos Serrano (National Banking Commission, Mexico), and the ADR team from the Bank of New York, among many others. The views expressed here are those of the authors and do not necessarily represent those of the World Bank.

globalization in LAC has continued to increase over the past decade according to widely used de facto measures, namely, the stock of foreign assets and liabilities and capital flows by domestic and foreign agents (gross flows). However, LAC corporations have not used foreign markets much as a source of new financing. Still, compared to the use of domestic capital markets, the issuance of bonds and equity abroad has been gaining momentum. This trend has been accompanied by increased liquidity abroad in equity markets. In contrast, bond financing by the public sector has been shifting to local markets. These trends in the use of foreign markets are closely related to the developments in domestic markets. Moreover, LAC countries have become net creditors in debt assets and net debtors in equity assets over time, a position that has been particularly beneficial during crises.

Introduction

There has been much talk about financial globalization over the past decades. Less is known, however, about whether the trend of rapid globalization that took place during the 1990s for most of the emerging world, and in Latin America and the Caribbean (LAC) in particular, has continued during the 2000s and whether the nature of financial globalization has changed over time. To the extent that they can help us understand the development of domestic financial systems, a deeper analysis of these trends is important. Financial development cannot be viewed in isolation. When an economy is open to financial flows, financial transactions can take place domestically and internationally. Moreover, the fact that foreigners can invest in a domestic market is an important aspect for any analysis of the availability of funds for investment in a local economy.

This chapter explores the interplay between a country's financial development and its participation in financial globalization. One aspect of globalization is related to financial diversification—that is, the availability of foreign funds that might help develop domestic markets as they seek international risk diversification. That aspect, however, needs to be understood in the context of domestic investors who are also investing abroad. This increased financing from foreigners can have many beneficial effects as risk is shared across borders, but it may also mean that shocks to foreign investors (reflected in the volatility of capital flows) can be imported into the local economy.

The second aspect of financial globalization is related to financial offshoring: that is, the use of foreign markets or foreign jurisdictions to conduct financial transactions by firms and governments.[1] In a world where assets can be traded at home and abroad, one needs to consider the activity abroad to grasp the full extent of financial development. We thus investigate how developments in domestic agents' use of foreign markets may be associated with the trends in the use of domestic markets. Our analysis can also shed light on the extent to which foreign markets are substitutes for or complements to domestic markets. For instance, foreign markets are substitutes when domestic financing activity actually migrates abroad. To the extent that such migration occurs, financial development is negatively correlated with financial globalization, for example, with firms' raising capital and trading their assets in international markets. Domestic and international markets may also be complements when they offer different financing choices. Foreign bond markets, for example, might typically be used for assets denominated in foreign currency, while domestic markets might offer financing in both domestic and foreign currency.

According to widely used de facto measures, such as the stock of foreign assets and liabilities and capital flows by domestic and foreign agents (or gross flows), financial globalization in LAC appears to have continued to increase over the past decade. Interestingly, developed countries have typically experienced a greater expansion of flows as a percentage of gross domestic product (GDP) and a significantly larger increase in the stock of foreign assets and liabilities than have emerging countries. This increased financial globalization has been a two-way process, with increased participation of both foreigners in local markets and residents in foreign markets. The recent patterns of financial globalization described in this chapter reaffirm the notion put forward in chapter 1 that financial systems remain relatively less developed in emerging countries than in advanced economies not because of insufficient available funds: significant evidence shows that foreigners are entering domestic markets and that domestic residents are saving more abroad by hoarding international reserves.

The increased participation of foreigners in local capital markets around the world has largely been as investors, as they typically do not seek financing in these markets. Emerging market residents, in contrast, use foreign markets as investors as well as borrowers, tapping a much wider range of instruments.

Still, over the past decade, LAC corporations have not generally expanded their use of foreign markets. Capital-raising activity in foreign markets has been relatively small and stable over time, in contrast to the growing depth of financial markets around the world. It has also been highly concentrated in a few firms. In other words, the increased globalization that has taken place over the past 20 years has tightened links across markets, with increased gross capital flows, but it has not been accompanied by an increased use of foreign capital markets as a financing source.

Furthermore, positive developments in local bond markets have been matched in maturity and currency by developments in foreign markets. For instance, bond maturities in LAC have been longer in the 2000s than in the 1990s for both the private and the public sectors in emerging countries. Moreover, some firms as well as governments have been able to place local currency bond issues abroad, although bonds typically remain almost exclusively denominated in foreign currency.

Although emerging countries have not used foreign markets much as a source of new financing, their issuance of bonds and equity abroad has been gaining ground over the use of domestic capital markets, particularly among LAC7 countries (Argentina, Brazil, Chile, Colombia, Mexico, Peru, and Uruguay). Furthermore, this apparent migration of equity financing to foreign markets has been accompanied by increased liquidity abroad for many LAC countries, possibly suggesting a shift of equity trading to foreign markets. In contrast, bond financing by the public sector has been shifting to local markets.

These trends in the use of foreign markets by the public and private sectors of LAC countries in fact reinforce the developments in domestic markets. As argued in chapters 1 and 3 in this volume, financial markets in emerging countries have typically been expanding, although not as fast as expected. A possible explanation for the underdevelopment of local markets for the financing of the private sector could be the use of financial services abroad, as agents might get better financing terms in foreign markets.

We also find that emerging economies have typically become net creditors in debt assets and net debtors in equity assets. Such a composition of foreign assets and liabilities is particularly beneficial in times of turbulence, as balance sheet effects work in their favor. For example, if their currencies depreciate, the local currency value of their external assets would increase, while that of their debt liabilities would shrink. In addition, as observed during the global financial crisis of 2008–09, with the collapse in economic growth and in equity markets, the local currency value of emerging economies' equity liabilities can also contract. Hence, another interesting feature of the process of financial globalization over the past decade is the safer international integration of many emerging countries arising from the changing structure of their external assets and liabilities.

The rest of the chapter is organized as follows. The next section documents and gives a broad overview on where LAC stands on commonly used and simple measures of financial globalization. The following section evaluates the relative size of domestic and foreign capital markets for financing the public and private sectors. The chapter then analyzes whether and how the nature of financial integration has changed over time and concludes with a discussion of some issues for further research.

Extent of Financial Globalization

As documented in Lane and Milesi-Ferretti (2007) and others, de facto financial integration measures suggest increasing globalization. For instance, both developed and emerging countries, especially the former during the 2000s, have been expanding their ties to financial systems around the world as seen by increased foreign assets and foreign liabilities, a standard measure of the extent of financial integration (figure 4.1a). The extent of financial integration is much greater in developed countries than in emerging markets. Foreign assets and liabilities represented about 300 percent of GDP in developed countries in the 2000s, whereas they were less than half that in emerging markets, at around 130 percent in emerging Asian, Eastern European, and LAC7 countries.

Foreign direct investment (FDI) and bank flows capture the bulk of foreign liabilities, particularly in emerging markets, where they are more than 70 percent of total foreign liabilities in Asian, Eastern European, and LAC7 countries. In contrast, foreign assets are concentrated in international reserves for a number of emerging economies. For example, reserves accounted for 52 percent of the total foreign assets of emerging Asian countries and about 37 percent in Eastern Europe in the 2000s. For LAC7 countries, reserves accounted for 24 percent over the same period (figure 4.2). In developed economies, direct investments and other investments typically represent about 50 percent of the total foreign assets and liabilities.

This expansion of the stock of foreign assets and liabilities might reflect not only increased gross capital flows but also valuation effects; as many have argued, capital gains and losses on outstanding holdings of foreign assets and liabilities can be sizable.[2] Just as important, capital inflows by foreign residents and capital outflows by domestic residents have been on the rise, particularly in developed countries, where not only are foreign residents investing more in local markets but also domestic residents are expanding their use of foreign markets (see figure 4.1b).

This increase in gross capital flows over the past decade points toward an increased globalization of world financial markets with greater participation of residents from developed and emerging countries as investors in global markets. In fact, the developments of domestic markets documented in chapter 1 in this book might have benefited from the increased participation of foreign investors in domestic markets. A broader base of investors may lead to increased liquidity and larger analyst coverage of corporations, which would improve the quality and amount of information available to market participants. Furthermore, the scrutiny of foreign investors and analysts may increase transparency and promote the adoption of better corporate governance practices, thus reducing agency problems (Stulz 1999; Errunza 2001).

However, foreigners invest mostly in emerging markets, but they typically do not raise capital in these local markets. For instance, foreign firms issuing either equity or bonds in local markets in LAC countries account for less than 3 percent of total firms raising new capital in these markets and less than 2 percent of the total amount raised during the 2000s. Yet, in comparison to the 1990s, foreign firms have been seeking more financing in emerging markets. One possibility behind these patterns

Figure 4.1 Financial Integration in Selected Countries and Regions, 1980–2007

a. Stock of foreign assets and liabilities

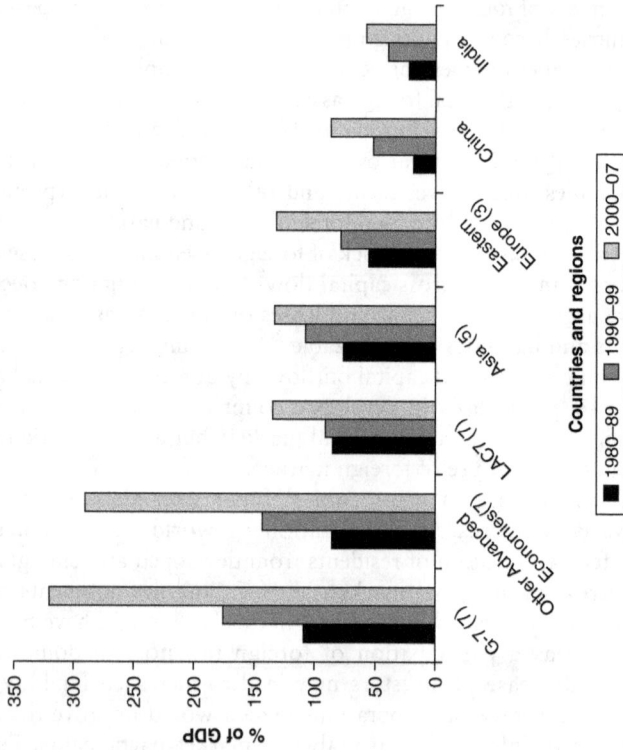

(continued next page)

Figure 4.1 (continued)

b. Gross capital flows

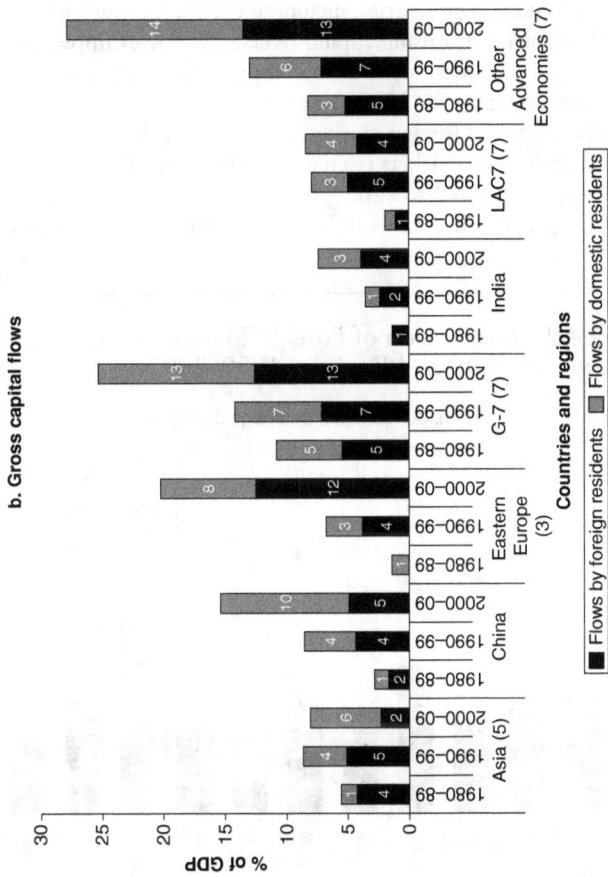

Source: Lane and Milesi-Ferretti 2007; IMF's BOP.
Note: Numbers in parentheses show the number of countries in each region. GDP = gross domestic product.

is that within emerging countries, firms look for financing alternatives in more developed—that is, relatively deeper and more liquid—markets.

Emerging market residents, however, not only invest but also borrow in foreign markets. In fact, they use a wider range of instruments than foreign investors locally. However, the participation of residents from emerging countries in foreign markets as borrowers is somewhat limited, particularly for the private sector. Figure 4.3 presents data on borrowing in foreign markets, including syndicated loans, bond issues, and equity issues. As the figure shows, emerging countries, including LAC7, are much less active than developed countries in raising capital overseas.[3] For example, new capital raised through syndicated loans abroad represented more than 2 percent of GDP on average during the 2000s for a number of emerging markets, and so did new bond issues in foreign markets for many countries. Not surprisingly, bond issues in foreign markets from corporations in emerging countries are typically heavily skewed toward government financing, with the private sector playing a much smaller role. New capital raising through equity

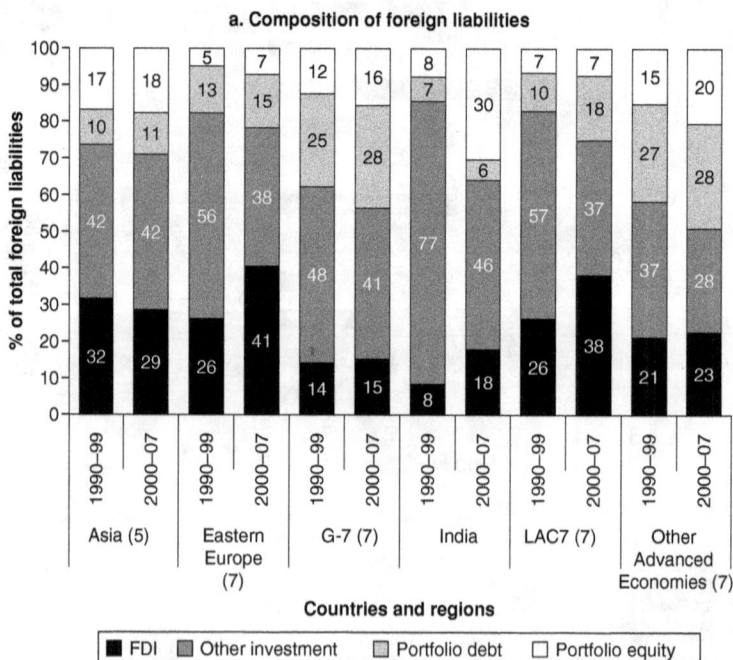

Figure 4.2 Composition of Foreign Liabilities and Assets in Selected Countries and Regions, 1990–2007

a. Composition of foreign liabilities

(continued next page)

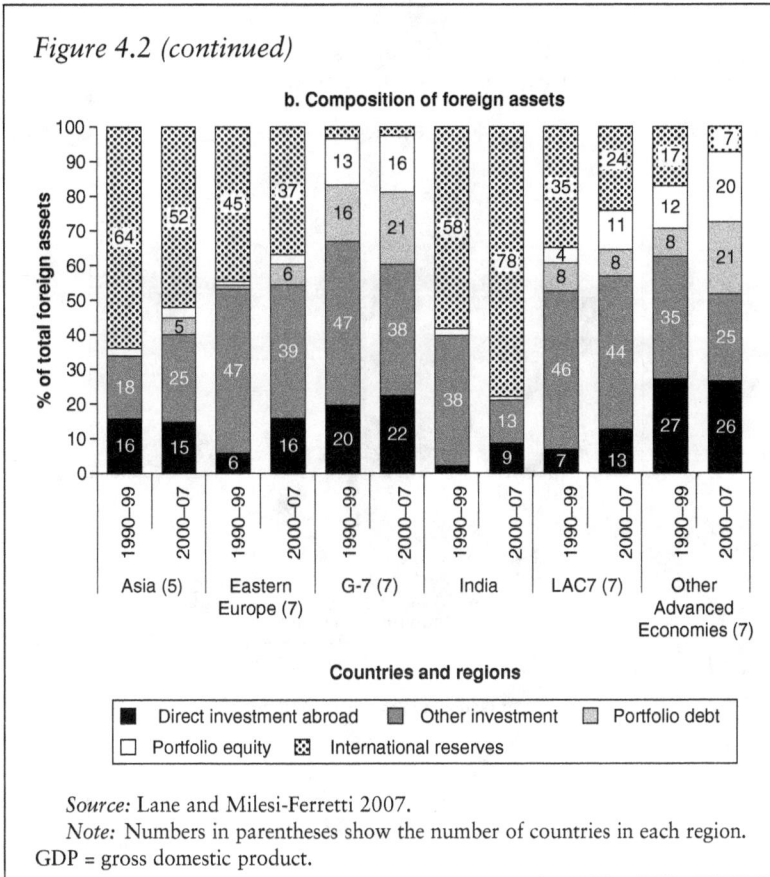

Figure 4.2 (continued)

b. Composition of foreign assets

Source: Lane and Milesi-Ferretti 2007.
Note: Numbers in parentheses show the number of countries in each region.
GDP = gross domestic product.

issues is also relatively limited, representing on average 0.2 percent of GDP
per year across emerging economies. The figure also shows a mixed picture
of capital-raising activity in foreign markets over the past decade. While
syndicated loans expanded between 1990–99 and 2000–08, international
equity financing declined in many emerging regions, as did international
bond financing, largely because of lower activity in the private sector.
In contrast, in Eastern Europe and India, both public and private sector
international bond issuance expanded, as did international equity issues.

Financing through Capital Markets: Domestic and Foreign Markets

In this section, we explore the extent to which foreign markets are substitutes
or complements to domestic financial markets in emerging countries. As
shown above, the private sector of emerging countries has a relatively small

Figure 4.3 New Capital-Raising Issues in Foreign Markets in Selected Countries, Regions, and Economies, 1991–2008

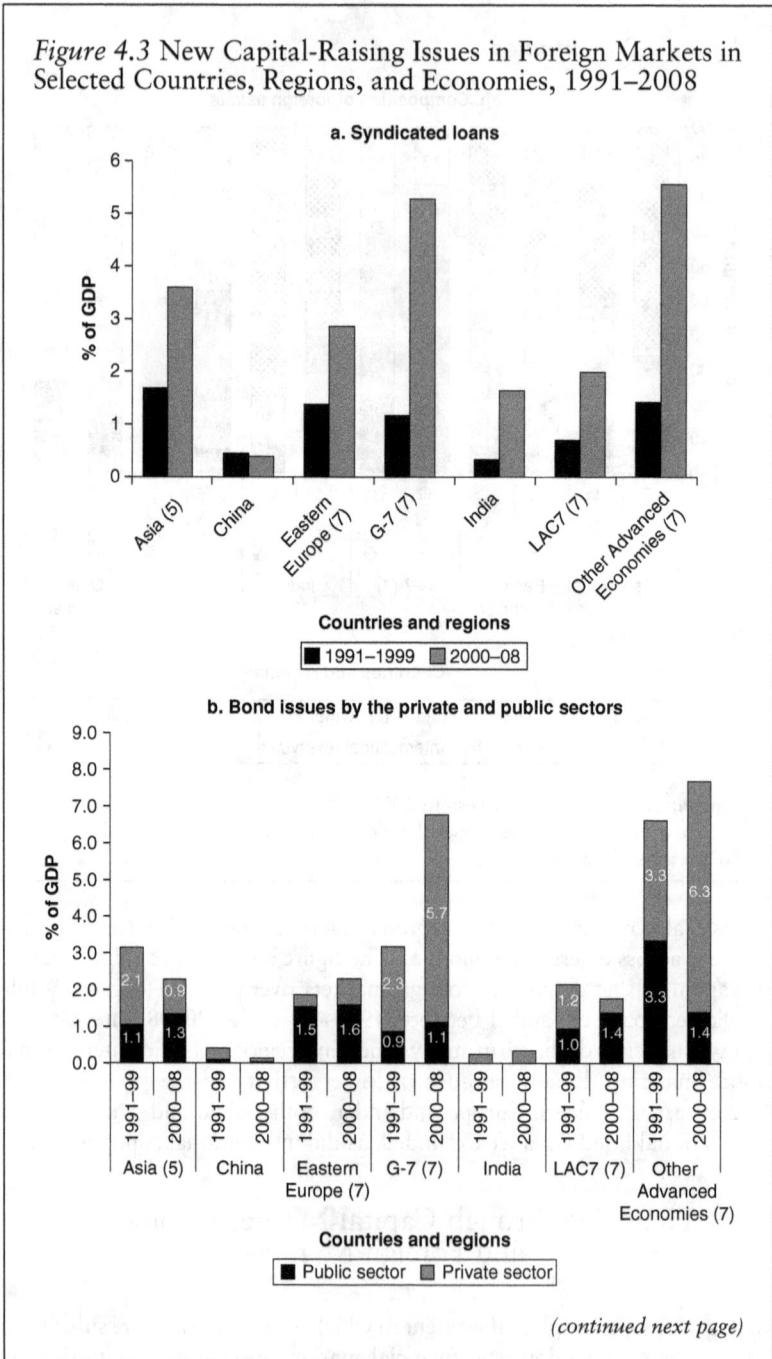

a. Syndicated loans

Countries and regions

■ 1991–1999   ▨ 2000–08

b. Bond issues by the private and public sectors

Countries and regions

■ Public sector   ▨ Private sector

(continued next page)

Figure 4.3 (continued)

c. Equity issues

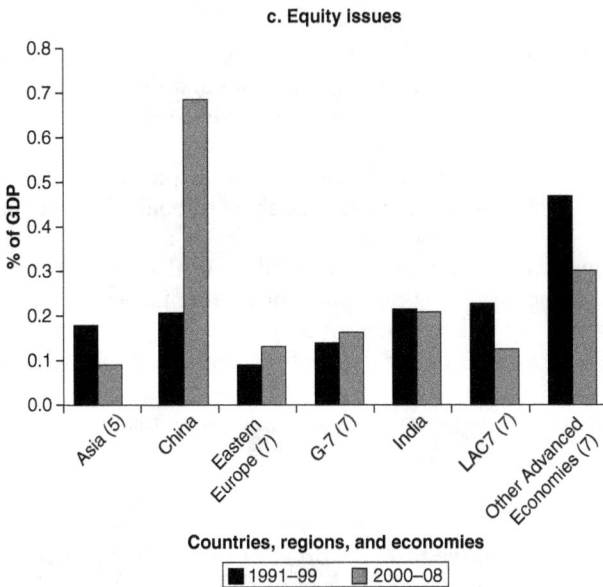

Countries, regions, and economies

■ 1991–99   ▨ 2000–08

Source: SDC Platinum.
Note: Numbers in parentheses show the number of countries in each region.
GDP = gross domestic product.

and stable capital-raising activity abroad. Nevertheless, in comparison to new issues in domestic markets, issuance of bonds and equity abroad has been increasing for many countries. Insofar as foreign markets have substituted for domestic financial markets—perhaps because local firms get better financing terms there—then one may expect to see such adverse outcomes as segmentation, where larger firms have access to foreign capital markets while smaller firms are limited to local financing sources. The substitution of foreign for domestic financial markets may reduce not only the liquidity of the remaining firms in local markets but also their ability to raise capital, thereby jeopardizing the sustainability of domestic capital markets. In sharp contrast, bond financing by the public sector has shifted to local sources, consistent with the deeper domestic markets documented in chapter 1 in this volume. We now explore in more detail these shifts in the use of domestic and foreign markets across emerging and developed countries.

Despite the small volume of financing activity taking place abroad, emerging economies, and especially LAC7 countries, still rely more on foreign markets than developed countries do; for example, about 30 percent of outstanding government bonds were issued abroad during the 2000s for LAC7 and Eastern European countries, compared to only 6 percent by G-7 countries (figure 4.4a). Notably, the share of international bonds issued by the public sector in emerging countries has declined, suggesting that public financing is shifting toward domestic markets. Such a decrease is particularly sharp among LAC7 countries and those in emerging Asia, a trend consistent with the significant expansions of local markets for government bonds and, at the same time, with a reduction in foreign indebtedness of many of these countries (see chapter 1).

For the private sector, however, the share of bond financing in foreign markets typically increased for both developed and emerging countries. For example, issues abroad represented more than 50 percent of total outstanding bonds during the 2000s for Eastern European countries and India as well as "other advanced economies" (figure 4.4b). For LAC7 countries, the share is one of the smallest among emerging regions, and it has remained relatively stable at around 35 percent over the past 20 years, suggesting that domestic markets are an important source of funding for

Figure 4.4 Relative Size of Foreign Capital Markets in Selected Countries and Regions, 1990–2009

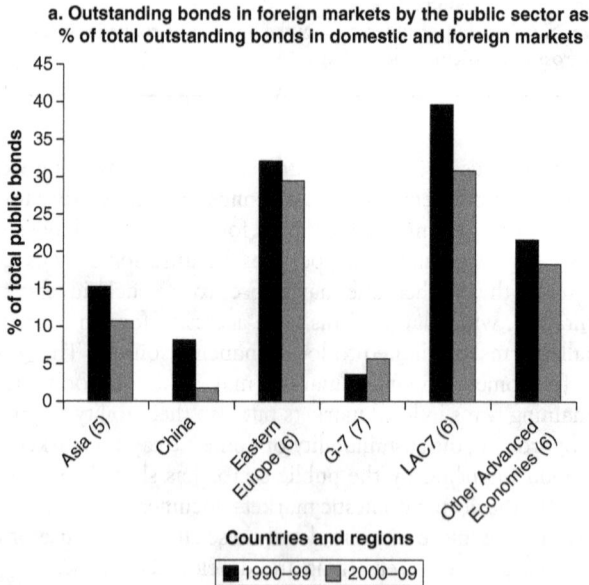

a. Outstanding bonds in foreign markets by the public sector as % of total outstanding bonds in domestic and foreign markets

(continued next page)

Figure 4.4 (continued)

b. Outstanding bonds in foreign markets by the private sector as % of total outstanding bonds in domestic and foreign markets

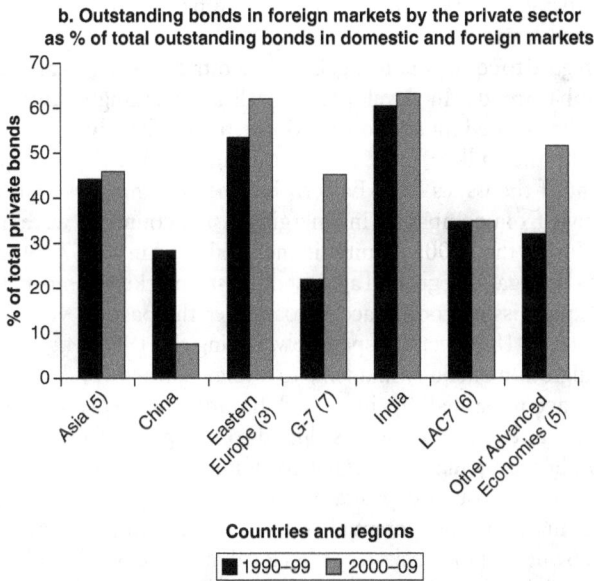

Countries and regions

■ 1990–99 ■ 2000–09

c. Amount raised in foreign equity markets as % of total amount raised through equity issues in domestic and foreign markets

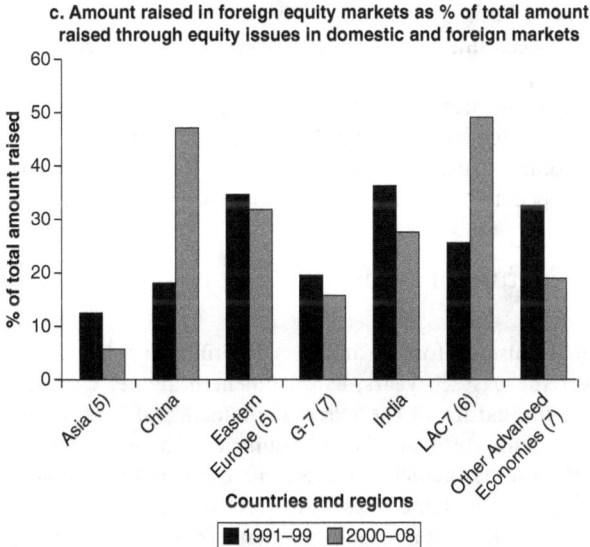

Countries and regions

■ 1991–99 ■ 2000–08

Source: Bank for International Settlement (BIS); SDC Platinum.

Note: International debt securities reported in 4.4a and 4.4b are defined as those that have not been issued by residents in domestic currency and targeted at resident investors. Numbers in parentheses show the number of countries in each region.

the private sector. Nevertheless, domestic bond markets are relatively small and concentrated in a few firms in LAC7 countries, indicating that bond financing is a restricted option for the private sector more broadly in these countries.

With regard to equity financing, LAC7 countries and China are exceptions to the global trends. In developed as well as emerging countries, equity financing has shifted mostly toward domestic markets, which increasingly account for the bulk of new capital-raising activity. For instance, only 30 percent of the issues from Eastern European companies and 6 percent of the issues from companies in emerging Asian countries were in foreign markets during the 2000s. Equity financing abroad in LAC7 countries and China has been gaining ground against domestic markets: almost 50 percent of their equity issues took place abroad over the past 10 years, up from 26 percent and 18 percent, respectively, during the 1990s (figure 4.4c).

This migration of equity financing to foreign markets for LAC7 countries has been accompanied by increased liquidity abroad, suggesting the possibility that equity trading has shifted to foreign markets. The issuance of equity abroad by many emerging economies has usually taken the form of cross-listings through depositary receipts (DRs), which are particularly useful for analyzing this potential shift of liquidity in stock markets. DRs represent ownership of stocks traded in local markets, but they also trade on the New York Stock Exchange, NASDAQ, and the London Stock Exchange, among others. Firm-level trading activity for LAC7 countries shows that liquidity has been shifting to foreign markets. In fact, it represents the bulk of the trading for a number of firms in these countries (figure 4.5). This trend suggests an increased internationalization of equity financing, with borrowers and lenders migrating to foreign markets and a diminishing role for domestic markets in LAC7, which have remained relatively underdeveloped and illiquid compared to those in other emerging regions.

Nature of Financing in Foreign Markets

Although the use of foreign markets for financing has been relatively stable over the past 20 years, as documented above, we have observed changes in the nature of the external financing of both the public and the private sector for a number of countries. These changes may reflect tighter links among financial markets in a more globalized world. In fact, positive developments in domestic markets are being matched by positive developments in foreign markets. For example, the maturity of public and private sector bonds in LAC7 countries has typically lengthened, and local currency bond financing abroad has expanded, although it still remains very limited. Nevertheless, there is a long road ahead for emerging markets in increasing the depth and breadth of external financing. Private bond and equity markets remain on average small and highly concentrated

Figure 4.5 Equity Trading in Domestic and Foreign Markets by Selected Countries and Regions, 2000–09

Share of value traded abroad as % of total value traded

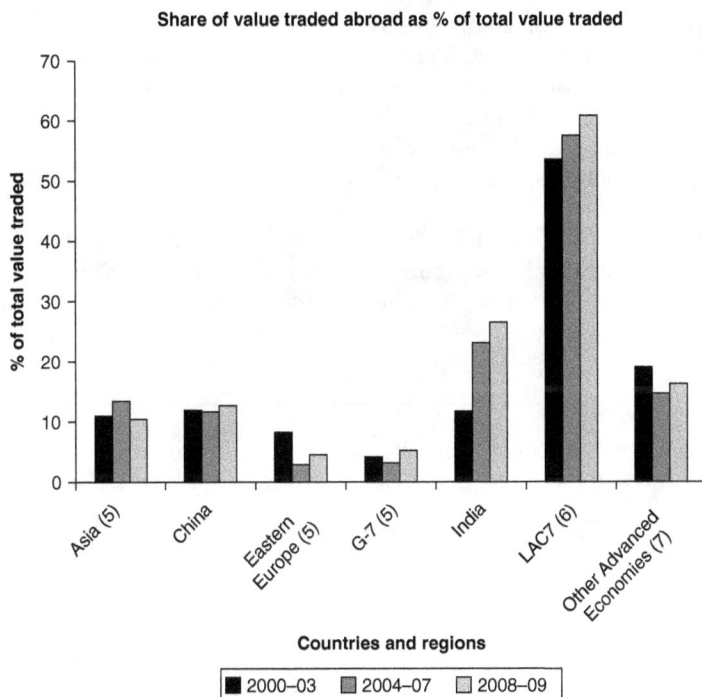

Source: Bank of New York; Bloomberg.

Note: This figure shows the cross-country averages of firm-level value traded in depository receipts over total value traded (in domestic markets and depository receipts). All depository receipts identified in the Depository Receipt Directory of the Bank of New York, with trading data reported in Bloomberg, are considered in this figure. Numbers in parentheses show the number of countries considered in each region.

in large firms, reinforcing trends in local markets. We now review more systematically these qualitative developments in firm financing abroad in light of the trends in domestic activity.

Bond Markets

While total bond issuance in foreign markets has not increased for most emerging countries, these countries have, on average, made a conscious effort to try to reduce currency and maturity mismatches, mitigating concerns about rollover difficulties. As in domestic bond markets, and most likely as a consequence of a series of financial crises in the 1990s, the maturity profile of both public and private sector bonds abroad has lengthened during the 2000s for a number of emerging markets, and especially for LAC7 countries. For example, relative to the 1990s, the average maturity of LAC7 private sector foreign bonds has increased by almost 12 months on average, whereas that for the public sector has increased from 7.7 to 13.2 years (figure 4.6).

At the same time, both the public and the private sector in many emerging countries have been able to issue bonds in local currency in foreign markets. For example, 7 percent of the LAC7 private sector bonds and 11 percent of the public sector bonds issued abroad in the 2000s were denominated in local currency, whereas there were virtually none in the 1990s. Of course, these percentages are small compared to the

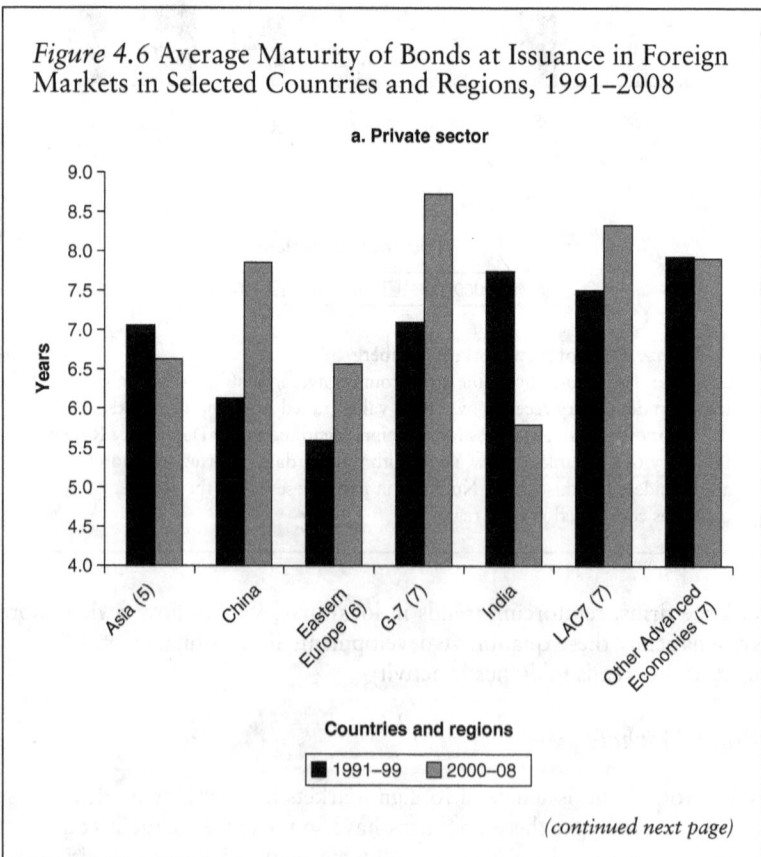

Figure 4.6 Average Maturity of Bonds at Issuance in Foreign Markets in Selected Countries and Regions, 1991–2008

a. Private sector

(continued next page)

Figure 4.6 (continued)

b. Public sector

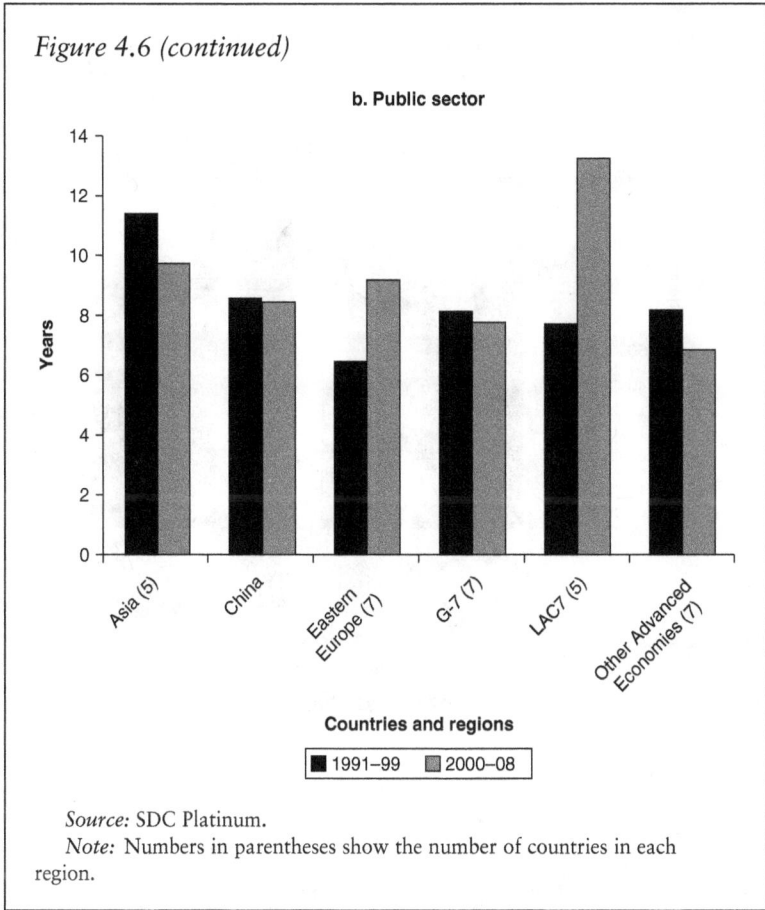

Source: SDC Platinum.
Note: Numbers in parentheses show the number of countries in each region.

capacity of advanced economies to issue local currency bonds in foreign markets (figure 4.7).

Despite the positive changes in the terms of the bonds issued abroad, access and concentration in foreign markets are still concerns for many emerging countries. Only a small number of firms use foreign bond markets for new capital in comparison to developed countries. In fact, the number of firms in LAC7 and emerging Asian countries that raise capital in foreign bond markets has declined considerably during the 2000s compared to the 1990s (figure 4.8a). At the same time, markets remain largely concentrated, with top issuers representing a significant fraction of new bond financing abroad. In the past 10 years, this concentration has even increased over the previous decade for most emerging markets, including LAC7 countries. In other words, only a few firms still seem to capture the bulk of the market (figure 4.8).

Figure 4.7 Ratio of Foreign Currency Bonds to Total Bonds at Issuance in Foreign Markets in Selected Countries and Regions, 1991–2008

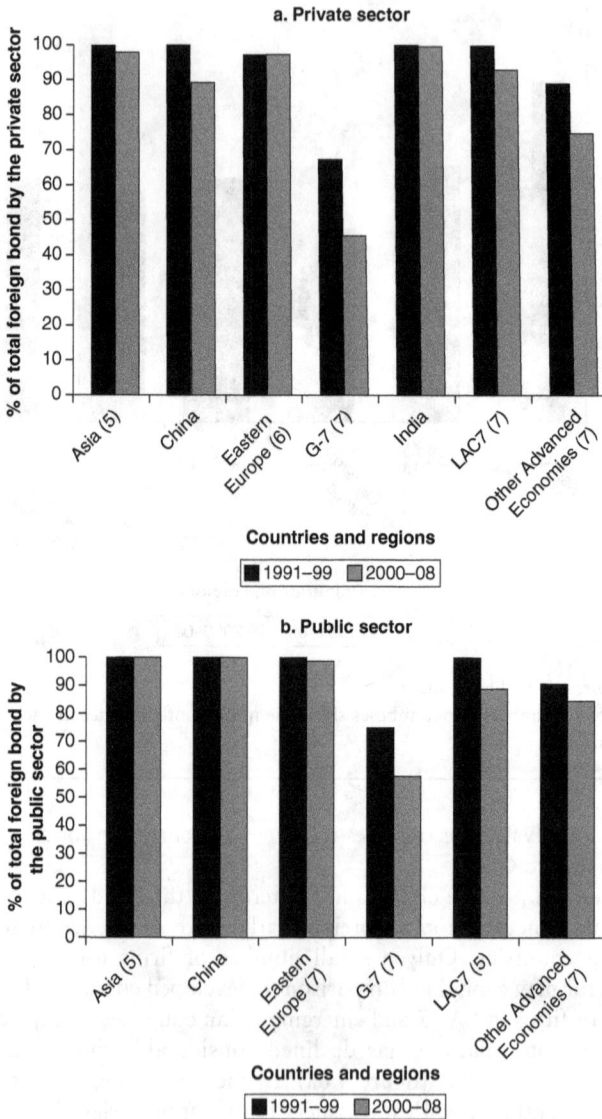

a. Private sector

y-axis: % of total foreign bond by the private sector

x-axis (Countries and regions): Asia (5), China, Eastern Europe (6), G-7 (7), India, LAC7 (7), Other Advanced Economies (7)

Legend: ■ 1991–99 ■ 2000–08

b. Public sector

y-axis: % of total foreign bond by the public sector

x-axis (Countries and regions): Asia (5), China, Eastern Europe (7), G-7 (7), LAC7 (5), Other Advanced Economies (7)

Legend: ■ 1991–99 ■ 2000–08

Source: SDC Platinum.

Note: Numbers in parentheses show the number of countries in each region.

Figure 4.8 Issuance Activity in Foreign Private Bond Markets
in Selected Countries and Regions, 1991–2008

a. Average number of firms issuing bonds abroad per year

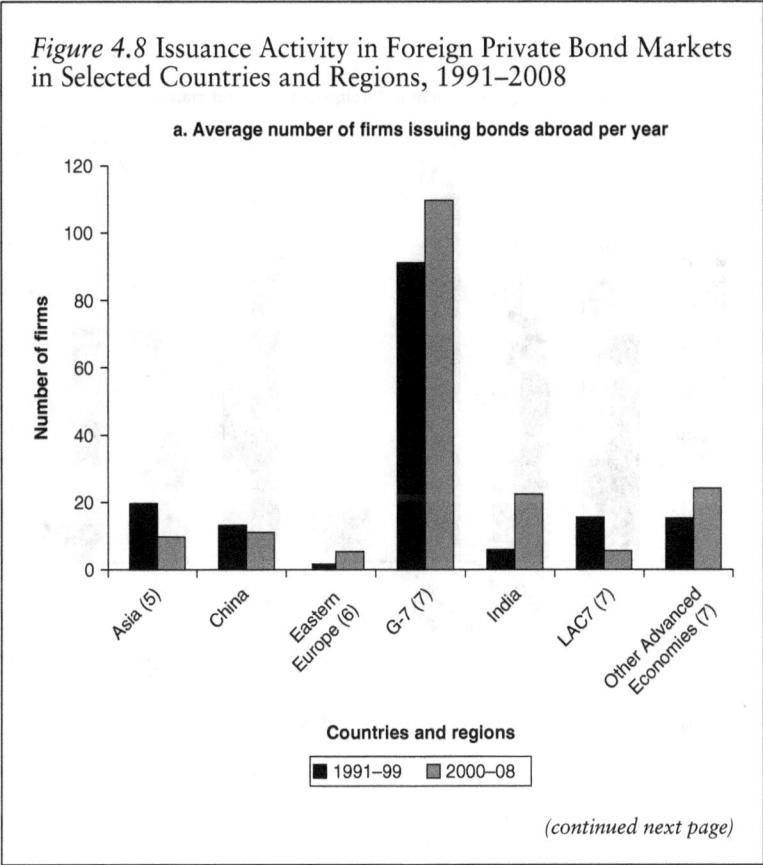

Countries and regions

■ 1991–99   ■ 2000–08

(continued next page)

Equity Markets

Like bond markets, foreign equity markets remain a limited option for firm financing among emerging economies. Compared to developed countries, the number of firms using foreign equity finance on a regular basis is rather small in emerging markets. For instance, in LAC7 and Asian countries, about two firms on average issued equity in any given year during the 2000s, while over 15 firms did so in developed countries. Moreover, the average number of firms raising capital in equity markets has declined significantly for many emerging economies, including those in LAC7, whereas it has actually increased for developed countries over the same period (figure 4.9a). At the same time, equity financing in foreign markets has been highly concentrated in a few issues. The share of the total amount raised abroad by the largest five issues has, in fact, increased

Figure 4.8 (continued)

b. Concentration in foreign private bond markets

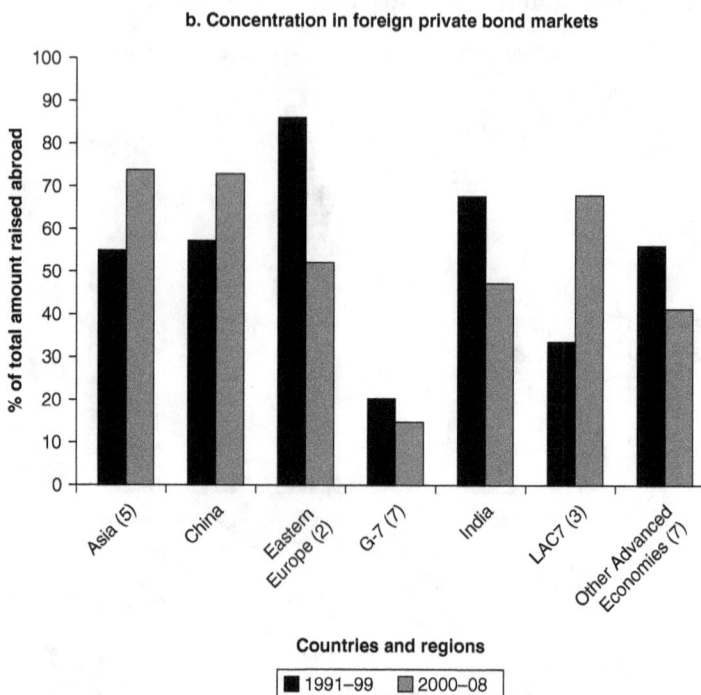

Source: SDC Platinum.

Note: 4.8b shows the amount raised by the top five bond issues by corporations as a percentage of the total amount raised by the private sector in foreign markets between 1991 and 2008. Only country-years with at least five issues were considered in this figure. Numbers in parentheses show the number of countries in each region.

for LAC7 and a number of other emerging countries (figure 4.9b). Trading in foreign equity markets is also highly concentrated in a few firms, with the top five firms from LAC7 countries capturing more than 90 percent of the total trading abroad for these countries (figure 4.9c).

Firms Using Foreign Markets

It is well known that larger firms have greater access to domestic capital markets, due at least in part to cost and liquidity considerations. In practice, these considerations render the minimum issue size rather

Figure 4.9 Issuance Activity in Foreign Equity Markets in
Selected Countries and Regions, 1991–2008

a. Average number of firms issuing equity in foreign markets per year

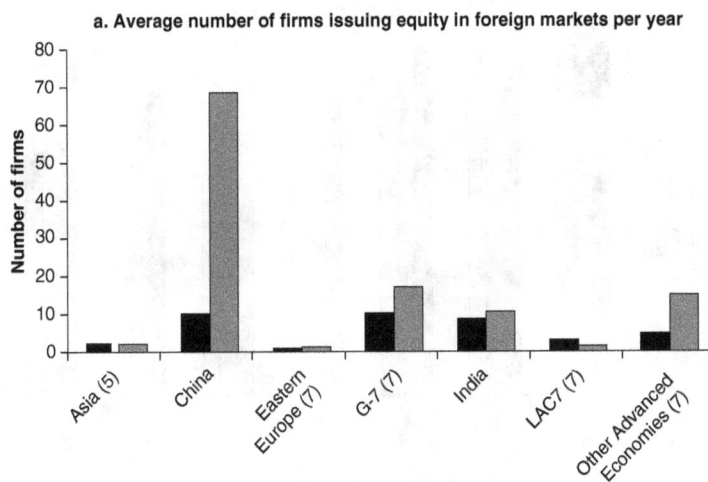

Countries and regions

■ 1991–99   ▨ 2000–08

**b. Share of amount raised by the top five issues as % of total
amount raised abroad**

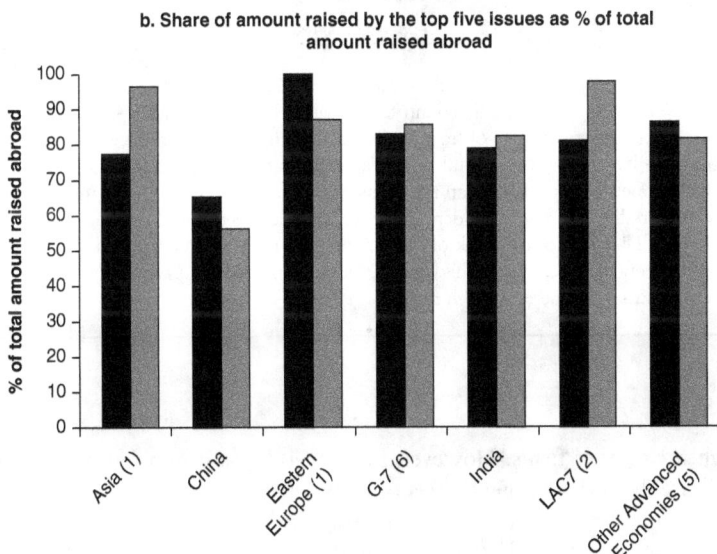

Countries and regions

■ 1991–99   ▨ 2000–08

(continued next page)

Figure 4.9 (continued)

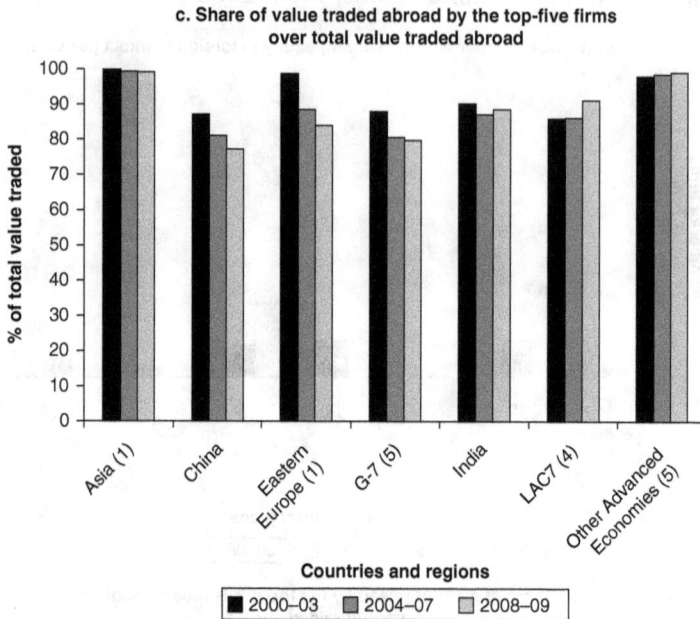

c. Share of value traded abroad by the top-five firms over total value traded abroad

Countries and regions

■ 2000–03   ■ 2004–07   □ 2008–09

Source: SDC Platinum; Bank of New York; Bloomberg.

Note: 4.9b includes only country-years with at least five issues. 4.9c shows the cross-country average of firm-level value traded in depository receipts for the top-five firms over the total value traded in domestic and foreign markets. Only countries with more than five firms with depository receipt programs were considered in this figure. All depository receipts identified in the Depository Receipt Directory of the Bank of New York, with trading data reported in Bloomberg, are included in this figure. Numbers in parentheses show the number of countries considered in each region.

high for smaller firms. However, firm-level data on publicly listed firms indicate that even among this set of relatively large firms, only a few firms have made use of capital market financing abroad. Typically, firms from developing countries that raise capital in foreign financial markets are larger, with faster-growing sales and more liquidity (cash-to-current-assets ratios), than firms that do not issue bonds or equities abroad. The fact that only a restricted set of firms uses capital markets can be explained at least in part by supply factors; as documented in a number of papers and mentioned in chapter 3, institutional investors tend to invest in larger and more liquid firms, hence limiting the supply of funds available to smaller and less liquid firms.

Safer Integration

Over the past 20 years, the composition of foreign assets and foreign liabilities has been shifting, and this change has given rise to a safer form of financial integration among emerging markets. Many of these countries have steadily reduced their debt liabilities and increased their equity liabilities. At the same time, having learned the lessons of the Asian currency crises of the late 1990s, they accumulated large amounts of international reserves, which contributed to their improved macroeconomic and financial stances. Thus emerging economies have become net creditors to the rest of the world in debt contracts and net debtors in equity contracts (particularly through FDI) (figure 4.10).

Figure 4.10 Net Foreign Assets: Equity and Debt Positions in Selected Countries and Regions, 1990–2007

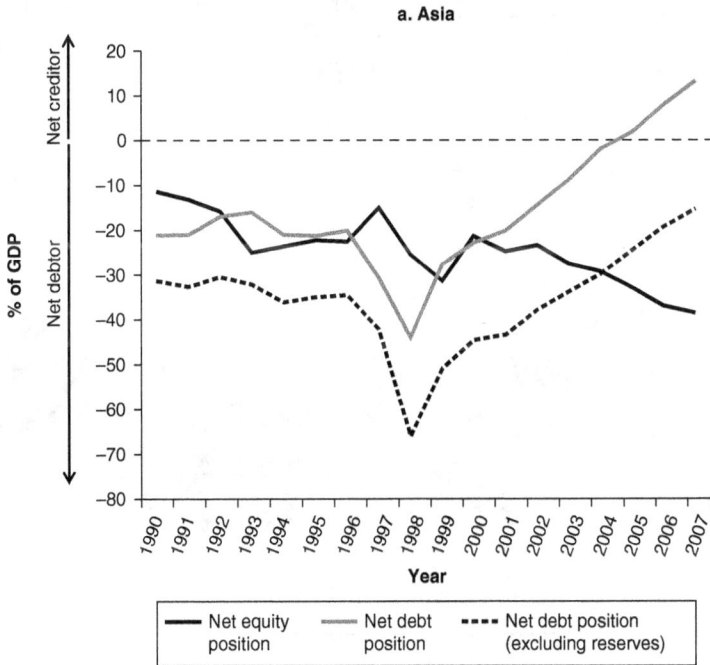

a. Asia

Legend:
- Net equity position
- Net debt position
- Net debt position (excluding reserves)

(continued next page)

Figure 4.10 (continued)

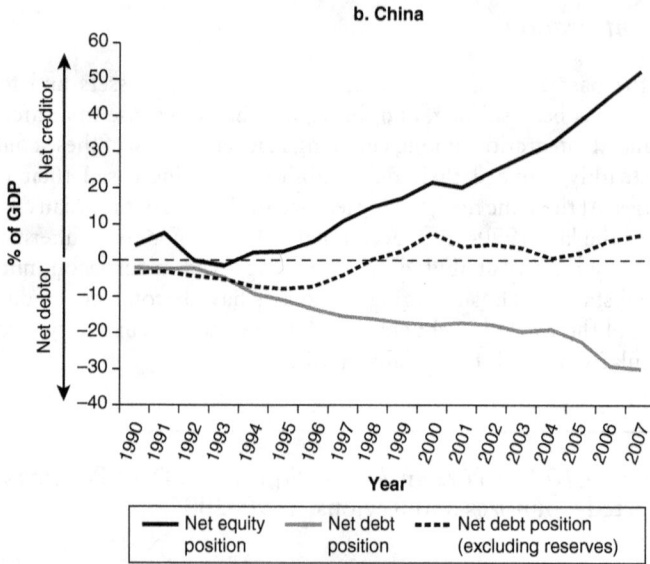

b. China

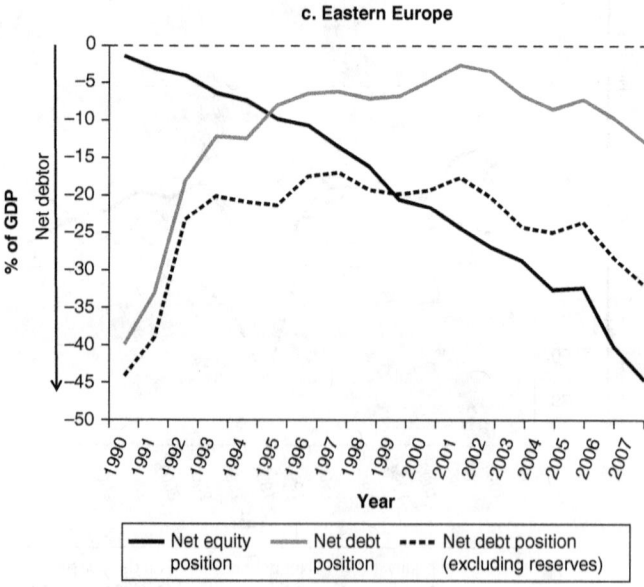

c. Eastern Europe

(continued next page)

Figure 4.10 *(continued)*

d. G-7

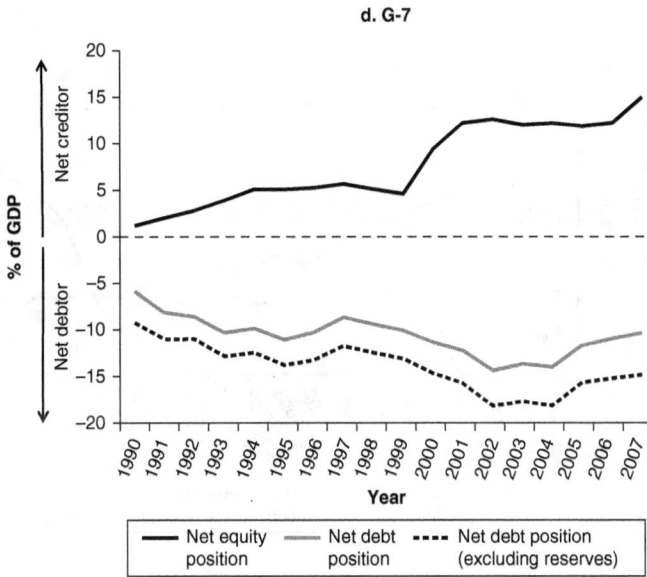

e. India

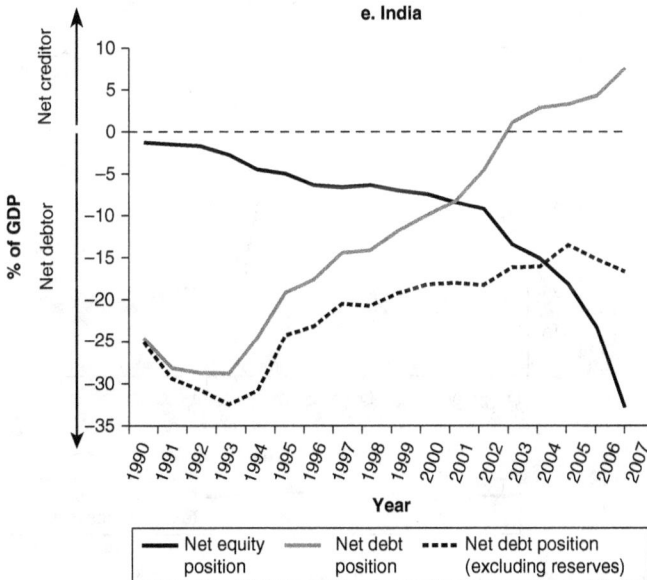

(continued next page)

Figure 4.10 (continued)

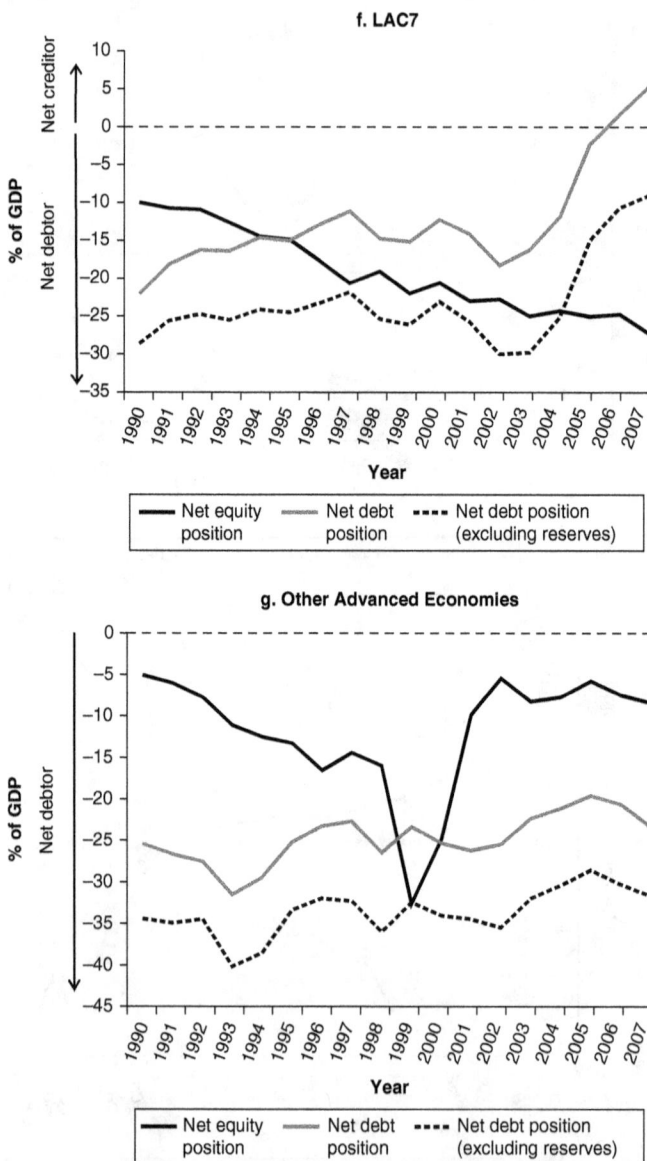

f. LAC7

g. Other Advanced Economies

Source: Lane and Milesi-Ferretti 2007.

Note: Net equity and net debt positions are reported as a percentage of GDP. GDP = gross domestic product.

These changes in the structure of emerging countries' external assets and liabilities may play a role in avoiding the downside risks of financial globalization. For instance, compare the experience of the 2008–09 global financial crisis with that of earlier crises. In earlier episodes, the devaluations that typically ensued tended to increase the burden of foreign debt issued in foreign currency; in addition, market shutdowns triggered rollover crises because of the high incidence of short-term debt. During the 2008–09 crisis, in contrast, the devaluations implied an improvement in the external positions of emerging economies (when measured in local currency) due to their net creditor status (see Didier, Hevia, and Schmukler 2012). Moreover, the external liability was reduced as equity prices plummeted around the world and the net debtor equity position shrank. The large pool of international reserves also played an important role in emerging countries: it slowed down the appreciation of the domestic currency during the precrisis expansionary period, and it served as a self-insurance mechanism during the crisis, deterring currency and banking panics. In fact, when the global crisis erupted, many emerging countries held international reserves in excess of their stock of short-term foreign liabilities. In practice, this eliminated concerns about debt rollover difficulties, giving investors fewer incentives to attack domestic currencies.

Conclusions

LAC has continued its financial globalization in recent years. De facto financial integration as measured by the stock of foreign assets and liabilities and by gross capital flows has continued to increase. While this increase has been significant, LAC has not been alone in the process. Many other regions of the world, developed and emerging countries alike, have also deepened their globalization. This trend has been particularly pronounced in developed countries, where the stock of foreign assets and liabilities on average almost doubled in the 2000s relative to the 1990s. In contrast, emerging countries typically experienced increases of about 50 percent over the same period, with Eastern European countries and China slightly ahead of the others.

LAC has not used international capital markets extensively for firm financing purposes, although it did so for equity trading purposes. The public sector, however, has increasingly used domestic markets. These two markets have alternatively served firms and governments, and their developments are tightly linked. Probably because of past crises, LAC has used this globalization process to integrate with the rest of the world in a safer manner.

The picture of financial globalization presented here is admittedly somewhat incomplete and requires more research, as the measures we study capture only part of the financial integration process. Other important aspects are the ability to trade assets across countries, the capacity of financial institutions to operate in different jurisdictions (most notably foreign banks operating at home), and the equalization of asset prices and returns across borders (even without actual transactions taking place). Furthermore, the evidence on the expansion of the stock of foreign assets and liabilities might reflect not only increased gross capital flows, as shown here, but also valuation effects. Capital gains and losses on outstanding holdings of foreign assets and liabilities can be sizable indeed. These caveats suggest caution in interpreting the evidence. Indeed, according to some alternative measures of globalization, LAC countries and other emerging markets have not increased the extent of their financial integration significantly in recent years (chapter 5).

For policy makers, the continuing integration of LAC with the international financial system raises many questions. First, what are the net effects of globalization? On the positive side, it allows agents to diversify risk and tap into other investment opportunities; it also allows firms and governments to reduce the cost of capital by accessing funds that would otherwise be harder to obtain. On the negative side is the potential migration of financing activity to international markets, which may reduce such activity at home and thus slow domestic financial development. However, the underdevelopment of local markets is unlikely attributable to the globalization process alone, since countries from other emerging regions have witnessed greater development of local markets as well as more financial globalization. Another potentially negative effect comes from the shocks to international investors, which might introduce more volatility into domestic economies.

Second, does financial globalization entail more risk? The answer on the equity side appears to be no. On the debt side, financial globalization may carry exchange rate risk if debt securities are issued in foreign currency. It may also entail maturity risk if it allows shorter forms of financing. To the extent that domestic markets provide local currency financing, they would play an important role.

Third, what is the relation between domestic and international markets? In particular, do domestic and international capital markets act as complements or substitutes? This chapter has provided some evidence suggesting that they are complements. Fourth, is financial globalization just a search for more and cheaper capital from segmented markets? Is it a quest for better corporate governance? The literature has put forward arguments supporting both perspectives, and some evidence suggests that the former cannot be rejected. Fifth, since several of the trends documented here are similar across countries, what is the role for domestic policy making, given these secular forces?

Notes

1. See Ceballos, Didier, and Schmukler (2012a, 2012b) for a more extended discussion of these two aspects of globalization.

2. See, for example, Lane and Milesi-Ferretti (2001, 2007), Gourinchas and Rey (2007), and Gourinchas, Govillot, and Rey (2010).

3. Notice that figure 4.3 shows the total amount raised in foreign markets, without any distinction of issuance activity taking place in developed or developing markets. Given their limited participation in developing - country markets, firms from developed countries thus typically raise capital in foreign developed markets.

References

Bank of New York. http://www.bnymellon.com/.

BIS (Bank for International Settlements). http://www.bis.org/.

Bloomberg. http://www.bloomberg.com/.

Ceballos, F., T. Didier, and S. Schmukler. 2012a. "Different Facets of Financial Globalisation." VoxEU.org, August 28.

———. 2012b. "Financial Globalization in Emerging Countries: Diversification vs. Offshoring." In *New Paradigms for Financial Regulation: Emerging Market Perspectives,* edited by Mario B. Lamberte and Eswar Prasad, 110–28. Washington, DC: Brookings Institution; Tokyo: ADBI.

Didier, T., C. Hevia, and S. Schmukler. 2012. "How Resilient Were Emerging Economies to the Global Crisis?" *Journal of International Money and Finance* 31 (8): 2052–77.

Errunza, V. 2001. "Foreign Portfolio Equity Investments, Financial Liberalization, and Economic Development." *Review of International Economics* 9: 703–26.

Gourinchas, P. O., N. Govillot, and H. Rey. 2010. "Exorbitant Privilege and Exorbitant Duty." Mimeo. London Business School.

Gourinchas, P. O., and H. Rey. 2007. "International Financial Adjustment." *Journal of Political Economy* 115 (4): 665–703.

IMF (International Monetary Fund). http://www.imf.org/external/index.htm.

———. Balance of Payments Statistics (BOP). http://www.imf.org/external/np/sta/bop/bop.htm.

Lane, P. R., and G. M. Milesi-Ferretti. 2001. "The External Wealth of Nations: Measures of Foreign Assets and Liabilities for Industrial and Developing Countries." *Journal of International Economics* 55: 263–94.

———. 2007. "The External Wealth of Nations Mark II: Revised and Extended Estimates of Foreign Assets and Liabilities, 1970–2004." *Journal of International Economics* 73: 223–50.

SDC Platinum. http://thomsonreuters.com/sdc-platinum/.

Stulz, R. 1999. "Globalization, Corporate Finance, and the Cost of Capital." *Journal of Applied Corporate Finance* 12: 8–25.

5

Financial Globalization in Latin America and the Caribbean: Myth, Reality, and Policy Matters

Eduardo Levy-Yeyati and Tomás Williams

Abstract

Financial globalization, defined as global links through cross-border financial flows, has become increasingly relevant for Latin American markets as they have integrated financially with the rest of the world. This chapter characterizes the evolution of financial globalization in the region across countries and relative to other comparison groups. In particular, the chapter shows that, because of the way financial globalization is often measured, the available evidence has led to the misperception that it has been growing in recent years. Contrary to conventional belief, in the 2000s financial globalization both in Latin America and in other emerging markets has grown only marginally and

Eduardo Levy-Yeyati is a professor at Universidad de Buenos Aires and Universidad Torwato Di Tella, and a Director at Elypsis Partners. Tomás Williams is at Universitat Pompeu Fabra, Barcelona. They want to thank seminar participants at the World Bank and, particularly, Tito Cordella, Augusto de la Torre, Alain Ize, and Sergio Schmukler for their valuable comments and suggestions, as well as Mariana Barrera for excellent research assistance. The material for this chapter borrows extensively from Levy-Yeyati and Williams (2011).

much more slowly than in more advanced markets. In turn, international portfolio diversification (a welfare-improving source of consumption smoothing) has been limited at best and has been declining over time. The chapter also revisits the recent empirical literature on the implications of financial globalization for local market deepening, international risk diversification, and financial contagion. It finds that, whereas financial globalization has indeed fostered the deepening of domestic markets in good times, it has yielded neither the dividends of consumption smoothing nor the costs of amplifying global financial shocks.

Introduction

For a number of reasons, financial globalization, understood as the deepening of cross-border capital flows and asset holdings, has become increasingly relevant for the developing world, including the consequences of its changing composition, its role in the transmission of global financial shocks, its benefits of international risk sharing and business cycle smoothing, and its implications for monetary, exchange rate, and macroprudential policies.

In this chapter, we focus on these issues from a conceptual and empirical perspective, building on, updating, and adapting the existing literature to the case of emerging economies and customizing the discussion to Latin America and the Caribbean (LAC) in particular.

The second section of the chapter looks at alternative measures of financial globalization, how they evolved over the recent period for a group of advanced, emerging, and frontier markets and where we see it moving forward in intensity, direction, and composition. The third section tackles two key trade-offs highlighted in the debate on financial globalization—that between financial globalization, on the one hand, and financial development (understood as the depth of local markets) and financial stability, on the other. The chapter concludes with some normative implications of the empirical analyses presented in the previous sections.

Financial Globalization at First Glance: Is LAC Different?

How do we measure financial globalization?[1] Despite being the subject of a rich and growing literature, the concept of financial globalization has been defined in various, often uncorrelated ways in the academic research.[2] As a result, assessing a country's integration with international financial markets remains a complicated and controversial task.

Indeed, there is a general consensus about the need to distinguish at least between two alternative interpretations of the concept: de jure and de facto financial globalization and associated measures. While the former is based on regulations, restrictions, and controls over capital flows and asset ownership, the latter is related to the intensity of capital flows and cross-market correlation and arbitrage. It is well accepted by now that the extent to which globalization affects asset prices and, more generally, economic performance is related to the intensity and sensitivity of the cross-border flows, that is, de facto financial globalization, typically measured based on foreign asset and liability holdings.

A first, more conventional look at the data is provided by figure 5.1, which compares the evolution of financial globalization for a group of more financially integrated LAC countries (LAC7, which includes Argentina, Brazil, Chile, Colombia, Mexico, Peru, and Uruguay) and other LAC countries, throwing in a sample of non-LAC emerging markets and a group of peripheral core economies that are more readily comparable to the emerging markets. The figure shows the traditional "stock" proxy—foreign assets plus foreign liabilities over gross domestic product (GDP), broken down into equity, debt, and foreign direct investment (FDI)

Figure 5.1 Financial Globalization Measures in Selected Economies, 1990–2007

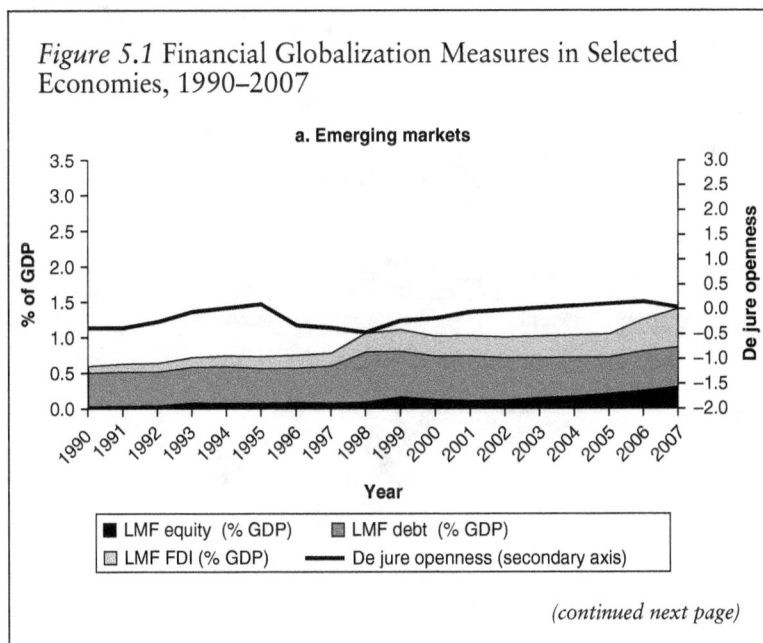

a. Emerging markets

| LMF equity (% GDP) | LMF debt (% GDP) |
| LMF FDI (% GDP) | —— De jure openness (secondary axis) |

(continued next page)

Figure 5.1 (continued)

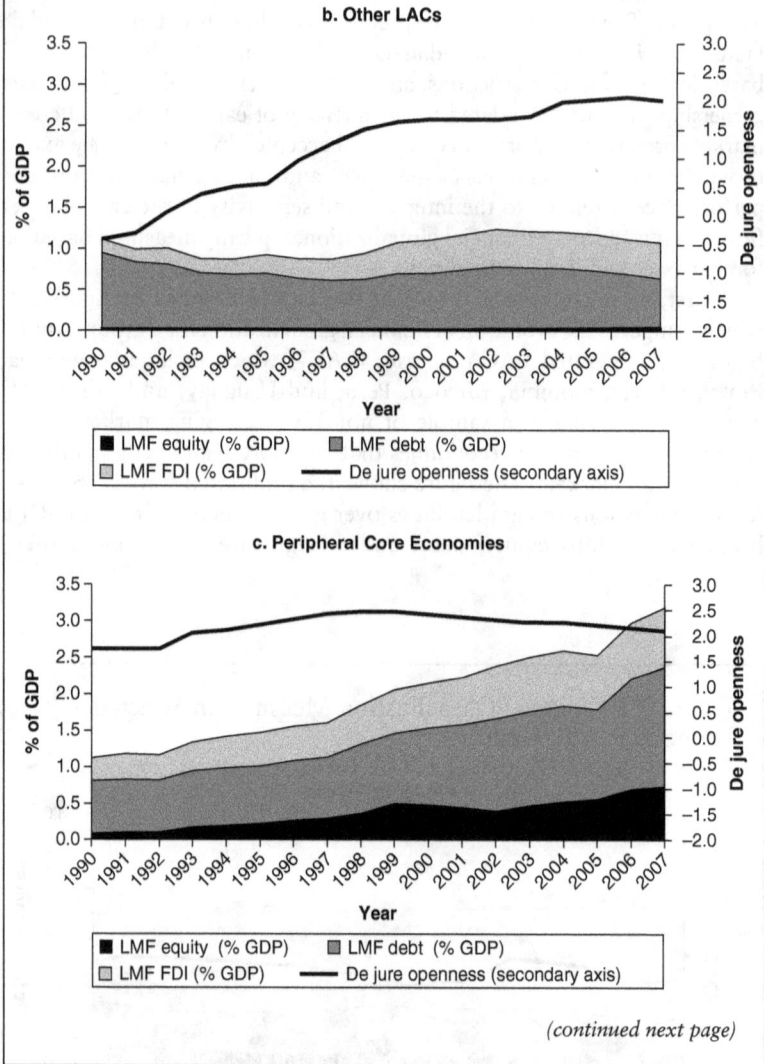

b. Other LACs

c. Peripheral Core Economies

(continued next page)

Figure 5.1 (continued)

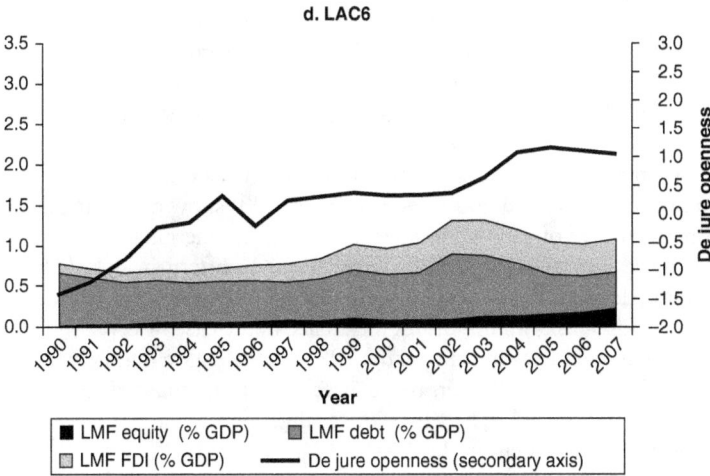

d. LAC6

Sources: Lane and Milesi-Ferretti 2008;WDI; Chinn and Ito 2007.
Note: This figure shows country group averages of de facto financial globalization measures over GDP and de jure measures of financial globalization for balanced panel data. LAC = Latin America and the Caribbean; FDI = foreign direct investment; LMF = Lane and Milesi-Ferretti.

holdings—based on Lane and Milesi-Ferretti's (2007) data, as well as on Chinn and Ito's (2007) de jure measure of financial globalization for comparison.[3]

A few nontrivial aspects emerge from the figure. First, the correlation between de jure and de facto measures of financial globalization is far from perfect. LAC appears to be the only group for which, in the past two decades, de jure financial globalization (higher than for its emerging-market peers) outpaced de facto financial globalization—particularly for non-LAC6 countries (Argentina, Brazil, Chile, Colombia, Mexico, and Peru), where de facto and de jure measures of financial globalization seem to go in opposite ways. De facto financial globalization increases despite a stable de jure financial globalization both for emerging markets and for the more globalized peripheral core economies.

Second, LAC, while not very different from other emerging markets, lags the latter in financial globalization. In LAC, a relatively stable ratio of financial globalization to GDP masks the increasing role of FDI. And more recently, equity markets have become the main vehicles for cross-border investments. These developments, coupled with a marked decline in debt liabilities, offer possible explanations for part of the lag in financial globalization.

This lag can be readily seen in figure 5.2, which compares the cumulative change in foreign stocks for the three different instruments (equity, debt, and FDI) over the periods of 1990–99 and 1999–2007, distinguishing between asset and liability holdings. Again, LAC underperformed emerging markets and peripheral core economies in the 1990s, with the exception of the growth in FDI liabilities, where LAC6 outdid the emerging-markets group, and non-LAC6 ranked above the rest. The 2000s show a similar picture of the performance of LAC economies relative to the emerging-markets group. The figure also shows the already mentioned pattern in debt securities: declining debt liabilities coupled with growing reserve assets, although this combination masks an important difference in the case of LAC: the greater incidence of debt restructuring in the 1990s in the region that helped reduce the debt burden, as well as the real depreciation trend that boosted the ratio of reserves to GDP due to valuation changes—two "supporting" factors that were largely absent in the 2000s.

Figure 5.2 Changes in de Facto Financial Globalization Measures in Selected Economies, 1990–2007

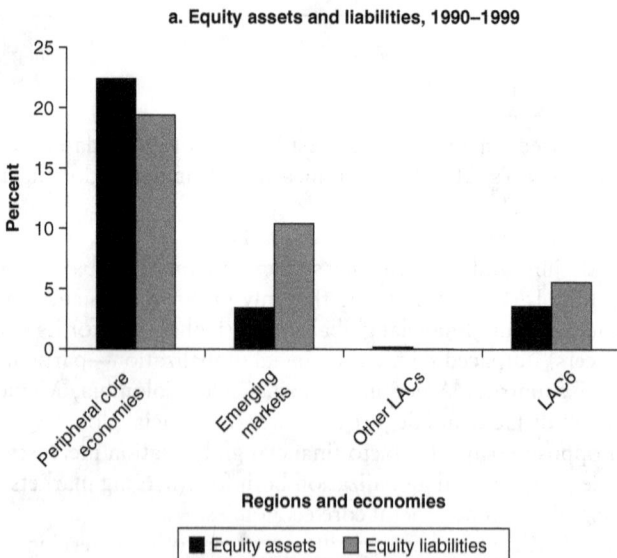

a. Equity assets and liabilities, 1990–1999

Regions and economies

■ Equity assets   ▨ Equity liabilities

(continued next page)

Figure 5.2 *(continued)*

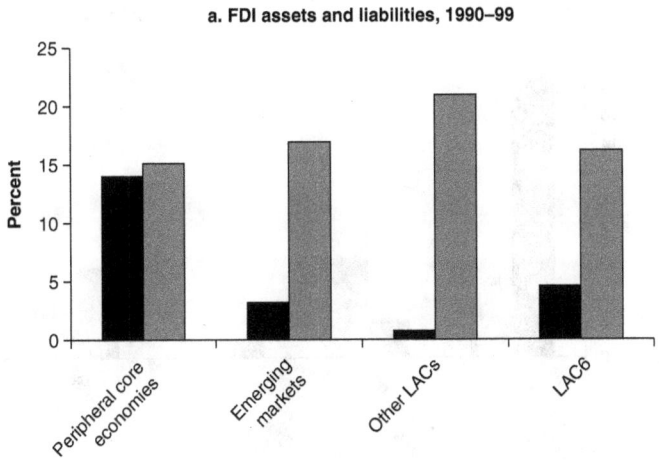

a. FDI assets and liabilities, 1990–99

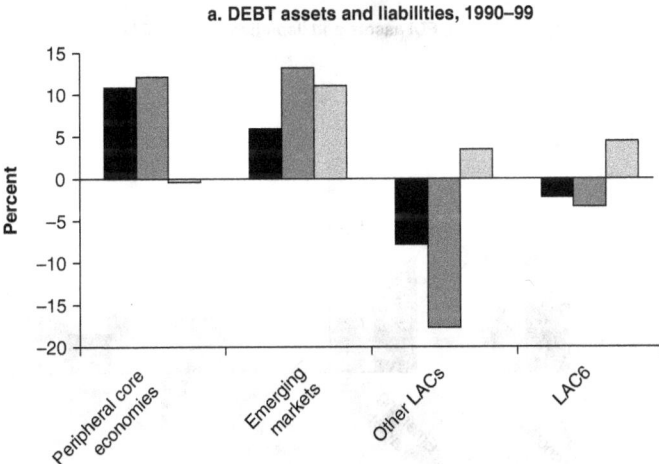

a. DEBT assets and liabilities, 1990–99

(continued next page)

212

Figure 5.2 (continued)

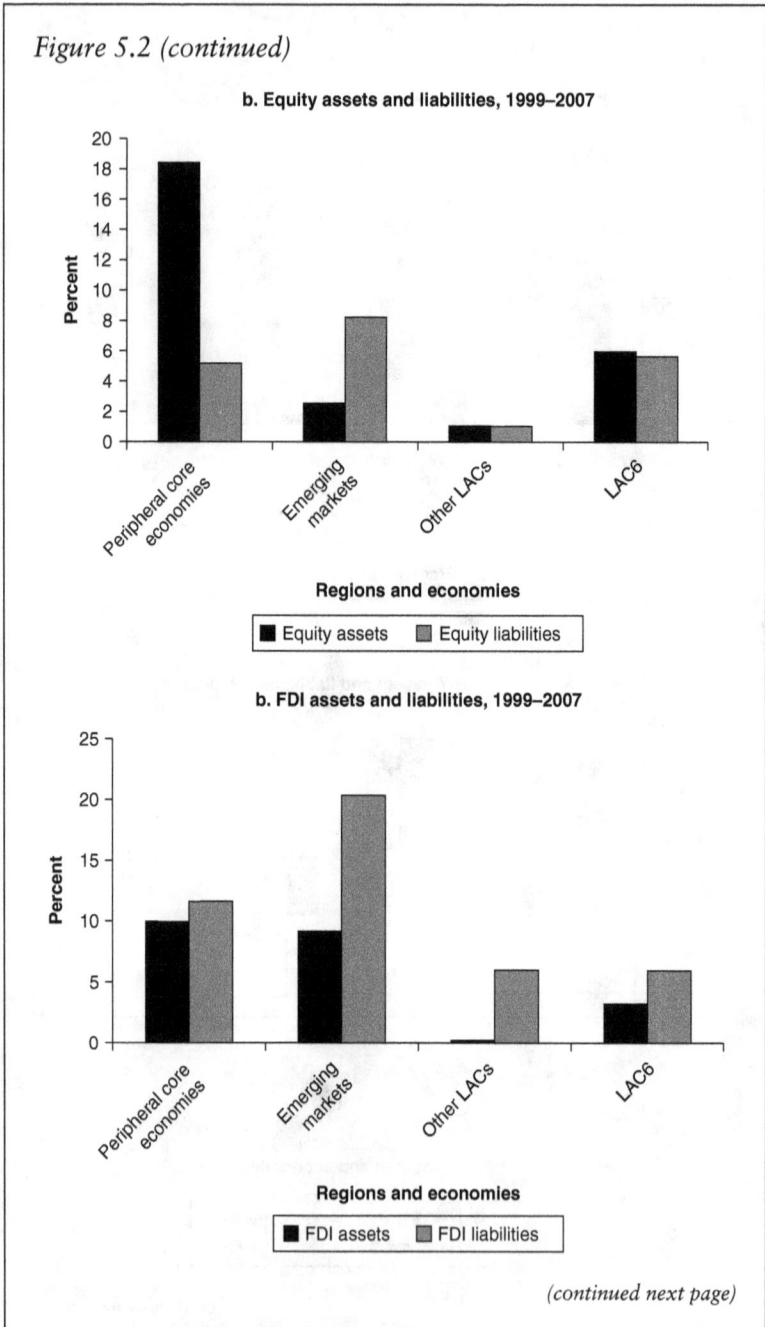

b. Equity assets and liabilities, 1999–2007

Regions and economies

■ Equity assets　■ Equity liabilities

b. FDI assets and liabilities, 1999–2007

Regions and economies

■ FDI assets　■ FDI liabilities

(continued next page)

Figure 5.2 (continued)

b. DEBT assets and liabilities, 1999–2007

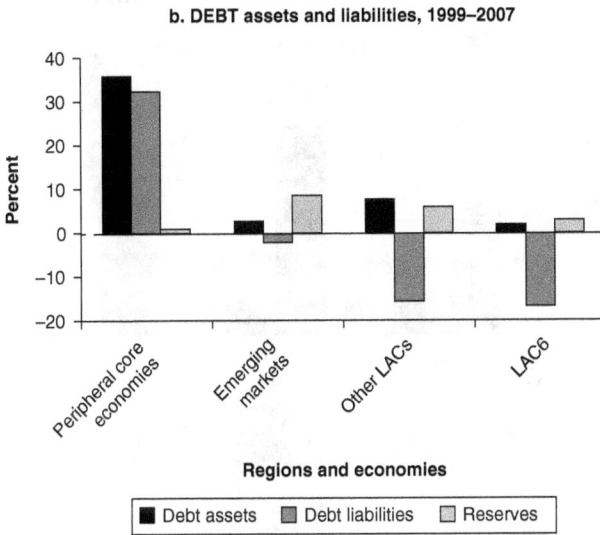

Source: Lane and Milesi-Ferretti 2008; WDI.
Note: This figure shows changes in de facto financial globalization measures from LMF (2008) over GDP. PCE = peripheral core economies; EM = emerging markets; GDP = gross domestic product; FDI = foreign direct investment.

Figure 5.3 offers an alternative cut of the same data on foreign equity and debt liabilities for the 2000s, this time normalizing by the host market capitalization, to focus on the question about whether a growing financial globalization (over GDP) is a sign (and, possibly, a consequence) of greater foreign participation or whether it just reflects (and responds to) the autonomous deepening of domestic markets, including the persistent price rallies.[4] The renormalization shows that the deepening of domestic markets played a central role in explaining the increase in the ratio of financial globalization to GDP, especially for LAC6 equity markets where the ratios of financial globalization to market capitalization (marcap) remained virtually unchanged for the latest period. In turn, a large part of this equity market "deepening" (more precisely, the increase in the ratio of the marcap to GDP during the period) was mechanically driven by price increases rather than by new issuance.

Finally, figure 5.4 looks at the evolution of data on capital flow from the balance of payments statistics, again showing the breakdown into equity and debt securities and FDI, normalizing by the country's GDP.

Figure 5.3 Different Normalizations for Financial
Globalization in Selected Economies, 1999–2007

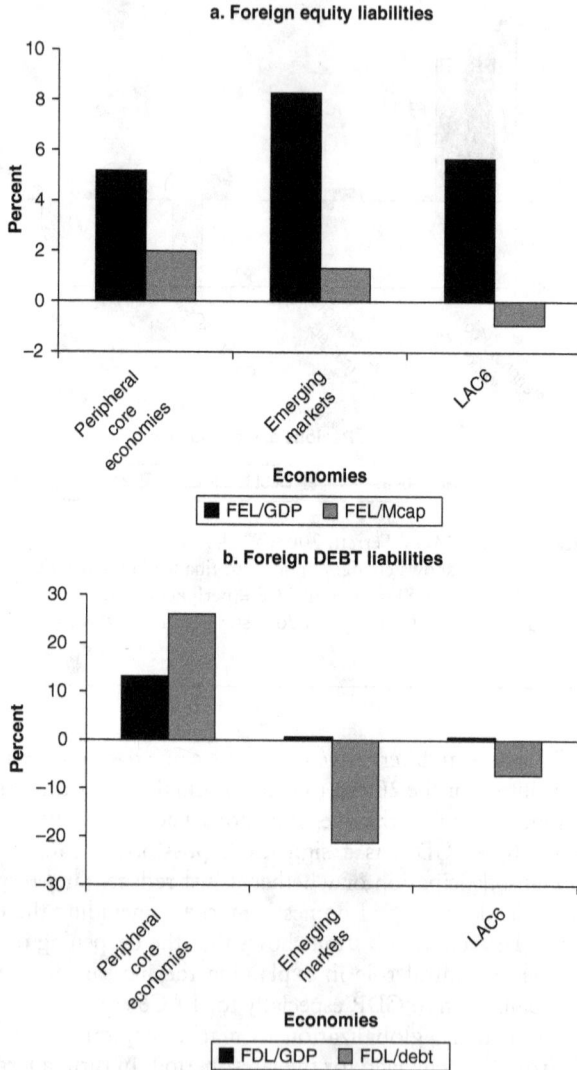

a. Foreign equity liabilities

b. Foreign DEBT liabilities

Source: Lane and Milesi-Ferretti 2008; WDI; BIS.
Note: This figure presents changes in the ratio of foreign equity to market
capitalization and in the ratio of debt liabilities to total debt. Changes are from
1999 to 2007. PCE = peripheral core economies; EM = emerging markets;
LAC = Latin America and the Caribbean; FDL = foreign debt liabilities; GDP =
gross domestic product; FEL = foreign equity liabilities.

Figure 5.4 Financial Globalization Flows in Selected Regions and Economies, 1990–2009

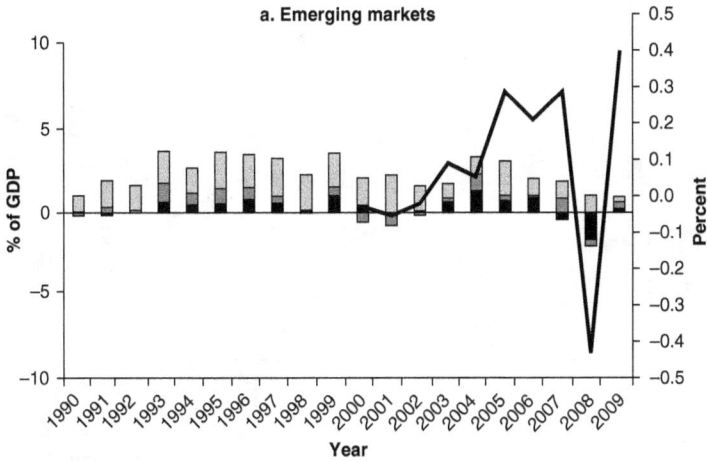

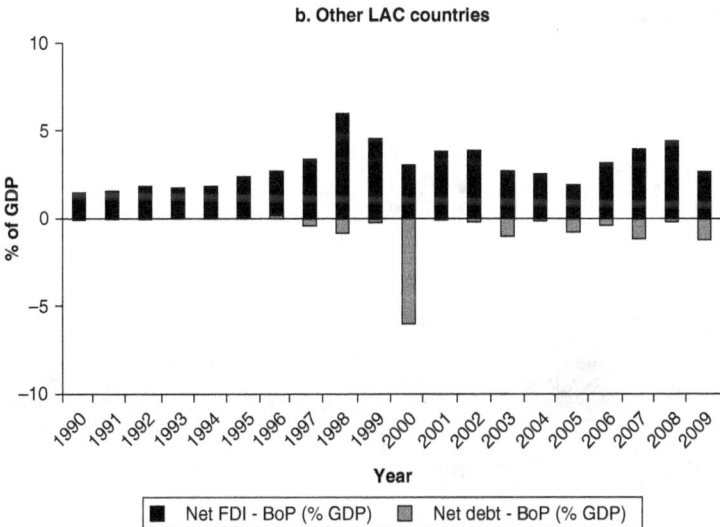

a. Emerging markets

Legend:
■ Net equity - BoP (% GDP) ▨ Net debt - BoP (% GDP)
□ Net FDI - BoP (% GDP) ▬▬ AUM flows (see right axis)

b. Other LAC countries

Legend:
■ Net FDI - BoP (% GDP) ▨ Net debt - BoP (% GDP)

(continued next page)

Figure 5.4 (continued)

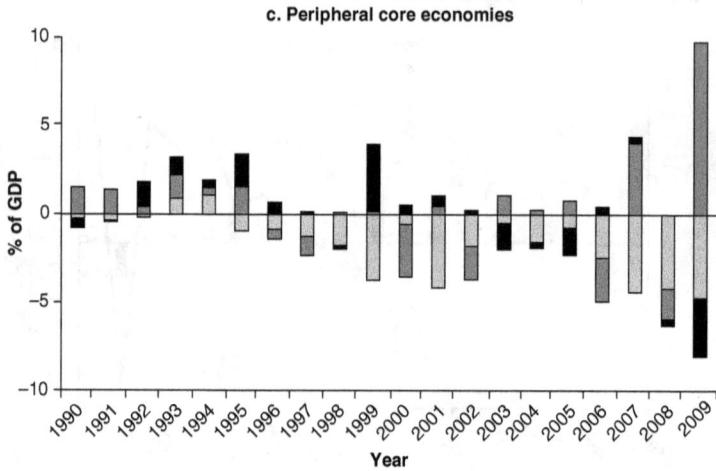

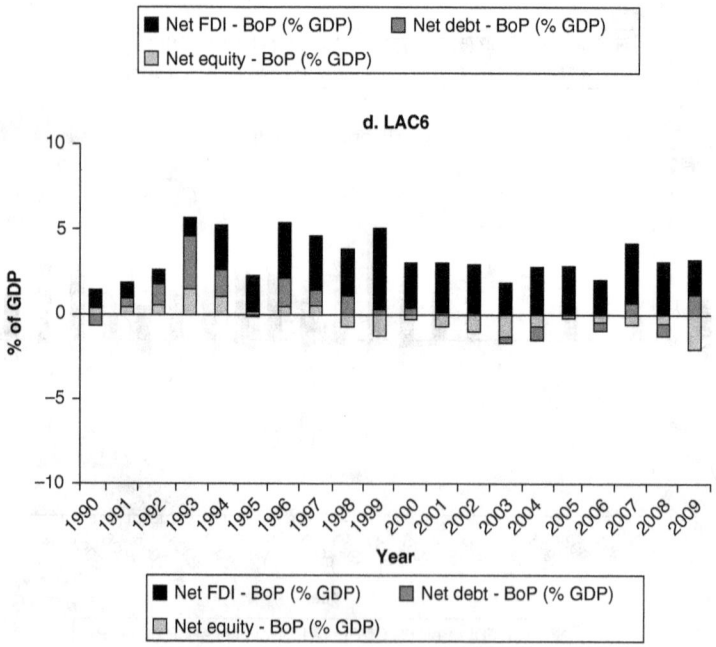

c. Peripheral core economies

d. LAC6

Source: IFS; WDI.
Note: This figure shows country group averages of flow data over GDP for balanced panel data. FDI = foreign direct investment; AUM = assets under management; BoP = balance of payments; GDP = gross domestic product; LAC = Latin America and the Carribbean.

The figure, which illustrates the positive net inflows for the emerging-markets group for most of the period of study, highlights the comparatively smaller portfolio inflow to LAC6: for all the recent debate on hot money and portfolio flows, FDI continues to be the most important (and stable) source of external finance for the group in general. This fact is also true for the emerging-markets group during the early period, although portfolio inflows have matched FDI inflows in recent years. A second aspect to note is the negative debt flow into LAC6, in line with the holdings data, and an indication that the declining foreign debt liability position owes more to the sovereign debt deleveraging process than to a deepening of the domestic corporate debt market. Finally, and perhaps more important, flow data show that financial globalization in emerging markets in general—and LAC in particular, as represented by net cross-market equity and debt flows—clearly lags behind comparable advanced economies.

How correlated are holdings with flows? Is a higher ratio of stock of foreign assets and liabilities to GDP (as financial globalization is typically measured in the economic literature) associated with larger flows of capital in and out of the economy? Note that the previous question goes beyond the mechanical exercise of assessing the extent to which alternative definitions of financial globalization refer to the same economic phenomenon. As noted above, one of the controversial aspects of financial globalization is its influence on local market development and the domestic business cycle through the composition, quality, and intensity of capital flows. At its best, that influence enhances market liquidity and productivity growth in capital-constrained economies and, at its worst, may lead to procyclical overheating, asset inflation, and overindebtedness. From this perspective, are countries with larger foreign holdings more prone to these influences? Can traditional stock measures of financial globalization tell us something about the size of capital flows? As shown in Levy-Yeyati and Williams (2011), the empirical answer is yes, to varying degrees.

Table 5.1 presents a simple illustration with a focus on LAC. Regressing the *absolute value* of balance of payments flows on the beginning-of-the-period holdings (see Lane and Milesi-Ferretti 2007) and controlling for time effects to eliminate common time trends, we find a significant link between holdings and flows, predictably stronger for FDI and equity cross-border flows (a large part of which are traded through benchmarked funds that allocate new flows or liquidate positions in proportion to local market share in the benchmark). Figure 5.5 shows the corresponding partial regression plots.

In short, the first pass at the data on financial globalization provides a few preliminary findings. First, there seems to be less financial globalization in LAC than usually thought. More precisely, if financial globalization in emerging markets lags that in peripheral core economies, LAC6 clearly lags emerging markets *even when financial globalization is measured in GDP*. However, financial globalization in less financially

Table 5.1 Capital Flows and Initial Holdings by Instrument in LAC and Other Emerging Markets, 1990–2007

Variables	EM FE Equity Liab. Flows	EM BE Equity Liab. Flows	LAC6 FE Equity Liab. Flows	LAC6 BE Equity Liab. Flows	Other LACs FE Equity Liab. Flows	Other LACs BE Equity Liab. Flows
Stock of foreign equity liabilities	3.74***	10.49**	2.59*	-7.85	0.00	0.00
	(0.84)	(3.37)	(1.05)	(0.00)	(0.00)	(0.01)
Observations	279	279	102	102	102	102
R^2	0.21	0.82	0.44	0.98	0.17	0.33
Countries	19	19	6	6	6	6

Variables	EM FE Debt Liab.Flows	EM BE Debt Liab.Flows	LAC6 FE Debt Liab.Flows	LAC6 BE Debt Liab.Flows	Other LACs FE Debt Liab.Flows	Other LACs BE Debt Liab.Flows
Stock of foreign debt liabilities	1.97	2.44*	0.10	8.19	0.01	0.00
	(2.41)	(1.20)	(1.81)	(4.36)	(0.02)	(0.03)
Observations	289	289	106	106	101	101
R^2	0.07	0.73	0.17	0.72	0.24	0.60
Countries	18	18	6	6	6	6

Table 5.1 Capital Flows and Initial Holdings by Instrument in LAC and Other Emerging Markets, 1990–2007 *(continued)*

Variables	EM	EM	LAC6	LAC6	Other LACs	Other LACs
	FE	*BE*	*FE*	*BE*	*FE*	*BE*
	FDI Liab. Flows	*FDI Liab. Flows*	*FDI Liab. Flows*	*FDI Liab. Flows*	*FDI Liab. Flows*	*FDI Liab. Flows*
Stock of foreign FDI Liabilities	22.89**	17.30***	−0.90	10.10***	0.04**	0.11**
	(8.84)	(3.71)	(3.74)	(1.21)	(0.01)	(0.03)
Observations	327	327	108	108	102	102
R^2	0.46	0.64	0.44	0.96	0.33	0.80
Countries	19	19	6	6	6	6

Note: Robust standard errors in parentheses. FG stock variables are lagged one period. All estimations include time dummies and capital account openness as additional control. *, **, and *** indicates significance at the 10 percent, 5 percent, and 1 percent level, respectively. LAC = Latin America and the Caribbean; EM = emerging markets; FDI = foreign direct investment; FE = fixed-effects estimation; BE = between estimation.

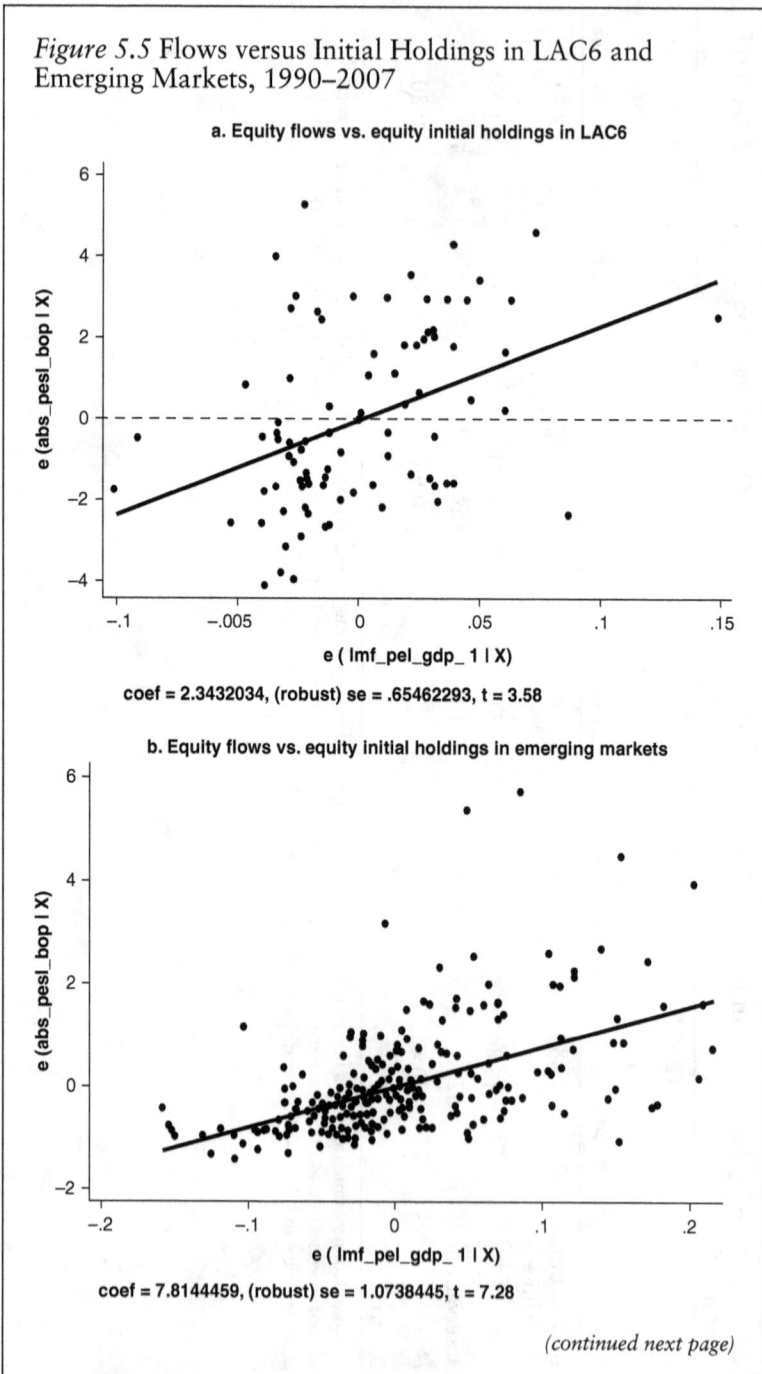

Figure 5.5 Flows versus Initial Holdings in LAC6 and Emerging Markets, 1990–2007

a. Equity flows vs. equity initial holdings in LAC6

coef = 2.3432034, (robust) se = .65462293, t = 3.58

b. Equity flows vs. equity initial holdings in emerging markets

coef = 7.8144459, (robust) se = 1.0738445, t = 7.28

(continued next page)

Figure 5.5 *(continued)*

c. Equity flows vs. equity initial holdings in other LAC countries

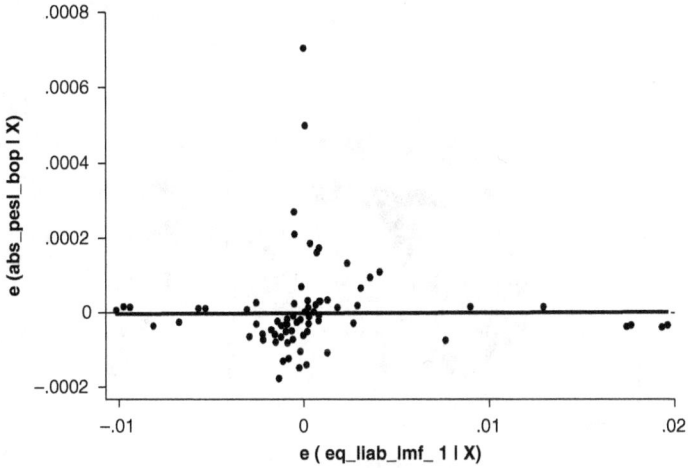

coef = .00021331, (robust) se = .00081951, t = .26

d. Debt flows vs. debt initial holdings in LAC6

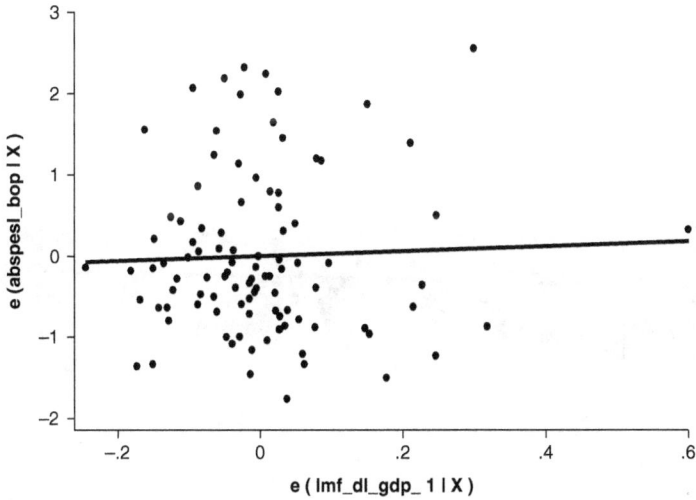

coef = .30657937, (robust) se = .90986862, t = .34

(continued next page)

Figure 5.5 (continued)

e. Debt flows vs. debt initial holdings in emerging markets

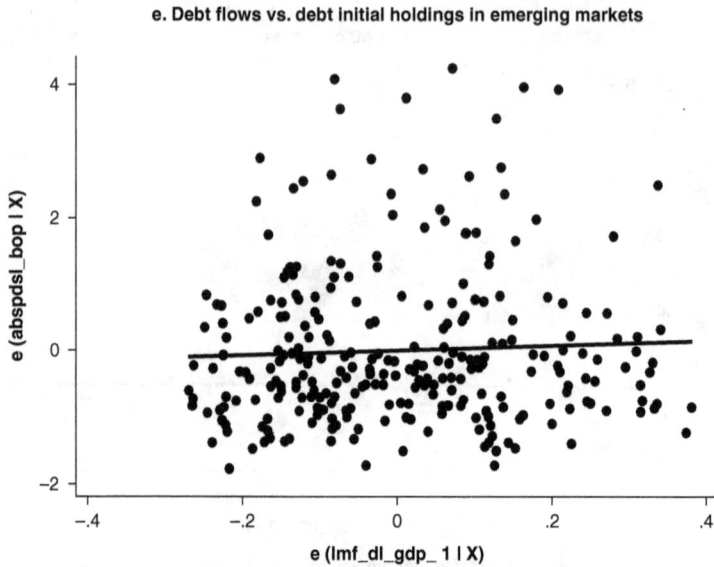

coef = .39341483, (robust) se = .42572822, t = .92

f. Debt flows vs. debt initial holdings in other LAC countries

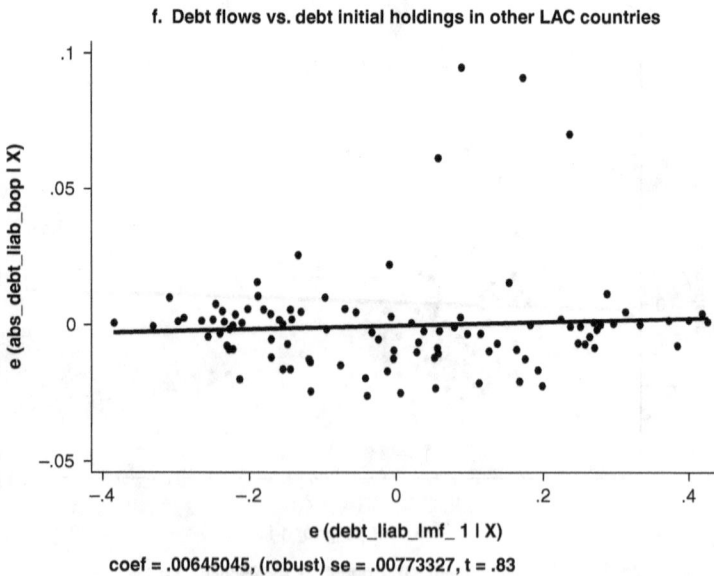

coef = .00645045, (robust) se = .00773327, t = .83

(continued next page)

Figure 5.5 *(continued)*

g. FDI flows vs. FDI initial holdings in LAC6

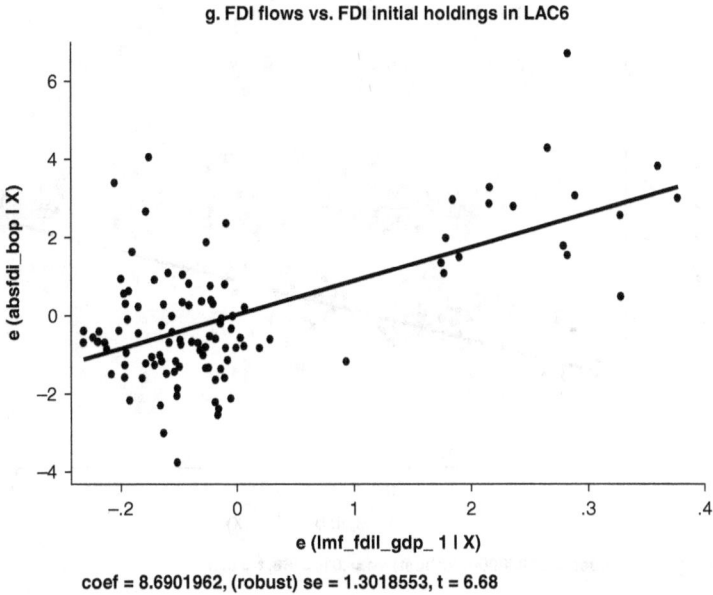

coef = 8.6901962, (robust) se = 1.3018553, t = 6.68

h. FDI flows vs. FDI initial holdings in emerging markets

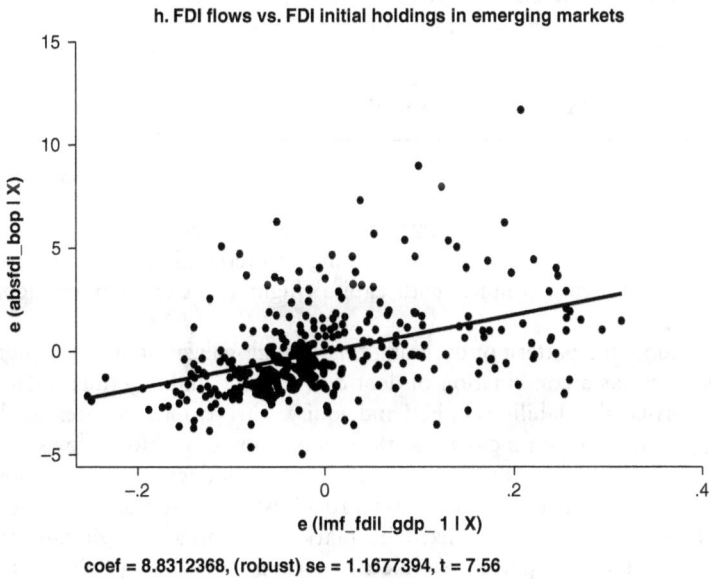

coef = 8.8312368, (robust) se = 1.1677394, t = 7.56

(continued next page)

Figure 5.5 (continued)

i. FDI flows vs. FDI initial holdings in other LAC countries

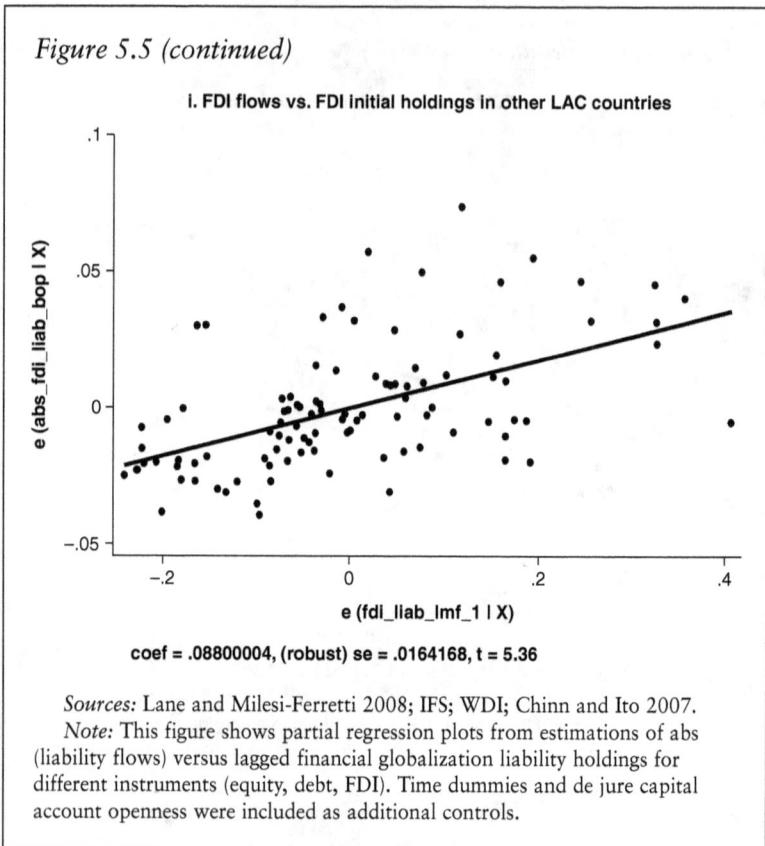

coef = .08800004, (robust) se = .0164168, t = 5.36

Sources: Lane and Milesi-Ferretti 2008; IFS; WDI; Chinn and Ito 2007.
Note: This figure shows partial regression plots from estimations of abs (liability flows) versus lagged financial globalization liability holdings for different instruments (equity, debt, FDI). Time dummies and de jure capital account openness were included as additional controls.

integrated LAC, while higher, is dominated by FDI and debt securities (the latter likely reflecting the offshoring of intermediation: external sovereign borrowing coupled with capital flight to external fixed-income securities).

Second, the pattern of declining financial globalization in LAC7 in the 2000s masks a combination of debt deleveraging and a gradual increase in cross-border liabilities in FDI and equity. This pattern has been used in the past to argue for a change in the composition of portfolio flows (from fixed- to variable-income instruments) more conducive to international risk sharing, as equity liabilities tend to adjust countercyclically.

However, when normalized by market size, financial globalization reveals a different pattern. While the pattern of declining debt persists, and is even more marked for emerging markets as a whole, the growing trend in equity holdings weakens and fully disappears for emerging LAC.[5] This result tells us that the often-cited increase in cross-border equity liabilities in LAC, rather than a proactive relocation of international capital, has largely mirrored the growing depth of local markets, which in turn have been boosted more by price increases before the crisis than by new (primary) issuance.[6]

Unlike in advanced economies, the flow composition of financial globalization is still dominated by FDI, particularly in LAC, a finding in line with its relatively less dynamic equity markets. And while in emerging markets equity flows have been gradually taking over debt flows as their main portfolio vehicle, in the 2000s net equity inflows in emerging LAC continued to be mostly negative, in line with the fall in foreign liability holdings over marcap. All of this contributed to a picture at odds with the globalizing story immediately brought to mind by the media hype and the precrisis boom in the Brazilian stock market.

However, there seems to be little (if any) correlation between de jure and de facto measures. While this finding does not come as a surprise, it warns us that these measures represent different economic aspects and that, at the very least, they should not be used interchangeably. That lack of correlation is also the rationale for our focus on de facto financial globalization in the rest of the chapter.

Finally, for FDI and equity instruments, there seems to be a significant correlation between liability holdings and the corresponding flows, suggesting that, while not interchangeable, larger stocks lead to larger flows, a link relevant to the discussion of financial globalization and financial stability below.

Why Do We Care about Financial Globalization?

Conventional wisdom tells us that financial globalization, by attracting sophisticated investors and considerable liquidity, should foster the development of domestic financial markets.[7] However, deeper, more liquid markets are expected to attract the foreign inflows and larger, more sophisticated investors that require a minimum trading scale.

Indeed, as we have shown above, while ratios of financial globalization to GDP have been on the rise for most emerging markets, ratios of financial globalization to marcap have remained relatively stable. Are the former (the key exhibit behind the conventional view of the ever-rising financial globalization in the emerging world) simply the indication that international investors are catching up, belatedly, with local market developments? Moreover, intuitively, tighter financial integration could foster the transmission of shocks in financial centers to peripheral advanced and developing markets, creating an exogenous source of financial (and ultimately real) instability. In what follows, we review and build on the empirical literature on the causes and consequences of financial globalization.

Does Financial Globalization Foster Financial Depth?

The drivers of financial globalization have not received much attention, despite the increase in financial integration in the past two decades. Many studies acknowledge the link between trade and financial openness, on the one hand, and the link between financial integration and domestic financial development on the other. However, many questions remain unanswered. Does the *composition* of financial integration matter? Is the link instrument specific (that is, does a deep domestic equity market lead to more financial globalization in the equity market, as opposed to financial globalization in general)? How do these links vary across different groups of countries? Finally, and perhaps more important, does financial development cause financial globalization, or is it the other way around?

One can think of a number of portfolio considerations that intervene in the degree and intensity of cross-market investment. For starters, investors tend to maximize risk-adjusted returns across different markets, balancing yield equalization against diversification and risk pooling (the less correlated national markets are, the stronger that tendency of investors). But there are a number of aspects (broadly grouped as *transaction costs*) that are not included in the asset price quotation but may end up being more relevant than attractive yields or hedging benefits. These aspects include not only financial innovation that reduces transfer and settlement costs and facilitates monitoring and transparency but also access to specialized analysis (which, in turn, requires a minimum market size to justify specialization costs) and a rich menu of instruments to cater to specific investors, both of which require a minimum market size to justify specialization and standardization costs. Market size is also critical to liquidity risks, which may keep big players away.

Thus, even in the face of a decline in credit risks (due to enhanced fiscal solvency, for example) or to a decline in currency risk (due to an improved balance of long currency positions or a reduced risk of a speculative attack on the currency), local markets may fail to fully develop scale until they gain a minimum scale. This rather circular logic highlights the simultaneity problem noted above: if, a priori, market depth is a condition of foreign participation and foreign participation fosters market deepening, how can we tell one link from the other?

To shed light on the complex—and possibly bidirectional—connection between financial development and financial globalization, we first build on work by Lane and Milesi-Ferretti (2008) on the drivers of financial globalization, which reports a positive cross-country correlation between their measure of financial globalization (foreign asset plus foreign liabilities over GDP) and financial development (proxied by bank deposits and the ratio of stock market capitalization to GDP), for a sample of emerging markets and advanced markets. We extend their exercise to the period 1995–2007 (the latest year covered by Lane and Milesi-Ferretti (2007), include frontier markets in the sample, and run panel regressions for financial globalization as a whole and broken down into equity, debt, and FDI. In addition, we include time dummies to capture common factors such as global liquidity, risk aversion, or fund reallocations relative to core markets,[8] and GDP per capita as a broad proxy for economic (and domestic financial) development.[9] Last, but not least, the way in which financial globalization is measured is not irrelevant: an improvement in local market conditions should be correlated with an increase in gross (and net) foreign *liabilities* (locals bringing money back; foreigners bringing money in), rather than the standard measure of financial globalization used in Lane and Milesi-Ferretti (2008).

A somewhat telling finding from the results (table 5.2) is the correlation between de jure and de facto financial globalization (the lower the restrictions, the higher Chinn-Ito's index), which is generally not significant or of the opposite sign—yet another reason to focus on de facto measures. Note also that, while the literature that looks at the globalization-financial development link often treats foreign assets and liabilities similarly (as in the standard Lane and Milesi-Ferretti 2007 measure), there is in principle no reason why capital *outflows* should be *positively* related to local market development. By the same token, a deep equity market should attract equity flows but not necessarily other unrelated flows. As expected, there is a stronger connection between the depth of the local equity market and foreign investment in equity.

The results for a sample of equity markets in developing countries show a closer link between local stock market development and foreign equity liabilities than the sum of assets and liabilities used in the original paper. The link between financial development and financial globalization is weaker across countries and stronger over time, where financial development is proxied by the sum of equity market capitalization and bank deposits over GDP as in the original specification in Lane and Milesi-Ferretti (2008) (table 5.2, columns 1 and 2). In addition, the relationship between financial development and financial globalization (column 3) in LAC countries is not unique. After that, we split our financial development proxy and consider bank deposits and equity market capitalization as different variables instead of their sum. Columns 4 and 5 show that financial globalization (as the sum of total foreign assets and liabilities) has a stronger link with bank deposits than with stock market capitalization and still does not show a differential effect for LAC economies. Furthermore, columns 7 and 8 confirm our hypothesis that a deep domestic equity market is strongly linked to more financial globalization in the equity market, as opposed to financial globalization in general. Interestingly, while this relationship is strong among emerging markets, LAC countries do not seem to have experienced the same link (column 9).

Table 5.2 Financial Globalization and Financial Development in Emerging Markets and LAC, 1990–2007

Group of countries	EM	EM	EM+other LACs	EM	EM	EM+other LACs	EM	EM	EM+other LACs	EM	EM
Type of estimation	BE	FE	FE	BE	FE	FE	BE	FE	FE	External GMM	Internal GMM
Variables	(FG)	(FG)	(FG)	(FG)	(FG)	(FG)	(equity liabilities)	(equity liabilities)	(equity liabilities)	(equity marcap)	(equity marcap)
Trade	0.20	0.19	0.15	0.32*	0.18	0.17*	−0.24	−0.26	−0.63		
	(0.14)	(0.13)	(0.11)	(0.16)	(0.12)	(0.09)	(0.41)	(0.54)	(0.67)		
Financial development	0.14	0.38***	0.45***								
	(0.11)	(0.07)	(0.09)								
Financial development*LAC			−0.16								
			(0.14)								
Equity mcap_GDP				0.16*	0.09**	0.07**	0.65**	0.49**	0.65***		
				(0.09)	(0.04)	(0.03)	(0.23)	(0.22)	(0.23)		
Equity mcap_GDP*LAC						−0.02			−0.63*		
						(0.06)			(0.36)		
Bank deposits_GDP				−0.19	0.43***	0.60***	0.63	−0.64*	−0.12		

Table 5.2 Financial Globalization and Financial Development in Emerging Markets and LAC, 1990–2007 *(continued)*

Group of countries	EM	EM	EM+other LACs	EM	EM	EM+other LACs	EM	EM	EM+other LACs	EM	EM
Type of estimation	BE	FE	FE	BE	FE	FE	BE	FE	FE	External GMM	Internal GMM
Variables	(FG)	(FG)	(FG)	(FG)	(FG)	(FG)	(equity liabilities)	(equity liabilities)		(equity marcap)	(equity marcap)
Bank deposits_ GDP*LAC				(0.19)	(0.12)	−0.31 (0.22)	(0.48)	(0.36)	0.19 (0.43)		
Foreign equity liab_ GDP									(1.52)	0.40*** (0.11)	0.41*** (0.13)
GDP per capita PPP	0.14 (0.10)	0.00 (0.21)	−0.12 (0.21)	0.14 (0.10)	−0.14 (0.24)	−0.27 (0.24)	0.21 (0.25)	1.47* (0.85)	0.10 (0.77)	0.41 (0.74)	0.54 (0.79)
KA openness	0.11* (0.06)	−0.01 (0.02)	−0.01 (0.02)	0.09 (0.06)	−0.01 (0.02)	0.00 (0.02)	−0.01 (0.16)	0.09 (0.10)	0.06 (0.11)		
Constant	−2.58** (1.14)	−2.43 (1.94)	−1.08 (1.78)	−2.75** (1.13)	−1.40 (2.15)	0.22 (2.01)	−7.37** (2.87)	−14.95* (7.28)	−3.59 (7.75)		
P-value joint test	0.24			0.24	0.00***	0.00***	0.00***	0.03**			

230

Table 5.2 Financial Globalization and Financial Development in Emerging Markets and LAC, 1990–2007 (continued)

Group of countries	EM	EM	EM+other LACs	EM	EM	EM+other LACs	EM	EM	EM+other LACs	EM	EM
Type of estimation	BE	FE	FE	BE	FE	FE	BE	FE	FE	External GMM	Internal GMM
Variables	(FG)	(FG)	(FG)	(FG)	(FG)	(FG)	(equity liabilities)	(equity liabilities)	(equity marcap)	(equity marcap)	(equity marcap)
Observations	326	326	375	326	326	375	326	326	342	323	323
Countries	27	27	32	27	27	32	27	27	30	27	27
R-squared within	0.55	0.58	0.57	0.59	0.58	0.58	0.74	0.54	0.47		

Note: Robust standard errors in parentheses. BE = between estimation; FE = fixed-effects estimation. All variables are in log terms except KA openness (capital account openness). All variables are lagged one period except for the foreign exchange variables. All estimations include time dummies. Joint test is FD_1 = FD_2=0. GMM = dynamic GMM estimation, and in parentheses is the type of instruments used. External instruments is the regional (EM) stock of the financial globalization (FG) variable excluding the corresponding country.

*, **, and *** indicate significance at the 10 percent, 5 percent, and 1 percent level, respectively. LAC = Latin America and the Caribbean; EM = emerging markets; GDP = gross domestic product; FG = financial globalization; PPP = purchasing power parity; GMM = generalized method of moments; marcap = market capitalization.

As noted, the strong relationship between financial globalization and financial domestic development comes with a severe endogeneity problem: foreign flows to equity and local debt markets, by definition, add to these markets' liquidity and depth. Is it the domestic market depth that draws foreign inflows, or is it instead the foreign inflows that foster the deepening of domestic markets? The connection between financial globalization and domestic financial markets has been noted by Rajan and Zingales (2003), who emphasize the impact of financial globalization and trade liberalization on the size of the domestic financial sector. In the same direction, the dynamic Generalized Method of Moments (GMM) estimates with internal instruments of Baltagi, Demetriades, and Law (2009) suggest that both financial globalization and trade openness *cause* greater financial development (measured separately as private credit and local stock market capitalization).

This causality problem is best approached by looking at foreign liabilities and the domestic depth of the equity market.[10] In line with Baltagi, Demetriades, and Law (2009), we estimate a GMM, albeit with a few changes. We focus on the more homogeneous emerging-markets group and compute, for each country-year, equity averages excluding its own ratio, as an external instrument. We do this under the assumption that financial globalization, highly correlated across emerging markets (the median correlation between individual equity liability holdings and their emerging-market group aggregates is 0.86), can affect financial development only in the host country.[11] The results indicate that equity inflows, indeed, appear to foster the deepening of the equity market (table 5.2, columns 10 and 11).

What can we conclude from this preliminary evidence? While foreign capital does seem to flow to larger, deeper markets, there is at least some indicative evidence that it also has contributed to developing the corresponding local market. For example, growing foreign holdings of emerging-market equity (rather than broader measures of financial globalization) led to growing equity markets in developing countries. Ultimately, in this regard, foreign capital is not different from domestic capital: it is attracted to liquidity in the marketplace, and it attracts liquidity in the marketplace.

Financial Globalization and International Risk Sharing

In past theoretical research studies, the implications of financial integration and macroeconomic volatility were clear: countries with greater financial globalization should reduce consumption relative to output volatility through international risk sharing.

In theory, one of the most important benefits of financial globalization comes by allowing more efficient international risk sharing in a country. As stated in the literature, more efficient international risk sharing may help reduce consumption volatility. Standard theoretical open-economy models yield clear testable implications for the role of financial integration in risk sharing: the further the country is from financial autarky, the lower the correlation is between consumption and domestic output, and the greater the correlation is of consumption across (financially integrated) countries. Furthermore, models with complete markets predict that the correlation of the growth of consumption with the growth of world output (or, equivalently, world consumption) would be higher than that with domestic output.

Recent empirical studies have failed to validate this premise. Kose, Prasad, and Terrones (2007) analyze output and consumption growth rates and their volatilities for the period 1960–2004 and find little evidence of a beneficial effect from financial globalization on international risk sharing (as captured by a smoothing out of output changes in the consumption pattern, once common global shocks are filtered out). In particular, following a standard risk-sharing measure they measure risk sharing as the consumption betas estimated from

$$\Delta\log(c_{it}) - \Delta\log(C_t) = \alpha + \beta(\Delta\log(y_{it}) - \Delta\log(Y_{it})) + \varepsilon_{it}, \qquad (5.1)$$

where $c_{it}(y_{it})$ is country i's purchasing-power-parity (PPP)-adjusted per capita consumption to GDP ratio and $C_t(Y_{it})$ is the world's per capita consumption to GDP ratio.[12] C_t and Y_{it} are, respectively, measures of aggregate (common) movements in consumption and output. Since it is not possible to share the risk associated with common fluctuations, the common component of each variable is subtracted from the corresponding national variable. The difference between the national and the common world component of each variable captures the idiosyncratic (country-specific) fluctuations in that variable. In this specification, under complete markets and perfect international risk sharing, the left-hand side of the equation should be zero.

In turn, to assess the influence of financial globalization on international risk, they estimate

$$\Delta\log(c_{it}) - \Delta\log(C_t) = \alpha + \mu(\Delta\log(y_{it}) - \Delta\log(Y_{it})) +$$
$$\lambda FG_i(\Delta\log(y_{it}) - \Delta\log(Y_{it})) + \varepsilon_{it}, \qquad (5.2)$$

where FG_i is a measure of the country's financial globalization over the period, and the degree of risk sharing is measured by $(1 - \mu - \lambda FG)$, where a negative λ would indicate higher risk sharing for higher financial globalization. The study focuses on three measures of financial integration—gross holdings (the sum of foreign assets and liability holdings), assets holdings, and liability holdings—and finds that financial globalization improves risk sharing only for the late period (1987–2004), the one most closely associated with an advance in financial globalization, and only for advanced economies.[13]

The data do not support these premises. The figures shown in table 5.3 indicate that consumption volatility generally exceeds that of output. Moreover, the same figures suggest that, for more financially integrated economies, the volatility of consumption growth relative to that of output has increased in past decades, while it has decreased for less financially integrated economies.

At first glance, the data indicate that this pattern has continued to prevail and that LAC economies are no exception. Table 5.3 presents descriptive statistics of growth and consumption volatility for 1995–2007 (and the subperiod 2000–07), across our selected country groups, which indicate that, in recent years, output volatility and economic growth seem

Table 5.3 Economic Growth and Volatility (group median)

| | Full sample | | | Late period | | |
| | 1995–2007 | | | 2000–07 | | |
	Volatility Y	*Volatility C*	*Ratio*	*Volatility Y*	*Volatility C*	*Ratio*
Full	2.05	2.32	1.13	1.57	1.85	1.18
sample	(1.72)	(2.36)		(1.55)	(2.20)	
AM	1.20	1.10	0.92	1.23	1.00	0.81
	(0.46)	(0.77)		(0.38)	(0.91)	
EM	3.21	4.30	1.34	1.95	2.35	1.21
	(1.78)	(2.22)		(2.00)	(2.48)	
FM	2.11	3.53	1.67	1.97	3.11	1.58
	(1.27)	(2.29)		(0.59)	(1.93)	
LAC7	3.23	3.36	1.04	2.13	2.18	1.03
	(1.76)	(2.16)		(2.72)	(3.16)	
MFI	2.88	4.66	1.62	1.70	2.96	1.74
	(1.82)	(2.43)		(2.37)	(2.74)	
LFI	2.20	3.36	1.53	2.05	2.12	1.03
	(1.65)	(1.98)		(0.86)	(1.86)	

Sources: WDI; World Bank data; Lane and Milesi-Ferretti 2008.

Note: More financially integrated (MFI) economies are economies that are above our median sample for financial openness (as measured by the stock sum of foreign assets and liabilities) but are not part of the advanced markets (AM) group. The same applies for less financially integrated economies (LFI) but for economies that are below our median sample value for financial openness. Full sample is 1995–2007, and the late period is 2000–07. Standard errors appear in parentheses. EM = emerging markets; FM = frontier markets.

to have moved hand in hand. Emerging markets exhibit the highest output volatility, advanced economies the lowest, and frontier markets lie in between. Interestingly, growth volatilities in LAC7 are comparable to those of emerging markets, but consumption volatilities range much lower.

Overall, the ratio of consumption to growth volatility ranks according to priors: the lower for presumably more financially integrated advanced markets, followed by emerging markets and frontier markets. However, when, following Kose, Otrok, and Prasad (2006), we divide the developing group (emerging markets plus frontier markets) into more financially integrated economies and less financially integrated economies (according to whether the ratio of financial globalization to GDP lies above or below the sample median), the link is much less clear: in contrast with less financially integrated economies, more financially integrated economies do not appear to have benefited from smoother consumption volatility, despite the marked decline in growth volatility.[14]

Figure 5.6a offers another glance at the same evidence: the country-specific sensitivity of consumption to output growth (relative to global values), estimated based on annual data, appears to have remained stubbornly close to 1 in the past two decades.

To measure the impact of financial globalization on risk sharing in LAC more rigorously, we proceed in two steps. We first estimate, for the period 1995–2007, "consumption betas" country by country using equation (5.1). Next, we run a regression of estimated betas on alternative measures of financial globalization.[15] The standard financial globalization proxy appears negatively correlated with betas for the whole sample (figure 5.6b), but the link is not significant (and changes sign for emerging markets). Interestingly, LAC countries appear closer to the pattern of advanced markets.[16]

Why this disappointing result? Kose, Prasad, and Terrones (2007) address and discard a number of potential explanations (measurement errors, country characteristics, composition of financial globalization), to propose two hypotheses: (a) a threshold effect, namely, the idea that countries need to achieve a minimum degree of integration to reap the diversification benefits (a proposition prompted by the better results they find for advanced markets); and (b) the procyclicality of capital flows in emerging markets, which in principle may offset the risk-sharing benefits of financial globalization.

While the first hypothesis is virtually impossible to verify, a casual look at the data suggests that a simple threshold cannot explain the whole story. The fact that emerging economies today exhibit levels of financial globalization comparable to those exhibited by advanced markets in the past begs the question, Do developing countries with advanced market–level financial globalization have a better risk-sharing pattern? Figure 5.6c shows consumption and GDP growth pairs within the developing group for the period 1995–2007, broken into high and low financial

Figure 5.6 Consumption Smoothing and Financial Globalization

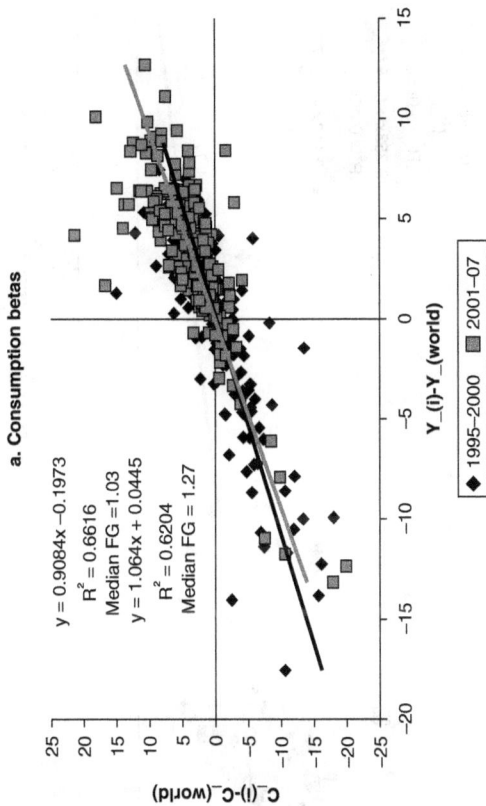

a. Consumption betas

y = 0.9084x −0.1973
R^2 = 0.6616
Median FG =1.03
y = 1.064x + 0.0445
R^2 = 0.6204
Median FG = 1.27

C_(i)−C_(world)

Y_(i)−Y_(world)

◆ 1995–2000   ■ 2001–07

(continued next page)

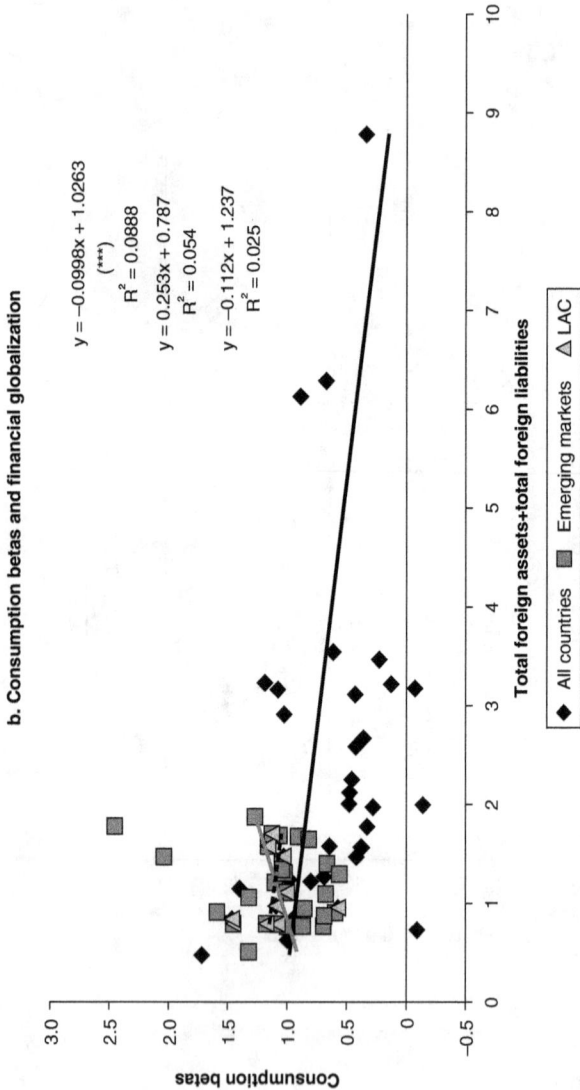

Figure 5.6 (continued)

b. Consumption betas and financial globalization

$y = -0.0998x + 1.0263$
$(***)$
$R^2 = 0.0888$

$y = 0.253x + 0.787$
$R^2 = 0.054$

$y = -0.112x + 1.237$
$R^2 = 0.025$

Consumption betas

Total foreign assets+total foreign liabilities

◆ All countries   ▪ Emerging markets   △ LAC

(continued next page)

Figure 5.6 (continued)

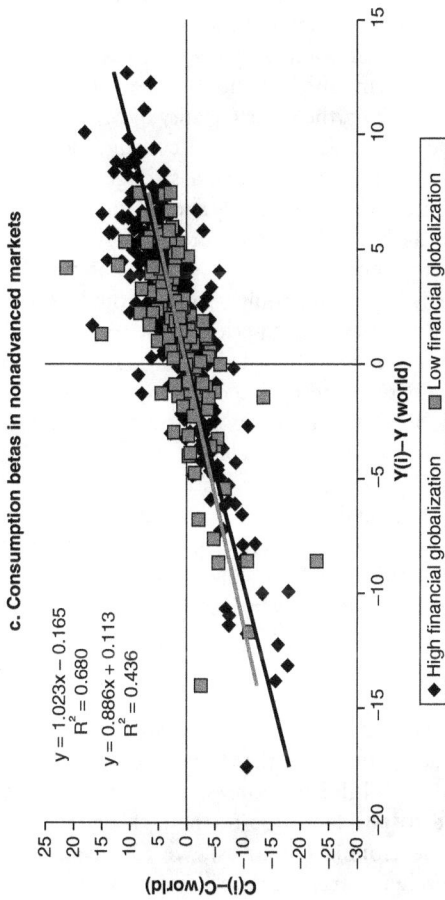

c. Consumption betas in nonadvanced markets

$y = 1.023x - 0.165$
$R^2 = 0.680$

$y = 0.886x + 0.113$
$R^2 = 0.436$

♦ High financial globalization   ■ Low financial globalization

Source: WDI; Lane and Milesi-Ferretti 2008.

Note: 5.6a shows a scatterplot of consumption and output growth during 1995–2000 and 2001–2007. $X_(i)$-$X_(World)$ refers to the domestic variable minus the world variable. C and Y represent consumption and output growth per capita. Financial globalization is determined by economies above the median sample of the ratio of foreign assets and liabilities to GDP. 5.6b presents a scatterplot of consumption betas as measured by the slope of $C_(i)$-$C_(World)$ to $Y_(i)$-$Y_(World)$ vs FG/GDP. 5.6c shows a scatterplot of consumption and output growth dividing the sample into high and low financial globalization, determined by the lower bound of financial globalization in advanced markets. If the country is above the lower bound, it belongs to the high financial globalization group.The sample in 5.6c excludes advanced markets. Financial globalization is sum of total assets and liabilities from LMF over gross domestic product. FG = financial globalization; LAC = Latin America and the Caribbean; EM = emerging market.

*** denotes significance at the 1 percent level.

globalization, according to whether the level of financial globalization of a given pair lies within the range of advanced markets for the same period. As can be seen, the results, if anything, contradict the hypothesis: high financial globalization pairs display higher consumption betas.

The second hypothesis is also hard to substantiate in the data. For starters, the diversification benefits of financial globalization as measured in the literature (in terms of international portfolio diversification) should in principle work through a decoupling of residents' income from the domestic economic cycle. By borrowing and investing abroad, residents benefit from income from their foreign assets that is uncorrelated with the domestic cycle, while sharing the ups and downs of the domestic cycle with foreign lenders. In this light, the procyclicality of capital flows should a priori have little to do with risk sharing and consumption smoothing: indeed, to the extent that capital flows have a stronger impact on GDP growth than on the consumption pattern, they should increase "measured" risk sharing. Moreover, as Kose and coauthors suggest, the recent shift away from procyclical fixed-income securities (most notably, bonded debt) to variable-income vehicles (FDI and equity flows) should have mitigated capital flow procyclicality in the recent period, which is at odds with the persistently high consumption betas found in recent data (figure 5.6a).

Therefore, we highlight two alternative reasons that, we believe, may explain why higher financial globalization does not lead to a smoother consumption pattern. The first one is related, again, to measurement considerations. If consumption smoothing is the result of a diversified portfolio, the standard financial globalization measure may not be the best gauge. The discussion of the price effect in equity markets is a good illustration of the limits of financial globalization over GDP as a proxy for portfolio diversification: as equity prices rise, the share of foreign equity over GDP also rises, regardless of whether the foreign share of the residents' equity portfolio changes. Thus, we may be seeing increased diversification when there is none.

More generally, by looking only at the standard proxy for financial globalization, we miss domestic assets that typically represent the largest part of residents' wealth. While the domestic-foreign composition or physical assets are hard to estimate (due to the lack of reliable data on capital stock for most developing countries), we can measure portfolio diversification as the foreign share of the representative resident's equity and debt security portfolio by combining Lane and Milesi-Ferretti and market capitalization figures, such that:

$$PD \text{ (equities + debt securities)} = FEA + FDA/[(FEA + \text{equity market cap} - FEL) + (FDA + \text{total debt} - FDL)],$$

where FEA and FEL (FDA and FDL) are foreign equity (debt) assets and liabilities.

This new measure has two advantages for our purposes: it tells us the degree of portfolio diversification and tracks its evolution over time, filtering out time trends such as equity price cycles. Figure 5.7a illustrates the first aspect: note the stark contrast between advanced economies and the rest. If financial globalization leads to risk sharing, the degree of portfolio diversification in the developing world appears at first sight to be too low to have a meaningful impact. LAC6 scores slightly higher than the average emerging market—perhaps because of the characteristic offshoring of local savings due to sovereign risk (see Levy-Yeyati 2007)—but still well short of advanced markets. Moreover, despite the increase in financial globalization, both in emerging markets and in LAC6, portfolio diversification has been declining over time (perhaps the reflection of local market development and the undoing of offshoring).[17] At any rate, both the limited diversification and the lack of time correlation between standard measures of financial globalization and the external domestic composition of residents' portfolios could explain why financial globalization has not been accompanied by a better global risk-sharing pattern.

Reassuringly, substituting this new measure (portfolio diversification) for the standard measure of financial globalization in figure 5.8, we obtain a better fit and a negative slope for emerging markets, although the result is still not significant, possibly because of the limited range of portfolio diversification exhibited by the group (figure 5.7b). Now LAC seems to be in line with emerging markets, with portfolio diversification displaying only a very weak correlation with consumption betas.

While the use of portfolio diversification brings the analysis conceptually closer to a risk-sharing test and the data empirically closer to the expected negative correlation between globalization and risk sharing, the actual result is still far from the theoretical result. This should not be surprising, given the rather low degree of diversification in the developing world. Moreover, the menu of financial assets in middle to- low-income countries is often limited and accessible only to a small population of high-income households.

What if financial assets were made available to the middle class with savings capacity, the class often associated with more advanced economies? And why is risk sharing so limited in the developed world where financial sophistication and access should not be such a problem? An additional reason why the global diversification of financial portfolios does not immediately translate into smoother (less cyclical) consumption patterns, independent of portfolio composition and financial access, lies in the fact that financial assets tend to move very close to each other, particularly during extreme events. In other words, the international diversification margin may have been declining along with a steady process of financial recoupling—a subject to which we turn next.

Figure 5.7 Portfolio Diversification and Risk Sharing in Selected Countries and Economies, 1999 and 2007

a. Portfolio diversification

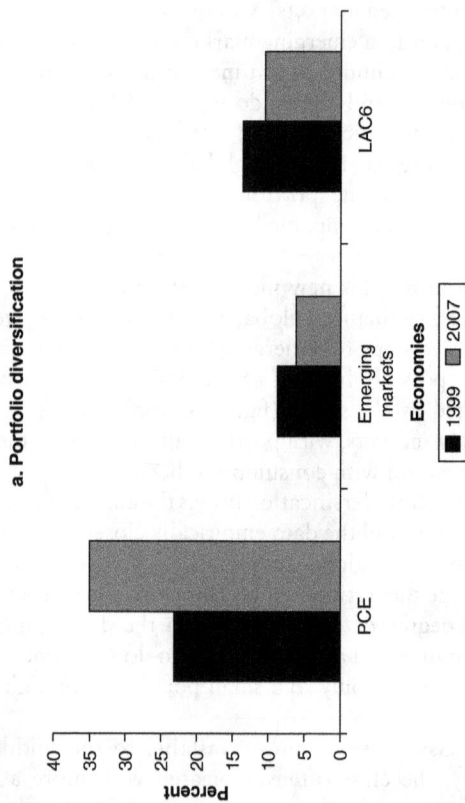

(continued next page)

Figure 5.7 (continued)

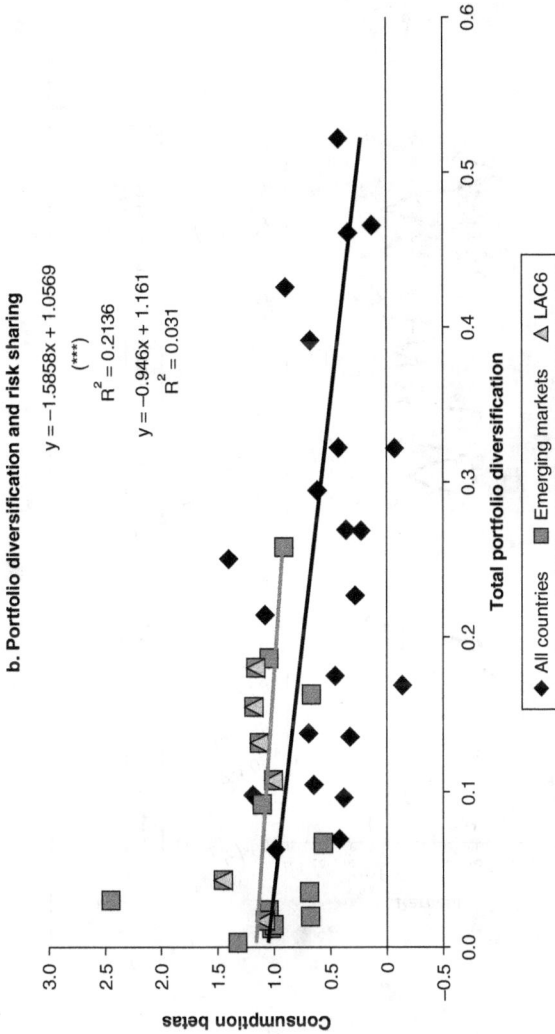

b. Portfolio diversification and risk sharing

$y = -1.5858x + 1.0569$
$(***)$
$R^2 = 0.2136$

$y = -0.946x + 1.161$
$R^2 = 0.031$

Consumption betas

Total portfolio diversification

◆ All countries   ■ Emerging markets   △ LAC6

Source: Lane and Milesi-Ferretti 2008; WDI; BIS.
Note: 5.7b presents a scatterplot of consumption betas as measured by the slope of $C_{-}(i)\text{-}C_{-}(World)$ to $Y_{-}(i)\text{-} Y_{-}(World)$ vs. portfolio diversification. Portfolio diversification is measured as $(FEA+FDA)/(NFEA+NFEA+Mcap+Total Debt)$. FEA = foreign equity assets; FDA = foreign debt assets; NFEA is net foreign equity assets; NFDA is net foreign debt assets.
   *** denotes significance at the 1 percent level.

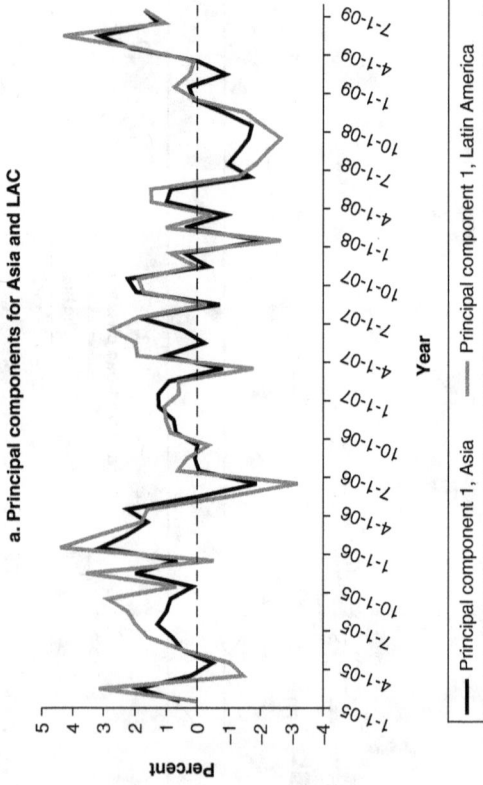

Figure 5.8 Equity Flows from Global Funds in Selected Regions and Countries, 2005–09

a. Principal components for Asia and LAC

(continued next page)

Figure 5.8 *(continued)*

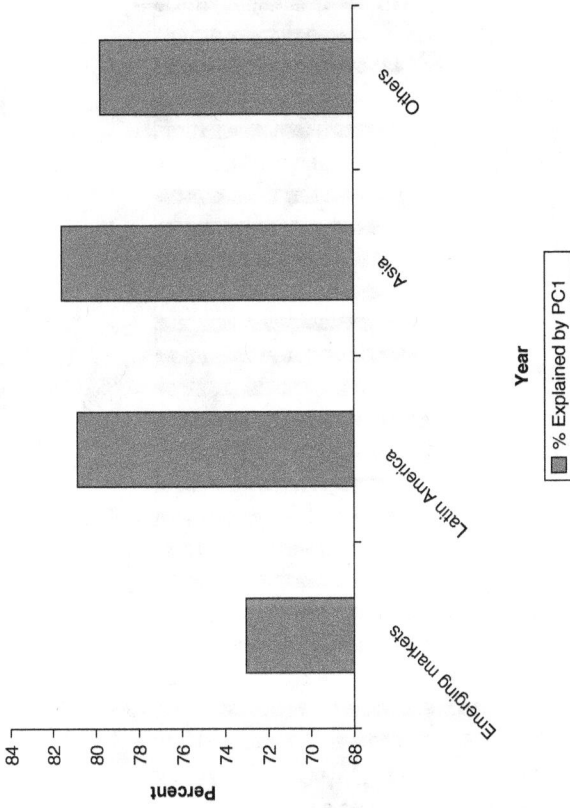

b. Percentage of global fund flows explained
by the principal component

(continued next page)

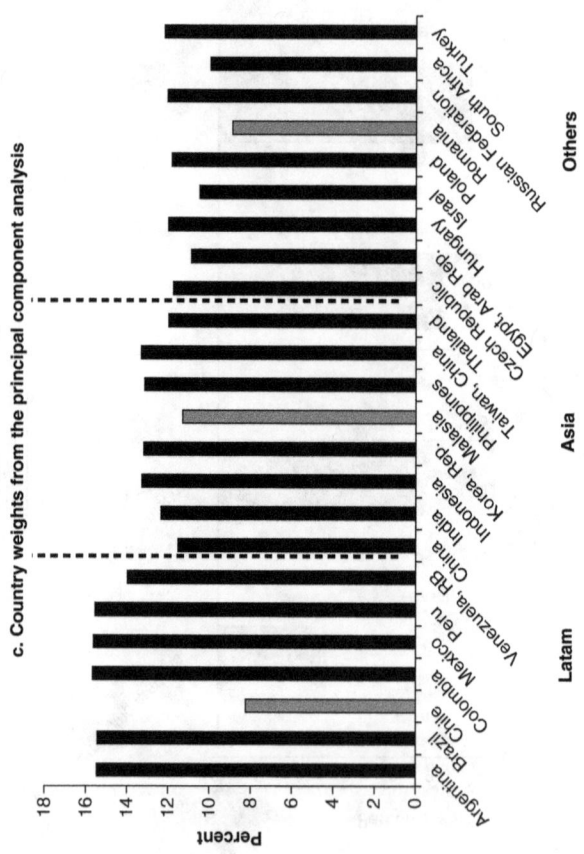

Figure 5.8 (continued)

c. Country weights from the principal component analysis

Source: Authors' calculations based on EPFR Global.

Note: 5.8a indicates the ratio of global fund flows over assets under management (AUM) (the latter lagged one period). The series are created from the weights of the first principal component for each region. 5.8b shows the percentage of flows' variance for each group explained by its first principal component. 5.8c indicates the weights from the first principal component of the AUM flows/AUM stocks ratio (computed separately for each region). PC1 = first principal component.

Financial Globalization and Asset Market Comovement: A Decade of Financial Recoupling

The debate on real decoupling in emerging markets—the comovement of national and global output cycles—has been receiving increasing attention in the literature. While there are arguments that favor the view that emerging economies have decoupled from industrial or advanced countries (see, for instance, Kose, Otrok, and Prasad 2008), others have argued that the decoupling evidence is not so robust (Rose 2009 or Wälti 2009, for example). An alternative account emphasizes that emerging markets have decoupled from core economies as a result of their strengthening ties with China, particularly in commodity-exporting LAC7 (Levy-Yeyati and Williams 2011).

However, the idea that this real decoupling, founded in a newly gained policy autonomy and macroeconomic resilience to external shocks, has enhanced the importance of a country's fundamentals as drivers of asset performance at the expense of global factors is a common misperception. Indeed, the degree of comovement of asset prices in emerging markets (estimated as the share of time variability explained by the first principal component, PC1) is considerable and has been growing over time (even before the 2008–09 sell-off) (figure 5.9a).[18] In turn, PC1 is highly correlated with global asset returns, as captured by the S&P 500 and the Morgan

Figure 5.9 Financial Recoupling

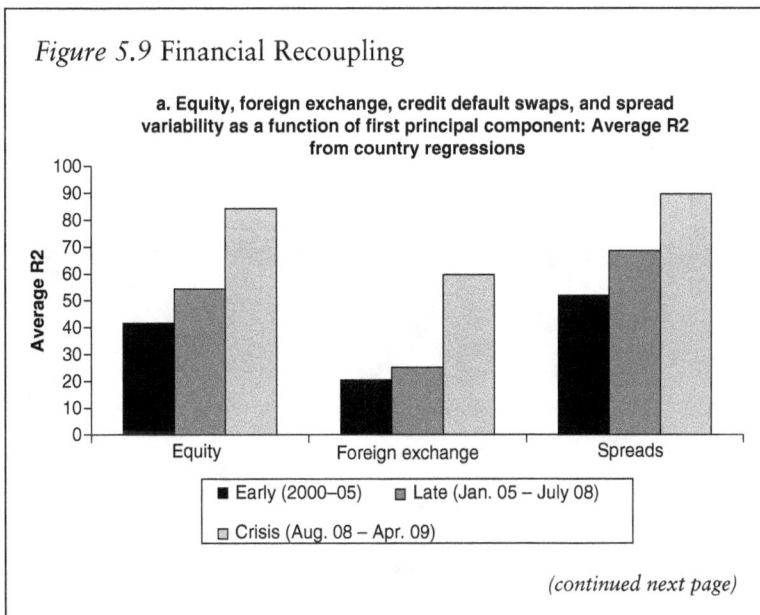

a. Equity, foreign exchange, credit default swaps, and spread variability as a function of first principal component: Average R2 from country regressions

Legend: ■ Early (2000–05) ■ Late (Jan. 05 – July 08) □ Crisis (Aug. 08 – Apr. 09)

(continued next page)

Figure 5.9 *(continued)*

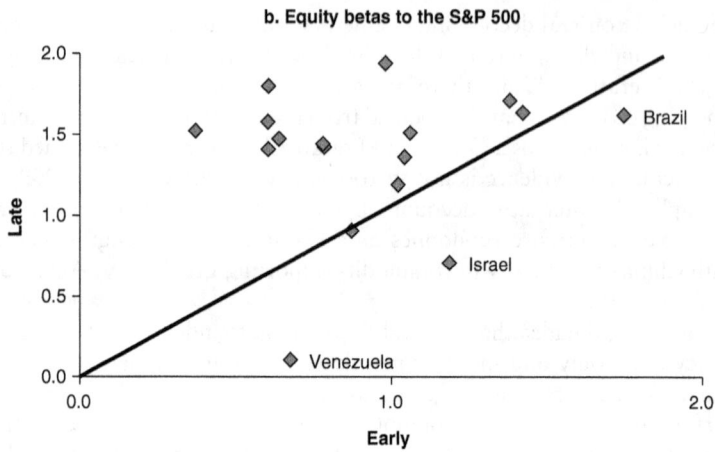

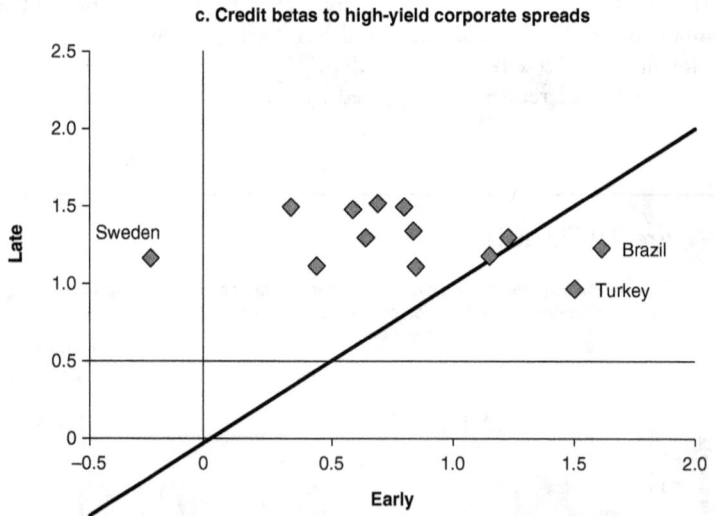

b. Equity betas to the S&P 500

c. Credit betas to high-yield corporate spreads

(continued next page)

Figure 5.9 (continued)

d. Currency betas to the DXY

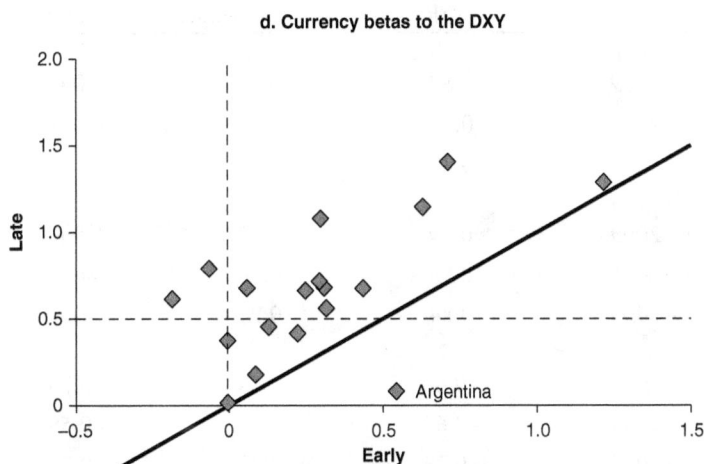

Source: Authors' calculations based on Bloomberg Data.

Note: 5.9a reports the average R-squared of the following regressions: country-specific equity, foreign exchange returns and sovereign credit spreads versus time series for the first principal component. The time series for the first principal component are computed by taking a weighted average of the changes in the country-specific equity, foreign exchange returns and sovereign credit spreads, where the weight for country i equals the i-principal component weight divided by the sum of all the principal component weights. 5.9b reports, for emerging countries, the median betas from the following regressions: MSCI vs. S&P, EMBI vs. HYM, and FX vs. DXY. These are based on monthly data: Early period (January 2000–December 2004); late period (January 2005–December 2009). MSCI = Morgan Stanley Capital International; EMBI = Emerging Markets Bond Index; HYM = high yield us corporate index; FX = foreign exchange; DXY = U.S. dollar index.

Stanley Capital International (MSCI) equity indexes and the spread on high-yield U.S. corporate debt (see table 5.4), indicating that most of the comovement displayed by emerging-market assets comes from global influences or globally synchronized shocks. Finally, it is easy to show that emerging-market equity and credit default swaps (as well as exchange rates betas to the relevant global risk factors) have mostly increased in the second half of the 2000s (figure 5.9a).[19]

That this comovement is directly related to financial globalization (specifically, cross-border flows) is readily seen in figure 5.9a, where we plot the first principal component of global fund flows to the two main emerging regions (Latin America and Asia) to show how they closely mimic

Table 5.4 Correlations: First Principal Component versus Global Indexes, 2000–09

	S&P	MSCI Developed	HY
PCE - Equity			
2000 – 2009	0.84	0.94	−0.69
2000 – 2004	0.83	0.92	−0.62
2005 – 2009	0.87	0.96	−0.73
EM - Equity			
2000 – 2009	0.79	0.85	−0.65
2000 – 2004	0.73	0.76	−0.65
2005 – 2009	0.84	0.91	−0.66
EM-CDS			
2000 – 2009	−0.66	−0.70	0.75
2000 – 2004	−0.62	−0.65	0.59
2005 – 2009	−0.73	−0.76	0.79
LAC6 - Equity			
2000 – 2009	0.67	0.75	−0.61
2000 – 2004	0.56	0.60	−0.55
2005 – 2009	0.77	0.85	−0.66
LAC6 - CDS			
2000 – 2009	−0.72	−0.74	0.71
2000 – 2004	−0.63	−0.63	0.59
2005 – 2009	−0.77	−0.78	0.76

Source: Bloomberg.

Note: This table reports the correlation of global index vs. the first principal component. The time series for the first principal component is computed by taking a weighted average of the changes in the country-specific equity and sovereign credit spreads, where the weight for country i equals the i-the principal component weight divided by the sum of all the principal component weights. Hy = high yield us corporate index; CDS = credit default swaps.

each other. Moreover, the first principal component explains roughly 80 percent of the monthly variability of global fund flows (figure 5.9b), and its link with individual countries is remarkably even across the board (figure 5.9c), which shows that PC1 is roughly similar to a simple average of individual changes. All of this clearly indicates that global fund flows are governed by common factors rather than by local idiosyncratic aspects—a simple reflection of the benchmarked nature of most of these funds and the flipside of similar findings for price performance as illustrated in table 5.4 and figure 5.9c.

The resemblance between asset price and flow comovements suggests that cross-border flows may explain at least part of the recent financial recoupling. In principle, stable to higher betas could be seen as the natural consequence of financial globalization, to the extent that the latter tends to increase the global nature of emerging markets' investor base, thereby making it more homogeneous. As global investors diversify into emerging-market assets, the importance of global factors coming from the developed world should increase accordingly. To explore this hypothesis, we focus on cross-border equity flows, in principle the ones that should reflect economic performance (hence, real decoupling) more closely and where the real contrast between financial decoupling and financial recoupling is more puzzling.

Did financial globalization indeed play a role? More generally, does foreign participation, measured as foreign holdings over local market capitalization, increase the market betas to global asset returns? Does financial globalization amplify the response of cross-border flows and asset prices to global shocks in times of global turmoil? Here, the findings are mixed. Although, in principle, there appears to be a significant link between U.S. residents' equity holdings and equity betas around the date of Lehman Brothers' collapse (Didier, Love, and Martínez Pería 2010), a closer look reveals that this finding is entirely accounted for by the frontier markets group (table 5.5), which, curiously enough, appears to be sensitive to global equity shocks while its more financially globalized peers do not (columns 2–4), directly contradicting this hypothesis. Alternative specifications using countries' MSCI instead of the local stock market index reveal a larger equity beta to the S&P (not surprisingly, given that the MSCI comprises stocks under the global investors' radar) but also fail to find a role for financial globalization (column 4). Similarly, no association is found when using the Lane and Milesi-Ferretti (2007) version of the ratio of financial globalization to GDP (column 5).

Not all results are negative, however: the sensitivity to global shocks increases significantly with the presence of global equity funds, both captured by the absolute value of fund flows (recall that we are trying to proxy the intensity of cross-border flows, not their direction) and by assets under management, although the S&P coefficient remains large and close to 1. A quick look at the differential response to positive and negative shocks during the late period (table 5.5, columns 10 and 11) reveals that the incidence of global fund flows is restricted to the sell-offs, in line with the view that, in the event of a liquidity crunch (such as the post–Lehman Brothers' panic), benchmarked global funds tend to liquidate everywhere in proportion to the market's index weight and regardless of the country's fundamentals. Are these large fund flows in bad months the endogenous result of a rush to the exit in the midst of a crisis? To control for this potential reverse causality (that is, the hypothesis that global funds pull out faster from countries with bigger price declines), we replicate the

Table 5.5 Comparison of Two Studies on Financial Recoupling and Financial Globalization

	Didier et al. 2010					Levy-Yeyati 2010, Crisis period			
Country group	All countries	AM	EM	FM	EM	EM	EM	EM	EM
Variable	1	2	3	4	5	6	7	8	9
FG variable	U.S. equity holdings	U.S. equity holdings	U.S. equity holdings	U.S. equity holdings	U.S. equity holdings	LMF equity liabilities	Fund flows	Fund AUM	Fund flows
SPX*U.S. holdings	0.01***	-0.01	0.00	0.04**	0.00	0.00	2.64***	0.03*	2.33***
	(0.09)	(0.40)	(0.86)	(0.03)	(0.59)	(0.35)	(0.00)	(0.10)	(0.00)
SPX	0.85	1.12***	1.07***	0.75***	1.49***	1.27***	1.11***	1.21***	1.17***
	0.00	0.00	0.00	0.00	0.00	0.00	0.00	0.00	0.00
FG proxy							-6.47		8.24***
							(0.20)		(0.00)
R-squared	0.35	0.69	0.49	0.27	0.58	0.58	0.62	0.59	0.54
Observations	1,628	308	374	858	408	408	323	408	935
Time dummies	No	No	No	No	No	No	No	No	No
Countries	74	14	17	39	17	17	17	17	17

Table 5.5 Comparison of Two Studies on Financial Recoupling and Financial Globalization (continued)

	Levy-Yeyati (2010), late period					Levy-Yeyati (2010), late period, GMM		
Country group	EM	EM	EM	EM	EM	EM	EM	EM
Variable	10	11	12	13	14	15	16	17
FG variable	Fund AUM	Fund flows	Fund AUM	Fund flows (Positive S&P)	Fund flows (Negative S&P)	Fund flows	Fund flows (Positive S&P)	Fund flows (Negative S&P)
SPX*U.S. holdings	0.03*	2.46***	−0.02	0.06	3.35***	4.43***	2.13	3.87***
	(0.10)	(0.00)	(0.38)	(0.95)	(0.00)	(0.00)	(0.15)	(0.00)
SPX*U.S. holdings*LAC6		−0.42	0.05					
		(0.63)	(0.18)					
SPX	1.33***	1.17***	1.65***	1.46***	1.14***	0.87***	1.00***	0.88***
	(0.00)	(0.00)	(0.00)	(0.00)	(0.00)	(0.00)	(0.00)	(0.00)
SPX*LAC6		0.00	−0.33					
		(0.98)	(0.18)					
FG proxy		8.36***		13.74***	12.06	9.69***	10.35***	24.06***
		(0.00)		(0.00)	(0.10)	(0.00)	(0.00)	(0.00)

Table 5.5 Comparison of Two Studies on Financial Recoupling and Financial Globalization *(continued)*

	Levy-Yeyati (2010), late period					Levy-Yeyati (2010), late period, GMM		
Variable	10	11	12	13	14	15	16	17
Country group	EM	EM	EM	EM	EM	EM	EM	EM
FG variable	Fund AUM	Fund flows	Fund AUM	Fund flows (Positive S&P)	Fund flows (Negative S&P)	Fund flows	Fund flows (Positive S&P)	Fund flows (Negative S&P)
R-squared	0.50	0.54	0.50	0.30	0.48			
Observations	1020	935	1020	544	391	935	544	391
Time dummies	No	No	No	No	No	No	No	No
Countries	17	17	17	17	17	17	17	17

Note: This table presents estimations on the effect of financial globalization on financial recoupling. The first four columns follow Didier Love, and Martínez Pería (2010). The returns are normal local returns, filtered out of outliers, and U.S. holdings are normalized by substracting its sample average and dividing by its sample standard deviation. The crisis period is defined as June 2007 to April 2009 as opposed to the 2008–2009 crisis period used in this paper. From columns 5 to 17, stock data are from MSCI country indexes,and FG variables are not normalized. Fund flows are in absolute value. GMM indicates Arellano Bond in-difference estimator using lagged gund AUM as instruments. *p*-values are in parenthesis. *, **, *** denote significance at the 1 percent, 5 percent, and 10 percent levels, respectively. AM = advanced markets; EM = emerging markets, FM = frontier markets; FG = financial globalization; AUM = assets under management; GMM = generalized method of moments; SPX = S8P500.

Source: Bloomberg; Barclays Capital; TIC; LMF.

estimation using GMM techniques and instrumenting equity fund flows using, as before, flows associated with the remaining emerging markets in the sample. Results remain unaltered.

Thus, global fund activity appears to amplify the asset price response to a sell-off in the S&P 500 (or, alternatively, an adverse global shock such as a peak in risk aversion or a liquidity crunch), although it does not fully explain the roughly one-to-one response of emerging-market equity prices to global shocks. Whether the unexplained part of the comovement is related to some measurement problem or some missing explanatory factor, the global comovement of asset prices remains an interesting puzzle in need of further research.

Financial Globalization and Global Event Risk: The Test of the Global Financial Crisis

If the benefits of financial globalization for international risk sharing and output and consumption smoothing are, at best, elusive, what about the tail risks of a global systemic shock? Does financial globalization amplify the adverse impact of generalized external shocks in a situation in which no risk sharing is available? Do external crises propagate more when the domestic economy is financially linked with the crisis epicenter?

The 2008 global financial crisis offers a perfect event for evaluating this question empirically. A good starting point is provided by Didier, Hevia, and Schmukler (2011), who analyze both the correlation between the growth collapse and the subsequent recovery in different countries and a few variables, including financial globalization proxies. Based on a definition of growth collapse as the 2009–07 growth differential, they find that middle-income countries fared only marginally better than high-income ones against what seems to be the conventional view in some quarters. We reproduce this exercise in figure 5.10a, where we also add our four country groups (advanced markets, emerging markets, LAC7, and other LAC countries). Interestingly, our emerging-market sample—which differs significantly from the middle-income group, in particular because of their higher degree of financial globalization—appears to have done slightly *worse* than advanced markets in the collapse of growth. The LAC universe is no exception: LAC7 contracted by less than manufactures-exporting emerging Asian economies or currency-imbalanced emerging Europe but by more than other, less financially integrated LAC countries. Moreover, figure 5.10b gives an interesting first glimpse, showing that the collapse in growth, both in emerging markets and particularly in advanced markets, seems to be negatively associated with financial globalization (greater globalization being associated with sharper drops in the growth rate). But a closer look at the evidence for LAC, which shows a positive but ultimately insignificant correlation, warns against the easy interpretation of financial globalization as a source of global exposure.

Figure 5.10 The Global Financial Crisis, the Collapse in Growth, and Financial Globalization, LAC and Selected Economies

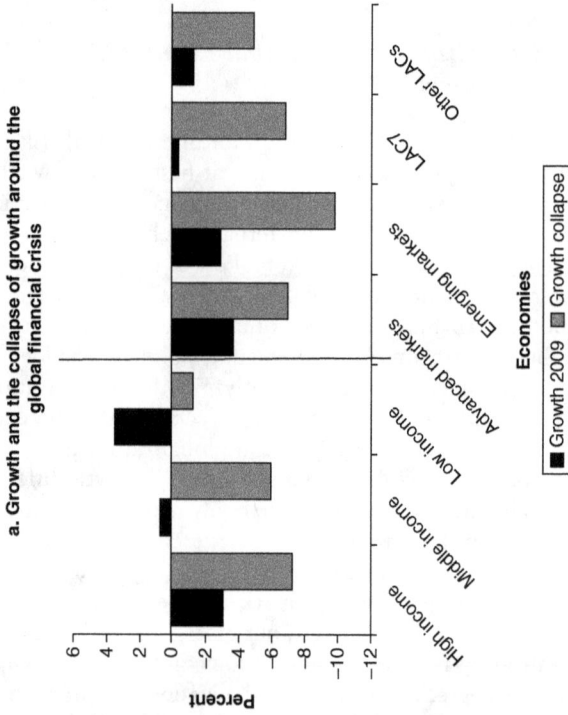

a. Growth and the collapse of growth around the global financial crisis

(continued next page)

Figure 5.10 (continued)

b. The global financial crisis and financial globalization

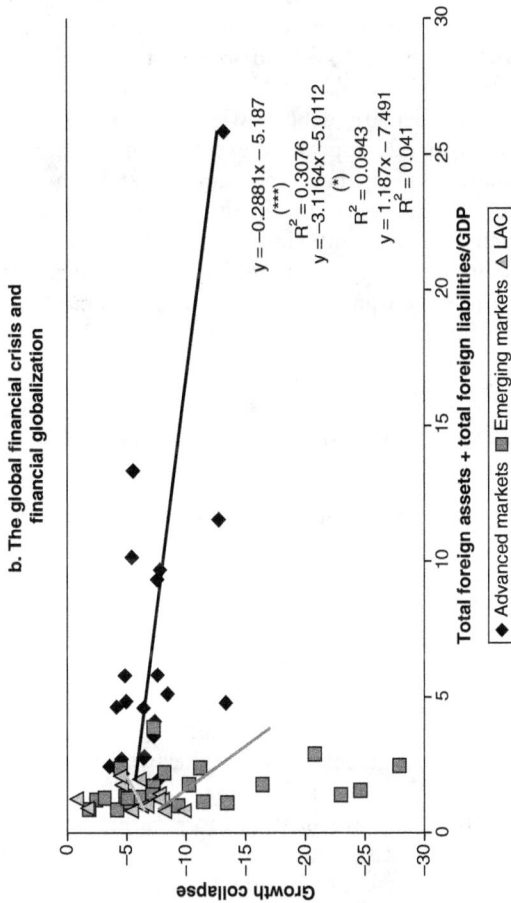

$y = -0.2881x - 5.187$
$(\ast\ast\ast)$
$R^2 = 0.3076$
$y = -3.1164x - 5.0112$
$(\ast)$
$R^2 = 0.0943$
$y = 1.187x - 7.491$
$R^2 = 0.041$

Growth collapse

Total foreign assets + total foreign liabilities/GDP

◆ Advanced markets ■ Emerging markets △ LAC

Sources: WDI; WEO IMF; Lane and Milesi-Ferretti 2008.

Note: Growth collapse is measured as 2009 growth minus 2007 growth. Income classification is from World Bank's July 2010 classification. In our sample (AM, EM, FM), growth collapse is measured as growth in 2009 minus the average growth rate in the 2003–07 period. Figure 5.10b presents a scatterplot of growth collapse versus financial globalization. Growth collapse is measured as growth in 2009 minus average growth in 2003–07. LAC is LAC6+Other LACs. GDP = gross national product; AM = advanced markets; EM = emerging markets; LAC = Latin America and the Caribbean.

Is the relatively light debt liability position of LAC countries the reason behind the difference between LAC and the rest?

Because the differential sensitivity to the global shock could be attributed to many factors other than financial globalization, for a more formal analysis along these lines, we build on Didier, Hevia, and Schmukler's (2011) cross-section regressions of growth collapses on financial integration (table 5.6). Results are rather mixed—not surprisingly, given the simultaneous, hard-to-identify effects of the many events that characterized the crisis period. The emerging-markets dummy appears negative (in line with figure 5.10a), and so does the standard financial globalization proxy, but significance is poor to nonexistent. It is the stock of foreign liabilities, particularly debt, however, that is associated with a harder collapse, whereas FDI appears to exert a benign influence during the crisis (particularly for advanced economies). While any conclusion from a test based on a cross-section of observations corresponding to a period populated with so many simultaneous systemic shocks must be viewed with caution, it appears that financial globalization played no systematic role in the output response to the global crisis beyond its correlation with the hard currency liquidity needs of liquidity-constrained, heavily indebted countries.

Taking Stock: From Positive to Normative

Perhaps the main takeaway from the previous empirical examination of financial globalization is its most pedestrian finding: for all the academic and media coverage that the concept has received in recent years, *financial globalization in the developing world appears to have been vastly overstated.* Rather than growing in the 1990s and 2000s as usually argued based on standard GDP ratios, de facto globalization has accompanied (and, to some extent, supported) a more secular process of financial deepening (in emerging markets and elsewhere), temporarily slowed down by the recent global crisis. In other words, once measured in a way that minimizes the various biases that plagued the most popular empirical proxies, financial globalization looks rather stable and well below advanced country levels.

This finding is critical to an agenda that often investigates the causes and consequences of financial globalization, starting from the false premise that financial globalization has actually strengthened over the years. Instead, the globalization process during the 1990s (which almost defined emerging markets as a financial concept) came to a halt in the 2000s. This is particularly so for the specific case of LAC7, where financial globalization levels lag those in their emerging peers and have fallen in the 2000s, reflecting in part the sovereign deleveraging trend in the region.

Table 5.6 Financial Globalization and the Global Financial Crisis

Variables	All countries' growth collapse	All countries' growth collapse	Emerging markets' growth collapse	Emerging markets' growth collapse	Emerging markets' growth collapse	EM+other LACs' growth collapse
Emerging markets	-1.76	-3.22*				
	(1.29)	(1.64)				
FM	1.25	-0.22				
	(1.13)	(1.56)				
Trade	-0.04**	-0.04*	-0.01	-0.01	-0.03	-0.02
	(0.02)	(0.02)	(0.03)	(0.03)	(0.03)	(0.04)
Financial globalization		-0.37	-3.34			
		(0.33)	(2.78)			
FG assets				6.34	1.74	-0.96
				(4.73)	(4.94)	(5.11)
FG liabilities				-10.67**		
				(5.17)		
Equity liabilities					5.40	11.73
					(10.80)	(12.36)

257

Table 5.6 Financial Globalization and the Global Financial Crisis (*continued*)

Variables	All countries' growth collapse	All countries' growth collapse	Emerging markets' growth collapse	Emerging markets' growth collapse	Emerging markets' growth collapse	EM+other LACs' growth collapse
FDI liabilities					5.13	4.13
					(4.99)	(5.59)
Debt liabilities					−19.93***	−15.44***
					(3.43)	(4.88)
Debt liabilities*LAC7						0.47
						(9.11)
Debt liabilities*other LACs						0.86
						(14.90)
Constant	−3.10**	−1.72	−2.14	−1.86	−1.77	−3.00
	(1.36)	(1.49)	(2.92)	(3.20)	(2.47)	(3.93)
Observations	72	72	29	29	29	32
R-squared	0.14	0.15	0.15	0.25	0.51	0.44

Note: This table presents estimations on the relationship of growth collapse and financial globalization during the global financial crisis. Robust standard errors are in parentheses. All financial globalization variables are normalized by GDP. Emerging markets and frontier markets are dummies indicating country group. *, **, and *** denote significance at the 10 percent, 5 percent, and 1 percent level, respectively. EM = emerging markets; LAC = Latin America and the Caribbean; FDI = foreign direct investment; FM = frontier markets; FG = financial globalization.

Significantly, the degree of financial globalization may have been further overstated by measurement problems, because part of the offshored financial intermediation of developing-country residents is reported as foreign, both because of the domicile of the investment vehicles (for example, global funds and exchange-traded finds) and because of tax evasion (which causes residents to misreport transactions booked in financial centers).

That said, it is true that the ratio of foreign liabilities to GDP has been on the rise, and the current enthusiasm for emerging markets continues to elicit overweight portfolio positions from benchmarked investors in the region, plus an increasingly active speculative turnover. All of this begs the question of whether cross-border holdings—particularly easy-to-unwind foreign portfolio liabilities—are good or bad or, more generally, whether policy makers should view them with concern. As noted, measurement limitations and the short time span of financial globalization should caution us to take any normative conclusion with a grain of salt. That said, the data examined here offer a few important policy implications and suggest issues that deserve to be addressed by additional research.

Financial Globalization: Good or Bad?

To the extent that financial globalization appears to play a positive role in domestic market deepening and that the latter has been a driving force in the "onshorization" of financial intermediation and the financial de-dollarization process, it can be said that financial globalization has played a supporting role in increasing the resilience of the developing world, particularly in emerging markets. Nowhere is this claim more pertinent than in the case of LAC7, a group previously plagued by currency imbalances, external dependence, and crisis propensity and today exhibiting low debt ratios and long foreign currency positions that have allowed them to exploit exchange rate flexibility in a countercyclical way.

On the negative side, there is evidence that financial globalization amplified the post–Lehman Brothers' asset sell-off (particularly through benchmarked global equity funds, although the same should apply, almost by construction, to bond funds). Similarly, the procyclical nature of portfolio inflows, which return to core markets in episodes of flight to quality (or, by arbitrage, move out of and into core markets in sync with the interest rate cycle in advanced economies) may amplify the effect of the global cycle on the emerging world in an undesirable way.

A second issue concerning financial globalization and currencies can be broadly denoted as the "financial Dutch disease"[20] associated with excessive capital inflows—in turn, a potential result of financial globalization.

The concern about the negative consequences of procyclical capital flows—and its counterpart, cyclical appreciation followed by sharp depreciations in the downturn—has recently come to the forefront because of the fear that globalized speculative capital may channel the excess global liquidity into emerging markets, with potentially adverse consequences for exchange rate overshooting and excess volatility and, more generally, for asset inflation and bubbles. However, the procyclical nature of international portfolio capital has been a topic of debate in the emerging-market literature as early as the mid-1990s, with the capital-inflow boom in Latin America, triggered by a combination of events (the creation of the Brady bond market, global liquidity, and the first wave of reforms), a pattern that also seems to apply to a lesser extent to FDI flows.[21] Not surprisingly, cross-border inflows are typically both negatively correlated with the cycle in the source country and positively correlated with the cycle in the host country. In this way, they may be seen either as speeding up the convergence toward new levels of real exchange rate equilibrium or as exacerbating short-lived deviations from them. Thus, for good or bad, to the extent that flows are positively associated with cross-border liabilities, financial globalization may strengthen this pattern.

To what extent does financial globalization contribute to this concern? A priori, the positive relation between cross-border stocks and flows documented above suggests that globalized countries are likely to face larger flows in either direction, but that positive relation does not say much about how it influences the cyclical nature of these shocks. To assess that influence in a simple way, in unreported results we run a panel regression of portfolio liability and asset flows on GDP growth rates, where the latter are interacted with a financial globalization proxy (the stock of foreign liabilities and the stock of foreign assets over GDP, respectively, both the ratio and a *high* dummy indicating values above the sample median). We control for common contemporaneous factors (like global liquidity or risk aversion) through time dummies. The evidence is inconclusive. Inflows display a significant (albeit weak) cyclical nature, however, amplified by financial globalization, whereas the same exercise fails to yield results for the case of outflows.

Too Much of a Good Thing?

As highlighted in the first two chapters of this volume, for all the market and media excitement about emerging economies, Latin America displays rather modest progress on increasing its financial depth, sophistication, and variety. Capital flows in search of yields in times of poor growth and low rates at the center can easily lead to temporary exchange rate overvaluation followed by a depreciation in the periphery. This pattern—in principle a natural way of sharing the burden of the down cycle in a flexible exchange rate environment—may have deleterious effects on relatively illiquid LAC markets, particularly when capital flows weaken or revert. At any rate, the ultimate challenge remains how to foster the liquidity of domestic markets by inviting long-term inflows, while filtering noisy short-term flows.

How much can monetary policy do (through financial stability considerations in interest rate decisions) to make a positive difference? There is growing consensus that a policy framework aimed at attenuating procyclical swings is much needed. Such a framework requires, however, a procedure for evaluating the persistence of the shock. Only with a clear understanding of the cyclical component of capital flows and exchange rate movements can *prudential macromeasures* be calibrated without risking stifling the markets unnecessarily.[22] The fact that flows and exchange rates display cyclical components should be clear from the illustrations of comovements and of the correlation between common factors and global drivers documented above. But from there to estimating a target exchange rate range (more specifically, determining whether exchange rate appreciation is overshooting its fundamental level due to cyclical forces) is far more complicated, not only because the persistence of the shock cannot be easily determined but also because the multilateral real exchange rate depends on other currencies that are also subject to the same transitory shock.

In turn, there seems to be a need to complement leaning-against-the-wind foreign exchange intervention with truly prudential macromeasures such as Tobin taxes, as well as other less popular and heavily studied recommendations such as reserve requirements (as the ones once imposed on banks' dollar liabilities in heavily dollarized economies such as Peru, or the more selective type recently imposed on foreign exchange forwards in Israel) or the use of reserve requirements in lieu of interest rate hikes (as currently in Turkey), both aimed at reducing the interest rate differential perceived by foreign investors and at discouraging speculative flows. In addition, the alleged cost of sterilized intervention calls for rethinking reserve management over longer horizons (emulating sovereign wealth funds) to increase their return above and beyond the typical short U.S. Treasury. At any rate, the challenge for the region, now as it was in the mid-1990s, is to learn how to respond to foreign and local enthusiasm for domestic assets to ensure that capital comes in search of a resident permit rather than a short tourist visa.

Notes

1. This section touches upon a number of issues already covered in the previous chapter. The present analysis, however, expands on the one in the previous chapter and introduces alternative ways to measure financial globalization. The overlap is necessary to give the reader a more comprehensive view.

2. In what follows, and for the sake of concision, we focus primarily on equities, where betas have been more consistently high, but the results are easily generalized to currencies.

3. See appendix I in Levy-Yeyati and Williams (2011) for a detailed analysis of de jure versus de facto measures of financial globalization and alternative data sources used.

4. Non-LAC6 economies are excluded due to insufficient data on local market capitalization.

5. In addition, equity holdings in peripheral core economies (PCE) have looked relatively stable for the past 10 years and with levels that are comparable to those in emerging markets—which indicates that the larger financial globalization to GDP levels in PCE simply reflect the deeper markets in advanced economies.

6. Note that this is not inconsistent with LAC equities' representing a larger share of the global portfolio: a passive (benchmarked) investor would increase the weight of LAC equities whenever the price of LAC equities grows relative to other equities.

7. For instance, Kose, Prasad, and Terrones (2007, 38) state: "There is a large body of theory suggesting that foreign ownership of banks can, in principle, generate a variety of benefits. First, foreign bank participation can make a country's access to international financial markets easier. Second, it can help improve the regulatory and supervisory frameworks of the domestic banking industry. Third, it can improve the quality of loans as the influence of the government on the financial sector should decline in more open economies. Fourth, in practice, foreign banks may introduce new financial instruments and technologies which can increase competition and improve the quality of financial services. The presence of foreign banks can also provide a safety valve when depositors become worried about the solvency of domestic banks."

8. See appendix table A3 in Levy-Yeyati and Williams (2011) for a detailed list. Advanced markets are the 28 advanced countries used in Lane and Milesi-Ferretti (2008). All variables are lagged and included in logs, except capital account openness.

9. As Lane and Milesi-Ferretti note in their paper (2008), "The level of economic development can also be an important factor in explaining domestic residents' propensity to engage in cross-border asset trade." We prefer to include it here more specifically as an indicator that subsumes many of the transaction costs listed above.

10. Cross-border holdings and flows could influence the depth of the banking sector, albeit in a less straightforward way, to the extent that flows are largely intermediated by banks.

11. We run a parsimonious version of the previous specification, dropping trade and other financial development proxies that are generally not significant, to gain observations at a minimum loss of information.

12. Growth in world output and consumption is measured as follows: $\Sigma \Delta \log (x_{it})^* \text{Share}_{AM}$, where x_{it} is either real per capita consumption or output in country i (where the country belongs to the advanced markets subsample), and Share_{AM} is the share country i represents of advanced markets' consumption or GDP measured by PPP current prices.

13. These results expand on previous findings by Kose, Prasad, and Terrones (2007) along the same lines, for the period 1960–95.

14. Financial globalization is measured here, as usual, as the sum of foreign assets and liabilities over GDP.

15. Note that this is similar to allowing μ to vary across countries in Kose, Prasad, and Terrones's (2007) panel estimation—and that their risk-sharing measure for country i would equal to $1-b_i$.

16. Using FDI holdings, or the sum of equity plus debt holdings, over GDP as financial globalization proxies yields comparable results.

17. Naturally, this is simply a reflection of the stylized facts shown when discussing the normalization over market cap.

18. For figure 5.8, we regress country-specific equity returns and credit default swaps spread changes on the first principal component constructed based on equity returns and spread changes for all emerging markets. Significantly, while the analysis in this section is based on monthly data, the comovement is also there for longer horizons.

19. Betas are estimated based on country-by-country regressions of monthly log changes in Morgan Stanley Capital International Index country equity indexes on log changes in the S&P 500, and log credit spreads on the U.S. high-yield corporate spreads, respectively. Results are similar when we use quarterly and annual changes instead. Much as in the case of real decoupling discussed above, the drawbacks of using standard correlations to estimate market interdependence have been repeatedly highlighted in the finance literature, most notably Forbes and Rigobon (2002).

20. See http://www.brookings.edu/research/reports/2011/04/08-blep-cardenas.

21. See, among other, Calvo, Leiderman, and Reinhart (1994) and Levy-Yeyati (2009) on the procyclical nature of net private capital flows (including FDI) to developing countries.

22. We prefer this term to the more broadly used *macroprudential measures*, which is often mistaken for traditional, bank-level microprudential measures that partially internalized the presence of systemic (macroeconomic) risk, as in the recent Basel III (see Cárdenas and Levy-Yeyati 2011).

References

Baltagi, B. H., P. O. Demetriades, and S. H. Law. 2009. "Financial Development and Openness: Evidence from Panel Data." *Journal of Development Economics* 89 (2): 285–96.

Barclays Capital (database). http://etfdb.com/index/barclays-capital-us-aggregate-bond-index/.

BIS (Bank for International Settlements). http://www.bis.org/statistics/.

Bloomberg (database). http://www.gsb.stanford.edu/sites/default/files/bloomberg_0.pdf.

Calvo, G. A., L. Leiderman, and C. M. Reinhart. 1994. "The Capital Inflows Problem: Concepts and Issues." *Contemporary Economic Policy* 12 (3): 54–66.

Cárdenas, Mauricio, Karim Foda, Camila Henao, and Eduardo Levy-Yeyati. 2011. *Latin America Economic Perspectives: Shifting Gears in an Age of Heightened Expectations.* Washington, DC: Brookings Institution.

Chinn, M., and H. Ito. 2007. "Price-Based Measurement of Financial Globalization: A Cross-Country Study of Interest Rate Parity." *Pacific Economic Review* 12 (4): 419–44.

———. 2008. "A New Measure of Financial Openness." *Journal of Comparative Policy Analysis* 10 (3): 309–22.

Didier, Tatiana, Constantino Hevia, and Sergio L. Schmukler. 2011. "How Resilient and Countercyclical Were Emerging Economies to the Global Financial Crisis?" Policy Research Working Paper 5637, World Bank, Washington, DC.

Didier, T., I. Love, and M. S. Martínez Pería. 2010. "What Explains Stock Markets' Vulnerability to the 2007–2008 Crisis?" Policy Research Working Paper 5224, World Bank, Washington, DC.

Forbes, K. J., and R. Rigobon R. 2002. "No Contagion, Only Interdependence: Measuring Stock Market Comovements." *Journal of Finance* 57 (5): 2223–61.

IFS (International Financial Statistics) (database). International Monetary Fund. Washington, DC. http://elibrary-data.imf.org/.

Ize, A., and E. Levy-Yeyati. 2003. "Financial Dollarization." *Journal of International Economics* 59 (2): 323–47.

Kose, A., C. Otrok, and E. Prasad. 2006. "Financial Globalization: A Reappraisal." CEPR Discussion Paper 5842, Centre for Economic Policy Research, London.

———. 2008. "Global Business Cycles: Convergence or Decoupling?" NBER Working Paper 14292, National Bureau of Economic Research, Cambridge, MA.

Kose, A., E. Prasad, and M. Terrones. 2007. "How Does Financial Globalization Affect Risk Sharing? Patterns and Channels." IMF Working Paper 07/238, International Monetary Fund, Washington, DC.

Lane, P. R., and G. M. Milesi-Ferretti. 2007. "The External Wealth of Nations Mark II." *Journal of International Economics* 73: 223–50.

———. 2008. "The Drivers of Financial Globalization." *American Economic Review* 98 (2): 327–32.

Levy-Yeyati, E. 2007. "Dollars, Debts, and the IFIs: Dedollarizing Multilateral Lending." *World Bank Economic Review* 27 (1): 21–47.

———. 2009. "Optimal Debt? On the Insurance Value of International Debt Flows to Developing Countries." *Open Economies Review* 20 (4): 489–507.

Levy-Yeyati, E., and T. Williams. 2011. "Financial Globalization in Emerging Economies: Much Ado about Nothing?" Policy Research Working Paper 4770, World Bank, Washington, DC.

———. 2012. "Emerging Economies in the 2000s: Real Decoupling and Financial Recoupling." *Journal of International Money and Finance* 31 (8): 2102–26.

Rajan, R. G., and L. Zingales. 2003. "The Great Reversals: The Politics of Financial Development in the 20th Century." CEPR Discussion Paper 2783, Centre for Economic Policy Research, London.

Rose, A. 2009. "Business Cycles Become Less Synchonised over Time: Debunking 'Decoupling.'" *Vox EU.* http://www.voxeu.org/article/debunking-decoupling.

Treasury International Capital System Database. https://sites.google.com/site/economicfeel/economic-indicators-1/foreign-trade/treasury-international-capital-system.

Wälti, S. 2009. "The Myth of Decoupling." Mimeo. Swiss National Bank.

WDI (World Development Indicators). World Bank, Washington, DC. http://data.worldbank.org/data-catalog/world-development-indicators.

WEO (World Economic Outlook) (database). International Monetary Fund, Washington, DC. http://www.imf.org/external/data.htm.

6

Institutional Investors and Agency Issues in Latin American Financial Markets: Issues and Policy Options

Claudio Raddatz

Abstract

Institutional investors have become more important in Latin America in the past 20 years. The rise of these financial intermediaries has increased the scope for agency problems in their interaction with individual investors, corporations, and regulators. This chapter describes these agency problems and discusses their relevance for Latin American countries in light of the existing data. The evidence shows that the incentive schemes used for dealing with agency problems matter for the

The author works for the World Bank in the DECMG unit and for the Central Bank of Chile. e-mail: craddatz@worldbank.org. The author would like to thank Augusto de la Torre, Alain Ize, Sergio Schmukler, Ana Fernanda Maiguashca, Manuel Luy, and participants at the author's workshop on the financial development in Latin America flagship organized by the Office of the Chief Economist of Latin America and the Caribbean for valuable comments. He is also grateful to Matias Braun, Pablo Castañeda, Heinz Rudolph, Carlos Serrano, and Fuad Velasco for useful discussions and to Alfonso Astudillo, Ana Maria Gazmuri, Carlos Alvarado, and Luis Fernando Vieira for outstanding research assistance. The views expressed in this chapter are the author's only and do not necessarily represent those of the World Bank, its executive directors, or the countries they represent.

asset allocation, risk taking, and portfolio maturity of institutional investors and have led them to favor low-risk and short-term assets. The source of the incentives varies across institutional investors. While pension funds respond mainly to incentives set by their regulators, mutual funds respond to the injections and redemptions of their individual investors and to a weak competitive environment. The resulting combination of structure and maturity of portfolios may entail lower returns for individual investors. This effect should be considered in the design of regulatory frameworks that trade off maintaining incentives and giving managers scope to undertake long-run arbitrage opportunities. In addition, according to the scarce available evidence, the concentrated corporate ownership of institutional investors in Latin America may give rise to problems of conflict of interest, related lending, and regulatory capture.

Introduction

The structure of Latin American financial markets has started to change in the past 20 years, with nonbank financial intermediaries like pension funds, mutual funds, and insurance companies playing an increasing role in credit provision and asset management and with bonds and equities becoming more prominent sources of credit for firms and means of investment for households.

The rise of nonbank intermediaries and their ancillary institutions (credit rating agencies, trading platforms, and the like) is increasing the complexity of Latin American financial systems. While in the past banks interacted directly with borrowers and lenders through relationship lending, several institutions—including financial analysts, financial advisers, asset managers, rating agencies, and underwriters—are now participating in the intermediation of savings and the allocation of credit through arm's-length markets. At the same time, the financial products offered to savers have also become more complex. While bank deposits used to be the main savings vehicle, a saver now faces a large set of risky securities whose evaluation requires detailed information on the issuers' prospects and on macroeconomic conditions.

The complexity of financial instruments and the intermediation process increases the number of interactions between agents in conditions of asymmetric information, giving rise to agency problems that are unfamiliar to individuals used to operating in bank-based systems. Since gathering information on the prospects of securities is costly, individuals that wish to invest in them may rely on the opinion of a financial analyst to guide their decisions or may delegate the management of their funds to a portfolio manager, trusting the manager to have superior information about those prospects. Of course, whether such agents do have superior knowledge about the securities is unknown to the individuals but not to the agents themselves. Similarly, asset managers that wish to invest on behalf of their clients will also rely on the opinion of credit-rating agencies and financial analysts that may have superior information about the products and firms.

Regulatory systems also have to adapt to this changing financial architecture, especially because, for the reasons stated above, they may be in charge of representing the interests of numerous and diverse individual investors in different segments of highly interconnected financial markets.

This chapter describes the main agency problems that arise with the emergence of nonbank financial intermediaries and discusses their relevance for Latin American countries in light of the current and future conditions of these intermediaries. In the process, the chapter also takes stock of the lessons learned in countries where these intermediaries have become systemically important (most notably the United States).

The chapter illustrates the discussion with examples and data from the region to the extent possible. However, the paucity of data and the scarcity of rigorous systematic analysis of the characteristics and workings of institutional investors in the region unavoidably temper the strength of the conclusions that can be reached. For this reason, the chapter has a dual goal. First, it aims to show that the increased importance of nonbank financial intermediaries raises a series of relevant agency problems that may, based on the existing data, have important real consequences for the returns to private savings and for financial market development. Second, it aims to convey the message that these potential consequences are important enough to warrant further systematic data-gathering efforts and detailed analysis of the workings of regulated and unregulated institutional investors in the region. Only an accurate characterization of the environment and behavior of these important market players will lead to proper and timely regulation.

The rest of the chapter is structured as follows. It first describes the changing landscape of financial intermediation in Latin America, showing banks' relative decline in importance and the increased importance of different institutional investors. It also characterizes the structure of the financial sector in Latin America, including its competitive structure, corporate structure, and portfolio composition. Next, the chapter describes the changes in the process of financial intermediation associated with this new landscape and the agency problems that arise from those changes. It then looks at the consequences of these agency problems for Latin American countries, taking into consideration the conceptual characteristics of each agency issue and the specific workings of the region's financial intermediaries. In the conclusion, the chapter raises some policy issues arising from the discussion.

The Changing Landscape of Financial Intermediation in Latin America

In many Latin American countries, the financial landscape in the 2000s is different from that of the 1990s. In the past, most intermediation in Latin America occurred in a banking system that was small relative to gross domestic product (GDP). In recent years, two phenomena have occurred. First, financial intermediation has deepened, and, second, a larger volume of intermediation is occurring in institutional investors outside banks. These institutions now intermediate a much larger fraction of aggregate savings. Figure 6.1 shows this evolution for LAC7 countries (Argentina, Brazil, Chile, Colombia, Mexico, Peru, and Uruguay). Among these countries, the average ratio of bank assets to GDP was about 37 percent in the 1990s, while in the 2000s it has reached 42 percent. Most of that growth has occurred outside the banking sector, where assets of nonbank financial institutions (pension funds, mutual funds, and insurance companies) have doubled as a share of GDP. Banks have also grown as a share of GDP, as a sign of the deepening of Latin America's financial markets, but in most countries, their relative size has fallen in the 2000s. Nonetheless, it is clear that while the landscape has changed, banks still dominate Latin American financial systems, both directly and indirectly.[1]

In nonbank financial intermediation, pension funds have been dominant in the region, both in the 1990s and the 2000s (figure 6.1). For instance, in LAC7, for which there are comparable data across the two decades, pension funds represented 7 percent of GDP and 14 percent of financial assets in the 1990s, and 17 percent and 21 percent, respectively, in the 2000s. They have also been the main drivers of the expansion of the nonbank financial sector, growing 58 percent from the 1990s to the 2000s.

Insurance companies are smaller than pension and mutual funds in Latin American financial markets, but they are present in almost every country. With the exception of a few countries (Chile and Peru), the insurance industry has experienced much slower growth than pension and mutual funds. The mutual fund industry expanded significantly between the 1990s and the 2000s; for all practical purposes, though, it has a meaningful size only in Argentina, Brazil, Chile, and Mexico.[2]

According to anecdotal evidence, an important component of intermediation in Latin America also occurs through personal asset management services provided by banks and other financial institutions. This form of intermediation, which does not occur through an institutional investor, combines some aspects of traditional relationship banking with delegated portfolio management and is analogous to the *separately managed accounts* offered by financial companies in the United States. Because this industry is unregulated in Latin America, there is little information on its size; but according to some estimates, in the United States

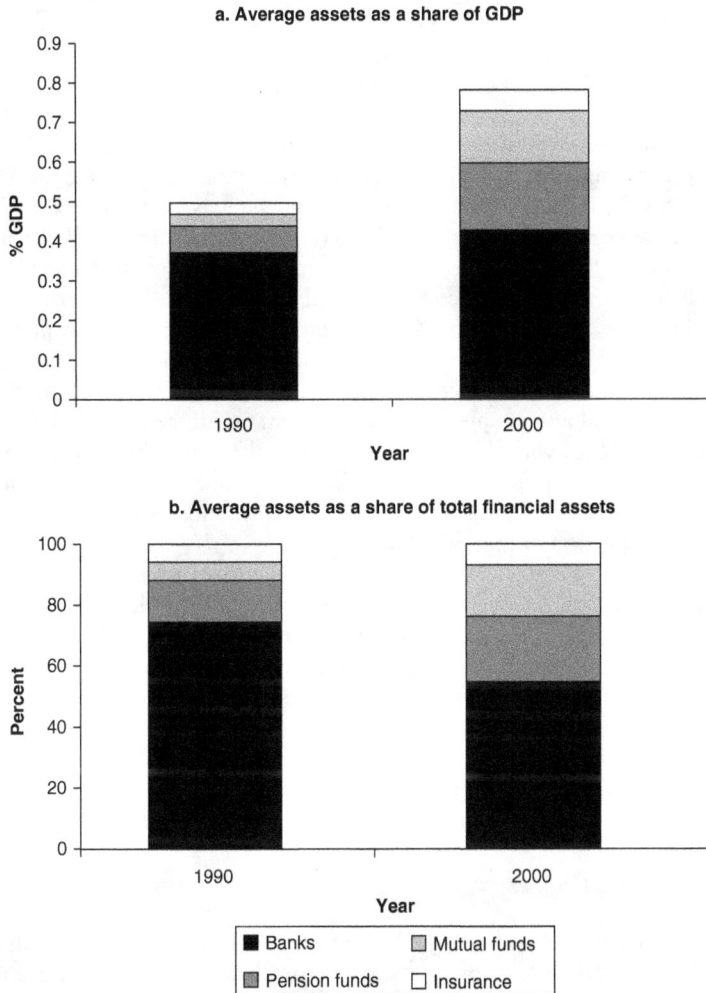

Figure 6.1 Evolution of Main Financial Market Players in Selected Latin American Countries, 1990 and 2000

Source: Based on data from FinStats; Beck, Levine, and Loayza 2000; Yermo 2000; Cheikhrouhou et al. 2007.

Note: Only countries with good coverage are taken into account (Argentina, Brazil, Chile, Colombia, Mexico, Peru, and Uruguay). GDP = gross domestic product.

personal asset management services are similar in size to the mutual fund industry.[3] Information on the size of this component of the industry is largely nonexistent in Latin America, but if the pattern is similar to that in the United States, an important segment of the financial intermediation industry could be seriously underreported.

Number of Firms and Market Concentration

Most countries experienced a market consolidation of pension funds and insurance companies between the late 1990s and the late 2000s (table 6.1). This was the case, for example, in countries such as Chile and Colombia (and Argentina before nationalization), where the number of pension fund administrators declined from nine and eight in 1998 to five and six, respectively, in 2008. Mexico experienced an inverted U-shaped pattern in this industry, with an increase in the number of administrators from 13 in 1998 to 21 in 2007 and down to 19 in 2008. The number of mutual funds available, however, increased in most countries between 1998 and 2008.[4] In funds per million people, Chile is the country with the highest incidence across industries with the exception of mutual funds, where Brazil has a higher penetration (not reported). Chile looks similar to the United States in mutual funds and insurance companies per million, while Brazil has a higher proportion of mutual funds.

Because of the small movements in the number of participants in the different markets, the concentration of the industries is still very high (table 6.2). The 10 largest mutual fund companies represent about 80 percent of the market in most Latin American countries with available data. The situation is similar among life insurance companies, with a little less concentration among general insurance companies. Among pension funds, the concentration is extremely high because many countries have fewer than 10 administrators operating; the table presents the share of the largest two companies, which in most cases is around 50 percent (Mexico being the only exception).

Corporate Structure

The relative decline of banks and the movement of intermediation outside the banking system do not necessarily mean that new players are becoming more prominent. Because of the prevalence of large business groups in Latin American countries, many of the large players among institutional investors have close ties to large banks. In some countries, they are directly part of the bank, while in others they belong to the same financial group. With the exception of Peru, most LAC7 countries allow banks to operate in the securities business. As of 2007, these activities were completely unrestricted in Argentina, Mexico, and Uruguay. Other countries impose some restrictions on the relations of banks with other segments of financial markets (Caprio, Laeven, and Levine 2007). In countries like Brazil

Table 6.1 Main Financial Participants in Financial Markets, 1998 and 2008

	Argentina	Brazil	Chile	Colombia	Mexico	Peru	Uruguay
			1998, absolute terms				
Banks	107	203[a]	30[a]	—	52[a]	19[a]	—
Pension fund administrators	15	—	9	8	13	5	6
Pension funds	—	—	—	—	—	—	—
Insurance companies	276	128	52	37	60	15	18
Mutual fund companies	—	—	—	—	—	—	—
Mutual funds	229	2,438[b]	102[b]	—	312[b]	—	—
			2008, absolute terms				
Banks	69	139	26	75	29	15	12
Pension fund adminstration	—	45	5	6	19	4	4
Pension funds	—	416	25	6	95	12	4
Insurance companies	178	187	52	42	98	13	16
Mutual fund companies	40	1,582	21	25	34	22	16
Mutual funds	200	7,130	418	—	502	54	—

(continued next page)

271

Table 6.1 (continued)

	Argentina	Brazil	Chile	Colombia	Mexico	Peru	Uruguay
	2008, per million people						
Banks	1.7	0.7	1.6	1.7	0.3	0.5	4.0
Pension fund administrators	—	0.2	0.3	0.1	0.2	0.1	1.3
Pension funds	—	2.2	1.6[d]	0.1	0.9	0.4	1.3
Insurance companies	4.5	1.0	3.3	1.0	0.9	0.5	5.3
Mutual fund companies	1.0	8.3	1.3	0.6	0.3	0.8	5.3
Mutual funds	5.0	37.5	26.1	—	4.6	1.9	—

Source: EIU country finance reports; How Countries Supervise Their Banks, Insurers and Securities Markets 2009; Local Superintendencies; AIOS; Based on the number of multifunds offered. FIAFIN. Population data were obtained from the World Development Indicators.

Note: The table shows the number of institutions in each category participating in financial markets for main Latin American countries.

— = not available.

Table 6.2 Market Share of Largest Companies and Funds in Selected Latin American Countries, 1998 and 2008

	Market share (%)				
	Argentina	Brazil	Chile	Colombia	Mexico
1998					
Banks: Largest 5	48	58	59	—	80
All insurances: Largest 10	—	67	—	—	100
Pension funds: Largest 2	53	—	62	77	45
2008					
Banks: Largest 5	51	67	73	64	77
Largest 10	74	76	94	86	92
Mutual funds: Largest 10	79	84	87	73	88
General insurances: Largest 10	54	—	—	78	—
Life insurance: Largest 10	82	62	73	61	88
Pension funds: Largest 10	—	60	100	100	92
Largest 2	—	—	55	52	33

Sources: Economist Intelligence Unit Country Finance Reports (various issues, 2009); Barth, Caprio, and Levine 2001; Yermo 2000; AIOS.
Note: — = not available.

and Chile, for example, banks can operate in securities markets through fully owned subsidiaries that are separated from the bank by some form of firewall, but they can use the same corporate name. The situation is somewhat different in the rest of Latin America, where restrictions on the operation of banks in different financial segments are more common.

Restrictions on the operations of insurance markets are more common in the region, with only two LAC7 countries permitting it with minimum requirements, three imposing tougher restrictions, and two countries prohibiting this activity. These differences might result from the initial strength of the insurance industry in the region (which may have opposed the incursion of banks into their segment) during the period of financial reforms in the 1990s.

Regarding ownership, most countries permit nonbank financial firms to own banks, while there are more restrictions on bank ownership of nonfinancial firms. This arrangement leaves room for the operation of financial conglomerates with complex ownership structures common in the region.

The ownership concentration of different segments of the financial sector by conglomerates has been noted and discussed since the origins of the pension fund system. Yermo (2000), for example, noted that the ownership of pension funds "is not very diversified, with large financial

institutions, especially banks and financial conglomerates, holding large
stakes in pension fund administrators." This concentration remains high
across all market segments.[5] Table 6.3 gives a rough view of the association
of the 10 largest institutions in several segments of the financial sector with
one of the 10 largest banks in selected Latin American countries. The association has been determined, in most cases, by comparing the corporate
name. This method thus gives a lower bound to the true degree of ownership concentration because it captures only obvious links. The complexity
of ownership structures in Latin America that include control pyramids
and cross-holdings suggests that the downward bias may be important.[6]

There is a large degree of ownership concentration in pension and
mutual funds and among investment banks. With the exception of Brazil,
where pension funds work differently from the rest of the region, about
40 percent of the 10 largest pension funds and 55 percent of the assets of

Table 6.3 Ownership Concentration in Selected Latin American
Countries, 2008

Percentage of 10 largest institutions related to 10 largest banks					
	Argentina	Brazil	Chile	Colombia	Mexico
Insurance					
General	10	—	30	30	40
Life	10	50	40	30	50
Pension funds	—	10	40	33	50
Mutual funds	70	60	80	—	80
Investment banks and brokerages					
Investment banks	0	90	60	33	—
Brokerages	—	70	—	—	30
Share of assets of 10 largest institutions related to 10 largest banks					
Insurance					
General	6		34	21	23
Pension funds	—	2	53	53	64
Mutual funds	56	67	91	—	94
Investment banks and brokerages					
Investment banks	0	98	52	83	—
Brokerages	—	87	—	—	30

Source: Economist Intelligence Unit (various issues).
Note: — = not available.

pension funds are directly related to some of the 10 largest banks in the country (that is, they share the name). In the case of mutual funds, the concentration is even higher, with 73 percent of the 10 largest funds and 77 percent of mutual fund assets related to large banks.

This concentration of ownership is also found in the Latin American banking sector. Caprio, Laeven, and Levine (2007) report that, among LAC7 countries, only 10 percent of the banks are widely held and that in 70 percent of the cases with concentrated ownership the controller is a family. In the rest of the world, the share of widely held banks is 27 percent, and only 33 percent of the banks are family owned.

The low number of firms in all segments of financial markets, the high concentration of ownership in banks, and the high degree of cross-ownership between banks and other financial institutions suggest that Latin American financial markets are still highly concentrated and controlled by a few important business conglomerates. In such environments, the competitive pressures on the banking sector from the development of other credit providers are likely to be limited, and, as will be discussed below, the potential for conflicts of interest is enlarged.

How Do They Invest?

The composition of institutional investors' portfolios gives an overview of their risk-taking behavior within and across countries. Do they invest mainly in government bonds, corporate bonds, or equity? Do their allocations relate to their investment horizons? Do they trade actively?

Portfolio composition is more widely available on pension funds. The evolution of the portfolio composition in the first and second half of the 2000s is reported in figure 6.2. The figure shows an increase in equity, foreign investments, and corporate bonds and a decline in financial institutions' assets and government bonds. This trend is similar to data from 1998. Thus, compared to the late 1990s, pension funds are investing a larger fraction of their portfolio in riskier assets. Nonetheless, government bonds and deposits still make up about 60 percent of pension fund portfolios, although this figure varies greatly across countries.

Data on the portfolio composition of insurance companies are harder to obtain. Figure 6.3 shows the composition of insurance companies' portfolios in seven Latin American countries in 2007, as reported by the Asociación de Supervisores de Seguros de Latinoamérica (ASSAL). The categories are different from those used for pension funds, and the time coverage is limited (reaching back only to 2004), but the data show a pattern consistent with that of pension funds. Thus, these data show that two of the largest institutional investors in the region allocate a large percentage of their portfolios to government debt.

Data on mutual fund portfolio composition are available for only a subset of Latin American countries. Figure 6.4a shows that mutual funds in Brazil invest most of their assets in government debt. Although the share of this debt declined significantly between 20003–04 and 2009–09, from 73 to 48 percent, much of this decline was accounted for by securities backed by government debt, and only a minor reallocation occurred for equity. The situation in Mexico is similar but with less variation over time (figure 6.4d).

A few studies have looked at the trading behavior and maturity structure of the portfolios of institutional investors in Latin America. Olivares and Sepulveda (2007) document the presence of "herding" in equity trades among Chilean pension funds, the situation in which funds trade simultaneously in similar assets. Raddatz and Schmukler (2008) confirm the presence of herding among pension funds within several asset classes,

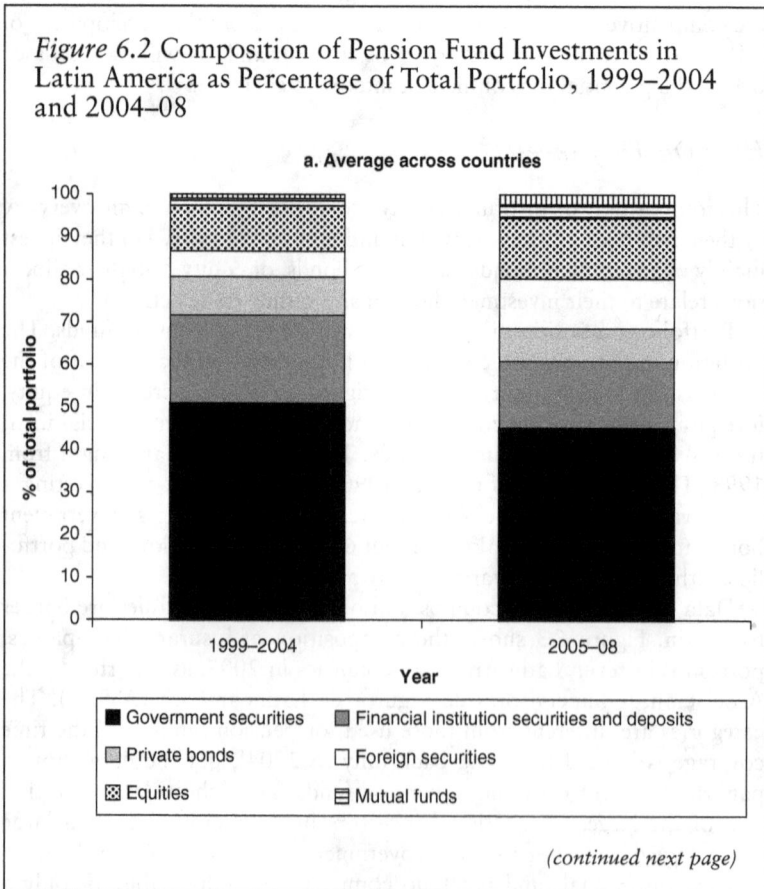

Figure 6.2 Composition of Pension Fund Investments in Latin America as Percentage of Total Portfolio, 1999–2004 and 2004–08

(continued next page)

Figure 6.2 (continued)

b. By country

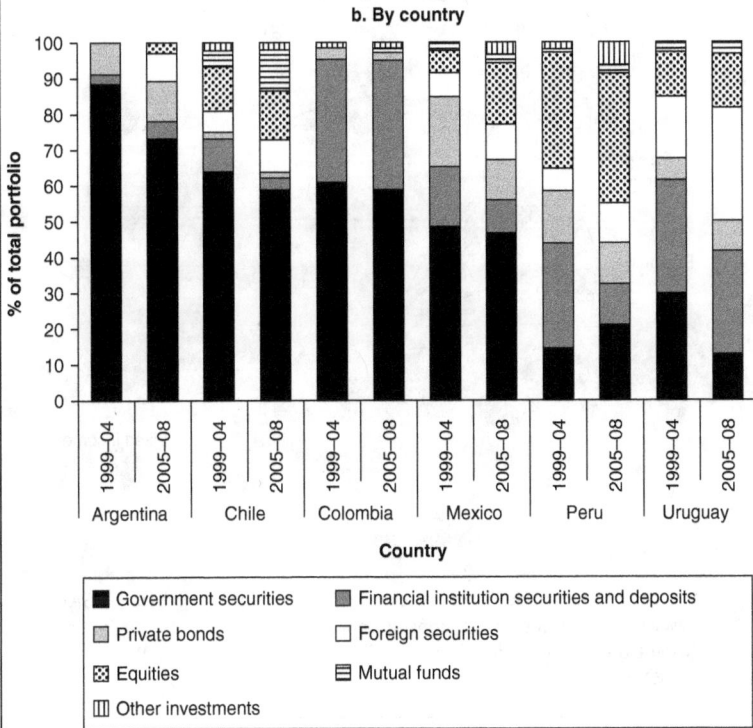

Legend:
- ■ Government securities
- ■ Financial institution securities and deposits
- □ Private bonds
- □ Foreign securities
- ▨ Equities
- ☰ Mutual funds
- ▥ Other investments

Source: Calculations based on data from FinStats; Beck et al. 2000; Yermo 2000; and Cheikhrouhou et al. 2007.

Note: Figure 6.2 shows the composition of pension fund investments as a share of the total portfolio between 1999 and 2008. Panel a shows average portfolio composition. Panel b shows the portfolio composition in each country.

especially among those that are relatively more opaque; but they also show that pension funds trade little (they mostly buy and hold assets) and that in several cases they follow momentum strategies (for example, a fund may buy assets that experienced an increase in price). Opazo, Raddatz, and Schmukler (2009) show that Chilean pension and mutual funds invest a large proportion of their assets in short-term securities (60 percent at less than three years) and that only insurance companies invest a larger fraction at long horizons. While all this evidence comes from only one country, Chile is one of the most financially developed countries in the region, and the patterns may likely be present in other countries as well.

Figure 6.3 Composition of Insurance Companies' Portfolios in Selected Latin American Countries, 2007 *(% of total portfolio)*

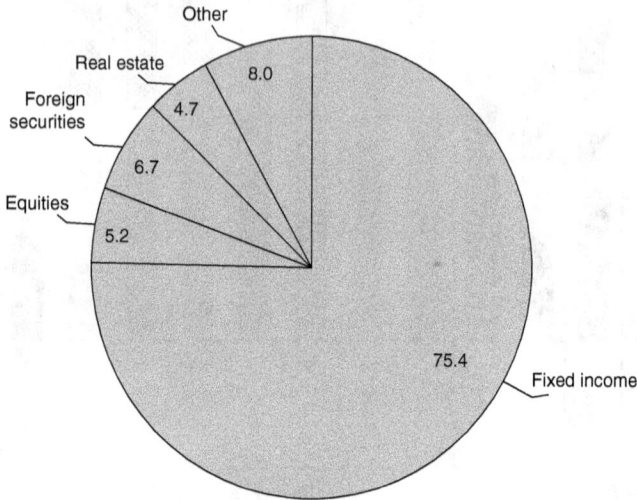

Other

Real estate

8.0

Foreign securities

4.7

6.7

Equities

5.2

75.4

Fixed income

Source: Asociación de Supervisores de Seguros de Latinoamérica (ASSAL), http://www.assalweb.org/index_consulta.php.

Note: Countries include Argentina, Chile, Colombia, Mexico, Peru, and Uruguay.

The Process of Financial Intermediation and Resulting Agency Problems

As intermediation gradually moves outside the banking system in Latin America, individuals increasingly rely on asset management companies, such as institutional investors, and absorb greater direct risks by becoming shareholders instead of insured debt holders. The movement of funds outside the relationship-based banking system introduces new challenges arising from the need to deal with agency problems on multiple layers. As folk wisdom indicates, the more participants involved in a transaction, the larger the potential for agency problems.

Financial intermediation through institutional investors raises several agency problems that are different from those resulting from the interaction between savers and banks. As noted by Diamond and Rajan (2001), financial institutions such as mutual funds are fundamentally different from banks because they do not create liquidity; and, as asset managers

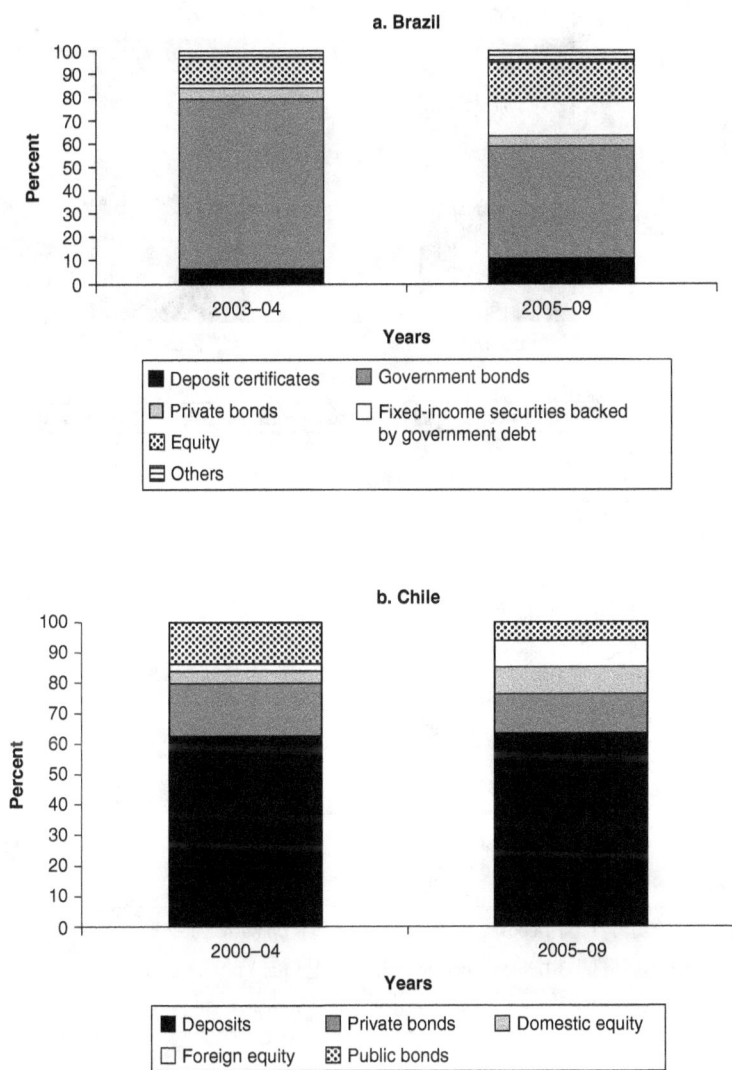

Figure 6.4 Composition of Mutual Fund Portfolios in Selected Latin American Countries *(% of total assets)*

(continued next page)

Figure 6.4 *(continued)*

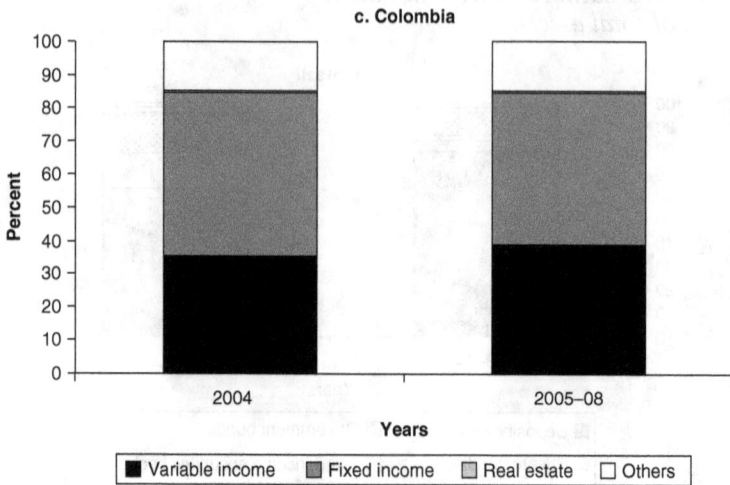

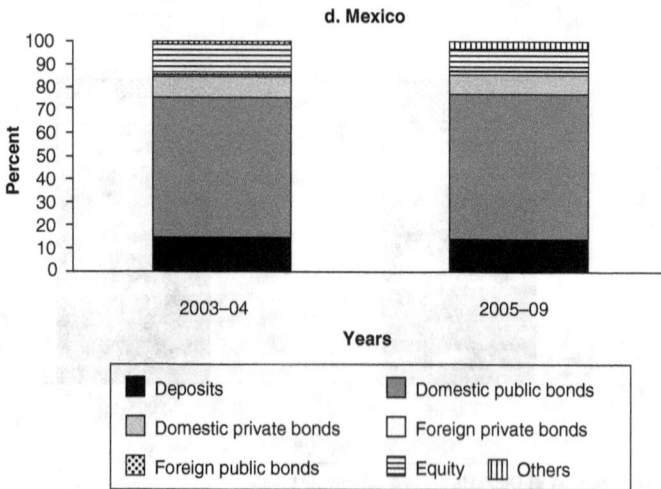

c. Colombia

Legend: ■ Variable income   ■ Fixed income   ■ Real estate   □ Others

d. Mexico

Legend: ■ Deposits   ■ Domestic public bonds   ■ Domestic private bonds   □ Foreign private bonds   ▨ Foreign public bonds   ▤ Equity   ▥ Others

(continued next page)

Figure 6.4 (continued)

e. Peru

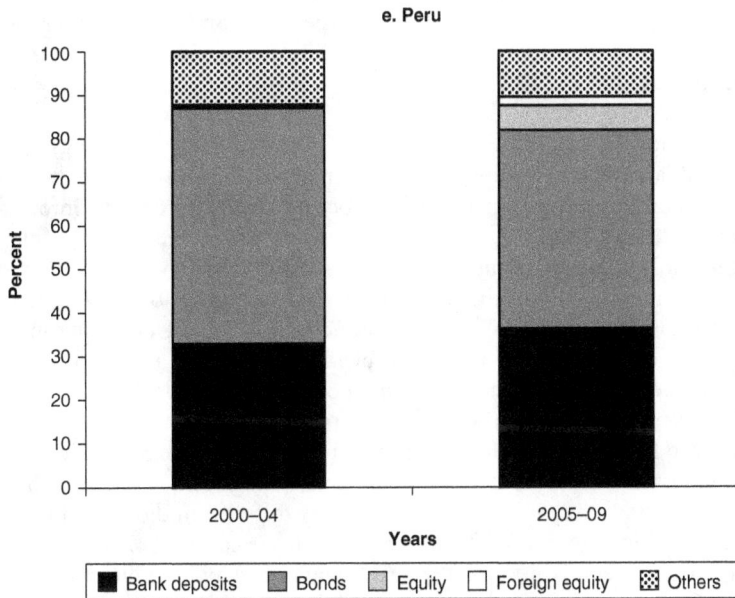

Bank deposits ■ Bonds ■ Equity □ Foreign equity ▨ Others

Source: IMF's IFS; FGV-Rio; Conasev; Superfinanciera; Andima; Banxico.
Note: For all countries, the original data are in current US$ millions.
In the case of Brazil, we had to adjust to current values (using the IGP-M
index), once the data come in constant terms. For Peru, we aggregated Fondos
Mutuos with Fondos de Inversiones. Equity includes "acciones de capital" and
"acciones de inversion" for fondos mutuos, while in the case of investment
funds, equities are composed by "acciones de capital," "fondos de inversion,"
and "otras participaciones" until 2002, and "derechos de participacion
patrimonial" from 2004 on. In the case of Colombia, Fondos Vigilados and
Fondos Controlados are reported in different tables for 2002. Period averages
are calculated using simple averages.

only, they do not have hard liabilities, and claim holders do not have
strong incentives to run in case of distress. Thus, because the structure
of liabilities and the threat of a run do not provide enough incentives for
asset managers, these incentives have to be provided through compensation schemes. To set up a road map for the rest of the chapter, this section
provides a simple description of the agents involved in the intermediation
process and discusses the potential agency problems arising from their
different interactions.

The process of financial intermediation through an institutional investor has some characteristics that are common across markets and others that are particular to each type of investor and to each country. Figure 6.5 shows the relation among agents involved in the operation of a prototype institutional investor. The figure does not aim to be exhaustive, but only to highlight the main interactions among the different players.[7]

As shown in figure 6.5, institutional investors gather savings from individuals (underlying investors) and invest them on their behalf. This delegation of the investment decision occurs under asymmetric information and gives rise to agency problems from "delegated portfolio management." These problems relate to the effort made by asset managers to gather information about securities and to the action they take on that information (portfolio selection and risk taking). Underlying investors can deal with these agency problems by imposing market discipline through compensation schemes and, in open-ended funds, by choosing to leave the manager (outflows). This divergence of interests may also occur between firm management and asset managers within the company, and it is addressed through compensation schemes with specific evaluation horizons and other types of incentives that may differ from those used by the individual investors in their interaction with the company. A related, but slightly different, issue is that the asset manager may have direct interests in some of the firms available in the market. Those interests may further bias the portfolio selection *(related lending)*.

Institutional investors are usually regulated, and those regulations will affect their operations. The regulator acts under asymmetric information with respect to the institutional investor, and there may also be a divergence of interests between the regulator and the individual investor. In this relationship, regulators will impose requirements on institutional investors to help address the delegated portfolio management problems, and institutional investors will lobby to obtain regulation better suited to their preferences and to capture the regulator *(regulatory capture)*.

Regulations may require risk-rating agencies to rate securities that can be purchased by institutional investors. There is also some degree of asymmetric information between the rating agency and the asset manager on the true quality of the issuance and on the relation between the agency and the issuer, which may result in inappropriate ratings *(conflict of interest, rating shopping)*.

It is rare that individual investors independently select asset managers and asset management companies. Most typically, these investors learn about the products through the sales and distribution channels of these companies. Again, the salesperson may have better information about the quality and nature of the services being offered to investors, which leaves scope for aggressive sales practices based on partial information *(predatory practices)*.

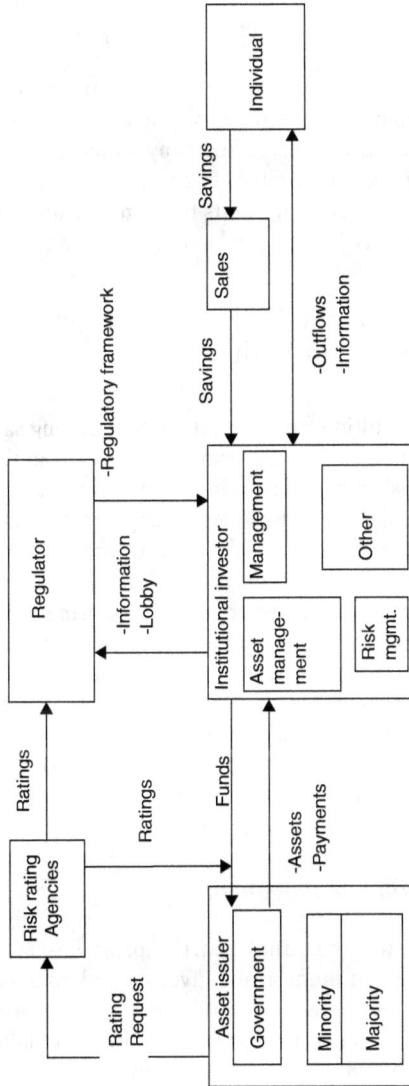

Figure 6.5 Prototype Institutional Investor Operation

Source: Asociación de Supervisores de Seguros de Latinoamérica (ASSAL), http://www.assalweb.org/index_consulta.php.
Note: Countries include Argentina, Chile, Colombia, Mexico, Peru, and Uruguay.

During their operation, institutional investors may acquire control rights as shareholders of companies. This situation exposes them to the standard agency problems among shareholders, debt holders, and management. Since institutional investors are larger and more sophisticated than individual investors, they are in a better position to address the agency problems related to corporate governance in representation of their investors.

Finally, the boundaries of institutional investors may include the sales and distribution channels and other segments of the financial markets. The investors are also connected to many other segments. As a result, some of them may become too big or too interconnected to fail and may anticipate government action if events turn unfavorable. This expectation will likely affect their risk-taking behavior.

Dealing with Agency Problems and the Consequences in Latin America

The agency issues resulting from the interaction among savers, firms, governments, and institutional investors are different from those present in a traditional relationship-based banking system. In these interactions, the compensation schemes faced by asset management companies and asset managers within these companies play a central role. Without the contract structure used by banks, based on demand deposits, these compensation schemes provide incentives to exert effort in information acquisition and to take risk.[8] Furthermore, the competitive and corporate structure of the financial system in Latin American countries would also caution us to pay close attention to the issues of related lending and regulatory capture.

The following section gives a detailed description of each of these agency issues and discusses their importance for Latin American countries based on existing evidence. The focus is on delegated portfolio management, related lending, regulatory capture, and moral hazard (too-big-to-fail).[9]

Delegated Portfolio Management

An extensive literature has analyzed the problems resulting from the relationship between an uninformed investor and an asset manager with better information on the returns of different risky securities than the client whose assets he or she is managing. The literature labels this problem the *delegated portfolio management* problem.[10]

The main question underlying the delegated portfolio management literature is how individual investors (or their representatives) can provide appropriate incentives for asset managers and the consequences of popular incentive schemes for taking risk and eliciting effort. The following discussion distinguishes between direct incentives provided to asset managers either by individuals or by the companies where they work, indirect incentives resulting from the decision of investors to move their savings across funds, and regulatory incentives set by the authority in representation of individual investors. In each case, the discussion focuses on the conditions in Latin American countries and on the main institutional investors in the region.

Direct Incentives An important part of the theoretical literature on delegated portfolio management focuses on how the direct incentives embedded in sharing rules and compensation schemes affect the efforts of asset managers to gather information about risky assets and invest optimally based on that information. While the literature typically assumes a direct interaction between the individual investor and the asset manager, in practice asset managers typically work for an asset management company (AMC). The individual investors pay fees to the AMC that vary across funds, and the AMC pays the managers for their work. Although in many cases the structure of fees may correspond to the manager's compensation arrangement, this does not need to be the case. One can think about compensation schemes as having two layers, one between the individual investor and the AMC and another between the AMC and the manager. This distinction may be especially important for the type of pension funds in Latin America, where the law regulates the fee structure charged by AMCs.

Pension Funds In most Latin American countries with a fully capitalized, privately managed, individual-contribution pension system,[11] future pensioners pay management fees corresponding to a percentage of the contributions to the fund during the accumulation phase. For instance, the contribution and management fees may be set to 5 percent and 1 percent of the worker's gross income. The worker would thus be paying a fee corresponding to 20 percent of the contribution. The fees currently charged by pension fund administrators (PFAs) in different Latin American countries and their structure are shown in table 6.4.

Under the typical Latin American fee structure based on a percentage of the inflows, a worker pays the PFA upfront for the management of the funds associated with his or her contribution. The PFA does not charge again for managing the funds that entered in the past. These upfront fees are not returned to the workers if they decide to move to a different PFA, and thus the new PFA would only benefit from the fees resulting from future contributions made by the workers, while having to administer the full stock of the workers' assets.

Evidently, this type of fee structure is not directly related to the PFA's absolute or relative performance (with the exceptions of Costa Rica and the Dominican Republic). A worker pays the same amount to the PFA regardless of the gross return obtained by the fund and of its performance relative to its peers. Thus, any impact of the fee structure on the behavior of PFAs will necessarily come from indirect or regulatory incentives.

Table 6.4 Fees Charged by Pension Fund Administrators in
Selected Latin American Countries, as Percentage of Workers'
Gross Income, 2006
(percent)

Country	Capitalization account	Fund administrator commission	Subtotal	Disability insurance	Total
Argentina	4.41	1.22	5.63	1.37	7.00
Bolivia	10.00	0.50	10.50	1.71	12.21
Colombia	11.00	1.55	12.55	1.45	14.00
Costa Rica	4.25	a	4.25	b	4.25
Chile	10.00	1.36	11.36	1.06	12.42
El Salvador	10.30	1.40	11.70	1.30	13.00
Mexico	5.24	1.26	6.50	c	6.50
Peru	10.00	1.83	11.83	0.91	12.74
Dominican Republic	7.00	0.50	7.50	1.00	8.50
Uruguay	11.95	2.03	13.98	1.02	15.00

Source: Federación Internacional de Administradores de Fondos de Pensiones
(FIAP), *Tasas de Cotización y Topes Imponibles en los Países con Sistemas de
Capitalización Individual.* March 2007. http://www.fiap.cl/prontus_fiap/site/
artic/20070608/asocfile/20070608111120/asocfile120070404111944.doc.

a. Commissions are charged on a different basis from percent of gross income.

b. Disability insurance is covered by the Public Program that has a cotization rate
of 7.5 percent.

c. Disability insurance is financed by the worker (0.625 percent), employer (1.75
percent), and state (0.125 percent), but it is administered by the Instituto Mexicano de
Seguridad Social.

It may be the case that although the fees charged by the PFAs to workers
do not contain direct incentives, the compensation schemes offered by the
PFAs to their asset managers do. Although there are no systematic data on
the types of asset managers' compensation schemes, anecdotal evidence
suggests that their compensation increases according to how they rank
among their peers in gross returns, with some extra compensation for
persistent good rankings, and that there are tight controls on risk taking to keep them from hitting the band of minimum returns imposed by
the regulator.[12] These schemes balance two forces. First, compensation
based on ranking is nonlinear in returns and convex.[13] It may be highly

nonlinear if there is only a bonus for reaching first place in the ranking. Although the theoretical literature has shown that convexity in compensation is not necessarily related to more risk taking, the empirical evidence suggests some relation in this direction (Chevalier and Ellison 1997; Elton, Gruber, and Blake 2003). Second, compensation schemes based on a tracking error—the percentage deviation of returns with respect to a benchmark—tend to reduce the incentives for risk taking relative to the benchmark, since risk makes it more likely to end up with a higher tracking error than the allowed amounts. The incentives for herding around a benchmark become even stronger if there is a serious penalty for hitting a given threshold below the benchmark, as is believed to be the case in countries like Chile.

The balance between these two opposite forces will depend on their relative strength: that is, how important the incentives are for risk taking resulting from ranking-related bonuses relative to the incentives for herding resulting from tracking errors and penalties for below-average returns. The explicit quantitative controls on risk taking in cases like Chile suggest that the balance is tilted against risk taking. This balance is not surprising because the PFA sets these internal incentives, and they likely depend on the impact that a high ranking and a low relative return may have on its income. As we will see below, there is little evidence that net inflows respond to performance, even when performance is measured by a fund's ranking. As we will also see below, however, PFAs may face serious regulatory costs if their returns are too far below average.

Available empirical evidence on PFAs' investment behavior seems to confirm this prediction. Several studies have documented the presence of herding in trading among PFAs in Chile (Olivares 2004; Raddatz and Schmukler 2008). Also using data from Chile, Opazo, Raddatz, and Schmukler (2009) show that PFAs invest a large part of their portfolios in bank deposits and other short-term assets that face very little short-term risk. They conclude from a series of counterfactual experiments that this behavior is due to the PFAs' incentives to herd in short-term returns.

According to the available evidence, then, the PFAs face weak direct incentives, and the incentives these PFAs give to their asset managers bias them toward conservatism. The rationale for this bias will be further clarified in the discussion of indirect and regulatory incentives.

Mutual Funds Existing evidence indicates that mutual fund fees in Latin America are high (Edwards 1996; Maturana and Walker, 1999; Borowik and Kalb 2010; Yermo 2000). Their structure, however, is relatively standard. Table 6.5 compares the simple average of the fees charged by a sample of equity, fixed income, balanced, and money market funds in six Latin American countries.[14] The table shows that the main type of fee charged by Latin American mutual funds is a fixed annual fee proportional to the assets under management (AUM). This fee is typically

Table 6.5 Mutual Fund Fees in Selected Latin American Countries

	Annual fixed fee (% Assets under management [AUM])	Funds with performance fee (% of funds)	Entry fees (% amount deposited)	Exit fees (% AUM)	Exit fees (% funds with sliding scale)	Office expenses fees (% AUM)	Funds with minimum investment (% of funds)	Sample of funds
Balanced funds								
Argentina	2.6	0	0.005	0.50	0	0	50	2
Brazil	2.0	70	0	0.50	0	0	100	10
Chile	4.8	0	0	2.38	60	0	80	5
Colombia	1.9	0	0	0.00	20	0	100	5
Mexico	4.2	0	0	0.00	0	0.008	50	4
Peru	3.0	0	0	1.17	0	0	100	3
Average	3.1	12	0.001	0.76	13	0.0013	80	
Bond funds								
Argentina	2.6	0	0.002	3.00	20	0	80	5
Brazil	2.4	0	0	0.00	0	0	100	10
Chile	1.5	0	0	0.00	40	0	100	5
Colombia	1.6	0	0	0.00	0	0	100	4
Mexico	3.2	0	0	0.00	0	0	60	5

Table 6.5 (continued)

	Annual fixed fee (% Assets under management [AUM])	Funds with performance fee (% of funds)	Entry fees (% amount deposited)	Exit fees (% AUM)	Exit fees (% funds with sliding scale)	Office expenses fees (% AUM)	Funds with minimum investment (% of funds)	Sample of funds
Peru	2.5	0	0	1.92	0	0	100	3
Average	2.3	0	0.0003	0.82	10	0	90	
Equity funds								
Argentina	3.9	0	0.002	0.40	20	0	80	5
Brazil	2.3	40	0	0.50	0	0	100	10
Chile	4.4	10	0	0.00	70	0.004	70	10
Colombia	0.6	0	0	0.00	0	0	100	1
Mexico	3.7	0	0	0.00	0	0.002	20	5
Peru	3.2	0	0	1.83	0	0	100	3
Average	3.0	8	0.0003	0.46	15	0.001	78	
Money market funds								
Argentina	1.2	0	0.002	3.00	20	0	80	5
Brazil	2.1	0	0	0.00	0	0	100	10
Chile	1.3	0	0	0.00	0	0	80	5
Colombia	1.2	0	0	0.00	0	0	100	4

(continued next page)

Table 6.5 (continued)

	Annual fixed fee (% Assets under management [AUM])	Funds with performance fee (% of funds)	Entry fees (% amount deposited)	Exit fees (% AUM)	Exit fees (% funds with sliding scale)	Office expenses fees (% AUM)	Funds with minimum investment (% of funds)	Sample of funds
Mexico	4.0	0	0	0.00	0	0	80	5
Peru	2.2	0	0	0.08	0	0	100	3
Average	2.0	0	0.0003	0.51	3	0	90	

Source: Based on information from mutual fund prospectuses in each of the countries.

larger for balanced and equity mutual funds and smaller for bond and money market mutual funds. Performance fees are rare and occur in only a fraction of Brazilian and Chilean equity and balanced funds.[15] Bond and money market funds do not charge performance fees. There are typically no entry fees (front-end loads), but exit fees are slightly more common, with funds charging an exit fee either at all events (back-end loads) or conditional on a minimum stay (so-called contingent differed sales charge).[16] Most funds in the region, across types, also require a minimum investment to enter, similar to that charged by mutual funds in developed countries.

As shown in table 6.5, a widespread aspect of compensation embedded in the funds' fee structure is that performance fees are rarely used and that, when used, they do not make a distinction between alpha and beta—the component of returns related to a manager's ability and risk taking, respectively—but depend on gross returns. Thus, alpha-generating managers earn fees similar to those who get returns from taking risk. This could give incentives to take more systemic risk rather than increase alpha, since boosting the latter requires actual selection abilities.[17] Nonetheless, the ultimate incentives for risk taking will depend on the responsiveness of managers' compensation to relative performance, which is believed to be small.[18]

Furthermore, there seems to be little long-term consequences to performance. Manager turnover is high, and actual portfolio management is usually an entry-level position in a financial firm. As a result, asset managers in the region are unlikely to have strong career concerns. The impact of this combination on risk taking is ambiguous, but together with the use of tracking error and a small response to overperformance, it may induce a conservative bias. Based on the circumstantial evidence discussed above, this is likely to be the case in Latin America.[19]

As previously mentioned, the provision of personalized portfolio management services to wealthy individuals is believed to be large in Latin America. In fact, even in the United States this industry has assets under management similar to the mutual fund industry. These services are unregulated, and little information is available on their operations; but they seem to follow a fee structure similar to that of mutual funds based on a fixed fee on assets under management. These services are also typically provided by the same banks and financial institutions that offer mutual funds, so that they probably provide similar incentives to the asset managers. The sales force, however, plays a more important role here than in the distribution of standardized products like mutual funds. Compensation to the distribution channel may be very important. In fact, anecdotal evidence from Mexico indicates that 70 percent of collected fees in this industry go to distributors and 30 percent to asset managers.

Overall, mutual fund fees in Latin American countries are typically high and do not include direct incentives linked to performance. Some anecdotal evidence indicates that asset managers are weakly rewarded for performance and that direct incentives are unlikely to play a major role in inducing risk taking.

Insurance Companies The assets of insurance companies consist mainly of portfolios of securities, but insurance companies do not charge management fees to insured persons. Unlike other institutional investors, insurance companies face substantial scope for asymmetric information on the side of the insured (moral hazard and adverse selection), so that contracts are structured to minimize this asymmetric information problem (for example, by requiring deductibles) without the goal of disciplining the insurance company.[20] Regrettably, there is little or no information on the type or structure of the fees insurance companies pay for asset management. In the cases in which asset management is internal to the company, confidential internal compensation policies provide the incentives for asset managers, in conjunction with the internal supervision carried out by the risk management function and other internal control systems. When asset management is external to the company, fee structures are likely to be similar to those charged by mutual fund companies; but, based on existing evidence, the fees charged by these companies to institutional investors are significantly lower and not subject to front- or back-loaded fees.

The discussion above indicates that fees charged to insured individuals offer no direct incentives for the insurance company. Instead, the companies' incentives come directly from their liability structure. Conditional on solvency, these incentives lead companies to monitor the allocation of assets properly. However, the equity of company shareholders declines if the value of the assets falls below the value of their expected liabilities (minus reserves). Similar to any firm that issues debt, these liabilities result in a convex payoff structure—a return below the value of liabilities results in no income for shareholders, but they are the residual claimants of any return in excess of that value—for shareholders. This convexity may induce shareholders to take excessive risk, but we will see that under normal conditions, regulatory constraints will significantly reduce the possibilities and incentives to do so.

Indirect Incentives Even if the direct compensation schemes do not provide high-powered incentives, the response of investors to performance can provide them. For instance, since mutual funds typically charge fees corresponding to a percentage of assets under management, the behavior of inflows and outflows is crucial for the profitability of fund administrators. Moreover, being a fraction of assets under management, these indirect incentives are convex,[21] so that they could affect the attitude of managers toward risk. The rest of this section discusses the role of these types of incentives in the main asset management industries in Latin America.

Pension Funds In many Latin American countries, fees charged by PFAs are typically a percentage of a worker's monthly contribution. Assuming that management costs increase along with assets under management, this fee structure makes workers with a low stock of assets much more profitable than those with a higher stock. Economies of scale would reduce the cost differential between these two types of workers, but it is unlikely to reverse it. For the high-flow worker, the PFA is collecting today the fees for future administration of the contributions and their future returns, while incurring little costs. In contrast, for a worker with a high stock already paid to the PFA for administration, the PFA is incurring a higher current management cost than the income it gets from the current fees. Since the fees collected for past contributions do not move with the worker when he or she moves to a different PFA, a PFA that captures relatively younger workers will have a higher income flow than one that serves mainly older workers close to retirement.

This structure could create a bias toward high-flow, low-asset clients, such as young workers, and the behavior of these workers might guide PFAs' behavior. For instance, if young workers are less risk averse than older ones, PFAs may be tempted to increase returns by taking more risk to attract this segment. In addition, since pension benefits are far in the future for young workers, they may respond more strongly to current transfers coming from the PFAs.[22]

Whether the types of fees charged by PFAs provide incentives to adjust performance depends crucially on whether workers (especially young ones) respond to any measure of PFAs' performance when deciding to change administrators. Most of the available evidence suggests that net inflows to PFAs do not strongly respond to performance or to management fees. Instead, they respond to the number of salespersons deployed by PFAs. The deployment of a large number of salespersons increases net transfers and the elasticity of these transfers to returns and fees (see Berstein and Micco 2002; Berstein and Ruiz 2004; Berstein and Cabrita 2007; García-Huitrón and Rodríguez 2003; Meléndez 2004; Armenta 2007; Masías and Sanchez 2006; Chisari et al. 1998). Some evidence shows a positive correlation between inflows and performance, when the latter is measured as obtaining a first-place ranking in profitability across PFAs, but the magnitude is small (Cerda 2006).

There are several possible explanations for this lack of market discipline on PFAs. A simple possibility is that in many countries workers may find regulatory barriers to changing administrators. These barriers, however, are typically temporary and should not preclude movements resulting from persistent differences in performances or fees.[23] It is also possible that workers lack the appropriate information to decide whether it is convenient for them to change PFAs. Some of the evidence discussed above on the impact of the sales force on increasing the price elasticity of transfers points in this direction.[24] There are also some behavioral explanations for the workers' lack of responsiveness to performance. For instance, Yermo (2000) argues that the compulsory nature of the contributions, which are deducted from payroll, reduces the ownership that workers have over the funds. Workers may correctly or incorrectly assume that the compulsory nature of contributions makes the government implicitly accountable for providing them a pension, and the existence of minimum return guarantees in many countries may undermine workers' incentives to exert market discipline if there is not much variation in performance (as seems to be the case) and there are fixed costs of monitoring.

Mutual Funds Indirect incentives likely play a larger role in mutual funds than in PFAs for two reasons. First, mutual funds typically charge fees as a percentage of assets under management. Thus, net inflows into (out of) funds have a direct impact on fees, without the considerations about stocks versus flows that are relevant for pension funds. Second, even if net inflows do not respond to returns, a higher return increases the assets under management and therefore increases fee income.

While the relationship between performance and net inflows in U.S. mutual funds has been extensively studied, there is virtually no evidence of that relationship for Latin American mutual funds. Some evidence comes from Opazo, Raddatz, and Schmukler (2009), who find a significant correlation between a fund's lagged short-run excess returns (one to three-month lagged return relative to the industry average) and net inflows of assets to medium to long-term Chilean mutual funds. The slope of the relation estimated is small; a (large) 10 percent excess return will result in inflows equivalent to only 2 percent of assets. With the average fees, this would result in a fee income of 0.3 percent of the assets under management.[25] Interestingly, Opazo, Raddatz, and Schmukler (2009) find that inflows depend significantly only on short-term returns, indicating that market discipline on mutual funds in Chile imposes a bias toward short-term performance (there are no money market funds in their sample).[26]

In this regard, the evidence for Latin America is similar to that for the United States, which shows that the relation between performance and inflows imposes some indirect incentives and market discipline on managers. However, Opazo, Raddatz, and Schmukler (2009) also document that outflows in Chilean mutual funds are more volatile than in similar U.S. mutual funds. This finding may result from a higher volatility of returns but may also be the outcome of more volatile investor behavior. There are some grounds for this second possibility. Proper market discipline requires transparent, timely, and comparable information, which is typically lacking in Latin American mutual fund markets. Although there is relative standardization in the reporting of information by PFAs, the information produced by mutual fund companies in Latin America is harder to compare because there are more mutual funds than PFAs and products are not as standard as those offered by pension funds.[27]

In sum, indirect incentives and market discipline may play a larger role in the behavior of mutual funds than in pension funds in Latin America, making the former less conservative and more prone to risk taking than PFAs. However, the response of inflows to performance in mutual funds is still small and based mainly on short-term performance. Given the importance of mutual funds in today's Latin American financial markets, systematic data on portfolio compositions, fee structures, returns, and inflows are urgently needed, and the analysis of these data is of first-order importance.

Insurance Companies There is typically little market discipline in some lines of insurance like life and health, where shifting insurance providers may even be counterproductive for the insured (because of preexisting conditions). In other lines, like property and casualty, there is more scope for market discipline, but it is typically related to the premiums and deductibles rather than to the return on the portfolio of investments, since the latter is immaterial to the claim holder as long as the company does not go bankrupt. To the best of my knowledge, there is no systematic analysis of the impact of reduced asset profitability on the total value of policies held by a company (even outside Latin America). Most incentives on the investment side come from regulation and will be discussed next.

Regulatory Discipline There are several reasons for the regulation of institutional investors. One of the most important relates directly to the information asymmetries that give rise to the problem of delegated portfolio management discussed above. The rest of this section discusses the specific regulations imposed on each of the main institutional investors and their likely impact on incentives.[28]

Pension Funds PFAs are heavily regulated, especially in countries with compulsory retirement contributions.[29] Although the regulatory burden has declined in recent years, in most countries PFAs still face quantitative restrictions aimed at reducing risk taking along several dimensions (default risk, liquidity risk, and exchange rate risk), at increasing diversification, and at reducing potential conflicts of interest. The regulation typically has broad scope and a large number of constraints at the macrolevel. In all countries, there are also regulatory constraints on the amount that can be invested in specific assets, depending on the relationship of the issuer to the fund, the liquidity of the issuance, and so forth. Given the high number of regulatory constraints faced by an asset manager, the payoff to asset discovery—that is, to gathering information about investment opportunities—is limited.

Fund administrators are usually required to guarantee a minimum return and to put equity capital in each fund that can be used to top off funds when the return achieved is below the minimum. In most countries, this requirement is implemented through a minimum return based on an industry average or a benchmark.

Tight regulation on portfolio composition reduces the return to asset discovery. For instance, managers have little room to improve returns by gathering information on private companies when funds are required to invest a large percentage of their assets in government bonds. Furthermore, restricting the set of private companies to those that meet minimum market capitalization, liquidity, and bond ratings may result in a very limited set of potential securities in which PFAs can invest, especially in countries with underdeveloped capital markets where a small proportion of firms is listed and even a smaller proportion has issued debt.

In addition, minimum return bands reduce the incentives to take risk and favor keeping a low-return variance, especially when considering the evidence of a small return elasticity of inflows discussed above. A fund that outperforms the industry will experience at most a small increase in inflows and fees, but if the fund underperforms and is unable to meet the minimum guaranteed return, it will have to use equity capital to compensate affiliates. In Chile, for example, where the amount of equity capital is 1 percent of the value of the fund, a performance 1 percent below the band will wipe out equity and require new capital injections.[30]

Pension fund administrators have to report information to regulators and workers on a monthly basis, and regulatory bands are computed over relatively short periods. Even if outflows are not very responsive to performance, the emphasis on short-term reporting and evaluation periods increases incentives for funds to reduce short-term risk. One way to achieve this is by having short-term investment horizons and investing in short-term assets.[31] Evidence from Opazo, Raddatz, and Schmukler (2009) suggests that these incentives matter for PFAs' investments. They show that Chilean PFAs invest a large share of their portfolio in short-term assets such as bank deposits and short-term central bank bonds (akin to T-bills). For other countries, there is no evidence on the maturity composition of investments, but the composition of portfolios (see figure 6.2 above) shows that a large percentage of pension funds' assets is invested in government bonds and financial deposits. Coupled with the evidence of the relatively short maturity of Latin American government bonds (Broner, Lorenzoni, and Schmukler 2010), this finding is consistent with the prevalent short-termism documented for Chilean PFAs across Latin America.

The structure of regulatory incentives for Latin American pension fund administrators will likely lead them to be conservative in risk taking, especially when considering the low responsiveness of flows to performance. This conservatism shows up not only in the bias toward the selection of relatively safer types of assets (such as government bonds and bank deposits) but also in their short-term maturity. This conservative behavior may be what the regulator had in mind, but it is hard to reconcile the emphasis on short-term performance in an industry that is supposedly aiming to provide for retirement and that should therefore be better prepared to hold onto assets and take advantage of long-term opportunities.

Mutual Funds Mutual funds are much less heavily regulated than PFAs in Latin America. Nonetheless, in many countries they face restrictions on the quality of assets in which they can invest (minimum ratings); on the maximum amounts they can invest in individual corporations, in equity shares, or in bond issuances; and on regulatory information requirements. Some of these regulations aim at separating different types of mutual funds. For instance, they stipulate the thresholds for the composition of mutual fund portfolios for classification as a bond fund or an equity fund. There are also some restrictions on the amounts that can be invested in shares of related companies. These restrictions are lighter than those on pension funds, and it is unclear whether they are binding for portfolio decisions.

Regulation may have some effect on market discipline by defining and controlling the type of information provided to fund shareholders and by imposing constraints on the compensation schemes that can be used. On the first front, the information that funds are required to report, after the prospectus, is relatively sparse and is limited to the value of the fund share, the returns, and the monthly fees charged. Investment styles and segments that could be used for comparisons seem not to be standardized, and, for most countries, there are no independent companies tracking and benchmarking local funds (as Morningstar does for funds in several developed countries). Funds also have to report transactions and portfolios on a regular basis to the regulator. For instance, in Brazil, Chile, and Mexico, funds have to report the detailed composition of their portfolios on a monthly basis (Brazil permits some aggregation in cases where revealing positions may affect the fund's investment strategy).[32] On the second front, some countries specify the type of fees that funds can charge. The rules here also seem to be broad, mainly restricting the type of services that can be charged but imposing little structure on the fees. While some countries like Brazil explicitly allow performance fees, others like Mexico do not specify in their regulation the base over which fees can be paid. These broad regulations are unlikely to impose serious constraints on the behavior of mutual funds or to offer these funds effective incentives.

In contrast to PFAs, there is no minimum guaranteed return on mutual funds. The mutual fund manager and administrators are liable only for misconduct. This is also the case for managers of personal portfolios, who are largely unregulated and subject to rules against misconduct. At most, these managers are required to be registered with the supervisor.

Overall, while there are some light regulatory constraints on the risks that mutual funds' can take, the type of fees that funds can charge, and the information they have to report, no clear regulatory incentives are imposed on Latin American mutual funds. Thus, incentives will come mainly from direct and indirect market discipline.

Insurance Companies Insurance companies are usually tightly regulated to ensure that they can meet their liabilities. Among the many regulations, they are required to manage their investments in a sound and prudent manner (establishing a clear investment policy and the mechanisms to monitor its conduct) and to maintain certain minimum technical provisions, capital, and reinsurance coverage to cover expected and unexpected liabilities. Many Latin American countries explicitly establish limits on the types and quantities of assets in which insurance companies can invest. Regulators enforce these rules through information gathering and on- and off-site inspections, and the regulator may intervene in companies that do not meet these thresholds.[33]

In many jurisdictions, there is some form of protection or special status assigned claims on insolvent insurance companies, but the detailed implementation of this coverage of last resort varies. For instance, in the United States there is a fee charged ex post to other insurers within the state to cover policies with a bankrupt insurance company up to a cap. In Latin American countries, policyholders enjoy preferential debtor status, but there is no government-provided fund. Nonetheless, many countries allow for the possibility that regulators will transfer portfolios from distressed insurance companies before they reach bankruptcy.

Overall, insurance companies face restrictions on the composition of their portfolios and are expected to conduct due diligence on their management, but they do not have to meet minimum return requirements or pay other fines related to underperformance. Thus, there are no strong regulatory incentives to engage in strategic portfolio allocation, but regulatory supervision and punishments are in place to ensure that companies adhere to prudent asset management policies.

Related Lending and Portfolio Biases

Most institutional investors in Latin America belong to local business groups or financial conglomerates. There is, therefore, the legitimate concern that the resources managed by these investors may be used to benefit related companies or banks.[34] This issue is not specific to institutional investors, since it applies equally to banks that belong to business groups. However, given the structure of bank liabilities and the additional layers of agents involved in the operation of institutional investors, the problems may be more prevalent and harder to detect within institutional investors. For instance, they may place deposits in banks that lend to related companies, thus providing funds in an indirect way. In addition, institutional investors may favor subscribing for securities underwritten by related banks, thus boosting banks' underwriting spreads.

A substantial literature has explored the benefits and problems arising from the impact of business groups on corporate control. In fact, in most countries business groups are the prevalent form of corporate organization. In that regard, the United States is largely an exception (La Porta, Lopez-de-Silanes, and Shliefer 1999). Most typically, these groups are organized as control pyramids, especially in Latin America.

Control pyramids and other corporate groups may have positive effects by helping overcome market frictions prevalent in developing countries, providing insurance across firms within the pyramid, and facilitating monitoring of individual business units. These structures, however, also entail potential problems. Some of the most important are those related to the agency issues and conflicts of interest that arise from the separation of cash flow and control rights typical of these corporate structures.[35] One of the agency issues arising from the presence of business groups in Latin American financial sectors relates to the possibility of *tunneling*. The literature uses this term to refer to the movement of resources from firms in the corporate structure (where the controller has relatively few cash-flow rights) to firms where cash-flow rights are higher. These movements may take the form of business transactions or the provision of capital at below market prices.

Tunneling may clearly be a problem in the relationship between banks and related firms, and it may also be a problem for institutional investors. These investors could bias their portfolios toward related firms beyond what is consistent with risk-return maximization, easing their placing of shares or bonds and, therefore, their access to credit. Regulation typically tries to contain this type of portfolio bias by placing caps on the portfolio share a fund can invest in related firms. Latin American countries are no exception, with most of them containing some form of restrictions on these types of activities. However, the complexity of the ownership structures in many Latin American countries, which mix control pyramids with horizontal and vertical cross-holdings, makes the enforcement of these rules difficult (Yermo 2000; Morck, Wolfenzon, and Yeung. 2005; Khanna 2000). Whether Latin American supervisors have the regulatory capacity to control this possible behavior needs to be addressed on a case-by-case basis.[36]

In addition to portfolio biases, there are other, more subtle ways in which tunneling may occur. For instance, while most regulations restrict the amount a fund can invest in the securities of related companies, the amounts placed as deposits in different banks are much less restricted. Therefore, a fund that has a relationship with a bank, as is common in Latin America, may privilege this bank when investing in deposits, despite differences in interest rates, or may decide to invest more in deposits than recommended for the management of short-term liquidity needs. Thus, a pension or mutual fund could serve as a liquidity provider for related banks, increasing their operating margins.[37] There is no systematic evidence of this behavior, but the large amount held in bank deposits by Chilean pension and mutual funds (see tables 6.6 and 6.7) indicates that this could be a potentially important problem (Opazo, Raddatz, and Schmukler 2009).[38] In addition, as shown in figure 6.2, the instruments of financial institutions (mainly deposits) also represent a large percentage of pension fund portfolios in other Latin American countries.

Beyond liquidity provision or direct purchases of the securities issued by related parties, there are multiple other ways that institutional investors can use their assets under management to benefit related financial companies. For instance, they can boost the profitability of the underwriting arms of related banks by subscribing for the issues where these banks are involved. This type of bias would unlikely be affected by most regulatory frameworks because the issuer is an unrelated company, but it could increase the underwriting spread obtained by the investment bank. This

Table 6.6 Share of Deposits in Portfolios of Chilean Pension Fund Administrators, by Pension Fund Category, 2002–05

	Mean (%)	Minimum (%)	Maximum (%)
Fund A (40 percent<equity<80%)	12.4	8.5	15.7
Fund B (25 percent<equity<60%)	17.8	13.8	20.3
Fund C (15 percent<equity<40%)	18.8	13.3	24.0
Fund D (5 percent<equity<20%)	20.3	13.8	26.3
Fund E (equity=0%)	17.0	11.0	28.8
All	17.3	n.a.	n.a.

Source: Based on data from Raddatz and Schmukler 2008.

Table 6.7 Share of Deposits in Portfolios of Chilean Mutual Funds, by Type of Fund

	Mean (%)	Minimum (%)	Maximum (%)	Cumulative share of total assets
Money market funds	78.0	8.2	98.0	40.0
Medium- and long-term funds	30.7	0.0	88.9	75.1
Short-term maturity funds	65.5	21.9	93.1	86.8
Capital market funds	0.7	0.0	2.8	92.3

Source: Chilean Superintendency of Values and Insurance.
Note: Types according to circular number 1578; http://www.svs.cl/normativa/cir_1578_2002.pdf.

problem may be particularly acute for unregulated individual portfolio managers where the financial adviser and the portfolio manager are both part of a bank or a bank subsidiary. In the case of pension funds, they can also use their influence on providers of annuity services to favor related companies to the detriment of their clients. This bias can be subtle; for instance, the funds probably have firsthand information on the time to retirement of their clients and may "tip" annuity sellers from related companies to capture them. In addition, in countries where pension and mutual funds hire distribution and operation services, the existence of ties with other financial institutions may also bias the hiring decisions.[39]

Overall, the high and complex degree of ownership connections between players in the Latin American financial markets makes the problem of related lending potentially significant. The main barrier to this behavior is regulation. It is important that regulatory enforcement be able to detect and sanction this type of behavior in an environment where ownership relations are opaque. Special attention should probably be paid to the management of liquidity and to the purchase of assets underwritten by related investment bank arms, in addition to portfolio composition. The importance of unregulated intermediation through individual portfolio management is also an area of concern. Some rules regulating or disclosing the allocation of assets underwritten by the institution that is managing the funds could at least increase the transparency of these practices.

Regulatory Capture

Regulation could help address the agency and coordination issues related to the information asymmetry in delegated portfolio management or the problem of portfolio biases. In fact, the rationale for regulation is typically based on the premise that small and dispersed investors lack the expertise and incentives to discipline managers properly (Dewatripont and Tirole 1994). This is the public interest view of regulation (Pigou 1932; Noll 1989). Complementary to this view is also a broad literature that sees regulation as the outcome of a game between regulators and the regulated industries, where both parties use regulation to further their private interests (for example, Stigler 1971; Noll 1989; Kroszner 1998; La Porta, Lopez-de-Silanes, and Shleifer 1999). According to this view, regulated industries frequently capture the regulators, and regulation ends up favoring the interests of the industry. Examples of these types of regulations are those that directly or indirectly restrict competition or benefit certain segments of society at the expense of another. These two views indicate that regulators may act as agents for the general population or may instead favor the regulated industry. In fact, most recent theoretical models of government action see the government's preferences as trading off public and private interests (see Grossman and Helpman 2002).

Although there is little evidence on the role and importance of private interests in the shaping of regulation in Latin America, some results from cross-country studies suggest that the issue should not be ignored.[40] For instance, several Latin American countries in the sample of Djankov et al. (2002) have very high barriers to entry and corruption levels. Dal Bó and Rossi (2007) find that electric companies are more inefficient in Latin American countries where regulators are easier to capture. Braun and Raddatz (2010) find numerous connections between politicians and banks in major Latin American countries. It is impossible to draw solid conclusions without hard evidence, and hard evidence that private interests determine regulatory outcomes is difficult to produce because proper identification of a causal link between private interests and regulation requires finding shocks to the relative strength of parties involved in the determination of regulation.

Public and private interest explanations can certainly account for the extent and scope of the regulation of institutional investors in Latin America. For instance, most countries restrict entry into the pension fund industry by imposing minimum capital requirements and, in some cases, by imposing costs on switching from one PFA to another (for example, in Mexico transfers are limited to one per year). While these restrictions can be explained by the need to guarantee that the players have "skin in the game" and to reduce the overhead cost resulting from excessive switching, they are clearly convenient for incumbents. Whether these restrictions bind and restrict competition is still an open question.[41]

Restrictions on the set of instruments in which institutional investors can invest also represent a barrier to entry to capital markets. Firms that are "investment grade" under local regulations benefit from much cheaper access to funds than smaller and younger firms. Again, safety considerations can easily motivate this type of restriction, although it is somewhat odd that these restrictions are typically stronger for pension funds that theoretically have longer investment horizons and would benefit from investing in "growth" firms. Finding evidence of the motivation behind this type of regulation is even harder than in other cases because the strength and lobbying ability of firms are likely to be highly correlated with their size and rating.

The structure of financial markets in Latin America might lead one to believe that the capturing of regulators through the revolving-door phenomenon (that is, regulators becoming industry participants and vice versa) is potentially more important in this region than in developed countries. First, the high concentration of economic and political power in Latin American countries creates closer ties between politicians and incumbents. Second, the relative scarcity of human capital reduces the set of potential candidates for technical positions that do not have ties to the industry. The smaller number of financial specialists in academia than in the private sector, for example, makes it hard to find candidates for regulatory positions that have no connections to the industry.[42] Third, the concentration of the financial sector makes it easier to lobby and to punish hostile regulators with limited future career prospects. Although the failure of most Latin American countries to impose "cooling-off" periods on regulators does not constitute formal proof of regulatory capture, it is a puzzling omission.[43]

Beyond regulatory capture, even a public interest view of the world may entail a conflict of goals between the regulators of institutional investors and the underlying investors. For instance, regulators may have secondary goals such as fostering capital market development or increasing financial stability that are not necessarily in the best interest of those putting money in pension or mutual funds. Even if these goals are welfare enhancing, there may be a nontrivial distributive component from the underlying investors in these funds to those benefited by financial stability or capital market development.

As stressed by Kroszner (1998), it is crucial to understand the incentives associated with the regulatory structure. The incentives given to regulators have a powerful impact on the implementation of policies. Are regulators trying to increase the size of the regulatory agencies as a way to increase their political influence? Are they trying to please higher-ranking politicians or potential contributors to improve their political careers? Are they trying to please the regulated industry to pursue a career in the private sector? Answering these questions will lead to a better understanding of the performance of the institutional investor industry and its impact on investor welfare.

Moral Hazard (Too Big to Fail)

The recent crisis has again brought to our attention the moral hazard issues resulting from ex post government rescues of financial institutions. One of the differences between previous incarnations of this argument and the current one has been the latter's emphasis on too-big-to-fail as a rationale for rescuing financial institutions in trouble.

Latin America fared relatively well during the recent crisis. However, it is important not to be complacent. One reason to worry is the degree of concentration in Latin America's financial sector, where in almost all countries there is significant concentration across financial markets. Furthermore, in many cases the same institutions are present as the main players across markets, either through subsidiaries or through business groups. As a result, the share of financial assets in the hands of the largest institutions is much larger than it was in the United States before the crisis.

While safeguards exist to limit the interaction between related financial institutions and to limit risk taking, even the unlikely event of the failure of one of these large financial players may have disastrous consequences. For instance, many mutual funds use related banks as distribution channels. Thus, even if safeguards operate properly (and this is an important *if*) problems with a bank may impair the ability of related mutual funds to raise money. Similarly, in some countries pension funds can invest money in mutual funds. Problems with these funds will affect the health of pension funds. Furthermore, pension and mutual funds keep large amounts of assets in bank deposits: if those funds have problems that require them to liquidate their banks deposits, an important source of bank funds may dry up on short notice. Alternatively, problems with the bank will affect the deposits that pensions and mutual funds hold (typically noninsured) and spread the malaise to those markets, too.

Considering these links and the within- and across-market concentration in most markets, Latin American financial markets seem to be more exposed than U.S. markets to institutions that are too big to fail; those institutions may rationally believe that they will be rescued if trouble arises and take on too much risk on that account. This potential problem is clearly seen in table 6.8, which shows the importance of the largest three banks, insurance companies, and pension and mutual fund companies in selected Latin American countries and compares them to similar segments in the United States before the recent crisis. The three largest banks in Latin America are much more important relative to the economy than the three largest banks in the United States. On average, the largest banks in the region are 50 percent more important than in the precrisis United States, and in cases like Brazil and Chile the difference is even larger. Insurance and mutual funds are typically less systemically important in Latin America than in the United States, but with some exceptions: insurance companies in Brazil and Chile seem particularly large. Where the difference in size of the largest institutions relative to those in the

Table 6.8 Too Big to Fail? Largest Three Institutions in Selected Countries as a Percentage of GDP, 2010–11

	Banks	Insurance	Mutual funds	Pension funds
Argentina	8.7	0.7	0.5	—
Brazil	41.9	2.6	24.4	8.2
Chile	43.2	4.5	12.5	34.2
Colombia	18.0	0.7	—	7.4
Mexico	20.2	0.6	4.7	2.8
Average LAC	26.4	1.8	10.5	13.1
United States[a]	17.6	1.9	31.0	3.9
Ratio of LAC to the United States	1.5	1.0	0.3	3.4

Source: Based on Economist Intelligence Unit data (various issues).
a. 2006.

United States is abysmal is in pension funds. In Chile, the three largest funds have assets corresponding to almost 35 percent of GDP.

Clearly, the sheer size of these intermediaries, their social role in the case of pension funds, and their interconnections with the rest of the financial system make them the "poster child" for too-big-to-fail institutions, with the consequent implications for moral hazard. It seems, therefore, important to take on the lessons of the recent U.S. subprime crisis and properly monitor these institutions, perhaps under a systemic approach. However, regulation is still segmented in many Latin American countries.

In a context of highly interconnected markets and ownership, like in Latin America, a piecemeal approach to regulation not only risks missing the two layers of connections between firms but also opens the possibility of indirect regulatory arbitrage in which financial institutions transfer assets to sectors with softer or easier-to-overcome regulations. For instance, as discussed above, pension funds may use mutual funds or banks to increase their allocation of assets to certain firms beyond what is feasible under regulatory constraints. The heavy use of bank deposits by these institutions may hint at the presence of this type of situation.

Conclusions

As institutional investors develop in Latin America, the agency issues discussed in this chapter will become increasingly more relevant. The evidence and discussion suggest that the incentives of institutional investors and other financial intermediaries matter for their asset allocation, maturity structure, risk taking, and investment horizon. In Latin America, so far these incentives have led investors to favor low-risk and short-term assets.

Restrictions on the supply of riskier or long-term assets are unlikely to fully explain this behavior, especially 10 or more years after institutional investors such as pension funds started playing a quantitatively important role in the region. First, supply and demand are inextricably linked. If an issuer anticipates low demand for long-maturity bonds, it may prefer to issue securities of shorter maturity rather than paying a hefty maturity premium. Second, there are assets that are not tapped by institutional investors, even within those that are permitted by regulation. Furthermore, the supply explanation is much weaker for mutual funds that can invest in foreign assets. Finally, some investors, like domestic insurance companies, do invest more heavily in longer-maturity assets.

Without an appropriate theoretical benchmark, which the literature lacks, it is impossible to say whether the conservative behavior of the main institutional investors is optimal. However, it is hard to explain why institutional investors such as pensions and mutual funds, which theoretically should have different investment horizons and optimal portfolios, would end up investing in similar assets. According to the evidence presented in this chapter, the reason is that they face similar incentives to invest in relatively safe, short-term assets. Furthermore, regardless of the optimality of these behaviors, it is clear that their investment choices have implications for the expected role of institutional investors as active players in the development of financial markets. Beyond the initial impetus that institutional investors gave to these markets in the 1990s, their contribution to lengthening the maturity of the yield curve and to the discovery of profitable new investment opportunities seems to be limited.

As discussed above, regulatory incentives appear to play an important role versus direct and indirect market incentives, especially for pension funds. This may be an endogenous outcome: in the presence of an active regulator, individuals may optimally decide not to exert market discipline. The initial regulation may also have determined the competition scheme followed by administrators, and the coordination of industry benchmarks may persist even after the regulations are relaxed.

Nonetheless, regardless of the causality, the evidence suggests that regulation of institutional investors forces trade-offs that may not have been completely obvious during the design phase. Among them, the trade-off between monitoring and returns is probably among the most important. Institutional investors, like pension funds, have the ability and means to acquire investments that are profitable in the long run, even if they may not be so in the short run. For instance, they could invest in growth firms, private equity, or long-term assets. Such investments could significantly increase returns for their underlying investors. However, in an environment of asymmetric information and conflict of interests, a trade-off appears. On the one hand, giving fund managers leeway to make long-run bets exposes investors and regulators to the possibility of realizing too late that managers did not collect sufficient information and that long-run investments thought to be good were really unprofitable, risky bets even from an ex ante perspective. On the other hand, subjecting managers to continuous short-run monitoring may reduce their willingness to undertake long-run investments, may lead them to rely excessively on short-term assets, and may reduce returns for underlying investors. Policy makers and regulators need to decide where to draw the line in this trade-off, according to the individual market's characteristics of their countries. For instance, countries with a strong guarantee of a minimum replacement rate may allow pension funds more leeway in choosing long-term investments. Nonetheless, the evidence presented in the chapter suggests that the current focus may be tilted too much toward short-run monitoring across the board, even in countries with a strong public component in their pension payments (a so-called first pillar). Circumstantial evidence on the returns to assets with different maturities suggests that shifting portfolios toward longer-term investments may have a positive impact on the long-run returns of investors, but clearly more research is needed to inform policy choices in this area. Furthermore, if institutional investors were more willing to invest in long-term assets, the demand for these instruments would increase the access of firms (and governments) to long-term financing.

In sum, the use of industry benchmarks such as minimum return bands may interact with market conditions to tilt incentives toward low-risk and short-term investments. This result may reduce short-term fluctuations in returns but may also entail important long-run costs for pensioners that need to be considered in the trade-off. Using these types of instruments to protect pensioners may not be a second-best solution. Strengthening the first-pillar components and giving more leeway to funds to engage in long-term investment opportunities may be a better way to combine safety with long-run returns, offer a good replacement rate, and foster capital market development. Clearly, more research is needed on these options.

The conservatism of institutional investors in Latin America seems to have paid off during the recent crisis. Their reliance on government bonds and bank deposits dampened the impact that declining equity prices had on the value of their portfolios. But it is important to realize that the situation could have been different if some domestic banks had been in trouble during the crisis or if the fiscal situation of any Latin American country had been questioned, as recently happened for European banks. In these cases, the heavy exposure of all institutional investors to financial sector and country risk could have resulted in large losses for these investors and even in problems for the whole Latin American financial sector because of the degree of interconnections in the region.

The discussion in the chapter also emphasizes the importance of conflicts of interest and related lending in the region. The concentrated corporate ownership structure and the prevalence of financial conglomerates operating in several financial services areas make these issues particularly important for Latin American countries. The prevalence of financial conglomerates in the region also implies that too-big-to-fail considerations are probably more important in Latin American countries than they were in the United States before the crisis. Arguably, even with firewalls, troubles in one segment of the operations of a financial conglomerate may spread to other segments through contingent credit lines, equity values, or brand association, causing a systemic impact. A systemic approach to regulation that considers these interconnections would help reduce the possibility of tunneling, regulatory arbitrage, and systemic shocks to the financial system, all of which favor the owners of the conglomerates at the expense of investors. Several countries have formally and informally moved in this direction. Further steps can be taken, though, and other countries still need to start thinking about ways to address the challenges of a large, tightly interconnected financial sector.

Because of the relative scarcity of human capital, the size of the financial industry relative to the whole economy, and the presence of large financial conglomerates, the possibility of regulatory capture also seems more likely in Latin American countries than in the United States. Considering that recent accounts of the crisis suggest that regulatory capture was important in shaping the attitude of the government toward regulation in the United States, this is an issue that needs attention, even if no actual evidence of capture exists. Addressing this concern is not easy in countries where specialized human capital may find a natural place in the regulated industry and few other comparable opportunities are available. Cooling-off periods paid by the government could contribute to reducing the scope and intensity of the revolving-door channel of capture.

While the current situation in the region is promising, it is important to remain alert to the interaction of large foreign capital inflows with the incentives of domestic institutional investors. At the end of the day, many economists now agree that it was the quick expansion of credit and the incorrect incentives of financial institutions that triggered the recent crisis. It is possible that access to cheap money may increase the risk appetite of mutual funds, where incentives are not so heavily tilted against risk taking as in pension funds, or of other less heavily regulated investors (like the nascent hedge and private equity fund industry, which are relatively large in countries like Brazil). While one may argue that risk taking by these institutions may have a limited impact because they are not leveraged, their strong connections with leveraged institutions (banks) pose risks that should not be ignored.

The scarcity of evidence, research, and discussion on the role of investors' incentives in the region is worrying, especially because theoretical models are ambiguous about the design of optimal incentive schemes in these industries. In the United States, there was much more evidence and research on the relationship between incentives and risk taking among financial market participants before the crisis. Yet the crisis still occurred. Not having a deep understanding of these issues is potentially risky. It is at this stage, when institutional investors are growing but are still developing, when it is appropriate to start thinking about the issues highlighted in this discussion.

Notes

1. A caveat with the figures comparing the assets of banks and other financial intermediaries is that these intermediaries typically hold an important fraction of their assets in bank deposits. Netting out those deposits, the relative importance of banks would be larger, but the changes in relative importance would be similar or larger because institutional investors used to have larger levels of bank deposits in the past.

2. Pension funds also dominate other nonbank institutional investors in a broader set of Latin American countries. Outside LAC7, pension funds have

64 percent of nonbank financial assets, but there are important differences within the region. Nonbank institutional investors are much smaller in Central American and Caribbean countries, reaching only half the share of GDP in LAC7 countries (14.2 percent versus 31.3 percent). Furthermore, in the Central American and Caribbean region, the insurance industry is larger than the mutual fund industry, as could be expected from the inclusion of Panama and Jamaica in this group.

3. "Are Unified Accounts the Next Big Trend?" *Wall Street Journal*, November 10, 2010.

4. This does not necessarily entail an increase in competition because the extent of competition may be more closely related to the number of fund adminis-tration companies.

5. Impavido, Lasagabaster, and Garcia-Huitron (2010) also mention that "the governance structure varies among countries, including private providers often sponsored by large financial holding companies [in Latin America]."

6. For instance, in Chile, Banco Santander owns the PFA Suma through a holding company. The criterion used above to estimate the fraction of PFA market associated with the largest banks would not detect a case like this in which the name of the PFA and the bank are different.

7. In figure 6.5, the boundaries of the different components have been set arbitrarily, but they may vary across types of investors and across companies. For instance, in the case of (mandatory) privately run pension funds, in many countries the distribution and collection take place within the company.

8. Because the absence of hard liabilities in many institutional investors may decouple the process of information acquisition (finding out about good invest-ment opportunities) and risk taking (allocating money to these opportunities), it is possible to have outcomes where appropriate risk taking occurs with inefficient information acquisition and vice versa (Stracca 2006).

9. The working paper version of this chapter (Raddatz 2011) includes a brief discussion on predatory practices (consumer protection) and aggregate risk taking.

10. Refer to the working paper version (Raddatz 2011) of this chapter for a review of this literature.

11. This section benefited greatly from discussions with Heinz Rudolph and Pablo Castañeda.

12. In Chile, the middle office controls the tracking error of the portfolios, and the back office exerts further control on the transactions to ensure that the tracking error remains within boundaries.

13. The nonlinearity comes from the stepwise functional form that ranking-based rules have. An increase in returns that does not change a manager's ranking does not increase payoffs, but an increase of the same amount that results in a jump in rankings raises these payoffs importantly. The convexity comes from these incentives having a zero return for reaching a very low ranking.

14. This evidence is not fully systematic because the sampling design is not representative. In each country and type of funds, the sample includes a number of funds equal to the minimum between 10 funds and 1 percent of the universe of funds, with a lower bound of 5 funds. Only in segments with fewer than 5 bonds was a smaller number permitted. These funds were selected from among those administered by the largest fund administrators in the country.

15. This may occur because some Brazilian balanced funds actually corre-spond to hedge fund–like structures.

16. An exit fee charged at all events is applied whenever an investor liquidates her position in the fund, regardless of how long she has held the position. A mini-mum stay fee is applied only when the investor liquidates her position before a predetermined amount of time.

17. For this reason, we may not need to worry much that U.S. funds are creating fake alpha. Furthermore, the instruments that were used to falsely increase alpha in the buildup to the recent crisis, such as CDSs (credit default swaps) with fat tails, are still not prevalent in Latin American markets, and in many cases are not within the set of assets in which the mutual funds can invest.

18. As in the case of pension funds, there is no systematic evidence on mutual fund managers' direct compensation schemes, and because of the larger number of players relative to the pension industry, anecdotal evidence is probably less informative. A simple extrapolation from the U.S. experience would suggest that it is likely that managers' compensation relates to the fees charged by the fund, but some anecdotal evidence suggests that this is not always the case. In countries like Chile, it is not uncommon for managers to be paid a fixed wage plus a bonus according to gross returns. Industry participants state that the slope of the bonus is small and tracking error is sometimes used. It is hard to reach a conclusion without further systematic evidence, but if the small slope is prevalent, there would be small incentives for risk taking.

19. The portfolio composition of Latin American mutual funds described in figure 6.4, highly biased toward government bonds and bank deposits—generally considered the safest types of assets available to these institutional investors—seems to confirm this conservatism. Furthermore, the relative importance of money market mutual funds that invest heavily in short-term, low-risk instruments probably leaves little scope for searching for yield among managers.

20. A type of adverse selection specific to insurance companies' interaction with other institutional investors is that arising from the option of buying annuities for retirement. Annuitization is voluntary in many countries. This opens the possibility of adverse selection in which people who expect to live longer annuitize their retirement income, while those with shorter expected life spans may decide to draw directly into their funds.

21. This is easily seen by noticing that assets under management are strictly positive. Thus, compensation is unbounded above but slowly converging to zero as assets deplete.

22. These transfers could take the form of gifts that PFAs have offered in some countries to attract new clients because regulation typically prohibits offering different rates based on age. It would be interesting to explore whether these gifts were mainly targeted to young workers, as this argument would suggest. Of course, with little mobility of workers across PFAs, from an intertemporal perspective each one would be collecting similar fees. Little mobility may result from reaching an equilibrium in which there are no large differences across PFAs in fees or products. In this regard, it is also interesting to note that in several countries the fees include penalties for quickly changing PFAs, thus further restricting mobility.

23. For instance, Chile, Colombia, and Mexico impose some type of restriction on the mobility of workers or salespersons.

24. Notice that the correlation between sales force and the elasticity could be spurious if firms with higher returns could deploy a larger sales force and also provide gifts that induce workers to move. Although there would be an apparent response of movements to returns, the actual movement would be driven by the gifts.

25. Although the U.S. literature has also explored the shape of this relation to determine if there is some extra convexity in incentives resulting from this shape, Opazo, Raddatz, and Schmukler (2009) only estimate linear relations, implicitly assuming a symmetric relation between net inflows and excess returns.

26. Regrettably, there is no evidence on these elasticities for different types of mutual funds that could be used to better assess the increase in fees and the impact on the bias toward safer assets.

27. As will be discussed next, mutual funds in Latin America are typically required to provide monthly information on gross returns and fees charged. According to market participants, performance comparison within the industry is difficult because, except for index funds, it is hard to define a set of peers or an appropriate benchmark relative to the fund's investment style. This requires a minimum of standardization within the industry, not necessarily resulting from regulatory constraints (for instance, the standardization of measurement may come from industry participants or financial advisory services), and a large number of peers in each investment style. The definition of benchmarks is also important for computing alphas and betas for individual funds that permit shareholders and potential investors if high returns are just the result of a high load on the benchmark (a beta higher than 1) or true value creation (a high alpha). As mentioned in the previous section, performance seems to be measured simply from gross returns, sometimes relative to nonstandard comparison groups, except for index funds. There are, therefore, few incentives for alpha creation, and beta loading may be an easier way of boosting returns under such circumstances.

28. Refer to the working paper version of this chapter (Raddatz 2011) for a detailed discussion of the rationale for the regulation of this sector.

29. Contributions are usually compulsory for salaried workers. For instance, Bolivia, Chile, Mexico, Peru, and Uruguay have compulsory contributions for these types of workers.

30. Furthermore, since the band is computed as a moving average, it is very likely that the fund will hit the band again next month and again have to put in equity capital. This scenario is very costly for a PFA and may even lead to bankruptcy. The situation is not specific to Chile; most Latin American countries with a defined-contribution pension fund system offer guaranteed minimum returns, either relative or absolute. For instance, Colombia, the Dominican Republic, El Salvador, Peru, and Uruguay guarantee these minimum returns, and funds are required to maintain reserves to meet these guarantees in case of underperformance. Among major reformers, only Mexico does not guarantee a minimum return.

31. Investing in assets with relatively high short-term volatility, such as long-term bonds, would expose funds to reporting very volatile returns to the underlying investors and regulators and would expose managers to volatility in their income.

32. These observations are based on the current norm in these countries.

33. For a comprehensive review of insurance regulation in Latin America, see OECD (2001) and International Association of Insurance Supervisors (1999).

34. For instance, the Central Bank of Colombia's (2009) *Financial Stability Report* referring to nonbank financial institutions states that "they are linked closely to other financial agents, either as counterparts in their market transactions or because they are part of a financial group. As a result, non-bank financial institutions can serve as systemic agents in certain contingencies."

35. Control pyramids also offer some advantages for the exercise of political control by commanding a large number of assets and activities across many sectors (Morck and Yeung 2004). Thus, they have resources to channel in many ways that do not raise suspicion. Furthermore, money from the bottom of the pyramid comes at a very cheap price because they are residual claimants of a small portion of it. Finally, dynasties can also make more credible promises for quid pro quo than managers that have relatively short tenures (Morck, Wolfenzon, and Yeung 2005), or they may be directly related to politicians (Claessens, Djankov, and Lang 2000; Johnson and Mitton 2003).

36. One way of constraining the ability of funds to bias their portfolios in favor of related enterprises that does not require strong regulatory monitoring is the imposition of diversification caps that constrain what a fund can invest in any

single firm (regardless of ownership relations). This type of practice is common in Latin America and most likely precludes extreme biases in favor of related firms. However, biases with respect to the optimal portfolio allocation may persist, and other inefficiencies may arise from these caps. The lack of appropriate instruments is another issue. Portfolio restrictions typically require funds to invest only in firms with reasonable market capitalizations, liquidity, and ratings. Few firms may meet these conditions in relatively underdeveloped financial markets, like many Latin American countries. If on top of that, funds cannot invest more than a certain share of their portfolio or of a security's issuance in specific assets, funds may quickly find themselves with no assets in which to place their money. It is unclear whether regulatory enforcement would be tight in a situation like this.

37. Of course, as mentioned above, the bank could also favor certain related firms in their lending activity. The fund could therefore use the bank to allocate funds to related firms indirectly and thus overcome regulatory constraints. If that were the case, larger amounts could be deposited in related banks than could be justified by interest rates. This may be especially problematic because banks enjoy an explicit or implicit government guarantee.

38. Because Chilean mutual funds are prohibited from investing in related banks, they typically do not hold large amounts of deposits in them. However, this does not preclude other types of arrangements through subscription of underwritten securities. Furthermore, two funds could arrange for depositing money in each other's banks. Since funds report their positions to the regulator frequently, these types of arrangements could be easy to enforce. In fact, the data show some positive correlation between the amounts that a fund family has in another family's banks.

39. For instance, in Mexico, mutual funds (sociedades de inversión) hire distributors and operators. Distributors are in charge of retailing the sale of shares of the fund to the public, and operators are in charge of asset management. In a situation like this, it is likely (as is the case in Mexico) that the sponsor of the fund, the distributor, and the operator will belong to the same financial group. This could be explained through gains in efficiency, but it may also end up being a barrier to competition and raise costs and fees for mutual funds' shareholders. A particularly interesting aspect of this case is that the directors of the sponsoring entity set the fees for the operators and distributors. In practice, however, there is overlap of directors in the three entities.

40. Two recent books that tackle the political economy of Latin America extensively analyze the characteristics of the policy-making process in Latin America and the interaction between the government players that are behind this process (Stein 2009) and the changes of paradigms in Latin American politics (Santiso 2007). Neither of them focuses on the interaction between regulators and the demand side of regulation.

41. It is a fact that some of these markets, such as that for pension funds, have extensively consolidated in many Latin American countries. There is also evidence that margins and profitability are high (Impavido, Lasagabaster, and Garcia-Huitron 2009). The persistence of high fees makes it difficult to explain the consolidation using efficiency considerations, but, of course, the counterfactual is ill defined.

42. In fact, as noted by Rajan (2010) and Johnson and Kwak (2010), even in the United States, the regulation of the financial sector requires expertise typically found only among market participants.

43. As mentioned above, the restrictions imposed on investment in government securities are also potentially consistent with a broad view of regulatory capture. In this interpretation, however, the regulator is not responding to the demand from industry incumbents but to the internal demand from within the government.

References

AIOS. http://www.aiosfp.org

Andima, Associação Brasileira das Entidades dos Mercados Financeiro e de Capitais. http://www.andima.com.br

Armenta, A. 2007. "Determinantes de los Traspasos de los Trabajadores en las Administradoras del Sistema de Pensiones en México: 2000–2006." BA thesis, ITAM.

Asociación de Supervisores de Seguros de Latinoamérica (ASSAL). http://www.assalweb.org.

Banxico, Banco de Mexico. http://www.banxico.org.mx

Barth, J. R., G. J. Caprio, and R. Levine. 2001. "The Regulation and Supervision of Banks around the World: A New Database." Policy Research Working Paper 2588, World Bank, Washington, DC.

Beck, T., R. Levine, and N. Loayza. 2000. "Finance and the Sources of Growth." *Journal of Financial Economics* 58 (1/2): 261–300.

Berstein, S., and C. Cabrita. 2007. "Los Determinantes de la Elección de AFP en Chile: Nueva Evidencia a Partir de Datos Individuales." *Estudios de Economía* 34: 53–72.

Berstein, S., and A. Micco. 2002. "Turnover and Regulation: The Chilean Pension Fund Industry." Working Paper 180, Central Bank of Chile, Santiago.

Berstein, S., and J. Ruiz. 2004. "Sensibilidad de la Demanda con Consumidores Desinformados: El Caso de las AFP en Chile." *Revista de Temas Financieros* 1.

Borowik, K., and S. Kalb. 2010. *Investment Fund Fees in Emerging Markets: A Comparison of Mutual Funds Fees in Brazil, Other Emerging Markets and OECD Countries.* London: London Business School.

Braun, M., and C. Raddatz. 2010. "Banking on Politics: When Former High-Ranking Politicians Become Bank Directors." *World Bank Economic Review* 24 (2): 234–79.

Broner, F., G. Lorenzoni, and S. Schmukler. 2010. "Why Do Emerging Economies Borrow Short Term?" *Journal of the European Economic Association* 11: 67–100.

Caprio, G., L. Laeven, and R. Levine. 2007. "Governance and Bank Valuation." *Journal of Financial Intermediation* 16 (4): 584–617.

Central Bank of Colombia. 2009. *Financial Stability Report.* Bogotá: Central Bank of Colombia.

Cerda, R. 2006. "Movilidad en la Cartera de Cotizantes por AFP: La Importancia de Ser Primero en Rentabilidad." *PUC Economics Institute Working Paper* 309. Santiago: Pontificia Universidad Catolica de Chile.

Cheikhrouhou, H., W. B. Gwinner, J. Pollner, E. Salinas, S. Sirtaine, and D. Vittas. 2007. *Structured Finance in Latin America: Channeling Pension Funds to Housing, Infrastructure, and Small Businesses.* Washington, DC: World Bank.

Chevalier, J., and G. Ellison. 1997. "Risk Taking by Mutual Funds as a Response to Incentives." *Journal of Political Economy* 105 (6): 1167–1200.

Chilean Superintendency of Values and Insurance. http://www.svs.cl

Chisari, O., P. Dal Bó, L. Quesada, M. Rossi, and S. Valdés Prieto. 1998. *Opciones Estratégicas en la Regulación de las AFJP: Modulo III—Costos, Comisiones y*

Organización Industrial del Régimen de Capitalización. Buenos Aires: Instituto de Economía, Universidad Argentina de la Empresa.

Claessens, S., S. Djankov, and L. H. Lang. 2000. "The Separation of Ownership and Control in East Asian Corporations." *Journal of Financial Economics* 58 (1/2): 81–112.

Conasev, Superintendencia del Mercado de Valores de Peru. http://www.smv.gob.pe

Dal Bó, E., and M. A. Rossi. 2007. "Corruption and Inefficiency: Theory and Evidence from Electric Utilities." *Journal of Public Economics* 91: 5–6.

Dewatripont, M., and J. Tirole. 1994. *The Prudential Regulation of Banks.* Cambridge: MIT Press.

Diamond, D. W., and R. G. Rajan. 2001. "Banks and Liquidity." *American Economic Review* 91 (2): 422–25.

Djankov, S., R. La Porta, F. Lopez-De-Silanes, and A. Shleifer. 2002. "The Regulation of Entry." *Quarterly Journal of Economics* 117 (1): 1–37.

Economist Intelligence Unit Country Finance Reports. Various issues.

Edwards, S. 1996. "Chile: Los Fondos Mutuos." *Regional Studies Report 39.*

Elton, E. J., M. J. Gruber, and C. R. Blake. 2003. "Incentive Fees and Mutual Funds." *Journal of Finance* 58 (2): 779–804.

FGV-Rio, Fundação Getulio Vargas, Rio de Janeiro. http://www.portal.fgv.br

FIAP (Federación Internacional de Administradores de Fondos de Pensiones). 2007. *Tasas de Cotización y Topes Imponibles en los Países con Sistemas de Capitalización Individual.* March.

FinStats (database). Interactive Data, United Kingdom. http://www.interactive-dataclients.com/content/view/38/155/.

García-Huitron, M., and T. Rodríguez. 2003. "La Organización del Mercado de Ahorro para el Retiro Mexicano Durante su Etapa de Acumulación." Mimeo.

Grossman, G. M., and E. Helpman. 2002. *Special Interest Politics.* Cambridge: MIT Press.

Impavido, G., E. Lasagabaster, and M. Garcia-Huitrón. 2010. *New Policies for Defined Contribution Pensions: Industrial Organization Models and Investment Products.* Washington, DC: World Bank.

International Association of Insurance Supervisors. 1999. *Supervisory Standard on Asset Management by Insurance Companies.* Basel: IAIS, Investments Subcommittee.

International Financial Statistics (database). International Monetary Fund, Washington, DC. http://elibrary-data.imf.org/FindDataReports. aspx?d=33061&e=169393.

Johnson, S., and J. Kwak. 2010. *13 Bankers: The Wall Street Takeover and the Next Financial Meltdown.* New York: Pantheon Books.

Johnson, S., and T. Mitton. 2003. "Cronyism and Capital Controls: Evidence from Malaysia." *Journal of Financial Economics* 67 (2): 351–82.

Khanna, T. 2000. "Business Groups and Social Welfare in Emerging Markets: Existing Evidence and Unanswered Questions." *European Economic Review* 44 (4/6): 748–61.

Kroszner, R. S. 1998. "On the Political Economy of Banking and Financial Regulatory Reform in Emerging Markets." *Research in Financial Services* 10: 33–51.

La Porta, R., F. Lopez-de-Silanes, and A. Shleifer. 1999. "Corporate Ownership around the World." *Journal of Finance* 54: 471–517.

Masías, L., and E. Sánchez. 2006. "Competencia y Reducción de Comisiones en el Sistema Privado de Pensiones: El Caso Peruano." *Revista de Temas Financieros III* (1): 65–103.

Maturana, G., and E. Walker. 1999. "Rentabilidades, Comisiones y Desempeño en la Industria Chilena de Fondos Mutuos." *Estudios Públicos* 73: 293–334.

Meléndez, J. 2004. *La Industria de las AFORE: Análisis de su Estructura y Recomendaciones de Política de Competencia y Regulación.* Mexico, DF: Instituto Mexicano del Seguro Social.

Morck, R., D. Wolfenzon, and B. Yeung. 2005. "Corporate Governance, Economic Entrenchment, and Growth." *Journal of Economic Literature* 43 (3): 655–720.

Morck, R., and B. Yeung. 2004. "Family Control and the Rent-Seeking Society." *Entrepreneurship: Theory and Practice* 28 (4): 391–409.

Noll, R. 1989. "Comment on Peltzman." *Brooking Papers: Microeconomics:* 48–58.

OECD (Organisation for Economic Co-operation and Development). 2001. *Insurance Regulation and Supervision in Asia.* Paris: OECD.

Olivares, J. A. 2004. "On the Chilean Pension Funds Market." PhD diss. University of Texas at Austin.

Olivares, J., and J. Sepulveda. 2007. "How Do Fund Managers Invest: Self Strategy or Herding in Private Pension Funds?" Working paper, Universidad del Desarrollo, Santiago.

Opazo, L., C. Raddatz, and S. L. Schmukler. 2009. "The Long and the Short of Emerging Market Debt." Policy Research Working Paper 5056, World Bank, Washington, DC.

Pigou, A. 1932. *The Economics of Welfare,* 4th ed. London: MacMillan and Co.

Raddatz, C. 2011. "Institutional Investors and Agency Issues in Latin American Financial Markets: Issues and Policy Options." Online working paper version, LAC Finance Development Flagship, Office of the Chief Economist for Latin America and the Caribbean, World Bank, chapter VI.

Raddatz, C., and S. L. Schmukler. 2008. "Pension Funds and Capital Market Development: How Much Bang for the Buck?" Policy Research Working Paper 4787, World Bank, Washington, DC.

Rajan, R. G. 2010. *Fault Lines: How Hidden Fractures Still Threaten the World Economy.* Princeton, NJ: Princeton University Press.

Santiso, J. 2007. *Latin America's Political Economy of the Possible: Beyond Good Revolutionaries and Free-Marketeers.* Cambridge: MIT Press.

Stein, J. C. 2009. "Presidential Address: Sophisticated Investors and Market Efficiency." *Journal of Finance* 64 (4): 1517–48.

Stigler, G. J. 1971. "The Theory of Economic Regulation." *Bell Journal of Economics* 2 (1): 3–21.

Stracca, L. 2006. "Delegated Portfolio Management: A Survey of the Theoretical Literature." *Journal of Economic Surveys* 20 (5): 823–26.

Superintendencia Financiera de Colombia. http://www.superfinanciera.gov.co

World Development Indicators (database). World Bank, Washington, DC. http://data.world bank.org/data-catalog/world-development-indicators.

Yermo, J. 2000. "Institutional Investors in Latin America: Recent Trends and Regulatory Challenges." In *Institutional Investors in Latin America,* 23–120. Paris: OECD.

7

Revisiting the Case for Public Guarantees: A Frictions-Based Approach

Deniz Anginer, Augusto de la Torre, and Alain Ize

Abstract

Based on a review of the theoretical foundations of public guarantees, this chapter concludes that the commonly used justifications for public guarantees based solely on agency frictions on un-internalized externalities are flawed. When risk is idiosyncratic, public guarantees can be justified only if there is risk aversion. The state can spread risk more finely than markets by coordinating atomistic agents that would otherwise not organize themselves to solve monitoring or commitment problems. When risk is systematic, the state adds value not by spreading the risk but by directly limiting it through better coordination among agents. In all cases, the analysis calls for exploiting more fully the natural complementarities between the state and the markets in bearing risk.

The authors work for the World Bank as, respectively, economist (danginer@worldbank.org), chief economist for Latin America and the Caribbean (adelatorre@worldbank.org), and senior consultant (aize@worldbank.org). The chapter benefited from valuable comments by Guillermo Babatz, Tito Cordella, Roberto Rocha, and participants in the December 2010 Authors' Workshop for the Flagship Study on Financial Development in Latin America. The views in this chapter are entirely those of the authors and do not necessarily represent the views of the World Bank, its executive directors, or the countries they represent.

In turn, this effort also requires overcoming agency frictions between the managers and the owners of development banks, a process that may entail a significant reshaping of development banks' mandates, governance, and risk management systems.

Introduction

The global financial crisis has brought public financial risk bearing to the forefront. Governments came to the rescue of troubled financial markets and institutions through large risk-absorption-of-last-resort operations involving outright asset purchases, capital injections, and a relaxation of collateral requirements for liquidity support. Some governments also absorbed large losses from the risk positions they had implicitly taken through their developmental commitments before the crisis. This was the case in particular for the U.S. government, which saw itself as obligated to absorb the losses of Fannie Mae and Freddie Mac, the two large government-sponsored mortgage companies.

In Latin America and the Caribbean (LAC), the global financial crisis has reawakened contentious issues one thought had been finally settled. The region was moving away from public financial risk bearing through the privatization of first-tier public banks and a refocusing of development banks toward second-tier lending, well-targeted guarantee programs, and temporary, catalytic developmental supports. However, development banks are now asking themselves whether they should grow bigger even in good times, so as to play a more forceful role in bad times. At the same time, the pressures of globalization and the important role played by Chinese public banks in aggressively funding enterprises have stimulated in many LAC countries an eagerness to revisit and rethink the role of public development banks in supporting the global competitiveness of the region's exporters, large or small.

In this context, interest in partial credit guarantee programs has surged. Some view the expansion of such programs as a desirable middle ground for expanding the risk-bearing role of the state while limiting the distortions resulting from its direct intervention in financial activities. However, the recent U.S. experience has also been a useful reminder that public guarantees can be quite costly, in both their potential fiscal costs and their impact on financial development and stability.

The concerns derived from the fiscal costs of public guarantees are compounded by the fact that the conceptual foundations of these programs are quite shaky. Guarantee programs are often justified based on social objectives. However, the rationale underlying the preference for state guarantees over other forms of public intervention is generally left unexplained. Alternatively, the need for state guarantees is based on the existence of market failures that need to be addressed.[1] The latter may be related to agency frictions (adverse selection, moral hazard, and lack of collateral) or to collective frictions (un-internalized externalities, free riding, and coordination failures). Again, however, once a sufficiently broad welfare criterion is adopted (one that fully internalizes the fiscal cost of the guarantees and the way it is allocated among taxpayers), it becomes unclear why public guarantees can succeed where markets failed. If guarantees are called for, why should they be public? And why can't private market participants fill in the gap? Similar questions seem to apply to nearly all forms of public financial risk bearing.

Despite the worldwide popularity of public sector credit guarantees[2]—typically granted through national and multilateral development agencies and banks—the theoretical economics literature has devoted rather scant attention to the issue. As argued in this chapter, the paper of Arrow and Lind (1970) presents the fundamental and most enduring rationale for public sector guarantees, which hinges on risk aversion and the government's superior capacity to spread risk across space and time. Curiously, however, this seminal paper has been generally ignored in scholarly work on public guarantees.

This chapter contributes to the policy debate by setting the underpinnings of credit guarantees on a sounder theoretical footing. It analyzes the foundations of public risk bearing from a perspective of financial paradigms, using the conceptual framework developed in de la Torre and Ize (2010, 2011), which emphasizes the irreducible, independent implications of four types of market failures, two of which (information asymmetry and enforcement costs) conform to the agency paradigms while the other two (collective action and collective cognition frictions) conform to the collective paradigms.[3] The chapter reaches the six following broad conclusions:

- When risk is idiosyncratic (hence is ultimately diversifiable), risk aversion is the key required justification for all forms of guarantees, whether private or public. In the absence of risk aversion among lenders, the case for guarantees cannot be made based on the traditional grounds of agency failures or externalities. Agency failures justify neither guarantees nor subsidies; externalities justify subsidies but not guarantees.
- The state can spread idiosyncratic risk more broadly than markets by coordinating and pooling atomistic agents that would otherwise not organize themselves to solve agency frictions. Agency frictions lead to risk concentration (reflecting the need for sufficient "skin in the game" to align principal-agent incentives) and thus get in the way of risk spreading. State guarantees may thus have an edge over private guarantees not because the state can better resolve the agency frictions but because it can better resolve the collective action frictions that disable the market's ability to overcome the agency frictions.

- Public guarantees can be justified on a transitory basis when financial systems are underdeveloped but only so long as such guarantees aim at crowding in (rather than crowding out) the private sector. However, the permanent use of public guarantees may also be justified, even in mature financial systems, when the idiosyncratic risk is excessively fat-tailed.
- The state can also put public guarantees to good use when risk is systematic (nondiversifiable), even in the absence of agency frictions.[4] This is because private individuals faced with endogenous risk and constrained by bargaining costs can fail to coordinate in a way that allows them to behave consistently with their collective interest. In this case, what matters is the direct coordinating (rather than the risk-spreading) ability of the state.
- While the state's comparative advantage in spreading risk should in principle allow it to take on riskier projects than the markets, this does not generally happen in practice. The high de facto risk aversion of public development banks is a reflection of shareholder-manager agency frictions that increase with the level of risk. The more risk a public banker takes, the more difficult it becomes for the state (ultimately, the taxpayer) to sort out whether losses were due to bad luck or poor risk management.
- This conundrum invites a major rethinking and reformulation of the mandate, transparency, governance, and risk management capabilities of public development banks.

The rest of this chapter is organized as follows. The chapter first addresses the case of pure agency frictions and no risk aversion. It then looks at collective action frictions but continues to assume away risk aversion. After introducing lenders' risk aversion, the chapter then expands by introducing managerial risk aversion motivated by agency frictions between bank managers and the owner (the state). In the following section, it broadens the discussion to the case of systematic risk. The final section concludes by reviewing key policy implications and issues.

The Pure Agency Paradigms

Consider first the case of idiosyncratic risk and pure agency frictions, assuming for now that lenders are not risk averse and that there are no collective action frictions (derived from externalities or coordination problems). As is well known in the literature, asymmetric information in credit markets, even without risk aversion, can lead to socially inefficient outcomes of either underlending or overlending. For example, Jaffee and Russell (1976) and Stiglitz and Weiss (1981) demonstrate the case for underlending by showing that asymmetric information can lead to adverse selection as higher interest rates attract riskier borrowers. They show that lenders may be better off rationing credit below the level that would be socially desirable.[5]

The appropriate policy response to these agency-driven market failures is not obvious, however. Most of the literature that finds that asymmetric information can justify state credit guarantees uses a partial equilibrium framework; that is, it does not consider the welfare effects of the taxes needed to finance the guarantees. Instead, the literature that uses a general equilibrium framework and applies an appropriately stringent welfare criterion (requiring revenue neutrality *and* taking into account the distributional implications of the taxes levied to finance the state guarantees) systematically concludes that, in the absence of risk aversion, state guarantees cannot improve the market outcome, except when the state has an informational or enforcement advantage over the private sector, which is, in general, hard to argue.[6]

To help understand what is at stake, consider the student loan model of Mankiw (1986). This model focuses on the information asymmetry problem of adverse selection and assumes that lenders are risk neutral. Students' honesty varies over the population. However, the lender knows less than the borrowing student; specifically, he or she knows the mean of the distribution but not each individual student's characteristics. Moreover, reflecting enforcement and informational frictions, the lender cannot force repayment and must thus raise the interest rate on all loans to cover the losses on the unpaid loans. But when the price of all loans rises, the dishonest (those who do not intend to repay) prevent the honest (those committed to repaying) from borrowing. Because it would have been socially desirable for the honest to borrow, society is worse off.

What can policy do about this? To answer this question, notice first that, in the absence of risk aversion, an unsubsidized guarantee (that is, a guarantee priced to cover expected losses) has no impact. While it reduces risk, that is of no consequence to a risk-neutral lender. The price of the guarantee matches the cost of the loan-loss provisions that the lender would have to incur in the absence of the guarantee. As a result, the fairly priced guarantee adds no value and, hence, will not affect the lender's behavior.

By contrast, if the state provides a fully subsidized credit guarantee (a 100 percent default guarantee with a price equal to zero), the risk-neutral lender saves the cost of loan-loss provisions and is thereby induced to lend to all students at the risk-free interest rate. From a partial equilibrium viewpoint, absent a requirement of revenue neutrality, the subsidized guarantee would, therefore, allow the social optimum to be reached. However, from a more stringent (and generally warranted) welfare perspective, the financing of the guarantee and the distribution of tax payments across the student population also matter. Unless the students who default also pay the tax, taxing only the nondefaulting students would make them worse off because they would end up paying for the defaulting students (see the proof in the annex). Thus, although a subsidized guarantee could be socially justified, the nondefaulting, tax-paying students (including those who would not borrow without the guarantee) would prefer to go without it.

Clearly, taxing only the defaulting students would lead to a Pareto improvement. But doing so amounts to assuming that one can enforce taxation where one cannot enforce a loan repayment. The optimality of the (subsidized) guarantee in a Mankiw-type student loan model of adverse selection hinges, therefore, exclusively on a *differential enforcement capacity*. This does not make sense in a political system in which the rule of law applies to states as well as to citizens. Any preferential loan collection capacity that states may have should be made readily available to everyone through improving the judiciary, as part of a more supportive enabling environment. For similar reasons, a private agent might consider offering his screening services to the lender if he or she was better informed (hence, better able to discriminate between the good loans and the bad loans) or better able to collect (hence, make the dishonest pay for their sins). However, an agent with such capabilities (for example, one who is able to benefit from economies of scale in putting together an effective sorting system for borrowers) would be in the business of selling services to banks, not in guaranteeing their loans.

Broadly similar arguments can be developed when, instead of adverse selection, the problem underlying the failure of risk-neutral creditors to lend to honest students is one of enforcement. Suppose, for example, that borrowers cannot obtain a loan because they lack good collateral and hence cannot credibly commit to repaying the loan. In this case, viable student borrowers without collateral would be excluded from the loan market, resulting again in a socially inefficient equilibrium. By replacing the missing collateral, it is often argued, a state guarantee could bring such borrowers back into the market. The problem with this argument is that, absent any change in the students' own skin in the game, they would confront the same commitment-to-repay problem. Thus, unless the guarantee is fairly priced (so as to cover the expected loan losses and other costs), the loan default losses would simply be shifted to the state (the guarantor). But if the guarantee is fairly priced, risk-neutral lenders would not pay for it because, by definition, they care only about expected losses and not about the variance of such losses. Unless the state has an enforcement advantage over private lenders—which, as we have already argued, is hard to justify—there is no case for a state guarantee.

The discussion in this section can be summarized as follows. In a world devoid of risk aversion and collective action frictions, agency frictions alone do not in general justify guarantees under a general equilibrium viewpoint that uses an appropriately restrictive welfare criterion. While the market outcome would be inefficient, a state that does not know more or enforce better than the private sector cannot improve the outcome through credit guarantees. Indeed, one would generally expect the state to have a comparative disadvantage in dealing with pure agency frictions rather than an advantage. If the state had a comparative advantage in this regard, the right policy would be to have only state-owned and state-run banks, which patently makes no sense.[7] More generally, in a world where distortions arise only from agency frictions, while the market equilibrium is inefficient, the state cannot improve on it by assuming risk, because there is no wedge between private and social interests—principals and agents want the same thing that society wants, namely, to overcome agency frictions and engage in mutually beneficial financial contracts. The only legitimate role left for the state in such a world is to improve the informational and enforcement environment so that markets can operate better.

Adding Collective Action Frictions

Let us now add collective action frictions that manifest themselves in the form of *social* externalities—for example, positive externalities to lending that are not internalized by the private lender are However, we continue to assume that risk is idiosyncratic and lenders are risk neutral. The literature generally concludes that, in the absence of information asymmetries, any credit policy, including guarantees, is ineffective in improving the equilibrium outcome unless subsidized (see, for example, Raith, Staak, and Starke 2006; Penner and Silber 1973; Lombra and Wasylenko 1984). Indeed, subsidies and taxes are generally shown to be the best policy responses to a market failure arising from un-internalized externalities. However, the literature concludes that it becomes significantly more difficult to design optimal subsidies where externalities and asymmetric information coexist.

To see what is at stake, notice first that in the Mankiw (1986) model of pure agency frictions, the dishonest inflict negative *informational* externalities on the honest. However, barring differential taxation or enforcement capacity, there is no way for the state to internalize such externalities. *There is no collective action failure.* The dishonest are simply getting away with mischief. Even if bargaining were costless, it would not pay for the honest to buy out the dishonest. Indeed, using the same reasoning as in the previous section, the honest would have to make a transfer payment to the dishonest that exactly matches the tax payments that would be required to cover a subsidized state guarantee or an interest rate subsidy. Similarly, even though it seems obvious that one should lend to every student whose return exceeds the social cost of funds, a state banker without an informational or enforcement advantage should not lend and behave exactly like a private banker.

How would adding social externalities and collective action frictions change this conclusion? Suppose lending to some targeted students (say, the ones studying to become primary school teachers) has positive social externalities (that is, a good basic education enhances the earning potential from college education in all fields of study). The market outcome would be inefficient even if private lenders could solve agency problems and properly identify all the creditworthy students. Private lenders, by pricing all loans uniformly, would fail to lend sufficiently to students planning to be primary school teachers because their earnings prospects are mediocre, even though those students can contribute the most to other students' earnings. The private lender does not internalize the externality. There is now a clear case of a *collective action* failure. If students of all generations and in all fields of study could get together, bargain an agreement, and enforce it at no cost, they would agree on setting aside part of the increase in their future earnings resulting from a better primary education to subsidize the interest rates on the loans to future primary school teachers.

However, in the presence of collective action frictions, students will not be able to coordinate their actions to ensure a socially beneficial outcome. Instead, where wage subsidies to school teachers are not an available option, the state can resolve this externalities-driven market failure by coordinating agents through an interest rate subsidy program favoring loans to the would-be teachers and paid for by all other students. Since informational frictions require that bankers screen potential borrowers and monitor their performance, and since such efforts are costly, targeted interest rate subsidies dominate targeted and subsidized guarantees. While both policy instruments can similarly expand the level of targeted lending, the interest rate subsidy is preferable because it is less likely to distort the lender's screening and monitoring incentives (the lender retains full skin in the game). This illustrates that, as long as there is no risk aversion, collective action frictions alone establish the case for tax and subsidy policy but not for state credit guarantees.

But there might also be cases in which the state's cost of monitoring private lenders to see whether they appropriately screen loan applicants according to the social criteria it set forth is greater than the cost of simply setting up a first-tier state bank that directly provides the subsidized loans.[8] In such cases, the state's assumption of the risks associated with financial activities can be justified on the basis of the state's capacity to address agency frictions (that is, ensuring that the loans are given to the most socially desirable borrowers). However, it is crucial to note that such agency frictions arise out of an underlying collective action failure that prevents markets from internalizing externalities.

The bottom line for this section is, therefore, as follows. When social externalities and collective action frictions are added to agency frictions in a world devoid of risk aversion, the case for state intervention becomes clear, but it is hardly in the form of credit guarantees. When these frictions are relatively light, the state might limit its intervention to that of a catalyst that brings together all interested parties and facilitates the transfers across parties required for a mutually beneficial equilibrium. When the frictions are harder to overcome, the state can circumvent them through a targeted tax-subsidy program, which internalizes externalities. However, the implementation of this program may run into agency frictions. Thus, depending on whether the state or the markets can better address these latter frictions, it might be optimal for the state to subsidize the loans provided by private lenders or to provide the loans directly through a first-tier state bank. Remarkably, however, the basic motivation underlying the state's intervention is always the need to address collective frictions, which introduce a wedge between private and social interests that markets cannot resolve on their own.

Adding Lenders' Risk Aversion

Let us now add risk aversion, first among private lenders. The paper of Arrow and Lind (1970) presents the fundamental and most enduring conceptual framework for understanding the role of the state in bearing risk when there is risk aversion. They first show that, when risk is spread in small amounts over large numbers of investors, capital can be priced at risk-neutral prices. They then argue that the state's intertemporal tax and borrowing capacity gives it a unique ability to spread risk across large populations. Thus, state guarantees (as opposed to subsidies or loans) are naturally called for to reduce the cost of risk bearing and to encourage private investment or lending in the face of high risk or high risk aversion.

Curiously, the literature on partial credit guarantees has mostly ignored the Arrow and Lind (1970) perspective. Moreover, in the scant literature on this subject, a dominant theme is a rebuttal of the proposition that there is anything unique in the state's capacity to spread risk. For example, Klein (1996) argues that if the state's advantage did not lie purely in its coercive taxation powers (that is, its capacity to oblige taxpayers to bear unwanted risk through the tax system), then markets would be able to spread risk just as efficiently. But as Arrow and Lind themselves suggest, it may not be possible for the private sector to be completely risk neutral, even when risk is spread through broad ownership. Since the controlling shareholders of a firm need to hold large blocks of stock and since such holdings are likely to constitute a significant portion of their wealth, the costs of risk bearing are not negligible, and the firm should behave as a risk averter. Thus, although Arrow and Lind hint at the existence of a link between risk aversion and agency problems (adequate monitoring implies large-stake exposures), they do not develop it, nor has the literature picked up on that theme.

To help analyze whether there is indeed something unique about the state's risk-bearing capacity, we introduce risk aversion into the well-known monitoring model of Calomiris and Khan (1989). An entrepreneur funds a risky project through a mixture of retail and wholesale funding. Projects that are doomed to fail can be liquidated—thereby salvaging some of their value—if they are so identified at an early stage through monitoring. Retail investors do not monitor because they have too small a stake in the project relative to the cost of monitoring. Instead, wholesalers can engage in monitoring because they can recoup their investments in failing projects. However, they will do so only if they have sufficiently large stakes in the project (sufficient skin in the game) to warrant incurring the monitoring costs. In the absence of risk aversion (the case analyzed by Calomiris and Khan), wholesalers do not need to be paid a premium to bear such risk. Hence, it is not socially costly for them to retain skin in the game. Entrepreneurs can therefore contract enough wholesale funding to allow wholesalers to fully recoup the cost of the socially efficient level of monitoring. An efficient equilibrium is therefore obtained where monitoring costs can be absorbed *without having to spread any risk*.[9]

But suppose now that wholesalers are risk averse. Having skin in the game raises the cost of wholesale funds, resulting in an inefficient equilibrium with insufficient wholesale funding, hence insufficient monitoring. A guarantor buying the risk that is concentrated in wholesalers and spreading it by reselling it in small amounts to retailers can therefore improve, in principle, the market equilibrium. In doing so, however, the guarantor faces and must solve three interrelated problems. First, since monitoring is costly, the guarantee undermines wholesalers' incentives to monitor the entrepreneur and his project. This is the standard moral hazard problem of insurance markets. To avoid distorting wholesalers' monitoring incentives, the guarantor can monitor wholesalers and adjust the premium of the guarantee according to how well they perform their monitoring. However, monitoring the monitor also has a cost. Second, the guarantor's capacity to resell the risk to retailers will itself depend on his capacity to convince them that he is doing a good job himself at monitoring wholesalers and, hence, is offering retailers a fairly priced risk-sharing deal. Retailers need therefore to be able to monitor the guarantor's own monitoring efforts. But this again has a cost. Third, to spread risk over a sufficiently large base, guarantors need to have a sufficiently broad clientele. However, even in the absence of informational frictions, retailers' participation may be limited due to un-internalized externalities (that is, individuals' failure to take into account that the social benefits of their participation exceed the individual net benefits) and other collective action frictions.

Because it is in the guarantors' own interest to have their monitoring certified (they will not be able to sell risk otherwise) and because they can include the certification cost in the price of their guarantee, guarantors can pay someone (say, a rating agency) to do the certifying. Retailers, in turn, need to be convinced that the rating agency has done a good job certifying guarantors. Market arrangements to monitor the rating agencies should eventually spring up, the costs being added to the other monitoring costs incurred at other levels of the monitoring pyramid. The compounded costs of monitoring should thus ultimately be factored into the price of the guarantee to be paid by wholesalers as part of the insurance premium.

As shown in the annex, for risk to be fully spreadable (hence, for full guarantees to restore the first best, fully efficient equilibrium), the compounded monitoring and marketing costs should thus be lower than the benefits of monitoring (the gains from early project liquidations). At the same time, the costs of monitoring the monitor should be lower than wholesalers' direct monitoring costs. Hence, there should be efficiency gains as one goes up the monitoring pyramid.

There is therefore, on the one hand, a basic correspondence between the market's capacity to spread risk and its capacity to limit monitoring costs through an effective monitoring pyramid (which includes rating agencies and other market analysts). There is, on the other hand, also a correspondence between the market's capacity to spread risk and its capacity to limit distribution and marketing costs through a sufficiently well-developed financial system (which includes deep capital markets and an efficient, multilayered intermediation chain of banks, institutional investors, brokers, dealers, and other specialized financial institutions). Indeed, in a well-developed financial system, the guarantor would not have to deal directly with depositors. Instead, an additional layer of agents—the asset managers (mutual funds, pension funds, hedge funds, and the like)—would pool retail investors for the guarantor, thereby reducing the costs of participation. Thus, the market's risk-spreading capacity is fundamentally a function of the reduction in information and participation frictions that are at the heart of financial development.

At the same time, a good argument can be made that private guarantors should generally be better able to deal with informational and other agency frictions than public guarantors. Thus, in a well-developed financial system where participation and other collective frictions are not significant, the comparative advantage of markets in dealing with agency frictions should dominate the state's comparative advantage in dealing with collective failures. Private guarantors should thus naturally emerge, leaving no role for public guarantees. The only remaining role for the state in these circumstances is to strengthen the enabling environment in a way that helps alleviate the informational (or enforcement) frictions that hinder risk spreading. In particular, the state may need to help close the monitoring pyramid through the provision of official oversight over the rating agencies (a public good). Indeed, as amply demonstrated in the global crisis, with collective action frictions, the necessary arrangements for monitoring rating agencies are unlikely to spring up by themselves.

Instead, in less developed financial systems, the costs of mobilizing the participation that is required to achieve sufficient risk spreading may be too high for private guarantees to be viable. This is precisely the point at which the state can help complete markets. Because a state guarantor does not have to market the risk (the risk spreading is taken care of through well-established frameworks of taxation and public choice), the quarantor may be able to lower the distribution costs sufficiently to resolve the participation failure. Thus, there is a clear infant-industry argument for *transitory* state guarantees when financial systems suffer from low participation.

If idiosyncratic risk is fat-tailed, however, state guarantees may also be justified on a more *permanent* basis, because even the developed financial markets may not be able to reach the scale of participation that would be needed to atomize and distribute the risk sufficiently.[10]State guarantees can spread the risk all the more finely because they can do so across currently living taxpayers as well as across generations within a given jurisdiction. Remarkably, even in the case of intergenerational risk spreading, the state has an edge because the political system is naturally designed (whether fairly or not) to conduct intergenerational burden sharing, not because it has a better "enforcement capacity."[11] Thus, the state's advantage derives again from its comparative advantage in addressing a collective action (participation) friction, rather than an enforcement (agency) friction.

The argument in this section can thus be summarized as follows. Unless risk is properly spread out, risk aversion, combined with agency frictions, introduces a deadweight cost (manifested in the form of a higher-than-necessary risk premium) that constitutes a first source of market inefficiency. A state guarantee may, therefore, be justified as a means of lowering the cost of capital by spreading risk more broadly. However, the guarantee introduces moral hazard, a second source of market inefficiency. Hence, for the monitoring pyramid to fully spread risk (through 100 percent guarantees) without weakening effort and monitoring incentives, it must be sufficiently efficient. If the costs of monitoring the monitor are low enough, the market solution can replicate the optimal solution by replacing a socially costly skin-in-the-game requirement with a more efficient (cheaper) pyramidal market-monitoring arrangement that enables greater risk spreading. In a well-developed financial system, the guarantees are likely to be provided more effectively by markets than by the state, especially if the idiosyncratic risk is normally distributed. Instead, in a developing financial system, there is a good argument for involving the state through transitory guarantees because it can pool atomistic investors (or taxpayers) that would otherwise not participate in underwriting the guarantee. Moreover, where idiosyncratic risks are one-time events or fat-tailed, permanent state guarantees may be justified, even in developed financial systems. Taxation should in this context be viewed not as a device to force unwilling taxpayers to share risks (as in Klein 1996), but rather as a simple, built-in coordination mechanism that facilitates the participation of all. In sum, the risk-spreading ability of the state, and hence the rationale for state guarantees, ultimately rest on the comparative advantage of the state in resolving collective action frictions, which is the traditional justification for public goods.

Adding Managerial Risk Aversion

The state's comparative advantage in risk spreading should naturally become more prominent as risk rises, hence as the risk distribution becomes flatter or its tails become fatter. Thus, one would expect the state's intervention to add more value (that is, to have more "additionality") when the public guarantor takes more risk than the markets and does so without subsidizing it. The logic of the argument should therefore lead the state to guarantee riskier projects or borrowers than those that markets are willing to finance and to do so at an actuarially fair price (one that covers expected losses).[12] In the past, there were many examples of politically captured public banks, driven by populist policies, which guaranteed or financed unviable but politically important projects at highly subsidized prices. At present, however, reflecting reforms aimed at improving the financial sustainability of public banks, public guarantee programs, and, more generally, public development banks are not typically constructed in this way. Instead, they tend to shy away from risk taking. Typical state-sponsored credit guarantee programs target well-defined, recurrent, limited risks instead of insufficiently understood risks or tail risks where the state's comparative advantage in risk bearing and spreading could be, in principle, more fully exploited. Indeed, many development banks proudly emphasize that they carefully screen their guarantees or their borrowers and concentrate on the least-risky projects and best-rated borrowers to minimize losses. At the same time, development bankers view a steady stream of positive profits as their best measure of stellar performance.

What explains this disconnect between theory and practice? The most likely explanation is an additional key agency friction that has so far been omitted from our analysis, namely, the friction between the bank owner (the state, acting as principal) and the bank manager (acting as agent). Unless appropriate governance and risk management arrangements are in place that allow the principal to sort things out (more on this in the next section), the more risk the manager takes, the more exposed he or she becomes to the risk of occasional losses due to bad luck interpreted as the outcome of bad management. Hence, the higher the risks the manager takes, the greater the chances of being fired. The shorter the time horizon that the political system uses to evaluate the manager and the more complex the risks involved, the more difficult it becomes to sort out bad from good managers: hence, the larger the manager's exposure and the higher the aversion to risk. This factor is typically compounded by the bias that favors penalizing mistakes over rewarding successes in evaluating the performance of development banks. The inadequate governance arrangement of development banks, or the limited capacity of the political system to understand or handle accidental losses, can therefore largely explain public bank managers' low risk appetite.[13]

Expanding the risk frontier is naturally unpalatable to both development bank managers and politicians insofar as they are held accountable. Indeed, parliaments in many regions of the world have strictly limited risk taking by development banks. At the same time, development bank managers protect their capital because they know that they will live or die by it.[14] The constraints that development banks face in avoiding losses often induce them to compete with commercial banks to reap high returns for low risks, rather than—as the risk-aversion rationale would suggest— to complement private activity by providing fairly priced risk insurance at the frontier.[15] State guarantees to small and medium enterprises or to target clienteles, such as those reached through low-income housing or student loan programs, look like safe bets when they are well within the risk frontier.[16] Why, then, not safely collect the low-hanging fruit instead of shooting for the moon? It is precisely such reasoning that largely explains the limited additionality of most public guarantee programs: that is, the fact that they tend to substitute for rather than crowd in private guarantees.

Systematic Risk

Consider, finally, the case in which risks are systematic, hence not diversifiable. State guarantees can be justified on a permanent basis in the presence of systematic risk, including that which is endogenously brewed in the process of financial development itself. The rationale in this case, however, no longer derives from the need to spread risk as broadly as possible but rather from the state's capacity to help coordinate agents' actions around an efficient risk-sharing equilibrium.

Systematic risk has three main threads. First, since systematic risk is correlated with consumption, wealth, and income, the risk-spreading argument in Arrow and Lind (1970) no longer holds, and agents may require a significant risk premium. Second, risk may become endogenous and prone to multiple equilibriums, turning into *systemic* risk, as in the typical bank run setting of Diamond and Dybvig (1983). Finally, systematic shocks may be associated with extreme uncertainty, inducing agents to abandon altogether the expected utility-maximizing framework and to choose instead a minimum-maximum criterion that minimizes their exposure to the maximum possible loss. In the latter case, the choices made by individual agents may cease to be fully rational, as each agent can behave as if he or she were affected more than the average.[17] In all of these cases, the Arrow-Lind risk-spreading argument no longer holds. When risk is endogenous or agents abandon the expected utility framework, the total cost of risk bearing remains the same as the population of taxpayers becomes large, making risk nondiversifiable. At the same time, because correlated risk applies to an investor deciding whether to invest in a private guarantee scheme as much as to a taxpayer deciding whether to vote for a state guarantee scheme, the state no longer has a natural risk-aversion advantage.

However, state guarantees are still useful because they help resolve collective action failures. When all agents minimize their exposure to a worst-case scenario, the state can be in some sense more rational than the agents it represents. By eliminating such a scenario, state guarantees effectively function as a coordination device, much as deposit guarantees and lender-of-last-resort facilities can eliminate self-fulfilling bank runs. In the case of correlated risk, state guarantees can still improve things by helping avert the collective action failures that magnify the impact of a systemic event. By coordinating agents' behavior around a collectively desirable outcome, state guarantees help reduce the risk of catastrophic downturns, thereby smoothing out private consumption, which, in turn, helps reduce the costs associated with risk aversion and lowers the required risk premium.

Toward a Rebalanced Policy

This chapter has emphasized three key messages:

- The role of the state in bearing risk reflects its comparative advantage in overcoming collective participation frictions, not agency frictions.
- Without risk aversion, there would be no role for public guarantees (nor, for that matter, for private guarantees).
- To shed their de facto risk aversion and hence exploit more fully their comparative advantage in bearing risk responsibly (hence at unsubsidized prices and without recurrent losses), development banks will most likely need a thorough overhaul of their mandates, governance, and risk management arrangements.

Each of these messages points to a specific set of policy implications. Let us take each of them in turn, starting with the state's comparative advantage in overcoming participation frictions. Instead of justifying government loan and guarantee programs based on goals, policy makers need to focus on *alternative means of achieving these goals*. This effort involves comparing social costs and benefits across alternative channels of state intervention that may or may not involve risk taking by the government. This in turn opens two broad avenues to explore. The first comprises policy interventions aimed exclusively at solving participation frictions—that is, achieving greater financial inclusion both along the intensive margin (the same players engaged in more transactions) and along the extensive margin (the incorporation of new players)—*without dealing directly with risk*. Rising financial inclusion makes it easier for the financial services industry to lower costs, expand market liquidity, and capture other positive spillovers associated with scale and network effects, thereby ultimately helping diversify risk. Increased financial inclusion can justify a catalytic role for the state in financial development, as well as the state's provision of basic infrastructure such as large-value payments and trading systems or other public goods such as the standardization of contracts.[18] Similarly, the creation of mandatory but privately administered pension funds can help promote the development of annuities, which in turn can help develop a market for spreading the risk associated with long-term instruments.

The second avenue deals with risk by *promoting risk-spreading arrangements among private agents*. This can be done through catalytic efforts or compulsory schemes. As an example of the first type, states can promote private sector participation in guarantee schemes, such as mutual guarantee associations funded by small local entrepreneurs, or guarantee schemes structured as joint stock companies with private participation. The experience across the world with such schemes has been generally positive, partly because they promote peer pressure, a purely private form of resolving collective frictions. Indeed, some evidence suggests that such associations work best when they remain purely private, as this fully preserves incentives for group monitoring and limits moral hazard.[19] As an example of the second type (compulsory risk-sharing arrangements), the state can mandate participation in health insurance schemes, as was recently the case in the United States.

Clearly, the two avenues above should be explored and exploited as a matter of priority. However, they may not suffice, not least because peer pressure or compulsory participation may not work in all cases and in all environments. A third avenue, more controversial and thorny, involves risk absorption and risk spreading by the state, whether through guarantees or long-term loans.[20] At this point, the second key message of this chapter comes into play. By construction, the rationale for such public risk-bearing programs should be tightly anchored on risk measurement, risk aversion, risk premiums, and differential costs of capital between public and private financial entities. These programs need to explain—based on risk aversion and hence on a careful evaluation of risk premiums and a comparison of costs of capital—why the state can achieve what markets cannot. And as soon as such cost differentials diminish with financial development, the public guarantee programs should be phased out or devolved to the private sector.

The correct pricing of the guarantees, to ensure that they properly reflect expected losses, also deserves more attention than it generally receives.[21]

The fact that private guarantees have not surfaced to replace public guarantees may reflect the existence of complex or hidden risks (fat-tailed or systemic) that free markets cannot handle well and that public guarantors would need to explicitly recognize and take into account. Unless this identification of possible hidden risk is done right and state guarantees are reasonably priced, state guarantees will likely end up subsidizing private risk-taking unduly, distorting incentives, and triggering unpleasant fiscal surprises (as well as political upheavals) once downsides materialize (the recent U.S. experience in the subprime crisis is, of course, the most obvious illustration).

This brings us to the third and last key message, the need to increase the additionality of public guarantees by carefully pushing out the risk frontier, the area where the state's comparative advantage in bearing risk is magnified. As suggested earlier, the key line of action to overcoming development banks' aversion to risk is to enhance the political system's capacity to discriminate between bad luck and poor management. That capacity implies a radical reshaping of the mandates, governance arrangements, risk management systems, and monitoring and evaluation procedures of development banks. It is important that their mandate allows them to take more risk without taking systematic losses, that is, to function as authentic development banks rather than as imperfect replicas of private commercial banks. To do so, of course, requires that development banks develop their capacity to assess and assume risk, not just their capacity to avoid it. Of course, this proposition is not trivial, and it is likely to involve at the same time a quantum improvement in development banks' analytical capacity as well as a quantum change in their board's focus of attention.

But the more one pushes out the risk frontier, the more difficult it becomes to properly estimate expected losses and sort out the risk premiums from the expected losses. Perhaps development banks cannot move too far beyond the risk frontier and should instead increase their risk taking at the margin (and in the shadow) of markets. For example, when loans are made directly by first-tier public banks, making sure the interest rates on the loans are above market rates can help ensure that public risk bearing does not crowd out private risk bearing.[22] At the same time, staying close to the risk frontier should allow development banks to use market signals, thereby facilitating risk discovery, and to share risk efficiently, thereby promoting and enhancing longer-term market development.[23] Staying close to (and working closely with) markets should also provide the natural guidelines and performance benchmarks that limit the risks of going wild as well as the risks of political or bureaucratic capture.

Finally, managers of development banks (the agents) will need to do a better job of explaining what they are doing to the political system and society at large (the principal). This task requires both accountability and transparency. Development banks need to be more transparent about

the risks (hence the possible losses) they are taking and the supporting
methodologies and processes they are using to assess and price those risks.
In this endeavor, the financial and academic communities should be able to
provide important help in validating, explaining, and contributing to these
choices and their associated implications.[24] Official supervision also has an
essential role to play. Just as for private commercial banks, supervisors should
test and certify the quality of risk management. However, development
banks' focus on the risk frontier—including more uncertain, less recurrent,
and often more complex risk—should naturally be taken into account by
supervisors. In addition, risk taking can be bounded in a variety of ways.
For example, capital earmarked for specific insurance or countercyclical risk
absorption can help development banks assume more risk in a responsible,
bounded manner while protecting their capital from depletion.[25] The political
evaluators of development banks, moreover, should stress the economy-
wide costs and benefits of public risk taking (whether through development
banks or special loan and guarantee programs) while encouraging rigorous
assessments of its additionality and impact.

Annex: Supporting Models

The Mankiw Model

Students borrow at an interest rate r and obtain a return R. Their
probability of repayment, p, is uniformly distributed between P_0 and P_1.
Only the sufficiently dishonest students will ask for a loan, with the
threshold such that

$$p < \frac{R}{r}. \tag{7A.1}$$

Hence, for an adverse selection equilibrium to prevail (where there are
honest students who cannot borrow), the return on the loan must not be
too high, such that

$$R < rP_1. \tag{7A.2}$$

The bank's cost of funds is the risk-free rate (social cost of funds) ρ.
The social benefit of education is assumed to be higher than its social cost:

$$R > \rho. \tag{7A.3}$$

If the mean repayment probability is π, the bank will set the lending
rate such that

$$r = \frac{\rho}{\pi}, \tag{7A.4}$$

where the average probability of repayment is

$$\pi = \frac{P_0 + R/r}{2} . \tag{7A.5}$$

Define $\overline{W}$ as the total social value created by the loans in the market equilibrium. It equals the difference between the social benefit per loan, R, and the social cost, ρ, times the number of loans:

$$\overline{W} = (R - \rho)\frac{R/r - P_0}{P_1 - P_0} . \tag{7A.6}$$

The value of the loans in the socially optimal solution where all students borrow would be W^* such that

$$W^* = R - \rho. \tag{7A.7}$$

In a comparison of (7A.6) and (7A.7), it immediately follows that $W^* > \overline{W}$ when (7A.2) is satisfied. Instead, a fully subsidized credit guarantee can induce the risk-neutral lender to lend to all students at the risk-free interest ρ. Absent a requirement of revenue neutrality, the subsidized guarantee would therefore allow the social optimum to be reached.

However, from a broader welfare perspective that imposes revenue neutrality and where the distribution of tax payments across the student population matters, such a guarantee is not optimal. With a guarantee, everyone borrows, and a share $(P_0 + P_1)/2$ of students (the honest students) repays the loans. Hence, the cost of the guarantee is $\rho - r\frac{P_0 + P_1}{2}$. If the honest students are the only ones who can be taxed to cover this cost, the tax per honest student will be

$$\tau = \frac{\rho - r(P_0 + P_1)/2}{(P_0 + P_1)/2} . \tag{7A.8}$$

The honest students will be better off paying the tax only if their excess return exceeds the tax:

$$R - r > \tau. \tag{7A.9}$$

Using (7A.8) in (7A.9) and rearranging terms leads to

$$\frac{R}{\rho} > \frac{2}{P_0 + P_1} . \tag{7A.10}$$

But for an adverse selection equilibrium to exist, (7A.2) also needs to be verified. In turn, since with (7A.4) and (7A.5)

$$\frac{R}{r} = \frac{R/\rho}{2 - R/\rho} P_0,$$

(7A.11)

then, with (7A.11), (7A.2) can be written

$$\frac{R}{\rho} < 2 \frac{P_1}{P_0 + P_1}.$$

(7A.12)

Putting together (7A.10) and (7A.12),

$$\frac{2}{P_0 + P_1} < \frac{R}{\rho} < \frac{2P_1}{P_0 + P_1}.$$

(7A.13)

This set of inequalities cannot be verified for $P_1 < 1$; hence, it is not possible to find an equilibrium in which there are honest students who are driven away from the market but would be better off with a guarantee.

Adding Risk Aversion to the Calomiris-Khan Model

There are three periods. In period one, entrepreneurs-bankers invest in projects that will yield X in period three with probability p, and 0 with probability $1-p$. The project is productive, so that $pX > 1$, and its maximum size is one. In period two, an imperfect signal $m \in [0,1]$ is obtained on the project's failure probability, such that if the signal indicates failure, failure will actually occur with probability m. Based on this signal, projects can be terminated in period two, yielding a liquidation value $L<1$ (if a project is liquidated in period three, its liquidation value is zero). Monitoring is costly, and better monitoring provides a better signal.

Bankers are risk neutral but are funded by an infinite population of ex ante identical risk-averse investors. Ex post, however, the investor population separates into two groups. Some investors (the "wholesalers") choose to invest big in the project (have skin in the game) and monitor, under the expectation that monitoring will allow them to exit early in the case of a bad project and thereby recoup their investment. The lumpiness of wholesalers' investment, which is needed to make monitoring cost effective, prevents them from diversifying, making them risk averse. The other investors (the "depositors") choose to fully diversify by limiting their investment to an atomistic amount. Because of this, and assuming projects' probability of success is not systemically correlated across projects or to investors' income, the "depositors" remain de facto risk neutral.

Having skin in the game raises the cost of wholesale funds, which may result in insufficient monitoring. A risk-neutral guarantor buying the risk that is concentrated in wholesalers and spreading it by reselling it in small amounts to depositors can therefore improve in principle the market equilibrium. The risk transfer takes the form of bonds whose payoff is contingent on the project's failure. In keeping with the binomial structure of the model, we assume that partial guarantees cover uncertain full repayments (with probability $v \in [0,1]$) rather than certain partial repayments. Guarantees are priced fairly.

However, guarantors face three types of costs. First, since monitoring is costly, the guarantee undermines wholesalers' incentives to monitor the entrepreneur and the project. This is the standard moral hazard problem of insurance markets. To avoid distorting wholesalers' monitoring incentives, the guarantor can monitor wholesalers and adjust the premium of the guarantee according to how well they perform their monitoring. However, this monitoring of the monitor also has a cost. Second, the guarantor's capacity to resell risk to depositors depends on the capacity to convince them that the quarantor is doing a good job at monitoring wholesalers and, hence, is offering depositors a fair deal. To certify the good quality of the bonds they sell to the public, guarantors must therefore hire another, credible monitor (say, a rating agency), which implies another monitoring cost. Third, to pulverize the risk, guarantors need to have a sufficiently broad clientele of depositors. However, depositors' participation may be limited due to un-internalized externalities (that is, a failure to take into account the social benefits of their participation) and other frictions, including collective cognition frictions (that is, the cost associated with becoming aware of the deal and understanding it).[26] To overcome such frictions, guarantors must therefore incur a marketing cost aimed at promoting participation.

The possible states of the world are thus as follows:

- With probability p, the project succeeds, yielding X.
- With probability $(1 - p)m$, the project fails; however, given that a correct failure signal has been received, the project is terminated early and yields L; wholesalers get their investment back and retailers get the remainder.
- With probability $(1 - p)(1 - m)v$, the project goes on and fails; retailers lose their investment, but wholesalers recoup it through the guarantee.
- With probability $(1 - p)(1 - m)(1 - v)$, the project goes on, fails, and everybody loses their investment (the guarantee is not activated).

If δ is wholesalers' probability of getting their full return, it follows that

$$1 - \delta = (1 - p)(1 - m)(1 - v). \qquad (7A.14)$$

And the variance of the underlying binomial distribution, σ, equals:

$$\sigma = \delta(1 - \delta). \qquad (7A.15)$$

Wholesalers and retailers bid competitively on the amounts of wholesale and retail funding, W and D, respectively, which are set by the entrepreneur.

For notational convenience, we define $s = R^W W$ as wholesalers' total stake in the project, including interest payments. Bidding eliminates excess returns over the safe rate of return, which for simplicity is assumed to be zero.[27]

Wholesalers choose the amount of monitoring m, the rate of return on wholesale funding, R^W, and the extent of the guarantee, v, to maximize a mean-variance utility:

$$\underset{m,v,R^w}{Max}\, E\{U^W\} = [p + (1-p)m + (1-p)(1-m)v]s - W - \frac{a}{2}m^2 - \frac{\varepsilon\sigma}{2}s^2 - Y = 0. \quad (7A.16)$$

In this expression, a measures the cost that wholesalers' incur in monitoring entrepreneurs, ε is the degree of risk aversion, Y is the premium on the guarantee, and σ is the variance of project outcomes, that is, a measure of risk. As in any insurance contract, there is moral hazard. Wholesalers have an incentive to shirk, which depends on the extent to which the guarantee internalizes "deviant behavior." Because it is costly for the guarantor to fully discriminate between wholesalers, the quantor sets fees partly on a collective basis and partly on an individual basis. Thus, while he does charge for all bad behavior collectively, he can do it only to a limited extent on an individual basis. Thus, each individual wholesaler internalizes only a fraction μm ($\mu \in [0,1]$) of the cost of the guarantee, taking the rest, $(1-\mu)\hat{m}$, where $\hat{m}$ is collective monitoring, as given. Thus, from the individual wholesaler's point of view, the premium he is charged is

$$Y = (1-p)vs[\mu(1-m) + (1-\mu)(1-\hat{m})] + \frac{b}{2}\mu^2 + c + d, \quad (7A.17)$$

where $\frac{b}{2}\mu^2$ is the cost to the guarantor of monitoring wholesalers (which is assumed to increase quadratically with the extent of internalization, which in turn reflects the quality of the monitoring), c is the monitoring fee charged by the rating agency, and d is the guarantor's marketing cost.

Replacing (7A.17) in (7A.16),

$$\underset{m,v,R^w}{Max}\, E\{U^W\} = [p + (1-p)m + (1-p)(1-\mu)(\hat{m}-m)v]s$$

$$- W - \frac{a}{2}m^2 - \frac{b}{2}\mu^2 - \frac{\varepsilon\sigma}{2}s^2 - c - d = 0. \quad (7A.18)$$

Thus, the guarantee has two impacts. It reduces the variance of the distribution (σ), hence the risk premium, which is good. But, unless there is full internalization ($\mu = 1$), it also affects m, hence undermining monitoring incentives, which is bad.

Since guarantors are risk neutral and the guarantee market is fully competitive, guarantors set μ so as to minimize the premium on the guarantee, which through market arbitrage will equal its expected cost. Since from their perspective $m = \hat{m}$, this amounts to setting Y such that

$$\underset{\mu}{Min}\, Y = (1-p)(1-m)vs + \frac{b}{2}\mu^2 + c + d. \tag{7A.19}$$

Because they are fully diversified, depositors behave as if they were risk neutral; hence they maximize:[28]

$$\underset{R^D}{Max}\, E\left\{U^D\right\} = (pR^D - 1)D + (1-p)m[L(D+W) - R^W W] = 0. \tag{7A.20}$$

Entrepreneurs, who are also risk neutral, maximize their expected profits:

$$\underset{W,D}{Max}\, E\left\{\pi^B\right\} = p[D(X - R^D) + W(X - R^W)]. \tag{7A.21}$$

Entrepreneurs internalize the participation constraints of wholesalers and retailers when setting W and D. Hence, pDR^D and $pR^W W$ can be replaced in (7A.21) using their values extracted from (7A.18) and (7A.20), which gives

$$\underset{W,D}{Max}\, E\left\{U^B\right\} = [pX - 1 + (1-p)mL](D+W)$$

$$+ (1-p)(\hat{m} - m)(1 - \mu)vs$$

$$- \frac{a}{2}m^2 - \frac{b}{2}\mu^2 - \frac{\varepsilon\sigma}{2}s^2 - c - d \geq 0. \tag{7A.22}$$

Maximizing (7A.22) with respect to W and D is equivalent to maximizing with respect to $D + W$ (the total size of the investment) and s (the composition of the funding). In turn, as $pX > 1$, it is obvious that entrepreneurs should choose the maximum size of the investment; hence,

$$D + W = 1. \tag{7A.23}$$

Since risk-averse wholesalers and risk-neutral depositors just meet their participation constraints (they have zero excess returns), finding the guarantee that maximizes social welfare is equivalent to maximizing bankers' profits while taking into account that guarantees are priced fairly (that is, removing moral hazard):

$$\underset{W,D}{Max}\, E\{U^B\} = [pX + (1-p)mL - 1]$$

$$-\left(\frac{a}{2}m^2 + \frac{b}{2}\mu^2 + C\right) - d - \frac{\varepsilon\sigma}{2}s^2 \geq 0 \cdot \qquad (7A.24)$$

Notice that there are four groups of terms on the right hand side of this expression. Hence, searching for the social optimum is equivalent to maximizing the total size of the surplus pie, as determined by the total expected excess returns of the project, $pX + (1 - p)mL - 1$, minus the *sum of monitoring costs* along the entire monitoring pyramid $\left(\frac{a}{2}m^2 + \frac{b}{2}\mu^2 + c\right)$, the *participation costs*, d, and the deadweight cost of risk taking, $\frac{\varepsilon\sigma}{2}s^2$. It follows from this expression that the socially optimal level of monitoring is obtained by differentiating the right hand side of (7A.24) with respect to m:

$$m^* = \frac{(1-p)L}{a} \qquad (7A.25)$$

In contrast, the market-determined level of monitoring is obtained by deriving the first-order conditions with respect to s, m, v and μ. Maximizing (7A.22) with respect to s gives

$$\left[(1-p)(L-(1-\mu)vs) - am - \frac{\varepsilon s^2}{2}\frac{\partial\sigma}{\partial m}\right]\frac{\partial m}{\partial s} = \varepsilon\sigma s \qquad (7A.26)$$

The first-order condition of (7A.18) with respect to m yields

$$am = (1-p)[1-(1-\mu)v]s - \frac{\varepsilon s^2}{2}\frac{\partial\sigma}{\partial m} \qquad (7A.27)$$

Using (7A.27), (7A.26) can be rewritten as

$$(1-p)(L-s)\frac{\partial m}{\partial s} = \varepsilon\sigma s. \qquad (7A.28)$$

From which

$$s = \frac{L}{1 + \varepsilon\sigma s/[(1-p)\partial m/\partial s]} \cdot \qquad (7A.29)$$

Deriving m, however, from the first-order condition of (7A.18)

$$m = \frac{(1-p)(1-(1-\mu)v)s + \varepsilon s^2(1-p)(1-v)[1-(1-p)(1-v)]}{a - \varepsilon s^2(1-p)^2(1-v)^2}. \qquad (7A.30)$$

The first-order condition of (7A.19) can be written

$$b\mu = (1-p)vs\frac{\partial m}{\partial \mu}, \qquad (7A.31)$$

or, using (7A.9),

$$\mu = \frac{(1-p)^2 v^2 s^2}{ab - b\varepsilon s^2(1-p)^2(1-v)^2}. \qquad (7A.32)$$

Finally, the first-order condition of (7A.18) with respect to v is

$$b\mu\frac{\partial \mu}{\partial v} + \frac{\varepsilon s^2}{2}\frac{\partial \sigma}{\partial v} = 0. \qquad (7A.33)$$

Or, using (7A.32), (7A.14), and (7A.15) and after some algebraic manipulations:

$$\mu v = \frac{\varepsilon(2\delta - 1)(1-m)}{4(1-p)}\frac{[a - \varepsilon s^2(1-p)^2(1-v)^2]^2}{a + \varepsilon s^2(1-p)^2(1-v)v}. \qquad (7A.34)$$

Consider first the case where wholesalers are risk neutral ($\varepsilon = 0$). From (7A.19) and (7A.21), it can be readily inferred that $\mu = v = 0$; that is, no guarantees are demanded. It therefore follows from (7A.16) that $s = L$ (wholesalers take the largest position that can be recovered in the liquidation), and from (7A.17) that $m = (1-p)L/a$. Hence, the market-determined level of monitoring coincides with the socially optimal level of monitoring. This is the Calomiris-Khan classical result.

The intuition behind this result is straightforward. By appropriating the proceeds from the liquidations, risk-neutral wholesalers fully internalize the social benefits of their monitoring. At the same time, they do not need to be paid a risk premium to bear the risk associated with holding sufficiently large stakes in the project (sufficient skin in the game) to warrant incurring the monitoring costs. Since it is not socially costly for these wholesalers to retain large stakes, bankers can therefore contract enough wholesale funding to allow wholesalers to fully recoup the cost of the socially optimal level of monitoring. An efficient equilibrium is thus obtained where monitoring costs can be absorbed *without having to spread any risk*. Hence, fairly priced (unsubsidized) guarantees add no value.

But suppose now that wholesalers are risk averse ($\varepsilon > 0$). Consider in this case under which conditions the market solution leads to full internalization of the moral hazard associated with the guarantee $\mu \geq 1$. From (7A.32), this condition can be written:

$$ab \leq (1-p)^2 s^2 [v^2 + b\varepsilon(1-v)^2]. \tag{7A.35}$$

If internalization is complete, wholesalers will always prefer a full guarantee to a partial guarantee since the former eliminates the risk premium term in (7A.5) but results in the same monitoring costs. Using (7A.29) and (7A.30), a full guarantee ($v = 1$) then implies

$$s = L \tag{7A.36}$$

$$m = \frac{(1-p)L}{a}. \tag{7A.37}$$

Thus, as in the case of the market solution without risk aversion, the full guarantee–full internalization solution with risk aversion replicates the socially optimal solution: risk is fully spread out. However, for risk to be fully spreadable, a number of conditions need to be met. Notice first that (7A.35) reduces to

$$(ab)^{\frac{1}{2}} \leq (1-p)L. \tag{7A.38}$$

This is a straightforward cost-benefit condition: the (geometric) average of the monitoring costs incurred by wholesalers and guarantors should be lower than the maximum possible benefit of monitoring, which equals the full expected value of the liquidations.

At the same time, given that the direct monitoring costs, a, should be sufficiently high to justify imperfect monitoring ($m < 1$), it follows from (7A.37) and (7A.38) that the full internalization–full guarantee equilibrium should also be such that

$$b < (1 - p)\, L < a. \tag{7A.39}$$

This is an efficiency condition: the cost to the guarantors of monitoring wholesalers, b, should be lower than wholesalers' cost of monitoring bankers, a. Hence, there should be "efficiency gains" as one goes up the monitoring pyramid.

Finally, using (7A.37), the participation constraint for bankers can be written:

$$c + \frac{b}{2} + d \leq (pX - 1) + \frac{(1-p)^2 L^2}{2a}. \tag{7A.40}$$

This is a broad economic feasibility condition in dispersing the risk. The sum of the guarantor's monitoring cost associated with a full guarantee, $b/2$, plus the rating agency's monitoring cost, c, plus the guarantor's marketing cost, d, must be more than covered by the expected surplus value of the project, $pX-1$, plus the expected liquidation value for the optimal level of wholesaler monitoring, which is itself a declining function of the wholesalers' monitoring cost, a. In other words, for risk to be spreadable, the total costs of distribution and monitoring (both direct and indirect) must be sufficiently low.

Notes

1. See, for instance, Jaffee and Russell (1976), Stiglitz and Weiss (1981), Mankiw (1986), Smith and Stutzer (1989), Bernanke and Gertler (1990), Innes (1991), Benavente, Galetovic, and Sanhueza. (2006), and Arping, Loranth, and Morrison (2008). As discussed below, the papers that analyze government guarantees in a general equilibrium setting typically have focused on adverse selection problems and unanimously conclude that these problems do not justify guarantees (see Greenwald and Stiglitz 1986; Gale 1990; Williamson 1994; Lacker 1994; Li 1998).

2. As documented, for instance, in Honohan (2008) and Beck, Klapper, and Mendoza (2010).

3. The framework developed in de la Torre and Ize (2010, 2011) considers four paradigms, labeled *costly enforcement* (CE), *collective action* (CA), *asymmetric information* (AI), and *collective cognition* (CC). Two of these paradigms (CE and AI) give rise to bilateral (agency) market failures, while the other two (CA and CC) are associated with multilateral (social) market failures. At the same time, two paradigms (CE and CA) are founded on full information and full rationality while the other two (AI and CC) are based on informational and learning frictions, possibly leading to bounded rationality.

4. Systematic risk refers to aggregate undiversifiable market risk. A systematic shock may lead to systemic risk, where the entire financial system becomes affected and where risk is compounded by agents' endogenous responses and interdependencies.

5. Likewise, overlending can occur: when projects that would be equally profitable if successful have different probabilities of success, low interest rates can induce borrowers with low success probabilities to borrow, even though their expected returns are below the social rate of return. See de Mezza and Webb (1987, 1999) and Beck and de la Torre (2006).

6. The partial equilibrium literature that does not require revenue neutrality finds that state guarantees can improve things by increasing credit (for example, Mankiw 1986; Smith and Stutzer 1989; Innes 1991; Benavente, Galetovic, and Sanhuenza 2006; Arping, Loranth, and Morrison 2010). The literature that takes a general equilibrium view (and hence imposes revenue neutrality) can be classified

into two groups. The first group uses a Kaldor-Hicks welfare criterion that simply looks at the total size of the pie but not at its distribution across the population. With such a criterion, some papers predict that state guarantees can lead to an improved equilibrium (for example, Ordover and Weiss 1981; Bernanke and Gertler 1990; Innes 1992; Athreya, Tam, and Young 2010). However, others do not (for example, Li 1998; Gale 1990; Williamson 1994). The second group of papers incorporates the welfare impacts of tax redistribution. The papers in this latter group (for instance, Greenwald and Stiglitz 1986; Lacker 1994) uniformly conclude that, without an informational advantage and the ability to cross-subsidize, it is not possible for state guarantees to produce a Pareto improvement.

7. Notice, however, that multilateral development banks that lend to public sectors to finance investment projects may enjoy informational advantages over private lenders, such as knowing more than private lenders about state processes and procedures. This may justify multilateral development bank guarantees even in a world characterized by pure agency failures with no risk aversion.

8. The argument that the state may be able to provide incentives to public lenders more easily than to private ones is in line with Holmstrom and Milgrom's (1991) result that increasing the incentives along a measurable performance dimension (costs or profitability) reduces the incentives along nonmeasurable dimensions.

9. This is indeed the main result in Calomiris-Khan. However, Huang and Ratnovski (2011) challenge this result by showing that in the presence of noisy public information, wholesalers may have an incentive to free ride on this information and run early when needed rather than to monitor.

10. In principle, the Arrow and Lind argument continues to apply: no matter how lumpy the risk, it can still be distributed atomistically, provided there are enough retailers over which the risk can be spread. In Arrow and Lind, the number of retailers can go all the way to infinity. In practice, however, there is an important difference between a large number and an infinite number. Moreover, and perhaps more important, participation frictions limit market depth even in well-developed financial systems. Thus, the number of retailers over which risk can be spread, even if large, may not be sufficient. That is why there may be a point at which a permanent public guarantee may be needed, even in mature systems, to bound the risk associated with unpredictable returns or where there is some probability, even if very small, of very large losses. Knightian uncertainty—decision makers cannot determine the probabilities of events (see Epstein 1999)—is likely to have an effect similar to fat tails. The more uncertain the risk, the more finely it needs to be distributed, which, in principle, makes more of a case for public guarantees.

11. Indeed, trying to depict the inability of markets to contract across generations from a pure enforcement perspective is rather futile. Since it is not possible to write bilateral contracts with someone unborn, "enforcing" such contracts is meaningless.

12. Needless to say, the state should charge a premium that fully offsets the expected losses. Hence, over the longer term or over a sufficiently large number of borrowers, the law of large numbers should come into play, and the state should not take significant losses.

13. The link between managerial risk aversion and governance can be easily visualized in a Bayesian inference setting where the bank manager cannot signal the quality of risk management to the bank owner.

14. Development banks in Mexico, for instance, are regulated and supervised on par with commercial banks and are required by law to preserve the real value of their capital.

15. The tension between development banks' actual risk aversion, on the one hand, and their social mandate (which pressures them to move into relatively lower

return–higher risk activities) can result in an unstable equilibrium that has been dubbed "Sisyphus Syndrome" (de la Torre, Gozzi, and Schmukler 2007). Pulling in the opposite direction of the mentioned risk aversion can be a political drive to unduly and imprudently expand lending or credit guarantee programs, in lieu of strengthening the appropriate social protection systems, as a convenient way to relieve some of the build-up political pressures associated with social inequities (Rajan 2010).

16. Such programs appear to pay for themselves (hence are fiscally safe) when well priced and well designed. See Honohan (2008) and Beck, Klapper, and Mendoza (2010).

17. See Diamond and Dybvig (1983) and the more novel contributions of Caballero and Krishnamurthy (2008) and Caballero and Kurlat (2009) on the role of public guarantees under uncertainty. More generally, one could also argue that the state could behave collectively in a more rational way than individuals when the latter are subjected to systematic behavioral biases.

18. This can also justify mandated—or gently coerced—participation, as in the case of the payment of state employee wages through accounts in banks that participate in a shared, open-architecture platform for retail payments.

19. On the experience of mutual guarantee associations in Europe, see Columba, Gambacorta, and Mistrulli (2010). Lebanon provides an interesting example of a seemingly successful and profitable guarantee scheme structured as a joint stock company.

20. A long-term finance commitment can be viewed as a funding (liability) guarantee that provides protection against liquidity risk and price volatility, instead of protection against credit default.

21. This is indeed one of the main conclusions reached in recent reviews of existing public guarantee programs. See Beck, Klapper, and Mendoza (2010) and Saadani, Arvai, and Rocha (2011).

22. Some lending and guarantee programs by development banks in high-income countries are structured in this way. The Business Development Bank Canada small business loan guarantee program is a prime example. See Gutierrez, et al. (2011).

23. One possible approach to facilitating risk discovery is to auction the guarantees according to their coverage or price. This is the approach followed in Chile by FOGAPE. See Benavente, Galetovic, and Sanhueza (2006) and de la Torre, Gozzi, and Schmukler (2007). By setting volumes rather than prices, guarantors can better protect themselves against the risk of major mispricing. At the same time, volumes may be adjusted to meet countercyclical objectives.

24. For example, recurrent assessments by independent evaluation units or occasional, more strategic reviews by blue-ribbon committees should help.

25. Alternatively, to align incentives, development banks can assume a limited part of the risk, the rest being covered by the fiscal authorities through earmarked capital or other means.

26. Participation externalities occur when the gains in participating in an activity depend on the number of other agents participating as well (see Diamond 1982 and Pagano 1989). By hindering coordination, participation frictions prevent agents from internalizing such externalities.

27. Since the risk coverage instruments are priced fairly, they do not appear in depositors' utility.

28. However, Huang and Ratnovski (2011) challenge this result by showing that in the presence of noisy public information, wholesalers may have an incentive to free ride on this information and run early when needed rather than monitoring.

References

Arping, S., G. Loranth, and A. D. Morrison. 2010. "Public Initiatives to Support Entrepreneurs: Credit Guarantees versus Co-funding." *Journal of Financial Stability* 6 (1): 26–35.

Arrow, K. J., and R. C. Lind. 1970. "Uncertainty and the Evaluation of Public Investment Decisions." *American Economic Review* 60 (3): 364–78.

Athreya, K., X. S. Tam, and E. R. Young. 2010. "Loan Guarantee Programs for Unsecured Consumer Credit Markets." Working paper, University of Cambridge, Cambridge, UK.

Beck, T., and A. de la Torre. 2006. "The Basic Analytics of Access to Financial Services." Policy Research Working Paper 4026, World Bank, Washington, DC.

Beck, T., L. Klapper, and J. C. Mendoza. 2010. "The Typology of Partial Credit Guarantee Funds around the World." *Journal of Financial Stability* 6 (1): 10–25.

Benavente, J. M., A. Galetovic, and R. Sanhueza. 2006. "Fogape: An Economic Analysis." Working Paper 222, University of Chile, Department of Economics, Santiago, Chile.

Bernanke, B., and M. Gertler. 1990. "Financial Fragility and Economic Performance." *Quarterly Journal of Economics* 105 (1): 87–114.

Bhattacharya, J. 1997. "Credit Market Imperfections, Income Distribution, and Capital Accumulation." *Economic Theory* 11 (1): 171–200.

Caballero, R. J., and A. Krishnamurthy. 2008. "Collective Risk Management in a Flight to Quality Episode." *Journal of Finance* 63 (5): 2195–230.

Caballero, R. J., and P. Kurlat. 2009. "The 'Surprising' Origin and Nature of Financial Crises: A Macroeconomic Policy Proposal." Presentation prepared for the "Jackson Hole Symposium on Financial Stability and Macroeconomic Policy," Jackson Hole, Wyoming, May 18.

Calomiris, C., and C. Himmelberg. 1993. *Directed Credit Programs for Agriculture and Industry: Arguments from Theory and Fact.* Washington, DC: World Bank.

Calomiris, C., and C. M. Kahn. 1991. "The Role of Demandable Debt in Structuring Optimal Banking Arrangements." *American Economic Review* 81 (3): 497–513.

Columba, F., L. Gambacorta, and P. E. Mistrulli. 2010. "Mutual Guarantee Institutions and Small Business Finance." *Journal of Financial Stability* 6 (1): 45–54.

de la Torre, A., J. C. Gozzi, and S. Schmukler. 2007. "Innovative Experiences in Access to Finance: Market Friendly Roles for the Visible Hand?" Working Paper 4326, World Bank, Washington, DC.

de la Torre, A., and A. Ize. 2010. "Regulatory Reform: Integrating Paradigms." *International Finance* 13 (1): 109–39.

———. 2011. "Containing Systemic Risk: Paradigm-Based Perspectives on Regulatory Reform." *Economia* 11 (1): 25–64.

de Mezza, D., and D. C. Webb. 1987. "Too Much Investment: A Problem of Asymmetric Information." *Quarterly Journal of Economics* 102 (2): 281–92.

———. 1999. "Wealth, Enterprise and Credit Policy." *Economic Journal* 109 (455): 153–63.

Diamond, D. W., and P. H. Dybvig. 1983. "Bank Runs, Deposit Insurance, and Liquidity." *Journal of Political Economy* 91 (5): 401–19.

Epstein, L. 1999. "Are Probabilities Used in Markets." RCER Working Paper 464, University of Rochester Center for Economic Research, Rochester, NY.

Gale, W. G. 1990. "Collateral, Rationing, and Government Intervention in Credit Markets." In *Asymmetric Information, Corporate Finance, and Investment*, edited by R. Glenn Hubbard, 43–62. Cambridge, MA: National Bureau of Economic Research.

Greenwald, B., and J. E. Stiglitz. 1986. "Externalities in Economies with Imperfect Information and Incomplete Markets." *Quarterly Journal of Economics* 101 (2): 229–64.

Gutierrez, E., H. Rudolph, T. Homa, and E. Beneit. 2011. "Development Banks: Role and Mechanisms to Increase Their Efficiency." Policy Research Working Paper 5729, World Bank, Washington, DC.

Holmstrom, B., and P. Milgrom. 1991. "Multitask Principal-Agent Analysis: Linear Contracts, Asset Ownership, and Job Design." *Journal of Law, Economics and Organization* 7: 24–52.

Honohan, P. 2008. "Partial Credit Guarantees: Principles and Practice." Paper presented at the World Bank Conference "Partial Credit Guarantee Schemes: Experiences and Lessons," Washington, DC, March 13–14.

Huang, R. and T. Ratnovski. 2011. "The Dark Side of Bank Wholesale Funding." *Journal of Financial Intermediation* 20 (2): 248–63.

Innes, R. 1991. "Investment and Government Intervention in Credit Markets When There Is Asymmetric Information." *Journal of Public Economics* 46 (3): 347–81.

———. 1992. "Adverse Selection, Investment, and Profit Taxation." *European Economic Review* 36 (7): 1427–52.

Jaffee, D. M., and T. Russell. 1976. "Imperfect Information, Uncertainty, and Credit Rationing." *Quarterly Journal of Economics* 90 (4): 651–66.

Klein, M. 1996. "Risk, Taxpayers, and the Role of Government in Project Finance." Policy Research Working Paper 1688, World Bank, Washington, DC.

Lacker, J. 1994. "Does Adverse Selection Justify Government Intervention in Loan Markets?" *Economic Quarterly* (Winter): 61–95.

Li, W. 1998. "Government Loan, Guarantee, and Grant Programs: An Evaluation." *Economic Quarterly* (Fall): 25–52.

Lombra, R. E., and M. Wasylenko. 1984. "The Subsidization of Small Business through Federal Credit Programs: Analytical Foundations." *Journal of Economics and Business* 36 (2): 263–74.

Mankiw, N. G. 1986. "The Allocation of Credit and Financial Collapse." *Quarterly Journal of Economics* 101 (3): 455–70.

Ordover, J., and A. Weiss. 1981. "Information and the Law: Evaluating Legal Restrictions on Competitive Contracts." *American Economic Review* 71 (2): 399–404.

Pagano, M. 1989. "Trading Volume and Asset Liquidity." *Quarterly Journal of Economics* 104 (2): 255–74.

Penner, R. G., and W. L. Silber. 1973. "The Interaction between Federal Credit Programs and the Impact on the Allocation of Credit." *American Economic Review* 63 (5): 838–52.

Raith, M., T. Staak, and C. Starke. 2006. "The Goal Achievement of Federal Lending Programs." FEMM Working Paper 19, Faculty of Economics and Management, Magdeburg, Germany.

Rajan, R. 2010. *Fault Lines: How Hidden Fractures Still Threaten the World Economy*. Princeton, NJ: Princeton University Press.

Saadani,Youssef, Zsofia Arvai, and Roberto Rocha. 2011. "A Review of Credit Guarantee Schemes in the Middle East and North Africa Region." Policy Research Working Paper 5612, World Bank, Washington, DC.

Smith, B. D., and M. J. Stutzer. 1989. "Credit Rationing and Government Loan Programs: A Welfare Analysis." *Real Estate Economics* 17 (2): 177–93.

Stiglitz, J. E., and A. Weiss. 1981. "Credit Rationing in Markets with Imperfect Information." *American Economic Review* 71 (3): 393–410.

Williamson, S. D. 1994. "Do Informational Frictions Justify Federal Credit Programs?" *Journal of Money, Credit and Banking* 26 (3): 523–44.

8

Recent Trends in Banking Supervision in Latin America and the Caribbean

Socorro Heysen and Martín Auqui

Abstract

This chapter examines the ratings of compliance with the Basel Core Principles in 31 countries in Latin America and the Caribbean in absolute and relative terms. It also discusses the specific measures taken by several LAC countries in 10 key areas of bank oversight. The analysis of ratings in absolute terms provides a picture of the effectiveness of oversight, whereas the analysis in relative terms uses econometric tools to compare the effectiveness of oversight relative to a benchmark of LAC countries' peers across the world. We show that progress in prudential oversight has been broad based and includes aspects as diverse as the institutional framework, authorization processes, supervision of other risks, internal controls, and market discipline. However, progress has been uneven in two key respects. First, the LAC region still performs poorly on the independence of supervisors, capital adequacy, supervision of risks, and consolidated supervision. Second, there are

Socorro Heysen is an independent consultant and served previously as superintendent of banks for Peru. Martín Auqui is on the staff of the Superintendency of Banks, Insurance and Pension Funds Administrators of Peru.

significant disparities within the region. While LAC7 countries show acceptable supervisory frameworks, both absolute and relative to their peers in the rest of the world, countries in the rest of LAC tend to exhibit a much lower absolute and relative performance in several areas, especially those associated with supervision of other risks, capital, and consolidated supervision. Thus, while the region is better prepared to face the oversight wars of today, outstanding weaknesses pose certain challenges. LAC supervisors need to continue working toward frameworks that increase the effectiveness of bank capital and liquidity buffers during adverse situations, both on a consolidated basis and on one that takes into account all relevant risks.

Overview

Most countries in Latin America and the Caribbean (LAC) sailed through the 2008 global financial crisis essentially unharmed. Rather than examining the reasons for the resilience of LAC banking systems during the crisis, the purpose of this chapter is to highlight the common weak spots in LAC supervisory frameworks and to present recent efforts to address them. However, the question of LAC's resilience inevitably remains in our minds. We believe that while the improvement in bank regulation and supervision played a role in reducing the vulnerabilities of the region's banking systems, the main reasons for their resilience lay elsewhere. For instance, macroeconomic fundamentals were more solid than in previous crises, allowing several countries to implement countercyclical financial policies. Credit growth was high in the years before the crisis, but the credit boom was shorter and smaller than in other regions and also shorter and smaller than the credit booms that had preceded previous banking crises in the region. Moreover, most LAC banking systems still run on a traditional banking and funding model, which provided some insulation from the significant losses related to global financial volatility.

The progress achieved in prudential oversight over the past two decades nevertheless deserves some of the credit. The pace of credit growth cannot be dissociated from the prudent supervisory frameworks that required high capital, liquidity, and provisioning buffers as well as sound credit-granting policies. The financial crises that occurred in several LAC countries during the 1990s and early 2000s[1] had triggered efforts from governments, regulatory agencies, and financial institutions to prevent subsequent crises. At a time when supervisors in some developed countries seemed to focus on creating institution-friendly regimes by diluting prudential buffers and expanding the range of the banking business, many LAC countries moved in the opposite direction and concentrated on strengthening bank soundness (see box 8.1). In addition,

Box 8.1 Analysis of the 2007 World Survey of Bank
Regulation and Supervision

Regressions were run for 56 of the questions on the 2007 Survey of Bank
Regulation and Supervision around the World (BRS). The BRS database is available on the World Bank website (www.worldbank.org) and
includes responses from 142 countries to more than 300 questions. The
regressions explain differences for LAC countries, controlling for gross
domestic product (GDP) per capita. Two specifications were run with
each question as a dependent variable. The first one includes a dummy
variable for the LAC region and the second one for the LAC7 countries
(Argentina, Brazil, Chile, Colombia, Mexico, Peru, and Uruguay).

The analysis focuses on the sign of the coefficients of the significant
explanatory variables. Positive coefficients are associated with better and
stronger supervision, with the exception of variables COURTINV and
LOANCS. Table B8.1.1 presents the results of the most relevant regressions with LAC DUMMY and LAC7 DUMMY, respectively, and defines
the dependent variables of those regressions. The main conclusions are
the following:

- A higher per capita GDP is generally associated with a greater financial freedom, specifically with regard to shareholder and conglomerate structure, and incursion into nonbanking business (insurance,
  securities, and real estate). Countries with higher GDP per capita
  also tend to have less stringent regulatory systems on loan provisions. However, these countries are likely to have a greater financial
  transparency, a lower participation of the public sector in the financial system, and greater financial intermediation. In this context,
  banks in LAC countries usually have more restrictions on engage-
  ment in a variety of financial intermediation and investment banking activities such as securities underwriting, brokering and dealing,
  mutual funds, insurance, and real estate investment than their peers
  and also stricter provisioning rules; in addition, the LAC region lags
  in the adoption of internationally accepted accounting standards.
- The regressions are generally consistent with the findings of the
  BCP assessments and support the following findings:
  - *Legal protection of bank supervisors.* Bank supervisors in the
    LAC region are more likely than their peers in the rest of the
    world to be held personally liable for damages caused by their
    actions or omissions as bank supervisors.
  - *Independence of bank supervisors.* Supervisors in LAC are also
    more exposed to political decisions than their peers in other

(box continued next page)

Box 8.1 Analysis of the 2007 World Survey of Bank Regulation and Supervision *(continued)*

Table B8.1.1 Results of Regression Analysis of the Banking Regulation Survey

| Endogenous variables | Regressions with LAC dummy | | | Regressions with LAC7 dummy | | | Description of endogenous variables | Source |
| | Coefficients | | | Coefficients | | | | |
	LGDPPC	LAC	R2	LGDPPC	LAC7	R2		
CONG10B	1.3290	31.8200***	0.12	-0.0381	30.8700***	0.04	The percentage of capital in the 10 largest banks that is owned by commercial/industrial and/or financial conglomerates.	BRS2.4
OVER3AR	0.4010***	1.1440**	0.19	-0.4160***	-0.0190	0.14	The extent to which banks may engage in aspects of the mutual fund, insurance, and real state industries.[a]	BRS4.1–4.3
BONF	-0.1470***	0.6170***	0.18	-0.1540***	0.3990	0.11	The extent to which banks may own and control nonfinancial firms.[a]	BRS4.4

(box continued next page)

Box 8.1 Analysis of the 2007 World Survey of Bank Regulation and Supervision *(continued)*

Table B8.1.1 Results of Regression Analysis of the Banking Regulation Survey *(continued)*

Endogenous variables	Regressions with LAC dummy			Regressions with LAC7 dummy			Description of endogenous variables	Source
	Coefficients		R2	Coefficients		R2		
	LGDPPC	LAC		LGDPPC	LAC7			
OSPOWER	-0.2700*	0.9390**	0.06	-0.2980**	1.3530**	0.06	Whether the supervisory authorities have the authority to take specific actions to prevent and correct problems.[c]	BRS5.5, 5.6, 5.7, 6.1, 10.4, 11.2, 11.3.1, 11.3.2, 11.3.3, 11.6, 11.7, 11.9.1, 11.9.2, 11.9.3
DIPOWER	-0.0014	0.5260***	0.04	-0.0087	0.4920***	0.01	Whether the supervisory authorities have the power to declare a deeply troubled bank insolvent.[c]	BRS11.6, 11.7
COURTINV	0.1050**	-0.1950	0.07	0.1080**	-0.2970**	0.07	The degree to which the court dominates the supervisory authority.[b]	BRS11.12–11.14

(box continued next page)

Box 8.1 Analysis of the 2007 World Survey of Bank Regulation and Supervision (*continued*)

Table B8.1.1 Results of Regression Analysis of the Banking Regulation Survey (*continued*)

Endogenous variables	Regressions with LAC dummy				Regressions with LAC7 dummy				Description of endogenous variables	Source
	Coefficients				Coefficients					
	LGDPPC	LAC	R2		LGDPPC	LAC7	R2			
LOANCS	−23.3200	−112.4000**	0.06		−23.4000	−62.1000	0.03		The minimum number of days beyond which a loan in arrears must be classified as substandard, then doubtful, and finally loss.[b]	BRS9.2.1–9.2.3
PSTRING	−8.2480**	−4.5470	0.09		−8.0140**	−28.0500	0.11		The minimum required provisions as loans become sub-standard, doubtful, and loss.[d]	BRS9.3.1–9.3.3
INDPOLI	0.0352	−0.2050**	0.04		0.0379	−0.1650	0.02		The degree to which the supervisory authority is independent within the government from political influence.[c]	BRS12.2, 12.2 (c)

(box continued next page)

Box 8.1 Analysis of the 2007 World Survey of Bank Regulation and Supervision *(continued)*

Table B8.1.1 Results of Regression Analysis of the Banking Regulation Survey *(continued)*

| Endogenous variables | Regressions with LAC dummy | | | Regressions with LAC7 dummy | | | Description of endogenous variables | Source |
| | Coefficients | | | Coefficients | | | | |
	LGDPPC	LAC	R2	LGDPPC	LAC7	R2		
INDBANK	−0.0041	−0.4590***	0.15	0.0023	−0.5260***	0.08	The degree to which the supervisory authority is protected by the legal system from the banking industry.[c]	BRS12.10
INDSA	0.0106	−0.7460***	0.11	0.0285	−1.0350***	0.09	The degree to which the supervisory authority is independent from the government and legally protected from the banking industry.[c]	BRS12.2, 12.2 (c), 12.10, 12.2.2
FUNDID	2.6870**	10.7700	0.06	2.4810**	26.2500**	0.10	The percentage of the commercial banking system's assets that is funded with insured deposits.	BRS7.10.1

(box continued next page)

Box 8.1 Analysis of the 2007 World Survey of Bank Regulation and Supervision (continued)

Table B8.1.1 Results of Regression Analysis of the Banking Regulation Survey (continued)

Endogenous variables	Regressions with LAC dummy			Regressions with LAC7 dummy			Description of endogenous variables	Source
	Coefficients			Coefficients				
	LGDPPC	LAC	R2	LGDPPC	LAC7	R2		
GOVBANK	4.1750***	0.8260	0.08	-4.1660***	16.7100**	0.11	The fraction of the banking system's assets is in banks that are 50% or more government owned.	BRS3.8.1
FSTRANS	0.1720***	0.1100	0.07	0.1700***	0.3740**	0.08	The transparency of bank financial statements practices.[e]	BRS10.1, 10.3, 10.4.1, 10.5, 10.6, 10.1.1
ACCTPRA	-0.0011	-0.4600***	0.18	0.0057	-0.5580***	0.11	Whether or not international financial reporting standards or USGAAP is used for all banks.[e]	BRS3.10, 3.11

(box continued next page)

Box 8.1 Analysis of the 2007 World Survey of Bank Regulation and Supervision (continued)

Table B8.1.1 Results of Regression Analysis of the Banking Regulation Survey (continued)

Endogenous variables	Regressions with LAC dummy			Regressions with LAC7 dummy			Description of endogenous variables	Source
	Coefficients			Coefficients				
	LGDPPC	LAC	R2	LGDPPC	LAC7	R2		
BNKDEV	0.2190***	−0.1930**	0.44	0.2200***	−0.3020**	0.44	Private credit by deposit money banks to GDP.	Financial structure data from World Bank; Beck, Demirgüç-Kunt, and Levine(2006)

Note: Numerals refer to BRS questions. All explanatory variables used were lac_dummy: 1 when it is a country of Latin America and the Caribbean or 0 otherwise; lac7_dummy: 1 when the country is Argentina, Brazil, Chile, Colombia, Mexico, Peru, or Uruguay or 0 otherwise; cons: constant. Exogenous variables are considered significant when they have a p value < 0.05 (whereas regressions R2 is in general low). The variable constant is not shown in these tables (because it is not relevant to this analysis). The table B8.1.1 shows only the main regressions for the purpose of this analysis. LAC = Latin America and the Caribbean; BRS = Banking Regulation Survey; GDP = gross domestic product; USGAAP = U.S. Generally Accepted Accounting Principles.

*** p<0.01, ** p<0.05, * p<0.1.

a. Higher values indicate greater restrictiveness.

b. Lower values indicate greater stringency and independence.

c. Higher values indicate greater power and independence.

d. Higher values indicate greater stringency.

e. Higher values indicate transparency and monitoring.

(box continued next page)

Box 8.1 Analysis of the 2007 World Survey of Bank
Regulation and Supervision *(continued)*

regions, as their removal is likely to require just a decision by
the president, prime minister, or the minister of finance, rather
than congressional approval.

- *Remedial powers of supervisors.* LAC supervisors tend to have
greater powers to impose corrective actions on supervised institutions. They are also more likely to be able to declare a bank
insolvent or to resolve a bank without a court order. Moreover,
in the LAC7 countries supervisors are more likely to be able to
appoint a liquidator or supersede shareholders' rights without
court intervention.

The structures of LAC banking systems are also different from those in
other regions, including a lower bank intermediation and more conglomeration. LAC7 countries show a higher government participation and a
higher proportion of insured deposits in bank funding, as well as greater
financial transparency than their peers in the rest of world.

---

these efforts were inspired by the development of international standards
for bank supervision and actively supported by technical assistance from
multilateral financial organizations. The outcome of these efforts was
the notable improvements in the regulatory and supervisory frameworks
in most countries. The assessments of compliance with the Basel Core
Principles for Effective Banking Supervision (BCP)—carried out by the
International Monetary Fund (IMF) and the World Bank in the context
of the Financial Sector Assessment Program (FSAP)—are evidence of the
progress in all countries that have been through an update. The review of
the selected topics and countries included later in the chapter also indicate
that progress. At the same time, in many countries, these crises prompted
banks to strengthen risk management and become more responsive to the
supervisors' prudential requirements by, for instance, reinvesting a higher
share of profits and building up larger voluntary liquidity, provisioning,
and capital cushions.

Overall, the region is better prepared to face the systemic oversight
wars of today, but outstanding weaknesses in complex issues, such as
consolidated supervision and the supervision of key risks, suggest that
there is still a long road ahead for most countries. Even for the countries
with the strongest supervisory frameworks, complacency would be
dangerous. Full compliance with Basel Core Principles is not sufficient to
keep up with an evolving international setting. Particular challenges are
the innovations in the financial industry, the implementation of improved

international standards (such as the forthcoming changes in the Basel Core Principles for Banking Supervision—the Basel II and III Capital Accords), and the need to pay more attention to macroprudential and perimeter issues to determine if some unsupervised types of entities pose material risks to the financial system and thereby justify legal reforms to bring them under the umbrella of supervisory oversight. With this in mind, banking supervisors should continue working toward establishing regulatory and supervisory frameworks that increase the effectiveness of bank capital and liquidity buffers during adverse situations, taking into account the size and complexity of the risks and their systemic importance. Overcoming these challenges, in conjunction with the adoption of sound macroeconomic policies, would help strengthen the financial system's resilience to future crises even further.

The chapter is organized as follows. The next section describes the status of LAC's compliance with the Basel Core Principles, both quantitatively and qualitatively and relative to other regions. The following section discusses 10 selected issues related to LAC's progress in banking supervision. The final section offers some conclusions.

Assessments of Compliance with the Basel Core Principles in LAC Countries

The analysis in this section is based on quantitative as well as qualitative evidence. On the quantitative side, we proceed along two dimensions. First, we compare the principle-by-principle ratings obtained by LAC countries in the BCP assessments conducted in the region as of December 2010. This assessment provides a picture of the absolute effectiveness of oversight, pointing out weaknesses that are common in the region or in specific subregions. Second, we conduct an econometric analysis to compare and benchmark the region's progress in relation to the rest of the world, using the BCP assessments conducted globally (see box 8.2). On some principles, the region is not performing very well; yet this finding is not unexpected, given that most countries are having difficulties with them. For other principles, however, the region is not only performing poorly in absolute terms but also lagging its peers. These principles clearly require even more attention. The quantitative evidence is complemented in the next section with a more qualitative, expert-based review of the main oversight reforms recently introduced, as well as an assessment of the most important remaining issues.

Between 1999 and 2010, assessments of compliance with the Basel Core Principles were conducted in 31 countries in the LAC region.[2] Eight countries have been assessed twice, and Peru has been assessed three times. These assessments, conducted in the context of the FSAP, reveal weaknesses common to a large number of the countries in the region (on average,

37 percent of the core principles were rated as not compliant or materially noncompliant). The assessments also show significant differences, as a group of higher-middle-income countries exhibits strong compliance with most core principles, while, in contrast, several countries continue to have broadly ineffective regulatory and supervisory frameworks. Because many LAC countries have used the results (and accompanying recommended action plans) of the BCP assessments to plan regulatory and supervisory reforms, it is no surprise that in general second and third assessments show noticeable improvements in compliance; and it is likely that an updated assessment of countries where an FSAP has not recently taken place would evidence improvement as well. Thus, a strong caveat for the analysis in this section is that only 11 of the 31 LAC countries in the sample had had assessments during the previous five years.

Since 2007, the BCP assessments have been based on the more demanding 2006 BCP methodology and are not strictly comparable with earlier assessments (8 of the 31 most recent LAC assessments). As stated in box 8.2, table B8.2.1 presents the lists of original and revised BCPs, organized to allow a comparison of the assessments conducted using the two BCP versions.

Analysis of the Absolute Effectiveness of Banking Oversight

The BCP assessments point toward four challenges common to a large number of LAC countries: the supervision of banking risks, consolidated supervision, capital requirements, and the independence of bank supervisors. These challenges (in absolute terms) are associated with core principles on which fewer than 50 percent of the countries scored a rating of compliant or largely compliant in their most recent BCP assessment. One of these, supervision of banking risks, is associated with several core principles, including comprehensive risk management (CP 7), country risk (CP 12), market risk (CP 13), liquidity risk (CP 14), operational risk (CP 15), and interest rate risk in the banking book (CP 16) (see figure 8.1).

Supervision of Banking Risks Only a third of the LAC countries had an effective supervisory framework that could determine whether banks have adequate risk management policies, processes, and strategies according to their size and the nature of their activities (CP 7). Banks in many LAC countries do not have a comprehensive risk management process that addresses all their material risks and assesses their capital adequacy in relation to their risk profile. With regard to specific risks, while most countries had a general framework for supervising credit risks, they did not have the capacity to effectively supervise some of the other key risks. In particular, more than two-thirds of LAC countries lacked an effective framework for supervising market risk (CP 13), and nearly half of them lacked a framework for supervising country risks (CP 12). The original

Box 8.2 Explaining Country Differences in BCP Ratings: An Econometric Analysis

Regressions were run for a universe of 167 BCP assessments (133 countries, 31 belonging to LAC). The analysis sought to explain the BCP ratings assigned to the countries as a function of per capita GDP, of dummy variables identifying LAC regions, of whether the ratings corresponded to a first assessment or to an update, and of whether the assessment was carried out with the original or with the revised BCP methodology (BCBS 2006a). The principles were grouped in 10 categories: institutional framework, authorizations, capital, credit risk, other risks, internal controls, supervision, market discipline, corrective actions, and consolidated supervision. Table B8.2.1 maps the lists of original and revised BCPs to allow a comparison of the assessments conducted using the two BCP versions.

The dependent variables take values 1–4 as follows: 1 (compliant), 2 (largely compliant), 3 (materially noncompliant), and 4 (noncompliant). Thus, negative coefficients are associated with better ratings and stronger bank supervision. The results should be taken with a caveat: BCP compliance ratings have a subjective element, so that cross-country comparisons could also reflect differences in the assessors' views.

The main conclusions are summarized from table B8.2.2:

- Higher-income countries score better in all groups of principles, showing that supervision improves as countries develop. The regressions also control for nonlinearity by introducing the square of per capita GDP. This variable is also significant in all regressions, and its coefficient varies significantly in size across principles. This finding suggests that some principles are either less relevant to simpler systems (hence not a real source of concern for these countries) or just tougher to fulfill (hence still a source of concern, but one that is relatively understandable). Thus, the corresponding regression coefficient can be used to score and rank the principles by order of complexity. As expected, the groups on other risks and consolidated supervision appear to be the most complex (see figure B8.2.1).

- Update assessments produce better ratings for five groups of principles (institutional framework, authorizations, other risks management, internal controls, and market discipline) but not for the other five (capital, credit risk, supervision, corrective actions, and consolidated supervision); the evidence is thus mixed for the view that BCP assessments are a useful tool for motivating efforts to improve bank supervision.

(box continued next page)

Box 8.2 Explaining Country Differences in BCP Ratings:
An Econometric Analysis (*continued*)

Table B8.2.1 Basel Core Principles for Effective Banking
Supervision, 1997 versus 2006

1997 Basel Core Principle	Core Principles, by Group	2006 Basel Core Principle
Institutional		
1.1	Responsibilities and objectives	1.1
1.2	Independence, accountability, transparency	1.2
1.3	Legal framework	1.3
1.4	Legal powers	1.4
1.5	Legal protection	1.5
1.6	Cooperation[a]	1.6
Authorizations		
2	Permissible activities	2
3	Licensing criteria	3
4	Transfer of significant ownership	4
5	Major acquisitions	5
Capital		
6	Capital adequacy	6
Credit risk		
7	Credit risk	8
8	Problem assets, provisions, and reserves	9
9	Large exposure limits	10
10	Exposures to related parties	11
Other risks		
-.-	Risk management process	7
11	Country and transfer risks	12

(box continued next page)

Box 8.2 Explaining Country Differences in BCP Ratings: An Econometric Analysis (*continued*)

Table B8.2.1 Basel Core Principles for Effective Banking Supervision, 1997 versus 2006 (*continued*)

1997 Basel Core Principle	Core Principles, by Group	2006 Basel Core Principle
12	Market risks	13
13	Liquidity risk	14
13	Operational risk	15
13	Interest rate risk in the banking book	16
Internal controls		
14	Internal control and audit	17
15	Abuse of financial services group[a]	18
Supervision		
16	Supervisory approach	19
17	Supervisory techniques	20
18 & 19	Supervisory reporting	21
Market discipline		
21	Accounting and disclosure	22
Corrective actions		
22	Corrective and remedial powers of supervisors	23
Consolidated supervision		
20 & 23	Consolidated supervision	24
24 & 25	Home-host relationships	25

Source: BCBS 2006a.

Note: This table shows the criteria for the construction of the endogenous variables used in the regressions presented in table 8.2.1. BCP = Basel Core Principle.[a]

Not included in BCP regressions.

(box continued next page)

Box 8.2 Explaining Country Differences in BCP Ratings: An Econometric Analysis (continued)

Table B8.2.2 Results of Regression Analysis of the Basel Core Principles Ratings (Principal Components)

						Endogenous variables					
	Explanatory variables	Institutional framework	Authorizations	Capital	Credit risk	Other risks	Internal control	Supervision	Market discipline	Corrective actions	Consolidated supervision
Regression 1	gdppc	−3.487***	−3.152***	−5.050***	−4.270***	−7.670***	−4.531***	−3.956	−4.711***	−4.534***	−5.510***
	gdppc_sq	3.618***	2.840***	4.219***	4.030***	7.783***	4.010***	5.184***	4.061***	4.457**	5.665***
	update_asmt	−0.320**	−0.403**	−0.255	−0.213	−0.447**	−0.537**	−0.133	−0.476**	−0.312	−0.262
	new_bcp	0.172	0.225	0.099	0.060	0.102	0.194	0.199	0.335	0.015	0.199
	lac	3.539**	1.808	4.227**	1.538	1.625	2.135	4.084***	1.867	2.322	2.559
	lac_gdp	−3.633	−4.859	14.812*	12.132	15.618	2.757	1.489	6.334	3.546	−8.689
	lac_update	−0.453	2.255	−1.735	0.194	−0.703	1.725	−2.297	1.821	−2.472	−1.116
	Constant	1.939***	1.973***	2.359***	2.303***	2.991***	2.373***	1.976***	2.224***	2.438***	2.437***
Regression 2	lac_7	−0.618	−6.001***	1.459	−4.406*	−6.346*	−4.315	−2.027	0.442	1.039	−5.686**
	lac_7_update	2.094	5.478***	−5.768	−1.263	−4.224	1.712	−3.224	−8.090***	0.755	0.918
Regression 3	caribbean	3.799***	2.863**	7.635***	6.262***	6.637***	4.308	5.286***	2.875	2.509	6.702**
	caribbean_update	0.858	−0.772	−0.997	−2.794	−2.049	3.352	−1.732	4.291	−2.780	−1.705

(box continued next page)

Box 8.2 Explaining Country Differences in BCP Ratings: An Econometric Analysis *(continued)*

Table B8.2.2 Results of Regression Analysis of the Basel Core Principles Ratings (Principal Components) *(continued)*

	Explanatory variables	Endogenous variables									
		Institutional framework	Authorizations	Capital	Credit risk	Other risks	Internal control	Supervision	Market discipline	Corrective actions	Consolidated supervision
Regression 4	rest_lac	4.053	3.986*	2.963	1.443	3.271	3.432**	5.149***	2.160	2.574	4.411
	rest_lac_update	−2.627	2.157	1.335	4.109	3.035	0.176	−0.980	4.594	−3.003	−3.530
	Observations	159	167	167	167	151	167	167	167	166	122
Average observed score	LAC	2.016	1.931	2.512	2.268	2.741	2.293	2.146	2.171	2.317	2.376
	LAC7	1.802	1.379	2.222	1.691	1.957	1.778	1.637	1.889	2.333	1.727
	Caribbean	1.991	1.916	2.588	2.426	2.821	2.353	2.191	2.118	2.176	2.533
	Rest of LAC	2.172	2.279	2.600	2.434	3.121	2.533	2.402	2.400	2.467	2.589

Note: Regressions were run for a universe of 167 BCP assessments (133 countries, 31 belonging to LAC) carried out by the International Monetary Fund and the World Bank in the context of the Financial Sector Assessment Program (1999–2010).

Regression 1: The explanatory variables were gdppc: GDP per capita; gdppc_sq: square of GDP per capita; update_asmt: equals 0 for the first BCP assessment and 1 otherwise; new_bcp: equals 1 when 2006 methodology was used and 0 otherwise; LAC: equals 1 for BCP assessments of LAC countries and 0 otherwise; lac_gdp: combination of lac and gdppc; lac_update: combination, of update asmt and lac dummy; and the constant. (3) Regressions 2, 3, and 4: The explanatory variables were gdppc; gdppc_sq; update_asmt; new_bcp; lac_7 (equal 1 for BCP assessments of Brazil, Chile, Colombia, Mexico, Peru, and Uruguay and 0 otherwise; Argentina is not included because it had no BCP assessment by end 2010)/Caribbean (equals 1 for BCP assessments of Anguilla, Antigua and Barbuda, Bahamas, Barbados, Bermuda, British Virgin Islands, Dominican Republic, Eastern Caribbean Central Bank, Haiti, Jamaica, Montserrat, St. Vincent and the Grenadines, Trinidad and Tobago, Turk, and Caicos and 0 otherwise)/rest_lac (equals 1 for BCP assessments of Belize, Bolivia, Costa Rica, Ecuador, El Salvador, Guatemala, Guyana, Honduras, Nicaragua, Panama, Paraguay and 0 otherwise); update lac dummies (combination of the lac dummies with the update_asmt dummy); and the constant. Table B8.2.1 shows only the coefficients of lac dummies and update lac dummies (regressions 2, 3 y 4). BCP = Basel Core Principles; GDP = gross domestic product; LAC = Latin America and the Caribbean.

Coefficients (cells) are shaded when variables were explanatory. *** p value <0.01, ** p value <0.05, * p value <0.1.

(box continued next page)

Box 8.2 Explaining Country Differences in BCP Ratings: An Econometric Analysis *(continued)*

Figure B8.2.1 GDP Square Parameter Value

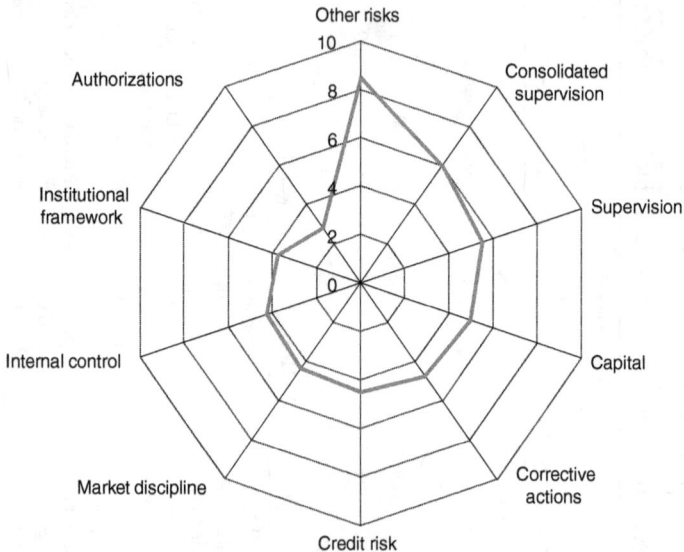

Note: Figure shows the coefficients of GDP square variable in regression 1 (see table 8.3). GDP = gross domestic product.

- Evidence does not support the conclusion that the 2006 BCP methodology significantly raised the bar for compliance relative to the 1997 one, as assessments prepared on the basis of the 2006 BCP do not result in significantly worse ratings.
- The LAC countries tend to have worse ratings than their peers in the rest of the world for three key groups of principles: institutional framework, capital, and supervision.
  There are strong disparities across the LAC region:
  - LAC7 outperforms its peers on four groups of principles (authorizations, credit risk, other risks, and consolidated supervision) and matches their performance on the other groups, with the exception of market discipline, where it underperforms.
  - The Caribbean countries tend to underperform their peers in the rest of the world, with the exception of the groups on internal control, market discipline, and corrective actions, where their performance matches their peers.

(box continued next page)

Box 8.2 Explaining Country Differences in BCP Ratings:
An Econometric Analysis *(continued)*

- The rest of the LAC region (countries not in the above-mentioned groups) tends to match its peers in the rest of the world, with the exception of the groups associated with supervision, authorizations, and internal control, where it underperforms.
- The progress of bank oversight achieved by the LAC region between two assessments does not differ significantly from progress achieved by supervisors in the rest of the world.

Figure 8.1 Percentage of 31 Countries in Latin America and the Caribbean That Were Compliant or Largely Compliant with the Basel Core Principles

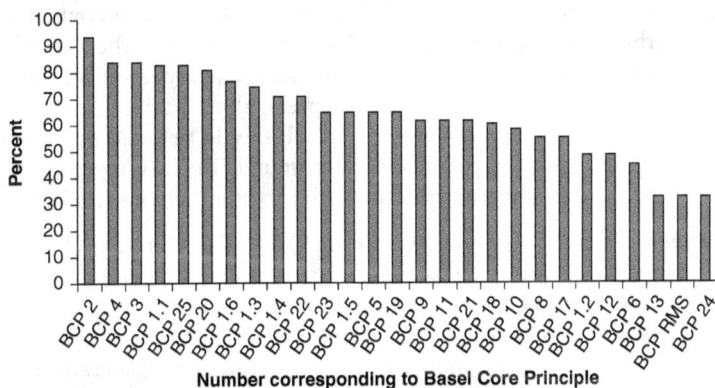

Note: Basel Core Principle assessments were carried out by the International Monetary Fund and the World Bank in the context of the Financial Sector Assessment Program (1999–2010). The chart displays the last assessment of compliance with the BCP conducted for each country. The list of core principles corresponds to the 2006 methodology. The assessments under the original 1999 BCP methodology are mapped into the revised 2006 methodology list of core principles (see table B8.2.1). BCP = Basel Core Principle; BCP RMS = four principles of the supervision of risks that were part of principle 13 in the 1997 BCP methodology—risk management process (CP 7), liquidity risk (CP 14), operational risk (CP 15), and interest rate risk (CP 16).

1997 methodology did not dedicate a specific principle to operational, liquidity, and interest rate risks, and thus the BCP ratings do not help in identifying the proportion of countries with weaknesses in these areas. However, it is known that the supervision of interest rate and operational risk there yet to be effectively implemented in most countries. The regression analysis shows these weaknesses particularly for the Caribbean countries, which underperform their peers in the rest of the world on those dimensions (see box 8.2).

Consolidated Supervision (CP 24) Only a third of LAC countries effectively supervised the financial conglomerates that operate within their jurisdiction. The supervision of financial conglomerates is perhaps the most complex task that a supervisor faces. The fact that only 2 of the 31 countries were rated fully compliant in the assessment of this principle illustrates the complexities of this task. The absence of legislation granting the powers to conduct consolidated supervision of these conglomerates or lack of a comprehensive regulation including key prudential requirements on a consolidated basis are not the only relevant problems. Inadequate supervisory powers, insufficient cooperation among domestic and foreign supervisors, scope for regulatory arbitrage, and difficult conglomerate structures are common problems. It is generally because of a combination of these that many countries cannot effectively supervise their conglomerates on a consolidated basis. The econometric analysis shows that the Caribbean countries underperform their peers, albeit a select group within LAC outperforms their peers (see box 8.2). It should be noted that compliance with this principle is particularly important in the LAC region because of its higher level of conglomeration relative to other regions (see box 8.1).

Minimum Capital Requirements (CP 6) Over 50 percent of LAC countries had capital requirements that did not meet the minimum international standards. To comply with the BCP, countries are not expected to implement the Basel II capital standard; satisfying the Basel I standard would suffice. Lack of compliance with this principle is generally associated with the absence of capital charges to cover some risks and the lack of supervisory powers to ensure that capital charges reflect the risk profile of all banks, but also with lower weights for some asset categories and differences in the components of capital and the deductions from capital. In a few countries, the lack of compliance with this BCP is also associated with the existence of some form of regulatory forbearance that has allowed weak banks to maintain effective capital adequacy below the formal requirements for prolonged periods. Regression analysis shows that the LAC region as a whole (and particularly the Caribbean subregion) underperforms its peers on this core principle (see box 8.2).

Independence of Bank Supervisors (CP 1.2) In more than half of LAC countries, bank supervisors lacked the operational or budgetary independence to do their job. Lack of independence could be de jure or de facto. It is de jure when the legal framework does not grant independence to bank supervisors by, for instance, allocating some of the supervisory powers or decisions to a different government body, such as the ministry of finance. Common aspects allocated to a different agency are the budget of the supervisory agency, the decision to issue or withdraw a banking license, and the power to issue prudential regulation. It is de facto, when, in spite of having legal independence, the capacity of the supervisory agency is limited by other means, including political interference or industry capture. The process for appointing or removing the head of the supervisory agency and the governance structure of this agency may facilitate political interference or industry capture. Regression analysis shows that the LAC region as a whole underperforms its peers in institutional aspects (see box 8.2). These weaknesses are also highlighted in the BRS survey results presented in box 8.1, as removing the head of supervision by executive decision without congressional approval is more likely in the LAC region than in the rest of the world. Independence is one of the preconditions for effective supervision; and lack of it, one way or another, may affect the ability of supervisors to do their job, including their capacity to require an adequate minimum capital to cover banks' risks and to impose timely remedial actions whenever deemed necessary.

There are important regional differences within the LAC area. Other challenges are relevant to one region but not to the LAC countries as a group:

- *Legal protection for bank supervisors (CP 1.5).* Lack of legal protection is particularly important in Central and South America.[3] but, does not seem to be a significant problem in the Caribbean, where more than 90 percent of supervisors have it. Less than half the supervisors in Central America and South America, however, have legal protection. Box 8.1 shows that bank supervisors in LAC are more likely to be personally liable for damages caused by their actions or omissions than their peers in the rest of the world. This problem, coupled with the lack of independence of the supervisory agencies, would clearly hamper the effectiveness of bank supervision in these countries.
- *Exposures to related parties (CP 11).* The Caribbean countries tend to have weaker supervision of related-party exposures, relative to South and Central America. Only a third of countries in the Caribbean have adequate supervision of related-party exposures, compared to 90 percent of the countries in South America and more than two-thirds in Central America. Most countries in the latter two regions that have experienced banking crises, triggered in part by such exposure, have made legal and regulatory amendments to address the issue, and perhaps it is becoming a problem of the past.

- *Internal controls and audit (CP 17)*. Less than half the countries in the Caribbean had effective supervision of internal control and audit.
- *Three additional core principles (8, 10, and 19)*. Challenges associated with three additional core principles (supervision of credit risk, CP 8; large exposures, CP 10; and the supervisory approach, CP 19) were relevant in Central America, as less than half the countries were rated as compliant or largely compliant. The regressions presented in box 8.2 show that countries in the LAC region tend to have lower ratings on the core principles pertaining to supervision than their peers in the rest of the world.

The assessments also show significant differences that cut across subregions within LAC. Nearly a third of LAC countries have highly effective supervisory frameworks, with ratings of compliant or largely compliant on 85 percent or more of the core principles. For these countries, the road ahead requires that they fine-tune their already strong supervision of key risks, strengthen consolidated supervision, implement the Basel II-and III-related reforms recently proposed by the Basel Committee on Bank Supervision (BCBS), ensure that an adequate framework to address systemic risks is in place, and continue monitoring the new risks arising from financial innovations taking place within their jurisdictions. At the other end of the spectrum, nearly a third of the countries have ratings of compliant or largely compliant on less than 50 percent of the core principles. These countries need to implement ambitious reform plans that address the significant weaknesses in their regulatory and supervisory frameworks. It must be noted that there are countries with highly effective supervisory frameworks and countries with weak supervision in the three LAC subregions (Central America, South America, and the Caribbean).

The BCP assessments provide evidence of improved compliance in the countries that experienced assessment updates. The before and after scores of the nine LAC countries that have more than one BCP assessment show that the percentage of BCPs rated as compliant or largely compliant increased from about 50 percent to about 75 percent. All nine countries showed improvements. The principles with the greatest improvements are home-host relationships (CP 25), major acquisitions (CP 5), cooperation between agencies inside each country (CP 1.6), abuse of financial services (CP 18), and capital requirements (CP 6) (see figure 8.2). In one area, comprehensive risk management (CP 7), the assessments indicate a step backward. The explanation for this finding is that the revised core principles imply a much higher bar for achieving compliance with the new CP 7 than for achieving compliance with the old CP 13. In spite of the strong evidence of progress, our regression analysis shows that the progress LAC countries made between assessments is by no means exceptional, as countries in the rest of the world made similar progress (see box 8.2).

Figure 8.2 Financial Regulation and Supervision Progress in Nine Latin American Countries, 2000–10

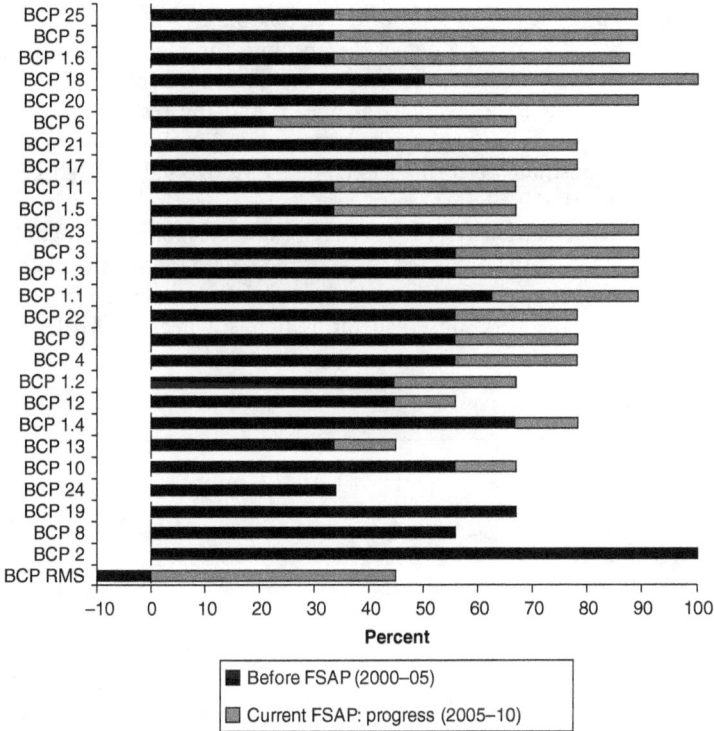

Note: The chart displays data from Barbados, the Dominican Republic, El Salvador, Guatemala, Honduras, Mexico, Nicaragua, Peru, and Trinidad and Tobago. FSAP = Financial Sector Assessment Program; BCP = Basel Core Principle; BCP RMS = four principles of the supervision of risks that were part of principle 13 in the 1997 BCP methodology—risk management process (CP 7), liquidity risk (CP 14), operational risk (CP 15), and interest rate risk (CP 16).

Advanced implementation of the BCP is not enough to prevent banking crises. The 2008 crisis, which affected countries with high compliance with the BCP, has exposed weaknesses in the supervisory standard delineated by the system. The BCBS is working on a new revised version of the BCP methodology. It is expected that the revised BCP will imply, at a minimum, tightened capital and liquidity requirements, along the lines of the Basel III proposals, a clear macroprudential framework, and stronger risk management and governance requirements, in which the incentives of banks' management and board can be better aligned with prudent risk management.

Analysis of the Relative Effectiveness of Banking Oversight

The econometric analysis supports the claim that there are strong disparities in compliance with the BCP across LAC as well as between the LAC region and the rest of the world (see box 8.2).

Figures 8.3, 8.4, and 8.5 depict the absolute and relative performance of LAC supervisory frameworks. The three figures correspond to the three subregions of LAC: LAC7, the Caribbean, and the rest of LAC.[4] The average ratings of LAC countries shown in the vertical axis (SCORE) represent the absolute performance, while the horizontal axis reflects the relative performance of LAC with respect to a benchmark of its peers (GAP). The GAP is the difference between the corresponding benchmark, which is defined as the predicted value of the regression for the countries with similar characteristics (in per capita GDP and the other control variables), and the LAC observed rating. Thus a negative GAP means

Figure 8.3 BCP Assessments of LAC7 Countries, Average Score and GAP

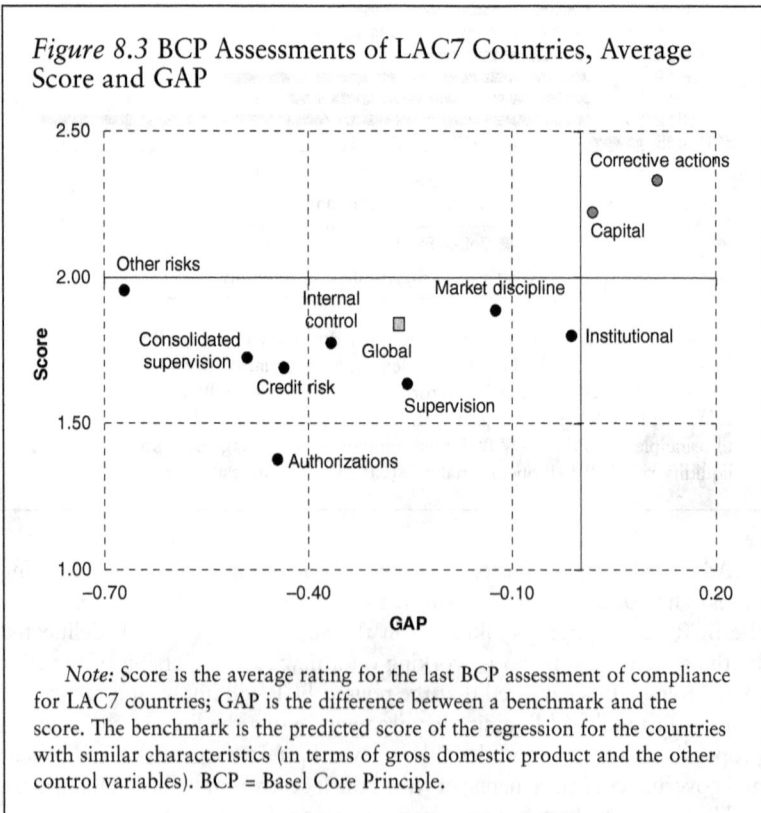

Note: Score is the average rating for the last BCP assessment of compliance for LAC7 countries; GAP is the difference between a benchmark and the score. The benchmark is the predicted score of the regression for the countries with similar characteristics (in terms of gross domestic product and the other control variables). BCP = Basel Core Principle.

Figure 8.4 BCP Assessments of Caribbean Countries, Average Score and GAP

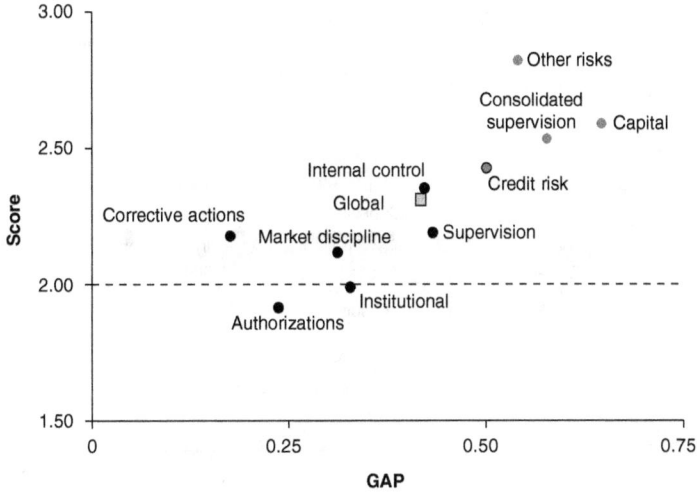

Note: Score is the average rating for the last BCP assessment of compliance for Caribbean countries; GAP is the difference between a benchmark and the score. The benchmark is the predicted score of the regression for the countries with similar characteristics (in terms of gross domestic product and the other control variables). BCP = Basel Core Principle.

that LAC countries have better ratings than their peers across the world. In turn, a rating of two or lower on the variable SCORE shows an acceptable absolute performance. This presentation allows us to consider four quadrants (see table 8.1).

Because the analysis is carried out for the 10 groups of principles considered in the econometric analysis, some of the fine results obtained for individual principles are lost in this exercise. Nonetheless, the results are revealing:

- For most groups of principles, LAC7 countries show adequate absolute compliance with the BCP, and they outperform their peers. The exceptions are the principles on corrective actions and capital, where LAC7's compliance with the BCP is less than adequate in absolute terms and relative to their peers. The overperformance of LAC7 on the supervision of other risks is remarkable, showing that these countries have made strides in tackling a particularly

Figure 8.5 BPC Assessments for the Rest of LAC, Average Score and GAP

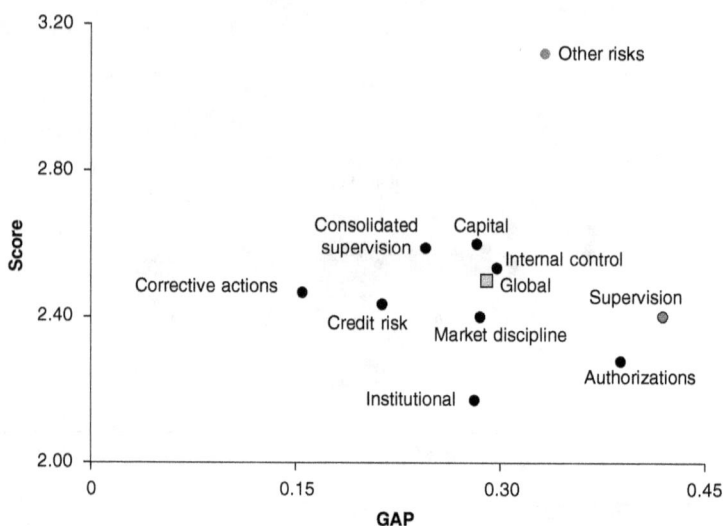

Note: Score is the average rating for the last BCP assessment of compliance for rest of LAC; GAP is the difference between a benchmark and the score. The benchmark is the predicted score of the regression for the countries with similar characteristics (in terms of gross domestic product and the other control variables). BCP = Basel Core Principle.

Table 8.1 A Measure of Absolute and Relative Performance

Absolute performance	Relative performance	
	GAP < 0	GAP > 0
Score > 2	Absolute underperformance and relative overperformance	Absolute and relative underperformance
Score < 2	Absolute and relative overperformance	Absolute overperformance and relative underperformance

challenging issue for all supervisors around the world. Other groups of BCPs on which LAC7 shows an important overperformance are consolidated supervision, authorizations, and supervision of credit risk (see figure 8.3).

- For most groups of principles, the average compliance of the Caribbean countries shows absolute and relative underperformance. The only exceptions are authorizations and institutional framework, where the Caribbean countries display a slight absolute overperformance (see figure 8.4).
- The rest of LAC exhibits underperformance, both in absolute and in relative terms, for all the groups of principles. While the absolute performance of the rest of LAC tends to be worse than the Caribbean, the rest of LAC performs better than the Caribbean relative to their peers (see figures 8.4 and 8.5).

What Have Countries Done during the Past Decade?

This section reviews the progress in strengthening bank supervision made by LAC countries during the past decade. The focus is on 10 selected issues. The first four are the weakest links in LAC countries' supervisory frameworks, as evidenced by the BCP ratings (independence of supervisors, capital, risk management framework, and consolidated supervision). The next three are associated with the bread and butter of bank supervision (credit risk, loan classification and provisioning, and the supervisory approach). These are particularly relevant for traditional banking systems, which prevail in most LAC countries, and have been highlighted in recent years as the weak supervisory practices that were at the root of the 2008 global financial crisis. Traditionally overlooked by regulators and supervisors alike, the last three issues became the center of attention with the 2008 global crisis (macroprudential framework, the perimeter of regulation, and consumer protection). We do not present an in-depth analysis of these issues but instead analyze some success stories from some of the countries with the strongest supervisory frameworks. This section generally covers progress as of mid-2011. However, the implementation of Basel II and III in the LAC7 countries has been updated to 2012.

Independence and Legal Protection of Supervisors

The independence of bank supervisors has proved difficult to achieve in LAC. Efforts to undertake legal reforms addressing this matter are under way in several LAC countries, including Chile and Colombia, but laws have not yet passed. Nevertheless, a few countries have strengthened supervisory governance and independence. Mexico, for instance, has recently reassigned to the National Banking and Securities Commission (CNBV) most of the regulatory powers previously held by the Ministry of Finance, including the authority to issue and withdraw licenses for banks and bank subsidiaries and to set prudential regulations. In addition, the CNBV was granted decision-making powers for assessing ownership changes in and investments by banks, powers that had also been held by the Ministry of Finance.[5] However, regrettably, the Mexican reform does not go as far as granting the CNBV full budgetary independence, stipulating the minimum term of appointment for its head, or providing that he can be removed from office only for causes specified in law. As for Colombia, in 2012 it sought to strengthen the regulatory process by establishing a more autonomous and stronger regulatory unit, the Unidad de Regulacion Financiera, with a board that includes a delegate from the Superintendencia Financiera de Colombia, even thought that unit is still under the umbrella of the Ministry of Finance.

Some countries have granted legal protection to bank supervisors. The Dominican Republic introduced provisions that grant comprehensive legal protection to all supervisory staff. Specifically, the Dominican law states that no civil or criminal action can be brought against staff of the central bank or the Superintendency of Banks for acts carried out in the performance of their duties. Peru has extended the scope of legal protection against criminal actions provided by the banking law to former superintendents and their deputies and introduced legal protection from civil suits for all supervisory staff, by stipulating that suits against them can be admitted only if the responsibility of the Superintendency of Banking, Insurance and Pension Fund Administrators has previously been established by the judicial system. Chile has recently introduced limited protection by requiring that the superintendency cover the cost of the legal defense of the superintendent, when legal actions are initiated for his actions or omissions as superintendent.

Capital Requirements

During the past decade, LAC countries have focused on establishing larger and better buffers to protect their banking systems. Legal or regulatory reforms to conform to the Basel I capital standard were undertaken by many countries. Many LAC countries have implemented minimum capital requirements well in excess of the Basel standards (12 percent in El Salvador; 11 percent in Brazil; 10 percent in Honduras, Nicaragua, and Peru; and 9 percent in Colombia, for example). Capital charges for market risks have been implemented (Argentina, Brazil, Colombia, Peru, and Trinidad and Tobago). Some countries apply these charges to cover only foreign exchange risks (Nicaragua), as exposure of banks to other market risks is considered rather limited. In turn, Argentina and Peru have a capital requirement for interest rates in the banking book.

Only a few countries have moved forward with the implementation of Basel II (BCBS 2006b). Brazil, Mexico, and Peru have implemented the capital requirements under pillar 1. The default option for the calculation of the capital requirements for credit risk is the standardized approach, but the use of internal models (basic and advanced) is possible with prior authorization of the supervisor. As of end-2010, only Mexico had authorized these. All three require capital for market and operational risks consistent with pillar 1 of Basel II. The remaining LAC7 countries have made some progress in the implementation of Basel II since 2010. For example, Argentina and Uruguay have established capital requirements for operational risk (see table 8.2).

Progress with the implementation of pillars 2 and 3 of Basel II is even more limited. Only Brazil has established detailed guidelines requiring banks to develop a process for assessing their capital adequacy, taking into account all risks under pillars 1 and 2. Peru requires banks to submit an annual self-assessment of capital adequacy and, since 2012, has required capital for portfolio concentration, and the four largest banks have capital charges for market concentration. In Chile, supervisors review a bank's capital planning process, in the context of establishing its overall risk profile. Brazil and Mexico have also initiated their implementation of pillar 3. Both of them require banks to publish detailed information on their risks and risk policies, methodologies, and other relevant measures to manage each of their risks. These two countries have also initiated a well-defined plan for the implementation of the International Financial Reporting Standards.

Some countries are strengthening their capital requirements along the lines of the most recent BCBS revisions to Basel II. Starting in December 2011, banks operating in Brazil were required to have additional capital to cover losses generated during moments of stress, on the basis of the stressed value-at-risk methodology considered in the BCBS document on revisions to the Basel II Market Risk Framework (BCBS 2009a as modified in June 2010). Brazil also issued a regulation to adopt the adjustments to the Basel II capital requirements proposed by the BCBS (BCBS 2009b) by 2012, in line with the internationally agreed deadline (Central Bank of Brazil 2010).

Most LAC7 countries have been working on the implementation of the Basel III reforms, which, according to the BCBS schedule, are to be implemented between 2013 and 2019. Argentina, Colombia, Mexico, Peru, and Uruguay have issued regulations that address some aspects of Basel III. Argentina, Colombia, Mexico, and Uruguay have also established a minimum common equity ratio (4.5 percent). Mexican regulations include an additional conservation buffer equivalent to 2.5 percent, which should be covered by common equity. Peruvian regulations include a countercyclical buffer (on average, 2.0 percent of risk-weighted assets) but have not established minimum common equity ratios. Brazil has published

Table 8.2 Capital Adequacy Requirements for LAC7 Countries

	Argentina	Brazil	Chile	Colombia	Mexico	Peru	Uruguay
Capital adequacy ratio (% of risk-weighted assets)	8	11	8	9	8	10	8
Standard	Basel II	Basel II	Basel I	Basel I	Basel II	Basel II	Basel II
Authorization for Basel II internal models	No	Yes	No	No	Yes	Yes	No
Power to require a higher capital adequacy ratio to individual banks based on the supervisory risk assessment	Yes	Yes	Yes	Yes	Yes	Yes	Yes
Capital charges for							
Credit risk	Yes	Yes	Yes	Yes	Yes	Yes	Yes
Interest rate risk in the trading book	Yes	Yes	No	Yes	Yes	Yes	Yes
Foreign exchange risk	Yes	Yes	No	Yes	Yes	Yes	Yes
Other market risks (commodities, equity)	Yes	Yes	No	Yes	Yes	Yes	Yes
Operational risks	Yes	Yes	No	No	Yes	Yes	Yes
Basel II: pillar 2	No	Yes	In progress	No	No	In progress	No
Basel II: pillar 3	No	In progress	No	No	In progress	No	No
Basel III							
Common equity tier 1	Yes	No	No	Yes	Yes	No	Yes
Capital conservation buffer	No	No	No	No	Yes	No	No
Capital countercyclical buffer	No	No	No	No	No	Yes	No

a draft regulation aligned with Basel III for consultation, which includes all three concepts: minimum common equity ratio, conservation buffer, and countercyclical buffer. Chile, the only LAC7 country that has not recently published revisions to its capital regulations, has strong preexisting capital regulations, however, that in practice include a leverage ratio, requiring that the ratio of capital to assets, net of required provisions (including off-balance-sheet items), be larger than 3 percent; and over the past decade, this ratio has always exceeded 6 percent (IMF 2011). In addition, Chile has a system of regulatory incentives for banks to maintain capital in excess of the required minimum.

Risk Management Framework

Many LAC countries have issued norms or guidelines on banks' risk management. In the 1990s, the few LAC countries that addressed risk management issues focused mainly on the allocation and segregation of responsibilities, regulatory limits (to control some risk exposures), and risk buffers (provisions or capital). Over the past five years, many LAC countries have issued broader risk management regulation, more in line with the 2006 BCP (CP 7). They cover the whole risk management process—including strategies, policies, methodologies, and procedures—and all its stages (identification, measurement, mitigation, control, reporting, and monitoring). However, some of these countries have yet to develop the necessary supervisory capacity to effectively assess bank governance and board and management oversight of risk management and to ensure that all risks are adequately managed, with sufficient financial buffers in place. The supervisory capacities for assessing the adequacy of risk models and the interconnections among the various risks are matters that need further work in all countries. The establishment of a comprehensive risk management regulatory framework and the strengthening of these supervisory capacities are essential conditions for the implementation of effective risk-based supervision.

There are differences in the scope and depth of risk management regulation and the implementation of supervisory processes. Some LAC banking supervisors (Mexico and Peru) have established comprehensive minimum standards and guidelines for overall risk management. Some countries (Brazil, Colombia, and Mexico) have issued detailed independent regulation on the management of all the main banking risks (credit, liquidity, market, and operational). Other LAC countries have established standards on most, but not all, of the individual risks. For instance, Argentina and Peru have not yet established a comprehensive regulation on market risk and credit risk, respectively. Chile has adopted a less prescriptive, but not less effective, approach. It has not issued enforceable standards on risk management but has established a bank-rating system that includes criteria for the evaluation of risk management, covering all main risks. Thus, in Chile, weaknesses in risk management affect a bank's rating and, consequently, the supervisory behavior. Many countries have not yet issued standards or developed effective supervisory processes on most of the key risks, as evidenced by the BCP assessments.

The attention paid to ensure the suitability of banks' boards of directors with regard to risk management has increased. In line with international standards, most LAC countries have assigned these boards the primary responsibility for establishing appropriate risk management systems and the oversight for them. In this regard, the board is responsible for approving the risk strategies, policies, methodologies, manuals, and procedures and for ensuring that these are adequately applied by management. The board is also responsible for attention to banks' risk exposures so that they can take timely corrective actions. Therefore, the challenge for supervisors is to ensure that board members have the experience and capacity to carry out these new functions (especially in the local banks), through effective regulation and supervision. Chile has made the most progress by establishing a strong, very proactive, risk-based framework for the supervision of governance and risk management.

Some countries have recently established criteria for banks' staff compensation systems to align incentives with prudent risk management, along the lines of the principles established by the Financial Stability Board (see Financial Stability Forum 2009). The regulations issued by Brazil and Mexico in November 2010, for example, are based on four basic criteria. First, the "variable retribution" must be based not only on short-term results but also on medium-term risks and results. Second, part of the retribution must be deferred to future years and must be contingent on those years' results. Third, the compensation of risk management staff must be based on their own risk management objectives, not on business results. Last, the compensation system must be reviewed annually by an independent committee to assess its impact on business decisions and risk taking. The Mexican regulation covers the retribution system for all bank staff, while the Brazilian one focuses on all management staff of all financial institutions (with the exception of credit unions and microfinance institutions). In Brazil, at least 50 percent of the variable compensation must consist of stock-based instruments, consistent with creating value in the long term, and at least 40 percent of the variable compensation must be deferred by at least three years. In Argentina and Mexico, banks have to publish their compensation policies on their web pages. A more general regulation had been established earlier by other countries (Peru), in which the banks' boards are required to establish staff compensation policies with adequate incentive systems, consistent with proper risk management and prudent risk taking.

Consolidated and Cross-Border Supervision

LAC countries have worked toward strengthening their legal frameworks and supervisory processes for consolidated supervision, but efforts have generally fallen short of achieving an effective consolidated supervision of financial conglomerates. Brazil has one of the most comprehensive legal and supervisory frameworks. Other countries have also implemented a strong supervisory framework for the supervision of conglomerates, but these frameworks have some limitations that could pose supervisory risks. Peru, for instance, has a strong downward consolidation of financial conglomerates and—through moral suasion and regulations, including one in 2010[6]—has circumvented some of the limitations of its legal framework. But the fact is that the SBS in Peru, as in many other countries in LAC, does not have effective authority over the holding companies domiciled abroad. Most countries have limited access to information on parallel-owned banks.[7] set up in other jurisdictions (Mexico and Peru).

Gutierrez and Caraballo (2011) identify important weaknesses in the consolidated supervision frameworks on the basis of a survey conducted in the LAC region. They note that in 40 percent of LAC countries, banking groups or financial conglomerates exclude nonfinancial groups. They also note that supervisors can generally presume which companies belong to the financial conglomerates (80 percent), but in only 30 percent of the respondent countries does a financial holding company have to be created to control all of its financial sector activities. Moreover, a financial holding company can in most cases be created abroad, in which case it would be under foreign supervision.

Supervisors in the LAC region generally lack sufficient power to conduct an effective consolidated supervision. A number of flaws are common across LAC:

- Inadequate definition of *financial conglomerate* that leaves important sources of risk outside the scope of supervision.
- Insufficient access to information, in which some supervisors have the power to request consolidated financial statements but do not have access to other information about the financial conglomerate, including data on the nonfinancial entities of the group that could pose risks to the conglomerate.
- Limited power to conduct on-site examination of some of the entities in the group.
- Lack of a risk management framework for conglomerates.
- Lack of prudential requirements for conglomerates: more than half the countries do not have consolidated capital requirements (Gutierrez and Caraballo 2011). Most countries report having some sort of consolidated limits on large exposures and connected parties.

However, in many cases consolidated requirements cover only part of the conglomerate. Other countries have implemented requirements and limits but do not have the capacity or the supervisory processes to effectively verify compliance.

- Lack of enforcement powers for conglomerates or for holding companies (many supervisors have access to information, can conduct on-site examinations, and have prudential requirements; however, they do not have sufficient legal powers to enforce corrective actions for conglomerates or holding companies).
- Insufficient authority to prevent the establishment of cross-border operations or investments that would entail risks for the conglomerate or in countries with important limitations on access to information.
- Lack of powers to require changes in the conglomerate structure when it is an obstacle for effective consolidated supervision.
- Insufficient supervisory powers to mitigate local or international regulatory arbitrage (such as requiring high provisions or reserves on operations located or booked in lightly regulated countries or sectors or when access to information is restricted).

Gaps in the supervision of financial conglomerates may remain, even when supervisors are granted all the necessary powers. The supervision of financial conglomerates, for example, requires that supervisors use individual and consolidated supervision as complementary tools to ensure that all material risks are covered. This task requires a careful consideration of processes, organization, and coordination, which is a work in progress in many countries. As a result, in many countries supervisors lack an adequate understanding of the groupwide risks within financial conglomerates, including some of the risks arising in entities directly under their supervision. Moreover, many of these conglomerates lack adequate groupwide management systems. Serious vulnerabilities may exist in this context, as material risks can remain undetected and conglomerates may have insufficient capital and liquidity buffers to cover them.

Domestic coordination with supervisors of the nonbanking sectors continues to be a problem in many countries. A silo approach is still predominant. While some countries face legal restrictions on cooperation among supervisors, the most common problem is the lack of an effective operational framework for cooperation, in some cases associated with an unwillingness of domestic supervisors to cooperate, especially in countries where the incentives of the supervisory bodies do not foster a culture of cooperation. Coordination problems are highlighted when the supervisors of the different sectors are separate entities. To address this problem, in 2005 Colombia established a unified financial supervisor in charge of supervising banks, securities, and insurance. In Colombia and Peru, the organizational structure of the financial supervisor includes a department responsible for the supervision of financial conglomerates.

However, coordination problems could also arise when all sectors are supervised by separate areas of the same institution. Mexico and Uruguay, for example, have recently reformed the organizational structure of the agency responsible for supervision to address internal problems of coordination and to close supervisory gaps. In Mexico, the CNBV was recently restructured so that every financial institution that is part of a financial group is supervised by the same team within CNBV, except pension funds and insurance companies. This reorganization is expected to allow inspectors to better assess the overall risk position on a consolidated basis. In Uruguay, a legal amendment that unifies all financial supervisors into one Superintendency of Financial Services within the central bank was approved,[8] thereby favoring a comprehensive and more homogeneous supervision of the financial system.

Cross-border cooperation is a major challenge. Significant improvements have taken place in this area. Most countries have lifted obstacles to cooperation and have signed bilateral and multilateral memorandums of understanding (MOUs) as a framework for cooperation. In other cases, cooperation effectively takes place, even without an MOU. Colleges of supervisors have been established to supervise the largest international conglomerates operating in the LAC region. All these have allowed most countries to obtain favorable ratings on cross-border cooperation during BCP assessments. However, important remaining limitations need to be addressed, some of which are not adequately captured by the Basel Core Principles Assessments. First, the MOUs are generally devised by bank supervisors, essentially to deal with the supervision of banking groups, and are not very effective in coordinating plans and actions for nonbanking groups and for the nonbank entities of a banking group. Second, they do not include an effective cooperation framework for problem banks, and the recent global crisis has shown that cross-border coordination has been insufficient in actual cases of problem banks and nonbanks. Third, LAC countries that are host of subsidiaries or branches of large international banking institutions—which are large for the host country but small for the home country—have frequently seen their valid concerns ignored or downplayed by the home supervisors. Finally, many home and host supervisors of LAC conglomerates are dissatisfied with the scope, depth, and timeliness of the information shared by their counterparts within the region in the context of the signed agreements.

Cross-border coordination for the supervision of regional conglomerates has improved in Central America and the Caribbean, but more is needed. Cooperation in these regions takes place within the framework of multilateral MOUs signed in 2007. In Central America, the coordination is entrusted to a technical committee with representatives of all the countries; the committee meets regularly, exchanges information, and coordinates supervisory plans. In the Caribbean, colleges of supervisors have been established for all regional groups and meet semiannually. Some on-site exams have been conducted in both regions, but not all important groups have been examined. A common problem throughout both regions is that the scope of the exams conducted by home supervisors often mirrors the exams conducted by the host supervisor, thus duplicating efforts, with limited value added.

Supervision of Credit Risk

Many LAC countries have adopted a comprehensive approach to the supervision of credit risks. A decade ago, the supervision of credit risks in most LAC countries focused mainly on establishing criteria for loan classification and provisioning and on reviewing borrower files to verify compliance with these norms. Several countries had also set individual limits on large exposures and related-party lending. Nowadays, many countries have regulation and supervisory processes that address a broad range of issues related to comprehensive credit risk management and cover all stages of the credit process. This is a fundamental change in the supervision of the most important risk that banks face, as many supervisors now suggest risk management improvements before excessive risks have been taken. Colombia and Mexico have issued very detailed comprehensive regulations covering all stages of the credit process and all components of credit risk management, along the lines of the Enterprise Risk Management approach of the Committee of Sponsoring Organizations of the Treadway Commission.[9] The norms issued by Brazil and Chile are also comprehensive but less prescriptive and do not go into detail about procedures or best practices. Other countries, including Argentina, Honduras, Nicaragua, Peru, and Trinidad and Tobago, have issued regulations covering several, but not all, aspects of credit risk management.

Supervisors are also developing the capacity to conduct stress tests, and several require banks to conduct regular tests to assess their credit risks. One of the important products of the FSAP is the stress test that exposes the vulnerabilities of financial institutions to key risks. Many countries have followed up on the FSAP basic tests, and some have developed their own models and conduct regular analyses of vulnerabilities of supervised institutions. Brazil, Chile, Colombia, Mexico, and Peru require banks to conduct regular stress tests to evaluate the credit risks in their books. Most important, in some of these countries the tests are fully integrated into the supervisory strategies and into the banks' management systems. In Brazil, for instance, banks are explicitly required to use them to review their risk management policies and limits.

Some supervisors have taken specific measures to control the risks of overindebtedness. Countries that have issued credit risk regulation usually require banks to assess the solvency of potential borrowers by examining variables such as their level of indebtedness and the ratio of their leverage to equity or their ratio of debt service to income (Argentina, Colombia, Mexico, and Peru). In the Peruvian regulation, banks are explicitly required to monitor the overall indebtedness of their borrowers, and the SBS can require an additional provision equivalent to 1 percent of their portfolio of highest-rated retail loans to any bank whose management of this risk is considered deficient.

Many countries have established supervisory procedures for assessing concentration risks of financial institutions. In addition to individual limits, some countries (Argentina, Brazil, Colombia, and Mexico) have also established global limits on large exposures. The analysis of concentration risks now generally goes beyond the verification of compliance with limits on large exposures and related parties. Banks are expected to establish internal limits to control the risks of concentration by sector, region, or other highly correlated exposures, and supervisors must have effective procedures for evaluating the adequacy of banks' systems to control their concentration risks. But limiting the exposure is not sufficient. Continued efforts are necessary to mitigate this risk, since this is still one of the main banking risks in most LAC countries. The relative small size of local banking systems relative to the size of the economies and the concentrated income distribution create natural barriers to the diversification of the portfolios. Under Basel II (pillar 2), banks should be capable of properly pricing that risk. In this regard, Peru is considering capital requirements for concentration risk, along the lines of pillar 2 of Basel II.

Most partially dollarized countries in LAC have taken measures to address the credit risks associated with borrowers' currency mismatches. These measures include special prudential requirements, such as higher capital or provisions, and risk management systems capable of controlling exchange-rate-induced credit risk. Peru and Uruguay have the most comprehensive frameworks, which consider all of these measures. Both countries require capital to cover this risk by applying a higher risk weight to the relevant foreign exchange exposures, but the additional buffer is significantly higher in Uruguay because of a higher risk weight (102.5 percent in Peru and 125 percent in Uruguay) and also a broader exposure base.[10] In addition, both Peru and Uruguay require specific provisions to cover exchange-rate-induced credit risk, but again, the added provisions are higher in Uruguay, as they are determined on the basis of a larger exchange rate shock (a depreciation of 10 to 20 percent in Peru compared to a depreciation of 20 to 60 percent in Uruguay). In both countries, borrowers, whose capacity to repay was affected after the largest of the two shocks, cannot be classified in the first category. Peru requires additional provisions of up to 1 percent of the highest-rated foreign currency loans to banks that have not implemented adequate systems to manage this risk. Some countries with a low degree of dollarization have also focused on this issue. Chile, for instance, instructed supervised institutions in the early 2000s to pay attention to their clients' foreign exchange risks, regardless of whether their own positions were well hedged (Marshall 2010).

Loan Classification and Provisioning

Several countries have tightened their loan classification and provisioning rules and practices. Among these, the Dominican Republic, El Salvador, and Honduras improved their rating on this principle, from materially noncompliant to largely compliant, during their last assessment of compliance with the BCP.

The most advanced LAC countries are moving toward a forward-looking approach to loan classification and provisioning. Loan classification and provisioning systems follow three alternative approaches. The first one, which is applied by most LAC countries, is essentially prescriptive, with criteria for classification and minimum provisioning rates for each category established by regulation and with no room for using internal models. Typically, commercial loans are classified on the basis of predetermined criteria to establish the borrowers' capacity to repay; and consumer, mortgage, and microcredit loans are classified on the basis of the payment record. Brazil and Peru, two countries that have moved forward with the implementation of Basel II, follow this approach. However, in these two countries, the regulator has stipulated that the entities that use internal models for the calculation of capital charges for credit risk also have to use these models to estimate expected losses, to compare the results with the provisions prescribed by the regulation, and to treat the differences according to the procedure established in Basel II. The second approach, currently used by Colombia and Mexico, is a mixed approach. Under this approach, the regulator establishes the rules for loan classification, which are generally forward looking, but also allows the financial institution to use internal models, with prior authorization of the supervisor. In Mexico, for instance, CNBV shifted provisioning regulations for consumption and mortgage loans to an expected-loss from an incurred-loss approach (FSB 2010). The third approach, based on internal models, has been used by Chile since 2011. Under the Chilean regulation, financial institutions are required to develop and apply internal models to estimate expected losses for the retail portfolio, whereas expected losses for corporate loans are derived on the basis of requirements set by the regulator. The move from an incurred-loss to an expected-loss approach could contribute to better underwriting standards and more sustainable credit growth in the future.

Bolivia, Colombia, Peru, and Uruguay have adopted dynamic provisioning rules that vary during an economic cycle. The rules require financial institutions to accumulate provisions during the expansionary phase of an economic cycle and allow a reversal of these provisions during a contraction. In Colombia, for instance, the additional buffer is determined by applying a higher probability of default for performing loans during the expansionary phase. The higher default probabilities result from provisioning rates that are on average about 1 percent higher during that phase. The timing of the accumulation and reversal is determined by each financial institution on the basis of the annual growth of its loan portfolio, the quarterly growth of its outstanding provisions, and its quarterly expenses on provisions. Intuitively, the goal is to accumulate more provisions when credit is expanding and provisions are falling or stable. In Peru, the provisioning buffer is determined by directly applying a higher provisioning requirement for all the highest rated loans. A simple average indicates that the provisioning buffer is about 0.65 percent. The timing of the accumulation and drawdown is announced by the supervisor, on the basis of the annual GDP growth. The new Chilean regulation, effective in 2011, also includes a cyclical component based on internal models and establishes a minimum ratio of provisions (0.5 percent) to total the highest-rated loans rated as 1.

Supervisory Approach and Risk-Based Supervision

LAC countries have undertaken reforms to implement a risk-based supervision, but the scope and depth of these reforms and their degree of implementation are diverse. Some countries have well-defined risk-based systems that are fully integrated into the supervisory processes and are used to prepare supervisory plans, defining, for instance, the intensity and scope of supervisory oversight and specific supervisory actions (for example, Argentina, Brazil, Chile, Colombia, Mexico, and Peru). To this end, these countries have strengthened their supervisory capacities by incorporating staff with the necessary set of skills and improving information systems and supervisory processes. Generally, these countries complement their risk-based systems with a strong compliance environment. Other countries, like Nicaragua and Trinidad and Tobago, that have also developed risk-based ratings need further work to incorporate all key risks into the framework and to better integrate these ratings into their supervisory processes and plans. Yet a third group—including Bolivia, the Dominican Republic, Honduras, and Paraguay—is at the early stages of implementing risk-based supervision. To a large extent, the latter two groups have yet to undertake the necessary investment in human resources, supervisory processes, and information systems needed for an effective implementation of risk-based supervision. At least during its initial stages, risk-based supervision makes heavy demands on human resources, as it involves making a comprehensive risk analysis of all banks to establish supervisory priorities.

The way in which the risk-based system is integrated into supervisory actions also varies across countries. The risk-based systems determine the risk profile of a financial institution by establishing its exposure to the main financial and nonfinancial risks and the quality of risk management (thereby quantifying the residual risks). The overall risk rating generally results from a combination of this analysis with the results of the evaluation of solvency, profitability, corporate governance, and business strategy. In some of these countries, the rating methodology is public (Chile), and the supervisor reveals the rating to the financial institution (Argentina, Brazil, Chile, and Ecuador). In some cases, the rating system has been formally incorporated into the legal and regulatory framework (Argentina, Chile, and Peru). In Argentina, the capital requirements for credit risk vary according to the entity rating, found by multiplying the required capital by a factor of 0.97 to 1.15 associated to these ratings. Since 2000, Chilean banks have been required to conduct a self-assessment of their risk profile on the basis of this rating methodology, and this self-assessment is an input for the supervisory work. In other countries, the supervisor does not reveal the rating to the financial institution, only the corrective actions that need to be taken (Colombia, Mexico, and Peru).

Macroprudential Framework

The macroprudential framework is a relatively new area of policy development in which there is substantial scope for improvements in the LAC region. The recent global crisis showed that various decisions that might be efficient for individual institutions can create risks for the system as a whole, thereby amplifying the effects of shocks, creating havoc in markets, and damaging financial stability. These need to be addressed with a macroprudential framework, which should include prudential and risk management requirements to contain these risks, state clear responsibilities, and ensure effective coordination among the government agencies that have a role in the preservation of financial stability. A survey conducted in the region identifies various hindrances to the capacity of countries to conduct effective systemic supervision, including the following: (a) the lack of proper staff skills; (b) poor coordination with other domestic supervisors; (c) inadequate legal powers, protection, and independence of supervisors; and (d) insufficient use of market data (Gutierrez and Caraballo 2011).

Nevertheless, some LAC countries are working to strengthen their systemic supervision:

- Several countries have put in place a framework to strengthen coordination between authorities involved in the preservation of financial stability (central bank, ministry of finance, supervisory agencies, and deposit protection). In 2010, for instance, Mexico established the interagency Financial System Stability Council to monitor and assess systemwide risks.
- Many central banks have an analytical framework for assessing the risks to the financial system; and some of them issue a public report

on financial stability (Brazil, Colombia, Mexico, Peru, and Uruguay). Brazil has developed tools and methodologies to help the central bank improve its monitoring of the financial system's stability and to take corrective actions. Brazil established the New Monitoring System of Markets to provide more safety and efficiency in monitoring market and liquidity risks, and in 2009 it improved the Credit Information System to enrich the quality of the credit information used by the central bank.

- Several countries have established cyclical buffers accumulated during the expansion phase to be reversed during the downward phase. The buffers have been built up through cyclical provisions (Bolivia, Chile, Colombia, Peru, and Uruguay), through a voluntary reserve equivalent to 40 percent of the 2008 profits (Colombia) and through specific additional capital charges (Peru).
- Some countries are considering a systemic capital surcharge for the largest banks in the economy (Peru).
- Many countries have issued standards on the liquidity risk of banking institutions that require banks to control their maturity mismatches and funding and concentration risks, to stress their liquidity needs under extreme scenarios, and to prepare contingency plans to mitigate liquidity risks under these scenarios. Several countries require banks to have significant liquidity buffers to ensure that they cover their liquidity needs under systemic liquidity pressures. These buffers, which are particularly large in countries with high dollarization (Bolivia, El Salvador, Peru, and Uruguay), were lowered during the recent global crisis to provide adequate liquidity to the banking system.

Countries have also worked to strengthen their financial safety nets. Several countries, particularly those that experienced a banking crisis in the past decade, have strengthened their financial safety nets (Argentina, the Dominican Republic, Ecuador, Peru, and Uruguay). Ecuador, with technical assistance from the Inter-American Development Bank, overhauled its safety net in 2008, and introduced new legislation on a financial system liquidity fund, deposit insurance, and bank resolution. With the exception of the fully dollarized countries of El Salvador and Panama, the central bank acts as a lender of last resort in all Central and South American countries. In the case of Ecuador, the central bank acts as a fiduciary agent for a liquidity fund. With the exception of Costa Rica and Panama, all countries in Central and South America have deposit insurance. Coverage can go from US$2,500 in Guatemala to US$127,000 in Mexico (Guerrero, Focke, and Rossini 2010). Safety nets in many countries include provisions to address systemic problems (Colombia, the Dominican Republic, Honduras, Mexico, Nicaragua, and Peru) (Bolzico, Gozzi, and Rossini 2010).

Crisis simulations, including all the agencies that would be involved in crisis management, have been conducted since 2008, with the support of the World Bank, in several countries (Colombia, Guatemala, and Peru); and a regional exercise took place in Central America. Crisis exercises are also under preparation in El Salvador and Mexico.

Perimeter of Regulation

Some LAC countries are identifying gaps in the regulation and supervision of their financial system and markets. The recent global crisis exposed gaps in the regulatory and supervisory framework of major financial centers around the world. Mexico, for instance, has identified several types of institutions, markets, and products that are likely to need greater oversight. The institutions include large cooperatives and nonbank financial institutions, such as *sofoles* and *sofomes*. Asset-backed securities have been identified as needing closer oversight. The regulatory framework for asset-backed securities has been strengthened in several ways: (a) a mandatory requirement for issuers to maintain a subordinated bond as a percentage of total issuance; (b) enhanced information and analytical tools available to investors; and (c) increased requirements on trustees and portfolio administrators. Closer monitoring of derivatives markets is another area on which some countries are working (Brazil and Peru).

Financial institutions that were previously under the regulatory radar are being subject to prudential supervision. Mexico, for example, expanded the perimeter of regulation by placing the large cooperatives under the supervision of the CNBS in 2009. In addition, it is considering implementing greater oversight over two types of nonbank financial institutions, *sofoles* (limited-purpose financial companies) and *sofomes* (multiple-purpose financial companies), which have expanded significantly in the past few years and have experienced serious deterioration in their loan portfolios and liquidity. In this regard, the Mexican authorities are seeking to better define systemically important financial institutions and are moving forward with a plan to expand the regulatory perimeter to include large *sofomes* and *sofoles*. Peru, in turn, is working to bring large cooperatives under the supervision of the SBS, pending approval by Congress. Paraguay has initiated a technical assistance project aimed at strengthening the regulation and supervision of its large cooperative sector.

Consumer Protection

During the past decade, several LAC countries have strengthened the protection of the consumers of financial services. Regulators have sought to establish market conduct rules to ensure that consumers have adequate information on the financial services they use and that financial institutions adhere to fair business practices, including timely and truthful information, freedom of choice, responsible processing of complaints, proper management of conflicts of interest, and customer education. For instance, banks must provide information on the effective cost of bank services, summarizing the costs in one single rate (Mexico and Peru). Regulations in Colombia, Mexico, and Peru define abusive contract terms and practices and declare them unlawful and invalid. Model contracts for financial transactions are publicly disclosed (Colombia, Mexico, and Peru); they must include a summary page that clearly presents the key aspects of the contract (Mexico and Peru), and they are reviewed and approved by a government agency (the Commission for the Protection of the Users of Financial Services in Mexico; and the Superintendency of Banks and Insurance in Peru). These countries have favored market mechanisms to promote a gradual reduction of lending rates and broaden access to financial services, as opposed to establishing price controls. In some countries, these actions are complemented with financial education programs conducted in public schools (Peru).

Conclusions

This chapter presents evidence of the notable improvements in the regulatory and supervisory frameworks of the LAC region during the past decade. The improvements, which were most likely motivated by the lessons of the recurrent and widespread financial crises that the region experienced during the 1990s and early 2000s, occurred at a time when many developed-country supervisors were bent on easing intermediation through more market-friendly regimes. Evidence shows that most LAC countries have reached adequate standards on the following aspects of bank oversight: authorizations (licensing criteria, ownership structure, and permissible activities), supervisory techniques, supervisor responsibilities and objectives, and home-host relationships.

Nevertheless, the evidence also shows that the progress is not homogenous and that significant supervisory gaps remain throughout the region. On four key dimensions, LAC performs poorly absolutely: independence of supervisors, capital adequacy, the comprehensive supervision of risks, and consolidated supervision. Moreover, on the first two, LAC countries also lag relative to their peers with similar income levels outside the region, which would indicate some issues that require special attention. Moreover, there is a considerable heterogeneity within the region: LAC7 countries perform well, both absolutely and relatively, while the other LAC countries underperform absolutely and relatively along most supervisory dimensions.

While the region is better prepared to face the oversight wars of today, outstanding weaknesses pose certain challenges. LAC supervisors, especially those in lower-income countries, need to continue working toward establishing regulatory and supervisory frameworks that increase the effectiveness of bank capital and liquidity buffers during adverse situations, both on a consolidated basis and on one that takes into account all relevant risks. Complacency would be dangerous, even for the countries with the strongest supervisory frameworks. Supervisors in the most developed financial systems must continue moving forward to keep up with an evolving international setting. Particular challenges are the innovations in the financial industry, the implementation of improved international standards (including the forthcoming changes in the Basel Core Principles for Banking Supervision and the Basel II and III Capital Accords), and the need to pay more attention to macroprudential and perimeter issues. Overcoming these challenges, in conjunction with the adoption of sound macroeconomic policies, could greatly strengthen the financial system's resilience to future crises.

Notes

1. Banking crises have recently occurred in the following LAC countries: Argentina (1995 and 2001), Bolivia (1994), Brazil (1994), Colombia (1998), Costa Rica (1994), the Dominican Republic (2003), Ecuador (1996, 1998), Haiti (1994), Honduras (1999), Jamaica (1996), Mexico (1994), Nicaragua (2000), Paraguay (1995), Peru (1998), Uruguay (2002), and Venezuela (1994).

2. Anguilla, Antigua and Barbuda, the Bahamas, Barbados, Belize, Bermuda, Bolivia, the British Virgin Islands, Brazil, Chile, Colombia, Costa Rica, the Dominican Republic, the eastern Caribbean, Ecuador, El Salvador, Guatemala, Guyana, Honduras, Jamaica, Mexico, Montserrat, the Netherlands Antilles, Nicaragua, Panama, Paraguay, Peru, St. Vincent and the Grenadines, Trinidad and Tobago, Turks and Caicos, and Uruguay.

3. For the purposes of this analysis, Mexico is included in South America.

4. LAC7 encompasses the large, medium-income LAC economies: Argentina, Brazil, Chile, Colombia, Mexico, Peru, and Uruguay. For the analysis in this section, however, Argentina is not included, since it had not undergone a BCP assessment by the end of 2010.

5. Amendments to the banking law in February 2008.

6. Resolution SBS No. 11823 of 2010, September 2010.

7. "Parallel banks are defined as banks licensed in different jurisdictions that, while not being part of the same financial group for regulatory consolidation purposes, have the same beneficial owner(s), and consequently, often share common management and interlinked businesses. The owner(s) may be an individual or a family, a group of private shareholders, or a holding company or other entity that is not subject to banking supervision." See Bank for International Settlements, http://www.bis.org/publ/bcbs94.htm.

8. These supervisors were previously organized as separate areas within the Central Bank. The reform was included in the New Central Bank Chart (Law No. 18.401 of 2008).

9. The Committee of Sponsoring Organizations of the Treadway Commission (COSO), Enterprise Risk Management Framework. The framework approach considers eight components of risk management: internal environment, objective

setting, event identification, risk assessment, risk response, control activities, information and communication, and monitoring.

10. In Peru, exposures that are sensitive to exchange-rate-induced credit have a higher risk weight, whereas in Uruguay the higher risk weight is applied to all foreign currency exposures in the nonfinancial sector.

References

Barth, J., G. Caprio, and R. Levine. 2008. "Bank Regulations Are Changing: For Better or Worse?" Policy Research Working Paper 4646, World Bank, Washington, DC.

Basel Committee on Bank Supervision (BCBS). *Core Principles for Effective Banking Supervision*. Basel: BCBS.

———. 2006a. *Core Principles Methodology*. Basel: BCBS.

———. 2006b. *International Convergence of Capital Measurement and Capital Standards, A Revised Framework Comprehensive Version*. Basel: BCBS.

———. 2009a. *Revisions to the Basel II Market Risk Framework*. Basel: BCBS.

———. 2009b. *Enhancements to the Basel II Framework*. Basel: BCBS.

———. 2010. *The Basel Committee's Response to the Financial Crisis: Report to the G20*. Basel: BCBS.

Beck, T., A. Demirgüç-Kunt, and R. Levine. 2000. "A New Database on Financial Development and Structure." *World Bank Economic Review* 14 (3): 579–605.

Bolzico, J., E. Gozzi, and F. Rossini. 2010. "Financial Safety Nets in American Countries: A Comparative Analysis." http://www.fitproper.com/documentos/propios/FSN_American_countries.pdf.

Central Bank of Brazil. 2010. *Relatorio de Estabilidade Financeira* 9 (2).

COSO (Committee of Sponsoring Organizations of the Treadway Commission). 2003. "Enterprise Risk Management Framework." http://www.coso.org/default.htm.

Financial Stability Forum. 2009. *Financial Stability Board Principles for Sound Compensation Practices*. https://www.financialstabilityboard.org/activities/compensation/.

———. 2010. *Country Review of Mexico: Peer Review Report*. http://www.financialstabilityboard.org/publications/r_100927.pdf.

Guerrero, R. M., K. Focke, and F. Rossini. 2010. "Redes de Seguridad Financiera: Aspectos conceptuales y experiencias recientes en América Latina y el Caribe." IDB TN-121, Inter-American Development Bank, Washington, DC.

Gutierrez, E., and P. Caraballo. 2011. "Survey on Systemic Oversight Frameworks in LAC: Current Practices and Reform Agenda." Policy Research Working Paper 5941, World Bank, Washington, DC.

IMF (International Monetary Fund). 2011. "Chile: Financial Stability Assessment." IMF Country Report 11/261, International Monetary Fund, Washington, DC.

Marshall, Enrique. 2010. "The Central Bank's Contribution to Financial Stability: The Experience of Chile." Speech given at the Central Bank of Bolivia's First Financial Workshop "Macroregulation and Financial Stability," La Paz, September 29.

Wezel, T. 2010. "Dynamic Loan Loss Provisions in Uruguay: Properties, Shock Absorption Capacity and Simulations Using Alternative Formulas." IMF Working Paper 10/125, International Monetary Fund, Washington, DC.

World Bank. 2007, 2008. *Banking Regulation Survey.* Washington, DC: World Bank. http://econ.worldbank.org/WBSITE/EXTERNAL/EXTDEC/EXTRESE ARCH/0,,contentMDK:20345037~pagePK:64214825~piPK:64214943~theSit ePK:469382,00.html.

9

Macroprudential Policies over the Cycle in Latin America

César Calderón and Luis Servén

Abstract

The recent global financial crisis has highlighted the need for a policy framework to manage the financial cycle and particularly to contain the buildup of systemic risk in its expansionary phase. A comparative analysis of financial cycles reveals that they should be a bigger policy concern in Latin America and the Caribbean than elsewhere: they are more pronounced and more likely to end in crashes, and these are costlier when they do occur. The evidence also suggests that policy makers might view credit growth as a rough proxy for the buildup of systemic risk over the cycle. The primary objective of macroprudential policy is the management of systemic risk. It should not aim to eliminate the financial cycle but to counter the procyclicality induced by inadequate financial regulation and unaddressed externalities across private agents. Macroprudential regulation of the financial system is the key resource available to policy makers for this purpose. A variety of regulatory tools have been proposed, and some have been deployed in emerging markets; but their effectiveness in containing systemic risk—and the

The authors work for the World Bank as, respectively, senior economist in FPDVP and research manager in DECRG. The authors are grateful to Stijn Claessens, Augusto de la Torre, Alain Ize, and Luiz Pereira da Silva for their comments and suggestions. The views expressed in this paper are those of the authors and do not necessarily reflect those of the World Bank or its board of directors.

costs incurred—is largely unknown. Furthermore, there is increasing evidence that monetary policy and fiscal policy also have significant effects on financial stability. This opens the possibility of a two-handed approach that combines regulatory and macroeconomic policy tools for macroprudential purposes.

Introduction

The global financial crisis has provided a stark reminder of the devastating effects that boom-and-bust financial cycles can have on output and employment. While there is no unanimity among academics or policy makers on the causes of the crisis, there is broad agreement that an excessive buildup of aggregate risk in the financial system was one of the main forces—or, in the view of many qualified observers, the key force—behind the worldwide financial meltdown. An inadequate regulatory framework gave financial institutions distorted incentives for risk taking that fueled a vicious circle of asset bubbles, expanding credit, and rising leverage, which, in the view of some observers, was further encouraged by overly expansionary monetary and fiscal policies in advanced countries. The chaotic unraveling of the boom that started in 2007 brought the global financial system to the brink of collapse and triggered the biggest global recession in almost a century.

The crisis has underscored the need for a new policy framework to manage systemic risk and reduce the cost of boom-and-bust financial cycles. Systemic risk arises from common exposures and interconnectedness across financial institutions. It is not just the sum of the risks faced by individual institutions due to the presence of risk spillovers across them—that is, the negative externalities that each institution imposes on the rest, owing to the fact that the social cost of its illiquidity or insolvency exceeds the private cost to the institution in question. These spillovers operate through both financial links across institutions and links between the real and the financial sides of the economy. They create a "fallacy of composition," in that sound risk management of individual institutions does not ensure sound management of systemwide risk. Indeed, actions that enhance the stability of individual institutions may weaken systemwide stability. What for an institution is a prudent retrenchment to reduce its exposure may be a run for another—the so-called credit crunch externality (see, for example, Allen and Gale 2000). Likewise, asset sales by an institution to rebuild its balance sheet may weaken the balance sheets of other institutions through the ensuing fall in asset prices, forcing them to engage in further asset sales—the so-called fire-sale externality (see, for example, Shleifer and Vishny 2010). Through these mechanisms, risks taken by individual institutions are ultimately borne by the system as a whole.

Systemic risk follows a cyclical pattern; it is typically built in the upswing of the financial cycle, when credit, asset prices, leverage, and maturity mismatches all rise in a mutually reinforcing boom. The opposite happens (often more abruptly) in the downswing, in which a vicious circle arises among deleveraging, asset sales, and deteriorating lending portfolios. Moreover, the evidence shows that these credit cycles are larger, more persistent, and more asymmetric in emerging economies than in advanced economies (Mendoza and Terrones 2008). It also shows that financial crashes do not occur at random times; they almost invariably follow booms, as documented, for example, by Schularick and Taylor (2009). This empirical regularity is very familiar to emerging countries, and in particular to Latin American ones, which suffered a number of major financial crashes in the 1990s and early 2000s, in most cases in the aftermath of financial booms.

The primary objective of macroprudential policies is to manage systemic risk. It is useful to distinguish two dimensions of the latter. The cross-sectional dimension has to do with the correlated exposures of financial intermediaries and their vulnerability to common shocks. The time dimension, which is the focus of this chapter, relates to the evolution of systemic risk over the cycle and in particular the booms and busts in credit and asset prices.

This chapter reviews policy options for dealing with financial cycles and their real consequences. It takes stock of the recent academic and policy debates from the perspective of emerging countries and Latin America in particular. Much of the discussion is concerned with macroprudential regulation, especially over the cycle, but the role of macroeconomic policies is considered as well. Given the broad range of topics covered, the discussion is necessarily brief; further details can be found in Calderón and Servén (2011).

The chapter is organized as follows. The next section offers a comprehensive analysis of the empirical regularities that characterize financial cycles, taking a comparative perspective that contrasts the experiences of Latin America with those of middle-income economies in other world regions as well as industrial countries. The third section turns to macroprudential regulation. It summarizes policy proposals advanced in the recent literature, along with experience with the use of various regulatory tools. The chapter then discusses the potential contribution of macroeconomic policies to macroprudential objectives. The final section offers some concluding thoughts.

Characterizing Financial Cycles in Latin America

This section characterizes financial cycles in Latin America, drawing from a large sample of 79 countries with quarterly information over the period 1970–2010.[1] Using time-series techniques to date peaks and troughs in credit and asset prices, as well as to identify booms and busts in finance, we benchmark the cycles of credit, asset prices, and capital flows in Latin America and the Caribbean (LAC) with respect to two comparator groups: industrial countries and non-LAC emerging markets.

Empirically, we adopt the "classical" definition of business cycles to distinguish recession and recovery periods in real and financial variables (Burns and Mitchell 1946). The quarterly adaptation of the Bry-Boschan procedure (1971) implemented by Harding and Pagan (2002a, 2002b) is the methodological workhorse for identifying these episodes. This methodology has been extensively used in recent papers that characterize the properties of real and financial cycles on industrial countries and, to a lesser extent, in emerging market economies.[2] Our empirical assessment of financial cycles in LAC yields four stylized facts.

First, credit cycles are more protracted and more abrupt in LAC than elsewhere—especially during downturns. This may reflect the region's longer history of macroeconomic instability, as captured by unsustainable fiscal and external positions, high inflation episodes, and frequent banking and currency crises. In addition, the duration and amplitude of credit cycles in LAC countries are bigger in times of crisis than in noncrisis periods. In times of crisis, credit cycles are more violent in LAC than elsewhere, as measured by the slope of the cycle in either real credit per capita or the credit-GDP ratio. In line with these results, the leverage ratio of the banking system fluctuates more intensely in LAC countries than in other emerging market economies both in tranquil and in crisis times.

Second, credit is tightly synchronized with real output over the cycle in all country groups—and more so than for other financial variables such as leverage, stock, or housing prices. In fact, output and credit share the same cyclical phase more than 70 percent of the time for LAC, non-LAC emerging markets (EMs), and industrial countries. Interestingly, real output and capital flows spend more than 60 percent of their time in the same cyclical phase for LAC and for industrial countries—and this share rises to nearly 70 percent for other emerging markets (non-LAC EMs). Among financial variables, credit and housing price cycles show the largest extent of cyclical synchronization in both industrial and LAC countries—that is, they are in the same cyclical phase more than 70 percent of the time. Regardless of the sample of countries, real credit is more weakly aligned with either stock prices or the leverage ratio of the banking system. This result is consistent with the findings of Claessens, Kose, and Terrones (2011a, 2011b).[3] Next, capital flows are more synchronized with credit and stock prices than with other asset prices in LAC and non-LAC markets. Nearly 60 percent of the time, credit and capital flows as well as stock prices and capital flows share the same cyclical phase for these groups of countries. In contrast, capital flows have stronger comovements with stock prices and housing prices for industrial countries. Finally, we should point out that credit cycles tend to precede real output cycles in LAC—with peaks in real credit per capita anticipating those in real GDP. The same pattern of cyclical behavior is observed in asset prices—especially for stock prices and real exchange rates.

Third, few lending booms end in a full-blown financial crisis, in either industrial countries or emerging market economies. However, the likelihood that a lending boom will lead to a crisis is higher in LAC (more than 8 percent) than in industrial countries (4.6 percent) or non-LAC EMs (nearly 4 percent). Banking crises, though, are often preceded by a credit boom. In fact, the frequency with which banking crises follow a credit boom is fairly high (nearly 35 percent for either industrial countries or non-LAC EMs and approximately 45 percent for LAC countries). This finding is consistent with the evidence presented by Tornell and Westermann (2002) for middle-income countries.

Finally, credit upswings are good predictors of future crises. Not only does the duration of credit upturns matter in predicting a future banking crisis, but also the size of credit booms rather than the size of asset price or capital flow booms contains information that helps predict a crisis. In short, credit appears to be a summary statistic of financial conditions that help predict future crisis episodes.[4] This finding is consistent with recent evidence by Barajas, Dell'Ariccia, and Levchenko (2009), Schularick and Taylor (2009), and Jorda, Schularick, and Taylor (2011).

The Data

We have collected quarterly data for a wide array of real and financial indicators over the period 1970–2010 for a large sample of 23 industrial countries as well as for 56 emerging market economies.[5]

Real cycles are typically characterized by dating turning points in real output. Quarterly data on real GDP have been gathered from national data sources—and also from cross-country databases such as Haver Analytics, Datastream, and the Economist Intelligence Unit.

To characterize financial cycles, we examine the cyclical properties of credit and asset prices. Credit is measured by the claims on the private sector by deposit money banks (International Financial Statistics line 22d). We assess credit cycles using both real private credit per capita (as in Mendoza and Terrones 2008) and the ratio of credit to GDP, as in Gourinchas, Valdés, and Landarretche (2001) and Barajas, Dell'Ariccia, and Levchenko (2009). We also consider the leverage of the banking system (that is, the ratio of private credit to deposits). Deposits, in turn, are the sum of demand and time deposits (IFS lines 24 and 25, respectively). Asset price cycles are approximated using information on stock prices, housing prices, and the real effective exchange rate. Stock price information is collected from national sources and complemented with data from cross-country databases such as the IFS of the International Monetary Fund (IMF) (line 62), Haver Analytics, and the World Bank's Global Economic Monitoring. Housing price information was available from Igan et al. (2009) and Claessens, Kose, and Terrones (2011a, 2011b) and complemented by data from national sources as compiled by Haver Analytics.[6] Finally, the data on real effective exchange rates were collected from the IFS; higher values signal a real appreciation of the domestic currency.

Quarterly data on real output, credit, and asset prices are complemented with data on capital flows—say, total gross capital inflows (foreign direct investment, portfolio investment, and other investment liability flows). Capital inflows are normalized by the permanent component of gross domestic product (GDP). The data on capital flows are collected from the IMF's balance of payments statistics whereas GDP (in U.S. dollars at current prices) is gathered from the World Bank's World Development Indicators. The permanent component of GDP is computed using the Hodrick-Prescott filter.

Main Features of Financial Cycles in LAC

We use the quarterly adaptation of the Bry-Boschan algorithm (BBQ) to date turning points in real output, credit, asset prices, and capital flows and characterize the main features of real, financial, and capital flow cycles in Latin America.[7] Asset prices are expressed in real terms by dividing them (either stock prices or housing prices) by the consumer price index. Capital flows, however, are approximated by dividing annualized gross inflows by annualized GDP.[8] We benchmark the features of real and financial cycles in the region relative to two comparator regions: industrial countries and other emerging market economies (also called non-LAC EMs). Viewing the cyclical phases of real and financial indicators in the region provides a broad perspective on their average duration (in number of quarters), as well as on their (median) amplitude (as measured by the size of the cyclical phase) and slope (or intensity of the cyclical phase).

After dating peaks and troughs in real and financial indicators, we proceed to characterize downturns (peak-to-trough episodes) and upturns (trough-to-previous-peak episodes) as in Claessens, Kose, and Terrones (2011a, 2011b). We have identified 1,631 completed financial cycles for our dataset of 79 countries over the period 1970–2010 (of which 313 were experienced in Latin America). Our full sample shows 340 complete credit cycles, 421 stock price cycles, 170 housing price cycles, and 700 real exchange rate cycles. Our LAC sample yields 90 complete credit cycles, 55 stock price cycles, 17 housing price cycles, and 160 complete real exchange rate cycles. Note that the number of complete cycles is subject to the number of countries and time span of the corresponding data.

Table 9.1 presents the main features of real and financial cycles for industrial countries, Latin American countries, and non-LAC emerging markets for the full sample period (1970q1–2010q4) and for the more recent globalization period (1990q1–2010q4). This table shows the average duration (in quarters) of the upturn and downturn phase in real GDP, real credit per capita, the ratio of credit to GDP, bank leverage (as calculated by the ratio of bank credit to deposits), stock prices, housing prices, real exchange rates, and the ratio of gross capital inflows to GDP. The duration of the downturn is computed as the number of quarters that it takes the

Table 9.1 Main Features of Real and Financial Cycles in a Sample of 79 Countries, 1970–2010

	1970–2010						1990–2010					
	Average duration		Median amplitude (%)		Median slope (%)		Average duration		Median amplitude (%)		Median slope (%)	
	Upturn	Downturn	Upturn	Downturn	Upturn	Downturn	Upturn	Downturn	Upturn	Downturn	Upturn	Downturn
Real GDP												
Industrial countries	3.17	3.98	2.9%	-2.4%	0.6%	-0.6%	3.48	4.15	2.4%	-2.4%	0.5%	-0.7%
Latin America	3.36	3.76	5.6%	-5.5%	1.3%	-1.4%	3.27	3.52	5.8%	-3.9%	1.5%	-1.2%
Non-LAC MICs	3.34	3.61	7.5%	-5.1%	1.8%	-1.6%	3.43	3.32	7.5%	-5.8%	2.0%	-1.9%
Real credit per capita												
Industrial countries	5.08	6.12	3.9%	-4.4%	0.9%	-0.9%	5.38	6.30	3.2%	-3.0%	0.8%	-0.7%
Latin America	4.40	7.10	9.9%	-17.7%	2.4%	-2.8%	4.87	6.70	9.9%	-15.9%	1.9%	-2.4%
Non-LAC MICs	4.39	5.31	7.4%	-7.1%	2.2%	-1.8%	4.43	5.30	6.8%	-6.1%	2.1%	-1.6%
Credit:GDP ratio												
Industrial countries	4.56	7.15	3.5%	-5.5%	0.9%	-1.0%	4.53	6.82	3.3%	-4.4%	0.8%	-1.0%
Latin America	4.94	8.31	7.6%	-15.9%	2.0%	-2.5%	5.64	8.70	8.7%	-14.4%	2.2%	-2.5%
Non-LAC MICs	4.03	6.53	5.2%	-7.4%	1.2%	-1.3%	4.70	7.24	4.3%	-7.5%	1.1%	-1.3%

Table 9.1 Main Features of Real and Financial Cycles in a Sample of 79 Countries, 1970–2010 (continued)

	1970–2010						1990–2010					
	Average duration		Median amplitude (%)		Median slope (%)		Average duration		Median amplitude (%)		Median slope (%)	
	Upturn	Downturn	Upturn	Downturn	Upturn	Downturn	Upturn	Downturn	Upturn	Downturn	Upturn	Downturn
Bank leverage												
Industrial countries	4.31	10.33	3.3%	−11.3%	0.9%	−1.5%	4.38	8.42	3.3%	−10.7%	0.9%	−1.4%
Latin America	3.42	14.64	4.9%	−31.4%	1.9%	−3.3%	3.76	9.65	5.1%	−21.5%	1.4%	−2.9%
Non-LAC MICs	3.29	13.13	3.7%	−20.4%	1.3%	−2.6%	3.53	10.20	3.7%	−17.9%	1.4%	−2.5%
Stock prices												
Industrial countries	3.99	6.23	19.3%	−35.9%	5.3%	−7.0%	4.41	5.50	20.2%	−41.2%	5.9%	−8.4%
Latin America	4.09	6.42	36.3%	−56.7%	8.9%	−11.2%	4.00	5.98	38.2%	−55.9%	8.9%	−11.4%
Non-LAC MICs	4.08	6.21	33.4%	−55.4%	7.2%	−8.9%	4.02	6.15	33.2%	−59.0%	7.7%	−9.6%
Housing prices												
Industrial countries	3.94	7.06	2.9%	−4.5%	0.9%	−0.9%	3.55	6.83	2.9%	−4.6%	0.9%	−1.0%
Latin America	4.50	8.33	6.8%	−19.7%	2.4%	−2.7%	4.50	7.63	6.8%	−19.2%	2.4%	−2.7%
Non-LAC MICs	3.91	7.89	3.5%	−8.1%	1.0%	−1.4%	3.94	7.75	3.5%	−8.3%	1.2%	−1.4%

Table 9.1 Main Features of Real and Financial Cycles in a Sample of 79 Countries, 1970–2010 *(continued)*

	1970–2010						1990–2010					
	Average duration		Median amplitude (%)		Median slope (%)		Average duration		Median amplitude (%)		Median slope (%)	
	Upturn	Downturn	Upturn	Downturn	Upturn	Downturn	Upturn	Downturn	Upturn	Downturn	Upturn	Downturn
Real effective exchange rate												
Industrial countries	4.05	5.45	3.5%	-6.7%	1.0%	-1.3%	4.53	5.21	3.1%	-6.8%	0.9%	-1.3%
Latin America	3.94	6.01	6.4%	-12.3%	2.1%	-2.3%	3.57	5.11	4.8%	-9.1%	1.7%	-1.8%
Non-LAC MICs	3.72	5.89	5.4%	-9.8%	1.5%	-2.0%	3.60	5.33	5.7%	-8.4%	1.6%	-1.6%
Gross capital inflows (ratio to GDP)												
Industrial countries	3.29	5.17	3.7%	-5.3%	0.9%	-1.1%	3.09	4.89	5.7%	-8.2%	1.4%	-1.8%
Latin America	3.45	5.20	3.0%	-4.2%	0.6%	-1.0%	3.43	5.07	3.1%	-4.4%	0.7%	-1.1%
Non-LAC MICs	3.23	4.98	3.0%	-4.4%	0.8%	-1.0%	3.24	4.69	3.4%	-4.7%	0.9%	-1.2%

Note: We report the average duration of the different cyclical phases (downturns and upturns) for real and financial variables. The statistics for amplitude and slope refer to sample median across episodes (note that averages for those statistics are not reported but are available from the authors upon request). The duration of downturns (recessions or contractions) is the number of quarters between peak and trough. Upturns (or recoveries), however, are defined as the early stage of the expansion that takes place when either the real or the financial indicator rebounds from the trough to its previous peak. The amplitude of the downturn is the distance between the peak in real output and its subsequent trough while that of the upturn is computed as the four-quarter cumulative variation in real output following the trough. The slope of the downturn is the ratio of the peak-to-trough (trough-to-peak) phase of cycle to its duration. GDP = gross domestic product; LAC = Latin America and the Caribbean; MIC = middle-income country.

403

corresponding variable to travel from peak to trough, while that of upturns is the number of quarters that it takes to rebound from its trough to its previous peak. The table also shows the amplitude of downturns and upturns. The size of the downturn is measured by the distance of each corresponding variable from its peak to the subsequent trough. In contrast, the amplitude of the upturn or recovery phase is calculated as the four-quarter-cumulative change in the corresponding variable from its trough. Note that we use this definition rather than the distance from trough to previous peak (as in the measurement of duration). This latter definition was suggested by Sichel (1994) and widely used in the empirical literature (see Claessens, Kose, and Terrones 2009, 2011a, b).[9] Finally, the intensity of the phases of the cycle is measured by the slope—that is, the amplitude of the phase divided by its duration (see Claessens, Kose, and Terrones 2011 a, b).

There are no major differences in the duration of recessions or recoveries in real economic activity across groups of countries, with recessions lasting on average between 3.2 and 3.3 quarters (that is, almost 10 months) and recoveries taking between 3.5 and 4 quarters. Contractions and surges in capital flows also tend to have the same duration across groups of countries (on average, 3.3 and 5.1 quarters, respectively). However, credit recoveries tend to be shorter in emerging markets—and, in particular, in the LAC region—than in industrial countries (4.4 quarters for either LAC or non-LAC EMs in contrast to 5.1 quarters for industrial countries), while credit downturns tend to be longer in emerging markets, most notably in LAC. Contractions in real credit (per capita) tend to last, on average, 7.1 quarters in LAC—that is, one and two quarters longer than downturns in industrial countries and non-LAC EMs, respectively.

Downturns in real economic activity are larger in size and also more intense in emerging markets—and, particularly, in LAC countries. For instance, the median amplitude of the downturn in real GDP in LAC is 5.5 percent, and it more than doubles that of industrial countries (2.4 percent). Larger contractions in output imply that subsequent output recoveries may also be longer (the "rebound" effect). Indeed, the amplitude of the upturn phase is greater in developing countries (5.6 percent for LAC and 7.5 percent for non-LAC EMs) than in industrial countries (2.9 percent).

As stated above, the cyclical phases of credit are more pronounced in LAC (in size) than in industrial countries or non-LAC EMs. The median drop in real credit per capita during peak-to-trough phases is approximately 18 percent, which is significantly larger than the median decline in industrial countries or in non-LAC EMs (4.4 percent and 7.1 percent, respectively). The amplitude of credit upturns (as measured by the four-quarter cumulative variation from the trough) is indeed larger for LAC countries (9.9 percent) than for industrial countries or non-LAC EMs.

Finally, we should note that these qualitative features of cycles in real credit per capita also hold for the ratio of private credit to GDP and bank leverage. That is, downturns and upturns are larger and more intense in

LAC than elsewhere. In addition, downturns in either the ratio of credit to GDP or the leverage (as defined by the ratio of credit to deposits) last longer in LAC than elsewhere.

As for the cyclical features of asset prices, there are no major differences across groups in the duration of their downturn and upturn phases. However, it should be noted that downturns in housing prices (8.3 quarters) tend to be longer than those in stock prices or real exchange rates (6.4 quarters and 6 quarters, respectively). Despite the shorter availability of data for LAC countries, the same result holds for industrial countries and non-LAC emerging markets.

The median size of the drop from peak to trough in stock prices, housing prices, and real exchange rates is larger in LAC than in industrial countries and, to a lesser extent, in non-LAC EMs. The behavior is symmetric for upturns in (real) asset prices—with stock prices and housing prices recovering at a stronger pace in LAC and with LAC currencies strengthening at a slightly higher rate than non-LAC EMs or industrial countries. The joint behavior of duration and amplitude allows us to infer that asset price busts and booms are more intense in LAC than in industrial countries or non-LAC EMs.

Evolution of LAC Credit Cycles over Time Figure 9.1 presents the main features of the credit cycles in industrial countries, LAC countries, and non-LAC emerging market economies by decade: 1980–89, 1990–99, and 2000–10. In general, we observe that the amplitude and slope of credit cycles have declined over 2000–10 relative to 1990–99 across all groups. And, particularly for Latin America, not only has the duration of credit cycles monotonically declined over time, but also the downturns have become smaller (in size) and less intense (that is, a lower slope). The lower volatility of fluctuations in credit cycles around the world over time can be partly attributed to the "great moderation." Institutional and structural changes—especially, in industrial countries—have effectively reduced the business cycle volatility in industrial countries.[10] In Latin America, improved macroeconomic policy frameworks, a lower debt burden, and reduced currency mismatches have not only lowered the volatility of output cycles over time but also made the region more resilient to global shocks. The macroeconomic stability brought about by this silent revolution in macroeconomic policy frameworks, as pointed out in de la Torre et al. (2010), has also fostered the development of local-currency debt markets.

Financial Downturns and Crisis Financial downturns typically become more protracted and abrupt in times of crisis. Figure 9.2 depicts the duration, amplitude, and slope of financial indicators during peak-to-trough phases of the cycle that end in a banking crisis versus those phases that do not coincide with a banking crisis.[11] To identify the banking crisis episodes, we use the recent database by Laeven and Valencia (2008). They define systemic banking crises as situations in which the following four

Figure 9.1 Evolution of the Main Features of Credit Cycles over Time, 1980–2009

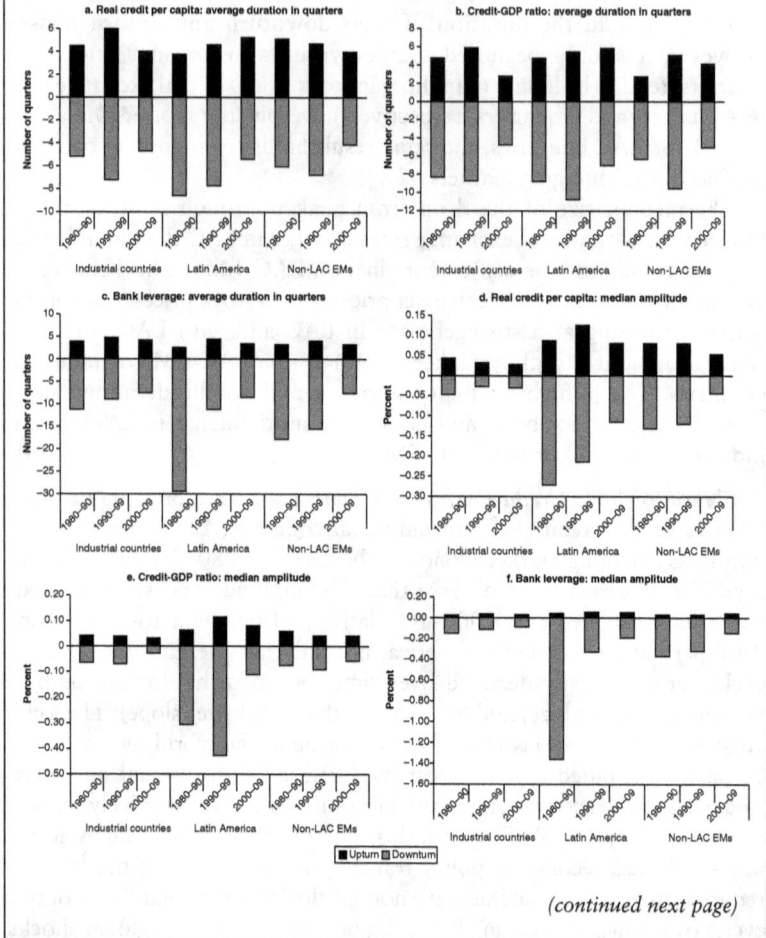

a. Real credit per capita: average duration in quarters

b. Credit-GDP ratio: average duration in quarters

c. Bank leverage: average duration in quarters

d. Real credit per capita: median amplitude

e. Credit-GDP ratio: median amplitude

f. Bank leverage: median amplitude

■ Upturn ▧ Downturn

(continued next page)

Figure 9.1 (continued)

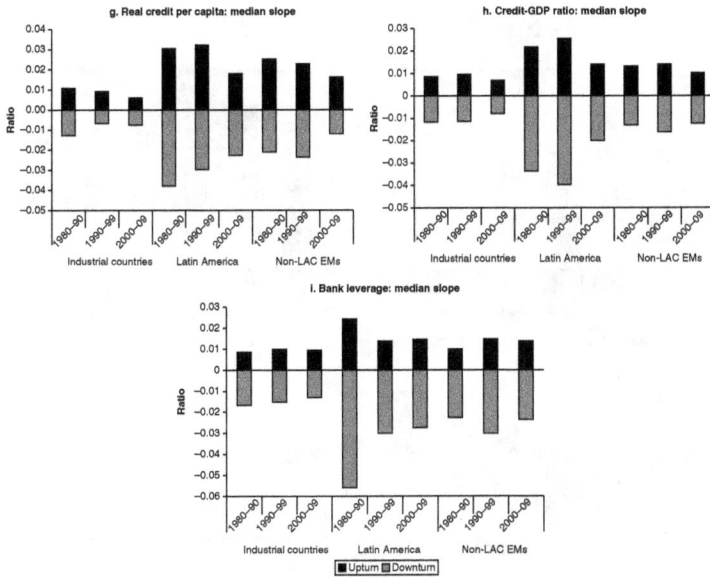

g. Real credit per capita: median slope

h. Credit-GDP ratio: median slope

i. Bank leverage: median slope

■ Upturn ▨ Downturn

Note: We report the average duration of the different cyclical phases (downturns and upturns) for real and financial variables. The statistics for amplitude and slope refer to sample median across episodes (note that averages for those statistics are not reported but are available from the authors upon request). The duration of downturns (recessions or contractions) is the number of quarters between peak and trough. Upturns (or recoveries), however, are defined as the early stage of the expansion that takes place when either the real or financial indicator rebounds from the trough to its previous peak. The amplitude of the downturn is the distance between the peak in real output and its subsequent trough while that of the upturn is computed as the four-quarter cumulative variation in real output following the trough. The slope of the downturn is the ratio of the peak-to-trough (trough-to-peak) phase of the cycle to its duration. LAC = Latin America and the Caribbean; EM = emerging market.

conditions are met: (a) rising nonperforming loans exhaust a bank's capital; (b) asset prices collapse on the heels of run-ups before the crisis; (c) real interest rates are sharply raised; and (d) there is a reversal or slowdown in capital flows.

On average, credit downturns that end in a banking crisis tend to be longer than regular credit downturns—and this difference is larger for non-LAC emerging markets, where regular credit downturns last only 4.8 quarters while those associated with banking crisis episodes can last

Figure 9.2 Main Features of Credit Cycles and Financial Crisis in Industrial Countries, Latin America, and Non-LAC Emerging Markets, 1970–2010

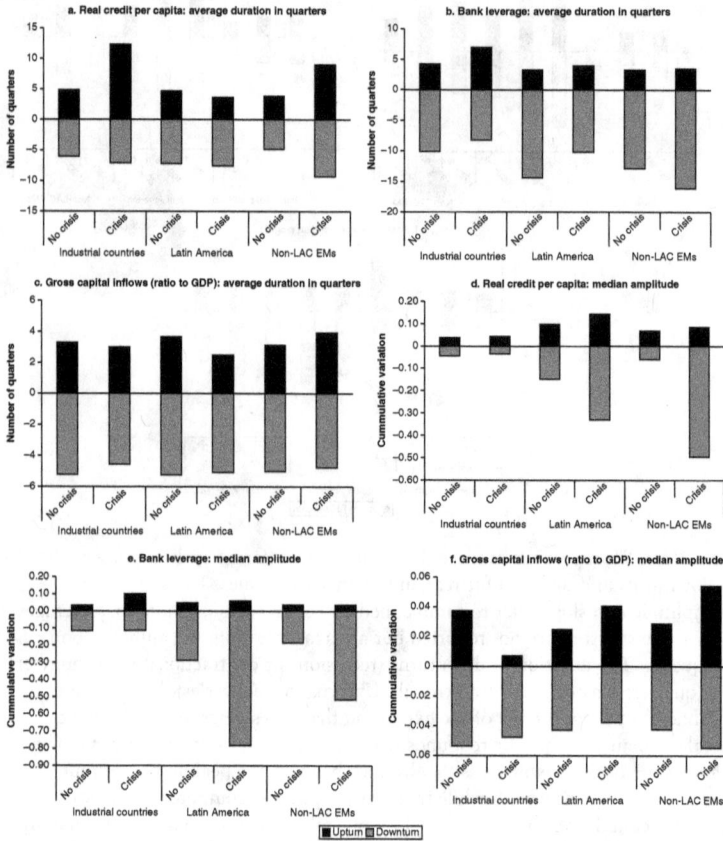

a. Real credit per capita: average duration in quarters

b. Bank leverage: average duration in quarters

c. Gross capital inflows (ratio to GDP): average duration in quarters

d. Real credit per capita: median amplitude

e. Bank leverage: median amplitude

f. Gross capital inflows (ratio to GDP): median amplitude

■ Upturn ▨ Downturn

(continued next page)

Figure 9.2 *(continued)*

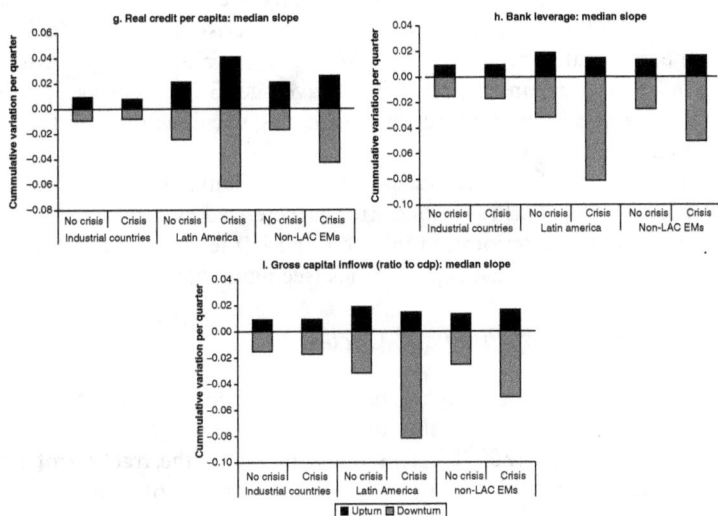

g. Real credit per capita: median slope

h. Bank leverage: median slope

i. Gross capital inflows (ratio to cdp): median slope

■ Upturn ▣ Downturn

Note: We report the average duration of the different cyclical phases (downturns and upturns) for credit indicators per region. The statistics for amplitude and slope refer to sample median across episodes. The definition of the different phases of the cycle and all main cyclical features can be found in the footnote of Figure 9.1. We distinguish the downturns and upturns in credit associated with financial crisis form regular downturns and upturns Financial crisis episodes are defined as in Laeven and Valencia (2008).

more than 9 quarters. As for their size, credit cycles that coincide with a banking crisis tend to be larger and more intense in EMs, especially in Latin America. Note that while the median drop in real credit per capita for non-LAC EMs is 4.2 percent per quarter, it rises to 6.1 percent per quarter in LAC countries. In addition, the contraction in the leverage ratio in crisis times is also remarkable in LAC when compared to either industrial countries or non-LAC EMs. Finally, we observe that the size of upturns and downturns in capital flows (in percentage points of GDP) in LAC during noncrisis times is comparable to that of non-LAC EMs, while that of capital flows in times of crisis is slightly smaller in LAC (relative to non-LAC EMs). However, we can argue that—given that average gross inflows to non-LAC EMs are larger than those of LAC countries—the percentage decline is greater in LAC than elsewhere.

However, there is a clear fall in (real) asset prices (that is, stock and housing prices) in times of crisis relative to regular downturns in industrial economies and non-LAC EMs. The same applies to LAC countries, except in the case of equity prices—where the drop in times of crisis is not larger than in normal downturns but is nevertheless more abrupt (as indicated by its higher slope) in times of crisis. Finally, we should point out that the collapse of the exchange rate in times of crisis is notable in LAC. The median real depreciation of LAC during peak-to-trough episodes associated with a banking crisis is, on average, 32 percent as opposed to a real depreciation of 11 percent during regular downturns in the real exchange rate.

In sum, financial downturns associated with banking crises in the LAC region, as well as in other regions, are characterized by protracted, larger, and more intense deterioration in credit and in the leverage ratio as well as longer and sharper real depreciations (see figure 9.2).

Synchronization of Financial Cycles

We examine the degree of synchronization in financial cycles as well as in financial and real cycles using the concordance index as proposed by Harding and Pagan (2002b). This index measures the fraction of time that two real financial indicators are in the same phase of their respective cycles. If the concordance index is equal to 1 (0), we can argue that the series are perfectly procyclical (countercyclical).

Table 9.2 reports the synchronization of financial cycles and output cycles as well as the financial and capital flow cycles for the sample of industrial countries, LAC countries, and non-LAC emerging market economies over the 1990–2010 period.[12] We report the median of the synchronization between these two variables for each country in our sample.[13]

Before describing the comovement in financial indicators, we examine the synchronization of real and financial cycles in our sample of countries. The extent of synchronization between output and credit cycles is larger than the concordance of output and asset prices or output and capital flows regardless of the sample of countries. In fact, output and credit share the same cyclical phase nearly 75 percent of the time for industrial and non-LAC EMs according to cross-country medians. That percentage declines slightly to 73 percent for LAC countries. The concordance of output and housing price cycles is smaller than that of credit (0.72 for industrial countries and 0.65 for non-LAC EMs) but higher than the concordance of either output and stock prices or output and the real exchange rate.[14] However, we should note that the synchronization between real output and the leverage ratio is negligible for industrial countries and even negative for LAC and non-LAC EMs. Real output and capital flow cycles share upturn and downturn phases more than 60 percent of the time in both industrial and LAC countries. Interestingly, the concordance of output and capital flows is larger for non-LAC EMs (0.7). Finally, we should point out that, in general, the synchronization of real and financial cycles is stronger in industrial countries than in emerging markets (and within this group, it is typically

Table 9.2 Synchronization of Real and Financial Cycles in a Sample of 79 Countries, 1970–2010

	Cross-country sample medians		
Concordance	Industrial countries	Latin America	Non-LAC emerging markets
(Real output, credit)	0.747	0.726	0.747
(Real output, bank leverage)	0.469	0.325	0.422
(Real output, stock prices)	0.639	0.607	0.610
(Real output, housing prices)	0.723	0.464	0.645
(Real output, real exchange rates)	0.560	0.590	0.604
(Real output, gross inflows)	0.627	0.612	0.695
(Credit, bank leverage)	0.572	0.538	0.575
(Credit, stock prices)	0.571	0.578	0.542
(Credit, housing prices)	0.711	0.722	0.579
(Credit, real exchange rates)	0.571	0.554	0.571
(Stock prices, housing prices)	0.581	0.422	0.613
(Stock prices, real exchange rates)	0.452	0.583	0.529
(Housing prices, real exchange rates)	0.563	0.571	0.536
(Credit, capital inflows)	0.548	0.617	0.600
(Bank leverage, capital inflows)	0.518	0.472	0.479
(Stock prices, capital inflows)	0.615	0.571	0.604
(Housing prices, capital inflows)	0.584	0.410	0.568
(Real exchange rate, capital inflows)	0.530	0.554	0.584

Note: The figures presented in this table represent the concordance statistics for the cycles of the corresponding pair of variables (Harding and Pagan 2002b). The corcordance index takes values between 0 and 1 and measures the proportion of time that the two cycles are in the same cyclical phase. The concordance figures presented in the table are computed over the period 1990q1–2010q4. Concordance measures over the full sample period, 1970q1–2010q4, are computed but not reported, and they are available from the authors upon request. Although we do not report the cross-country averages, they yield qualitatively similar results. GDP = gross domestic product.

higher in non-LAC EMs than in LAC countries). As Claessens, Kose, and Terrones (2011a) argue, the greater synchronization of real and financial cycles in industrial countries can be attributed to differences in financial development, with credit and asset price channels of transmission operating more efficiently in the industrial countries than in emerging markets.

Claessens, Kose, and Terrones (2011b) document the synchronization of financial cycles across industrial countries and find that the comovement of credit and housing prices is stronger than that of credit and stock prices and that the degree of synchronization tends to be higher during the globalization period. Our evidence for industrial countries is consistent with the findings of Claessens, Kose, and Terrones (2011b): credit and housing price cycles are more synchronized than cycles of credit and stock prices (0.71 and 0.57, respectively). However, the difference between the degree of synchronization of credit and housing prices and of credit and stock prices is negligible for non-LAC EMs.

In contrast, we also find that the synchronization of the credit cycle and the output cycle is stronger than between output and stock prices and between output and housing prices for all our groups of countries. In LAC, output and credit have a strong direct comovement (0.73), while the concordance is weaker for output and stock prices (0.61) and negligible for output and housing prices (0.46). We should point out, though, that the concordance between credit and leverage is approximately 0.57 for both industrial economies and non-LAC emerging market economies—whereas that for LAC countries is slightly weaker (0.54). Note that the results reported in table 9.2 for industrial countries and non-LAC EMs are qualitatively similar to those reported in Claessens, Kose, and Terrones (2011a).

Finally, we investigate the synchronization of financial cycles and capital flow cycles. We are interested in assessing the degree of comovement between gross inflows and credit as well as gross inflows and asset prices. We find that the synchronization of credit and capital flows as well as credit and stock prices is stronger than that of capital flows and either housing prices or real exchange rates. For instance, the concordance index between real credit and capital flow cycles in LAC is 0.62, whereas that of stock prices and capital flows is 0.57.

Do Financial Indicators Lead the Real Output Cycle? As mentioned above, the concordance index measures the proportion of time that two series tend to share the same cyclical phase. This measure may signal the strength of the contemporaneous comovement between two variables. However, it does not provide information on whether financial cycles tend to precede real cycles.[15] More specifically, we run regressions of (year-on-year) growth in credit and asset prices on a 17-quarter window centered on the peak of real GDP (T). The period from $T-8$ to T represents the run-up to the downturn in real economic activity. On average, the period from T to $T+4$ may capture the downturn in real output, whereas that after $T+4$ may capture the start of the recovery period. In short, we would like to detect whether peaks in real credit or in asset prices tend to precede peaks in real output (T). Figures 9.3 and 9.4 plot the estimated coefficients of these regressions.

Figure 9.3 depicts the behavior of real credit and (real) asset prices around peaks in real GDP and compares the dynamics of financial indicators in the

Figure 9.3 Behavior of Credit and Asset Prices during Downturns in Real Economic Activity: Real Downturns Associated with Banking Crises as Opposed to Other Real Downturns in Selected Countries, 1970–2010

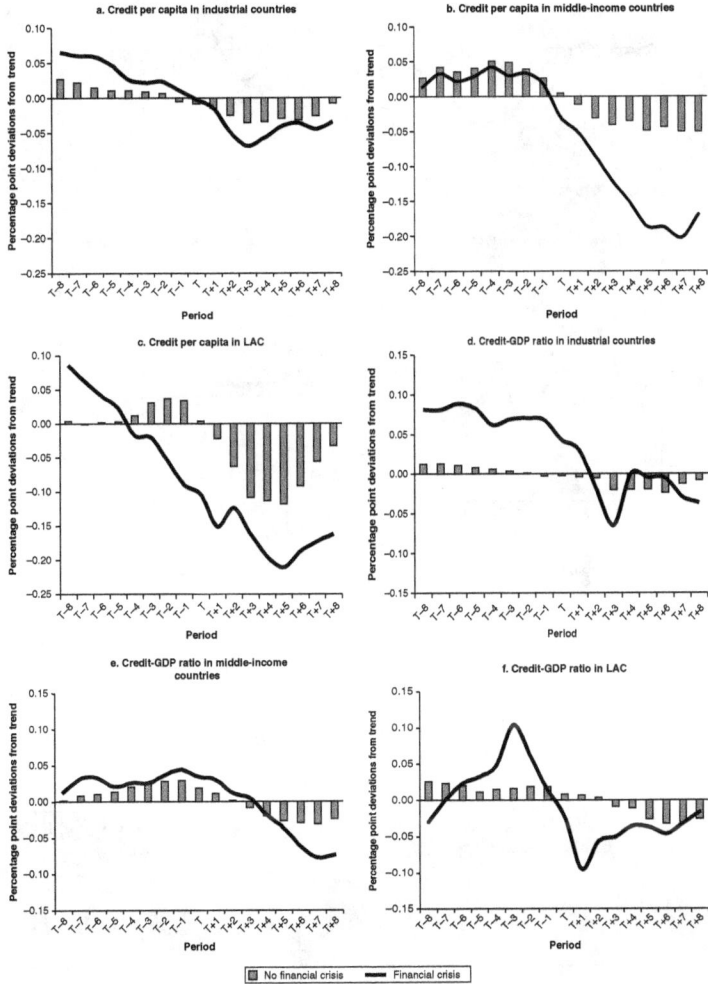

(continued next page)

Figure 9.3 *(continued)*

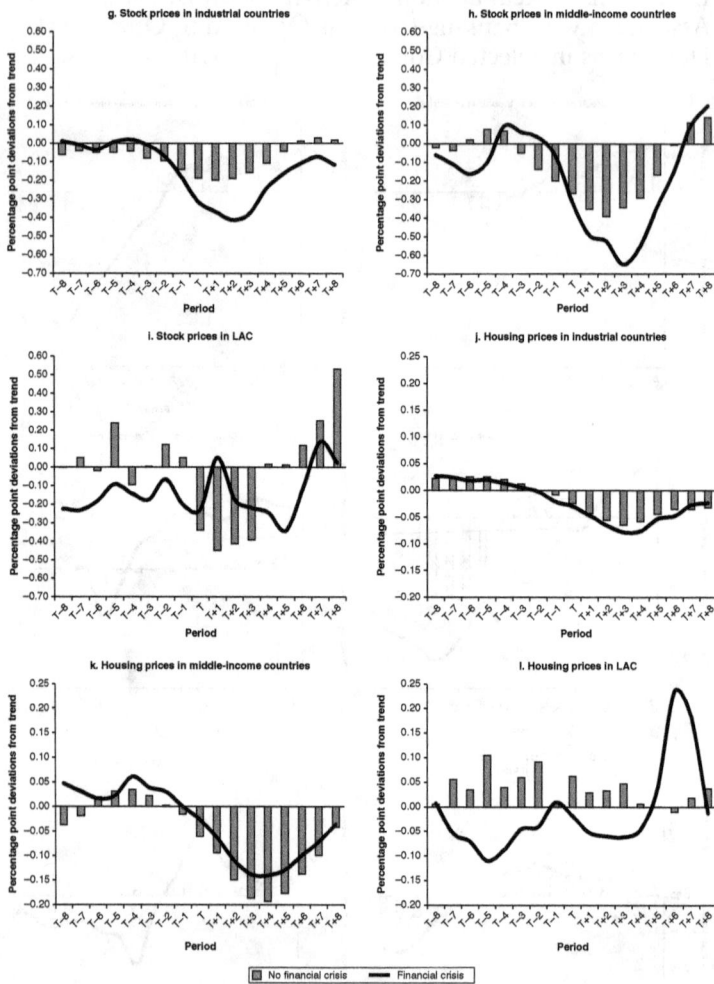

g. Stock prices in industrial countries

h. Stock prices in middle-income countries

i. Stock prices in LAC

j. Housing prices in industrial countries

k. Housing prices in middle-income countries

l. Housing prices in LAC

No financial crisis — Financial crisis

(continued next page)

Figure 9.3 *(continued)*

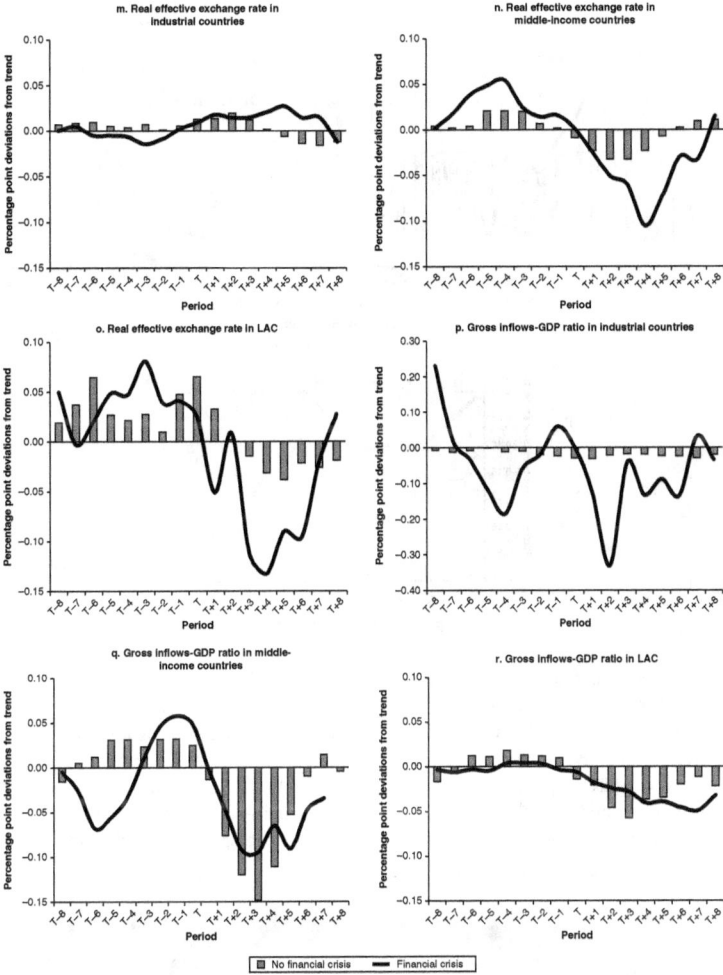

m. Real effective exchange rate in industrial countries

n. Real effective exchange rate in middle-income countries

o. Real effective exchange rate in LAC

p. Gross inflows-GDP ratio in industrial countries

q. Gross inflows-GDP ratio in middle-income countries

r. Gross inflows-GDP ratio in LAC

☐ No financial crisis   ▬ Financial crisis

(continued next page)

Figure 9.3 (continued)

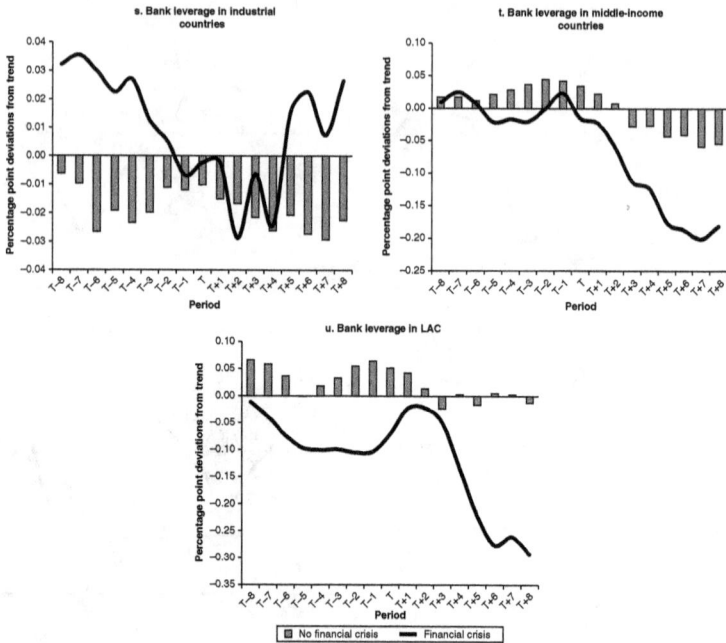

Note: This figure depicts the year-on-year growth rate (or variation) in credit and asset prices around 17-quarter windows centered on peaks in real GDP (T). The period T when the peak in real GDP takes place is identified using the Bry-Boschan quarterly algorithm (Harding and pagan 2002a). Note that the figures reported distinguish peaks in real GDP associated with episodes of banking crisis (as defined in Leaven and Valencia 2008) from other peaks. GDP = gross domestic product; LAC = Latin America and the Caribbean.

run-up to regular output downturns versus the dynamics in real economic downturns associated with banking crises. Figure 9.3 shows that peaks in credit (as measured by either real credit per capita or the ratio of credit to GDP) tend to precede peaks in real GDP regardless of the sample of countries. The leverage ratio of the banking system does not strongly precede peaks in real GDP. In contrast to industrial countries and non-LAC EMs, the peak in bank leverage tends to occur after the peak in real output either in regular or in crisis-related economic downturns. Housing prices, however, tend to precede real cycles in non-LAC EMs, while they tend to lag the cycle in LAC countries. Finally, real exchange rates tend to appreciate

Figure 9.4 Behavior of Credit and Asset Prices during Downturns in Real Economic Activity: Real Downturns in the Current Cycle in Contrast to Average Historic Real Downturns in Selected Countries, 1970–2010

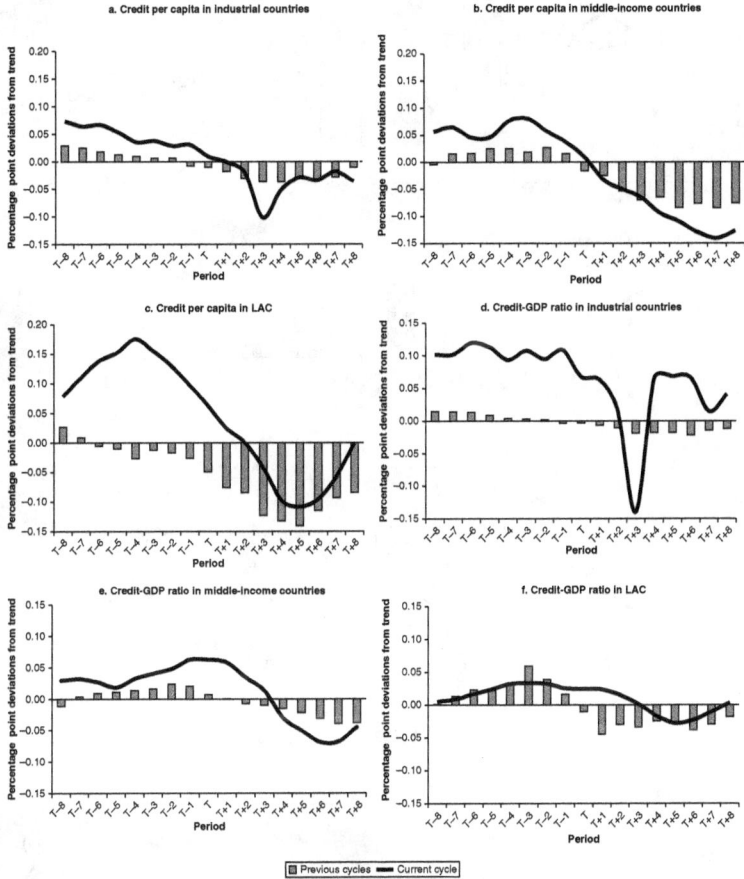

a. Credit per capita in industrial countries

b. Credit per capita in middle-income countries

c. Credit per capita in LAC

d. Credit-GDP ratio in industrial countries

e. Credit-GDP ratio in middle-income countries

f. Credit-GDP ratio in LAC

Previous cycles ▬ Current cycle

(continued next page)

Figure 9.4 (continued)

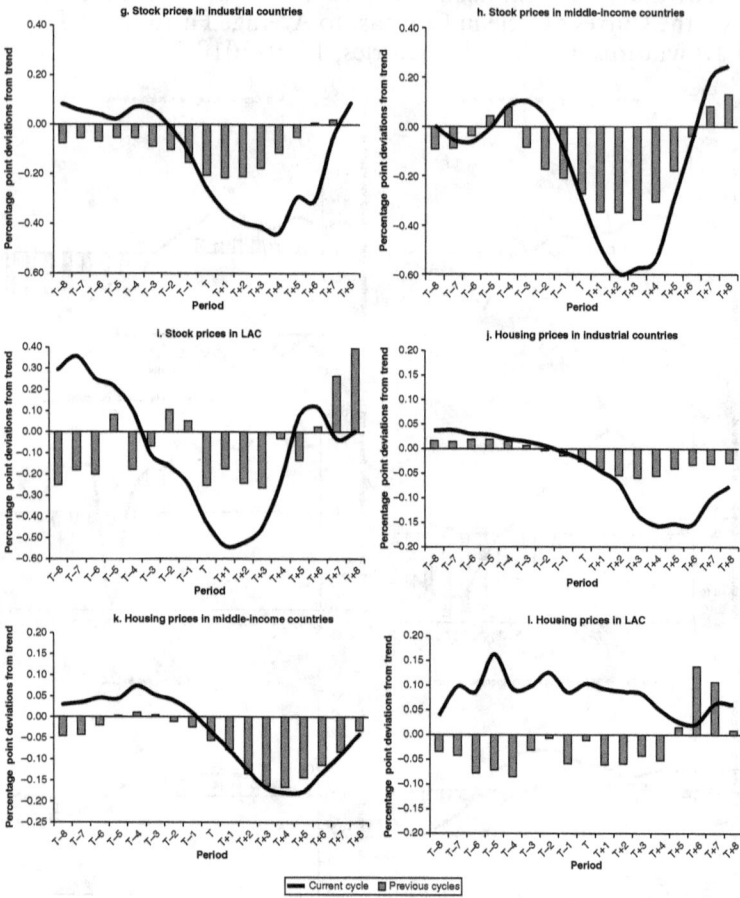

g. Stock prices in industrial countries

h. Stock prices in middle-income countries

i. Stock prices in LAC

j. Housing prices in industrial countries

k. Housing prices in middle-income countries

l. Housing prices in LAC

Current cycle   Previous cycles

(continued next page)

Figure 9.4 (continued)

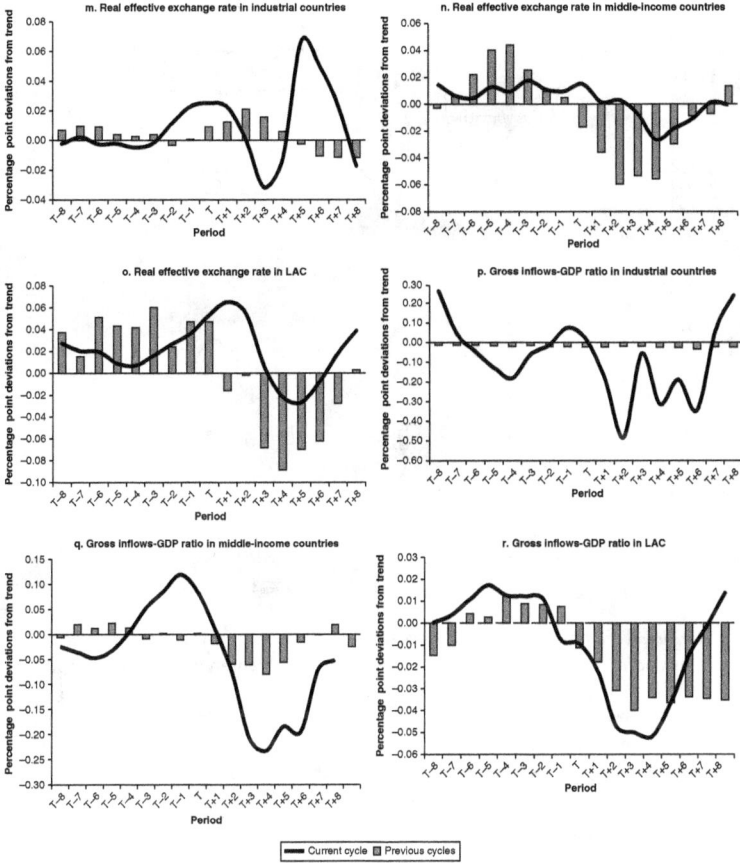

m. Real effective exchange rate in industrial countries

n. Real effective exchange rate in middle-income countries

o. Real effective exchange rate in LAC

p. Gross inflows-GDP ratio in industrial countries

q. Gross inflows-GDP ratio in middle-income countries

r. Gross inflows-GDP ratio in LAC

Current cycle   Previous cycles

(continued next page)

Figure 9.4 *(continued)*

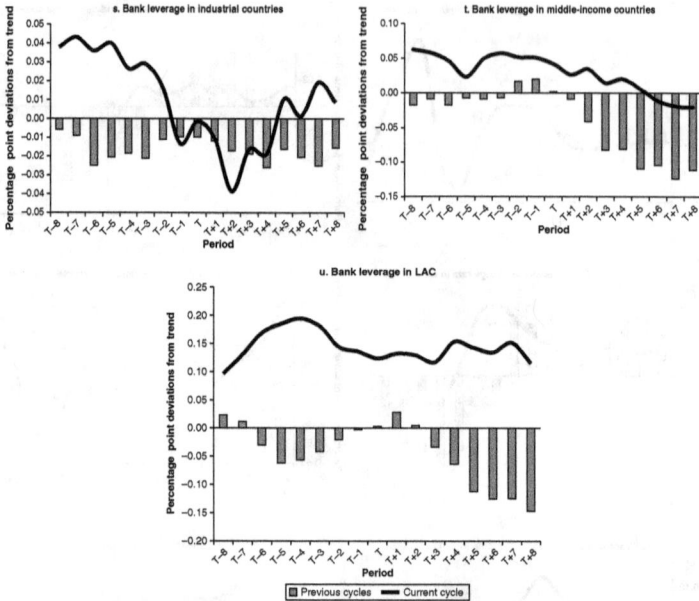

s. Bank leverage in industrial countries

t. Bank leverage in middle-income countries

u. Bank leverage in LAC

Previous cycles ▬ Current cycle

Note: This figure depicts the year-orvyear growth rate (or variation) in credit and asset prices around 17-quarter windows centered on peaks in real GDP (T). The period T when the peak in real GDP takes place is identified using the Bry-Boschan quarterly algorithm (Harding and Pagan 2002a). Note that the figures reported distinguish peaks in real GDP during the current cycle (2006–10) and the average of previous output cycles. GDP = gross domestic product; LAC = Latin America and the Caribbean.

in the run-up to real downturns for both LAC and non-LAC emerging markets. This pattern of behavior does not hold for industrial countries.

Figure 9.4, though, illustrates the dynamics of credit and asset prices around peaks in real GDP but compares the current cycle to the average of previous cycles (or what we call here "historical cycles"). It clearly shows that credit cycles precede real output cycles, and the peak in real credit (per capita) takes place at least four quarters before the peak in real output in the current cycle. Figures 9.4d through 9.4f also show the precedence of cycles in the ratio of credit to GDP. We find that stock prices in the current and previous cycles tend to precede real cycles in LAC and non-LAC EMs and that precedence is stronger for LAC countries in the current cycle (see figures 9.4g through 9.4i). Furthermore, note that leverage is also a leading indicator in the recent cycle (figures 9.4s through 9.4u). Finally, we should note that the stronger precedence of credit in the current cycle is partly reflected in the precedence of gross inflows in the current cycle—especially for non-LAC EMs (figures 9.4p through 9.4r). However, further tests are needed to make this case.

Financial Booms and the Likelihood of Crisis

We have already examined the main features of financial cycles (in duration, amplitude, and slope), their degree of comovement with the business cycle, and the amplification of these properties in times of crisis. So far, we have found that credit upturns and downturns are protracted, larger in size, and more abrupt in LAC than in industrial countries or non-LAC EMs. Credit cycles tend to precede output cycles in the region, and that pattern of behavior is stronger in the run-up to crisis-related recessions or in the run-up to the real downturn in the recent cycle.

We now focus our attention on financial booms and their relationship to banking crises. First, though, figure 9.5 reports the unconditional probability of banking crises as well as lending booms, asset price booms, and capital flow bonanzas. Banking crisis episodes are identified as in Laeven and Valencia (2008), and lending booms are defined as in Mendoza and Terrones (2008). They take place whenever the cyclical component of real credit per capita (constructed using the Hodrik-Prescott filter) exceeds a specific threshold.[16] We use the same criterion to define equity price booms, housing price booms, and capital flow bonanzas. To calculate these unconditional probabilities, we have taken as the threshold 1.75 times their standard deviation over the cycle. We find that banking crises are more frequent in LAC (with an unconditional probability of 4.6 percent) than in non-LAC emerging markets (3.4 percent) or industrial countries (2.7 percent). Lending and equity price booms are also more likely to happen in emerging markets than in industrial countries—and the differences between LAC countries and non-LAC EMs are negligible. Finally, capital flow bonanzas are more likely to happen in LAC countries (9.2 percent) than in industrial countries or non-LAC EMs (7.3 and 5.2 percent).

Table 9.3 computes the conditional probability that a banking crisis will take place within two years after the occurrence of a lending boom in our sample of industrial countries, LAC countries, and non-LAC emerging markets. The table clearly shows across country groups that the percentage of lending booms that ended in a banking crisis is much smaller than the percentage of banking crises that took place after a lending boom. This finding is consistent with those of Tornell and Westermann (2002) and Barajas, Dell'Ariccia, and Levchenko (2009): few lending booms lead to a financial crisis. More specifically, we find that only 4 percent of lending booms may end in a full-blown banking crisis in non-LAC emerging markets, while 4.6 percent is the probability for industrial countries. Although still small, the

Figure 9.5 Unconditional Probability of Booms and Crises in a Sample of 79 Countries, 1970–2010

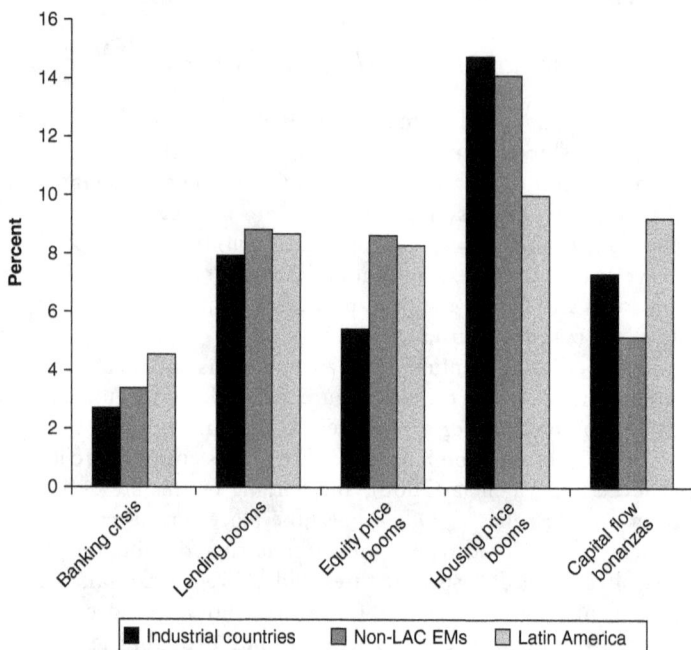

Note: This figure presents the frequency of banking crisis episodes in our sample of countries. We compute the unconditional probability of banking crisis as the number of years where as banking crisis takes place divided by the number of years in the entire sample of the country. Banking crisis episodes are identified as in Leaven and Valencia (2008). An analogous calculation is made for the frequency of lending booms, equity price and housing price booms, and capital flow bonanzas. Following Claessens et al. (2011a, b), we define these financial booms as the top quartile of of the upturn in credit, stock price, housing price, and gross capital inflow in our world sample.

conditional probability of a banking crisis almost doubles for LAC countries (8.3 percent). As argued by Tornell and Westermann (2002), excessive risk taking and cronyism characterize only a small share of lending booms.[17]

The evidence presented in table 9.3 suggests, in general, that a small share of credit booms or asset price booms will lead to a banking crisis. This implies that most financial booms may have a soft landing. Interestingly, the frequency with which financial booms end in a banking crisis is higher in LAC than in industrial countries or non-LAC EMs. For instance, the probability of a crisis in $(t, t+2)$ given that an equity price boom took place in period t is 4.2 percent for industrial countries and non-LAC EMs, but it is 14 percent for LAC countries. If a surge in the leverage ratio occurs in period t, the conditional probability of a crisis more than doubles in LAC (7.8 percent) relative to industrial countries (3.1 percent). However, it shows that banking crises are more likely to be preceded by financial booms in LAC than elsewhere. Nearly half of banking crisis episodes in LAC are preceded by lending booms, equity booms, housing price booms, strong currency appreciation, or capital flow bonanzas. Finally, more than one-third of banking crises are preceded by surges in the leverage ratio.

Panel B of table 9.3 examines whether there is an order of precedence among financial booms by computing the conditional probability of a financial boom. It indeed shows that most booms in asset prices or capital flow bonanzas may not end or come along with a lending boom. For instance, the probability of a lending boom in $(t, t+2)$ given that an equity price boom took place in t is approximately 8 percent for non-LAC EMs and 14 percent for LAC countries. However, lending booms are often preceded by other financial booms. One-third of lending booms were preceded by equity price booms for non-LAC EMs, and that frequency almost doubles for LAC countries. In addition, more than half of lending booms follow a capital flow bonanza in LAC, while that share is only a third for industrial countries and non-LAC EMs.

This notion of precedence of asset price booms and capital flow bonanzas is corroborated in figures 9.6 and 9.7, when we depict the dynamic behavior of asset prices and capital flows around peaks in real credit per capita. Figure 9.6 compares regular credit downturn episodes and crisis-related downturns, while figure 9.7 shows the behavior during the current cycle in comparison with previous ones. In most cases, we find that peaks in stock prices and housing prices tend to precede peaks in credit—especially during times of crisis or in the current credit cycle. Capital flow bonanzas clearly precede credit cycles for LAC and non-LAC emerging market economies (and this pattern of behavior is more notorious during the current cycle), while peaks in real exchange rates (that is, strong currency appreciations) tend to precede credit downturns more clearly in LAC during crisis times and in industrial and non-LAC EMs during the current cycle.

The Likelihood of Crisis and the Size of the Financial Boom: Probit Analysis So far, we have found that most lending booms have a soft landing and that banking crises are typically preceded by financial booms. We also find evidence that few asset price booms and capital flow bonanzas end in a lending boom, even though lending booms are often preceded by these other kinds of booms. Next, we look at whether the duration and amplitude of upswings in credit can help predict the likelihood of a banking crisis. To accomplish this task, we run probit models in which the dependent variable is a binary indicator that takes the value of 1 when there is a peak in credit that ends up in a crisis within a two-year period and 0 otherwise.[18]

Table 9.3 Conditional Probability: Financial Booms and Crises in a Sample of 79 Countries, 1970–2010 (percent)

Probabilities	Median amplitude (%)		
	Industrial countries	Non-LAC emerging markets	Latin America
Financial booms and crisis			
Prob [banking crisis (t)/lending boom (t–2, t–1, t)][a]	4.60%	3.96%	8.26%
Prob [lending boom/banking crisis (t–1, t)][b]	35.00%	36.00%	45.45%
Prob [banking crisis (t)/equity price boom (t–2, t–1, t)][a]	4.24%	4.23%	13.73%
Prob [equity price boom/banking crisis (t–1, t)][b]	23.81%	31.25%	55.56%
Prob [banking crisis (t)/housing price boom (t–2, t–1, t)][a]	4.55%	6.32%	10.00%
Prob [housing price boom/banking crisis (t–1, t)][b]	5.26%	60.00%	50.00%
Prob [banking crisis (t)/capital flow bonanza (t–2, t–1, t)][a]	7.85%	6.82%	8.64%
Prob [capital flow bonanza/banking crisis (t–1, t)][b]	68.18%	56.25%	53.85%
Prob [banking crisis (t)/leverage surge (t–2, t–1, t)][a]	3.13%	4.66%	7.76%
Prob [leverage surge/banking crisis (t–1, t)][b]	33.33%	39.13%	36.00%
Prob [banking crisis (t)/strong RER appreciation (t–2, t–1, t)][a]	2.84%	5.61%	7.33%
Prob [strong RER appreciation/banking crisis (t–1, t)][b]	33.33%	40.74%	42.31%

Table 9.3 Conditional Probability: Financial Booms and Crises in a Sample of 79 Countries, 1970–2010 (continued)

(percent)

Probabilities	Median amplitude (%)		
	Industrial countries	Non-LAC emerging markets	Latin America
Lending booms and other financial booms			
Prob [lending boom (t)/equity price boom (t−2, t−1, t)][c]	12.73%	8.15%	14.29%
Prob [equity price boom/lending boom(t−1, t)][d]	31.58%	33.33%	62.50%
Prob [lending boom (t)/housing price boom (t−2, t−1, t)][c]	10.00%	9.57%	11.11%
Prob [housing price boom/lending boom (t−1, t)][d]	25.64%	42.86%	33.33%
Prob [lending boom (t)/capital flow bonanza (t−2, t−1, t)][c]	13.91%	12.60%	7.14%
Prob [capital flow bonanza/lending boom (t−1, t)][d]	33.33%	35.29%	55.56%

Note: GDP = gross domestic product; RER = Real Exchange Rate. a. The table reports the frequency of booms in credit, asset prices, or capital flows occurring in t, t−1, or t−2 that end up in a banking crisis in period t. b. It is also computed the probability of financial booms have taken place within the same year or the year before a banking crisis occurred. c. We compute the frequency of asset price boom, or capital flow bonanza occurring in t−2, t−1, or t that end up in a lending boom in period t. d. We report the frequency of asset price booms or capital flow bonanzas that have taken place within the same year or the year before a lending boom took place. Finally, we should note that booms and bonanzas are defined as cyclical components of the corresponding financial variables exceeding 1.75 times their standard deviation. Banking crises are defined as in Laeven and Valencia (2008).

Figure 9.6 Behavior of Asset Prices around Peaks in Real
Credit during Tranquil and Turmoil Periods, 1970–2010

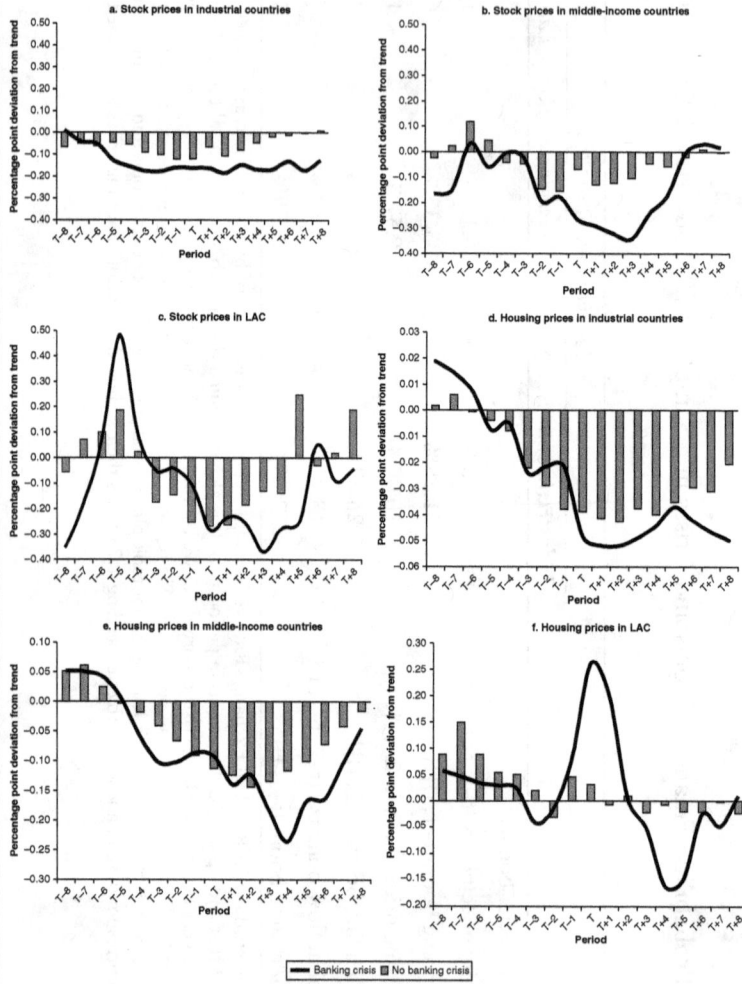

a. Stock prices in industrial countries

b. Stock prices in middle-income countries

c. Stock prices in LAC

d. Housing prices in industrial countries

e. Housing prices in middle-income countries

f. Housing prices in LAC

— Banking crisis ▣ No banking crisis

(continued next page)

Figure 9.6 (continued)

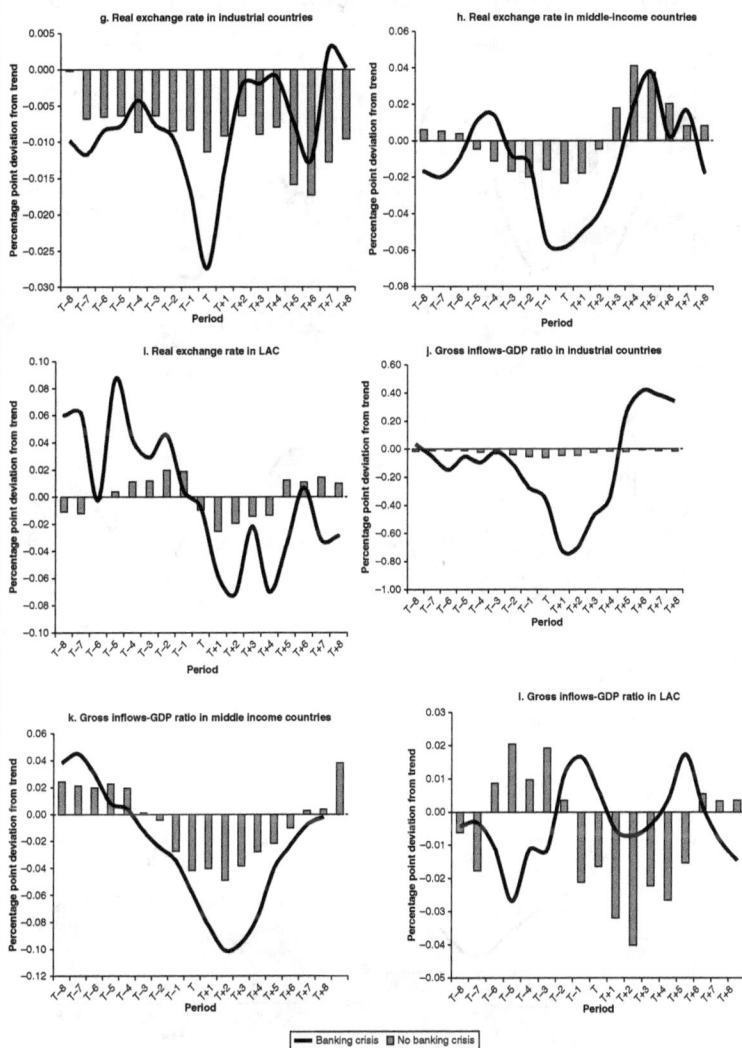

Note: This figure depicts the year-on-year growth rate (or variation) in asset prices and capital flow around 17-quarter windows centered on peaks in real credit per capita (T). The period T when the peak in real credit per capita takes place is identified using the Bry-Boschan quarterly algorithm (Harding and Pagan 2002a). Note that figures distinguish peak in real credit per capita associted with episodes of banking crises (as defined in Laeven and Valencia 2008). GDP = gross domestic product; LAC = Latin America and the Caribbean.

Figure 9.7 Behavior of Asset Prices around Peaks in Real Credit in the Current vis-à-vis Previous Cycles, 1970–2010

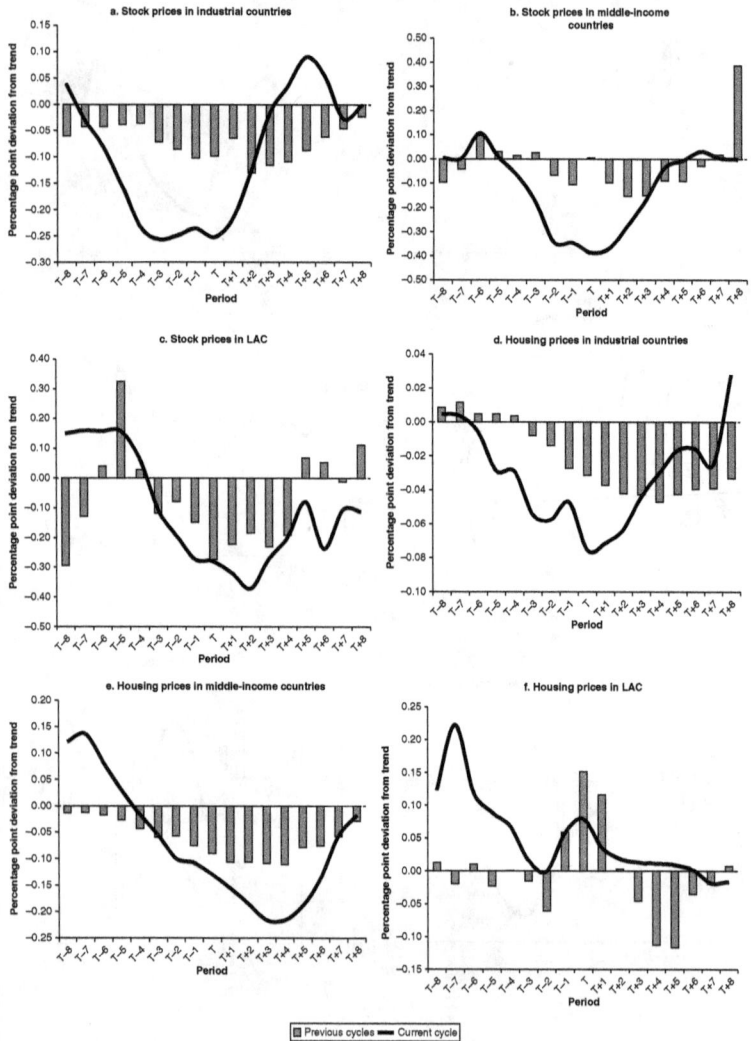

(continued next page)

Figure 9.7 (continued)

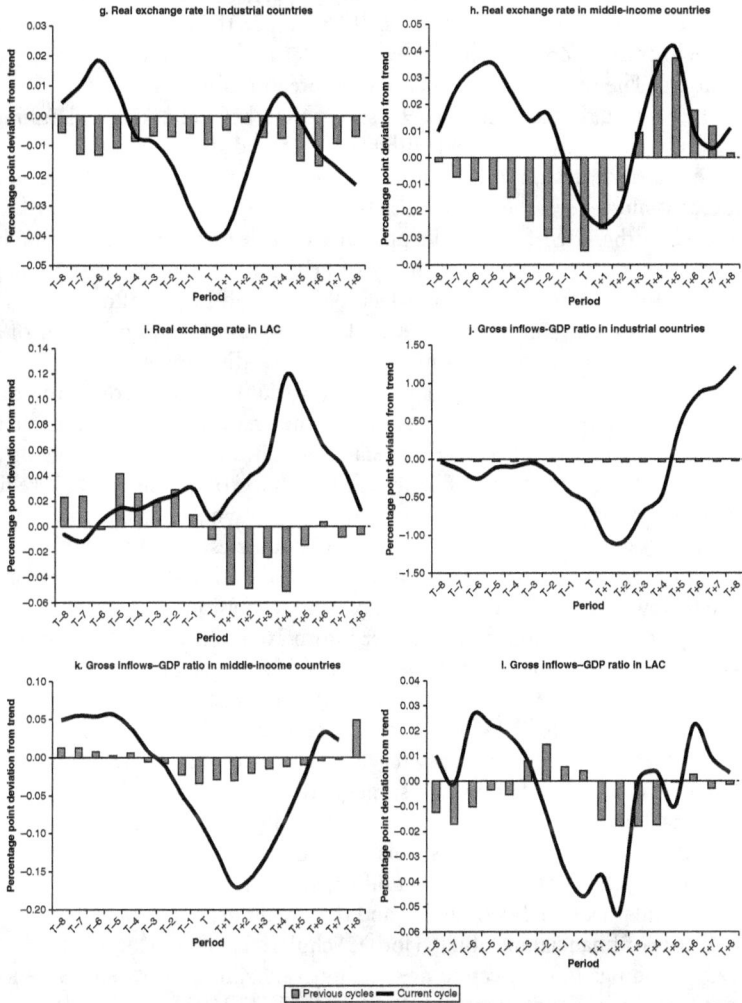

g. Real exchange rate in industrial countries

h. Real exchange rate in middle-income countries

i. Real exchange rate in LAC

j. Gross inflows–GDP ratio in industrial countries

k. Gross inflows–GDP ratio in middle-income countries

l. Gross inflows–GDP ratio in LAC

Previous cycles ▬ Current cycle

Note: This figure depicts the year-on-year growth rate (or variation) in asset prices and capital flows around 17-quarter windows centered on peaks in real credit per capita (T). The period T when the peak in real credit per capita takes place is identified using the Bry-Boschan quarterly algorithm (Harding and Pagan 2002a). Note that figures depict the evolution of the year-on-year growth in asset price capital flows in the current cycle (2006–10) vis-à-vis the average of previous cycles. GDP = gross domestic product; LAC = Latin America and the Caribbean.

Our variables of interest are the duration and amplitude of the preceding upturn in credit. In addition, we control for three specific conditions: (a) the presence of credit upturns with equity price booms, housing price booms, and capital flow bonanzas; (b) whether the downturn in credit is synchronized across countries worldwide; and (c) a dummy for LAC countries. The regression results are presented in table 9.4.

The evidence depicted in table 9.4 shows that the likelihood of a banking crisis is significantly associated with the length and size of credit upswings. A one-quarter increase in the duration of a credit upswing would lead to a 3 percent increase in the probability of a banking crisis, while a 1 percent increase in the size of the credit upturn would lead to an approximately 1 percent increase in the probability of crisis. This result is qualitatively similar to the findings of Barajas, Dell'Ariccia, and Levchenko (2009), in which the size and duration of the credit upturn are a good predictor of a crisis that follows a credit boom (that is, *bad* credit booms).

We should also note that the dummy variables that account for the presence of other financial booms during the credit upturns do not seem to affect the likelihood of a crisis-related credit downturn—except for a strong capital flow bonanza. Finally, the likelihood of a crisis-related credit downturn is higher when credit contractions are synchronized worldwide (as in the current credit cycle) or in LAC countries (vis-à-vis the rest of the sample). Taking this dimension into consideration drives the "strong capital flow bonanza" dummy out from the regression.

Table 9.5, in addition, tests whether information on credit booms as well as other financial booms (say, stock prices, real exchange rates, capital flows, or surges in leverage) helps signal an increasing risk of a banking crisis. Besides the amplitude of the upturn in credit preceding a banking crisis, we included the size of the upswing in asset prices (stock prices and real exchange rates), capital flows, and surges in the leverage ratio.[19] Our findings show that the amplitude in credit upturns is still a good predictor of crisis-related credit downturns. This is consistent with the findings in the literature that credit cycles contain significant information on the probability of future crisis (Schularick and Taylor 2009) and that credit growth is one of the best predictors of financial instability (Jorda, Schularick, and Taylor 2011).

Our findings in this section are qualitatively similar to recent evidence from Gourinchas and Obstfeld (2012) and IMF (2010a). Both studies find that financial crisis episodes are typically preceded by a significant buildup of domestic leverage (that is, an increasing ratio of domestic credit to output).[20] Moreover, Gourinchas and Obstfeld (2012) show that mounting leverage in industrial countries raised the likelihood of a financial crisis; more specifically, they find that the predicted (out-of-sample) probability of a financial crisis surged from 8 percent in 2003 to 72 percent in 2009. However, reflecting the buildup of buffers and sound macroeconomic policies in the run-up to the crisis, the same probability increased only from 1.8 percent in 2003 to 4.8 percent in 2009 for emerging markets.

Table 9.4 Probit Analysis: Main Features of the Credit Cycle and Probability of a Crisis in a Sample of 79 Countries, 1970–2010

	[1]	[2]	[3]	[4]	[5]	[6]
Features of trough-to-peak cyclical phase in credit						
Amplitude of credit upturns	1.0453**	0.8610*	0.9006*	1.0210*	0.9533*	1.0591**
	(0.507)	(0.527)	(0.528)	(0.535)	(0.529)	(0.530)
Duration of credit upturns	0.0383*	0.0395*	0.0382*	0.0387*	0.0353*	0.0229
	(0.020)	(0.020)	(0.022)	(0.022)	(0.021)	(0.022)
Credit upturns with						
Equity price booms	..	..	0.2986	0.2775	..	..
			(0.270)	(0.274)		
Housing price booms	..	..	−0.2874	−0.4146	..	..
			(0.616)	(0.635)		
Capital flow bonanzas	..	..	0.2586	0.1636	..	..
			(0.361)	(0.371)		
Strong equity price booms	..	..	..	..	0.1644	0.1620
					(0.430)	(0.430)
Strong housing price booms	..	..	..	..	0.6621	0.5823
					(0.822)	(0.870)
Strong capital flow bonanzas	..	..	..	..	0.8574**	0.6937
					(0.435)	(0.468)

(continued on next page)

Table 9.4 Probit Analysis: Main Features of the Credit Cycle and Probability of a Crisis in a Sample of 79 Countries, 1970–2010 (*continued*)

	[1]	[2]	[3]	[4]	[5]	[6]
Concordance in credit cycles						
Synchronized	..	..	..	0.3416*	..	..
				(0.203)		
Highly synchronized	..	..	..	..	..	0.6675**
						(0.285)
Regional factors						
Dummy: LAC	..	0.3296*	0.3471*	0.3610*	0.3950*	0.4136**
		(0.203)	(0.207)	(0.208)	(0.207)	(0.208)
Constant	-1.4295**	-1.5189**	-1.5760**	-1.7110**	-1.5887**	-1.6277**
	(0.151)	(0.163)	(0.172)	(0.193)	(0.170)	(0.173)
Observations	298	298	298	298	298	298
Log likelihood	-111.7	-110.5	-109.5	-108.1	-108.4	-105.7
Pseudo R^2**	0.0336	0.0448	0.0532	0.0654	0.0629	0.0855

Note: Numbers in parentheses represent robust standard errors. * (**) indicates that the coefficient is statistically significant at the 10 (5) percent level. LAC = Latin America and the Caribbean. We report the average duration of the different cyclical phases (downturns and upturns) for real and financial variables. The statistics for amplitude and slope refer to sample median across episodes (note that averages for those statistics are not reported but are available from the authors upon request). The duration of downturns (recessions or contractions) is the number of quarters between peak and trough. Upturns (or recoveries), however, are defined as the early stage of the expansion that takes place when either the real or the financial indicator rebounds from the trough to its previous peak. The amplitude of the downturn is the distance between the peak in real output and its subsequent trough while that of the upturn is computed as the four-quarter cumulative variation in real output following the trough. The slope of the downturn is the ratio of the peak-to-trough (trough-to-peak) phase of the cycle to its duration. GDP = gross domestic product; LAC = Latin America and the Caribbean; MIC = middle-income country.

Table 9.5 Probit Analysis: Size of Financial Booms and the Probability of a Crisis in a Sample of 79 Countries, 1970–2010

	Median slope (%)			
	[1]	[2]	[3]	[4]
Credit				
Real credit	1.1555**	1.3246	2.5876*	2.6228*
(amplitude of preceding upturn)	(0.518)	(1.027)	(1.364)	(1.405)
Capital flows				
Ratio of non-FDI inflows to GDP	..	–0.1269	–1.2177	–1.3084
(amplitude of preceding upturn)		(1.844)	(2.306)	(2.308)
Asset prices				
Real exchange rate	..	..	2.1246	2.2336
(amplitude of preceding upturn)			(2.208)	(2.291)
Stock prices (real)	..	..	0.1658	0.0984
(amplitude of preceding upturn)			(0.523)	(0.560)
Leverage				
Bank-deposit ratio	..	..	..	–0.3075
(Trough-to-peak amplitude)				(0.528)
Real effective exchange rate	–1.4536**	–1.3826**	–1.8141**	–1.7686**
	(0.163)	(0.256)	(0.345)	(0.366)
No. of observations	298	144	116	110
Gross capital inflows (ratio to GDP)	–108.4	–58.0	–38.3	–36.8
Pseudo R^2	0.0623	0.0581	0.2084	0.193

Note: Numbers in parentheses represent robust standard errors. * (**) indicates that the coefficient is statistically significant at the 10 (5) percent level. GDP = gross domestic product; FDI = foreign direct investment.

Macroprudential Policy and the Management of Financial Cycles

The preceding section shows that financial cycles exhibit a high degree of synchronization, both in financial variables (credit growth, asset prices, and leverage, for example) and in the real side of the economy. This synchronization reflects pervasive feedback effects across the financial system and between macroeconomic and financial variables. In the cyclical upswing, expanding credit puts upward pressure on asset prices and real activity, strengthening balance sheets and prompting further credit growth (Kiyotaki and Moore 1997; Adrian and Shin 2010; Bianchi and Mendoza 2011). Because the decisions of individual institutions ignore these feedback effects, the upswing is characterized by a socially excessive expansion of credit and leverage (Lorenzoni 2008; Jeanne and Korinek 2010). Credit, asset prices, and real activity all rise in a self-reinforcing loop, and lending standards weaken as credit is extended to marginal borrowers (Dell'Ariccia and Marquez 2006; Adrian and Shin 2010). These systemic fragilities created in the upswing deepen the downturn, in which feedback effects go in reverse and a vicious circle develops among deleveraging, asset sales, weakening loan portfolios, and deteriorating real activity.

In considering policies to manage systemic risk over the cycle, we need to keep in mind that the financial cycle itself reflects multiple factors. On the one hand, fundamentals are themselves procyclical: investment opportunities and credit demand rise in the upswing, while the riskiness of prospective borrowers declines. On the other hand, inadequate regulatory policies may accentuate the procyclical behavior of the financial system. Last, the cycle may also be amplified by externalities and spillovers across financial institutions as well as between the financial and real sides of the economy.

Ideally, policy should address the latter two sources of procyclicality, but not the first one. Nor should it seek to eliminate the financial cycle. Indeed, it is surely desirable to allow the financial system to respond to fluctuations in real fundamentals. Moreover, as described in the previous section, the evidence shows that most credit booms do not end in crashes— just about one in ten do.

Countercyclical Macroprudential Regulation: Some General Issues

The macroprudential perspective has motivated a number of proposed regulations whose primary aim is to manage risk along the financial cycle.[21] Most of those proposals involve adjusting regulatory instruments to the trends in risk over the cycle, essentially tightening regulation in the upswing and relaxing it in the downswing. This raises three major issues that affect virtually all proposals. First, should the adjustment be based on contingent rules or left to the regulator's discretion? Second, especially in the rules-based case, what cyclical variable(s) should govern the adjustment—that is, what indicators should trigger tightening or loosening of regulation over the cycle? Third, should the trigger be aggregate or institution specific?

None of these questions has been satisfactorily answered to date. Regarding the choice between rules and discretion, the limited experience with most proposals of countercyclical regulation, and the fact that many of them remain untested, suggests the need for wide regulator discretion.

However, countercyclical regulation faces big political-economy obstacles, which may be especially hard to overcome when it is left to discretionary decisions by the regulator. In the boom, when tighter regulation would be most needed, it will face strong opposition from both lenders and borrowers and even from policy makers, who credit the prosperity to their policy choices, leading to too little and too late action on the part of the regulator. In this regard, it is important to recall that countercyclical regulatory changes would have been possible in many countries in the run-up to the global financial crisis; yet very few made use of them. Instead, some degree of "set it and forget it" regulation, based on well-defined rules rather than on discretion—as well as regulator independence from government—is likely to help deflect pressure on the regulator.

In turn, macroprudential regulation over the cycle should be guided, at least in theory, by the trends in financial (in)stability. But the latter is a multidimensional concept and therefore difficult to measure and monitor, in contrast, for example, to monetary policy, whose objective—price stability—can be represented by a summary index. Ideally, regulatory tightness should vary according to some summary indicator(s) that provide a timely signal of the buildup of financial imbalances—in the dual sense that the signal should become available quickly and should offer an early indication of cyclical turning points, particularly at the beginning of the downturn.

A variety of options have been suggested for this purpose—from real variables such as GDP growth to financial variables like the rate of growth of credit, the credit-to-GDP ratio, and asset prices—with housing as the prime candidate.[22] As shown in the previous section, they all show a considerable degree of comovement over the cycle but differ in other respects. For example, information on GDP growth becomes available only with considerable lags. Also, the evidence in the previous section suggests that the rate of growth of real credit leads real GDP at cyclical turning points. Of course, adjusting regulation over the cycle according to a variety of financial and real variables should allow a more nuanced perspective and yield better outcomes than if the policy adjustment is conditioned on a single indicator, which by necessity must provide a very rough proxy for the cyclical changes in system risk. However, this approach would be hard to implement in a rules-based framework: it would be virtually impossible to design simple and transparent rules that condition regulation over the cycle to the evolution of a multiplicity of real and financial indicators.

A further issue of particular relevance to emerging countries concerns the distinction between trend and cycle. Sustained increases in the rate of real credit growth, or the ratio of credit to GDP, might reflect advancing financial development rather than signaling a cyclical boom. Mechanically gearing regulatory stance to changes in these variables could have the unintended result of retarding financial deepening. While in theory empirical methods exist to distinguish trend and cycle, they are all based on past information, and estimated trends can change substantially as new observations are added to the sample. By implication, a good deal of judgment on the part of the regulator is likely to be necessary when using financial aggregates to capture cyclical variations in risk.

The third question is whether the changes in regulatory stance over the cycle should be top down or bottom up—that is, guided by systemwide or by institution-specific indicators. Both alternatives have been defended in the literature,[23] and—as described below—both have been applied in practice. At first sight, aggregate triggers would seem more in line with the stated objective of countercyclical macroprudential regulation, namely, the management of systemwide risk. However, they might also encourage risky behavior to the extent that institutions perceive that their individual decisions have no effect on the aggregate indicator triggering regulatory tightening for the system as a whole. Indeed, conditioning regulatory stance on institution-specific indicators of risk buildup is conceptually the right approach, given that the need for intervention arises from the externalities that individual institutions impose on the system. It has the advantage of better aligning private and social incentives by enforcing tighter conditions on those institutions that contribute more to the accumulation of aggregate risk.

Implementing Countercyclical Macroprudential Regulation

A wide variety of proposals for countercyclical macroprudential regulation have been advanced in the academic and policy literature. Some have seen no actual use so far, but a number of schemes have been implemented in emerging markets in recent years, as illustrated in table 9.6.[24] These schemes can be categorized along different dimensions—for example, according to their design, that is, price versus quantity based, discretionary versus rules based, and so forth. Here we classify them into two broad categories according to their main objective: proposals whose primary objective is to build buffers in the upswing for use in the downswing and proposals that seek to contain risk taking during the expansion.

Of course, the distinction is somewhat arbitrary. Indeed, prudential charges or taxes on risk taking whose proceeds are used to create buffers may achieve both objectives at the same time; likewise, schemes for accumulation of buffers can (and arguably should) be designed so as to discourage risk taking by raising its cost to financial institutions. And successful implementation of proposals of either kind might result in an attenuation of the financial cycle, even if this may not be their primary objective. In practice, however, measures deployed by regulators have typically aimed (and enjoyed greater success) at one of these objectives rather than the other.

The key feature of buffers is that they need to become available to financial institutions in the downturn, when their lending portfolio and profitability deteriorate. Fixed "minimum requirements" (on capital,

Table 9.6 Some Experiences with Countercyclical Use of Macroprudential Tools in Emerging Markets

Measure	Non-LAC countries	LAC countries
Temporary adjustments to risk weights	Croatia, India, Malaysia, Turkey	
Countercyclical provisioning	China, India	Bolivia, Colombia, Peru, Uruguay
Caps on LTV ratios for property lending	China; Hong Kong SAR, China; Korea, Rep.; Malaysia; Singapore; Thailand; Turkey	
Caps on ratios of debt service to income for household lending	China; Hong Kong SAR, China; Korea, Rep.; Malaysia; Thailand	
Liquidity requirements on credit expansion	Croatia, Estonia	
Caps on lending	China, Indonesia, Korea, Rep.	
Taxes on lending	Turkey	
Reserve requirements	Multiple	Brazil, Colombia, Peru

Source: BIS 2010; Moreno 2011.
Note: LAC = Latin America and the Caribbean; LTV = loan to value; GDP = gross domestic product; SAR = special administrative region. Empty cells indicate no reported LAC experiences with the tools in question.

loan-loss provisions, and so on), however high, are not helpful in this regard, since they are out of reach for the institutions involved and remain at the exclusive disposal of the regulator (see, for example, Goodhart 2010b; Hellwig 2010). Conceptually, the ability to draw from buffers built in the upswing tends to weaken the fire sale and credit crunch externalities in the downswing by reducing the need for institutions to sell assets and restrict lending to meet regulatory requirements.

The two concrete proposals for buffers that have gained broadest support (Brunnermeier et al. 2009; Hanson, Kashyap, and Stein 2011) involve countercyclical variation of capital requirements and loan-loss provisions, scaling them up or down according to cyclical conditions.

Countercyclical Capital Buffers Countercyclical capital buffers have been advocated in both the academic and the policy literatures (Hanson, Kashyap, and Stein 2011; Shleifer and Vishny 2010, Brunnermeier et al. 2009; Goodhart 2011). Yet they have seen no actual use so far, and the closest experience is provided by a few cases of discretionary changes in risk weights introduced in some emerging economies during episodes of rapid growth of aggregate credit or when the growth of specific types of credit (such as housing) was deemed excessive.

Much of the appeal of countercyclical capital buffers is due to the perceived need to offset the procyclical effect of risk-weighted minimum capital requirements, as originally adopted under Basel II and recently reformulated under Basel III: capital needs decline in the boom, owing to the decline in measured risks and the improvement in borrowers' risk ratings, and rise in the slump (Gordy and Howells 2006; Repullo and Suárez 2009). This has the unintended effect of increasing the pressure for deleveraging in the downturn, to an extent that appears substantial according to available empirical estimates (Repullo, Saurina, and Trucharte 2010).

Different options have been offered to mitigate this regulation-induced procyclicality. Some involve cyclical adjustment of loan-level risk estimates, while others advocate rescaling of aggregate capital requirements on the basis of a suitable indicator of the real or financial cycle (Gordy and Howells 2006; Saurina 2011).[25] Instead, the option recently endorsed by the Basel Committee involves the separate creation of a new "countercyclical capital buffer," leaving untouched the procyclical bias built into conventional risk-weighted capital requirements (BCBS 2010). For the most part, the specifics of the new buffer are left to national regulators, although with the recommendation that the accumulation or release of the countercyclical buffer be geared to the ratio of credit to GDP (after suitable detrending).[26]

At present, there is limited analytical research, and no actual experience, on the design and effectiveness of countercyclical capital requirements. It is not clear how large the buffers would have to be to substantially contain deleveraging in the downturn, and it remains to be seen whether the 2.5 percent of assets recommended by the Basel Committee (see BCBS 2010) would be adequate for this purpose. Likewise, little is known about the likely contribution of countercyclical capital requirements to dampening aggregate volatility. A recent study by Angelini et al. (2011) simulates the effects of a Basel III–style countercyclical capital scheme on aggregate volatility in a variety of models. The main finding is that GDP volatility falls considerably, by as much as 20 percent relative to the no-buffer scenario, but much work remains to be done to assess the robustness of these results.

Dynamic Provisions Countercyclical provisioning has seen actual use in several countries, notably Spain, and more recently in Latin America and Asia. Like with countercyclical capital requirements, the objective is to build up buffers in the upswing so that they can be deployed when the performance of loan portfolios deteriorates in the downswing. The main difference is that provisions have been traditionally seen as buffers against risks that have already been recognized, while capital is intended as a buffer against risks that have not been recognized. In reality, however, the conceptual distinction gets blurred when capital requirements are linked to risk-weighted assets and hence to risks that have been partly recognized, as is the case under the Basel II system (Hellwig 2010).

The logic underlying the so-called dynamic provisions is that credit risk is incurred during expansions, when credit portfolios are being built up, even though the expected losses the provisions intend to cover have not yet been identified in *specific* loans. Of course, the introduction of dynamic provisioning requirements, in addition to traditional specific provisions, gives incentives for banks to extend loans more carefully in the upswing and also limits the growth in bank profits and capital, all of which may restrain credit expansion—at least for given bank leverage ratios. However, the primary purpose of dynamic provisioning is not to prevent credit booms per se, a task that might require prohibitively high provisioning rates.

There is considerable variation in the design and features of the dynamic provisioning systems adopted in different countries. Spain's system—the oldest one—was introduced in 2000 and modified in 2005. It defined a rules-based dynamic provision, additional to standard loan-loss provisions, calculated on the basis of each individual institution's rate of credit growth, following a parametric specification (defined by the regulator) calibrated to loan portfolio performance over past cycles. The rule implicitly allows substitution between dynamic and traditional specific provisions to ensure an overall level of provisions commensurate with risks averaged over the cycle. Dynamic provisions are separately disclosed in banks' financial statements, so that the latter accurately reflect both the income generated and the risks taken by banks.

The actual operation of the Spanish system is described in detail by Saurina (2011). Credit boomed in Spain between 2004 and the first half of 2007, while the economy's fast growth kept nonperforming loans at very low levels. By the second half of 2007, however, real growth and credit expansion began a sharp slowdown, and nonperforming loans quickly climbed (figure 9.8).

As the boom developed, banks built up the stock of dynamic provisions at a rapid pace, while conventional provisions grew little due to the good performance of credit portfolios. At the end of 2007 with the onset of the crisis, total loan provisions were around 1.3 percent of total assets. Dynamic provisions accounted for the bulk of this amount—over 1 percent of assets, or 80 percent of total provisions (figure 9.9).[27] The sharp deterioration in portfolio performance that followed led to a rapid rise in conventional provisions, but much of it was offset by a decline in the stock of dynamic provisions as banks made use of the buffer accumulated in the preceding years. As a result, while the stock of conventional provisions increased more than fivefold relative to total loans by June 2010, the overall stock of provisions rose by just 50 percent.

The dynamic provisioning scheme had a significant impact on banks' income account. During the boom, it absorbed around 15 percent of their net operating income—which helps explain banks' less-than-enthusiastic

Figure 9.8 Lending Cycle and Nonperforming Loans in Spain, 2000–10

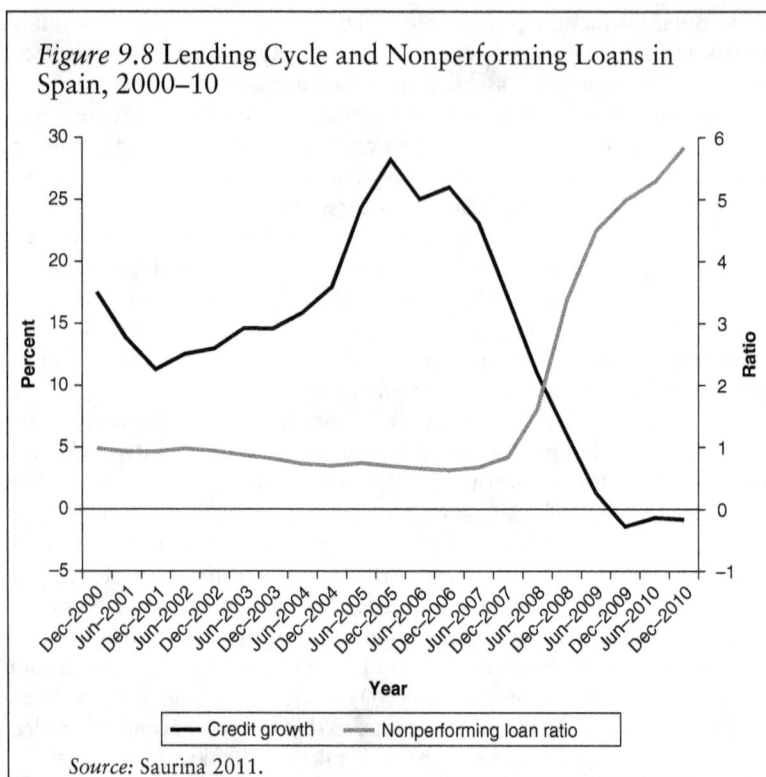

Source: Saurina 2011.

support for the system at the time. But in the downturn, the release of the accumulated buffers—which amounted to almost 25 percent of banks' core capital—supported banks' income to an even greater extent, thus limiting the erosion of their capital as nonperforming loans escalated (figure 9.10).

In retrospect, Spain's countercyclical provisioning scheme was not enough to tame the lending cycle or to prevent the boom in real estate prices. However, it is impossible to establish the counterfactual, and it can be argued that had the scheme been absent, the credit boom and the real estate bubble might have been even bigger. Furthermore, the stock of dynamic provisions accumulated in the boom will likely prove insufficient to cover all the nonperforming assets revealed by the crash. Still, most observers agree that the scheme succeeded in helping Spanish banks weather the downturn better and enhanced their resilience in the crisis.[28]

Apart from Spain, countercyclical provisioning schemes have also been employed in emerging markets in recent years. In China and India, for example, the authorities have resorted to discretionary increases in provisioning requirements in the context of rapid credit growth. But the phenomenon has been especially widespread in Latin America, where

Figure 9.9 Ratio of Banks' Cumulative Provisions to Total Loans in Spain, 2000–10

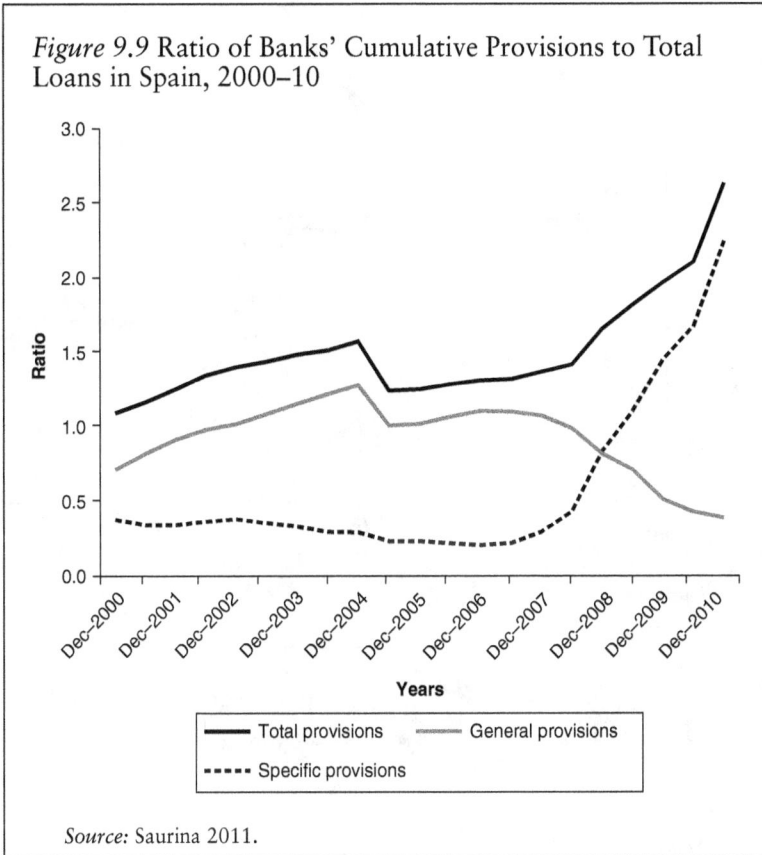

Source: Saurina 2011.

Bolivia, Colombia, Peru, and Uruguay have implemented different systems of dynamic provisioning. Only Uruguay's provisioning, established in 2001, has been in operation for a significant length of time. The systems vary considerably in design.[29] The Uruguayan system is broadly modeled after Spain's. The two main differences are that Uruguay's scheme allows substitution between dynamic provisions and realized loan losses (rather than specific provisions in the Spanish case) and lacks an additional provisioning requirement for the expected losses of new loans that is included in the Spanish system (see Wezel 2010).

The Peruvian system is based on GDP growth: cyclical provisioning is activated when GDP growth exceeds a certain threshold. This triggers an additional "generic" provisioning requirement. At times of growth deceleration, the requirement is deactivated, and banks can use the accumulated stock of additional generic provisions to offset increases in specific provisions.

Figure 9.10 Flow of Dynamic Provisions over Banks' Net Operating Income, 2001–10

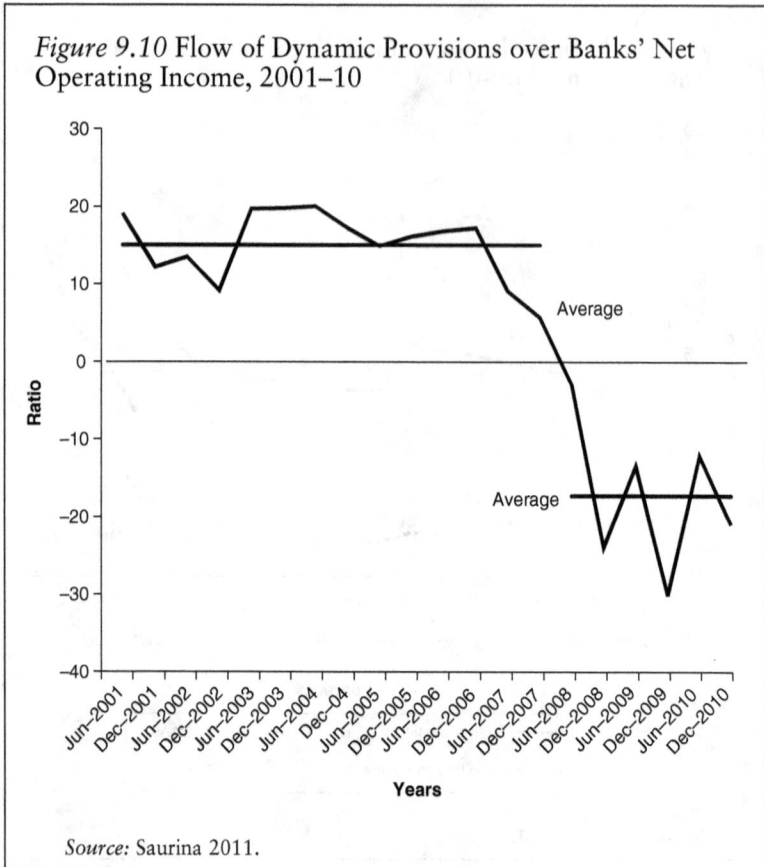

Source: Saurina 2011.

The Colombian system was introduced in 2007 and modified in 2010. Initially, the system relied on a two-scenario setting, with the countercyclical provisioning requirement operative in the "good scenario" and its amount determined by the authorities according to prespecified loan default probabilities. The provisions, however, were attached to individual loans, thus offering coverage for a potential deterioration in the performance of the loan in question—and only for that one loan. In the "bad" scenario, which became the prevailing one at the authorities' discretion, the entire stock of countercyclical provisions became available to all banks, regardless of the health of their portfolios. After the 2010 reform, the accumulation and release of the provisions have been linked to bank-specific portfolio performance—including the rate of expansion of their loans. The amounts to be accumulated or released are still defined by prespecified default probabilities, and the provisions remain attached to individual loans.

Finally, in Bolivia the cyclical provision *(previsión cíclica)* was established in 2009. It is accumulated at rates specified by the regulator, which vary across loan categories. Release of the buffer is linked to institution-specific portfolio performance but also requires authorization from the supervisor, which in turn may be dependent on macroeconomic developments.

Comparisons among these systems as well as with Spain's reveal some important differences and highlight the uncertainties that surround the proper design of anticyclical provisioning schemes. After the reform of Colombia's system, all the schemes are, to varying extents, rules-based but differ in many respects. The accumulation of buffers is linked to institution-specific credit growth in Uruguay (the same as in Spain), to their portfolio performance in Bolivia and Colombia, and to aggregate GDP growth in Peru.[30] Another relevant dimension is the choice between gradual and on-off schemes. For example, the Uruguayan system fits the former type, while Peru's fits the latter. A gradual system is likely to result in less abrupt fluctuations in financial conditions than an on-off system.

Counterfactual simulation of these various schemes can help clarify their differences and similarities. Wezel (2010), for example, reports on simulations of the different systems using Uruguay's loan data. In the results, two facts separate the Spanish system from the rest. First, only the Spanish formula yields a substantial correlation between total provisioning flows and aggregate credit growth. This seems a desirable feature to the extent that fast credit expansion signals future credit distress, as suggested by the empirical results in the previous section. Second, only the Spanish system features a relatively stable ratio of total provisions to credit over the cycle. The reason is the strong substitution between dynamic and specific provisions built into the Spanish model. While this feature may seem appealing, its desirability is not obvious on conceptual grounds. This underscores the fact that there really is no clear metric, nor is there sufficient international experience, for assessing the relative merits of different schemes of countercyclical provisioning.

In summary, there seems to be a consensus, especially in light of the evidence from Spain, that countercyclical provisioning arrangements can allow banks to enter the downswing in more robust shape than they would otherwise. However, the Spanish experience (as well as that of Uruguay, as argued by Wezel 2010), also shows that the burden on banks' profitability in tranquil times can be considerable. It is much less clear, however, if such arrangements have a major effect on the credit cycle, and their ability to shelter the financial system from large adverse shocks appears limited.[31]

Containing the Buildup of Risk Countercyclical buffers seek to self-insure the financial system against the buildup of systemic risk through the accumulation of precautionary balances. Another option is to try to contain the risk buildup itself—what is known as "self-protection" in the parlance of insurance theory (Ehrlich and Becker 1972). As already argued, aggregate risk is created in the boom, when credit grows rapidly, when financial institutions raise their leverage, and when their maturity mismatches widen through increased reliance on short-term borrowing to fund the expansion of balance sheets—a strategy encouraged by the steepening of the yield curve that characterizes the upswing (Brunnermeier et al. 2009; Adrian and Shin 2010). Rapid credit growth leads to a disproportionate increase in lending to lower-quality borrowers, while rising leverage and maturity mismatches likewise add to systemic risk. Higher leverage requires a bigger balance sheet contraction in the face of asset impairment in the downswing, which exacerbates the fire-sale externality, while excessive reliance on uninsured short-term funding likewise amplifies and propagates panic-driven asset sales.[32]

To address these risk spillovers, various observers have proposed measures to constrain financial institutions' leverage and short-term financing. Some observers have suggested a maximum leverage ratio that can be adjusted downward at the discretion of the regulator in times of rapid credit growth (for example, Goodhart 2010a). Leverage limits have been recently imposed in Switzerland and are expected to be endorsed by the global regulatory community as part of Basel III, but there is otherwise little experience with their use.

Different schemes have also been suggested to penalize maturity mismatches in intermediaries' balance sheets (Brunnermeier et al. 2009). These seek to remedy what from the point of view of systemic risk is a major omission in conventional regulation: if two institutions hold the same assets, but one is funded with long-term debt and the other by overnight borrowing, the contribution of the latter to systemic risk is much bigger than that of the former. However, regulation concerned with capital and loss provision requirements makes no distinction between the two situations, which gives banks an incentive to fund assets short-term when the yield curve is upward sloping—as is typically the case in a boom.

Conceptually, liquidity regulations—like other regulations—can take the form of quantity constraints, such as liquidity requirements against short-term funding, or (Pigouvian) taxes. The relative merits of both options have been recently analyzed by Perotti and Suárez (2011). One potentially important consideration is that time-varying taxes are likely to help counter the procyclical bias embedded in fixed ratios, whose shadow price to the institution varies endogenously over time depending on the fluctuations in the cost of liquidity over the cycle—hence exerting little discipline in the upswing and hardening it in the downswing, exactly the opposite of the desired effect. However, there is little empirical experience with schemes of this kind.

The financial upswing typically involves increased recourse by banks to noncore liabilities (Shin and Shin 2011). These usually take the form of borrowing from other financial institutions or wholesale markets.

They are acquired in the boom as the growth of bank assets outstrips that of the domestic deposit base, forcing banks to resort to other sources of funding to sustain the expansion of credit. Noncore liabilities are generally more volatile than deposits, and therefore more susceptible to runs, as seen in the global crisis. Thus, their volume may be viewed as reflective of systemic risk. This suggests the possibility of regulatory measures—quotas or regulatory charges—to discourage their issuance. Suitably varied over the cycle, such measures could provide an effective tool for preventing the buildup of risk.

A more direct approach to containing risk taking is to target credit growth over the cycle. As shown in the previous section, the incidence of financial crises is significantly associated with the occurrence of big credit booms, as measured by their duration and, especially, by their amplitude. In practice, credit expansion has often been implicitly taken as a summary statistic of the buildup of financial imbalances, and regulators have intervened in a variety of ways to tame credit growth deemed "excessive." For example, some Eastern European countries have introduced liquidity requirements on credit expansion in the form of mandatory holdings of government or central bank debt at below-market rates, which amounts to an implicit tax on credit creation.

In recent years, emerging markets have frequently resorted to changes in banks' cash reserve ratios (CRRs) to moderate credit cycles (table 9.7). Remarkably, this discretionary use of the CRR—raising it, or expanding its base, at times of rapid credit growth and conversely when credit growth slows down—has included a number of economies that had embraced inflation-targeting monetary regimes such as Brazil, Colombia, and Peru in Latin America, as well as the Republic of Korea and Turkey.[33] Typically, reserve requirements were lowered during the financial crisis in an attempt to alleviate the effects of the global liquidity crunch; most countries subsequently raised them as market liquidity was gradually restored.

But in most cases it is not clear if this resort to countercyclical use of the CRR reflected macroprudential concerns or an attempt by the monetary authorities to defeat the "Impossible Trinity"—that is, to pursue independent monetary policy, along with exchange rate targets, in a context of open capital accounts (Montoro and Moreno 2011). As a tool of monetary policy, the CRR is widely seen as a blunt instrument, which in inflation-targeting monetary regimes has been superseded by policy rates.[34] In recent years, however, the use of the latter has posed difficult policy dilemmas. Booming capital inflows in the run-up to the global crisis, and again since 2009, made the monetary authorities in a number of emerging markets reluctant to raise policy rates to contain inflation, for fear of exacerbating the pressure of capital inflows on the exchange rate. They resorted instead to tightening cash reserve requirements in an attempt to rein in rapid growth of credit and domestic expenditure.

Table 9.7 Use of Reserve Requirements in Emerging Markets, 1980–2011

Country	Year	Measures
Brazil	2008	Reduced time deposits' reserve requirement by 2 pp (to 13%).
	2009	Reduced time deposits' reserve requirement by 2 pp (to 13%).
Bulgaria	2004	Tightened reserve requirements (including measures as a higher deposit base, minimum ratio, etc.).
		Introduced a marginal reserve requirement for credit growth.
China	2005	Increased mortgage rates by 0.2 pp.
	2003–2004, 2006–07	Gradually increased reserve requirements from 6% to 14.5%, in either 0.5% or 1% point steps.
	2009	Raised the reserve requirement of 150 basis points since 2009 Q3 (as of October 5, 2010).
	2010	Raised the reserve requirements by 50 basis points, effective February 25, the second such increase on November 10.
	Jan. 2011	Raised the level of reserves by 50 basis points. Chinese major banks will have to set aside 19% of their deposits and small and medium banks will have to keep 15.5% of their deposits as reserves.
Colombia	2007, 2008	Created marginal reserve requirements on savings, checking, and CD deposits, up to 27%, and introduced reserve requirements on capital inflows.
Croatia	2003	Introduced reserve requirements for credit growth over 20%; made investment in central bank bills against excessive credit growth compulsory.
	2004, 2005, 2006	Introduced a 24% reserve requirement on marginal foreign borrowing, which rose 3 times up to 55%.
	2006	Required 55% marginal reserve on issuance of securities; increased the reserve requirement rates for credit growth.

(continued next page)

Table 9.7 Use of Reserve Requirements in Emerging Markets, 1980–2011 *(continued)*

Country	Year	Measures
Estonia	2006	Increased reserve requirements from 13% to 15%; introduced reserve requirements for housing loans and for banks' liabilities to foreign banks.
Greece	1990–2000	Introduced required nonremunerated deposits in line with excess credit growth.
India	2004, 2006, 2007	Increased in cash reserve requirements from 4.5% to 5%, 5.5%, and 6%.
	2008	Raised banks' reserve requirement 25 basis points; cut banks' cash reserve requirement by 1.5 pp to ease a cash squeeze.
	2009	Raised the reserve requirement 100 basis points since 2009 Q3 (as of October 5, 2010).
	2010	Raised the cash reserve ratio from 5% to 5.75%.
Indonesia	2009	Raised the reserve requirement 300 basis points since 2009 Q3 (as of October 5, 2010).
	Nov. 2010	Raised the reserve requirement of commercial banks from 5% to 8%.
	Mar. 2011	Raised the reserve requirement on foreign-currency accounts from 1% to 5%. A further increase to 8% was scheduled for June 2011.
Korea, Rep.	2006	Increased reserve requirements from 5% to 7% for demand deposits, money market deposit accounts, and other nonsavings deposits; reduced the reserve requirement from 1% to 0% for long-term savings deposits.
Latvia	2004, 2005, 2006	Increased reserve requirements from 3% to 4% (2004), then to 6% and 8% (2005); inclusion in the reserve base of banks' short-term liabilities to foreign banks (2005), and liabilities with the maturity of over two years (2006).

(continued next page)

Table 9.7 Use of Reserve Requirements in Emerging Markets, 1980–2011 *(continued)*

Country	Year	Measures
Malaysia	May 2011	Increased the statutory reserve requirement from 2% to 3%, effective from May 16, 2011.
Peru	2007	Raised reserve requirements for local and foreign-currency deposits.
	Jan. 2011, Apr. 2011	Increased by 100 basis points the reserve requirement rates on domestic and foreign-currency deposits and the remunerated portion of reserve requirements (currently 9% of deposits); reduced the reserve requirement on external foreign exchange liabilities with maturities under two years (from 75% to 60%) but extended their application to credit channeled through offshore branches of domestic financial institutions.
Romania	2008	Reduced the local currency reserve requirements from 9% to 6% (first a 1.5 pp cut, then 1 pp and 0.5 pp); reduced the marginal foreign-currency deposit requirements from 49% to 35%, and finally to 30%.
	2004–06	Increased the reserve requirement for deposits in foreign currency from 25–30% to 35–40%, alongside a reduction in that local currency from 18% to 16%.
Taiwan, China	Jan. 2011	Raised the reserve requirement on local currency accounts held by nonresidents to 90% on balances exceeding the outstanding balance on December 30, 2010. Balances below end-2010 levels were subject to 25% reserve requirement. Required reserves for such accounts are no longer remunerated.

(continued next page)

Table 9.7 Use of Reserve Requirements in Emerging Markets, 1980–2011 *(continued)*

Country	Year	Measures
Thailand	2006	Raise the foreign-currency reserve requirement to 30% on (a) investments in debt securities transacted from December 18, 2006, onward; (b) foreign-currency borrowings transacted from December 19, 2006, onward; and (c) foreign currencies bought or exchanged against baht for purposes other than those exempted in (b).
Turkey	2009	Reduced the local currency reserve requirement from 6% to 5%.
	2010	Raised the foreign-currency reserve requirement from 10% (Sept. 2010) to 11%; increased the reserve requirement by 50 basis points to 6% (Nov. 2010).
	2011	Increased the reserve rate to 12% for immediate-access deposits and 10% for accounts with terms of up to one month (Jan. 2011); raised the reserve requirement for one-month deposits from 10% to 15% (Mar. 2011); raised the reserve requirement on deposits with maturities of less than six months by up to 5 pp (Apr. 2011).

Source: Authors' elaboration based of table 3 of Borio and Shim 2007; IMF 2010a, 15–16. IMF 2010c, 63–64; IMF 2011c, box 2.2; IMF 2011a, table 1.2; Asian Development Bank 2011, 186; Bank Negara Malaysia (http://www.bnm.gov.my); Bank of Thailand News (http://www2.bot.or.th/FIPCS/eng/PFIPCS_List.aspx). pp = percentage points; GDP = gross domestic product; Q = quarter.

How effective are CRR changes in influencing credit growth? The CRR is primarily a tax on deposits (or, more broadly, on reservable liabilities, which in some countries also include certificates of deposit and other items). Hence, the main effect of CRR increases is to discourage banks' deposit funding and to widen the loan-deposit interest rate differential. The consequences for banks' loan supply depend on the same conditions that shape the traditional lending channel of monetary policy, namely, the extent of banks' access to nonreservable sources of funding and their ability to substitute between lending and other assets. The bigger the scope for substitution along these two margins, the smaller is the effect of CRR changes on bank lending. If banks can easily raise nondeposit financing by, for example, issuing market debt or equity, borrowing from the central bank, or selling government bonds, the main effect of CRR changes is to alter the composition of bank financing without much consequence for their total volume of lending.[35] Whether this is the case depends primarily on the degree of development of financial markets. Broadly speaking, more developed financial markets make it easier for banks to issue other liabilities to finance their lending and thereby offset the increased cost of deposit financing following a CRR increase.

In particular, in an inflation-targeting regime, CRR changes may have little effect on the supply of bank credit if the monetary authority stands ready to supply whatever amounts of financing are demanded by the system at the going policy rate.[36] Still, central bank loans may not provide a good substitute for deposit financing if, as is usually the case, the maturity of central bank loans is shorter than that of bank deposits, and future monetary policy—and hence the cost or availability of central bank funds—is uncertain. In such conditions, substitution of central bank loans for deposits widens banks' maturity mismatch and their exposure to interest rate risk. Under standard value at risk (VaR)–based risk management, this can lead to a contraction in banks' loan supply.[37]

Overall, the conclusion is that financial frictions enhance the effect of CRR changes on banks' loan supply, even when policy rates are left unchanged.[38] However, the quantitative importance of this mechanism, as well as its implications for the cost and quality of lending, remains to be established.[39] Last, the contribution of CRR increases to containing financial cycles has to be weighed against the cost of financial disintermediation that follows from the higher burden of deposit taxation that CRR rises imply.

Specific Risks Actions aiming to contain specific types of risk—that is, those associated with particular economic sectors or financial instruments—have focused on two main areas: the housing sector and foreign exchange exposures. Concern with the housing sector is well justified by the fact that housing price cycles are closely synchronized with credit cycles and that in emerging markets housing booms precede the majority of financial crises, as shown in the empirical section of this chapter.[40] A variety of tools have been deployed in Asian emerging markets in recent years at times of rapidly growing property lending and housing prices. Among them, caps on loan-to-value ratios (LTVs) have seen considerable use. Limits on the ratio of debt service to income (DTI) have been likewise applied in several countries.

Loan-to-value ratios can be an important source of financial system procyclicality when the valuation of collateral follows a strong cyclical pattern—as is typically the case. As asset prices, especially housing, rise in the boom, a given LTV allows the extension of more credit in the upswing than in the downswing. Further credit expansion feeds back into additional asset price rises, and so on. In addition, the higher the LTV is, the bigger the marginal effect on credit creation of a given increase in collateral prices, and the effect is compounded if competition among lenders leads to procyclical variation of LTVs, as appears to be the case (Borio, Furfine, and Lowe 2001). A similar reasoning applies to DTIs, owing to the procyclical behavior of personal income.

LTV ceilings have been imposed in some countries, and repeatedly lowered in a few cases, to dampen these procyclical pressures.[41] DTI limits have analogously been tightened to contain lending to lower-quality borrowers. These adjustments have sometimes been accompanied by other ad hoc measures, such as increases in risk weights applied to property lending for the calculation of regulatory capital (a step taken, for example, in India in 2005), as well as by direct controls such as credit ceilings, actively employed in some countries (notably China) to restrict bank lending to housing.

In many cases, these adjustments have been only loosely related to quantitative indicators of risk, and in virtually all cases they have relied on judgment rather than on quantifiable relationships. On the whole, there is little systematic evidence on the extent to which they have been effective at restraining housing booms[42]—although there is some anecdotal evidence that such measures may have increased banks' resilience to falling property prices.

Currency risk is the other area that has attracted particular attention from regulators. Financial institutions' foreign-currency exposure represents an important source of aggregate risk, as shown by the experience of the emerging market crises of the 1990s and 2000s and, more recently, by the global financial crisis, especially in Eastern Europe. In these episodes, abrupt real depreciations had a devastating impact on the balance sheets of foreign-currency borrowers, including in most cases the financial system. In some instances, banks' currency mismatches had been hidden by the fact that their foreign-currency liabilities were matched on paper by foreign-currency lending to borrowers without foreign-currency assets or incomes, who in reality were unable to meet their debt obligations in the face of large real depreciations.

The rationale for macroprudential intervention in connection with currency risk arises for reasons analogous to those underlying the fire-sale and credit crunch externalities. As shown in the previous section, the real exchange rate appreciates in the boom, strengthening the balance sheets of institutions indebted in foreign currency and prompting them to expand their lending and thereby increase aggregate demand, which encourages further appreciation. In the downturn, the mechanism goes into reverse: real depreciation weakens balance sheets, forces sales of domestic assets and credit, and causes aggregate demand to contract, adding further to real depreciation. The role of this force in emerging market crises has been highlighted by numerous observers (Krugman 1999, for example).

Individual foreign-currency borrowers fail to internalize their contribution to these aggregate spillovers, and, as a result, they engage in socially excessive foreign-currency borrowing in good times, which causes excessive credit contraction in bad times. This calls for policy intervention in the form of Pigouvian taxes or, alternatively, quantitative limits on foreign-currency exposure (Korinek 2010). Following this logic, many emerging markets have imposed limits on financial institutions' foreign-currency exposure or have additional reserve requirements on their foreign exchange deposits; see Terrier et al. (2011) for details.

Increasing notice is also being taken of the "indirect" foreign-currency exposures of financial institutions that arise through the currency mismatches of their borrowers. Several countries impose higher capital or loan-loss provisioning requirements on foreign-currency loans than on domestic-currency loans, and some (Argentina, for example) even prohibit foreign-currency lending to borrowers without foreign-currency earnings or assets. In the same vein, many emerging-country governments, especially in Latin America, have shifted their sovereign borrowing away from foreign currency in recent years and hence have reduced their vulnerability to real exchange rate depreciation.

Finally, it is important to keep in mind that deployment of macroprudential regulatory tools is not devoid of costs. On the one hand, additional constraints or charges on lenders' financing choices necessarily lead to an increase in their cost of funding, which will be duly reflected in the terms of their lending—although the magnitude of this effect may be dampened if the regulation succeeds in reducing the fragility, and thus the perceived riskiness, of financial institutions (Hellwig 2010). On the other hand, the costs of macroprudential policy tend to be highly visible and to materialize immediately, while its benefits—in the form of reduced incidence of crises—may become evident only in the long run. Finally, the deployment of macroprudential tools will impose additional informational and capacity requirements on regulators. And the increased regulatory pressure in the boom will surely encourage migration of financial activity to less-regulated instruments, institutions, and jurisdictions, adding yet new complexities to regulators' task (Goodhart 2010a).

The Role of Macroeconomic Policies

While the global crisis put macroprudential regulation in the spotlight, too little is still known about the proper design of its tools, and the experience with their use is very limited. Systematic evidence is still lacking on the effectiveness of different tools in containing systemic risk and the costs that they may impose in doing so.

However, prudential tools are not the only ones available to policy makers for managing systemic risk. Macroeconomic policies also have a potentially important impact on the financial cycle and the buildup of aggregate risk. In the future, they may have to do more than in the past to support financial stability, especially in countries with relatively limited supervisory capacity and less-developed financial systems.

Monetary Policy and Financial Stability

The global crisis has revived interest in the powers of monetary policy to aid financial stability. What really matters from a macroprudential perspective is its effect on the growth of systemic risk. This has been the focus of a recent literature that underscores the key role of financial intermediaries' capital and risk management strategies in the transmission of monetary policy through what has been termed the "risk-taking channel," described by Adrian and Shin (2010).[43] Short-term policy rates are inversely related to the term premium and hence to the profitability of intermediaries engaged in maturity transformation. Lower policy rates boost forward-looking measures of their capital, augmenting their risk-taking capacity as dictated, for example, by standard VaR risk management strategies. Banks respond by expanding their lending, specifically by reducing hurdle rates, so that marginal loans that were not made earlier now become feasible with their increased risk-bearing capacity. In this way, monetary policy affects the rate of expansion of intermediaries' balance sheets, their leverage, the market price of risk, and the quality of their lending.

Empirical evidence offers support for this view. In particular, recent studies of the effect of monetary policy on the quality of bank credit confirm the notion that monetary loosening allows banks to relax lending standards and increase their risk taking; see in particular Jiménez et al. (2008) for the case of Spain; Ioannidou, Ongena, and Peydró (2009) for Bolivia; and Delis and Kouretas (2011) for the Euro Area. These studies find that lower policy rates encourage banks, especially those less capitalized, to expand credit to riskier firms and lend to new and riskier applicants in larger quantities and longer-term conditions. The implication is that timely monetary tightening might be effective not only in containing the cyclical expansion of credit but also in maintaining lending standards during the upswing, thereby limiting the eventual deterioration of banks' credit portfolio during the downswing and the extent of deleveraging required to confront it.

Given these facts, the natural question is whether monetary policy *should* be formulated with the objective of aiding financial stability by leaning against the financial cycle—the so-called lean versus clean question.[44] Such strategy runs counter to the conventional view that monetary policy should focus exclusively on inflation of goods' prices and not react to asset prices or other financial variables—in particular, not attempt to counter the buildup of financial imbalances, except to the extent that conventional Taylor rules dictate such a course of action in light of inflation and output gap trends (see, for example, Bernanke and Gertler 2000). In the conventional view, it is very difficult to establish in a timely manner whether asset prices are out of line with fundamentals when intervention might help. Moreover, not much is known about the timing and magnitude of monetary policy impacts on asset prices—massive tightening, with considerable collateral damage, might be required to halt an asset price boom.[45] Thus, the authorities should adhere to the "Tinbergen principle," gearing monetary policy to the stability of goods' prices and macroprudential regulation to financial stability—a view that prominent advocates of inflation targeting have reasserted after the crisis (for example, Svensson 2010).

However, an emerging view that is gaining broad support holds instead that monetary policy should take into account the buildup of risk in the financial system. Notwithstanding the Tinbergen principle, such strategy would be justified by the fact that the proper design and effectiveness of macroprudential tools remain to be established. In this view, monetary policy would be set taking into account indicators of the financial cycle—for example, the rate of credit expansion, leverage, or measures of the price of risk, such as the credit premium (Woodford 2010). In effect, what matters is not whether assets are overvalued—which may be hard or impossible to establish—but rather the degree to which positions taken by leveraged intermediaries pose a risk to financial stability. The guiding principle should be to deter them from assuming extreme levels of leverage and maturity transformation (Woodford 2012). Central banks and regulators usually have timely information for determining whether lenders have weakened their standards, if risk premiums are unusually low, or if lending is rising at an abnormally fast pace.

How such strategy should be articulated is hotly debated. One way in which considerations of financial stability could help guide monetary policy makers without compromising their commitment to price stability is to allow such considerations to affect the short-run transition path to the (prespecified) medium-run inflation objective. Even for countries pursuing inflation targeting—as is the case in major Latin American economies—this would not represent a major departure from current practice, that is, what is known as "flexible inflation targeting." Inflation should thus be temporarily allowed to undershoot its normal target when financial imbalances are building up, and conversely to overshoot in the downswing of the financial cycle—a strategy that could be articulated through price-level (as opposed to inflation) targeting (Woodford 2012).

The more radical option of systematically gearing the conduct of monetary policy to financial stability objectives, in addition to price stability objectives, would face virtually insurmountable challenges. The two objectives could well demand policy changes in opposite directions; in fact, the optimal policy setting for price stability and the optimal setting for financial stability would generally differ from each other. This conflict would repeatedly force the authorities to make very difficult choices between the two objectives. It would also detract from the transparency and predictability of monetary policy, potentially sowing confusion on the central bank's commitment to price stability—a critical concern especially for countries still in the early stages of establishing their monetary policy credibility.

Thus, monetary policy is not a good substitute for macroprudential regulation. Still, they are sufficiently connected with each other—because monetary policy affects risk taking and macroprudential policy affects monetary transmission—to require close coordination. In the wake of the global crisis, this connection has prompted calls for the central bank to assume both tasks (for example, Mishkin 2011; Claessens, Kose, and Terrones 2009). This is already the case in many countries, but it is much less frequent in Latin America.

Fiscal Policy

Aside from monetary policy, appropriate deployment of fiscal policy might also contribute to financial stability in two ways: mitigating the amplitude of the cycle and better aligning private and social incentives for risk taking.

Countercyclical deployment of fiscal policy weakens the feedback loop among credit growth, asset prices, and output by containing the response of aggregate expenditure to changing financial conditions. In this way, fiscal tightening in the upswing can moderate the expansion of balance sheets and risk taking, thus dampening the financial boom. It also helps build buffers that can be deployed in the bust to contain its adverse real effects. Yet the crisis has also shown that discretionary countercyclical deployment of fiscal policy often faces considerable delays, which limit its ability to counteract a sudden crash in a timely manner. This problem underscores the need to build up self-deploying automatic stabilizers, still weak in most developing countries, including Latin America (Debrun and Kapoor 2010; Claessens, et al. 2010).

The second major way in which fiscal policy can contribute to financial stability is by helping align incentives. As discussed earlier, the buildup of systemic risk in the upswing of the cycle can be traced to the failure of individual agents to take into account the implications of their choices for systemic vulnerability. Conceptually, this creates room for Pigouvian taxes to align private incentives with social costs in connection with credit expansion (Jeanne and Korinek 2010), maturity mismatches (Perotti and Suárez 2011), or noncore liabilities (Shin and Shin 2011).[46] Cyclical taxes on borrowing could help deter excessive leveraging in the upswing and thus contain fire sales in the downswing; ideally, the taxes should be higher when leverage, and thus financial fragility, is rising, to induce agents to increase precautionary saving (Bianchi and Mendoza 2011). Likewise, taxes on financial intermediaries' short-term funding would contribute to reducing systemic vulnerability to creditor runs—that is, the credit-crunch externality. These taxes are analogous to the regulatory constraints on financial intermediaries examined earlier but offer the added advantage of generating revenues that could be deployed by the authorities to cover the costs of emergency intervention in times of distress. Moreover, taxes could be linked to specific types of instruments or transactions and would thus affect all intermediaries (or borrowers), not just those covered by regulation.

However, in spite of the solid theoretical justification for these kinds of taxes, little is known about their likely effectiveness in practice, how tax rates should be set, or the extent to which they should be varied over the cycle. And their optimal design is likely to require detailed real-time information on the asset-liability position of nonfinancial private agents and financial institutions, as well as the marginal cost of borrowing they face.

A simpler step in the same direction would be the removal of fiscal incentives that favor debt financing over equity financing. In the end, the fundamental source of financial fragility is the fact that intermediaries engaged in maturity transformation hold too little capital; equivalently, their leverage (or that of their borrowers) is too high. One key reason is that debt is perceived as being cheaper than equity, and this is so partly because the former receives a more favorable fiscal treatment than the latter in income taxation. This is the case in most countries, including Latin America. Qualified observers have argued that removal of tax incentives to debt could have a major effect on the resilience of the financial system (Hellwig 2010; Goodhart 2011).

Capital Controls

As shown in the empirical section, capital flows and credit growth show a significant degree of comovement over the cycle, and financial crises in emerging markets have been frequently preceded by capital flow booms. However, as also shown earlier, the vast majority of capital flow booms do not end in financial crashes, and the occurrence or magnitude of a capital flow boom has no predictive power for the occurrence of crises once credit booms have been taken into account.

Capital controls for dealing with inflow booms have often been advocated, and introduced, based on macroprudential concerns. This scenario has recurred recently as flows to emerging countries have escalated in the wake of the global crisis, with Latin America among the top destinations. From the macroprudential perspective, the danger is that inflows may worsen financial institutions' currency and maturity mismatches, so that a sudden inflow reversal may amount to a run on domestic institutions coupled with an abrupt real depreciation, with potentially devastating real effects—as witnessed, for example, in the East Asian crisis.

Banks' liabilities to foreign investors, especially short-term liabilities, can be viewed as part of their overall noncore liabilities, which, as already discussed, are typically accumulated in the boom and can be taken as a proxy for systemic risk (Shin and Shin 2011). In this context, macroprudential use of capital controls has sought to change the composition of inflows toward less risky forms—without necessarily seeking to reduce their overall volume. The typical objective is to limit short-term inflows other than foreign direct investment, as direct investment flows are widely perceived as less risky to the destination economy.

Conceptually, however, the distinguishing feature of capital controls as opposed to other prudential tools is that they discriminate on the basis of the residency of the asset holder—that is, between residents and nonresidents (Ostry et al. 2011). This is in contrast to the prudential measures to contain exchange rate or maturity mismatches reviewed earlier, whose application is based on the features of the assets themselves—that is, the currency of denomination and maturity, respectively—regardless of who holds them.

It is not easy to think of many situations, or types of transactions, in which the risks faced by financial institutions depend primarily on the residency of their creditors. If the risk posed by foreign borrowing stems instead from the foreign-currency denomination or short maturity of the loans, it follows that capital controls represent only a potentially useful instrument when conventional tools for dealing with currency or maturity mismatches are ineffective. One such situation could arise if capital inflows bypass regulated financial institutions and directly accrue to the nonfinancial private sector. Short-term external borrowing by large nonfinancial firms could be a systemic concern if they are also heavily indebted to the domestic financial system. To the extent that in this scenario the borrowers are not subject to financial regulation, there might be scope for direct controls on their borrowing from abroad. Alternatively, capital controls might be the only option if conventional instruments for limiting the currency and maturity risk of financial institutions are inoperative due to weak regulatory or supervisory capacity.[47]

The effectiveness of capital controls in altering the volume or composition of capital flows has been the focus of a massive empirical literature (see Demirgüç-Kunt and Servén 2010 and Ostry et al. 2011 for references). There are few robust findings, however, largely owing to the almost insurmountable difficulty of establishing the counterfactual scenario. An effect on the maturity or composition of inflows is found in some instances, but even then it is very hard to determine the extent to which it is due to a genuine change or merely to relabeling the flows in favor of those less affected by the controls.

One lesson from the use of capital controls is that they quickly develop leaks. The more advanced the domestic financial markets are, and the deeper their integration with world markets, the greater is the likelihood of such leaks. Strategies to evade the controls tend to develop rapidly, especially in the case of selective controls targeting specific kinds of flows. Uniform restrictions are somewhat easier to enforce, but they are obviously incapable of targeting the composition of flows, which is the key issue from the macroprudential perspective.

Conclusions

The global crisis serves as a reminder that boom-and-bust financial cycles can have devastating macroeconomic consequences. This fact is already familiar to Latin American countries—which underwent major episodes of financial turmoil in the 1990s and early 2000s—and underscores the need for a policy framework to manage the financial cycle and in particular the buildup of systemic risk in its expansionary phase.

A thorough comparative analysis of financial cycles reveals that they are generally more pronounced in Latin America than in other emerging and industrial countries. They also show a high degree of synchronization of financial variables; for example, credit, capital inflows, and housing prices move closely together over the cycle. Moreover, the financial and the real cycle display a high degree of concordance: credit growth and output growth are highly synchronized over the cycle. However, credit tends to precede output at turning points, particularly at the beginning of the downswing.

Financial crashes have occurred more frequently in Latin America than in other regions. Many of them have been preceded by financial booms—in credit, housing prices, or capital inflows. However, the vast majority of financial booms end in soft landings rather than financial crises; indeed, this is the case for 90 percent or more of observed booms. Yet the frequency of crash landings is higher in Latin America than in other emerging or industrial regions, and, when crises have occurred, their real cost has been bigger, too.

While credit booms are not invariably followed by crises, the empirical analysis shows that the scale of the boom is a significant predictor of the occurrence of crises: bigger booms are more likely to end badly. Moreover, credit growth appears as a sufficient statistic in this regard: once the magnitude of the credit upturn is taken into consideration, the occurrence (or the magnitude) of booms in other financial variables does not contribute significantly to the prediction of financial crises.

From the policy viewpoint, these results imply that macroprudential management of financial cycles should be a bigger policy concern in Latin American countries than elsewhere—they end in turmoil more frequently, and when they do, they have bigger real costs than in the other regions analyzed. The results also suggest that policy makers might view credit growth as a proxy for the buildup of systemic risk over the cycle. This is in line with the analytical and empirical literature arguing that rapid credit expansion is typically associated with rising financial fragility, owing to increased leverage, widening maturity mismatches, and deteriorating lending standards in the boom. The implication is that large-scale credit booms will often signal the need for macroprudential action. Identifying such booms, however, may be trickier than it seems, especially in emerging markets, where it requires disentangling short-term credit accelerations from the advancing process of financial deepening.

This does not imply that policy makers should attempt to eliminate the financial cycle—even if such a task were feasible. There are good fundamental reasons why financial variables should display cyclical fluctuations. Instead, policy should be concerned primarily with the procyclicality induced by inadequate financial regulation and unaddressed externalities across private agents.

The primary objective of macroprudential policy is to manage systemic risk. The recent academic and policy debates have focused on macroprudential regulation of the financial system as the key resource at the disposal of policy makers for achieving that objective. A wide variety of regulatory tools have been proposed—from rules-based countercyclical accumulation of precautionary buffers (in the form of capital, provisions, or liquidity) to direct measures deployed in a discretionary manner to contain risk taking, as captured by different financial indicators such as credit growth, loan-to-value ratios, leverage, or maturity and currency mismatches. Some of these tools have been deployed in emerging markets; in particular, several Latin American countries have adopted dynamic provisioning rules, and some have also made active countercyclical use of reserve requirements, while a number of Asian countries have engaged in countercyclical adjustment of loan-to-value and debt-to-income ratios. However, many tools remain untested, and the effectiveness at containing risk of those that have been deployed—as well as the costs incurred in so doing—is largely unknown.

Even though the spotlight is on macroprudential regulation, there is increasing evidence that macroeconomic policies—especially monetary policy—also have significant effects on financial stability. This suggests the possibility of a two-handed approach combining regulatory and macroeconomic policy tools for macroprudential purposes. In fact, in countries with more limited capacity for regulatory policy design and implementation, macroeconomic policy may have to bear much of the burden of containing boom-and-bust cycles.

In this regard, because there is solid evidence that monetary policy has significant effects on credit growth and risk taking, policy setting should not ignore financial stability considerations. However, it does not necessarily follow that monetary policy should take an activist role by systematically leaning against the financial cycle—for example, attempting to deter asset price booms—as some observers have proposed. Too little is known at present about the likely magnitude of its effects, and the "collateral damage" inflicted on real activity could be too large. Moreover, such a strategy would unavoidably face difficult policy dilemmas between financial stability and price stability or other monetary policy objectives. These dilemmas are particularly severe in financially open countries with restricted exchange rate flexibility, as the recent experience of a number of emerging markets has shown. In addition, the attempt to pursue multiple objectives could detract from the hard-earned credibility and transparency of monetary policy. Ultimately, monetary policy and financial stability policy have different objectives and instruments, and thus the former cannot serve as a substitute for the latter.

Countercyclical deployment of fiscal policy might also provide some help to financial stability—by dampening fluctuations in borrowers' incomes and asset prices, thus weakening the feedback loop between financial and real fluctuations and building buffers in the upswing that can be deployed in the event of a crash. But an even more straightforward option would be the removal of tax incentives for debt financing. They are widespread across Latin America and encourage both financial institutions and other private agents to raise their leverage and thereby increase systemic fragility.

To a large extent, macroprudential risk management involves a precautionary tightening of policies—whether macroeconomic or regulatory—in the upswing, in exchange for relaxation in the downswing. This strategy will inevitably face major political-economy challenges, as amply demonstrated by the experience with fiscal policy in emerging markets. Rules-based fiscal policy has proven more resilient to those challenges than discretionary policy, as exemplified by Chile's structural fiscal rule. The rule targets the cyclically adjusted fiscal balance, which allows the fiscal authorities to implement countercyclical responses without jeopardizing the sustainability of the fiscal position over the long term. The same lesson is likely to apply to countercyclical macroprudential regulation, although in this case some room for discretion seems unavoidable, given the uncertainties still surrounding the effectiveness of tools that have seen little practical use so far.

Notes

1. The sample of countries is constrained by the availability of rather long quarterly series, and it consists of 23 industrial countries and 56 developing countries—of which 15 countries belong to the LAC region. Our sample of LAC countries includes Argentina, Bolivia, Brazil, Chile, Colombia, Costa Rica, the Dominican Republic, Ecuador, El Salvador, Mexico, Panama, Paraguay, Peru, Uruguay, and Venezuela.

2. A brief outline of the sample, methodology, and goal of these papers can be found in Calderón and Servén (2011).

3. Across countries, the concordance analysis shows that market integration is higher among credit and stock markets than among housing markets in LAC. The same result holds for industrial countries and non-LAC emerging markets—that is, in the same spirit as Claessens, Kose, and Terrones (2011a, 2011b).

4. This is consistent with the fact that more than a third of lending booms followed asset price booms or capital flow bonanzas among industrial and emerging markets. For LAC, almost two-thirds of lending booms followed equity price booms, and more than half the lending booms followed capital flow bonanzas.

5. Our panel data are unbalanced for most industrial countries, having data from the early 1970s, whereas information for developing countries starts, on

average, around the second half of the 1970s (large EMs), the second half of the 1980s (medium-size EMs), and the 1990s (for most countries in Europe and Central Asia). Details on the sample of countries can be found in Calderón and Servén (2011).

6. We are highly indebted to Stijn Claessens for sharing his dataset on housing prices.

7. See Harding and Pagan (2002a, b) for a thorough description of the BBQ algorithm.

8. Our indicator of capital flows is the ratio of the annualized amount of gross inflows in period t divided by the HP-filtered trend component of the annualized real GDP. As in Cowan et al. (2008), detrending the normalization factor allows us to focus on the cycles of capital flows.

9. We focus on characterizing upturns or recoveries rather than on expansions to put emphasis on the short-term or cyclical forces driving credit or asset prices. Focusing on expansions instead would mix short-term fluctuations with long-term financial development trends.

10. The literature argues that the great moderation was achieved thanks to a combination of drivers such as (a) improved macroeconomic policy frameworks; (b) financial innovation and international financial integration; (c) improved inventory control and supply chain management; and (d) a favorable external environment—say, higher commodity prices (Benati 2008; Davis and Kahn 2008).

11. As we find later in this chapter, not all financial downturns end in crisis. This finding is consistent with the evidence presented in Tornell and Westermann (2002) and Barajas, Dell'Ariccia, and Levchenko (2009).

12. Note that the concordance indexes were computed for the full sample period, 1970–2010.

13. Although not reported, the differences between cross-country medians and averages in the degree of concordance are negligible. Hence, the degree of cycle synchronization is not driven by outliers.

14. These findings are in line with those of Claessens, Kose, and Terrones (2011a).

15. In this section, we use event study analysis to evaluate this statistical precedence rather than calculating cross-correlogram functions.

16. Empirically, Mendoza and Terrones (2008) assume that country C is experiencing a lending boom when the condition $l_{c,t} \geq \varphi\sigma(l_{c,t})$ holds for contiguous dates. According to these authors, lending booms take place whenever credit creation over the business cycle exceeds the average expansion (at least) by a factor φ. Following Mendoza and Terrones (2008), we calculate the incidence of lending booms for different values of φ—say, 1.5, 1.75, and 2.

17. Tornell and Westermann (2002) found that the probability of a financial crisis in a given country-year conditional on a lending boom in middle-income countries was approximately 6 percent.

18. Note that the peak in credit associated with a crisis refers to the contractionary phase that follows a boom and ends up in a crisis.

19. We included in the regression the amplitude of the preceding real economic upturn, and its coefficient is negative and significant in most cases. That is, higher growth would be associated with a lower probability that a credit boom will end in a banking crisis. The full set of regression estimates is not reported but available from the authors upon request.

20. Gourinchas and Obstfeld (2011) find in the run-up to a banking crisis in industrial countries, first, that excess credit (relative to its trend) amounts to 25 percent of GDP at its peak (vis-à-vis 8.6 percent for emerging markets) and (b) that each unit of equity was leveraged 32 percentage points more in 2007 than in tranquil times. In contrast, IMF (2011a) shows that financial crises are more likely

to occur within the next year when bank leverage ratios (that is, credit-to-deposit ratios) are above 120 percent and the ratio of credit to GDP has risen by more than 3 percentage points.

21. Many other proposals focus on the cross-sectional dimension of systemic risk; see, for example, Brunnermeier et al. (2009).

22. On the choice of risk indicator, see, for example, Drehmann et al. (2010) and IMF (2011a, 2011b). However, as noted by Goodhart (2011), it is not clear whether the empirical regularities that favor one indicator over another would survive once regulation is allowed to change over the cycle, as this might induce behavioral changes on the part of financial intermediaries.

23. See, for example, Goodhart and Persaud (2008) and Drehmann et al. (2010).

24. CGFS (2010), Moreno (2011), and Terrier et al. (2011) survey emerging market experiences.

25. A simpler but more radical proposal is to eliminate risk weights from the calculation of regulatory capital requirements; see Hellwig (2010).

26. Empirically, however, the credit-to-GDP ratio does not appear to be a timely indicator of cyclical turning points; see Repullo and Saurina (2011) for details. Thus, the mechanical use of the credit-to-GDP ratio as a trigger for the countercyclical capital buffer could prompt the regulator to act in the wrong direction.

27. Figures 9.8 and 9.9 exhibit a step change in the volume of dynamic provisions in 2005. This reflects a methodological change in their calculation, due to the adoption of International Financial Reporting Standards in that year.

28. As stressed by Caprio (2010), other factors also helped, in particular the Bank of Spain's tough regulatory treatment of securitization and off-balance-sheet activities.

29. See Fernández de Lis and García Herrero (2010) for a comparative analysis of the cases of Colombia and Peru. Wezel (2010) provides a detailed description of the Uruguayan system.

30. To overcome the unavailability of timely GDP data, Peru has resorted to construction of a monthly GDP series, which might pose potential issues of reliability.

31. This is also shown by Fillat and Montoriol-Garriga (2010), who simulate the application of the Spanish system to U.S. banks. They conclude that had the system been in place in the United States, the countercyclical buffer would have been exhausted at the beginning of 2009.

32. Indeed, the global crisis has shown that short-term financing in wholesale markets can be a major source of systemic vulnerability, because it leaves intermediaries engaged in maturity transformation open to creditor runs. These are similar to classic bank runs, but—as in the events of 2008–09—can affect a much broader range of institutions. The failures of Bear Sterns, Lehman Brothers, and Northern Rock, for example, can all be traced to their massive reliance on short-term funding. Raddatz (2010) presents strong evidence that the impact of the crisis on banks across the world was highly correlated with their resort to wholesale markets.

33. Terrier et al. (2011) document the recent use of the CRR in these countries.

34. This trend had been particularly marked in Latin America, especially with the adoption of implicit or explicit inflation targeting regimes by most of the major economies in the region. See Mohanty and Turner (2008) and Jeanneau and Tovar (2008).

35. This is a particular case of the property known as *portfolio separation*— that is, the independence of banks' asset decisions from its liability decisions, akin to a bank-specific version of the Modigliani-Miller theorem.

36. In contrast, under a quantity-target regime in which the central bank represents banks' main source of nondeposit funding, and sets the amount of lending it is willing to supply to them (letting the market determine endogenously the interest rate), changes in the CRR do affect the size of banks' balance sheets and, if lending is close to being banks' only asset, their lending supply as well.

37. The same result may obtain if banks are risk averse, as argued by Betancourt and Vargas (2008). Conceptually, risk-return considerations give rise to an optimal diversification of bank funding between deposits and borrowing. Vargas et al. (2010) claim some empirical support for this mechanism in the case of Colombia.

38. Montoro and Tovar (2010) present a Dynamic Stochastic General Equilibrium model in which banks face collateral and leverage constraints. They find that this allows reserve requirements to help stabilize the business cycle in the face of demand shocks but not supply shocks.

39. Vargas et al. (2010) find that CRR increases lead to higher loan interest rates in Colombia and attribute that effect to this mechanism. It is important to keep in mind, however, that the short maturity of central bank loans relative to bank loans also makes banks care about future monetary policy when determining their loan supply. Hence, if CRR changes are perceived as signaling future changes in the policy rate, they may lead to changes in bank lending supply in the opposite direction; see Mitusch and Nautz (2001) and Huelsewig, Mayer, and Wollmershauser (2005).

40. Crowe et al. (2011) review policy options for dealing with real estate booms.

41. LTV ratios, in use since the 1990s, are among the most commonly employed instruments (IMF 2011b).

42. Using data from Korea, Igan and Kang (2011) find some evidence that tightening DTI and LTV ceilings is followed by declining transaction activity and, to a lesser extent, decelerating housing prices.

43. The term was coined by Borio and Zhu (2008).

44. See, for example, Mishkin (2011).

45. Using data from 17 advanced countries, Assenmacher-Weste and Gerlach (2008) find that the impact of monetary policy shocks on asset prices is roughly three times as large as that on GDP. Hence, policy tightening to bring asset prices down by 10 percent, say, could reduce real GDP by over 3 percent.

46. In a similar vein, Angeletos, Lorenzoni, and Pavan (2010) develop a model of asset price booms under information externalities in which procyclical asset taxes can improve welfare by narrowing the gap between market-determined prices of assets and their fundamental values.

47. Even in this latter scenario, however, enforcement of capital controls is likely to require close collaboration of financial institutions, which would itself demand sufficient supervisory capacity.

References

Adrian, T., and H. Shin. 2010. "Financial Intermediaries and Monetary Economics." In *Handbook of Monetary Economics*, edited by B. M. Friedmand and M. Woodford, 601–50. North-Holland: Elsevier.

Allen, F., and D. Gale. 2000. "Financial Contagion." *Journal of Political Economy* 108: 1–33.

Angeletos, G., G. Lorenzoni, and A. Pavan. 2010. "Beauty Contests and Irrational Exuberance: A Neoclassical Approach." NBER Working Paper 15883, National Bureau of Economic Research, Cambridge, MA.

Angelini, P., et al. 2011. "Basel III: Long-Term Impact on Economic Performance and Fluctuations." Document de Travail 323, Banque de France, Paris.

Asian Development Bank. 2011. *Asian Development Outlook.* Manila: Asian Development Bank.

Assenmacher-Weste, A., and S. Gerlach. 2008. "Ensuring Financial Stability: Financial Structure and the Impact of Monetary Policy on Asset Prices." CEPR Discussion Paper 6773, Centre for Economic Policy Research, London.

Barajas, A., G. Dell'Ariccia, and A. Levchenko. 2009. "Credit Booms: The Good, the Bad, and the Ugly." Washington, DC, International Monetary Fund. http://www.nbp.gov.pl/Konferencje/NBP_Nov2007/Speakers/Dell_Ariccia.pdf.

BCBS (Basel Committee on Banking Supervision). 2010. "Counter-Cyclical Capital Buffer Proposal." BIS Consultative Document, Bank for International Settlements, Basel.

Benati, L. 2008. "The 'Great Moderation' in the United Kingdom." *Journal of Money, Credit and Banking* 40 (1): 121–47.

Bernanke, B., and M. Gertler. 2000. "Monetary Policy and Asset Price Volatility." NBER Working Paper 7559, National Bureau of Economic Research, Cambridge, MA.

Betancourt, Y., and H. Vargas. 2008. "Encajes bancarios y la estrategia de inflación objetivo." Borradores de Economía 533, Banco de la República, Bogotá.

Bianchi, J., and E. Mendoza. 2011. "Overborrowing, Financial Crises and Macroprudential Policy." IMF Working Paper 11/24, International Monetary Fund, Washington, DC.

Borio, C., C. Furfine, and P. Lowe. 2001. "Procyclicality of the Financial System and Financial Stability." BIS Papers 1, Bank for International Settlements, Basel.

Borio, C., and I. Shim. 2007. "What Can (Macro-) Prudential Policy Do to Support Monetary Policy?" BIS Working Paper 242, Bank for International Settlements, Basel.

Borio, C., and H. Zhu. 2008. "Capital Regulation, Risk-Taking and Monetary Policy: A Missing Link in the Transmission Mechanism?" BIS Working Paper 268, Bank for International Settlements, Basel.

Brunnermeier, M., A. Crockett, C. Goodhart, A. Persaud, and H. Shin. 2009. "The Fundamental Principles of Financial Regulation." Geneva Reports on the World Economy 11. Geneva: International Center for Money and Banking.

Bry, G., and C. Boschan. 1971. *Cyclical Analysis of Time Series: Selected Procedures and Computer Programs.* New York: NBER.

Burns, A. F., and W. C. Mitchell. 1946. *Measuring Business Cycles.* New York: NBER.

Calderón, C., and L. Servén. 2011. "Macro-Prudential Policies over the Cycle in Latin America." Policy Research Working Paper, World Bank, Washington, DC.

Caprio, G. 2010. "Safe and Sound Banking: A Role for Countercyclical Regulatory Requirements?" Policy Research Working Paper 5198, World Bank, Washington, DC.

CGFS (Committee on the Global Financial System). 2010. "Macroprudential Instruments and Frameworks: A Stocktaking of Issues and Experiences." CGFS Paper 38, Basel.

Claessens, S., G. Dell'Ariccia, D. Igan, and L. Laeven. 2010. "Lessons and Policy Implications from the Global Financial Crisis." IMF Working Paper 10/44, International Monetary Fund, Washington, DC.

Claessens, S., M. A. Kose, and M. E. Terrones. 2009. "What Happens during Recessions, Crunches, and Busts?" *Economic Policy* (October): 653–700.

———. 2011a. "How Do Business and Financial Cycles Interact?" IMF Working Paper WP/11/88, International Monetary Fund, Washington, DC.

———. 2011b. "Financial Cycles: What? How? When?" In *NBER International Seminar on Macroeconomics 2010*, edited by L. Reichlin and K. West, 303–44. Cambridge: National Bureau of Economic Research.

Cowan, K., J. De Gregorio, A. Micco, and C. Neilson. 2008. "Financial Diversification, Sudden Stops, and Sudden Starts." In *Current Account and External Financing*, Vol. 12 of *Central Banking, Analysis, and Economic Policies*, edited by K. Cowan, S. Edwards, and R. Valdés, 159–94. Santiago: Central Bank of Chile.

Crowe, C., G. Dell'Ariccia, D. Igan, and P. Rabanal. 2011. "Options to Deal with Real Estate Booms." IMF Staff Discussion Note 11/02, International Monetary Fund, Washington, DC.

Davis, S., and J. A. Kahn. 2008. "Interpreting the Great Moderation: Changes in the Volatility of Economic Activity at the Macro and Micro Levels." *Journal of Economic Perspectives* 22 (4): 155–80.

de la Torre, A., et al. 2010. *Globalized, Resilient, Dynamic: The New Face of Latin America and the Caribbean*. Washington, DC: World Bank.

Debrun, X., and R. Kapoor. 2010. "Fiscal Policy and Macroeconomic Stability: Automatic Stabilizers Work, Always, and Everywhere." IMF Working Paper 10/111, International Monetary Fund, Washington, DC.

Delis, M., and G. Kouretas. 2011. "Interest Rates and Bank Risk-Taking." *Journal of Banking & Finance* 35: 840–55.

Dell'Ariccia, G., and R. Marquez. 2006. "Lending Booms and Lending Standards." *Journal of Finance* 61 (5): 2511–46.

Demirgüç-Kunt, A., and L. Servén. 2010. "Are All the Sacred Cows Dead? Implications of the Financial Crisis for Macro and Financial Policies." *World Bank Research Observer* 25 (1): 91–124.

Drehmann, M., et al. 2010. "Countercyclical Capital Buffers: Exploring Options." BIS Working Paper 317, Bank for International Settlements, Basel.

Ehrlich, I., and G. S. Becker. 1972. "Market Insurance, Self-Insurance and Self-Protection." *Journal of Political Economy* 80 (4): 623–48.

Fernández de Lis, S., and A. García-Herrero. 2010. "Dynamic Provisioning: Some Lessons from Existing Experiences." ADBI Working Paper 218, Asian Development Bank Institute, Tokyo.

Fillat, J., and J. Montoriol-Garriga. 2010. "Addressing the Procyclicality of Capital Requirements with a Dynamic Loan-Loss Provision System." Working Paper QAU10-4, Federal Reserve Bank of Boston, Boston.

Goodhart, C. 2010a. "Is a Less Pro-Cyclical Financial System an Achievable Goal?" *National Institute Economic Review* 211: 81–90.

———. 2010b. "How Should We Regulate Bank Capital and Financial Products? What Role for 'Living Wills'?" *Revista de Economia Institucional* 12: 85–109.

———. 2011. "The Emerging New Architecture of Financial Regulation." CFS Working Paper 2011/12, Center for Financial Studies, Frankfurt.

Goodhart, C., and A. Persaud. 2008. "A Party-Pooper's Guide to Financial Stability." *Financial Times*, June 4th.

Gordy, M., and B. Howells. 2006. "Procyclicality in Basel II: Can We Treat the Disease without Killing the Patient?" *Journal of Financial Intermediation* 15: 395–417.

Gourinchas, P., and M. Obstfeld. 2012. "Stories of the Twentieth Century for the Twenty-First." *American Economic Journal: Macroeconomics* 4 (1): 226–65.

Gourinchas, P. O., R. Valdés, and O. Landarretche. 2001. "Lending Booms: Latin America and the World." *Economia* 1 (2): 47–100.

Hanson, S .G., A. K. Kashyap, and J. C. Stein. 2011. "A Macroprudential Approach to Financial Regulation." *Journal of Economic Perspectives* 25 (1): 3–28.

Harding, D., and A. R. Pagan. 2002a. "Dissecting the Cycle: A Methodological Investigation." *Journal of Monetary Economics* 29: 365–81.

———. 2002b. "A Comparison of Two Business Cycle Dating Methods." *Journal of Economic Dynamics and Control* 27: 1681–90.

Hellwig, M. 2010. "Capital Regulation after the Crisis: Business as Usual?" *CESifo DICE Report* 8: 40–46.

Huelsewig, O., E. Mayer, and T. Wollmershauser. 2005. "Bank Loan Supply and Monetary Policy Transmission in Germany: An Assessment Based on Matching Impulse Responses." CESifo Working Paper 1380, Munich.

Igan, D., A. N. Kabundi, F. Nadal-De Simone, M. Pinheiro, and N. T. Tamirisa. 2009. "Three Cycles: Housing, Credit, and Real Activity." IMF Working Paper WP/09/231, International Monetary Fund, Washington, DC.

Igan, D., and H. Kang, 2011. "Do Loan-to-Value and Debt-to-Income Limits Work? Evidence from Korea." IMF Working Paper WP/11/297, International Monetary Fund, Washington, DC.

IMF (International Monetary Fund). International Financial Statistics CD-ROM. Washington, DC: International Monetary Fund.

———. 2010a. *World Economic Outlook*. Washington, DC: IMF.

———. 2010b. *Regional Economic Outlook: Asia and Pacific*. Washington, DC: IMF.

———. 2010c. *Regional Economic Outlook: Western Hemispnere*. Washington, DC: IMF.

———. 2011a. *Regional Economic outlook: Asia And Pacific*. Washington, DC: IMF.

———. 2011b. "Macroprudential Policy: An Organizing Framework." Background paper, Monetary and Capital Markets Department, International Monetary Fund, Washington, DC.

———. 2011c. *Regional Economic Outlook: Western Hemisphere*. Washington, DC: IMF.

Ioannidou, V., S. Ongena, and J. Peydró. 2009. "Monetary Policy, Risk-Taking and Pricing: Evidence from a Quasi-Natural Experiment." European Banking Center Discussion Paper 2009-04S, Tilburg, the Netherlands.

Jeanne, O., and A. Korinek. 2010. "Managing Credit Booms and Busts: A Pigouvian Taxation Approach." NBER Working Paper 16377, National Bureau of Economic Research, Cambridge, MA.

Jeanneau, S., and C. Tovar. 2008. "Domestic Securities Markets and Monetary Policy in Latin America: Overview and Implications." In *New Financing Trends in Latin America: A Bumpy Road towards Stability*, 140–63. Basel: Bank for International Settlements.

Jiménez, G., S. Ongena, J. Peydró, and J. Saurina. 2008. "Hazardous Times for Monetary Policy: What Do Twenty-Three Million Bank Loans Say about the Effects of Monetary Policy on Credit Risk-Taking?" Documento de Trabajo 0833, Banco de España, Madrid.

Jorda, O., M. Schularick, and A. M. Taylor. 2011. "Financial Crises, Credit Booms, and External Imbalances: 140 Years of Lessons." *IMF Economic Review* 59 (2): 340–78.

Kiyotaki, N., and J. Moore. 1997. "Credit Cycles." *Journal of Political Economy* 105: 211–48.

Korinek, A. 2010. "Excessive Dollar Borrowing in Emerging Markets: Balance Sheet Effects and Macroeconomic Externalities." Unpublished manuscript. University of Maryland, College Park, MD.

Krugman, P. 1999. "Balance Sheets, the Transfer Problem and Financial Crises." In *International Finance and Financial Crises*, edited by P. Isard, A. Razin, and A. Rose, 31–44. Amsterdam: Kluwer Publishers.

Laeven, L., and F. Valencia. 2008. "Systemic Banking Crises: A New Database." IMF Working Paper WP/08/224, International Monetary Fund, Washington, DC.

Lorenzoni, G. 2008. "Inefficient Credit Booms." *Review of Economic Studies* 75: 809–33.

Mendoza, E. G., and M. E. Terrones. 2008. "An Anatomy of Credit Booms: Evidence from Macro Aggregates and Micro Data." NBER Working Paper 14049, National Bureau of Economic Research, Cambridge, MA.

Mishkin, F. 2011. "Monetary Policy Strategy: Lessons from the Crisis." NBER Working Paper 16755, National Bureau of Economic Research, Cambridge, MA.

Mitusch, K., and D. Nautz. 2001. "Interest Rate and Liquidity Risk Management and the European Money Supply Process." *Journal of Banking and Finance* 25: 2089–101.

Mohanty, M., and P. Turner. 2008. "Monetary Policy Transmission in Emerging Market Economies: What Is New?" BIS Papers 35, Bank for International Settlements, Basel.

Montoro, C., and R. Moreno. 2011. "The Use of Reserve Requirements as a Policy Instrument in Latin America." *BIS Quarterly Review* (March): 53–65.

Montoro, C., and C. Tovar. 2010. "Macroprudential Tools: Assessing the Implications of Reserve Requirements in a DGSE Model." Unpublished manuscript. Bank for International Settlements, Basel.

Moreno, R. 2011. "Policymaking from a 'Macroprudential' Perspective in Emerging Market Economies." BIS Working Paper 336, Bank for International Settlements, Basel.

Ostry, J., A. Ghosh, K. Habermeier, L. Laeven, M. Chamon, M. Qureshi, and A. Kokenyne. 2011. "Managing Capital Inflows: What Tools to Use?" IMF Staff Discussion Note, International Monetary Fund, Washington, DC.

Perotti, E., and J. Suárez. 2011. "A Pigouvian Approach to Liquidity Regulation." CEPR Discussion Paper 8271, Centre for Economic Policy Research, London.

Raddatz, C. 2010. "When the Rivers Run Dry: Liquidity and the Use of Wholesale Funds in the Transmission of the U.S. Subprime Crisis." Policy Research Working Paper 5203, World Bank, Washington, DC.

Repullo, R., and J. Suarez. 2009. "The Procyclical Effects of Basel II." CEPR Discussion Paper 6862, Centre for Economic Policy Research, London.

Repullo, R., and J. Saurina. 2011. "The Countercyclical Capital Buffer of Basel III: A Critical Assessment." CEPR Discussion Paper 8304, Centre for Economic Policy Research, London.

Repullo, R., J. Saurina, and J. Trucharte. 2010. "Mitigating the Pro-cyclicality of Basel II." *Economic Policy* 25 (64): 659–702.

Saurina, J. 2011. "Working Macroprudential Tools." In *Macroprudential Regulatory Policies: The New Road to Financial Stability?* edited by S. Claessens, D. D. Evanoff, G. G. Kaufman, and L. E. Kodress, 157–80. Chicago: Federal Reserve Bank of Chicago.

Schularick, M., and A. M. Taylor. 2009. "Credit Booms Gone Bust: Monetary Policy, Leverage Cycles and Financial Crises, 1870–2008." NBER Working Paper 15512, National Bureau of Economic Research, Cambridge, MA.

Shin, H., and Y. Shin. 2011. "Procyclicality and Monetary Aggregates." NBER Working Paper 16836, National Bureau of Economic Research, Cambridge, MA.

Shleifer, A., and R. Vishny. 2010. "Fire Sales in Finance and Macroeconomics." NBER Working Paper 16642, National Bureau of Economic Research, Cambridge, MA.

Sichel, D. E. 1994. "Inventories and the Three Phases of the Business Cycle." *Journal of Business and Economic Statistics* 12 (3): 269–77.

Svensson, L. 2010. "Inflation Targeting." NBER Working Paper 16654, National Bureau of Economic Research, Cambridge, MA.

Terrier, G., et al. 2011. "Policy Instruments to Lean against the Wind in Latin America." IMF Working Paper 11/159, International Monetary Fund, Washington, DC.

Tornell, A., and F. Westermann. 2002. "Boom-Bust Cycles in Middle Income Countries: Facts and Explanation." *IMF Staff Papers* 49 (Special issue): 111–55.

Vargas, H., C. Varela, Y. Betancourt, and N. Rodriguez. 2010. "Effects of Reserve Requirements in an Inflation Targeting Regime: The Case of Colombia." *Borradores de Economía* 587, Banco de la República.

Wezel, T. 2010. "Dynamic Loan Loss Provisions in Uruguay." IMF Working Paper 10/125, International Monetary Fund, Washington, DC.

Woodford, M. 2010. "Financial Intermediation and Macroeconomic Analysis." *Journal of Economic Perspectives* 24: 21–44.

———. 2012. "Inflation Targeting and Financial Stability." NBER Working Paper 17967, National Bureau of Economic Research, Cambridge, MA.

10

Microsystemic Regulation: A Perspective on Latin America and the Caribbean

Mariano Cortés, Miquel Dijkman,
and Eva Gutierrez

Abstract

The global financial crisis has underlined the need for better monitoring and management of systemic risk. A macroprudential approach to oversight has been proposed with a view toward mitigating systemic risk and is now being developed. From a microsystemic risk perspective, such a framework aims to remove incentives for a cross-sectional accumulation of systemic risk. This goal, among others, calls for extending regulatory perimeters and homogenizing regulations across different intermediaries to avoid regulatory arbitrage. There are significant challenges associated with the resolution of too-big-to-fail financial institutions. The difficulties in resolving such large and

The authors work for the World Bank, as, respectively, lead financial sector economist in the LAC Region (mcortes1@worldbank.org), senior financial sector specialist in the Financial and Private Sector Development Vice Presidency (mdijkman@worldbank.org), and lead financial sector specialist in the LAC Region (egutierrez2@worldbank.org). The authors wish to thank Caroline Cerruti, Augusto de la Torre, Socorro Heysen, Alain Ize, Brian Langrin, Maria Laura Patiño, Sergio Schmukler, Mario Bergara, and the participants in the flagship authors' workshop for their comments.

complex financial institutions generate bailout expectations and induce moral hazard behavior that, in turn, prompt even greater accumulation of systemic risks. This chapter reviews some of the proposed measures in these areas, discusses their pros and cons, and reflects on what would be most appropriate for countries in Latin America and the Caribbean. In the current environment, financial systems may have to intermediate large capital inflows to the region through an evolving network of channels with the potential for a substantial buildup of systemic risk and compel policy makers to take decisive action.

Introduction

The global financial crisis has underlined the need for better monitoring and management of systemic risk. The current oversight framework with its focus on the safety and soundness of individual institutions, as opposed to systemic stability, has proved ill equipped to assess systemic risk. In addition, existing resolution tools have not dealt efficiently with large, complex financial institutions, especially cross-border ones. The crisis has also motivated policy makers to revisit the *scope* of regulatory and supervisory arrangements. As illustrated in the run-up to the crisis, differences in prudential requirements can trigger a process of regulatory arbitrage in which financial institutions push risk-taking activities toward segments of the financial system with lighter or absent prudential requirements. While this process was most evident in the U.S. shadow banking system, regulatory perimeter questions are universal.

Financial sectors in Latin America and the Caribbean (LAC) were able to weather the global financial crisis, with the notable exception of some Caribbean countries.[1] In contrast to other regions, LAC had not experienced a protracted credit boom before the crisis. The relatively simpler financial systems and commercialized products and a more hands-on approach to prudential oversight with wide regulatory perimeters may have contributed to LAC's resilience. In addition, LAC countries faced this latest global crisis with stronger public and private sector balance sheets, increased exchange rate flexibility, and substantial international reserves. However, as financial systems in the region continue to evolve and increase their complexity and interconnectedness, the occurrence of a financial crisis induced by the accumulation of systemic risk cannot be ruled out, and supervisors in the region are increasingly aware of this possibility. Regulatory arbitrage issues, both across the regulatory perimeter and within the perimeter, will become even more pressing than they already are.

Large cross-border conglomerates with complex structures and institutions that, because of their size or interconnectedness, can be considered systemically important already dominate the landscape in several countries.

Also during the crisis, new and unexpected channels of contagion among institutions and markets came to the surface. In Mexico, for example, a corporate default arising from exposure to exotic foreign exchange derivatives froze the commercial paper market and affected firms' refinancing capacity, which in turn could have prompted further corporate defaults. In Brazil, the central bank engaged in substantial liquidity injections, in part to counter the "drain" from banks' requirement for additional liquidity to cover higher margin calls in stock exchange positions.

Systemic risk is typically defined as "a risk of disruption to financial services that is (a) caused by an impairment of all or parts of the financial system and (b) has the potential to have serious negative consequences for the real economy"(IMF, BIS, and FSB 2009). Systemically important financial institutions (SIFIs) are those whose impending failure, inability to operate, or disorderly wind down could produce such effects. There are two dimensions to systemic risk; one relates to how risk is distributed in the financial system at a given point in time (the cross-sectional dimension) while the other relates to how risks evolve over time (the temporal dimension) (see Caruana 2009). This chapter deals with the former dimension, or microsystemic risk, that arises from exposures that can trigger a system failure because they are common to all institutions or because institutions are interconnected.

Going forward, a key challenge for LAC—as elsewhere—is reforming the current oversight and safety net arrangements to account for the accumulation of systemic risks. A macroprudential approach to oversight, which has been proposed for some time with a view toward managing systemic risk (see Crocket 2000), is now being developed. From a microsystemic risk perspective, such a framework aims to remove incentives for the accumulation of risks in certain types of intermediaries, including through the extension of regulatory perimeters and the homogenization of regulations across different intermediaries to avoid regulatory arbitrage. The solvency and liquidity buffers required of the individual financial institutions would need to be adjusted not only according to the phase of the economic cycle but also according to the contribution of the institution to systemic risks caused by its interconnections with the rest of the financial system or by its size. The presence of large, complex financial conglomerates in LAC, in many cases with cross-border operations, poses great challenges. In addition to regulatory arbitrage issues and the difficulty of calculating appropriate buffers, significant challenges are also associated with the resolution of such institutions so that their too-big-to-fail (TBTF) status does not induce moral hazard behavior that, in turn, prompts an even greater accumulation of systemic risks. This chapter reviews some of the proposed measures in these areas, discusses their pros and cons, and reflects on what is most appropriate for LAC countries.

The rest of the chapter is organized as follows: after a brief overview of the main features of LAC's financial systems and their prudential oversight, the chapter discusses regulatory perimeter issues that were forced to the surface by the global crisis. It considers the reform measures that have taken place in other countries and reform proposals under discussion that seek to address those issues. It also discusses their pros and cons and possible applicability to the LAC context. The chapter then focuses on the prudential regulation of SIFIs, noting the relevance of these discussions for LAC. Next, the chapter discusses the resolution of financial conglomerates and nonbank SIFIs, including the range of tools that could facilitate a more effective unwinding of these types of intermediaries. The following section takes up the issues surrounding the evolving channels of contagion and liquidity regulation. The chapter ends with some conclusions.

Main Features of LAC's Financial Systems and Current Regulatory Frameworks

Financial System Structure

Financial systems in LAC remain relatively underdeveloped in size, but the complexity created by the variety of intermediaries and services offered has increased over time.[2] The past decade saw substantial financial deepening, with financial sector assets increasing from 50 percent of gross domestic product (GDP) in the 1990s to about 80 percent in the 2000s, and bonds and equity markets experienced substantial growth (see chapter 6). Nevertheless, credit to the private sector as a share of GDP is lower, on average, in LAC countries than in countries in other regions with similar income levels. A variety of financial institutions have started to operate in most countries, including pension funds, mutual funds, securities brokers, insurance companies, credit card companies, and nonbank credit institutions such as credit cooperatives, finance and leasing companies, department stores, and microfinance institutions. While banks are still the largest financial institutions, a substantial amount of the increase in intermediation has taken place through nonbanks. For example, in Chile household credit from retailers accounts for 11 percent of household debt, and in Mexico mortgage finance companies provided about 13 percent of total mortgage credit in 2008, compared to 11 percent from commercial banks.[3] However, there are substantial differences across countries in the degree of development of nonbank financial institutions. In Central America, for example, with the exception of Panama, there is much less diversity of institutions than in the rest of LAC.

Large financial conglomerates—comprising banks, pension and mutual funds, securities brokers, and insurance companies—Dominate the landscape in many LAC countries. The regulatory framework has helped shape the industry structure, as many countries have adopted a silo approach to financial regulation, requiring different licenses for different intermediation activities. According to a joint World Bank–Association of Supervisors of Banks of the Americas (ASBA) survey (referred to as JWBAS) conducted in 2010 on systemic supervisory and regulatory issues in LAC countries,[4] a universal banking license is allowed in only 60 percent of the countries; however, the concept of universal banking is quite restricted, given that in no case does it include insurance activities. Instead of universal banks, financial conglomerates have flourished in LAC. In chapter 8 in this volume, Heysen and Auqui find that the percentage of capital in the 10 largest banks owned by financial or mixed industrial and financial conglomerates is higher in LAC than in other regions. Regulations on bank ownership of nonfinancial firms in LAC tend to be more restrictive; thus, real sector firms and other financial firms typically have the same owners as the bank, as opposed to being directly owned by the bank. Only 60 percent of countries require constitution of a holding company, and in most cases the holding company can be domiciled abroad.

Foreign financial groups are quite active in LAC. On average, foreign banks hold 40 percent of total banking sector assets, although in some countries participation is considerably higher. In El Salvador, for example, all private commercial banks are foreign owned. Most foreign banks operate as subsidiaries. Foreign groups also control pension funds and insurance companies. Until recently, most of the cross-border financial conglomerates operating in LAC were European or North American groups, although regional cross-border conglomerates have now developed, particularly in Central America and Colombia.

Regulation and Supervision

Financial intermediation (defined as lending activities to third parties with leverage funding) is typically regulated and supervised in most LAC countries, as indicated by the responses to the JWBAS. Nevertheless, exceptions exist. For example, finance companies[5] in El Salvador, Mexico, and Peru are not regulated (in El Salvador and Peru, not even a license is required to conduct such activities, although in Peru they are not prevalent due to taxation disadvantages). Microfinance institutions and credit cooperatives are also unregulated in some countries, or they become regulated (in the case of cooperatives) only after their activities reach a certain threshold (in Chile, for example). Safety net arrangements are in place in most countries, although in some of them, particularly in the Caribbean islands and Central American countries, there are no deposit guarantee schemes. Although regulatory perimeters are wide, safety net perimeters are much narrower, primarily covering commercial banks, while credit cooperatives are outside the safety net in most countries. In addition, in some countries the absence of an independent monetary policy severely restricts the operation of lender-of-last-resort facilities.

According to the responses to the JWBAS, regulations for institutions tend to comprise licensing, paid-in capital, exposure limits, provisions, and liquidity requirements. The latter, however, are less frequently applied than other requirements. Prudential norms are rarely set on the basis of activity alone, being mostly set by license or by taking into account both a license and the activity. About half the JWBAS respondents indicated that as systems in LAC continue to evolve, a crisis similar to that in the United States and some European countries cannot be ruled out under the current oversight framework.

Most countries have adopted the Basel I capital standard, and only a few countries have moved forward with the implementation of Basel II (mostly of pillar 1, allowing banks to adopt the standardized approach). In many countries, the minimum capital adequacy requirement exceeds the 8 percent level set by Basel. Four countries (Bolivia, Colombia, Peru, and Uruguay) have already implemented countercyclical provisions to deal with the temporal dimension of systemic risks, but, as elsewhere, prudential buffers do not reflect microsystemic concerns. Some countries have moved to adopt aspects of Basel III. Colombia had adopted its liquidity standards even before Basel issued its new recommendations. Mexico will adopt the Basel III minimum capital requirements ahead of schedule, as its banking system already had substantial capital buffers, but adoption of new liquidity standards is not yet envisioned. Likewise, Colombia has yet to adopt Basel III capital requirements but is working on adjusting its definition of capital. Peru is among the most advanced countries in the region in the adoption of new recommendations; it has already adopted liquidity requirements in line with Basel III as well as a new capital norm, which is in some aspects stricter than Basel III, as it contemplates additional capital buffers for concentration risks. However, most countries in the region have yet to begin preparation for the adoption of new standards.

The quality of prudential regulation and supervision has improved substantially in LAC during the past decade, although challenges in key areas remain. In chapter 8, Heysen and Auqui find that compliance with Basel Core Principles for Effective Banking Supervision (BCP) improved in the nine LAC countries for which an assessment update was conducted in the context of the joint International Monetary Fund–World Bank Financial Sector Assessment Program.[6] The banking crises experienced in several countries during the late 1990s and early 2000s, the development of international best practices, and the support from multilaterals in the implementation of reform contributed to strengthening regulatory and supervisory frameworks. Nevertheless, the authors point out that substantial progress is still needed in some key areas, including independence of bank supervisors, capital requirements, the supervision of banking risks, and the supervision of conglomerates.[7] Responses to the JWBAS also confirm some of these shortcomings; about 40 percent of supervisors do not have budgetary independence, 40 percent lack administrative independence to set salary scales, and 15 percent also report lack of operational independence.

The quality of regulation and supervision varies substantially in LAC countries. While one-third of the countries have compliant or largely compliant ratings in 85 percent or more of the core principles, another third are compliant or largely compliant with less than 50 percent. Heysen and Auqui (chapter 8) note that there are countries with highly effective supervisory frameworks and countries with weak supervision in the three LAC subregions (Central and South America and the Caribbean).

Overall, compliance with BCPs in LAC appears to be lower than in other regions. LAC countries, on average, score worse on the core principles related to capital, comprehensive risk management, internal control, and supervision. On all these principles, with the exception of capital, compliance in LAC countries rises according to income level.[8] Nevertheless, cross-country comparisons based on BCP compliance should be taken with caution as the quality of assessments may vary. In contrast, empirical analysis of countries' responses to the survey from Barth et al. (2013) results in a more favorable view of the state of regulation and supervision in LAC vis-à-vis other regions, although the identified deficiencies tend to coincide with the analysis from the BCP assessments. Supervisory authorities seem to have greater authority in LAC to take specific actions to prevent and correct problems and to have greater powers to declare a deeply troubled bank insolvent; but legal protection of supervisors is weaker. Also, the degree to which the supervisory authority is independent from political influence is lower in LAC.

Regulatory Perimeter Issues

The Case for Prudential Regulation

The case for financial sector regulation has been traditionally built around the following set of market failures: (a) anticompetitive behavior; (b) market misconduct; (c) information asymmetries; and (d) systemic instability (Carmichael and Pomerleano 2002; Dewatripont, Rochet, and Tirole 2010). These failures can impair the capacity of financial markets to deliver efficient outcomes and can justify regulatory intervention, provided that the benefits outweigh the costs. Regulation aimed at curbing anticompetitive tendencies is necessary to foster an efficient allocation of resources and intermediation of funds. Regulation to curb market misconduct is needed to ensure that participants act with integrity and that sufficient information is available to make informed decisions. It comes primarily in the form of requirements to disclose the information provided to borrowers and investors, conduct of business rules (including anti-money-laundering regulation), governance and fiduciary responsibilities, licensing requirements, and minimal standards for financial soundness.[9] Once these requirements are met, financial markets are essentially believed to be self-correcting, and there is no case for intervention by the prudential authority or other public sector agencies.

While the first two market failures give rise to inefficiencies that need to be resolved through *market regulation*, the last two underpin the case for *prudential regulation*. Information asymmetries have traditionally served as the main justification for prudential regulation. Asymmetric concerns arise when the assets and liabilities are sufficiently complex that disclosure by itself does not allow investors to make informed choices. Professional bankers possess expert knowledge, and, because obtaining such knowledge is time consuming and costly, financial intermediaries have incentives to take on excessive risk. The regulator may also seek to protect the small, unsophisticated depositor, who is ill equipped to evaluate the safety and soundness of banks.

The high social costs of systemic instability have provided a powerful justification for prudential regulation. Collective action and collective cognition frictions are the underlying market failure that can cause incentive gaps between individuals and society and failures of collective rationality. Such failures of collective rationality can materialize in various forms: herd behavior (when diverse investment categories are bucketed together in the same high-risk category), informational cascades (situations in which every agent chooses the same action, regardless of his own private information), or sudden reappraisals of economic fundamentals (so-called sunspots). The occurrence of these market failures is highly problematic considering the complex web of interconnections and the links that sustain financial institutions, markets, and infrastructures in the modern era. As a result, the social costs of failures can be prohibitive, particularly in the case of large, interconnected intermediaries, leaving policy makers with no option other than mobilizing support operations with taxpayers' money (see Dijkman 2010). At the same time, the financial crisis has highlighted the limitations of market discipline in mitigating systemic risk, as individual investors do not have incentives to internalize the negative externalities that accumulation of systemic risk or the failure of a financial institution can generate. Market discipline proved ineffective in taming risk taking by unregulated investment banks even though their main counterparties were the most sophisticated and professional investors. Credit-rating agencies failed to properly identify the risks involved in several innovative products. In the regulated segment of deposit-taking banks, where market discipline played a complementary role to prudential supervision, market participants also failed to signal the excessive risk taking by a number of prominent establishments; spreads of banks' credit default swaps were rather compressed during most of the precrisis years and started rising only in the advanced stages of the crisis.

The Global Crisis and the Perimeter of Regulation

As a result of the global financial crisis, policy makers worldwide have emphasized the role of prudential regulation and supervision in preventing the emergence of systemic risk. Part of the answer is to raise regulatory requirements, but G-20 leaders have also committed to revisiting the *scope* of regulation and supervision. This effort needs to be seen against the background of widespread regulatory arbitrage in the run-up to the crisis, facilitated by financial deregulation and financial innovation. The commitment of the G-20 leaders was exemplified by a general trend toward less intrusive supervision and the absence of new regulation for rapidly growing unregulated financial entities, instruments, and markets.

Underlying this approach was the notion of segmentation between the regulated and the unregulated (or less regulated) components of the financial system. By drawing a "line in the sand" and separating deposit-taking banks from other entities (including investment banks) and by placing risky activities in separate legal entities, such as special-purpose vehicles, it was expected that the prudentially regulated segment—primarily the deposit-taking banking sector—would be isolated from difficulties in the unregulated segment of the financial system populated by well-informed professional investors. However, the differential prudential treatment set in motion a process of regulatory arbitrage that shifted intermediation to a domain where oversight arrangements were less intrusive (see de la Torre and Ize 2011). While these developments were especially evident in the United States, questions about where and how to set the regulatory perimeters are to some extent universal. The case of the Mexican *sofomes* and *sofoles* is illustrative. The *sofoles* are nonbank, non-deposit-taking financial institutions with a sector-specific or a multiple-purpose lending authorization; the latter are commonly referred to as *sofomes*. Their rapid growth in the aftermath of the so-called Tequila crisis, particularly of mortgage *sofomes*, reflected public development policies as well as their increasing professionalization. Some of the mortgage *sofomes* were subject to licensing requirements but not to prudential regulation. The mortgage *sofomes* were especially hard hit by the global financial crisis, which was associated with a steep recession and a spike in market volatility. A sharp deterioration in the financial outlook caused significant liquidity difficulties in the sector, given its dependence on short-term debt and mortgage bonds for funding and the lack of cheaper funding alternatives (especially deposits). Home-loan provider Hipotecaria Credito y Casa SA, for example, collapsed due to soaring bad loans and difficulty in refinancing short-term debt, while Metrofinanciera SA, a major lender to builders, restructured under prepackaged bankruptcy protection after defaulting. Thanks to the intervention of development bank Sociedad Hipotecaria Federal, which provided credit lines to the sector, further defaults could be avoided.

As noted before, policy makers in Latin America have been faced with a rapid deepening of their financial systems, much of which has taken place outside the domain of the deposit-taking banking segment. However, the fact that the expansion took place mostly in segments of the financial system that are in fact subject to oversight regimes and prudential requirements gives credibility to benevolent explanations for the expansion of the nonbank financial institution sector. It seems to reflect a broadening of the menu of financial services on offer, rather than a concerted industry effort to escape the tight prudential requirements in the deposit-taking banking sector.

Issues in Extending the Perimeter

Experiences in the crisis have motivated policy makers worldwide to expand the regulatory sphere. Indeed, all the supervisory agencies that responded to the JWBAS indicated that they are considering extending the perimeter to hitherto unregulated or unsupervised intermediaries.

The regulatory perimeter can be extended in a number of ways. In descending order of comprehensiveness, options range from the following: (a) regulating *all financial institutions* or all financial institutions except for those very small ones below a prespecified threshold; (b) regulating all financial institutions but *delegating* regulation and supervision for certain types of financial intermediaries; (c) regulating all financial institutions *except those* financial intermediaries that borrow only from regulated institutions; and (d) regulating all those financial institutions that are considered SIFI. Within each model, the scope and strictness of prudential requirements will still vary according to the type of financial institution, with stricter requirements in place for leveraged than for unleveraged finance (investment vehicles such as mutual funds, for example), which in most cases would be subjected only to a set of liquidity requirements and some sort of circuit-breaker mechanism.

Extending the perimeter is not costless and may create its own risks, including among others the boundary problem that affects most of the options mentioned above. The very establishment of a perimeter, regardless of its coverage, leaves financial intermediaries with an incentive to cross the "line in the sand" in search of excess returns that can be obtained by escaping prudential requirements—and, in an extreme case, by engaging in illegal financial activities.[10] Extending the regulatory perimeter may also be associated with opportunity costs related to business forgone due to regulatory constraints (Caravajal et al. 2009). This issue is especially problematic for emerging economies with significant financial development needs; that is the case in many countries in Latin America, which are characterized by a combination of shallow financial markets, a low level of financial intermediation, and bank-centered financial systems.

Allowing for some "controlled" unregulated intermediation (option c above) reduces the scope for regulatory arbitrage while ensuring that risks are internalized in the intermediation chain through the capital charges applied to the regulated institutions that are the only lenders to the unregulated sector. This approach, proposed by de la Torre and Ize (2009), is similar to how oversight of hedge funds was structured after the failure of Long-Term Capital Management.[11] Still, its effectiveness in avoiding the emergence of systemic risk is debatable, as it did not prevent hedge funds from building up highly leveraged positions. The deleveraging that took place through hedge funds also increased downward pressure on asset prices, which interacted with mark-to-market valuation rules to generate wider fallout from the crisis. Effective implementation of such an approach would require that capital charges applied to exposures to unregulated intermediaries account for such risks, which appears considerably more challenging than directly applying liquidity regulation to the unsupervised institutions.

Capacity and resource constraints may be important obstacles to expanding the regulatory sphere to include *all* financial institutions. Human and financial resources available for banking supervision are often already thin on the ground. Unless matched by a commensurate increase in resources, extending the regulatory perimeter could spread resources so thin that supervision may be compromised but still provide an unwarranted sense of comfort. Already, resource considerations have pushed a number of Latin American countries toward auxiliary models wherein regulatory responsibilities are delegated to nonsupervisory agencies, mostly industry associations. This model is especially popular for dealing with the cooperative sector, whose supervision is particularly labor intensive given the small average scale and geographical dispersion (for example, in El Salvador and Peru). While these and other models of auxiliary supervision usually entail incentives for such entities to cooperate with their regulators, the risk of a lack of regulatory independence and effectiveness looms large. This is the case at present in Paraguay in the supervision of cooperatives—a systemically important segment of the financial system—in which the board of the supervisory agency is selected by the industry.

Legal mandates and capacity to exert supervisory discretion are also critical considerations in extension of the perimeter. In Latin America, only a few countries are endowed with the statutory discretion to extend the perimeter to any systemically relevant financial entity. In most countries—Uruguay being the only exception in the region—this prevents the authorities from redrawing the "line in the sand" in the face of a rapidly changing financial landscape. Even if laws were to be amended empowering regulators to extend the perimeter, the regulator could be confronted with powerful pressures. About 40 percent of the JWBAS respondents indicated that political pressures and industry pressures were an important hindrance to the exercise of supervisory discretion.

Most G-20 members envisage a risk-based approach toward regulatory perimeter issues. Under this approach (akin to option d above), the risk that a particular segment of the financial sector poses to financial stability should guide the decision about whether it should be prudentially regulated and supervised or not. It thus reduces, but does not eliminate, the scope for regulatory arbitrage. Subsequently, the strictness of prudential requirements and the intrusiveness of supervisory arrangements should be proportional to the likely impact of a failure on the rest of the financial system and the real economy. This need highlights the importance of analytical tools and methodologies for judging the extent to which a particular intermediary or category of intermediaries is systemically relevant.

Measuring the systemic risk posed by individual financial institutions is, however, far from straightforward, in part because it evolves dynamically. Ultimately, depending on the overall condition of the system, even smaller institutions can be considered SIFIs, as illustrated by the Northern Rock experience.[12] Small British bank which suffered a bank run after having had to approach the bank of England for a loan facility to replace money market funding, during the global financial crisis in 2007. Troubles at Northern Rock created systemic financial instability Besides size, other factors—such as interconnectedness, complexity, and the ease with which a particular intermediary's functions can be taken over by other suppliers—determine systemic importance (see BCBS 2012). Nevertheless, size appears to be highly correlated with proposed composite indicators in Europe (see Goldstein and Veron 2011). Moreover, in many LAC countries, interbank markets do not yet play a key role in funding provision because banks' reliance on deposit mobilization and thus on financial interconnectedness through direct exposures remains limited, although in some countries deposits from pension funds constitute an important source of bank funding. Given the prevalence of conglomerates in the region, ownership links are a more relevant channel of contagion. Reputational spillovers can occur between the group members, while troubled parent companies may be inclined to skim solvency and liquidity buffers from their subsidiaries and vice versa. Similarly, exposures to common factors can leave the financial systems in LAC countries vulnerable to horizontal shocks. Methodologies for assessing the systemic risk posed by groups or categories of financial intermediaries that are currently under development are based on a measure for the joint tail dependence across financial institutions and their average comovement (IMF 2009).

Systemic risk may also emerge outside the domain of financial entities. Troubled nonfinancial companies may cause severe stress to the financial system, as illustrated by the difficulties of Comercial Méxicana, a Mexican hypermarket group, which at the height of the financial crisis suffered sharp losses in toxic foreign exchange derivatives. Its subsequent default in the autumn of 2008 triggered a breakdown in the Mexican commercial market paper, which represented a severe deterioration of the financial outlook for other corporations. If extending the perimeter to financial institutions is already challenging because of the trade-offs discussed above, extending it into the domain of nonfinancial corporations would seem infeasible. However, it is essential that the financial strength of households and nonfinancial companies be periodically assessed, through financial stability reviews, for example. It is also imperative for macroprudential oversight authorities to issue warnings on the accumulation of risks and to exert moral suasion, when deemed necessary, over systemically important agents in the nonfinancial sector.

Overall, Latin American policy makers seem to have struck a reasonable balance between their need for financial development and their need for financial stability: the wide regulatory perimeter has not prevented the emergence of financial intermediation outside the banking system, but most of it has occurred within the regulatory sphere. However, in the future, the obstacles that policy makers face in resetting the perimeter may prevent a timely regulatory response, given the structural changes in the financial system.

Scope for Arbitrage within the Perimeter

The global crisis also highlighted the room for regulatory arbitrage within the perimeter. By shifting activities between the investment and banking books, between on- and off-balance sheets, including through the use of conduits and special-investment vehicles, and across licenses, financial institutions have expanded the scope for regulatory arbitrage. Indeed, standard setters for the banking, insurance, and securities sectors have indicated that "there is room for greater consistency among each sector's core principles, as well as the standards and rules applied to similar activities conducted in different sectors."[13] The Basel Committee for Banking Supervision (BCBS) has issued guidance on the treatment of a range of exposures on- and off-balance sheet that seeks to harmonize their treatment. For example, the capital requirements for the trading book and complex securitization exposures have been raised.[14] In the region, the Brazilian regulator took measures to prevent regulatory arbitrage using affiliated entities by strengthening consolidation provisions.

Supervisors and monetary authorities in LAC also perceive substantial scope for regulatory arbitrage. The JWBAS results show that the most pressing perimeter issues relate to both cross-border and domestic risk shifting among entities of conglomerates. A vivid illustration of the potential severity of these problems was made evident by the failure of the CL group, a complex conglomerate operating in the Caribbean with interests in insurance, banking, and nonfinancial activities, including real estate. At least half the respondents to the JWBAS also perceived other perimeter issues associated with accumulation of opaque liabilities—including through derivatives by real sector corporations, over-the-counter trading of derivatives activities, and provision of services by unlicensed intermediaries—as important.

As previously discussed, a silo approach to financial regulation is prevalent in the region. But as financial systems develop and new products are commercialized, it becomes increasingly difficult to effectively separate intermediaries by activities. On the one hand, for example, the decision about which license (say, investment banks or insurance companies) should be the *only one* that authorizes the origination of derivative products that provide insurance against risks is by no means straightforward. On the other hand, convergence in the prudential treatment of similar financial intermediation activities across sectors is a tall order. Moreover, it is unclear how far the harmonization of regulations should go. Some favor regulating financial intermediation by activity as opposed to by license (see, for example, de la Torre and Ize 2011). However, it is debatable whether institutions such as insurance companies, which do not rely on short-term funding and are not subject to deposit runs, need to have the same level of capital and provisions for their assets as banks for that type of risk. Because solvency is a requirement for access to systemic liquidity facilities, demanding higher capital from those with access to such facilities could be seen as a means for dealing with liquidity fragility and for pricing such access. Moreover, if regulatory requirements were to be identical, banks would have a competitive advantage as they can obtain cheaper funding through insured deposits. Ultimately, identical regulations may lead to a universal license system, replacing the current silo approach.

There are several trade-offs involved in the silo versus universal license approach. The universal license approach eliminates the scope for regulatory arbitrage and could improve the efficiency of the system by allowing an intermediary room to exploit economies of scale and scope. The silo approach, however, increases the degree of modularity in the financial system by containing the loss of institutional diversity—as opposed to having a system in which all institutions have similar balance sheets and are exposed to similar risk factors—and therefore increases the system's resilience (Haldane 2009). In response to the global financial crisis, some countries are revisiting the issues involved in this trade-off (box 10.1). The prevalence of large, complex conglomerates in many LAC countries results in a type of hybrid structure in between silos and universal banks. The modularity is reduced, and the scope for interconnectedness increases as the identification of related parties becomes more complicated and reputational effects provide new avenues for contagion. The formation of conglomerates, though, raises system efficiency because they increasingly operate as integrated institutions, sharing information technology systems and central services.

Regulating by activity or harmonizing regulations across licenses to diminish the scope for regulatory arbitrage requires regulating according to the risk of the activity. Standard setters are committed to moving in this direction and are explicitly seeking to "develop common cross-sectoral standards where appropriate so that similar rules and standards are applied to similar activities" (see Joint Forum 2010, recommendation 3). The use of economic capital for prudential purposes across licenses could be an option. Economic capital is calculated by determining the amount of capital that the firm needs to ensure that its realistic balance sheet stays solvent over a certain time period with a prespecified probability. Therefore, economic capital is often calculated as value at risk. It already underpins the calculations of capital for banks under Basel II, and insurance regulation is moving in the same direction; "solvency II" is also an economic capital risk-based system that will determine solvency requirements for insurance companies operating in the European Union. Effective implementation of such regimes is, however, technically quite demanding and data intensive. In the region, very few countries have implemented Basel II. Chile, which has the largest insurance market in the

Box 10.1 Pros and Cons of Silos versus Universal Banking Licenses

Countries around the world are considering different approaches to the question of how broad the scope for banking activities should be. In the United States, the Dodd-Frank Act adopts the so-called Volcker rule whereby "banking entities, which benefit from federal insurance on customer deposits or access to the discount window, [are prohibited] from engaging in proprietary trading and from investing in or sponsoring hedge funds and private equity funds, subject to certain exceptions" (Financial Stability Oversight Council 2011).

In the United Kingdom, the Independent Commission on Banking, known as the "Sir Vikers Commission," has proposed putting the retail banking activities within a universal bank into a separately capitalized subsidiary—a "retail ring-fence"—that seeks to protect the latter's capital in time of distress (Morrision-Foerster 2011). In contrast, the Hong Kong Monetary Authority continues "to see merit in the model of universal banking," and the Swiss central bank notes the advantages of universal banking in attracting high-net-worth individuals and for risk diversification, while recognizing the need for stricter regulation of the largest banks because of their massive size relative to the Swiss economy (Chan 2011).

It is argued that universal banks (combining credit, investment, and securities businesses) can achieve better economic efficiency through economies of scale and better diversify risks through the cross-selling of a wide range of products and services. It is also argued that through economies of scope they are better able to service customers by providing a convenient one-stop financial supermarket, which in turn allows the bank to form a more comprehensive view of the risk characteristics of clients. Although lower thresholds have been identified, both cross- and time-series evidence points to an assets threshold of around US$100 billion, beyond which diseconomies appear. This value is well below the size of the larger banks both in the United States and in many countries around the world.

The extent of actual risk diversification achieved by universal banks and the systematic implications are points of contention. While individual institutions have diversified activities across business lines, the pursuit of return and the management of risk (using similar techniques) resulted in fairly homogeneous strategies and correlated returns for major financial entities. In the United States, this homogenization was facilitated by the repeal of the Glass-Steagall Act in 1999. While the financial system grew in complexity and interconnectivity, it became less diverse and therefore more fragile (Haldane 2009). Proponents of the silo approach seek to increase systemic resilience by fostering diversity. Policy makers in certain

(continued next page)

Box 10.1 (continued)

jurisdictions are prohibiting or severely limiting the joint conduct of certain financial intermediation activities (that is, adopting a silo), thus directly affecting the structure of the system to create more diversity of intermediaries.[a]

a. Separation may come in different guises. For example, Kay (2010) advocates for narrow banking while Kotlikoff (2010) for mutual fund banks (that is, full equity banks).

---

region associated with the annuities industry, is in the process of amending legislation to introduce a risk-sensitive solvency requirement for capital while overhauling its investment regime. Economic capital does not take into account liquidity risks, but there are several proposals under consideration for how to regulate different aspects of liquidity risk (see the section "Interconnectedness and New Risks" below).

Regulation and supervision of conglomerates also pose substantial challenges, which are compounded in LAC, given that supervisory powers to conduct consolidated supervision are not comprehensive. According to the responses to the JWBAS, most countries do not require creation of a financial holding company to control all the financial activities of conglomerates. In 40 percent of countries, banking groups or financial conglomerates exclude nonfinancial group entities. Moreover, in most cases financial holding companies can be created abroad and would thus be under foreign supervision. The home supervisor in such instances would have little interest in supervising the conglomerate, while the supervisor in the country where the conglomerate has its main activities lacks the powers to supervise the conglomerate effectively. In addition, there are important challenges of cross-border coordination in the LAC region. Lack of effective arrangements for cross-border information exchange and discussion of common issues is a very important concern for a significant majority of the respondents to the survey. Finally, most countries in the region do not have the power to impose capital requirements at the holding level. This gap, when combined with shortcomings in consolidated supervision, leaves open the possibility of double-gearing among different entities in the group or between an entity and the holding, particularly when it is an unregulated entity domiciled abroad. In these cases, judging the adequacy of capital commensurate with the risks being borne by the group as a whole is an extremely difficult undertaking and a source of systemic risk, given the interconnectedness and size of some of the groups operating in the region. These factors explain why the review of BCP compliance finds that only a third of LAC countries that underwent assessment supervise conglomerates effectively.

To be sure, efforts are under way to strengthen the institutional setup (both within and across countries) to strengthen oversight, and there are lively discussions on the most appropriate supervisory architecture. Different institutional arrangements can be found in the LAC region to address the challenges posed by financial conglomerates, from line supervisors with explicit coordinating mechanisms (Chile), to unified supervision under a single agency (Colombia), to unified supervision housed within the central bank (Uruguay). It is not clear that there is a best model, as the options have pros and cons. It is argued that a single supervisor is better at unifying the prudential treatment across different business lines with separate licenses, while separate supervisors could become more specialized in the sectoral business, which is a critical consideration as the sophistication of systems increases. However, the latter approach requires effective coordination, efficient information sharing, and so forth, which might be lacking at the moment. While efforts on these matters are welcome and could deliver improvements in the oversight of conglomerates, the fundamental challenge remains the need to achieve greater consistency across prudential regulation.

The Perimeter and Access to Systemic Liquidity

Experiences with the financial crisis not only underline the need to reset the regulatory perimeter but also illustrate the limitations of the current facilities for providing systemic liquidity. Central banks typically operate with a limited number of counterparties and with very little assumption of credit risks, in the expectation that liquidity will recycle through the market. However, in times of systemic distress, markets may cease to function, as occurred in the recent crisis. Thus, there is an emerging consensus that central banks need flexible operational frameworks to deal with stress situations (CGFS 2008; IMF 2010c). With financial intermediation increasingly taking place outside the banking sector, numerous central banks have either broadened the range of counterparties (both the number and type of financial counterparty firms) or contemplated doing so, and they have also expanded the range of eligible collateral to improve their ability to support systemic liquidity. The increasing links between financial intermediaries created by funding markets— that is, among banks but also between banks and nonbanks—also highlight the need for authorities to be able to support critically important funding markets rather than just individual liquidity-distressed financial institutions. In LAC, there have been instances in which similar actions have been adopted; for example, in the mid-2000s, an emergency decree allowed securities brokers in Colombia to repurchase their government securities directly at the central bank to address market disturbances. As central banks face trade-offs between effective liquidity provision and risks to their balance sheet, the appropriateness of pricing and risk management measures (such as haircuts and margin calls) that take into account credit and liquidity risks of financial assets will need to be reviewed.

The discussion of the scope of central bank liquidity support is particularly relevant for Latin America. Reflecting a background of frequent episodes of macroeconomic volatility and a history of high inflation, most central banks in the region operate under restrictive liquidity frameworks, especially those in countries that have adopted the U.S. dollar as their legal currency. Liquidity facilities are usually available for only a narrow range of financial intermediaries, notably deposit-taking banks, which constitute the backbone of LAC's financial systems. Nonetheless, the increasing importance of nonbank financial intermediaries and the growing interconnectedness among banks and between banks and nonbanks through funding markets would warrant a broader scope of intermediaries with acces to systemic liquidity facilities. Collateral eligibility frameworks also tend to be on the conservative side. Due to limitations imposed on central banks—at times in their charters—public banks have been used in some cases to provide liquidity. While there is a case for the state, including through public banks, to act as a risk absorber of last resort in cases of heightened risk aversion through the provision of lending or guarantees to the private sector, the responsibility for the provision of liquidity seems to be the natural realm of a central bank.

To their credit, the restrictions imposed by the current frameworks on central bank facilities have played an important role in disciplining monetary policy and fostering credibility. Many central banks in the region are therefore understandably reluctant to move toward more flexible arrangements. A balance could be struck by introducing liquidity frameworks that discriminate between normal times and times of crisis. The current framework would prevail under normal circumstances, but a temporary relaxation of counterparty and collateral eligibility requirements could be made under circumstances of severe distress. Putting in place an analytical and governance framework for assessing the extent to which a particular crisis situation represents systemic risk could further contain adverse credibility effects. Charging a user fee for the crisis liquidity facilities would be helpful in preventing overuse and could thus contribute to mitigating moral hazard. In addition, expanding the range of financial institutions with access to central bank facilities should be accompanied by an extension of the regulatory perimeter to limit moral hazard. Private liquidity pools can also facilitate access to systemic liquidity while containing negative credibility and moral hazard effects. Under these arrangements, institutions pay a liquidity insurance risk premium, which accumulates in a fund from which institutions can obtain liquidity in times of distress. Such arrangements are particularly attractive for dollarized countries because the central bank cannot issue currency to provide emergency liquidity.

Prudential Regulation of Systemically Important Financial Institutions

In addition to the presence of large, complex financial conglomerates, several institutions in many Latin American countries by themselves can be considered SIFIs. The largest bank in Argentina, Brazil, Chile, Colombia, and Mexico holds about 20 percent of total banking sector assets, while in Peru the largest bank holds 30 percent of the sector assets. According to Thomson (2009), any institution that holds more that 10 percent of banking sector assets or 5 percent of assets and 15 percent of total sector loans should be considered a SIFI in the United States, although he also proposes other indicators to measure interconnectedness and the role in key markets. According to this measure, LAC has the second-highest numbers of SIFIs in the emerging world (figure 10.1).

There is consensus on the need to adjust the regulation of SIFIs to take into account the contribution of these institutions to systemic risks. Several proposals have been discussed, including both price regulations (such as additional capital surcharges or taxes to discourage excessive risk taking) and quantity regulations that would limit the size of the institution or the range of activities institutions

Figure 10.1 Average Number of Banks with More Than 10 Percent of Total Assets of Banking Sector by Region, 2006–09

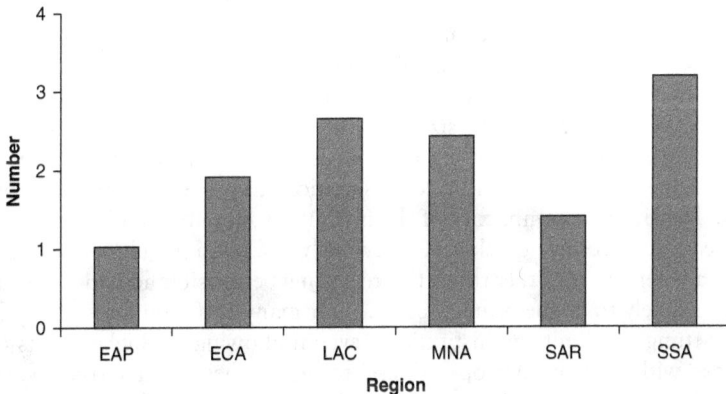

Source: *Bank scope.*
Note: EAP = East Asia and the Pacific; ECA = Europe and Central Asia; LAC = Latin America and the Caribbean; MNA = Middle East and North Africa; SAR = South Asia; SSA = Sub-Saharan Africa.

can undertake. The BCBS has recommended that global SIFIs have higher loss-absorbing capacity than other institutions, between 1 and 2.5 percent of risk-weighted assets, depending on how systemically important the institution is (see BCBS 2011). Domestic SIFIs should also have higher capital buffers as required by local authorities (see BCBS 2012). In addition, the resolution framework for these SIFIs is being revised so that they cease to be considered TBTF (see the section "Resolution of Financial Conglomerates" below).

Although ideally price regulations should incorporate the contribution that the SIFI makes to overall systemic risks, that calculation is challenging. The methodologies proposed estimate the incremental value at risk of the system induced by distress in one institution, which requires information on probabilities of default and loss given default for the whole bank portfolio or information on banks' equity and credit default swap prices.[15] Very few banks in LAC are regulated under the more sophisticated approaches of Basel II, and capital markets are relatively underdeveloped and illiquid. Consequently, such methods are not suitable for most countries in the region. Instead, price regulations could be linked in LAC countries to a set of indicators that proxy systemic risks such as size, leverage, and maturity mismatch, with all institutions being subject to certain charges depending on such ratios (as in France, with capital surcharges for systemic risk under pillar 2 of Basel II). The capital surcharge could apply to all institutions, increasing according to different thresholds to avoid creating a list of SIFIs that, in the absence of adequate resolution procedures, would exacerbate moral hazard. Capital surcharges have the advantage of creating buffers that reduce the probability of default, but Pigouvian taxes which tax activities generating negative externalities, could be used to address systemic risks in certain situations as a complement to regulation.

Although price regulations may discourage growth and provide buffers, they do not eliminate tail-risk problems posed by the existence of SIFIs, even if restricting the size of the institutions or their activities could hamper efficiency by limiting economies of scale and scope. However, efficiency concerns may need to be sacrificed to preserve financial stability. The size and complexity of the institution should be limited by what is feasible to resolve quickly. As previously discussed, regulations in LAC already tend to be rather restrictive regarding permissible activities, so that size is likely to be the primary concern for many LAC countries.

Setting size limits on institutions, even if allowing for higher limits on those with cross-border operations because of their greater risk diversification, is politically difficult. In the United States, the financial reform legislation introduced in 2010 does not set size limits although it empowers regulators to force a SIFI to sell activities deemed to contribute to excessive systemic risk.[16] At a minimum, if endogenous growth is not limited in LAC, exogenous growth could be limited by prohibiting mergers and acquisitions among the large institutions, with a possible exception in times of severe systemic distress to preserve financial stability. The U.S. reform, for example, prohibits insured depository institutions or systemically important nonbank financial companies from merging or substantially acquiring all the assets or control of another company if the resulting company's total consolidated liabilities would exceed 10 percent of the aggregate consolidated liabilities of all financial companies. To reduce systemic risk, competition policy has also been recently applied in Europe to limit the size of institutions that have received government funds. The European Commission's competition commissioner ordered the split of ING, the Dutch "bancassurance" conglomerate that received bailout funds and was consequently determined to have been given an unfair advantage under state aid rules. Government aid recipients in the United Kingdom such as the Royal Bank of Scotland and Lloyds reached an agreement with the government and the European Union competition authorities for significant divestments of the banks' businesses over four years.

Resolution of Financial Conglomerates and Nonbank SIFIs

The global financial crisis has emphasized the need to resolve financial institutions quickly, in particular SIFIs, and thus ensure the continuity of their economically vital functions while minimizing fiscal costs. The latter is particularly important in LAC in view of fiscal positions and given that no country in the region has the ability to issue a reserve currency. Ensuring that resolution costs of a SIFI are borne by shareholders and unsecured creditors not only reduces moral hazard behavior and systemic risk but also is key to preserving macroeconomic stability, as illustrated by the failure of Baninter in the Dominican Republic.

Following the financial crisis of the 1990s and early 2000s, bank resolution frameworks in many LAC countries were reformed to mitigate financial sector disruptions, although most of the reformed frameworks remain untested. The reforms give resolution authorities a range of tools for resolving depository institutions, including the transfer of assets and liabilities to an existing bank (purchase and assumption transactions) or to a new bridge bank established for resolution purposes. In some countries, such as the Dominican Republic, special powers were granted to authorities in case of systemic distress. However, it is unclear how effectively these resolution mechanisms can be implemented in practice, as in most countries the reforms focused on the legal modifications while operational aspects—such as guidance on how to implement the new resolution tools, standard contracts, and a list of potential counterparties in the transactions—still need to be developed. In addition, the fact that trust funds remain unregulated in many countries has created problems for resolution; institutions have constituted trusts to effectively fragment or remove assets from the liquidation pool, as in the case of a mutual bank in Ecuador in 2008.

Since 2008, financial crisis simulation exercises have been conducted in several LAC countries with the support of the World Bank and the FIRST initiative. In some countries, these exercises have found that the legal framework applicable to different financial institutions is unclear. In most cases, the exercises resulted in several specific findings: (a) the need for a framework to assess the potential systemic impact of failing institutions; (b) the need to improve operational readiness to resolve an institution through purchase and assumption or through bridge bank measures to avoid the simpler and better-known solution of nationalization; and (c) the need for better coordination between the different financial authorities and for a communication strategy to calm and reassure investors and the public.

Resolution of large, complex financial conglomerates like those operating in many LAC countries is far more challenging than bank resolution, in part because of difficulties in assessing the true level of bank capital and its liabilities. Moreover, in most LAC countries, resolution of financial institutions other than banks is still subject to the general bankruptcy framework. Thus, even in the few cases in which regulators can effectively *regulate* the conglomerate on a consolidated basis, they cannot *resolve* it on that basis. Such disparity in resolution frameworks poses substantial vulnerabilities, since the absence of effective procedures for resolving a nonbank could cause instability in other such institutions.

A consensus is emerging on the need to introduce legal reforms that grant authorities the necessary powers to conduct an orderly resolution of large, complex financial conglomerates and nonbank SIFIs.[17] Such powers include the ability to intervene quickly to restructure the institution— including the sale of business lines or units and rehabilitating part of the institution while winding down the rest—and to honor some contracts and invoke contingencies in others.

Resolution tools should help minimize fiscal costs and reduce moral hazard. The Financial Stability Board (FSB) has recommended that authorities consider several mechanisms for this purpose, including contingent capital and bail-in debt as well as statutory bail-ins.[18] Such securities or arrangements inject capital and reduce liabilities to facilitate the resolution of the institution by, for example, facilitating purchase and assumption transactions. Contingent capital would be converted first and then bail-in debt up to a certain amount. The BCBS is currently reviewing the role that contingent capital should play in the regulatory capital framework and has proposed that all newly issued capital instruments other than common equity should be, by contract design, converted to equity when (a) the regulator decides that the institution is no longer viable (although the bank can fail before the clause is triggered) or (b) the public sector provides support to make the institution viable (see BCBS 2010b, 2010c).

Contingent capital and bail-in debt or provisions would likely increase the cost of bank debt but arguably only because the "removal" of the TBTF advantage, which has hitherto unduly reduced banks' funding costs, gets priced in. Contingent capital seems a reasonable compromise with a stricter definition of regulatory capital, but it may not be enough to facilitate resolution of the institution. For these reasons, bail-in debt or provisions should be considered as well. Contractual clauses do not require modification of bankruptcy procedures, although in thin and illiquid securities markets, such as those in many LAC countries, introduction of such securities may be difficult to price and lead to further market segmentation. Very few institutions worldwide have issued contingent convertible bonds, but it is unclear to what extent such products can be commercially viable or how effective they would be in crisis conditions. Authorities may also be reluctant to trigger the clause on contingent capital and bail-in or to use statutory insolvency provisions to avoid contagion effects (as illustrated by the Irish experience).

Another tool that could be attractive for many LAC countries in reducing moral hazard while minimizing taxpayer costs is the constitution of prefunded resolution funds with charge to bank levies. The purpose of such funds is to enhance the effectiveness of the resolution framework by ensuring that funds are readily available; its rationale is akin to that of deposit insurance funds with resolution powers. To avoid bailout expectations, countries should constitute the fund only after a credible resolution framework for SIFIs has been introduced and should clearly restrict the possible uses of these resources. For example, funds can be used only in those resolution procedures in which shareholders and debtors bear losses, and in no case can they be used to provide liquidity before intervention. As such funds are part of the safety net, levies could be applied to all institutions within the regulatory perimeter on a home country basis. Rates could differ across institutions and be applied to uninsured nonequity liabilities and off-balance-sheet items (see IMF 2010b). Several European countries have already introduced such levies, and the European Council has endorsed their use (see EC 2010).

"Living wills" can be useful both in the supervisory and in the resolution process but can hardly be considered an alternative to integral resolution reform. To facilitate the resolution of complex institutions, the G-20 called upon SIFIs to "develop internationally-consistent firm-specific contingency and resolution plans," the so-called living wills. Such plans should include an assessment of the days necessary to resolve the firm without using regulatory intervention, steps to restructure the firm, and downside risks. The plans can help regulators distinguish between situations requiring intervention and those not requiring it and help guide them in the process if they decide to intervene. Drafting the initial wills may entail substantial costs for the institution, but the costs of updates and revisions would be much more modest. Moreover, besides helping regulators, these plans would help management and boards of directors to better understand the nature of a firm's operations and risks.

The introduction of a comprehensive resolution framework able to deal with complex financial conglomerates poses substantial technical, legal, and political challenges in LAC, but it is essential to ensuring financial and macroeconomic stability for the future. For one thing, introducing a special resolution framework in civil law countries is more complex than in Anglo-Saxon countries. In LAC, it is not sufficient to issue a framework law that can then be developed by judges who create the specific jurisprudence: any new law in LAC has to be comprehensive.[19] Moreover, the introduction of such a framework would create substantial political challenges in LAC. Being able to treat a group as a group "in death" requires being able to treat the group as a group "in life"; that is, the supervisor needs to have the powers to conduct effective consolidated supervision and regulation, a reform that has been politically difficult to pass in many countries. Passing regulation that also empowers authorities to resolve conglomerates will be an even greater challenge. However, countries in LAC can hardly afford not to adjust their resolution frameworks to the financial sector structure of the 21st century, as the economic disruptions caused by disorderly resolution of complex conglomerates and the fiscal costs of bailing out such institutions could have a serious negative impact on economic growth and poverty reduction. The adoption of a comprehensive resolution framework requires careful study and preparation and can be done only in times of low systemic risk, because the sudden adoption of some of the elements of the package (such as bail-in provisions) could precipitate a run on senior debt.

For most countries in LAC, this is the ideal time to start preparing for contingencies, as the region braces itself for protracted capital inflows that could trigger a sustained credit boom. The resolution framework introduced in the United States for SIFIs addresses several of the issues discussed. Title II of the Dodd-Frank Act creates an orderly liquidation authority aimed at reducing moral hazard associated with TBTF institutions. The authority allows the Treasury secretary to close and the Federal Deposit Insurance Corporation (FDIC) to unwind failing bank-holding companies or other financial companies that at the time of resolution are deemed systemically important by the Treasury secretary. The process pre-empts the bankruptcy code. The FDIC can use the resolution procedures it deems appropriate, including the sale of assets, merger with another company, purchase and assumption transactions, or creation of a bridge financial company. To help the FDIC in the liquidation process, Title I of the act requires that SIFIs submit living wills to the supervisory authorities. The FDIC is empowered to repudiate contracts or leases to which the company is a party under certain conditions, with damages recoverable against the FDIC limited to the counterparty's direct compensatory damages (that is, not including forgone profits or punitive damages). Shareholders and unsecured creditors bear losses, and management is removed. The FDIC has to promulgate regulations implementing Title II of the act with respect to rights and priorities of creditors and counterparties, harmonizing those to the extent possible with existing insolvency laws. Funds spent in the liquidation must be recovered from the assets of the company, and if not, other SIFIs will be charged the cost of the liquidation through assessments. The FDIC can issue debt to bridge funding for resolution costs. It would be interesting to see how the reform is further developed and applied.

Resolution of cross-border financial conglomerates requires not only adequate resolution powers by the national authorities but also enhanced harmonization of procedures in the jurisdictions in which the institutions operate. In LAC, regional and global conglomerates operate across borders usually through subsidiaries, which tends to facilitate the resolution process. Nevertheless, the lack of harmonized bankruptcy procedures or of burden-sharing agreements on how to cover the costs of the resolution of a conglomerate prompts local authorities to block flows among group entities in order to ring-fence assets. In Central America and the Caribbean, the two most financially integrated regions in LAC, cooperation and coordination need to extend from supervisory issues to resolution issues so that countries can be prepared to deal with the failure of a regional financial conglomerate. The failure of the CL group, the complex conglomerate operating in the Caribbean, underlines the importance of addressing these issues in the region. Harmonization of national frameworks granting adequate powers to the authorities to resolve institutions, a regional agreement on the procedures to follow in case a conglomerate fails, and how to share the resolution costs should be key elements of such frameworks. For countries in these regions, having a prefunded resolution fund with levies such as the ones described above is particularly attractive, as it would facilitate agreement on burden sharing and the resolution of the regional conglomerate. Again, regional coordination to avoid distortions and double taxation is necessary.

Interconnectedness and New Risks

As financial systems develop and become more sophisticated, the degree of interconnectedness significantly increases. New links between financial institutions, financial markets, and financial infrastructure are created, while existing ones may become increasingly important. Growing interconnectedness widens the scope for contagion. Banks, for instance, tend to become more interdependent in funding and liquidity management and more vulnerable to disruptions in key funding markets. Uncertainty about the distribution of subprime losses caused banks to hoard liquidity, with the main funding markets charging prohibitive spreads and coming to a near-standstill. Interconnections also increase as other wholesale markets such as over-the-counter derivatives markets develop.

Financial intermediaries also become more exposed to market risk as their investment activities grow in importance. Interruptions in key funding markets can be associated with severe liquidity stress in the banking system. Liquidity-constrained financial institutions may be tempted to generate cash by liquidating financial assets at fire-sale prices, which, through mark-to-market valuation rules, causes direct losses to other intermediaries that have similar exposures.

Interdependencies may also build up at the interface between financial institutions and financial infrastructure. Larger banks often provide smaller banks and other financial intermediaries with access to specialized payment services. They may act as system operators (beneficiary and payer service providers), correspondent banks (a domestic banking institution that handles payments on behalf of a foreign financial institution), and custodians (a bank that safe keeps and administers securities for its customers and often provides various other services, including clearing and settlement, cash management, foreign exchange, and securities lending). Disruptions at the level of the access providers may leave the end users cut off from effective payment services, especially in absence of backup providers. Counterparty clearing houses, while reducing the probability of direct contagion among institutions by ensuring that funds will be available to settle positions, can also act as a channel through which liquidity disturbances spread. In Brazil, for example, a drastic increase in the volatility of equity prices and foreign exchange rates led to a substantial hike in margin requirements at the stock and futures exchanges, necessitating a substantial posting of liquid collateral at a time of severe liquidity stress (Mesquita and Toros 2010).

As shown in the global crisis, liquidity creates disturbances in the system. However, until the crisis, very few countries had imposed funding requirements or numeric limits on liquidity. Liquidity regulation has been the subject of lively discussion. Some authors have proposed a Pigouvian systemic liquidity tax, proportional to a financial institution's maturity mismatch (see Brunnermeier et al. 2009). Others have argued that such regulation may increase systemic risk if it prompts institutions to shorten the maturity of assets as opposed to lengthening the maturity of liabilities and have proposed instead to tax short-term lending (see de la Torre and Ize 2009). Proposals have also been made for an approach that combines a mark-to-funding valuation rule and a capital surcharge (see Brunnermeier et al. 2009). In particular, this valuation rule provides a reprieve to intermediaries that might otherwise be forced—by the application of mark-to-market and fair value accounting rules—to reflect changes in the market value of assets (for which they hold adequate funding) directly on measured solvency.

Typical circuit breakers include suspension of deposit convertibility or mutual fund redemptions, stock trading suspension, short-selling bans, and, as noted, suspension of mark-to-market valuation rules.[20] In effect, a mark-to-funding approach introduces a circuit breaker to help arrest destructive downward price spirals and reduce contagion. Because application of such a rule may hamper market transparency, two sets of financial statements should be disclosed to palliate that concern, one using mark-to-market and the other mark-to-funding rules. Circuit breakers were used extensively during the crisis. For example, with key financial markets severely dislocated, banks made ample use of the opportunity granted by the International Accounting Standards Board to forgo substantial write-downs of financial losses, which helped them boost their net income (see Bischof, Brüggemann, and Holger 2010). Circuit breakers were also used in four LAC countries, but, according to the JWBAS, about 50 percent of supervisors and financial authorities are not considering introducing any type of circuit breaker.

Advanced countries are also tightening liquidity requirements. The proposed revisions of the Basel Accords on bank regulation known as Basel III envisage the introduction of the liquidity coverage ratio and the net stable funding ratio, which have yet to take effect as minimum standards. These prudential requirements aim to discourage excessive reliance on less stable funding sources, including the interbank market and other wholesale funding sources, thereby both reducing banks' exposure to adverse financial market developments and containing contagion risk.

It is expected that countries in LAC could meet the new prudential requirements with relative ease, particularly the liquidity requirements. Reflecting a more challenging operating environment, and—as is the case in Latin America—a history of macroeconomic volatility, most emerging markets have historically had comparatively conservative buffers. Even in countries where liquidity requirements are absent—as is the case in most Latin American countries—banks hold a large share of liquid assets, a reflection of reserve requirements and in some cases underdeveloped interbank markets.

Conclusions

Financial systems in LAC, aside from some Caribbean countries, have emerged from the global financial crisis largely unscathed. The region went into the crisis with strengthened economic policy frameworks, and wide regulatory perimeters kept the emergence of a "shadow" banking system in check. However, there were a few episodes of severe stress, perhaps early manifestations of how the evolving structure of interconnectedness is opening up hitherto unimportant channels of contagion in the region. The provision of financial services through conglomerates, in some cases of a mixed nature, is also gaining in relevance, and in a few countries they are already a dominant presence. Their sheer size and interconnectedness, including through reputational channels, make them a prime suspect for the potential buildup of systemic risk. In several countries in the region, a few banks hold a sizable fraction of their systems' total assets, "qualifying" them as SIFIs. While hard to predict with any certainty, systems in the region are likely to continue to develop in ways that create more specialized and interdependent intermediaries and to introduce new and more complex products. Developments already in progress and the likely trajectory of financial systems in the region point to the growing need to tackle the challenges posed by the increase in microsystemic risk. Results from the JWBAS show that both supervisors and monetary authorities in the region clearly acknowledge these challenges.

Tackling (both micro and macro) systemic risk calls for an eclectic approach that builds on ex ante prudential regulation and ex post safety net and resolution frameworks, overlaid with an effective macrosystemic oversight policy framework. Resolution frameworks that effectively and credibly deal with TBTF entities buttress the effectiveness of prudential regulation. For example, the credible prospect of an orderly resolution of those kinds of entities could act as a disciplining device for excessive risk taking, and the buildup of systemic risk may therefore be contained. The region faces important challenges in these matters, including the legal framework for bankruptcies of nonbank financial intermediaries. The crisis made clear the need to fundamentally rethink the financial system's safety net. It was simply not an option for central banks to stand idly by when key credit markets froze up in the belief that their liquidity injections through traditional counterparts would somehow be recycled to those markets. Various forms of interventions were applied to address those challenges. For the central banks in the region, the possibility looms that those types of challenges will become a reality down the road. But they are rightly cautious, given the not-too-distant memories of abusive resort to their balance sheets for assistance. At the same time, in the past decade many of them have built strong reputations for sound monetary policy making underpinned by strong inflation-targeting policy frameworks. They should carefully consider how best to "bank on" that reputational capital to revamp the liquidity safety net and introduce more flexibility. Building robust policy-making frameworks could help guide the creation of exceptional channels for providing liquidity in times of systemic distress in a transparent way.

The macroeconomic environment in which financial systems in the region will likely be operating in the next few years presents opportunities, such as widening financial inclusion, for example, but also poses substantial risks. Financial systems may be called on to intermediate large capital inflows to the region through an evolving network of channels with the potential for a buildup of significant systemic risk. Admittedly, it is not easy to get policy makers to reform the prudential and policy-making frameworks whose necessity may become evident only in the future. The challenge, however, is how not to be trapped by a possibly false sense that there is no need to change and to recognize the need to continue strengthening frameworks even in the face of "success." In many countries in the region, the latest reforms of the bank-insolvency regimes were undertaken in the midst of crisis, which is a rather difficult and frequently costly undertaking. Countries should heed those lessons and the more recent ones of European countries and start putting in place the required reforms in more favorable circumstances. Now is therefore the right time to push through the needed reforms, both to help deal more efficiently with the emerging challenges and to be better prepared to deal with an eventual downturn.

The process of revamping and adapting frameworks and systems is a complex and likely lengthy undertaking. International financial standards are changing in significant ways and are becoming rightly more demanding for both supervised entities and overseer authorities. The BCBS is allowing several years for the full phase in of strengthened prudential standards for the banking sector. In the region, the process will likely be evolutionary rather than "revolutionary," as countries refine and adapt regulation and institutional setups to their particular circumstances. Information gaps, for example, on the interconnectedness of entities should be addressed to provide a sounder basis for more effective macrosystemic oversight. While the process of achieving more consistency in the treatment of similar risks across standards advances, countries in the region would be wise to continue improving the frameworks to achieve more effective consolidated supervision and to fill the legal lacunae that constrain supervisors. The efforts to create robust cross-border frameworks—building on, for example, the multilateral memorandums of understanding among Central American supervisors—should be developed further and extended beyond prudential regulation into regional safety nets and harmonized resolution frameworks.

Notes

1. In the Caribbean, the failure of a complex regional insurance conglomerate that sold deposit-like products has impacted financial stability. In Jamaica, unregulated securities dealers experience financial distress due to maturity mismatches, in turn exacerbating problems in government securities markets.

2. See other chapters in this volume for a comprehensive discussion of financial sector developments in LAC.

3. Public sector institutions (Infovanit and Fovisste) provide most mortgage loans in Mexico.

4. See Gutierrez and Caraballo (2012) for details.

5. In these countries, finance companies are non-deposit-taking institutions that issue paper and borrow from banks to fund credit. In other jurisdictions, finance companies are allowed to mobilize non-sight deposits (for example, Paraguay).

6. The FSAP provides an overview of the stability and developmental needs of financial sectors in member countries.

7. Fewer than 50 percent of the 31 countries assessed scored a rating of compliant or largely compliant in those principles in their most recent BCP.

8. In chapter 8 in this volume, Heysen and Auqui estimate the correlation between the rating for each BCP principle and a LAC dummy, controlling for GDP per capita and population, as well as whether the assessment was conducted under the new BCP methodology introduced in 2005 and if it was an initial assessment

or an update of a previous one. Authors also controlled by a dummy variable that combines per capita GDP with the LAC region to explore differences in compliance in LAC countries depending on their income levels. The authors use the ratings for 118 assessments conducted in FSAPs.

9. See also de la Torre, Feyen, and Ize (2013) who present four conceptual paradigms, each of which leads to different policy implications for prudential regulation. at one extreme, in a world in which agents are fully informed and rational, and in which market failures are of a *bilateral* nature, there is no role for prudential regulation and supervision and only market regulation would be necessary. By contrast, in a world of widespread information asymmetries, bounded rationality, and *collective* market failures, the role of supervision and regulation is expanded considerably.

10. For supervisors in Colombia, one of the countries in LAC with the widest regulatory perimeter, preventing such developments is a key concern, especially following the collapse of several pyramid schemes in 2008.

11. At the time, the notion prevailed that prime brokers would exercise control on hedge funds via appropriate counterparty risk management, while regulators would concentrate on close supervision of the prime brokers.

12. Small British bank which suffered a bank run after having had to approach the Bank of England for a loan facility to replace money market funding, during the global financial crisis in 2007. Troubles at Northern Rock created systemic financial instability.

13. For example, the prudential regulation of credit risk held by banks and its transfer to an insurance company is treated very differently: a capital charge if held by the former, a technical provision if need by the latter. See Joint Forum (2010).

14. See BCBS (2009).

15. See IMF (2010a) for an overview of such proposals.

16. Goldstein and Veron (2011) caution that the extent to which this provision will be used in practice remains to be seen.

17. See, for example, Squam Lake Working Group on Financial Regulation (2009).

18. See FSB (2010). Contingent capital and bail-in debt are securities (subordinated in the first case and senior unsecured in the latter) that contain contractual clauses prompting conversion to common equity when the institution is no longer viable, diluting existing shareholders' equity and applying a haircut on debt holders. Contingent capital conversion could also be triggered when the prudential ratios of the institution begin to deteriorate as a form of automatic prompt corrective action. Statutory bail-in provisions empower liquidating authorities to write-down or convert debt into equity as part of the resolution procedure outside normal bankruptcy procedures.

19. For this reason, new bank resolution laws introduced in many countries defer in many aspects to what is contemplated in normal insolvency laws, which also has created problems as contradictions between the two norms may emerge.

20. A circuit breaker is considered prewired if it is already embedded in the contract and legal framework.

References

Barth, J., G. Caprio, and R. Levine. 2013. "Bank regulation and supervision in 180 countries from 1999 to 2011." NEBR working paper No. 18733. National Bureau of Economic Research Inc.

BCBS. 2009. *Enhancements to the Basel II Framework*. Basel: Bank for international settlements.

BCBS (Basel Committee on Banking Supervision). 2010a. *Report and Recommendations of the Cross-Border Bank Resolution Group*. Basel: Bank for International Settlements.

———. 2010b. *Proposal to Ensure the Loss Absorbency of Regulatory Capital at the Point of Non-Viability*. Basel: Bank for International Settlements.

———. 2010c. *Basel III: A Global Regulatory Framework for More Resilient Banks and Banking Systems*. Basel: Bank for International Settlements.

———. 2011. *Global Systemically Important Banks: Assessment Methodology and the Additional Loss Absorbency Requirement*. Basel: Bank for International Settlements.

———. 2012. *A Framework for Dealing with Domestic Systemically Important Banks*. Basel: Bank for International Settlements.

Bischof, J., U. Brüggemann, and D. Holger. 2010. "Relaxation of Fair Value Rules in Times of Crisis: An Analysis of Economic Benefits and Costs of the Amendment to IAS 39." Social Science Research Network Working Paper Series. http://ssrn.com/abstract=1628843 or http://dx.doi.org/10.2139/ssrn.1628843.

Brunnermeier, M., A. Crocket, C. Goodhart, A. Persaud, and H. Shin. 2009. "The Fundamental Principles of Financial Regulation." Geneva Reports on the World Economy, Preliminary Conference Draft. International Center for Monetary and Banking Studies.

Caravajal, A., R. Dodd, M. Moore, E. Nier, I. Tower, and L. Zanforlin. 2009. "The Perimeter of Financial Regulation." IMF Staff Position Note, SPN/09/07, International Monetary Fund, Washington, DC.

Carmichael, J., and M. Pomerleano. 2002. *The Development and Regulation of Nonbank Financial Institutions*. Washington, DC: World Bank.

Caruana, J. 2009. "The International Policy Response to the Financial Crises: Making the Macroprudential Approach Operational." Panel remarks at Jackson Hole, Wyoming, August 21–22.

Chan, Norma T. L. 2011. "Universal Banking—Hong Kong's Perspective." Keynote Address at the Opening Session of the Asian Banker Summit in Hong Kong, April 7.

Committee on Global Financial Stability. 2008. "Central Bank Operations in Response to Financial Turmoil." CGFS Paper 38, Committee on Global Financial Stability, Basel.

Crockett, A. 2000. "Marrying the Micro- and Macroprudential Dimensions of Financial Stability." BIS Paper 1, Bank for International Settlements, Basel.

de la Torre, A., E. Feyen, and A. Ize. 2013. "Financial Development: Structure and Dynamics." *World Bank Economic Review* (February). http://wber.oxfordjournals.org/content/early/2013/02/26/wber.lht005.short.

de la Torre, A., and A. Ize. 2009. "Regulatory Reform: Integrating Paradigms." Policy Research Working Paper 4842, World Bank, Washington, DC.

———. 2011. "Containing Systemic Risk: Paradigm-Based Perspectives on Regulatory Reform." Policy Research Working Paper 5523, World Bank, Washington, DC.

Dewatripont, M., J. C. Rochet, and J. Tirole. 2010. *Balancing the Banks: Global Lessons from the Financial Crisis*. Princeton and Oxford: Princeton University Press.

Dijkman, M. 2010. "A Framework for Assessing Systemic Risk." Policy Research Working Paper 5282, World Bank, Washington, DC.

EC (European Commission). 2010. "Commission Services Non-Paper on Bank Levies for Discussion at ECOFIN." September.

Financial Stability Oversight Council. 2011. "Study and Recommendations on Prohibitions on Proprietary Trading and Certain Relationships with Hedge Funds and Private Equity Funds." U.S. Treasury. http://www.treasury.gov/initiatives/documents/volcker%20sec%20%20619%20study%20final%201%2018%2011%20rg.pdf.

FSB (Financial Stability Board. 2010. Reducing the Moral Hazard Posed by Systemically Important Financial Institutions: Interim Report to G-20 Leaders.

Goldstein, M., and N. Veron. 2011. "Too Big to Fail: The Transatlantic Debate." Working Paper 11-2, Peterson Institute for International Economics, Washington, DC.

Gutierrez, E., and P. Caraballo. 2012. "Systemic Oversight Frameworks in LAC: Current Practices and Reform Agenda." Policy Research Working Paper 5941, World Bank, Washington, DC.

Haldane, A. 2009. "Rethinking the Financial Network." Speech delivered at the Financial Student Association, Amsterdam, April.

IMF (International Monetary Fund). 2009. "Detecting Systemic Risk." In *Global Financial Stability Report*, chapter 3, 111–49. Washington, DC: IMF.

———. 2010a. "Systemic Risk and the Redesign of Financial Regulation." In *Global Financial Stability Report*, chapter 2, 73–110. Washington, DC: IMF.

———. 2010b. *A Fair and Substantial Contribution by the Financial Sector: Final Report for the G-20*. Washington, DC: IMF.

———. 2010c. "Systemic Liquidity Risk: Improving the Resilience of Financial Institutions and Markets." In *Global Financial Stability Report*, chap. 2, 57–83. Washington, DC: IMF.

IMF, BIS, and Financial Stability Board. 2009. "Guidance to Assess the Systemic Importance of Financial Institutions, Markets and Instruments: Initial Considerations: Report to G20 Finance Ministers and Governors."

Joint Forum, BCBS. 2010. "Review of the Differentiated Nature and Scope of Financial Regulation: Key Issues and Recommendations." Press release, January 8.

Kay, J. 2010. "Should We Have 'Narrow Banking'?" In *The Future of Finance and the Theory That Underpins It*, chap. 8. London: London School of Economics.

Kotlikoff (2010). *Jimmy Stewart is Dead: Ending the World's Financial Plague Before it Starts Again. John Wiley and Sons Inc.*

Mesquita, M., and M. Torós. 2010. "Brazil and the 2008 Panic." In *The Global Crisis and Financial Intermediation in Emerging Market Economies*, 113–20. Basel: Bank for International Settlements.

Morrison-Foerster. 2011. "ICB Interim Report on UK Banking Reform." News Bulletin, April 29. http://www.mofo.com/files/Uploads/Images/110429-ICB-Report-UK-Banking-Reform.pdf.

Squam Lake Working Group on Financial Regulation. 2009. "Improving Resolution Options for Systemically Relevant Financial Institution." Council on Foreign Relations Working Paper.

Thomson, J. 2009. "On Systemically Important Financial Institutions and Progressive Systemic Risk Migration." Policy Discussion Paper 27, Federal Reserve Bank of Cleveland, Cleveland.

11

Systemic Supervision

Steven A. Seelig and Katia D'Hulster

Abstract

The financial crisis has highlighted the need for a broader vision of financial sector supervision that focuses on a more systemic view of risk. This approach requires supervisors to analyze macroeconomic developments, interconnectedness, market conditions, and contagion risks. The chapter first examines the current state of supervision in LAC countries and discusses the need for a more systemic perspective that entails the clever use of existing tools and instruments such as stress testing, mapping of interconnectedness, and the use of market indicators. The chapter then analyzes some typical issues confronting supervisors as they start to formulate this new vision. First is the definition of systemic supervision and regulation and how it can be distinguished from the more traditional supervisory and regulatory approaches. Second is the role of market discipline. The global financial crisis has revealed the pitfalls of excessive reliance on market discipline as well as its failure to curb the buildup of excessive risk in the system. Third is the balance between financial stability and financial development. When countries broaden supervisory responsibilities and powers to include systemic risks, they will have to make a delicate trade-off

The authors work for the World Bank. Steven A. Seelig is a consultant, and Katia D'Hulster is a senior financial sector specialist in the Financial Systems Department.

between rigorous financial supervision and financial development. The chapter then examines specific implementation issues associated with introducing systemic supervision. These include the retooling of supervision, the blending of top-down and bottom-up supervision, the roles of on-site and off-site supervision, the mechanisms that allow financial sector supervisors to coordinate both laterally and across borders, and additional powers and strong independence for systemic supervisors. We conclude with a list of major issues and steps that policy makers will need to focus on in reforming the supervisory process to incorporate a systemic vision.

Introduction

While markets punished weak institutions and countries during the recent crisis, Latin America managed to escape much of the financial contagion. However, it did not fully escape. Bank credit to the private sector decelerated but remained positive. Mexico faced the greatest contagion, likely because its financial system is more reliant on large multinational banks (see Cardenas 2011). Domestic funding markets were also affected by the crisis. Argentina saw the three-month overnight interbank spreads widen, and in Chile local peso money market rates were put under pressure. In response to these market pressures, Latin American central banks put in place policies to provide liquidity to the market, while at the same time trying to avoid stimulating inflationary pressures (see Jara, Moreno, and Tovar 2009).

As the global financial crisis continues to evolve, certain lessons for future policy have begun to crystallize. Among these is the need for a more systemic view of financial sector supervision. To address this need and to avoid the policy missteps that contributed to the crisis, policy makers in Latin America and the Caribbean (LAC) and elsewhere are considering a new model for financial sector supervision and the possible introduction of new structures and institutions to implement it. One of the lessons learned from the crisis is that regardless of the strength of microprudential supervision, it is necessary to identify, assess, and address developments that may have a systemic impact on the financial sector and ultimately on the economy as a whole.

Latin American and Caribbean financial systems are simpler than those in more developed countries, and many countries in the developing world take comfort from this fact, given that the crisis hit developed countries primarily. Nevertheless, Brazil, Chile, and Mexico reported adverse effects from the crisis, and other countries recognize that they are similarly exposed to systemic risks. Countries face both the risks of exposure to global systemic crises and to ones that are regional or locally generated. For example, the problems in some Caribbean countries did not stem from the global crisis but from problems at a large regional financial institution, CLICO. The current intermediate stage of financial development creates its own systemic challenges. A survey of supervisors and central bankers conducted by the World Bank and the Asociacion de Supervisores Bancarias de las Americas (ASBA) reveals that Latin American supervisors see the need for incorporating a systemic view into microprudential supervision. Specifically, they cite the necessity for adjusting prudential norms to better account for cross-sectional risk, for enhancing supervisory capacity to assess systemic risk and vulnerabilities, and for extending the supervisory authority to take discretionary action aimed at reducing systemic risk and vulnerabilities.

Traditional prudential supervision can be defined as a process of ensuring that institutions adhere to the minimum standards imposed by regulation and policy and by an institution's own policies, procedures, and controls. The establishment of minimum standards through regulation, policy, and international standard setting is typically thought of as prudential regulation. Systemic supervision, however, takes a broader view of institutional behavior and portfolio decisions. Systemic supervisors should monitor and control the buildup of systemic risk, which in turn could be defined as a risk that spreads to many (if not all) markets and institutions through asset or funding exposures that are similarly affected (highly correlated) by shocks or interconnectedness. Therefore, systemic supervision combines a holistic view of the financial system and macrodevelopments with a forward-looking approach applied to individual institutions and markets.

Systemic supervision can be thought of as taking a top-down view of systemic risk and blending it with bottom-up analysis. This process entails looking at macroeconomic developments, interconnectedness, market conditions, and risks of international contagion. Systemic supervision can involve stricter prudential standards, more intensive monitoring for systemically important institutions, and enhanced supervisory measures for all relevant financial institutions when systemic risks are prominent. It is clear that Latin American countries do not have systemic supervision, but then again neither do most other countries.

The chapter is organized as follows. The chapter first examines the state of supervision in Latin America. It then discusses the elements for formulating a new model for supervision and examines how traditional supervision is likely to change. The following section discusses the issues that are likely to arise as a country attempts to implement a new vision for financial sector supervision, particularly the coordination, organizational, and institutional issues. The chapter concludes with a list of major issues Latin American policy makers will need to address as they work toward a supervisory regime that includes systemic supervision.

The Current State of Supervision in Latin America and the Caribbean

Generally speaking, the Latin America and Caribbean region weathered the global financial crisis relatively well, and many LAC countries have not experienced significant direct effects from the crisis.[1,2] Among the wide variety of causes for this outcome are the reforms put in place by many countries in the region over the past decade to strengthen financial sector supervision. These reforms, which have fortified regional prudential frameworks, can be characterized by, among other things, improved legal frameworks for supervision, capital and liquidity regulations stricter than the Basel minimum standards, enhanced corrective action plans, and more robust bank resolution schemes. The high prudential buffers in the region were also probably remnants of past crises. In addition, financial institutions kept other cushions because the lending environment limited credit expansion. Moreover, during the crisis the region benefited from significant reliance on stable domestic funding and sound management of foreign currency liquidity risk, as well as from low direct exposures to securitization vehicles.[3] The latter is a reflection not only of the higher returns from more traditional banking operations resulting from relatively lower financial development but also of the prominence of strict regulatory frameworks in the region that limit bank exposures to complex derivatives and structured finance.

Despite this strong resilience of the LAC financial sector, a vast majority of respondents to the World Bank–ASBA survey believe that recent world events require a fundamental redefinition, or at least a partial broadening, of the role and functions of the supervisor. They are also of the opinion that supervisors should become more proactive. Only 4 respondents out of 22 believe that there is no real need to change and that the status quo is satisfactory. Hence, the survey reveals a clear consensus among LAC supervisors on the benefits of moving toward a more "early intervention" approach to supervision that takes into account systemic risks.

Such an approach requires revisiting the supervisory framework to establish a more intensive and effective presence at individual banks; conducting a more proactive dialogue with senior bankers on business models, strategies, and risks; and having broad powers for early intervention. Furthermore, a critical component of any supervisory framework should be the ability to combine a microprudential approach with a systemwide view of risks facing the industry and financial sector as a whole. Consequently, supervisors will need to build up their analytical capabilities. The following subsections look at where supervision stands on some of the key issues relating to the incorporation of a systemic view into supervision of the financial sector.

Independence of Supervisors

The review of the Basel Core Principles Assessments done for Latin American and Caribbean countries by Heysen and Auqui (2010) found that one of the remaining shortcomings for supervision is that more than half the bank supervisors lacked operational or budgetary independence. Seelig and Novoa (2009) found that the weaknesses in the independence of financial sector regulators and supervisors relate primarily to the ability to issue regulations and, in some cases, to take certain severe actions, such as license revocation. They also found, for example, that insurance industry representatives are more likely to be on the bodies that supervise the insurance industry than those that supervise banks or capital market firms. Legal protection is also a key element of independence. Heysen and Auqui note that this is particularly important in Central and South America but much less so in the Caribbean. It is also interesting to note that while two-thirds of financial sector supervisors worldwide believe they have legal protection, only 17 percent have that protection once they leave office. This lack of continuity of protection can have a serious chilling effect on supervisors if they know that legal action can be taken against them personally after they leave office. As the range of risks that supervisors are expected to address is broadened and the timeliness of their actions becomes more critical, these issues of independence and legal protection become even more important.

Consolidated Supervision

Consolidated supervision is an essential element of effective supervision. Given that many financial firms have bank and nonbank subsidiaries, a narrow stand-alone view of regulated entities does not give a full picture of their financial risks. The importance of consolidated supervision is confirmed by the core principles (CP24) for effective bank supervision promulgated by the Basel Committee. The remaining gaps in the legal and supervisory framework for consolidated supervision are important sources of risk in several countries. For example, according to the World Bank–ASBA survey in seven countries, the definition of *banking groups* or *financial conglomerates* under the local laws does not include nonfinancial group entities. It should be noted, however, that Brazil has a comprehensive legal and supervisory framework for supervising financial conglomerates.

In four countries, according to the World Bank–ASBA survey, supervisors do not have the capacity to presume which companies form part of the banking group or financial conglomerate. In some cases, parent companies or holding companies may also be excluded from the definition of a *group*. As a result, supervisors lack access to the information on the entities in the conglomerate or banking group that could posea risk of contagion to the group as a whole. These supervisory "blind spots" could allow significant risks to go undetected. On a purely technical basis, even when contagion risks can be identified, it remains very difficult to identify and assess qualitative risks, like reputational and strategic risks, coming from other entities in the group.

In addition, prudential norms in conglomerates or banking groups appear to be absent. Indeed, only eight countries reported having the power to impose a special capital requirement on a financial group. Related-party limits appear to be in place for most respondents, but ownership limits apply to only a bit over half the respondents. These differing regulatory frameworks and supervision practices raise concerns about regulatory arbitrage. Supervisory agencies appear to be well aware that it will require an effort to address this risk; 11 respondents state that their agencies' monitoring of regulatory arbitrage across groups or institutions with different licenses should be strengthened, while 4 admit that they do not monitor regulatory arbitrage at all.

The survey responses on the monitoring of off-balance-sheet risks were more encouraging. Sixteen respondents rate their monitoring as good, and only six state that they need strengthening. Most respondents also seem relatively comfortable with their ability to determine the risks inherent in sophisticated or newly orchestrated products and services; 17 respondents rate their ability as fair or good, while 9 state that it needs strengthening.

Cross-Border Cooperation

Significant improvements have taken place in Latin America in achieving greater multinational cooperation. Most countries have lifted legal obstacles to cooperation, allowing them to sign bilateral memorandums of understanding (MOUs) with other countries. Colleges of supervisors have been created to oversee the large multinational banks operating in Latin America. Nevertheless, the current approach has some significant weaknesses. First, these agreements are focused on banking groups and therefore do not include other financial firms. Second, these agreements (as is true in other regions) do not deal with the resolution of troubled cross-border banks. Third, a clearer division of labor and more frequent and intense communication to ensure that gaps and overlaps are avoided are desirable. Last, the home-host issue becomes even more challenging when the institution is systemically important in the host country but its foreign operations are small relative to the overall institution. This situation has complicated effective information sharing, and the concerns of the host country are frequently ignored by the home country. This latter issue was magnified on a global scale during the recent crisis.

Systemic Supervision

One of the issues emphasized by the global financial crisis is the importance of recognizing and addressing the interconnectedness of players in the financial sector. Traditional supervision has been based on the belief that strong individual banks typically lead to a strong banking system; but this firm-specific approach by itself has been shown to be insufficient. The recent crisis showed that the risk posed to the system was greater than the sum of the risks faced by individual institutions. Some Latin American and Caribbean supervisors recognize this fact and have attempted to address it in the inspection process. About 60 percent of the respondents report that the interconnectedness (in contrast to control) of financial institutions is part of their inspection process. That said, only four countries have taken this practice a step further and report on the interconnectedness within the financial system.

Fourteen respondents (78 percent) confirm that systemic concerns are integrated into the evaluation of the risk profile of individual institutions in a variety of ways. Among the practices cited most frequently are supervising systemically important entities more intensively, rating them differently, or addressing the systemic concerns in stress-testing exercises. One agency also reports that the systemic concerns are analyzed and approved by the top management of the agency before supervision teams are notified for further follow-up.

In the vast majority of cases (83 percent of respondents), the authorities do not explicitly require supervised institutions to report on their exposure to systemic risk. That said, some Latin American supervisory agencies report having started to build particular expertise in this area. The efforts are carried out by the supervisors or by the financial stability unit.

Most supervisory agencies include macroeconomic projections in their risk analysis of individual financial institutions, and only four supervisory agencies reported that they do not apply this practice. There is, however, a range of practices in incorporating these projections into the supervisory process. Some agencies include the results in their analysis of the inherent risks of individual institutions, for instance, when assessing and predicting risk trends, including the volatility of particular investments and the quality of the loan portfolio of a particular bank. Others use the projections in stress-testing exercises. A third practice is to make periodic presentations of the macroeconomic projections and their impact on the financial indicators of individual institutions to the agency's staff.

Latin American supervisors do not appear to rigorously monitor real sector markets for bubbles. Given the experiences in Ireland, Spain, and the United States, the survey asked about the monitoring of housing markets. Six countries indicated that there is no monitoring of the housing market, while 12 respondents believe that their agency's monitoring of the housing market needs strengthening. In this regard, it is interesting to note that close to 77 percent of the authorities do not have a housing price index available. Three countries reported having an index but believe it needs improvement. More than half the respondents do not monitor derivatives markets, but of those who do eight respondents assess their monitoring as good.

Table 11.1 A Sample of Macroprudential Measures in Selected Latin American Countries

	Limits on net open currency positions	Limits on interbank exposures	Limits on loan-to-value ratios and debt-to-income ratios in lending	Countercyclical provisioning
Argentina	X	—	X	—
Brazil	X	—	X[a]	—
Chile	X	X	X	X[b]
Colombia	X	X	X	X
Costa Rica	X	X	X	—
Mexico	X	X	—	X[b]
Peru	X	X	X	X
Uruguay	X	X	—	X

Source: Jacome et al. 2012.
Note: — = none.
a. Caps on loan-to-value ratios eliminated in December 2011.
b. Based on expected nonperforming loans.

Going forward, five respondents stated that they are considering a specific requirement for financial institutions to assess their exposure or contribution to systemic risk based on stress parameters provided by the supervisor. The institutions would then be required to adjust their capital and liquidity positions accordingly. Two countries stated that they already apply this procedure.

There is evidence, albeit limited, of movement toward macroprudential regulation in Latin America. The International Monetary Fund (IMF) conducted a survey of Latin American superintendencies and IMF desk economists during the period November 2010–January 2011.[4] The most commonly used tool has been to reduce exposure to foreign currency volatility by limiting open position exposures and exposures resulting from interbank lending. Other countries, ahead of Basel III, have adopted forms of countercyclical capital or provisioning requirements. Table 11.1 summarizes the results from the IMF survey. To a large extent, the introduction of these macroprudential indicators reflects the history of economic and banking crises in Latin America.

With the widespread adoption of Basel III throughout Latin America in the coming years, the focus on macroprudential policies will become sharper. While such policies aim to insulate banks from a broader range of shocks and to ensure that there is adequate capital in the system to mitigate crisis conditions, the region still needs to develop a more systemic approach to avoid crises.

Supervisory Capacity and Powers

Despite the recognized need to incorporate systemic issues into the supervisory process, countries in the region may not have the capacity and powers to carry out systemic supervision effectively. While 11 respondents to the survey rate their agency's current systemic supervision capacity as good relative to international standards and 5 rate it as fair, 10 respondents think it needs strengthening.

When survey respondents analyzed the obstacles to supervisory agencies' capacity to conduct systemic supervision, responses varied. The highest-rated obstacle is the development of proper staff skills, closely followed by the strengthening of powers, legal protection, and independence of the supervisor. Better coordination—including coordination with the central bank, foreign supervisors, and domestic agencies—also receives high scores, ranking it just above the better use of market data. The option of reconsidering the organization of the supervisory structure receives fewer votes, with only seven respondents considering this very important. Lowest in the overall ranking is the need to pay proper salaries to supervisors, with only eight respondents perceiving this as very important.

With regard to their agency's powers, most supervisors believe that their current authority to request that a financial institution increase its capital, provisions, or liquidity (based on a supervisory assessment of its exposure to systemic risks) is adequate. Only six agencies report that these powers are poor or nonexistent.

The use of systems that automatically trigger corrective action appears not to be widespread. Only one supervisory authority states that it has a fully operating system of automatic triggers. Although another three Latin American supervisors have such systems in place, they admit they need strengthening. Seven authorities have no system but do not rule out adopting one in the future. Another seven do not have automatic corrective triggers and are not planning on implementing them. The most common trigger for corrective action is the capital adequacy ratio. The point of intervention can be the minimum ratio or the breaches of a buffer held in addition to the minimum capital ratio. This illustrates the inevitable trade-offs between discretion and compliance approaches. Even when authorities use automatic triggering systems, they cannot fully avoid the use of supervisory judgment, for example, to set the capital buffer and to decide at which point the corrective action will be triggered.

One technique being used to address systemic risk is stress testing. Twelve respondents confirm that their agencies undertake regular systemic stress-testing exercises, while nine respondents perform this exercise only occasionally. The remaining seven countries do not perform system stress tests but do not rule them out for the future. When regular stress tests are carried out, the common practice appears to be to conduct them on a three to six-month cycle, but for the banking sector only. Authorities that do not perform regular stress tests themselves indicate that they rely on the stress tests conducted under the Financial Sector Assessment Programs.

Formulating a New Vision

Traditional prudential supervision focuses on monitoring the behavior of components of the financial sector (banking, insurance, and securities, for example) and intervening, when necessary, to ensure that individual firms are acting in compliance with the regulatory framework and policy. Prudential regulation consists of a body of laws and regulations that set out the rules of conduct and best-practice guidelines under which firms in the financial sector should operate to safeguard the safety and soundness of the individual players. However, this form of supervision focuses on the individual firm and does not take the forward-looking perspective necessary to assess systemic risk.

Systemic risks are risks to the financial system as a whole rather than risks that affect a single institution. These can arise from a macroeconomic shock, a liquidity crisis, or contagion from problems in one institution that undermine the financial position of the rest of the system, either through financial interrelatedness, common exposures and high correlations between asset classes, or a loss of public confidence in the domestic system. These shocks can arise from endogenous macrofinancial dynamics. However, as the global financial crisis has demonstrated, systemic disruptions to the financial sector in a single country can easily spill over to the rest of the economy and even to other countries. That said, one of the lessons from the Latin American and Asian financial crises in 1994–95 and 1997–98 is that "problems of individual banks can set off chain reactions, both because of the direct links between banks and because of the effects that bank collapses may have on borrowers' capacity to honor commitments" (see Stallings and Studart 2003, 7).

For the most part, past crises in Latin America were associated with unsustainable macrodynamics, often accompanied by the collapse of fixed-exchange-rate regimes. These crises, particularly in smaller Latin American countries, often originated as banking crises.[5] In many cases, the banking sectors in these countries had poor risk management and weak governance compounded by weak supervisory regimes. The global crisis, while not directly affecting much of Latin America, has highlighted a need for a broader approach to supervision. While in the past, international financial organizations, such as the IMF, the Inter-American Development Bank, and the World Bank, have recommended strengthening bank supervision, implementing stricter capital requirements and tightening other regulations, today there is global consensus that a new and broader supervisory vision is needed.

Recently, central banks or other national entities have been given a mandate for macroprudential regulation, meaning that the central bank, or a new body, would have the ability to issue regulations to curb practices that it views as a risk to the financial system. For example, if a credit-fueled housing bubble were developing, the central bank could tighten lending standards or capital requirements for mortgages and construction loans. It would be left to prudential supervisors to ensure that financial institutions follow the new regulations. More than two-thirds of respondents to the World Bank–ASBA survey in Latin American countries see a strong case for using macroprudential tools to curb credit and asset bubbles. In effect, for systemic reasons, the authorities could allocate credit away from certain sectors. However, some Latin American authorities have noted that it could be dangerous to use such tools to address economic downturns because they could also be used for purely political purposes. Many Latin American countries have used capital requirements to control credit booms, although the larger countries have resisted doing so.

While this approach to macroprudential regulation offers a way to deal with certain forms of systemic risk, it does not address interconnectedness and the systemic implications of problems at an institution deemed "too big to fail." Moreover, while only a few Latin American central banks publicly monitor financial stability, many central banks have only a limited ability to conduct macroprudential regulation in the absence of a mandate for financial stability.

Most Latin American countries, partly in response to their prior experience with crises, are perceived to have more "hands-on" supervision than is the case in many developed countries, especially in Europe. However, the majority of supervisors responding to the World Bank–ASBA survey believe that recent global events require a redefinition of the role and functions of supervisors. Supervisors acknowledged that this revised role would require them to be given broader powers, to strengthen off-balance-sheet supervision, to map interconnectedness, and to monitor the housing market.

Hence, framing this new vision for financial sector supervision requires identifying the tools currently missing from the microprudential toolbox but necessary for a more systemically focused approach. The primary vehicle for analysis of systemic issues has been the financial stability reports issued by several Latin American central banks.[6] Even with these reports, there is a question about whether they provide meaningful diagnostics of systemic risk.

New Tools

The tools missing from the current supervisory portfolio of most LAC countries include more robust stress testing and scenario analysis in supervisory reviews of institutional portfolios, a mapping of interconnectedness, full prudential and financial information on all financial institutions (consolidated prudential supervision), and the use of market-based indicators. While these tools are not "new," their use in a systematic assessment of systemic risk is.

Stress Testing

Stress testing was formally introduced into the microprudential supervisory process with the adoption of Basel II. Under Basel II, banks using sophisticated approaches to determine capital charges for credit and market risk have to have rigorous stress-testing programs in place. Some supervisors, such as Brazil, Chile, Mexico, and Peru, use stress testing as part of microprudential bank supervision. Its use, though, has tended to be limited to assessing market risk and the adequacy of bank capital.

Recently, stress testing has become recognized as a tool for macroprudential or systemic supervision. In 2009, the U.S. Federal Reserve introduced its own stress-test scenarios as a way to see whether the largest banks could withstand another systemic shock. U.S supervisors have viewed this as an approach to macroprudential supervision (see Hirtle, Scheurman, and Stiroh 2009) and have recently repeated these tests. Similarly, in 2009 the Committee of European Banking Supervisors conducted stress tests on the largest European banks. However, since banks that had supposedly passed the tests subsequently needed additional capital, the severity of the assumptions used was called into question. In mid-2010, the European Union (EU) announced its intention to conduct stress tests on its largest banks using scenarios developed jointly with the European Central Bank (Economist 2010).

While the use of bank-specific stress testing has advanced in some countries, there have been significant limitations affecting the ability to stress test for systemic events. To start with, financial firms have an inherent incentive to construct tests that show a need for less equity capital rather than more.

To better capture systemic risks with stress testing, models have to incorporate systemic shocks, despite these being low-probability extreme risks (those occurring at the tail of the probability distribution). With the benefit of hindsight, many stress tests did not capture these extreme market events. Historical information used in stress scenarios also reflected the long period of stability that preceded the global financial crisis. Moreover, many stress tests, and risk models alike, relied heavily on historical statistical relationships, like correlations, to assess risk. The crisis has shown that these relationships tend to break down in extreme market conditions. In addition, the stress-testing frameworks did not embody the extreme market reactions observed during the global financial crisis.

Forecasting the future based on the past is like driving a car on a winding mountain road while looking only through the rearview mirror. Hence, supervisors will need to specify well-planned scenarios that go far beyond the obvious and foreseeable risks. The discussions between supervisors and institutions will be difficult in this respect and not unlike those between the IMF and World Bank and the authorities during financial sector assessments.

When the technical capacity for sophisticated modeling is absent, supervisors should still undertake an empirical analysis of the ability of financial institutions to withstand shocks. Stress testing that uses spread-sheet techniques applied to relatively simple financial systems could still provide a useful tool for systemic supervision. However, as noted above, the interrelatedness of institutions and markets should be understood as part of this process. This undertaking should help identify the weakest links in the system without sophisticated modeling and can also be a useful check on the validity of models in a comparison of the findings under the two approaches.

The biggest problem with stress testing is that it is extremely hard to "connect the dots" and to foresee where a crisis might emerge and the channels through which it could spread. Therefore, before proper models can be designed, it is most important to understand how the system is wired and where the weakest link is. In the absence of this fundamental understanding, the result will be very sophisticated, but ultimately sterile, number crunching.

The global financial crisis has shown that, for systemic analysis, the models used in stress testing will have to be expanded in several ways. First, we need to understand the correlations and market reactions rather than focusing on individual events or risks. We must look not only at variances but also at covariances of possible events. Second, given the interconnectedness of the financial sector, it is no longer sufficient to estimate the outcome of scenarios on individual institutions without taking into account how problems at one institution affect others. Third, stress tests must be expanded beyond testing just for capital adequacy. One of the lessons of the crisis is that market liquidity and funding liquidity are equally important, and thus stress tests need to incorporate the impact of liquidity shocks on the ability of a bank to meet its obligations.

Mapping Interconnectedness

One of the key lessons from the recent crisis is that financial institutions and markets are interconnected and that this connection goes beyond links within an ownership group. While this may have been evident to knowledgeable observers, the extent and depth of the multiple interconnections, especially in complex financial systems, were not known. The spillover from the bankruptcy of Lehman Brothers in the United States clearly demonstrates that connectivity does not recognize national borders. For supervisors to map the interconnectivity of their financial sector, they must recognize the potential sources of risk that come from other institutions and markets, both domestic and international.

One can view interconnectedness as having three conduits: through balance sheets, through markets, and through ownership connections. Balance-sheet interconnectedness can be found both on the asset and on the liability sides of the ledger. Asset interconnectedness can arise from lending or investment concentrations, either by borrower or by industry.

Liability interconnectedness derives from excessive reliance on a limited number of parties for financing. Market interconnectedness results from a financial firm's reliance on wholesale funding or wholesale placement of assets, such as through securitization. Ownership interconnectedness, a common problem in Latin America, exists where bank and nonbank financial firms share common group or family ownership. If groups that own financial firms also have interests in the nonfinancial sector and these firms receive funding from the financial firms, the problem is compounded.

Financial systems in Latin America are highly interconnected through ownership. According to Powell (2010), many financial firms in LAC have such complex structures that it may be unclear how a subsidiary fits into the structure. Moreover, corporate structures and legal or regulatory structures may not match, thus raising questions of appropriate supervisory treatment.[7] Latin American financial firms may also face balance-sheet interconnectedness, given the economic concentration of real sector production activities in many of their countries. Financial firms face a real sector where borrowers are likely to be directly or indirectly connected with one another and cross-guarantees are ultimately tied to one family's resources. Moreover, given the heavy reliance of many Latin American economies on either agriculture or natural resources, financial firms face concentrated risks.

Market interconnectedness is less a problem in Latin America, given the level of financial development. However, as LAC countries increase the depth of their financial systems, supervisors will have to be more vigilant on these interconnectedness issues.

To map interconnectedness, one can evaluate institutions according to various criteria. Is the financial firm a branch or subsidiary of an offshore entity? Is it part of a group, whether a holding company or a single or family owner? How vulnerable are the asset and liability sides of the balance sheet to developments in other markets or institutions? How vulnerable is the institution's ability to fund itself to developments in markets or to developments affecting other institutions? Which ones? Can the financial firm's business that generates noninterest income (fees) and involves dealings with other financial institutions cause reputational risk? What are the paths of financial contagion within the system? Each of these questions is discussed below.

Offshore Entities Many Latin American countries are host supervisors to subsidiaries or branches of large foreign banks, including some in the United States that experienced difficulties during the crisis. Clearly, there is always the risk of contagion to the host bank following a parent bank's problems. The parent's ability to support its affiliate will also likely be constrained by the home country supervisor. Understanding the full dimensions of the parent organization is important, and cooperation with home supervisors is vital. Unfortunately, during the crisis, some home supervisors were unwilling, or unable, to share information with host supervisors in a timely way.

Group Entities The essence of consolidated supervision is viewing a financial group as a whole. In Latin America, this perspective may pose a greater challenge because family groups may own financial institutions in more than one country and because in many countries the connections between the financial and the nonfinancial parts of large family groups are not fully identified and understood. Nevertheless, institutions may fund activities within the group, transfer investment risk among firms within the group to escape capital restrictions, and even double-leverage investments in firms within the group. Supervisors will need to have a complete picture of the group and to coordinate with other supervisors to assemble a proper risk profile of the group and an understanding of the vulnerabilities of the entities in one sector and jurisdiction to actions affecting another part of the group.

Vulnerability to Risk from Another Institution Understanding the risks on the asset side of a financial institution's balance sheet emanating from another institution is a part of the mapping process. The recent crisis was to a large extent triggered by mortgage defaults in the United States. Latin American financial institutions did not take significant positions in assets related to the U.S. subprime mortgage market, perhaps because of both the abundance of high-yielding investment opportunities in Latin America and the shorter economic cycles. Alternatively, the high solvency and liquidity buffers observed in the region suggest that prudence and regulatory constraints may have been more important.

Funding of Financial Institutions How financial institutions fund themselves is critical to understanding the interconnectedness in the system. If financial firms fund themselves solely by taking deposits from the public in their home market, interconnectedness in funding is not a problem. However, if they rely on interbank markets, borrowings from other financial firms, funding from parent companies, heavy offshore funding, or even concentrated funding from domestic sources, the financial firm and potentially the system itself may be vulnerable to a shock that disrupts funding.

Reputational Risk As financial markets deepen, banks and other financial firms attempt to generate fee income to increase earnings. Inasmuch as these activities generally do not require that the firm hold additional capital, they generally are less costly than traditional financial activities and enhance earnings per share. In developed countries, such activities have taken the form of cross-selling of financial products to existing customers, originating loans for securitization, or elaborate investment and trading activities. Some of these activities, such as securitization, contributed to the crisis. More important, especially in countries where financial groups (formal or informal) exist, firms tend to engage in interfirm transactions that can expose one financial firm to the reputational risk caused by the actions of another firm. For example, if a bank sells insurance and the insurance company becomes insolvent, the bank may face a direct financial exposure or, at a minimum, a loss of reputation. Hence, as the financial system becomes more complex and interconnected, systemic risk increases.

Sources of Contagion One of the main purposes for mapping interconnectedness is to get an understanding of the sources of contagion. It is not enough to understand just the legal relationships between firms in the financial sector, but one must also understand the informal business relationships (such as loan participation and funding arrangements) that may give rise to contagion. Understanding concentrations, whether in the commercial or in the financial sectors, also serves to highlight potential sources of contagion. In many Latin American countries, given the concentrations of wealth, the financial sector may be directly affected by how well certain commercial groups do. Similarly, understanding cross-country contagion is critical. Empirical work has shown how closely connected some Latin American countries' economies are to their neighbors (see Sosa 2010). The risk of contagion is compounded when financial firms rely on citizens of the neighboring countries for a significant portion of their funding or income.

Market Indicators

Traditionally, prudential supervisors have paid little attention to financial markets' judgments on the health of financial institutions, except when market perceptions have triggered liquidity problems. In recent years, however, a number of instruments have been developed to capture some of the risks faced by financial institutions. Much of this has built on seminal work by Robert C. Merton (1974) and by Fischer Black and Myron Scholes (1973). However, it must be noted that for these indicators to provide useful information, a reasonably well developed capital market must exist.

Various instruments that have allowed investors to hedge against a broader range of risks can also provide supervisors with indicators of potential problems or growing risks. These indicators reflect the market's view of the outlook for nations, industries, firms, and financial institutions. These views directly affect firms' cost of borrowing and equity capital and thus allow markets to discipline firms. Markets have information different from supervisors, but, more important, market views and expectations directly influence the pricing and availability of funding. Central banks in several countries, such as Brazil, Chile, and Mexico, have been working to incorporate market-based measures into their financial stability analysis. However, most Latin American countries still rely on commodity and housing price indexes rather than on measures of market sentiment in their financial stability assessments.

One measure that can provide useful information to supervisors is the change in spreads on credit default swaps. This indicator identifies changes in the market's expectations that an entity will default on its bonds or other obligations. It can be viewed as a short-term leading indicator of market rates. Other measures are changes in stock prices and the volatility of traded equities (see Sharpe 1964). A more recent body of work, based on early work by Robert Merton, has incorporated finance theory, market data, and a contingent claims approach to examining financial stability risks (see Gray and Malone 2008). The Chilean central bank has used this approach (see Gray and Walsh 2008). A barrier to the use of market sentiment indicators faced by many smaller Latin American countries is the difficulty of obtaining market information like credit default swap spreads in the absence of well-developed local capital markets. Besides providing information to the markets, authorities may also initially need to provide quality institutional analyses to the market as a means of facilitating market development. As equity and debt markets develop in the region, more information on market sentiment will become readily available. In the meantime, however, larger institutions or groups may conduct securities, debt, or equity trading in regional or international markets, and the behavior of these instruments should provide information. In addition, credit default swap spreads are available for sovereign debt sold in international markets. Given LAC's history of financial sector problems translating into fiscal problems, these spreads will contain a view on the health of the banking sector.

Difference between Systemic Supervision and Regulation

Systemic regulation requires a legal framework implemented through rules that govern the allocation decisions and risk profiles of financial institutions. These rules apply to all institutions and are not specific to individual institutions. To discourage lending, for example, a systemic regulation might establish a maximum loan-to-value regulation in response to a housing price bubble.

Systemic supervision, however, tends to focus on individual firms and typically requires discretion on the part of the supervisor. It would entail examining the practices of individual institutions. In the case of a housing bubble, for example, if a supervisor determined that a lender either was being too lenient in underwriting loans or was extending an excessive volume of housing loans relative to its overall asset portfolio, that supervisor would order the institution to cease granting such loans or would require it to tighten underwriting standards beyond those spelled out in system-wide regulations.[8]

In a systemic context, there is an even greater need to deviate from a common rule (for example, raising capital requirements above the statutory limit across the board for all institutions) and to give supervisors the discretion to apply more rigid standards to individual institutions, either because they are systemically important or because their actions pose a risk to the system as a whole. Consequently, one can characterize the distinction between an approach in which supervision and regulation are based on a fixed set of rules and regulations and one that allows discretionary flexibility as a "rules-versus-discretion" debate.[9] The challenge is to build discretion into the supervisory process to allow supervisors to introduce systemic risk into supervision. This is a greater challenge in civil law countries, such as those in Latin America, where supervisors can usually take only actions that are specified in law and regulation. Consequently, these countries need to implement systemic regulations for supervisors to enforce but also to enact legislation that allows and encourages supervisory discretion.

While enhancing supervisory discretion is an admirable goal, there are issues that make the rules-versus-discretion debate delicate. Granting supervisors significant discretion requires confidence that the supervisor is independent from political pressure, has the expertise and technical capacity to make the judgments called for, and has the legal power to enforce those judgments. An alternative to placing all responsibility on the supervisor would be to have the systemic supervisory analysis reside with an entity other than the prudential supervisor. That entity could be the central bank or a council made up of different authorities.[10] However, to avoid abuse, it will likely be important to define a proper process of analysis, decision making, cooperation, and reporting, as has been done in many countries that have adopted inflation targeting.

Market Discipline

There has been a longstanding debate within the supervisory community on the efficacy of market discipline for the financial sector. Economists have supported greater reliance on capital market instruments, such as subordinated debt, as a means both to curb banks' appetite for excessive risk taking and to provide market feedback to supervisors. While there is an extensive body of literature (see Evanoff and Wall 2000) dating back to Horvitz (1983), it primarily revolves around requiring banks to issue subordinated debt to increase the market discipline of banks that have benefited from deposit insurance and possibly a wider implicit guarantee on their liabilities.

The global financial crisis, however, has uncovered some important flaws in this assumption, as market participants did not identify and adequately discipline in a timely manner firms that took excessive risks.[11] Once the crisis spread, market participants reacted as expected. That said, empirical evidence suggests that market discipline failed to operate early enough to prevent the buildup of systemic risks during the good times (Stephanou 2010). Despite this delayed response, market discipline manifested itself during the recent global crisis mainly through the short-term funding markets. Credit very rapidly became unavailable to Lehman Brothers, and, in the absence of measures to halt the buildup of risk, that lack of credit precipitated its downfall. Irish banks experienced outflows of wholesale deposits, at first partly in response to international nervousness over the bankruptcy of Lehman but subsequently in response to market concerns about the condition of these banks.

However, despite market signals of potential problems, market discipline alone did not curb the buildup of risk in the system. Only after the problems became apparent and the crisis was reality did market discipline become so severe that it forced regulatory and supervisory responses. The experience in Latin America and elsewhere suggests that market discipline may have been effective in triggering needed policy responses. While European and U.S. authorities were forced to take action to provide capital to troubled institutions and to resolve others, Latin American policy makers adjusted their monetary policies to minimize the disruption from the crisis but, given the financial position of their institutions, did not have to take the measures seen elsewhere.

The broader question arising from the crisis is not whether market discipline is good or bad but whether the markets have adequate information about financial institutions. Traditionally, supervisors felt that the information they collected from regulated financial firms should be kept confidential. In the United States, it was not until the mid-1970s that balance-sheet data collected by supervisors were made public. Today, most central banks and supervisory agencies around the world publish information about banks, generally on a bankwide consolidated basis but in some instances also on an individual basis. Less information is made available by insurance and securities supervisors. However, data and judgments contained in examination reports are usually kept confidential. Nevertheless, great strides have been made in providing additional information to markets in the Western Hemisphere. With the advent of risk-based deposit insurance premiums in the United States, analysts were readily able to estimate which banks were viewed as more risky by the Federal Deposit Insurance Corporation. In Uruguay, the banking supervisor (part of the central bank) publishes detailed financial information about each banking firm on a monthly basis with a degree of detail that allows analysts to completely understand the financial condition of individual banks. In fact, using the database, one financial reporter was able to predict when a small cooperative bank might become insolvent. While most supervisors make their ratings' methodology public, they do not disclose the actual ratings to the public. While in a sense supervisory information can be viewed as a public good that should be made available, such a practice could raise serious difficulties, particularly in market reactions. It could also distort incentives for supervisors to make rating changes and have up-to-date ratings, as any change would have to be justified to the outside world.

The key to "proper" market discipline is sound data and information on financial firms. Pillar 3 of Basel II is a step in this direction and should be applied beyond banks to a broader range of financial firms.

Striking a Balance between Financial Stability and Financial Sector Development

One of the key issues in formulating a new vision for supervision is striking the balance between financial stability and development. If supervisory responsibilities are to be broadened to include systemic risks, finding the appropriate trade-off between the restrictiveness of supervision and the stifling of the development of financial markets will be important. This is particularly true in Latin America, where many countries are only now beginning to develop markets in insurance and securities.

Chile is a good example of a country with a well-functioning and relatively developed financial sector that contributes to its economic growth. In their study of Latin American countries after the so-called tequila crisis, Stallings and Studart (2003) suggest that a more rigid supervisory and regulatory framework may be needed as financial systems begin to develop but that greater supervisory flexibility may be appropriate once markets have developed.

In studying some EU countries, Granlund (2009) found that stricter supervision was consistent with financial market development. However, in the EU countries he looked at, most of the supervisory changes were related to market stability and organizational changes in the supervisory structure. Thus, how supervision is made more stringent may be the more critical determinant to financial market development.

Given that the literature has shown financial development to be a key element of the economic development process (see Levine 1999; Kahn and Senhadi 2000), it becomes critical that supervisors not stifle financial innovation. As Musalem and Baer noted in their study of Latin American capital markets, "The key is to strike the right balance on the level of regulation and supervision to prevent financial crisis while not discouraging financial innovation and growth" (Musalem and Baer 2010, 3). When controlling for macroeconomic and other fundamentals that stimulate capital market development, de la Torre, Gozzi, and Schmukler (2006), in their econometric analysis, find that being a Latin American country has a negative and significant impact on financial market development. One possible explanation of these findings is that oversight and regulation in Latin America are more stringent than elsewhere.

While it is easy to blame financial innovation for the recent global crisis, supervisors, investors, and banks alike were more likely not to have understood the risk profile of some of the financial products, such as collateralized debt obligations, and the synthetic variations that were created to increase the size of the market, nor the risks associated with them. Requiring greater transparency, ensuring that adequate and timely information is made available to investors, and monitoring the risk positions of regulated investors are preferable to outright bans under the rubric of systemic supervision.

Implementing a New Model for Supervision

Systemic supervision looks at risks from a top-down perspective and blends this analysis with bottom-up analysis. Incorporating systemic risks into the supervisory process and increasing the powers of supervisors to take actions when these risks become a significant threat to the economy raise a number of implementation issues. These issues include coordination with other domestic and international supervisors and the central bank and with other economic policy bodies. Implementation also involves issues such as institutional capacity and skills, organizational structure (not only within existing agencies but also across the financial system), and the independence of systemic supervisors. More important, supervisors will need to recognize how their jobs fit into the overall macropolicy framework and that they need to incorporate a forward-looking macroperspective not only into their supervision of individual institutions but also into a view of the implications of macroeconomic developments for the financial sector as a whole. This change in vision entails significant implementation issues that are not specific to Latin America alone.

Is There a Need to "Retool" Supervision?

Systemic supervision can be viewed as a supplement to traditional microprudential supervision; however, it is not just a simple add-on. According to the World Bank–ASBA survey, five Latin American bank supervisors believe that they are, to some degree, incorporating systemic concerns into the risk profiles of individual banks, and those countries are considering asking financial institutions to assess their contribution to systemic risk based on stress parameters provided by the supervisor. While these are positive steps, they are not sufficient.

Latin American supervisory agencies should enhance their ability to address systemic risks. This effort will require access to increased analytical capabilities. It is worth noting that some of the Latin American countries that have made the greatest strides in using more advanced analytical tools are those where the supervisor is part of the central bank (Brazil, for example) or where the supervisory agency has recruited economists to staff a macroprudential unit, as in Mexico. However, many smaller countries have been slower to move in this direction.

The recent trend to require larger institutions to undertake stress tests, both as part of Basel II and as in the more recent response to the crisis by Europe and the United States, puts a burden on supervisors not only to define scenarios but also to have the technical capacity to evaluate the models being used by the institutions. Similarly, the necessity of paying more attention to market indicators will require staff to have a greater knowledge of finance theory and empirical techniques. Attracting qualified staff may be problematic, particularly in countries where salaries are limited to government pay scales.

If supervisors are unable to attract qualified staff, they can form cooperative arrangements with central banks where staff trained in econometrics are likely to reside. These arrangements can be informal or very structured. The supervisory and financial stability staffs will also need to show more cooperation, even when they are both housed in the central bank.

Can Top-Down and Bottom-Up Supervision Be Intermingled?

The question arises about whether and how a more systemwide approach can and should be combined with micro-oriented supervision. While all countries face this question, it may be made more complicated in civil law countries where the microprudential supervisory approach is more prescribed in law and supervisors have less flexibility than their counterparts in common law countries.

Traditional bottom-up prudential supervision focuses on assessing the financial condition and risk profile of a financial firm at a given point in time. The parameters and approaches used in making these assessments are spelled out in law and in the guidance, standards, and codes issued by the international standard setters for banking and insurance supervisors (the Basel Committee for Bank Supervision and the International Association of Insurance Supervisors). Typically, on-site inspectors examine the financial condition of an individual institution as well as the risks associated with its underwriting of loans or insurance and investments. The skill sets and approaches used for these activities are very different from those envisioned for systemic supervision. Following Basel II implementation, countries like Brazil, Mexico, and Peru require selected banks to use stress testing to help determine their capital adequacy (Heysen and Auqui 2010). As more countries in the region allow banks to use stress-test models to serve as an input into setting capital levels, supervisors will have to have the appropriate expertise to evaluate the banks' models and stress-testing methodologies critically.

The major benefit of intermingling bottom-up microprudential supervision with top-down systemic supervision is the information feedback loop that will allow for a sound assessment of systemic risks. Brazil has already taken steps in this direction. Since bank supervision is within the central bank, it has improved its ability to monitor financial stability and take corrective actions through the use of new tools that allow it to monitor the market risk and liquidity exposures of individual institutions (see Heysen and Aqui 2010). There are significant benefits from factoring the risk positions and strategies of individual institutions into macrolevel analysis. The best source of the latter information is the microprudential bottom-up supervisor.

For systemic supervision to be effective, supervisors need to understand the actions of individual institutions and their tolerance for various types of risks. One of the weaknesses in the financial stability analysis published by central banks has been the absence of the supervisors' perspective on what is happening at individual institutions. Hence, combining the bottom-up supervision with the top-down systemic supervision should provide synergies. Top-down supervisors will gain from the insights and information gathered by bottom-up supervisors, and the latter will gain new perspectives on potential risks that will enable them to refine and broaden their assessments. Moreover, with sufficient legal flexibility, microprudential supervisors will be able to incorporate these threats into their assessment of an institution's risk profile and assess the need for supervisory actions. For example, if excessive lending were deemed a systemic risk, supervisors could order banks to tighten underwriting standards or require higher provisions or capital buffers.

When top-down systemic supervision is separate from bottom-up micro-based supervision, it is very important that the two approaches be coordinated. In countries where bottom-up supervision is with the central bank, adding top-down systemic supervision should, in principle, make coordination issues much simpler. In reality, however, when top-down supervision and bottom-up supervision are housed in the same institution, coordination problems can still arise. For example, if the organizational structure divides responsibilities too finely or reporting lines lead to different senior managers, there tends to be a lack of coordination. In some central banks, the internal barriers between the financial stability staff and the bank supervisors are so great that financial stability analysis has ignored the findings of the on-site supervisors, resulting in a flawed analysis. Good coordination will require that the same deputy governor or governor take on the coordination role and the responsibility for total financial sector supervision. In countries where top-down supervision rests with the central bank and bottom-up supervision resides in one or more independent agencies, coordination has the potential to become more difficult. To address these challenges, countries will have to consolidate all supervision into a single agency, place bottom-up and top-down under the central bank, or create coordinating mechanisms at the highest level as well as at operational levels. Such mechanisms could take the form of a high-level systemic risk council. For further discussion of this issue, see below.

What Are the Roles for On-Site and Off-Site Supervision?

With the adoption of systemic supervision, the roles of on-site and off-site may need to be redefined. Prudential supervision has traditionally been a combination of on- and off-site supervision. In many countries, off-site supervision serves a monitoring function between full-scope inspections that occur only every one or two years. In other countries, both functions are fully integrated at the institutional level. In general, off-site supervision provides a review and analysis function in support of on-site supervision. Clearly, traditional on-site supervision can provide insights into systemic supervision, but the bulk of the work will be done off-site with a greater focus on systemwide analysis and research. The emphasis going forward needs to be on better understanding the risks faced by financial firms, and this effort will require that on-site supervisors have a role greater than just checking compliance with regulations.

Systemic supervision entails the identification of systemic risks. Those tasked with such supervision will therefore need to monitor macroeconomic trends, especially the potential for speculative bubbles. The latter is clearly manifested when financial firms are pressured by market forces to follow the strategies being pursued by other firms and a clear herd instinct has taken hold (in theoretical terms, there are coordination and other collective action failures in the market). The interconnectedness of the financial sector should be monitored, and links on the asset and liability sides of important institutions need to be monitored continuously. While much of the work can be done off-site, the continuous monitoring of the asset and liability links can best be verified by on-site inspectors. Last, there is a need for off-site monitoring of market indicators of risk, both to the system and to institutions considered systemically important.

How Should Supervisors Coordinate Laterally and across Borders?

Ensuring coordination among supervisors, both across agencies domestically and with international counterparts, is critical for effective systemic supervision. The World Bank–ASBA survey highlights the need to improve coordination among bank supervisors, other domestic financial sector supervisors, the central bank, and foreign financial sector supervisors. As discussed above, given the high degree of interconnectedness and the growing number of cross-border financial institutions in Latin America and the Caribbean, measures to ensure coordination are of utmost importance. In some countries, domestic supervisors have been cooperating less successfully, leading to problems and regulatory arbitrage by institutions. Even when the different parts of the financial sector are supervised within the same entity, internal coordination problems may arise. Both Mexico and Uruguay have recently reformed the organizational structures of the agencies responsible for supervision to enhance the supervision of cross-sectoral financial firms.

As shown below, the arguments for and against single supervisory agencies do not lead to an obvious conclusion, and thus the decision must be taken within the context of national characteristics. While there are arguments in favor of placing all financial sector supervision under the purview of the central bank and giving the central bank responsibility for systemic supervision, there are also arguments against doing so. Clearly, however, regardless of the structure chosen for supervision, the central bank must have ready access to the necessary prudential supervisory information and must maintain close coordination with the supervisory bodies. This coordination is easier said than done, given the natural tendency of bureaucracies to protect their own turf, even within an organization.

In the past, led by the United Kingdom, there was a movement toward single supervisory agencies as a means to enhance cooperation and address the specific risks from emerging conglomerates or from financial institutions active in different segments of the financial sector. This move was emulated in some emerging market countries, such as Colombia in 2005. However, the global crisis has led some European countries to rethink the single agency approach inasmuch as it did little to prevent the crisis, notwithstanding the supposed benefits from consolidation. There is a sense that the removal of supervision from the central bank resulted in less effective supervisory approaches and processes, possibly because the weakest supervisory framework within the single agency became the norm.[12] Masciandaro, Pansini, and Quintyn (2011), however, find that the degree of involvement of the central bank did not have any significant impact on the resilience of bank supervision. Whichever approach is taken, coordination issues will remain and are compounded by systemic supervision, since coordination is also needed with authorities responsible for macroeconomic policy and macroprudential regulation (if a different entity).

Garicano and Lastra (2010) have suggested some regulatory principles for the postcrisis world. The first of these is that the supervision (both prudential and market conduct) of banking, securities, and insurance should be further integrated to achieve greater coordination and reduce the costs associated with multiple regulators. According to Garicano and Lastra, the structure that would guarantee the maximum potential for coordination of prudential supervision and ensure a systemic perspective would be to place all financial sector supervision under the central bank. They argue that systemic supervision must be under the purview of the central bank. However, this proposal assumes that the central bank is responsible for financial stability and not just price stability. Aside from policy arguments in favor of this position, there may be practical arguments in developing countries, such as much of Latin America and the Caribbean, that support giving central banks this key role. In these countries, central banks typically have the greatest analytical capabilities, and their salaries are not constrained by government wages. The central bank would then also become the systemic regulator and have complete responsibility for managing systemic risk. While this arrangement would ensure the greatest potential for effective coordination, it would create an extremely powerful central bank that may not be fully consistent with political realities. Hence, there may be attempts to limit the independence of the central bank as a trade-off for its gaining systemic supervision responsibilities, thereby undermining the hard-fought gains in monetary independence.

Concentrating all financial regulation and supervision in one agency, however, may introduce an economic cost to the system. An argument for diversity in supervisors is to encourage innovation. Sah and Stiglitz (1986) have noted that in a centralized structure proposals for change will have to go through successive screens and that only those that make it through all the screens will be accepted. A system with multiple regulators allows for several independent screens, whereby if at least one agency accepts a proposal it gets through. Hence, if the goal is to encourage innovation in the provision of financial services, a diversity of agencies is preferred. However, aside from coordination costs, there is the risk of competition in laxity and a greater likelihood of forbearance toward systemically important institutions in the event of a liquidity crisis.[13]

In any case, in their lender-of-last-resort role, central banks must have real-time access to necessary prudential supervisory information on all financial firms.[14] The Bank of England's handling of Northern Rock during the early stages of the U.K. crisis highlights the outcome of poor coordination and the exclusion of central banks from such information. This episode drives home the point that a central bank, which is expected to provide emergency liquidity support to systemically important banks, needs immediate access to supervisory information—especially in a crisis—to perform its function as lender of last resort.

Rather than changing the basic structure of supervision, some countries have devised alternative mechanisms to bring about greater coordination in dealing with systemic risks. The United States established the Financial Stability Oversight Council made up of all major financial sector regulators with responsibility for determining which financial firms are "too big to fail." Similarly, in December 2010, the EU created the European Systemic Risk Board, an independent EU body responsible for macroprudential oversight of the financial system within the EU. The EU also established a joint committee of European supervisory authorities to ensure greater cooperation among supervisors. Latin American countries are wrestling with whether they should revise their structures. In some cases, measures have formalized existing arrangements that had grown out of previous experience with financial crises. For example, Uruguay has created a council made up of the superintendent of financial services, the president of the central bank, the head of the deposit insurance agency, and the minister of economy and finance to review developments and coordinate any necessary measures.

While in theory these structures should ensure greater coordination among policy makers, previous efforts have not always worked. Hence, within these structures there may be a need to ensure accountability and express authority to take necessary actions. The latter can be achieved by spelling out a clear decision-making process, whether by majority vote or by giving one party the final say. Nevertheless, less input has come from

LAC countries in shaping the international debate, perhaps because many LAC governments may not yet have come to a final view on the optimal structure for their countries.

Aside from ensuring lateral coordination domestically, countries need to develop mechanisms for coordination of cross-border systemic supervision. As noted earlier, Latin American and Caribbean countries are often served by international banks, regional banks, or banks that have common owners in other Latin American countries. Since systemic risks can spread across borders, it is imperative that systemic supervisors in Latin America have processes in place for adequate information sharing, for policy coordination during periods of stress, and for regular communication. In the past, prudential supervisors have used mechanisms such as colleges of supervisors or memorandums of understanding with their peers in other countries. However, the recent crisis showed that communications and information sharing broke down rather quickly. While the U.S. authorities may have communicated with their European counterparts, many developing countries with subsidiaries of Citibank, for example, felt that access to information was difficult.

In the absence of a simple solution to the coordination challenge, Latin American countries might be best off seeking a regional approach. This approach could ensure information sharing and coordination among regional systemic supervisors and would provide a unified front in dealings with home supervisors of institutions with a significant presence in Latin America. Whether the structure is a college of supervisors, a formal regional body (possibly under the auspices of an international financial institution), or an association of systemic supervisors similar to the International Association of Deposit Insurers is a political decision that needs to be worked out by regional consensus.

One of the barriers to meaningful information sharing on individual institutions both among domestic supervisors and with international counterparts is secrecy laws that limit the ability of supervisors to disclose certain types of financial information about individual institutions. In those countries where such laws block information sharing, amendments will be needed to allow prudential supervisors to share such information with domestic and international counterparts as well as with domestic and international systemic supervisors. This need becomes even more pressing in view of the growing interconnectedness of Latin American countries within the region and internationally.

Will Systemic Supervisors Need Additional Powers or Independence?

Systemic supervisors will require additional powers if they are to enforce systemic regulations. Included will be the need for the authority to order an institution to "cease and desist" from activities that pose a systemic risk. This authority may go beyond the "safety and soundness" orders used by some prudential supervisors. In the case of systemic risks, even though a practice or a transaction may not necessarily endanger the institution, it still may have systemic consequences. For example, securitization sheds risky loans from a bank's balance sheets but might transfer the risk to other institutions and have a systemic impact on, for example, pension funds.

The IMF has concluded that "in the absence of concrete methods to formally limit the ability of financial institutions to become systemically important in the first place—regardless of how regulatory functions are allocated—regulators are still likely to be more forgiving with systemically important institutions than those that are not" (see IMF 2010, 63). Systemic supervisors will need greater discretion in determining what poses a systemic risk and which institutions are systemically important and in taking appropriate actions. By their very nature, systemic risks cannot always be anticipated. Hence, it is difficult to catalog them ex ante in legislation. In addition, because to date no international standards or lists of risks exist, legislation cannot be written referencing such standards, as was done with Basel II. The implication is that Latin American authorities, faced with a civil law framework, will need to be creative in drafting legislation that gives the systemic supervisor sufficient discretion in both determining what poses a systemic risk and taking the necessary actions.

One of the lessons of the recent crisis is that countries need robust financial resolution frameworks that provide alternatives to reliance on corporate bankruptcy rules or, for banks, payouts by a deposit insurance scheme to depositors. The crisis highlighted the lack of adequate frameworks in Germany, Ireland, and the United Kingdom. While many of the Latin American countries that previously experienced banking crises (Argentina, Mexico, and Uruguay, for example) adopted resolution frameworks for banks, most countries do not have resolution frameworks for securities and insurance firms. Given their interconnectedness with the banking sector, as well as their own potential systemic importance, new financial sector resolution regimes will be needed. The United States recently adopted such a framework as part of the financial reform law passed in 2010. It will need to implement a broader resolution framework as part of a mandate to reduce systemic risks and avoid crises. The nature of the framework, the degree of authority given to systemic supervisors, and the methods of accountability are all policy issues that each country must tailor to its own needs.

What Role Can External Assessment Play in the Establishment of Systemic Supervision?

Besides calling for numerous changes to strengthen microprudential supervision of the financial sector, the G-20 leaders tasked the IMF, the Financial Stability Board, and the Bank for International Settlements to develop guidelines on how countries can assess the systemic importance of financial institutions, markets, and instruments. A report was presented to the G-20 finance ministers and central bank governors in November 2010. It covered the following main topics (see IMF 2010): the concept of what constitutes systemic relevance, the criteria for determining systemic importance, a toolbox of measures and techniques fpr operationalizing the assessment of systemic risk, and international guidelines for assessing systemic relevance, the form they may take, and their possible uses.

Given the difficult issues outlined in this chapter that countries will face in attempting to devise an appropriate scheme, a review and evaluation process should be helpful. Especially in Latin America, where economic power tends to be concentrated, giving authorities more powers and independence is likely to be politically contested.[15] Experience with the Reports on Standards and Codes performed by the World Bank and IMF as part of the Financial Sector Assessment Program has shown that many countries have used the criticisms in these peer reviews as arguments for strengthening their regimes. A review process can also help countries make some of the difficult decisions by introducing independent views. This would be most beneficial if the peer group contains persons with first-hand knowledge of what went wrong in other countries during the recent crisis.

Basel III and Latin America

Basel III combines macro- and microprudential supervision. The approach attempts to address risks across the financial sector as well as the evolution of risk over the economic cycle. Both the depth and the severity of the global financial crisis were amplified by inadequate and low levels of capital, excessive leverage, and insufficient liquidity (see Caruana 2010). As a result, the major regulatory focus of Basel III has been to improve both the quality and the quantity of capital, including a countercyclical component, and to require liquidity buffers.

The Basel Committee has strengthened the definition of capital by improving the quality of the capital base. There is a greater focus on equity capital, the definition of what counts as equity capital has been tightened, and deductions from capital come off of equity capital rather than tier 1 or tier 2 capital measures. The goal is to prevent banks from showing strong tier 1 capital while having eroded their equity base. In addition, as part of a move to require more capital, the minimum common equity level has been raised from 2 to 4.5 percent. The net effect of the change in the capital requirements is that banks will have to hold a minimum common equity of 4.5 percent of risk-weighted assets, tier 1 capital of 6 percent, and total capital of 8 percent. In addition, banks will need to hold a buffer of an additional 2.5 percent, comprising common equity, to cover cyclical risks. This latter buffer is called a capital conservation buffer and is to be used when losses mount. Moreover, as losses mount and capital moves toward the minimum requirements, supervisors should constrain discretionary distributions, such as dividends.

As noted earlier in this chapter, over the past decade supervisors in Latin America have made great strides in tightening their frameworks and in moving toward compliance with Basel I and Basel II requirements. Many countries benefited from assessments of their compliance with the Basel Core Principles for Effective Bank Supervision. In addition, many Latin American supervisors, recognizing the nature of the risks facing their banking sector, required capital in excess of the Basel requirements. These measures helped cushion Latin America from the effects of the recent crisis and softened the impact of tighter capital requirements on banks. A 2012 study by Galindo, Rojas-Suarez, and del Valle shows that banks in Bolivia, Colombia, Ecuador, and Peru will meet the Basel III capital requirements (see Caruana 2010).

Looking Ahead

While the global financial crisis has awakened much of the developed world to the realities of financial crises and has led to calls for improving supervision, Latin American countries have first-hand experience with crises caused by asset bubbles, hyperinflation, exchange rate instability, and liquidity pressures resulting from either loss of confidence in domestic banks or contagion from a neighboring country. As a result, they have made a concerted effort to strengthen bank supervision. While much work still needs to be done, LAC countries recognize the need to incorporate a more systemic view into microlevel prudential supervision.

The following are major issues and steps that policy makers need to focus on as they incorporate a systemic vision into their reform of financial sector supervisory processes:

- Given the risks facing Latin American economies, policy makers need to find the appropriate balance between financial stability and financial sector development when setting requirements.
- Ensuring that the agency tasked with systemic supervision has the resources and capability to attract appropriate staff is critical. Policy makers should adopt compensation and other policies that allow the agency to attract and retain staff with the necessary analytical skills.
- The role of market discipline and market indicators in systemic supervision in LAC countries needs to be considered. Policy decisions should be made about the role of the public sector in promoting market development and discipline and about how much

to rely on market discipline and indicators as part of the supervisory framework.

- Given the importance of ensuring proper coordination among the key players in the supervisory framework, countries need to decide on the appropriate organizational structure for systemic supervision. There is no clear "best-case model," and each country has to choose the option (create a new body, assign responsibility to the central bank or to the supervisory agency, or consolidate all prudential and systemic supervisory functions into one entity) that works best for it. In addition, if the preferred approach is to establish a systemic risk council, the country should ensure that the council is not just a façade for business as usual. The design issues for all these options are critical and in and of themselves raise political-economy issues.

- Improving coordination among domestic supervisors and central bankers is critical for systemic supervision. Hence, policy makers need to develop policies and mechanisms such as organizational changes, information-sharing rights, and incentives to achieve better coordination.

- Ensuring that supervisors have sufficient powers and independence to implement systemic supervision is critical. Countries should define their expectations for systemic supervision and then benchmark existing powers against these expectations.

- Successful systemic supervision depends on international cooperation, and thus the role of regional bodies needs to be adjusted and thought given as to whether to rely on existing bodies or to create a new one.

- Prudential supervision should be further developed and applied to capital market firms.

- Solvency standards that fully reflect the risks being taken by insurance firms should be developed.

All these issues and measures require a great deal of analysis and clearly involve economic and political trade-offs. Policy makers should put a great deal of effort into designing a framework that will work for their country. It is not clear that a "one size fits all" approach is appropriate.

Notes

1. This section draws heavily on the World–ASBA survey of supervisors and central banks conducted in 2010 and Heysen and Auqui (2010).

2. While Jamaica and Trinidad and Tobago suffered the failure of financial firms during the period of the crisis, these appear to be unrelated to the global crisis and were more linked to domestic or firm-specific factors.

3. Most Latin American banks hold capital in excess of requirements, averaging about 15 percent during the crisis period. See IMF (2010).

4. The results of this survey can be found in: Delgado and Meza (2011) and Jacome, Nier, and Imam (2012).

5. In some countries, e.g., Uruguay in 2002, liquidity pressures, resulting from a lack of confidence in banks, served as the triggering mechanism for the crisis.

6. For example, financial stability reports are issued by central banks in Brazil, Chile, Colombia, and Mexico. The Peruvian supervisor also conducts a systemic risk assessment.

7. One such example of a complex financial conglomerate that encountered difficulties is CL Financial in Trinidad and Tobago. This firm had subsidiaries in insurance, banking, real estate, and real sector commercial activities in nine countries.

8. This is especially true in countries with civil law frameworks.

9. The "rules vs. discretion" debate originated in the literature relating to monetary policy in the 1950s and 1960s. See, for example, Friedman (1959).

10. This has been done in the United States.

11. Pillar III of Basel II (Market Discipline), while not yet widely implemented, would have required commercial banks to publicly provide details of their risk management activities, risk rating processes, and the risk distribution of their portfolios.

12. Both the United Kingdom and Germany have proposed shifting bank supervision from a separate supervisory agency into the central bank. The French have moved toward creating a separate supervisory agency, under the auspices of the central bank.

13. For a discussion of forbearance incentives, see IMF (2010).

14. There is an extensive literature on this subject. See, for example, Goodhart and Schoemaker (1995) and Peek, Rosengren, and Tootell (1999).

15. The debate over the 2010 financial sector legislation in the United States is a good example of the politics that surface when there is a concerted effort to increase supervision and regulation, especially of the largest institutions.

References

Black, Fischer, and Myron Scholes. 1973. "The Pricing of Options and Corporate Liabilities." *Journal of Political Economy* 81 (3): 637–54.

Cardenas, Mauricio. 2011. "Latin America, the Global Financial Crisis, and the Velocity of Business." Speech delivered at the Brookings Institution "Latin America Private Equity Forum," Washington, DC, February 11.

Caruana, Jaimie. 2010. "Why Basel II Matters for Latin American and Caribbean Financial Markets." Speech given at the ASBA–FSI "High-Level Meeting," Antigua, Guatemala. November 19.

de la Torre, Augusto, Juan Carlos Gozzi, and Sergio L. Schmukler. 2006. "Capital Market Development: Whither Latin America?" In *Financial Markets Volatility and Performance in Emerging Markets*, edited by Sebastian Edwards and Marcio Garcia, 121–53. Chicago: University of Chicago Press.

Delgado, Fernando L., and Mynor Meza. 2011. "Developments in Financial Supervision and the Use of Macroprudential Measures in Central America." IMF Working Paper 11/299, International Monetary Fund, Washington, DC.

Economist. 2010. "Crash-Test Dummies." June.

Evanoff, Douglas D., and Larry D. Wall. 2000. "Subordinated Debt and Bank Capital Reform." Federal Reserve Bank of Atlanta Working Paper 2000-24, Atlanta.

Friedman, Milton. 1959. "The Demand for Money: Some Theoretical and Empirical Results." *Journal of Political Economy* 67: 327.

Galindo, Arturo J., Liliana Rojas-Suarez, and Marielle del Valle. 2012. "Capital Requirements under Basel III in Latin America." Center for Global Development Working Paper 296, Center for Global Development, Washington, DC.

Garicano, Luis, and Rosa M. Lastra. 2010. "Towards a New Architecture for Financial Stability: Seven Principles." *Journal of International Economic Law* 13 (3): 597–621.

Goodhart, Charles, and Dirk Schoemaker. 1995. "Institutional Separation between Supervisory and Monetary Agencies." In *The Central Bank and the Financial System,* edited by Charles Goodhart, 334–414. Cambridge, MA: MIT Press.

Granlund, Peik. 2009. "Supervisory Approaches and Financial Market Development: Some Correlation Based Evidence." *Journal of Banking Regulation* 11: 6–30.

Gray, Dale, and Samuel Malone. 2008. *Macrofinancial Risk Analysis.* Wiley Finance Series. West Sussex England: John Wiley and Sons.

Gray, Dale, and James P. Walsh. 2008. "Factor Model for Stress-Testing with a Contingent Claims Model of the Chilean Banking System." IMF Working Paper, International Monetary Fund, Washington, DC.

Heysen, Soccoro, and Martin Auqui. 2010. "Recent Trends in Latin America and the Caribbean." Draft paper prepared for the World Bank.

Hirtle, Beverly, Tiul Scheurman, and Kevin Stiroh. 2009. "Macroprudential Supervision of Financial Institutions: Lessons from the SCAP." Federal Reserve Bank of New York Staff Report 409, FRB, New York.

Horvitz, Paul. 1983. "Market Discipline Is Best Provided by Subordinated Creditors." *American Banker* (July): 3.

IMF (International Monetary Fund). 2010. *Global Financial Stability Review: Meeting New Challenges to Stability and Building a Safer System.* Washington, DC: IMF.

Jacome, Luis I., Erland W. Nier, and Patrick Imam. 2012. "Building Blocks for Effective Macroprudential Policies in Latin America: Institutional Considerations." IMF Working Paper 12/83, International Monetary Fund, Washington, DC.

Jara, Alejandro, Ramón Moreno, and Camilo Tovar. 2009. "The Global Crisis and Latin America: Financial Impact and Policy Responses." *BIS Quarterly Review* (June): 60.

Kahn, Mohsin, and Abdelhak S. Senhadi. 2000. "Financial Development and Economic Growth: An Overview." IMF Working Paper 00/209, International Monetary Fund, Washington, DC.

Levine, Ross. 1999. "Financial Development and Economic Growth: Views and Agenda." Policy Research Working Paper 1678, World Bank, Washington, DC.

Masciandaro, Donato, Rosaria V. Pansini, and Marc Quintyn. 2011. "The Economic Crisis: Did Financial Supervision Matter?" IMF Working Paper.

Merton, Robert C. 1974. "On the Pricing of Corporate Debt: The Risk Structure of Interest Rates." *The Journal of Finance* 29: 449–470.

Musalem, Alberto, and Fernando Baer. 2010. Introduction to *Capital Markets in the Southern Cone of Latin America,* edited by Alberto Musalem. Buenos Aires: Centro Para La Estabilidad Financiera, Prentice Hall.

Peek, Joe, Eric S. Rosengren, and Geoffrey M. B. Tootell. 1999. "Is Bank Supervision Central to Central Banking?" *Quarterly Journal of Economics* 114 (2): 629–53.

Powell, Andrew. 2010. "LAC Central Banks Ahead of the Curve? Financial Sector Regulation and Supervision." Presentation at the meeting of the Inter-American Development Bank in LACEA, Medellin, Colombia, April 10.

Sah, Raaj K., and Joseph E. Stiglitz. 1986. "The Architecture of Economic Systems: Hierarchies and Polyarchies." *American Economic Review* 76 (4): 716–27.

Seelig, Steven, and Alicia Novoa. 2009. "Governance Practices at Financial Regulatory and Supervisory Agencies." IMF Working Paper 09/135, International Monetary Fund, Washington, DC.

Sharpe, William. 1964. "Capital Asset Prices: A Theory of Market Equilibrium under Conditions of Risk." *Journal of Finance* 19: 425–42.

Sosa, Sebastian. 2010. "The Influence of 'Big Brothers': How Important Are Regional Factors for Uruguay?" IMF Working Paper 10/60, International Monetary Fund, Washington, DC.

Stallings, Barbara, and Rogerio Studart. 2003. "Financial Regulation and Supervision in Emerging Markets: The Experience of Latin America since the Tequila Crisis." CEPAL, Santiago de Chile.

Stephanou, Constantinos. 2010. "Rethinking Market Discipline in Banking: Lessons from the Financial Crisis." Policy Research Working Paper 5227, World Bank, Washington, DC.

Index

Boxes, figures, notes, and tables are indicated by b, f, n, and t following the page number.

ECO-AUDIT
Environmental Benefits Statement

The World Bank is committed to preserving endangered forests and natural resources. *Emerging Issues in Financial Development* is printed on recycled paper with 50 percent postconsumer fiber in accordance with the recommended standards for paper usage set by the Green Press Initiative, a nonprofit program supporting publishers in using fiber that is not sourced from endangered forests. For more information, visit www.greenpressinitiative.org.

Saved:
- 11 trees
- 5 million British thermal units of total energy
- 967 pounds of net greenhouse gases
- 5,245 gallons of waste water
- 351 pounds of solid waste

green press
INITIATIVE

www.ingramcontent.com/pod-product-compliance
Lightning Source LLC
Chambersburg PA
CBHW071144270326
41929CB00012B/1874